MW00787713

PHILOSOPHY OF PROBABILITY

'The philosophy of probability has had a venerable history, but recently it has especially stepped into the limelight, and it is flourishing nowadays. This volume brings together both classics and cutting-edge contributions to its literature. Antony Eagle does an excellent job of orienting the reader by grouping these articles thematically, and by providing a panoramic and incisive introduction to each of the themes. A terrific resource – that's a certainty'.

Alan Hájek, *The Australian National University, Australia*

Philosophy of Probability: Contemporary Readings is the first anthology to collect essential readings in this important area of philosophy. Featuring the work of leading philosophers in the field such as Carnap, Hájek, Jeffrey, Joyce, Lewis, Loewer, Popper, Ramsey, van Fraassen, von Mises and many others, the book looks in depth at the following key topics:

- subjective probability and credence
- probability updating: conditionalization and reflection
- Bayesian confirmation theory
- classical, logical and evidential probability
- frequentism
- physical probability: propensities and objective chances.

The book features a useful primer on the mathematics of probability, and each section includes an introduction by the editor, as well as a guide to further reading. A broad-ranging and highly accessible exploration of the subject, *Philosophy of Probability* is ideal for any student of formal epistemology, philosophy of science, metaphysics, or philosophy of mathematics.

Antony Eagle is Lecturer in Philosophy at the University of Oxford, UK, and William Kneale Fellow and Tutor in Philosophy at Exeter College, Oxford, UK.

Routledge contemporary readings in philosophy
Series Editor: Paul K. Moser,
Loyola University of Chicago

Routledge Contemporary Readings in Philosophy is a major new series of philosophy anthologies aimed at undergraduate students taking core philosophy disciplines. It is also a companion series to the highly successful *Routledge Contemporary Introductions to Philosophy*. Each book of readings provides an overview of a core general subject in philosophy, offering students an accessible transition from introductory to higher-level undergraduate work in that subject. Each chapter of readings will be carefully selected, edited, and introduced. They will provide a broad overview of each topic and will include both classic and contemporary readings.

Philosophy of Science
Yuri Balashov and Alex Rosenberg

Metaphysics
Michael J. Loux

Epistemology
Michael Huemer, with introduction by Robert Audi

Philosophy of Mind
Timothy O'Connor and David Robb

Ethics
Harry Gensler, Earl Spurgin and James Swindal

Philosophy of Psychology
José Luis Bermúdez

Metaphysics, Second Edition
Michael J. Loux

PHILOSOPHY OF PROBABILITY

Contemporary Readings

Edited by
Antony Eagle

Routledge
Taylor & Francis Group
LONDON AND NEW YORK

First published 2011
by Routledge
2 Park Square, Milton Park, Abingdon, Oxon OX14 4RN

Simultaneously published in the USA and Canada
by Routledge
270 Madison Avenue, New York, NY 10016

Routledge is an imprint of the Taylor & Francis Group,
an informa business

Typeset in Sabon by Glyph International Ltd.
Printed and bound in Great Britain by
CPI Antony Rowe, Chippeham, Wiltshire

British Library Cataloguing in Publication Data
A catalogue record for this book is available from the British Library

Library of Congress Cataloging in Publication Data
Philosophy of probability: contemporary readings / edited by
Antony Eagle.
p. cm. – (Routledge contemporary readings in philosophy)
Includes bibliographical references and index.
1. Probabilities–Philosophy. I. Eagle, Antony, 1976–
QA273.19.P4P45 2010
519.201–dc22   2010018087

ISBN 13: 978-0-415-48386-5 (hbk)
ISBN 13: 978-0-415-48387-2 (pbk)

TO MY TEACHERS

CONTENTS

CONTENTS

CONTENTS

ACKNOWLEDGEMENTS

Thanks to all those philosophers with whom I've discussed the philosophy of probability and to those who provided comments and feedback on the editorial matter, especially Al Hájek (who provided extensive comments on all the editorial matter), Bas van Fraassen, Branden Fitelson, John Cusbert, Grant Reaber, Seamus Bradley, the participants in my graduate and undergraduate courses on this material, and those who provided comments and suggestions on the proposed list of readings. I'd particularly like to thank those who gave their permission for pieces to be included: Steffi Lewis, Al Hájek, Bas van Fraassen, Adam Elga, Frank Arntzenius, Darren Bradley, Hannes Leitgeb, Branden Fitelson, Ronald Giere and Brian Skyrms. Lizzie's help was invaluable throughout, but I'm particularly grateful for her help with checking the page proofs.

PERMISSIONS

Part I: Degrees of belief

Part II: Updating degrees of belief:
Conditionalisation and reflection

7. Jeffrey, R. C. (1965) "Probability Kinematics". Originally published as Chapter 11 of *The Logic of Decision, 2nd edition*, University of Chicago Press: Chicago, 1983, pp. 164–180. Copyright © 1965 & 1983 The University of Chicago. Reproduced by kind permission.

8. van Fraassen, B. C. (1984) "Belief and the Will", *Journal of Philosophy* 81, pp. 235–256. Copyright © 1984 The Journal of Philosophy, Inc. Reproduced by kind permission of the author and The Journal of Philosophy.

9. Maher, P. (1993) "Diachronic Rationality". Originally published as Chapter 5 of *Betting on Theories*, by Patrick Maher. Cambridge University Press: Cambridge, 1993, pp. 105–129. Copyright © 1993 Cambridge University Press, reproduced with permission.

10. Elga, A. (2000) "Self-locating belief and the Sleeping Beauty problem", *Analysis* 60, pp. 143–147. Copyright © 2000 Adam Elga. Reproduced by kind permission of the author.

11. Arntzenius, F. (2003) "Some Problems for Conditionalization and Reflection", *Journal of Philosophy* 100, pp. 356–370. Copyright © 2003 The Journal of Philosophy, Inc. Reproduced by kind permission of the author and The Journal of Philosophy.

12. Bradley, D. and Leitgeb, P. (2006) "When Betting Odds and Credences Come Apart: more worries for Dutch book Arguments", *Analysis* 66, pp. 119–127. Copyright © 2006 Darren Bradley and Hannes Leitgeb. Reproduced by kind permission of the authors.

Part III: Evidence and probability: Bayesian confirmation theory

14. Howson, C. and Urbach, P. (1993) "Bayesian versus non-Bayesian Approaches to Confirmation", pp. 117–164 (omitting sections g, h.2, part of i, j.3, and the exercises). Reprinted by permission of open Court Publishing Company, a division of Carus Publishing Company, Peru, IL from *Scientific Reasoning: The Bayesian Approach, 2nd edition*, by Colin Howson and Peter Urbach. Copyright © 1989 & 1993 Open Court Publishing Company.

15. Glymour, C. (1980) "Why I am not a Bayesian". Originally published in Glymour Clark; *THEORY AND EVIDENCE*. Copyright © 1980 Princeton University Press. Reprinted by permission of Princeton University Press.

16. With kind permission from Springer Science+Business Media: *Philosophical Studies*, "Symmetries and Asymmetries in Evidential Support", 107, 2002, pp.129–142, Ellery Eells & Branden Fitelson. Copyright © 2002 Kluwer Academic Publishers.

Part IV: Evidence and probability: Evidential probability and principles of indifference

18. van Fraassen, B. C. (1989) "Indifference: the Symmetries of Probability". Originally published in *Laws and Symmetry*, by Bas C. van Fraassen. Oxford University Press, Oxford, 1989, pp. 293–317. Copyright © 1989 Bas C. van Fraassen. By permission of Oxford University Press.

19. Carnap, R. (1955) "Statistical and Inductive Probability". Originally published by the *Galois Institute of Mathematics and Art*, Brooklyn, 1955. Copyright © 1955 Rudolf Carnap.

20. Stove, D. C. (1986) "Is The Theory of Logical Probability Groundless?". Originally published in *Rationality of Induction*, by D. C. Stove. Oxford University Press, Oxford, 1986, pp. 178–189. Copyright © 1986 D. C. Stove. By permission of Oxford University Press.

Part V: Physical Probability: The frequency theory

22. von Mises, R. (1957) "The Definition of Probability", Originally published in *Probability, Statistics and Truth*, by Richard von Mises. Dover, New York, 1957, pp. 8–29 & pp. 81–103. Copyright © 1957 George Allen & Unwin Ltd. Reproduced by kind permission of Dover Publications, Inc.

23. Jeffrey, R. C. (1977) "Mises Redux". Originally published in *Basic Problems in Methodology and Linguistics*, eds. R. E. Butts and J. Hintikka. Kluwer Academic Publishers: Dordrecht, 1977, pp. 213–222. Copyright ©1977 Kluwer Academic Publishers. With kind permission from Springer Science+Business Media.

24. With kind permission from Springer Science+Business Media: *Erkenntnis*, "'Mises redux' – Redux: Fifteen arguments against finite frequentism", 45, 1996, pp. 209–227, Alan Hájek. Copyright © 1997 Kluwer Academic Publishers.

25. Hájek, A. (2009) "Fifteen Arguments Against Hypothetical Frequentism" Originally published in *Erkenntnis* 70, 2009, pp. 211–235. Copyright © 2009 Springer Science+Business Media B.V. Reproduced by kind permission of the author.

Part VI: Physical probability: Objective chance and propensities

27. Lewis, D. (1980) "A Subjectivist's Guide to Objective Chance". Originally published in *Studies in Inductive Logic and Probability* 2, ed. Richard C. Jeffrey. University of California Press, Berkeley, 1980. Copyright © 1980 David Lewis. Reproduced by kind permission of Stephanie Lewis.

28. Popper, K. (1959) "A Propensity Interpretation of Probability". Originally published in *British Journal for the Philosophy of Science* 10, 1959, pp. 25–38 (omitting the note and appendix). Copyright © 1959 The British Society for the Philosophy of Science. By permission of Oxford University Press.

29. Giere, R. N. (1971) "Objective Single-Case Probabilities and the Foundations of Statistics". Originally published in *Logic, methodology, and philosophy of science IV: Proceedings of the Fourth International Congress for Logic, Methodology and Philosophy of Science Bucharest 1971*, eds. P. Suppes, L. Henkin, G. C. Moisil, & A. Joja. Amsterdam: North-Holland, 1973, pp. 467–483. Reproduced by kind permission of the author.

30. Humphreys, P. W. (1985) "Why Propensities Cannot be Probabilities". Originally published in *The Philosophical Review* 94, 1985, pp. 557–570. Copyright © 1985 Sage

School of Philosophy at Cornell University. All rights reserved. Used by permission of the publisher, Duke University Press.

31. Loewer, B. (2004) "David lewis's Humean Theory of Objective Chance". Originally published in *Philosophy of Science* 71, University of Chicago Press: Chicago, 2004, pp. 1115–1125. Copyright © 2004 Philosophy of Science Association. Reproduced by kind permission.

32. Skyrms, B. (1977) "Resiliency, Propensities, and Causal Necessity", *Journal of Philosophy* 74, pp. 704–713. Copyright © 1977 Journal of Philosophy, Inc. Reprinted by permission of the author and The Journal of Philosophy.

Every effort has been made to trace and contact copyright holders but this may not have been possible in all cases. Any omissions brought to the attention of the publisher will be remedied in future editions.

PREFACE

Probability has long been thought to pose special philosophical challenges, but also to provide new philosophical resources. On the one hand, probabilities in successful scientific theories pose a challenge for the conceptual understanding of science, particularly because the integration of probabilities into existing pictures of the metaphysics of science is not straightforward. On the other hand, the probability calculus promises powerful and subtle new techniques for theorising about phenomena of considerable philosophical interest. Both sets of issues have spurred an enormous expansion in the amount of philosophical work on probability theory.

This volume attempts to provide a representative selection of this philosophical work on a number of core topics. I make no claim to completeness of coverage; I am aware of too many great pieces that I wish I could have included, but was prevented from doing so by lack of space. Anyone with any familiarity with the field will have their favourite pieces that they might wish had been included. But each of the pieces here provides a philosophically interesting take on a significant issue, and collectively they represent a useful diversity of opinion. The pieces included range from familiar to relatively obscure, and from the earliest recognisably contemporary philosophical discussions of probability to pieces only a couple of years old. The topics have all received a lot of discussion, and have reasonable claim to both importance and centrality.

There are two regrettable features in the selection. One is that I was unable to include pieces on decision theory, one of the main success stories involving the theory of credences. The other regrettable feature, which I could see no way to avoid, is the lack of pieces by women. It is an unfortunate fact that almost all of the literature concerning probability was written by men, up until quite recently. Thankfully, as the more recent items mentioned in the further readings show, this situation is beginning to change, as the field increasingly attracts able younger philosophers of both genders.

How to use this book

Philosophical interest in probability is indicated by the recent glut of textbooks in philosophy of probability—at least seven, by my count.[1] Obviously this book could be, and I hope will be, used in a classroom setting, so it overlaps to a certain extent with these textbooks. But for those who prefer to avoid using textbooks in teaching, or for those running higher-level classes for students who can and should read the original material, the present volume will provide a more useful adjunct to teaching. In the classroom context, then, this book could be used as a required text, supplemented if the instructor desires by their own additional favourites. A reasonably complete one-semester course in the philosophy of probability could quite easily be constructed from the present volume unsupplemented. And particular parts could be included in other courses; items from Parts I and II could, for example, be included in a course on epistemology that delves into formal aspects of the subject, and items from Parts III–VI are obviously relevant for courses in the philosophy of science and metaphysics. Much the same goes for courses at the graduate level; at this level the extensive further reading included in the introductions to each part will provide useful hints for supplementary reading, and suggestions for those who are looking to write research papers in the area.

The book is also designed to be useful for those who are pursuing self-guided study, including professional philosophers and graduate students who are looking to gain expertise in the field, and those who are experts in probability from related fields (such as mathematics or statistics), but who are looking to find out what philosophers have contributed to our understanding of probability. For those without extensive background in probability theory, the primer provides an overview of all the mathematics required to understand the papers in this book. The introductions to the parts provide an orientation, setting the readings in context and providing extensive pointers to the further directions in which the discussion of these topics has gone, as well as discussing the contribution of excellent pieces I was unable to include. Each introduction has a self-contained and annotated bibliography of relevant further reading.

Part I explores the proposal that there are degrees of belief, or credences, and that these credences, if rational, have the structure of probabilities. This provides the most notable example of a philosophically important application of probability in epistemology. Part II extends this account of credence from the static case of rational belief at a time to the dynamic case of rational shifts of belief. Part III applies the results of the first two parts to another application of philosophical interest, the confirmation of theories by evidence. Part IV discusses attempts to provide another account of the role of probability in confirmation, more 'objective' than the credence-based account of Part III. This objective role for probability is connected with familiar classroom explanations of probability as a kind of 'measure of possibility' of various outcomes, in cases like dice tossing. Consideration of these cases, and the appearances of probability in science, provide a prima facie case that not all uses of probability can be accounted for by credences, and there is a place for objective probability, or chance, too. The final two parts detail two attempts to provide accounts of objective probability. Part V discusses the once popular proposal that objective chances are relative frequencies; Part VI looks at non-frequentist accounts of chance, including accounts that draw on quite different metaphysical backgrounds, thus emphasising more broadly the ramifications of the philosophy of probability for philosophy.

Note

1 Including books by Maria-Carla Galvotti (*Philosophical Introduction to Probability*), Donald Gillies (*Philosophical Theories of Probability*), Ian Hacking (*An Introduction to Probability and Inductive Logic*), Colin Howson and Peter Urbach (*Scientific Reasoning: The Bayesian Approach*), Richard Jeffrey (*Subjective Probability: The Real Thing*), D. H. Mellor (*Probability: A Philosophical Introduction*), and Brian Skyrms (*Choice and Chance*).

PROBABILITY PRIMER

In this chapter, I'll provide an introduction to the mathematics of probability theory.[1] The philosophy of probability doesn't require much mathematical sophistication, at least not to get a good grip on the main problems and views. Nothing in this chapter is particularly complicated, and even the mathematically shy should, with a little effort, find it easy to follow. I do assume familiarity with the basics of an elementary logic course, and some basic facility with the notion of a set. If you lack these rudiments, some suggestions of textbooks to look at can be found in the Further Reading section at the end of this primer. References for most of the claims I make are also largely confined to the Further Reading.

Outcomes and algebras

What kind of thing has a probability? When probability is introduced, one normally sees examples like these:

(1) The probability of the coin coming up heads is one-half.
(2) The probability that I will win the lottery is one in a million.

In the first of these examples, what is said to have a probability is an *event*, namely, the coin landing heads. In the second example, what is said to have a probability is the *proposition* that I win the lottery. Events and propositions are quite different things, but there are correspondences between them. Obviously, events either occur or fail to occur, while propositions are either true or false. But for each event e, there is a proposition—the proposition that e occurs—which is true if e occurs, and false otherwise. And for each proposition p, there is an event—the event of p's being true—which occurs if and only if (henceforth, *iff*) p is true. This shows that there is a kind of structural similarity between events and propositions. We could choose to say that probabilities attach primarily to one or the other; but in fact, it doesn't make much difference whether we choose to say that events are the basic bearers of probabilities, or that propositions are.

What does matter is that both events and propositions have a similar *logical* structure. For each proposition p, there is another proposition $\neg p$ (the *negation* of p) which is true iff p is false. And so, for each event e, there is another event $\neg e$ which occurs iff e does not occur. For each pair of propositions, p and q, there is a *disjunctive* proposition $p \vee q$ which is true iff at least one of p or q is true; and there is a *conjunctive* proposition $p \wedge q$

1

which is true iff both p and q are true. So, too, for each pair of events, e and f, there is an event $e \vee f$ which occurs iff at least one of e and f occurs; and an event $e \wedge f$ which occurs iff both e and f occur. Finally, there is also a trivial proposition ⊤, the proposition which is trivially true (if you like, you can think of it as some arbitrary tautology, like 'p or not p'). Corresponding to this is the trivial event, often written Ω—this is the event which is sure to happen. It follows from what I claimed at the start of this paragraph that there is also the trivially false proposition, $\neg \top$ (sometimes written $\bot$), as well as the impossible event which is bound not to happen (sometimes written $\varnothing$).

Mathematical probability theory is usually based on set theoretic constructions, related to but distinct from the approach described in the last paragraph. Ω is taken to be the set of all 'elementary events'. Often what we have called a conjunctive event $e \wedge f$ will be described as the set-theoretic *intersection* of e and f, written $e \cap f$; our disjunctive events $e \vee f$ will be the *union* $e \cup f$; and the negation $\neg e$ will usually be the set-theoretic *complement* of e with respect to the set Ω, written $\Omega \backslash e$. The approach taken in the last paragraph and the majority of this primer avoids the vexed issue of precisely what an 'elementary event' might be, at least until it returns at p. 15ff.

We normally wish to assign probabilities to *possible outcomes* of some process. These might be the outcomes of a coin toss or another event about which we commonly gamble, but in general it might be any way that the world turns out to be. If some events e and f are possible outcomes, then what other possible outcomes are there? It is intuitively obvious that $e \vee f$, the event which happens if one or the other of e or f happens, is also a possible outcome; and that $\neg e$, the event which happens iff e fails to happen, is also a possible outcome. It is also obvious that the trivial event, the one that is bound to happen, is a possible outcome—we include its negation, the impossible event, as a possible outcome too, by courtesy and for simplicity. We can make these informal observations more precise by defining the following notion:

Definition 1 (Algebra). Assume that we have some set of events or propositions, or outcomes, A. A is an *algebra* iff these three conditions are satisfied:

1   ⊤ (or Ω) is in A.
2   For any member a of A, $\neg a$ is also in A.
3   For any members a and b of A, $a \vee b$ is also in A.[2]

The complex outcomes we have considered so far are finite logical compounds of other outcomes, but there is no reason to restrict ourselves to these. To that end, we introduce infinitary analogues of conjunction and disjunction. If $p_1, ..., p_n, ...$ are some (possibly infinitely many) propositions (or events), $\bigvee_i p_i$ is the proposition true iff at least one of the p_i's is true (or occurs), and $\bigwedge_i p_i$ is the proposition true iff all of the p_i's are true (or occur). (In the set-theoretic framework, the notions of union and intersection of a collection of sets are naturally extended to countable unions $\bigcup_i p_i$ and countable intersections $\bigcap_i p_i$ on a collection of sets $P = p_1, \{ ..., p_n, ...\}$.)

With these notions, we can introduce a special kind of algebra:

Definition 2 (σ-algebra). A set of outcomes A is a *σ-algebra* iff these three conditions are satisfied:

1   ⊤ (or Ω) is in $\mathcal{A}$.
2   For any member a of $\mathcal{A}$, $\neg a$ is also in $\mathcal{A}$.
3   For any (finite or countably infinite[3]) collection a_1, ..., a_n, ... of members of $\mathcal{A}$, $\bigvee_i a_i$ is also in $\mathcal{A}$.

The mathematical notion of an algebra makes the notion of a collection of possible outcomes rigorous. With it in hand, we can now say what it is that probabilities attach to. They attach to each member of an algebra of outcomes, so that for every member of the algebra, there will be an associated probability. As probabilities are numerical, probability is a function: a mapping that, for each member of some algebra, yields a number—which is the probability of that event or proposition.

Something which has been implicit in the present treatment, but which should be made explicit, is that because algebras are collections of outcomes, they aren't collections of sentences or descriptions of outcomes. If two outcomes are *equivalent*, they are true in just the same situations, and so are the same outcome. So, given that probability is a function from an algebra of propositions to numbers, sentences that express the same proposition must be given the same probability. This way of setting things up differs from one very common approach that takes an algebra of sentences (rather than propositions) to underlie the probability function. Some sentential treatments take probability to introduce an intensional context, in which co-referring names for outcomes may be given distinct probabilities, but here any expression that refers to the same outcome can be substituted into a probability function and receive the same probability. Some philosophically important issues, especially to do with the content of beliefs, turn on this, but will not be a major focus in what follows.

The laws of probability

There are many functions from outcomes to numbers (consider the function which tells us how many seconds have elapsed since the Big Bang until the time that a certain event first occurs). What makes a function a probability function? The first widely accepted answer to this question was proposed by A.N. Kolmogorov in 1933:

Definition 3 (Probability function). If $\mathcal{A}$ is some algebra of outcomes, and P is a function from $\mathcal{A}$ to the real numbers, then P is a *probability function* iff it obeys these conditions:

Normality $P(\top) = 1$ (or $P(\Omega) = 1$).
Non-negativity For all $p \in A$, $P(p) \geq 0$.
Additivity For any members p and q of A such that $p \wedge q$ cannot be true (or, $p \wedge q = \varnothing$), $P(p \vee q) = P(p) + P(q)$. (Propositions that cannot both be true together are called *mutually exclusive*.)

That's it. *Any* function on an algebra of outcomes that obeys these *Kolmogorov axioms* is a probability function. For a given algebra, there are many functions all of which are equally good as probability functions; which of those functions corresponds to the 'real' probabilities of the events in the algebra is not a question that mathematical probability theory attempts to answer.

Kolmogorov actually endorses a stronger version of the additivity axiom:

Countable additivity For any countable sequence of outcomes $p_1, \ldots, p_n, \ldots$ such that any two outcomes in the sequence are mutually exclusive, and each p_i is a member of a σ-algebra $\mathcal{A}$, which is the domain of the function P,

$$P\left(\bigvee_i p_i\right) = \sum_i P(p_i)$$

Countable additivity is almost always adopted in mathematical treatments of probability,[4] and is the key assumption in the assimilation of probability theory to abstract measure theory, but there has been considerable philosophical concern about its status. (See the further reading in Ch. 1, p. 27, for more details.) That said, we will adopt it from now on: all the probability functions we shall consider will be countably additive (and we will therefore only consider σ-algebras).

While Kolmogorov's general approach has received widespread acceptance in the philosophical community, and is virtually undisputed in mathematics, it should be noted that it may be challenged. A recognisably modern concept of probability first emerged in the middle of the seventeenth century (with Pascal, Huygens, the Port Royal *Logic*, and others), and over the next two hundred years the mathematical understanding of probability made significant advances even on this informal basis. Kolmogorov's axioms were an attempt to make this long-standing pre-theoretic notion of probability precise, in a way that preserved the substantial results of probability theory up to that point. But there are other ways that we could make the informal concept more precise (some of which will come up below; see pp. 13–4 and 19–21). There is by no means universal agreement that Kolmogorov's approach is better than these other approaches, if indeed there is a best approach at all.

Kolmogorov's approach makes probability theory a branch of measure theory, and probability itself a *normed measure*. All this means is that it is appropriate to use terminology from the theory of measurement to describe ideas from probability theory, in particular the idea of *proportion*.[5] We can think of probability, perhaps merely heuristically, as the proportion of possible situations in which a certain outcome obtains. Obviously the certain outcome obtains in 100% of cases, and all outcomes must obtain in at least 0% of cases, which accounts for the Normality and Non-negativity axioms. And outcomes that don't overlap in the cases in which they are true, when taken disjunctively, cover a proportion of cases which is the proportion covered by each of them added together—the Additivity axiom. This 'proportion of possible cases' way of thinking about probability has deep historical roots, and can be a useful guide, but be wary of relying on it too extensively.

Some theorems of probability theory

With the axioms defining probability functions in place, we can now prove a few theorems about probabilities. (In the following, let 'p', 'q', etc. stand for items drawn from some algebra of outcomes, with some probability function P defined on it.)

Theorem 1 (Negation). $P(\neg p) = 1 - P(p)$.

Proof. p and $\neg p$ are inconsistent; hence, by additivity, $P(p \vee \neg p) = P(p) + P(\neg p)$. But $p \vee \neg p$ is equivalent to $\top$, so $P(p \vee \neg p) = 1$. By elementary algebra, $P(\neg p) = 1 - P(p)$. $\square$

A simple corollary of this theorem is that $P(\bot) = 0$, since $P(\bot) = P(\neg \top) = 1 - P(\top) = 0$. Another simple corollary is that $0 \leq P(p) \leq 1$; Non-negativity shows that $0 \leq P(p)$. If we assume that for some q, $P(q) > 1$, it would follow that $P(\neg q) = 1 - P(q) < 0$, which contradicts Non-negativity; hence there is no such q.

Additivity dictates the probability of some disjunctions, but in general:

Theorem 2 (Arbitrary disjunctions). $P(p \vee q) = P(p) + P(q) - P(p \wedge q)$.

Proof. $p \vee q$ is equivalent to $(p \wedge q) \vee (p \wedge \neg q) \vee (\neg p \wedge q)$. All the disjuncts in this latter expression are mutually exclusive, so Additivity shows

$$P(p \vee q) = P(p \wedge q) + P(p \wedge \neg q) + P(\neg p \wedge q).$$

Elementary logic shows us that p is equivalent to this disjunction of mutually exclusive events: $(p \wedge q) \vee (p \wedge \neg q)$, so that $P(p \wedge \neg q) = P(p) - P(p \wedge q)$; similarly, $P(\neg p \wedge q) = P(q) - P(p \wedge q)$. Substituting:

$$P(p \vee q) = P(p \wedge q) + (P(p) - P(p \wedge q)) + (P(q) - P(p \wedge q)) = P(p) + P(q) - P(p \wedge q). \quad \square$$

Theorem 3 (Consequence). *If q is a consequence of p (or p entails q), $P(q) \geq P(p)$.*

Proof. q is equivalent to $(q \wedge p) \vee (q \wedge \neg p)$. If p entails q, then $q \wedge p$ is equivalent to p, so by substitution q is equivalent to $p \vee (q \wedge \neg p)$. This is a disjunction of mutually exclusive propositions, so that $P(q) = P(p) + P(q \wedge \neg p)$. By Non-negativity, $P(q \wedge \neg p) \geq 0$, so $P(q) \geq P(p)$. $\square$

We can apply these theorems to a simple case. Suppose we are considering a single toss of a fair die. The basic outcomes we're concerned with are the die landing with various numbers upwards, and can be represented as the set $\{1,2,3,4,5,6\}$. The set of all subsets of that set is an algebra, and we can define a probability function over that set. Since the die is fair, the natural probability function to choose over that set determines that $P(1) = 1/6$, and so on for each other outcome; since the die cannot land both 1 and 4, $P(1 \vee 4) = 1/3$. $P(\text{not } (3 \text{ or } 5)) = 1 - P(3 \text{ or } 5) = 1 - (P(3) + P(5)) = 1 - (2/6) = 2/3$. $P(\text{odd or less than } 4)$ is a little trickier, since those two outcomes aren't mutually exclusive; but by Theorem 2, we see that $P(\text{odd or less than } 4) = P(\text{odd}) + P(\text{less than } 4) - P(\text{odd and less than } 4) = 1/2 + 1/2 - P(1 \vee 3) = 1 - 1/3 = 2/3$.

Non-negativity and Theorem 2 together show that $P(p \vee q) \leq P(p) + P(q)$. We now show the arbitrary generalisation of this claim:

Theorem 4. *If $p_1, ..., p_n$ are some elements of the algebra, $P(\bigvee_i p_i) \leq \Sigma_i P(p_i)$.*

Proof. Proof is by induction on n. In the base case, $n = 1$, the claim is obvious. Now assume the theorem holds for $n - 1$. $\bigvee_{i=1}^{n} p_i$ is equivalent to $\bigvee_{i=1}^{n-1} p_i \vee p_n$, which is equivalent to $\bigvee_{i=1}^{n-1} p_i \vee (p_n \wedge \neg(\bigvee_{i=1}^{n-1} p_i))$. This last is a disjunction of mutually exclusive outcomes; so, by Additivity, and the induction hypothesis,

$$P\left(\bigvee_{i=1}^{n} p_i\right) = P\left(\bigvee_{i=1}^{n-1} p_i \vee \left(p_n \wedge \neg\left(\bigvee_{i=1}^{n-1} p_i\right)\right)\right)$$

$$= P\left(\bigvee_{i=1}^{n-1} p_i\right) + P\left(p_n \wedge \neg\left(\bigvee_{i=1}^{n-1} p_i\right)\right)$$

$$\leqslant \sum_{i=1}^{n-1} P(p_i) + P\left(p_n \wedge \neg\left(\bigvee_{i=1}^{n-1} p_i\right)\right).$$

Since p_n is a consequence of $p_n \wedge \neg(\bigvee_{i=1}^{n-1} p_i)$, theorem 3 entails that $P(p_n) \geq P(p_n \wedge \neg(\bigvee_{i=1}^{n-1} p_i))$. Therefore

$$p\left(\bigvee_{i=1}^{n} p_i\right) \leqslant \sum_{i=1}^{n-1} P(p_i) + P(p_n) \leqslant \sum_{i=1}^{n} P(p_i). \qquad \square$$

Now I prove a result which depends crucially on Countable Additivity. First, a useful definition:

Definition 4 (Partition). A countable set of outcomes $Q = \{q_1, \ldots\}$ is a *partition* of the outcome space iff (i) all the q_i's are pair-wise mutually exclusive, and (ii) $\bigvee_i q_i$ is equivalent to $\top$.

Theorem 5 (Impossibility of uniformity). *If $O = p_1, \ldots$ is a countably infinite partition, then there cannot be a number ϵ such that for all i, $P(p_i) = \epsilon$.*

Proof. By countable additivity and normality,

$$P\left(\bigvee_i p_i\right) = \sum_i P(p_i) = 1.$$

Suppose that all the p_is have the same probability, ϵ. If $\epsilon = 0$, then $\Sigma_i P(p_i) = 0 + 0 + \ldots = 0$, which is a contradiction. So $\epsilon > 0$; but $\Sigma_i P(p_i) = \epsilon + \epsilon + \ldots > 1$ (the infinite sum of the same finite term is larger than any finite number), so contradiction again. $\qquad \square$

This theorem shows we can't choose a positive integer from the set $\{1, 2, 3, \ldots\}$ completely at random (i.e., with the same probability of choosing each number).[6] A uniform probability function over the natural numbers is *not* in conflict with (finite) additivity; so this theorem also shows us that Countable Additivity is stronger than Additivity, and that there are finitely additive probability functions which aren't countably additive.

6

Reasoning probabilistically

The rules of probability set down above should be intuitive, and when they are laid out on the page they can seem obvious. Yet humans are surprisingly bad at probabilistic reasoning. In some very famous experiments, the psychologists Amos Tversky and Daniel Kahneman asked subjects to consider the following scenario, and a set of claims about it:

> Linda is 31 years old, single, outspoken and very bright. She majored in philosophy. As a student, she was deeply concerned with issues of discrimination and social justice, and also participated in anti-nuclear demonstrations.

> Linda is a teacher in elementary school.
> Linda works in a bookstore and takes Yoga classes.
> Linda is active in the feminist movement. (*F*)
> Linda is a psychiatric social worker.
> Linda is a member of the League of Women Voters.
> Linda is a bank teller. (*T*)
> Linda is an insurance salesperson.
> Linda is a bank teller and is active in the feminist movement. ($T \wedge F$)

By Theorem 3, the claim T that Linda is a bank teller must be assigned a probability at least as great as the conjunction $T \wedge F$. Yet in their experiments, Tverksy and Kahneman found that 88% of subjects judged that $T \wedge F$ was *more probable* than T; and, moreover, that this wasn't affected very much by the mathematical sophistication of the subject. The general sort of reasoning, of which the above reasoning concerning Linda is an example, has become known as the *Conjunction Fallacy*.

Their own explanation for this result was that intuitive judgements of probability of some statement often go by how *representative* the truth of that statement would be. In the case of Linda, the scenario allows the subject to build up a mental model of Linda. The conjunction $T \wedge F$ is often judged to be more representative of Linda, because it contains more features (i.e. the feature that Linda is a feminist) that match the mental model of Linda, whereas the claim that Linda is a bank teller T is not thought to be characteristic of the kind of person the scenario makes Linda out to be. Since people think the conjunction is more representative, they judge it to be more probable, in conflict with standard probability theory.

When this is pointed out, subjects almost invariably retract their initial assessment, and recognise the truth of the probabilistic laws, so people aren't irremediably flawed. Also, the Tversky and Kahneman tests were designed to elicit the conjunction fallacy, so they don't provide a good indication of how prevalent errors in probabilistic reasoning are ordinarily. Indeed, there seems to be some evidence that, when subjects are presented with the same case in a more explicitly probabilistic fashion, they reason in ways much more like those mandated by probability theory (Hertwig and Gigerenzer, 1999). Nevertheless, Tversky and Kahneman's results should give us pause: claims about probability that seem intuitively plausible to us at first glance could be incorrect, and only care and attention can ensure we do not fall into error. The proofs in the previous section were not motivated by masochism so much as the awareness that even elementary results of probability theory must be carefully checked.

ANTONY EAGLE

Conditional probability

The theory of probability we've discussed so far allows us to give an account of many probability claims of natural language, as the die example made clear. But what about claims of the form 'the probability of **6** *given* **even** is 1/3'? This is a claim concerning *conditional probability*, what the probability of some event is conditional on the occurrence of another event (as compared to the 'unconditional' probabilities we've discussed up until now). How can these be fitted into our framework? Let us adopt the notation $P(p|q)$ to represent the probability of p given q. (Sometimes this is written $P(p/q)$.)

Kolmogorov proposes to *define* conditional probabilities in terms of unconditional probabilities, by means of what has come to be called the ratio analysis:

$$P(p|q) = \frac{P(p \wedge q)}{P(q)}, \text{ when } P(q) > 0. \tag{Ratio}$$

The intuitive rationale behind this definition can be visualised by using the proportion imagery I discussed on page 4. $P(q)$ is the proportion of cases in which q obtains. In some of those cases, p also holds; the proportion of cases in which q holds which are also cases where p holds gives the probability that a q-case is also a p-case; this is the conditional probability. But it is also fairly clearly given by the equation in Ratio, at least when there are enough cases where q holds. Again, be cautious about using these proportion ideas, but this gives a fair idea of what makes Ratio so plausible as an account of conditional probability. Yet some controversy surrounds the Ratio analysis; we'll come to that in a later section (pp. 13–4).

With conditional probability in hand, we can define some useful notions:

Definition 5 (Independence). Two outcomes p and q, such that $P(p) > 0$ and $P(q) > 0$, are said to be *independent* iff $P(p|q) = P(p)$.

The idea is that p is independent from q just in case the probability of p is the same whether or not q happens to hold.

Definition 6 (Screening off). If $P(q|s \wedge p) = P(q|s)$, then s is said to *screen off* p from q.

The idea here is illustrated by this classic example: lightning strikes and barometer readings of 'Storm' are not independent, since the probability of a lightning strike given that the barometer says 'Storm' is much higher than the unconditional probability of a lightning strike (that is why barometers are useful). Yet since both of these events are effects of a common cause, the approaching storm, that common cause screens off the events from each other: the probability of lightning given a storm and the barometer reading 'Storm' is the same as the probability of lightning given the storm. When p and q are not independent, they may be *conditionally independent*, given an outcome that screens them off from one another.

Theorems involving conditional probability

Theorem 6 (Conditional probabilities are probabilities). *If c is held fixed (and $P(c) > 0$), and $P(p|c)$ considered as a function of p alone, it is a probability function.*

8

Proof. We need to show that $P(\cdot|c)$ obeys Definition 3 of a probability function. It is a function from an algebra of outcomes to numbers. It obeys Normality, since $P(\top \wedge c) = P(c)$, so $P(\top \wedge c)/P(c) = 1$. It obeys Non-negativity, since for any p, $P(p|q)$ is a ratio of non-negative real numbers. And it obeys Countable Additivity. Suppose p_1, ... is a countable set of pair-wise mutually exclusive outcomes. Then

$$P\left(\bigvee_i p_i|c\right) = \frac{P(\bigvee_i p_i \wedge c)}{P(c)}$$

$$= \sum_i \frac{P(p_i \wedge c)}{P(c)}$$

$$= \sum_i P(p_i|c) \qquad \square$$

We can therefore define conditional probabilities on conditional probabilities too:

Theorem 7 *If $P(c) > 0$ and $P(q|c) > 0$, then $P(p|q \wedge c) =_{df} P(p \wedge q|c)/P(q|c)$.*

Proof. By the definition of conditional probability,

$$P(p|q \wedge c) =_{df} P(p \wedge q \wedge c)/P(q \wedge c).$$

From the definition, $P(p \wedge q \wedge c) = P(p \wedge q|c)P(c)$; similarly, $P(q \wedge c) = P(q|c)P(c)$. Substituting and cancelling, we get the result. $\qquad \square$

Theorem 8 (Symmetry of independence) *If p is independent from q, then q is independent from p.*

Proof. Assume $P(p) = P(p|q)$. By the definition of conditional probability

$$P(p) = P(p \wedge q)/P(q), \quad \text{so} \quad P(q) = P(q \wedge p)/P(p) = P(q|p). \qquad \square$$

Theorem 9 (Multiplication). *If p and q are independent, $P(p \wedge q) = P(p) \times P(q)$.*

Proof. By definition of independence, $P(p) = P(p|q)$; by definition of conditional probability, $P(p) = P(p \wedge q)/P(q)$; by rearrangement, and the condition on independence that $P(q) > 0$, the result follows. $\qquad \square$

This is the usual multiplication rule for independent events. We can use this rule when we consider successive independent trials, say of tossing a fair die. The event of tossing **6** on the first throw is independent of tossing **odd** on the second throw; so the probability of the conjunctive event is the product of the individual probabilities, namely $1/6 \times 1/2 = 1/12$. Using the notion of screening off, we can prove an analogous multiplication theorem for conditionally independent outcomes:

Theorem 10 (Conditional multiplication). *If s screens off p from q, then $P(p \wedge q|s) = P(p|s) \times P(q|s)$.*

Proof. By theorem 7, $P(q|p \wedge s) = P(p \wedge q|s)/P(p|s)$. If s screens off p from q, $P(q|p \wedge s) = P(q|s)$. It follows that $P(p \wedge q|s)/P(p|s) = P(q|s)$, and by rearrangement we obtain the theorem. □

We can use the multiplication theorem to prove a very interesting result:

Theorem 11 (Probability 0 is not impossibility). *Some logically possible outcomes must be assigned zero probability.*

Proof. Consider an infinite sequence of independent tosses of a fair coin. The event of the ith toss landing tails is denoted t_i; the outcome of the first n tosses being tails is $\bigwedge_{i=1}^{n} t_i$. Since the trials are independent,

$$P\left(\bigwedge_{i=1}^{n} t_i\right) = \prod_{i=1}^{n} P(t_i) = 1/2^n.$$

If T is the event of all infinitely many tosses landing tails, i.e., $T = \bigwedge_{i=1}^{\infty} t_i$, then T has a probability, as it is an outcome in the σ-algebra over which P is defined. If $P(T) = \varepsilon > 0$, then some k is such that $1/2^k < \varepsilon$; therefore $P(\bigwedge_{i=1}^{k} t_i) < \varepsilon$. Since T entails $\bigwedge_{i=1}^{k} t_i$, there is a contradiction. So $P(T) = 0$.[7] Yet T is a logically (and metaphysically) possible outcome (it is a member of the σ-algebra of possible outcomes). So some possible events have probability zero. □

A quick corollary is that probability 1 is not necessity—the event $\neg T$ (i.e., at least one head occurs somewhere in the infinite sequence) from the previous theorem must have probability 1, but it could fail to come to pass, so isn't necessary.

In fact, it turns out that *every* infinite sequence of outcomes must be assigned probability zero, by the same reasoning. But suppose we guarantee that the coin will be tossed infinitely many times. It then turns out that, even though each of these sequences has probability zero, at least one of them must occur, so the 'disjunction' of all of them is equivalent to $\top$. This does not violate countable additivity, because there are *uncountably* many such sequences of outcomes, and it is a counterintuitive but true consequence of measure theory that the probability of the union of uncountably many outcomes doesn't depend on the probabilities assigned to the individual outcomes (we'll come back to this later, pp. 15–9, when we discuss probability densities).[8]

We now prove a very useful theorem involving conditional probability.

Theorem 12 (Total probability). *If $Q = \{q_1, ...\}$ is a partition, such that each for each i, $P(q_i) > 0$, then for any outcome p, $P(p) = \Sigma_i P(p|q_i)P(q_i)$.*

Proof. Since Q is a partition, $p \wedge q_i$ and $p \wedge q_j$ are mutually exclusive, for any distinct i, j. By logic, p is equivalent to $\bigvee_i (p \wedge q_i)$; by countable additivity, $P(\bigvee_i (p \wedge q_i)) = \Sigma_i P(p \wedge q_i)$. By the definition of conditional probability, noting that $P(q_i) > 0$, $P(p \wedge q_i) = P(p|q_i)P(q_i)$, and substitution gives us the result. □

The theorem of total probability is in practice extremely useful. What's the probability of going on a picnic tomorrow? Suppose the weather must either be sunny or rainy, and it can't be both. Then the probability of a **picnic** is the probability of **sun** multiplied by the probability of a **picnic** conditional on **sun**, plus the probability of **rain** multiplied by the probability of a **picnic** conditional on **rain**. The probabilities of **rain** and **sun** can be got from the weather; suppose $P(\textbf{sun}) = 0.4 = 1 - P(\textbf{rain})$. Suppose we will likely go on a picnic if it is sunny, but almost definitely not if it's raining: $P(\textbf{picnic}|\textbf{sun}) = 0.8$, but $P(\textbf{picnic}|\textbf{rain}) = 0.05$. Then the probability of a **picnic** is $0.4 \times 0.8 + 0.6 \times 0.05 = 0.32 + 0.03 = 0.35$.

The theorem of total probability can be understood intuitively as claiming that the probability of some outcome is like a 'weighted average': we see how probable the outcome is under various conditional assumptions, and weight those probabilities by how probable the assumptions are. In the case we just examined, going on a picnic was quite unlikely on the assumption that it was raining, but rain itself had a fairly high probability, so the overall probability of going on a picnic was significantly diminished.

Bayes' theorem

The most useful theorem involving conditional probability is important enough to warrant a section of its own:

Theorem 13 (Bayes' theorem). *Suppose $Q = \{q_1, \ldots\}$ is a partition, such that for each i, $P(q_i) > 0$. Then for any outcomes q_k and p*

$$P(q_k|p) = \frac{P(q_k)P(p|q_k)}{\sum_i P(q_i)P(p|q_i)}.$$

Proof. By the definition of conditional probability, $P(q_k|p) = P(q_k \wedge p)/P(p)$. By the definition of conditional probability again, the numerator (top line) of this fraction is equal to $P(q_k)P(p|q_k)$. By applying the theorem of total probability to the denominator (bottom line), we then get the result. □

One common way of understanding Bayes' theorem appeals to the notion of a complete family of rival *hypotheses* about some situation. These hypotheses are all the specific theories about what is true of some situation (maybe they are drawn from physics, or from a more restricted science). The set of hypotheses is a partition: one of them must turn out to be true, and each is inconsistent with the others because they are rivals. There are also other outcomes of interest, which will be the *evidence*. Theories, as accounts of the situation, make certain predictions about what evidence will come to pass. In many cases, these predictions will be probabilistic: so that each hypothesis h_i will give us a probability of some evidence e, given h_i (these are often called the *likelihoods* of the evidence on the hypotheses). Our antecedent views on how probable the hypotheses are, the *prior* probabilities of the hypotheses, can then be used, in conjunction with Bayes' theorem, to give probabilities for the various hypotheses conditional on the evidence (the *posterior* probabilities). And, in turn, many have thought that the posterior probability of a hypothesis, conditional on some evidence e that turns out to be actually observed, tells us which hypothesis is best supported by that evidence. (More on all this in Part III.)

A nice example of these ideas comes from medical tests. HIV is a dread virus, but a fairly rare one, and one that is relatively difficult to catch if one avoids obviously high risk behaviour. There are tests for HIV, but they are not perfect. There are both *false positives*, cases where the test comes back positive but the patient does not have HIV; and *false negatives*, cases where the test comes back negative but the patient does have HIV. HIV tests are pretty good; the false positive rate is about 1%, as is the false negative rate. So suppose a patient has an HIV test. How likely is it to come back positive? Let a be the outcome 'the patient has HIV', and let p be the outcome 'the test is positive'. The theorem of total probability tells us that $P(p) = P(p|a)P(a) + P(p|\neg a)P(\neg a)$. $P(p|a)$ is the known true positive rate, so we need to figure out $P(a)$. This is the *base rate*: how probable HIV is in general. In this case, we can identify $P(a)$ with the proportion of the population which has HIV. In southern Africa, the base rate for HIV in some countries in high-risk populations can be as much as 40%, but suppose our patient is a US college student, where the base rate is more like 1 in 200. Plugging in our values, we see that $P(p) \approx 0.99 \times 0.005 + 0.01 \times 0.995 \approx 0.0149$. Thus our patient has (knowing nothing more about them) about a 1.5% chance of a positive test.

Suppose the test does come back positive. Of considerable interest now is how probable it is that the patient has HIV, given that they have a positive test. We can use Bayes' theorem here. We know $P(p|a) = 0.99 = P(\neg p|\neg a)$, $P(a) = 0.005$. The relevant partition is $\{a, \neg a\}$. Plugging these results into Bayes' theorem, we see that $P(a|p) = 0.005 \times 0.99/0.005 \times 0.99 + 0.995 \times 0.01 \approx 0.33$. That is, even if the test is positive, our subject has only about a 33% chance of having HIV (again, knowing nothing more about them). This might seem counterintuitive; but it's really a product of the fact that the base rate is so low that more of the positive test results should be expected to be false positives than genuine cases. (Obviously, the more risky your behaviour, the higher the base rate for your group of the population will be, and the less likely it is to be swamped by the false positive rate.)

Another real example is the case of Sally Clark. Clark had two babies that died, and she was put on trial for murder, the thought perhaps being that while one dead baby was tragic, two was suspicious. The jury was required to evaluate whether, in light of the evidence, Clark was guilty. There were three hypotheses: that the babies were murdered m; that the babies died of natural causes n (most likely candidate was SIDS); and the catch all hypothesis $\neg(m \vee n)$; these obviously form a partition. The evidence e was the fact of two dead babies. Note that both hypotheses m and n entail the evidence, so the likelihoods are equal to 1. Plugging these values in to Bayes' theorem, we see that

$$p(m|e) = \frac{p(m)}{P(m) + P(n) + P(\neg(m \vee n))P(e|\neg(m \vee n))}.$$

The chance of the babies dying without either hypothesis being true (i.e., they were murdered by some outside party) is tiny; it is close enough to 0 to be negligible, and to render the last term of the denominator irrelevant.[9] So we obtain $P(m|e) \approx P(m)/(P(m) + P(n))$. Statistics seem to suggest that the base rate for double SIDS is about twice that of double murder, which means $P(m|e) \approx 1/3$. Thus it is not even more likely than not that Clark murdered her babies, let alone something a jury of reasonable people should believe. Yet Clark was convicted; the judge, lawyers and jury, noting how rare double SIDS was, neglected the fact that double murder is rare too—and that in this case it was known already that something rare must have occurred.

The failure of reasoning apparently shown by those involved in Sally Clark's case, as in the counterintuitive case of HIV testing, are examples of what is known as the *base rate fallacy*, where people neglect the base rate in favour of the likelihoods. This is another striking failure of probabilistic reasoning that was explored by Tversky and Kahneman. They asked subjects about a case quite similar to our HIV case: a very reliable test coming up against a low base rate (their case involved an eyewitness to a hit-and-run accident by a taxi). Most subjects formed their views about the hypothesis based solely on their judgements about the reliability of the test, and completely neglected the base rate, even though that made their judgements of probability wildly inaccurate.

Controversy over conditional probabilities

Logic tells us that if p and $p \rightarrow q$ ('if p then q') are true, then so must q be: p and $p \rightarrow q$ entail q, and the argument from those premises to that conclusion is *valid* (on every interpretation of the non-logical vocabulary in the premises, if the premises are true under that interpretation, the conclusion will be true too). The validity of this argument suggests that if we were to be certain of its premises, we could be certain of its conclusion. But sometimes we aren't certain of the premises; at best we can assign them some probability. So it interests us to know, given that the premises of a valid argument have some probability, how probable the conclusion of that argument is. Define the *uncertainty* of a proposition $U(p)$ as $1 - P(p)$. It turns out that, if $p_1, ..., p_n$ entail q, then $U(q) \leq \Sigma_{i=1}^{n} U(p_i)$. It is the province of *probability logic* to explore how tight this upper bound is—how often the uncertainty of the conclusion is close to the sum of the uncertainty of the premises—as well as other phenomena at the intersection between probability and logic.

But what is the probability of $p \rightarrow q$ in the argument we started with? One popular thought was that probabilities of conditionals are just the corresponding conditional probabilities. That is, for some conditional operator $\rightarrow$, $P(p|q) = P(q \rightarrow p)$. This proposal is attractive: after all, what is the probability that: I throw a six given that I throw an even number, if not the probability that: if I throw an even number, I get a six? And it fits well with what's become known as the *Ramsey test* for conditionals, the view that we evaluate a conditional $p \rightarrow q$ by adding, hypothetically, the antecedent p of the conditional to our beliefs, and seeing whether the consequent q holds under those augmented beliefs. But the conditional probability seems to involve much the same process, as it apparently tells us what the probability of q would be, given the truth of p.

Yet, for all this, the hypothesis that conditional probabilities are probabilities of conditionals is false. The argument, originally given by David Lewis and then considerably developed by others, is complicated. Here I will sketch part of his result, namely that the hypothesis cannot be true if $\rightarrow$ is the *material conditional $p \supset q$*. Recall that $p \supset q$ is equivalent to $\neg p \vee q$, so that $P(p \supset q) = P(\neg p) + (P(q) - P(\neg p \wedge q)) = P(\neg p) + P(p \wedge q)$ (by Theorem 2). So long as p doesn't have a trivial probability, it is easy to see that $P(q|p) = P(p \supset q)$ iff $P(p) = P(p \wedge q)$.[10] But since the hypothesis is supposed to be general, it applies to any pair of outcomes whatever; and it is just false that any pair of outcomes p, q are such that $P(p) = P(p \wedge q)$. Of course, a defender of the hypothesis could appeal to an alternative conditional, but, quite apart from the plausibility or otherwise of $p \supset q$ as an account of the indicative conditional, the results turn out not much differently for other conditionals. So there is no understanding of conditional probability by appealing to conditionals.

Others have sought to challenge Kolmogorov's claim that conditional probabilities are defined by the ratio analysis. While they agree that in many cases the ratio analysis gives the right account, they propose that in many other cases it goes awry. This is

particularly true of cases where $P(c) = 0$, but where $P(p|c)$ is nevertheless well-defined for
at least some outcomes p. The most comprehensive argument of this sort was developed
by Alan Hájek. His argument has two parts. First, he argues that almost every probability
function has many 'trouble spots'—cases where the unconditional probability of some
outcome is zero, or vague, or undefined, or otherwise problematic. The result we proved
in Theorem 11 supports part of the argument here, as it can be extended to show
that any infinite sequence of coin flips whatsoever must be assigned probability zero
(there are uncountably many such sequences, and at most countably many outcomes
can be assigned a non-zero probability). Then the second part of his argument kicks in,
where he argues that even in these trouble spots there are (intuitively) many well-defined
probabilities. Assuming that p is a probability zero event, Hájek (2003: 286) says:

> Indeed, here and throughout the paper, we hold this truth to be self-evident:
> the conditional probability of any (non-empty) proposition, given itself, is 1.
> I think that this is about as basic a fact about conditional probability as there
> can be, and I would consider giving it up to be a desperate last resort. Some
> others are comparably basic; in the case before us they include:
>
> $$P(\neg p|p) = 0,$$
> $$P(\top|p) = 1\ldots$$
>
> Less trivially, various conditional probability assignments based on judgments
> of independence are compelling—for instance:
>
> $$P(\text{this coin lands heads}|p) = 1/2.^{11}$$

If you agree with Hájek's intuitions, then you agree that the ratio analysis isn't the full
story about conditional probability. Kolmogorov actually recognised the problem posed
by intuitively well-defined conditional probabilities on probability-zero events, and he
gave a mathematically more sophisticated elaboration of his simple definition. Yet even
that revised definition fails for events that have vague or undefined probability; and yet
some outcomes still seem to have non-trivial probabilities conditional on such events.
If unconditional probability is basic, no other rival mathematical definition is even as
good as the ratio analysis (or its sophisticated descendant) at capturing our views about
conditional probability.

Hájek's response is to reject the idea that we have to give a definition of conditional
probability in terms of unconditional probabilities at all. He proposes that we could
take conditional probability to be the basic notion, and give axioms that characterise it
directly. If we need unconditional probabilities, we can define them:

$$P(p) =_{df} P(p|\top). \qquad \text{(Unconditional)}$$

In advocating this, Hájek returns to an older tradition, predating Kolmogorov, but
captured more recently as follows:

> every evaluation of probability, is conditional; not only on the mentality
> or psychology of the individual involved, at the time in question, but also,
> and especially, on the state of information in which he finds himself at that
> moment.
>
> (de Finetti, 1974: 134)

Probability distributions and random variables

An *elementary outcome* is one that is basic and not decomposable into further outcomes. In general the metaphysical problem of defining the class of absolutely elementary outcomes is quite difficult,[12] but there are many situations where the *relatively* elementary outcomes are easily discerned. These are the basic outcomes with respect to a given probabilistic process. So in the case of tossing a die, the elementary outcomes relative to that process will be the individual numbers landing uppermost. But of course a single such outcome includes many distinct outcomes that are more fundamental—for example, the outcome of **landing 1** includes the outcomes **landing 1 with 3 facing the thrower** and **landing 1 with 5 facing the thrower**, and many more besides.

Assume we have a process with a well-defined class of elementary outcomes relative to that process. Call the (countable) set of those outcomes $\Omega = \{\omega_1, \ldots\}$; as it includes all the elementary outcomes, $\bigvee_i \omega_i = \top$. The set of all subsets of Ω, call it $\mathcal{F}$, is a σ-algebra. If P is a probability function defined on $\mathcal{F}$, the triple $\langle \Omega, \mathcal{F}, P \rangle$ is an instance of what is known as a *probability space*.[13] If we define $\mathcal{P}(\omega) =_{df} P(\{\omega\})$ (i.e., the probability of a single elementary outcome), then it follows obviously (because Ω is a partition) that (i) $\mathcal{P}(\omega_i) \geq 0$, and (ii) $\Sigma_i \mathcal{P}(\omega_i) = 1$. Any function $\mathcal{P}$ which satisfies these two properties is known as a *probability distribution*. Every probability function on $\mathcal{F}$ generates a probability distribution over Ω, and vice versa. The special case where Ω is finite with n members such that $\mathcal{P}(\omega_i) = 1/n$ is called the *uniform distribution*; such distributions arise in many applications, and form the basis for the classical conception of probability (see Part IV).

Definition 7 (Random variable). A random variable is a function from the set of elementary outcomes to the set of real numbers.

Intuitively, a random variable corresponds to a physical quantity of unknown magnitude; the value it takes on each elementary outcome is the magnitude of the physical quantity if that outcome comes to pass. In the die rolling example, the random variable X such that $X(1) = 1$, $X(2) = 1$, $X(2) = 2$, etc., corresponds to the physical quantity 'number that lands uppermost', while the random variable that has the value 1 if either **1** or **2** occurs, and 0 otherwise, corresponds to the physical quantity 'a number less than three lands uppermost'. This latter random variable is an example of an *indicator* for a hypothesis; it is a variable which takes the value 1 if the hypothesis is true, and 0 otherwise.

Even if the actual value of a random variable X is unknown, there may nevertheless be values which are more probable than others. The *expectation* of a random variable is the average of the possible values on the elementary outcomes, weighted by how probable they are (note the role of the probability distribution):

Definition 8 (Expectation).

$$ex(X) =_{df} \sum_i X(\omega_i)\mathcal{P}(\omega_i).$$

Not every random variable has an expectation; if $\Omega = \mathbb{N}$, let $X(n) = 2^{n+1}$, and let $\mathcal{P}(n) = 1/2^n$. Then for each n, $X(n)\mathcal{P}(n) = 2$, and $\Sigma_{i \in \mathbb{N}} X(i)\mathcal{P}(i)$ is greater than any finite number, so has no well defined value. An obvious consequence of the definition of an expectation is that, if I_p is the indicator for p, $ex(I_p) = P(p)$.

Theorem 14 (Linearity). *If* $ex(X)$ *and* $ex(Y)$ *are defined, then* $ex(aX + bY) = a \cdot ex(X) + b \cdot ex(Y)$.

Proof.

$$ex(aX + bY) = \sum_i (aX(\omega_i) + bY(\omega_i))\mathcal{P}(\omega_i)$$

$$= \sum_i aX(\omega_i)\mathcal{P}(\omega_i) + \sum_i bY(\omega_i)\mathcal{P}(\omega_i)$$

$$= a\sum_i X(\omega_i)\mathcal{P}(\omega_i) + b\sum_i Y(\omega_i)\mathcal{P}(\omega_i) = a \cdot ex(X) + b \cdot ex(Y). \qquad \sqcup$$

If $p_1, \ldots, p_n$ are outcomes with the same probability ϵ, let I_{p_i} be the indicator random variable for p_i. The *success rate S* will be the number of outcomes that occur, so that $S = 1/n\Sigma_{i=1}^n I_{p_i}$. Then it follows that $ex(S) = \epsilon$, since, by linearity, $ex(1/n\Sigma_{i=1}^n I_{p_i}) = 1/n\ ex(\Sigma_{i=1}^n I_{p_i})$; by linearity again, the expectation of a sum is the sum of the expectations, so the latter quantity is equal to $1/n\Sigma_{i=1}^n ex(I_{p_i}) = 1/n\Sigma_{i=1}^n \epsilon = \epsilon$. Suppose that someone thinks some outcomes all have probability ϵ; this result shows that they should expect to think that ϵ proportion of the trials that might result in those outcomes will be successful. This has an obvious application to forecasting—forecasters announce each day what their probability for some type of outcome is, say $x\%$. Then all the days when they make this announcement are the relevant trials; they should expect that $x\%$ of those days are successes. To the extent that the actual success rate matches their expectation, the forecaster is said to be *well-calibrated*.

Let the notation $X = x$ represent the outcome of the random variable X taking on the value x. The expectation corresponds to the important statistical concept of the *mean* value of some physical quantity. The heuristic way of calculating the mean of some quantity in a population, where one adds all the individual values of the quantity and divides by population size, reduces to the definition of expectation where the probability of $X = x$ is the proportion of members of the population where it does take that value. (The *median* value of X will be defined as the value x such that $P(X \leq x) \geq 0.5$ and $P(X \geq x) \geq 0.5$.)

Theorem 15 (Chebyshev's inequality for expectation). *Where* $X \geq 0$ *and* $ex(X)$ *is defined,*

$$P(X \geq x) \leq \frac{ex(X)}{x}.$$

Proof. Let $\mathcal{X}_\geq = \{\omega : X(\omega) \geq x\}$. For every outcome in this set, $X(\omega)/x \geq 1$, so:

$$P(X \geq x) = \sum_{\omega \in \mathcal{X}_\geq} \mathcal{P}(\omega) \leq \sum_{\omega \in \mathcal{X}_\geq} \mathcal{P}(\omega)\frac{X(\omega)}{x}$$

$$= \frac{1}{x}\sum_{\omega \in \mathcal{X}_\geq} \mathcal{P}(\omega)X(\omega) \leq \frac{1}{x}\sum_{\omega \in \Omega} \mathcal{P}(\omega)X(\omega) = \frac{ex(X)}{x}. \qquad \square$$

With the expectation in hand, we can now define another important statistical concept:

Definition 9 (Variance). $var(X) = ex((X - ex(X))^2)$.

The variance is a measure of how much to expect some particular outcome value for X to differ in absolute terms from the expectation of X.

Theorem 16 (Chebyshev's inequality for variance). *If* $var(X) < \infty$, *then* $P(|X - ex(X)| \geq x) \leq var(X)/x^2$.

Proof. Let Y be the random variable $(X - ex(X))^2$. Obviously the outcome $|X - ex(X)| < x$ is the outcome $Y \geq x^2$. By Theorem 15,

$$P(|X - ex(X)| \geq x) = P(Y \geq x^2) \leq \frac{ex(Y)}{x^2} = \frac{var(X)}{x^2}. \qquad \square$$

We could go on now to define various other statistical concepts: covariance, correlation, etc. But I wish to turn instead to another treatment of the concept of independent trials. Suppose we have a finite space of outcomes $O = \{o_1, \ldots o_r\}$, with a probability distribution $\mathcal{P}(o_i) = \theta_i$. Let Ω_n be the set of all sequences of outcomes from O of length n, so that each $\omega \in \Omega = \langle p_1, \ldots, p_n \rangle, p_i \in O$. Define $P(\omega) = \Pi_{i=1}^n \mathcal{P}(o_i)$. It follows that $P(\omega)$ is a probability distribution over these sequences of outcomes, which generates a probability function P on the algebra generated by Ω. This space is the space of sequences of *independent identically distributed* (i.i.d) trials (independence comes from our invocation of Theorem 9 in defining the probability distribution). In the special case where O has only two members, these trials are called *Bernoulli* trials. The obvious model for a Bernoulli trial is a coin-tossing system, with two outcomes $O = \{H, T\}$, with probability distribution $\mathcal{P}(H) = \theta_H$, $\mathcal{P}(T) = \theta_T$.

Definition 10 (Binomial distribution). If random variable X takes integer values $0 \leq x \leq n$, and $P(X = x) = \binom{n}{x} p^x (1-p)^{(n-x)}$, the probability distribution $\mathcal{P}$ induced by P is called a *binomial distribution* with parameter p.

Repeated coin-tossing cases obviously give rise to binomial distributions, but so do many other cases. Let the indicator variable $I_i^{(j)}(\omega)$ be equal to 1 if $x_i = o_j$, and 0 otherwise. Let the random variable v_j on Ω represent the quantity, 'number of outcomes of type o_j that occur in the sequence of trials ω'; so $v_j(\omega) = \Sigma_{i=1}^n I_i^{(j)}(\omega)$.

Theorem 17 (v_j is binomially distributed). *The probability that* $v_j = k$ *is the number of ways of choosing k places out of n, times the probability of k occurrences of o_j in the sequence, times the probability of $n - k$ non-occurrences:*

$$P(v_j = k) = \binom{n}{k} (\theta_j)^k (1 - \theta_j)^{n-k}$$

Moreover, $ex(v_j) = n\theta_j$, *and* $var(v_j) = n\theta_j(1 - \theta_j)$.

Proof. See Sinai 1992: 18–21. $\qquad \square$

The actual achieved frequency of outcome o_j in a sequence of length n is v_j/n, while θ_j is the probability of outcome o_j. Can we say anything about the relationship between these two? It turns out we can:

Theorem 18 (Weak law of large numbers for i.i.d. trials). *For any* $\delta > 0$,

$$\lim_{n\to\infty} P\left(\bigvee_{1\le j\le r} |\tfrac{v_j}{n} - \theta_j| \ge \delta\right) = 0.$$

Proof. Any easy consequence of Chebyshev's inequality for variance:

$$P\left(|\tfrac{v_j}{n} - \theta_j| \ge \delta\right) = P(|v_j - n\theta_j| \ge \delta n)$$

$$= P(|v_j - ex(v_j)| \ge \delta n) \quad \text{(by Theorem 17)}$$

$$\le \frac{var(v_j)}{\delta^2 n^2} \quad \text{(by Theorem 16)}$$

$$= \frac{n\theta_j(1-\theta_j)}{\delta^2 n^2} \quad \text{(by Theorem 17)}$$

$$= \frac{\theta_j(1-\theta_j)}{\delta^2 n} \to 0 \text{ as } n \to \infty. \quad \text{(because } \theta_j, \delta \text{ are constants)}$$

Since the probability of each event for fixed j tends to 0, so does their disjunction. $\square$

The weak law of large numbers tells us that, as the number of trials in a sequence gets sufficiently large, the probability of there being a set difference between the observed frequency of an outcome and its probability gets arbitrarily small; for any number δ, the probability of the difference being greater than δ tends towards zero. The law does *not* provide any absolute guarantee that the observed frequency will converge to the real probability. There is a related but more difficult to prove theorem, the *strong* law of large numbers, which says that, with probability one, the limit of the frequency will be equal to the real probability:

Theorem 19 (Strong law of large numbers for i.i.d. trials). *For each outcome type* o_j, $1 \le j \le r$

$$P\left(\lim_{n\to\infty} \tfrac{v_j}{n} = \theta_j\right) = 1.$$

The strong law entails the weak law, but not vice versa. In both laws (bearing Theorem 11 in mind), the convergence is not necessary.

So far we have dealt only with countable sets of elementary outcomes. What if there are uncountably many outcomes in Ω? Examples abound here: any physical quantity which is real-valued and modeled by a random variable X will give rise to uncountably many events $X = x$. Assume that every elementary outcome $X = x$ has zero probability. There will be no probability distribution over the elementary outcomes that determines P (so P doesn't supervene on the probabilities assigned to the elementary outcomes). But we can define:

Definition 11 (Probability Density Function). If $\langle \Omega, \mathcal{A}, P \rangle$ is a probability space, with continuous random variable X, such that for any interval $[a, b]$, $P(a \leq X \leq b) = \int_a^b \mathcal{P}(x)dx$, we say X has probability density $\mathcal{P}$.

In many ways, though, probability densities are analogous to distributions. For example, random variables with probability densities have expectations and variances too: $ex(X) = \int_{-\infty}^{\infty} x\mathcal{P}(x)dx$, and $var(X) = \int_{-\infty}^{\infty} (x - ex(X))^2 \mathcal{P}(x)dx$.

Many interesting examples of probability density functions exist:

Uniform The *uniform density* on the interval $[a, b]$ is

$$\mathcal{P}(x) = \begin{cases} \frac{1}{b-a} & \text{if } x \in [a, b] \\ 0 & \text{otherwise} \end{cases}.$$

Normal (or Gaussian) The *normal density* is

$$\mathcal{P}(x) = \frac{1}{\sqrt{2\pi}} e^{-x^2/2}, \quad -\infty \leq x \leq \infty.$$

Exponential The *exponential density* is

$$\mathcal{P}(x) = \begin{cases} \lambda e^{-\lambda x} & x \geq 0 \\ 0 & x < 0. \end{cases}$$

The normal distribution, or bell curve, is particularly prominent, in part because it is particularly mathematically tractable (the expectation of a standard normally distributed random variable is 0, and its variance is 1), but largely because many natural distributions approximate it closely. The key result here is

Theorem 20 (Central Limit). *Suppose X_1, ..., X_n is a sequence of i.i.d. random variables each with finite expectation and variance (this models n repeated trials of some physical system). As $n \to \infty$, the sample average of these random variables convergences in distribution to the normal distribution, irrespective of the original distribution.*

Many natural quantities are i.i.d., and have finite variance—for example, large numbers of successive coin tosses—so the normal distribution models them well.

Alternatives to orthodox probability

Kolmogorov's approach has the advantage of mathematical tractability and power, making use as it does of the full resources of modern measure theory. It also suffices as a basis on which to develop all standard approaches to statistics, and captures a very large part of what we intuitively take to be characteristic of probability. Nevertheless there are commonplace views about probability that do not find a ready home in the Kolmogorov framework. Some of these have been developed into formal theories of probability that are alternative attempts to capture the pre-theoretical notion, that differ from Kolmogorov's approach to a greater or lesser extent. The approaches discussed on pages 13–4, which take conditional probability to be the fundamental notion, largely end up agreeing with the standard approach in assignments of unconditional probability, and propose just that there are some additional well-defined conditional probabilities. But some alternative approaches will add further axioms, dispute the ordinary laws of probability, or even challenge the range of probability functions. Here I'll just consider a couple of the more popular heretical views.

Many have found this thesis to be attractive:

Regularity $P(p) = 1$ iff p is (equivalent to) a tautology.

Regularity strengthens the normality axiom by saying that *only* tautologies should have probability 1. If a probability function violates Regularity, there are cases where possible outcomes are assigned zero probability; this can cause difficulties if (say) one of those outcomes comes to pass. By the ratio analysis, the probability of any hypothesis conditional on that outcome is undefined; we would have no guide at all as to which hypotheses were true on that assumption. This has struck many as problematic, and so they have wanted to uphold Regularity as a constraint on any reasonable probability function that we might adopt.

But what to say then about Theorem 11? The most popular diagnosis is that in those cases we have mistaken zero probability for *infinitesimal* probability. In non-standard analysis, an infinitesimal is a number greater than zero but smaller than any positive real number. Non-standard measure theory can be developed where there are non-standard numbers (in particular, infinitesimals) available to be the measure of an outcome as well as standard numbers, and we can develop probability theory as a branch of this theory, letting the range of the probability function include standard and non-standard infinitesimal numbers. If we do so, it has been thought (e.g., by Lewis, Chapter 27, p. 461) that we may be able to assign non-zero probability to any possible outcome. The proof of Theorem 11 breaks down just when we moved from saying that the probability of T couldn't be a standard number greater than zero to saying it must be zero; we neglected the possibility that the probability of T was a non-standard number. Infinitesimals aren't particularly well-behaved—there are *many* non-standard probability functions that approximate a given standard probability function, and we have no good way of getting a grip on any particular one of them, as they all differ merely infinitesimally from one another (Elga, 2004). Yet it may be thought a tolerable compromise to accept such unruly entities if doing so allows us to keep Regularity.

But infinitesimals in fact do not succeed in preserving Regularity in all cases. Many possible outcomes will *still* receive probability zero, as a recent argument by Tim Williamson shows. Consider an infinite sequence of outcomes of independent tosses of a fair coin, I. If the probability function is regular, I should receive some infinitesimal probability, i. If we now consider I^-, the infinite subsequence of I that includes all of I except the first toss, we should conclude that, as the coin is fair, the probability of I^- is twice i. But as the events of tossing I and I^- are structurally identical, and have the same measure, the probabilities of I and I^- are very plausibly the same. The only value of i, infinitesimal or otherwise, such that $2i = i$, is zero. So even here the possible event I must be assigned zero probability. Infinitesimals complicate the situation without resolving it, and the natural conclusion is that Regularity is false.

Another revision that has often been proposed is to liberalise the requirement that probabilities be single real numbers. For some propositions any perfectly precise probability might seem implausible, particularly when probability is used to represent firmness of opinion—take, for instance, my judgements of the probability that God exists, or that Labor will win the next Australian federal election. We may represent a vague probability as a set of precise probability functions, called the *representor*; a vague probability assigned to some outcome will be the set of the values assigned by functions in the representor. If the vague probability of p is about 0.5, then we can represent that by the set of all precise probability functions which assign a precise probability to p which is about 0.5.[14] The idea is that vagueness is something like ambivalence about the precise probabilities in question. If I judge nothing more than that p is more likely than not, then every probability function P_i such that $P_i(p) > P_i(\neg p)$ is consistent with what I judge, and should be included in the representor.

Should there by any further structure to the representor? It has been argued that, if the representor includes functions P_i and P_j, it should also include every *mixture* of P_i and P_j too.[15] A representor which includes the mixtures of any of its members is called *convex*. If the representor is convex, then for each proposition the possible precise probabilities it can have constitute an interval $[a, b]$ (for some a, b). In this case we can define the lower probability $P_*(p) = a$ and upper probability $P^*(p) = b$. If we impose the additional constraint that the lower probability of a disjunction $p \lor q$ is at least as great as the sum of the lower probabilities of each disjunct, minus the lower probability of their conjunction, lower probabilities are characterised by the Dempster-Shafer theory of belief functions.[16] This theory is a rival to standard probability theory, intended to capture the same kinds of phenomena about opinion and belief, but maintaining quite different principles to be true of those phenomena.

Further reading

There are many good textbooks on logic and set theory. Some I particularly like, for elementary logic, are Jeffrey (1991) and Barwise and Etchemendy (2002). Machover (1996) provides a rigorous overview of elementary set theory and logic with an emphasis on philosophical concerns, though for our purposes the exposition of set theory in Ch. 2 of Beall and van Fraassen (2003) is sufficient.

There are many textbooks on the mathematics of probability and statistics. The classic is Feller (1950), while an elegant modern introduction is Sinai (1992). Kolmogorov (1956) is his own account of the axiomatic approach. The basic elements of the theory of probability are also covered by a couple of philosophically informed texts: Hacking (2001: chs. 6–7) and Skyrms (2000: Ch. 6). A good account of the early history and development of probability theory can be found in Hacking (1975), while the modern history of the measure-theoretic approach is charted in von Plato (1994). Measure theory is covered by Halmos (1974); a good way of visualising the measure-theoretic approach to probability is the 'muddy Venn diagram' introduced by van Fraassen (1989: 161).

The conjunction fallacy is covered in Tversky and Kahneman (1983) (the quote comes from page 297); there they also discuss the lengths they went to in order to show that the problem didn't arise from confusing wording, or from carelessness on the part of the subjects. Some further discussion of possible mitigation of the fallacy is Hartmann and Meijs (forthcoming). The base rate fallacy is discussed by Tversky *et al.* (1982).

Bayes' theorem, despite its easy proof, is the foundation of so-called 'Bayesian' statistics and confirmation theory, covered in Part III of this book. The theorem was first brought to prominence by the Rev. Thomas Bayes (1764); a useful survey of alternative versions is Joyce (2008). The case of Sally Clark is discussed in Goldacre (2008: 254–6); the case of HIV is discussed in Fan *et al.* (2007: Ch. 8).

Probability logic is discussed in Adams (1998). The Ramsey test was proposed by Ramsey (1990). The Lewis triviality result against the hypothesis that conditional probabilities are probabilities of conditionals is in Lewis (1986), and later results that extend his are detailed in Eells and Skyrms (1994), particularly the papers by Hájek and Hall. Hájek (2003) contains his argument against the ratio analysis of conditional probability, and many references to the literature. He discusses Kolmogorov's elaboration of the ratio account in section 4.5. The most popular direct axiomatisation of conditional probability is in Popper (1959).

Textbooks of probability and statistics will also include discussion of probability distributions and random variables. An elementary discussion is Jeffrey (2004: Ch. 4). Some of the earliest work on probability, by Huygens, took the notion of expectation as basic, and defined probability in terms of it. The notion of calibration is discussed by van Fraassen (1983). The law of large numbers is one reason for thinking that probability and frequency are in some way connected; precisely how to understand this connection is a topic that will run through this book, particularly Parts V and VI. The central limit theorem is discussed by Feller (1945).

The term 'regularity' was introduced by Carnap (1962: 294); an argument that probabilistic coherence requires it was given by Shimony (1955). Non-standard measure theory is described in Bernstein and Wattenberg (1969). Elga (2004: 71) makes the point that principles we can reasonably adopt 'only very weakly constrain the probabilities [non-standard] functions assign to any individual outcome'. Williamson's argument against infinitesimal probabilities can be found in Williamson (2007). Vague probabilities as sets of precise probabilities are discussed in van Fraassen (1990) and Halpern (2005); the requirement of convexity is motivated in Levi (1980), and disputed by Jeffrey (1987) on the ground that independence judgements aren't closed under mixing. Imprecise probabilities are discussed more generally by Walley (1991), and belief functions are discussed by Kyburg (1987) and Shafer (1976).

Notes

1 *A Note on Notation.* The notation I've used in this primer is quite standard, but there are some common variations. For names of outcomes, I've used lower-case italic letters; these are also often written as upper-case letters. I've used $P(\cdot)$ to represent a probability function; one sometimes sees $p(\cdot)$ or $Pr(\cdot)$. In logic, occasionally one sees & for $\wedge$, and more frequently $\sim$ for $\neg$.

2 Algebras are sometimes called *fields.*

3 A collection is countable iff its members can be put into one-to-one correspondence with a (possibly improper) subset of the natural numbers—a countable set may be finite or of the same order of infinity as the natural numbers.

4 Sinai (1992: 5) maintains that 'only in the case of σ-algebras does an interesting theory arise'.

5 If you have ever used Venn diagrams to represent probability, you've used this measure-theoretic approach, where the diagram is basically a representation of the space of possible outcomes, regions of the diagram correspond to propositions, and the proportion of the diagram covered by a proposition corresponds to its probability.

   Another normed measure is *relative volume*; if we denote the volume of all liquid in the universe by V, we can re-express all volume measurements as proportions of V, ranging from 0 to 1. This is also additive: disjoint samples of liquid (with no common parts) have a volume which is the sum of their individual volumes. But while relative volume obeys the laws of probability, it is not a function from outcomes to numbers, so is not a probability function.

6 Suppose, on the other hand, that the probability of choosing n from $\{1, 2, 3, ...\}$ was $1/2^n$. Let p_i be the outcome, **choose number** i. Since $1/2 + 1/4 + 1/8 + ... = 1$, $\Sigma_i p_i = 1$, as required. So we can have a non-uniform assignment of probabilities.

7 You might wish to consider this alternative: $P(T) = \lim_{n \to \infty} P(\bigwedge_{i=1}^n t_i) = \lim_{n \to \infty} 1/2^n = 0$.

8 Note that the idea of a disjunction of uncountably many events is problematic; the set-theoretic notion of a union becomes the only safe approach to use in these types of case.

9 Even though the prior probability $P(\neg(m \vee n))$ is very high, since double SIDS and double murder are both very rare, the likelihood in this case is plausibly close enough to zero to render the product basically zero.

10 Assume $P(p) = P(p \wedge q)$; then $P(p \supset q) = 1$, as does $P(p \wedge q)/P(p)$. For the other direction, assume $P(p \supset q) = P(q|p)$. It follows that:

$$P(p \wedge q)/P(p) = P(\neg p) + P(p \wedge q)$$
$$P(p \wedge q)/P(p) = 1 - P(p) + P(p \wedge q)$$
$$(P(p \wedge q) - P(p))/P(p) = P(p \wedge q) - P(p).$$

Remembering that $P(p) \geq P(p \wedge q)$, either $P(p) = P(p \wedge q)$ or $P(p) > P(p \wedge q)$. Suppose the latter; then $P(p) = 1$, contrary to assumption in the main text. So $P(p) = P(p \wedge q)$.

11 I've altered his examples and notation slightly.

12 I think the most elegant proposal is to take entire *possible worlds* as elementary outcomes, but the philosophical perplexities of possible worlds hardly makes this proposal uncontroversial.

13 A probability space is a more general notion, since the algebra $\mathcal{F}$ needn't be the power set of Ω.

14 Here we neglect the possibility that it may be vague whether or not r is about 0.5.

15 P_m is a mixture of P_i and P_j iff there is some $0 \leq \alpha \leq 1$ such that for any outcome p, $P_m(p) = \alpha P_i(p) + (1 - \alpha)P_j(p)$.

16 i.e., $P_*(p \vee q) \geq P_*(p) + P_*(q) - P_*(p \wedge q)$. What is actually imposed is the generalisation of this claim to any finite disjunction $\bigvee_{i=1}^n p_i$, the principle known as *n-monotonicity*.

Bibliography

Adams, Ernest W. (1998), *A Primer of Probability Logic*. Stanford, CA: CSLI Publications.

Barwise, Jon and Etchemendy, John (2002), *Language, Proof and Logic*. Stanford, CA: CSLI Publications.

Bayes, Thomas (1764), 'An Essay toward Solving a Problem in the Doctrine of Chances'. *Philosophical Transactions of the Royal Society of London*, vol. 53: pp. 370–418.

Beall, JC and van Fraassen, Bas C. (2003), *Possibilities and Paradox*. Oxford: Oxford University Press.

Bernstein, Allen R. and Wattenberg, Frank (1969), 'Non-Standard Measure Theory'. In W. A. J. Luxemburg (ed.), *Applications of Model Theory to Algebra, Analysis, and Probability*, New York: Holt, Rinehart and Winston, pp. 171–185.

Carnap, Rudolf (1962), *Logical Foundations of Probability*. Chicago: University of Chicago Press, 2nd ed.

de Finetti, Bruno (1974), *Theory of Probability*. New York: Wiley.

Eells, Ellery and Skyrms, Brian (eds.) (1994), *Probability and Conditionals: Belief Revision and Rational Decision*. Cambridge: Cambridge University Press.

Elga, Adam (2004), 'Infinitesimal Chances and the Laws of Nature'. *Australasian Journal of Philosophy*, vol. 82: pp. 67–76.

Fan, Hung, Conner, Ross F. and Villarreal, Luis P. (2007), *AIDS: Science and Society*. Boston: Jones & Bartlett.

Feller, William (1945), 'The Fundamental Limit Theorems in Probability'. *Bulletin of the American Mathematical Society*, vol. 51: pp. 800–832.

—— (1950), *An Introduction to Probability Theory and its Applications*. New York: Wiley.

Goldacre, Ben (2008), *Bad Science*. London: Fourth Estate.

Hacking, Ian (1975), *The Emergence of Probability*. Cambridge: Cambridge University Press.

—— (2001), *Introduction to Probability and Inductive Logic*. Cambridge: Cambridge University Press.

Hájek, Alan (2003), 'What Conditional Probability Could Not Be'. *Synthese*, vol. 137: pp. 273–323.

Halmos, Paul R. (1974), *Measure Theory*. New York: Springer.

Halpern, Joseph (2005), *Reasoning About Uncertainty*. Cambridge, MA: MIT Press.

Hartmann, Stephan and Meijs, Wouter (forthcoming), 'Walter the Banker: The Conjunction Fallacy Reconsidered'. *Synthese*, URL http://philsci-archive.pitt.edu/archive/00004696/.

Hertwig, Ralph and Gigerenzer, Gerd (1999), 'The 'Conjunction Fallacy' Revisited: How Intelligent Inferences Look like Reasoning Errors'. *Journal of Behavioral Decision Making*, vol. 12: pp. 275–305.

Jeffrey, Richard C. (1987), 'Indefinite Probability Judgment: A Reply to Levi'. *Philosophy of Science*, vol. 54: pp. 586–591.

—— (1991), *Formal Logic: Its Scope and Limits*. New York: McGraw-Hill.

—— (2004), *Subjective Probability (The Real Thing)*. Cambridge: Cambridge University Press.

Joyce, James M. (2008), 'Bayes' Theorem'. In Edward N. Zalta (ed.), *The Stanford Encyclopedia of Philosophy*, Fall 2008 ed., URL http://plato.stanford.edu/archives/fall2008/entries/bayes-theorem/.

Kolmogorov, A. N. (1956), *Foundations of the Theory of Probability*. New York: Chelsea, 2 ed.

Kyburg, Henry E. (1987), 'Bayesian and non-Bayesian evidence and updating'. *Artificial Intelligence*, vol. 31: pp. 271–293.

Levi, Isaac (1980), *The Enterprise of Knowledge*. Cambridge, MA: MIT Press.

Lewis, David (1986), 'Probabilities of Conditionals and Conditional Probabilities'. In *Philosophical Papers*, vol. 2, Oxford: Oxford University Press, pp. 133–152.

Machover, Moshé (1996), *Set Theory, Logic, and their Limitations*. Cambridge: Cambridge University Press.

Popper, Karl (1959), *The Logic of Scientific Discovery*. London: Hutchinson.

Ramsey, F. P. (1990), 'General Propositions and Causality'. In *Philosophical Papers*, Cambridge, UK: Cambridge University Press, pp. 145–163.

Shafer, Glenn (1976), *A Mathematical Theory of Evidence*. Princeton: Princeton University Press.

Shimony, Abner (1955), 'Coherence and the Axioms of Confirmation'. *Journal of Symbolic Logic*, vol. 20: pp. 1–28.

Sinai, Yakov G. (1992), *Probability Theory*. Berlin and Heidelberg: Springer-Verlag. Translated by D. Haughton.

Skyrms, Brian (2000), *Choice and Chance*. Belmont: Wadsworth, 4 ed.

Tversky, Amos and Kahneman, Daniel (1983), 'Extensional versus intuitive reasoning: The conjunction fallacy in probability judgment'. *Psychological Review*, vol. 90: pp. 293–315.

Tversky, Amos, Slovic, Paul and Kahneman, Daniel (1982), *Judgment Under Uncertainty*. Cambridge: Cambridge University Press.

van Fraassen, Bas C. (1983), 'Calibration: A Frequency justification for Personal Probability'. In R. S. Cohen and L. Laudan (eds.), *Physics, Philosophy and Psychoanalysis*, Dordrecht: D. Reidel, pp. 295–319.

—— (1989), *Laws and Symmetry*. Oxford: Oxford University Press.

—— (1990), 'Figures in a Probability Landscape'. In J. Michael Dunn and Anil Gupta (eds.), *Truth or Consequences*, Dordrecht: Kluwer, pp. 345–356.

von Plato, Jan (1994), *Creating Modern Probability*. Cambridge: Cambridge University Press.

Walley, P. (1991), *Statistical Reasoning with Imprecise Probabilities*. London: Chapman and Hall.

Williamson, Timothy (2007), 'How Probable is an Infinite Sequence of Heads?' *Analysis*, vol. 67.3: pp. 173–180.

Part I

DEGREES OF BELIEF

1

INTRODUCTION

Partial belief

It is a truism that belief guides and explains action. If you want to eat a biscuit, then how you act so as to obtain that goal depends on what you believe is the best way to get a biscuit: baking one, perhaps. This simple kind of story about belief-desire psychology is good, so far as it goes. But it doesn't go far, as can be seen in a case where one believes that there is a possibility that acting in a certain way will not achieve the end in question. Since baking might not end up in eating a biscuit (you might burn it), and there is an alternative course of action (waiting for someone to give you one as a present) that might also end up with you eating a biscuit, there seems no *decisive* reason for acting one way rather than another: either act might succeed, and either might fail. Yet, all the same, we do explain people's actions even in such cases, and we do choose effectively and with good reason between these different courses of action.

The simplest explanation is that one's belief in the efficacy of a given action needn't be all or nothing. One should be guided not just by whether an action might lead to the desired outcome, but also by how *confident* one is that it will lead to that outcome. We can understand this notion of confidence by introducing the notion of *degree of belief*, or *credence*. This makes belief into a graded phenomenon, involving a range of attitudes to claims believed that represent how confident one is in the claim. These attitudes are partly captured in such English locutions as 'I am fairly confident that *p*', or 'I think *p* is more likely than not', or 'I'm (almost) certain that *p*'. The intelligibility of these locutions, and the fact that they are clearly not synonymous, supports the existence of such propositional attitudes as the various degrees of belief. While we introduced the idea by looking at beliefs about which actions will lead to certain outcomes, once we have it at our disposal we see it is fully general and applies to any belief, whatever the subject matter.

Some will say we can do without the notion of degree of belief. Kyburg in Chapter 3 argues that partial beliefs are a 'snare and a delusion' (p. 72), though he offers here no positive alternative theory. Among philosophers who do offer a positive account, a common suggestion is that partial confidence that *p* is really just full belief that *p* has a certain probability. But it is fairly easy to see this reduction won't succeed. For one thing, even people not in possession of the concept of probability, like small children, still seem to have more confidence in some opinions than others. Even if you have the concept of probability, you may have opinions about it that differ from your degrees of belief. For example, you might have middling confidence that Aboriginal people reached Australia 60,000 years ago, yet as that hypothesis about the past is already either true or false, you might also think the probability is either 1 or 0 that they did. A more contentious example concerns the future: some people believe that the past determines the future, so that (given the past) the only future probabilities are trivial: 0 or 1. Supposing you were one of these people, you might still be no more confident than not that it will rain tomorrow, even though you fully believe the probability that it will rain tomorrow is either 1 or 0. This reduction of degree of belief to full belief thus does not distinguish being certain that matters are objectively undecided from being uncertain about objectively decided matters.

The opposite reduction, of full belief to degree of belief is also controversial. Some have said that full belief is maximal degree of belief. This entails that I am equally confident in everything I fully believe, which doesn't seem right: I fully believe both that 'It is October' and '$1 + 1 = 2$', but I remain more confident in the latter than in the former. So most people wish to say that full belief in p involves having a degree of belief more than t in p, for some threshold t. Quite apart from the fact it is difficult to see what could dictate any particular choice of t, this proposal runs into problems with conjunction. It seems that if you fully believe p and fully believe q, then (assuming you draw the inference) you may fully believe $p \wedge q$. But suppose p and q are independent, and that your degree of belief in each of them is right on the threshold. It seems plausible that the degree of belief in their conjunction should fall below t. So even if you draw the inference, you don't fully believe the conjunction.

A final proposal is that one fully believes those propositions it is epistemically optimal to assert. This proposal involves more than just degrees of belief, as it also involves making use of decision theory to allow degrees of belief to bear on the evaluation of optimal courses of action. The proposal is subject to apparent difficulties: its use of decision theory seems to presuppose that belief might be a matter of voluntary decision, and it supposes an overly close connection between knowledge and actual assertions. In light of these troubled proposals, the best suggestion may be to take full belief and degree of belief both to be real, and to have each a distinctive role to play in epistemology.[1]

Bets and beliefs: measuring degrees of belief

The previous section shows why we need the notion of degree of belief. But we are still ignorant of what properties degrees of belief have and how to tell what our degrees of belief are. Introspection of how strongly we feel about a belief doesn't help; as Ramsey points out in Chapter 2, 'no one feels strongly about the things he takes for granted' (p. 54). So we need a good way to measure—or better yet, define—credences.

Ramsey attempts to do just that. Noting the connection between belief and potential action (p. 56), Ramsey makes the point that in the specific action of *betting* we get fairly good access to a person's credences. Not perfect: because the same amount of money matters different amounts to different people (more to a poor person than a rich one), the bettors on either side of the bet may have distorted opinions about the real value of the bet. For that reason, Ramsey proposes to use what he calls 'goods', the ultimate objects of our desire, which are ordered by how much we desire to have them. This induces an ordering of *utility* on these goods. It may be that utility more or less tracks money in the case of those goods we can purchase for sufficiently little, but utility is the fundamental notion. Betting distorts our true opinions in another way too, as some people are attracted to gambling for its own sake and so are readier to bet than others—perhaps ready enough to take a bet for worse odds than they would really regard as fair. Still, if the money values are sufficiently trifling, we can (as Ramsey hints but does not show) demonstrate that, using bets,

1   Credences can be assigned numerical values;
2   On pain of a certain kind of inconsistency, those values should conform to the probability calculus.

We will show the first claim in this section, leaving the second for the following one.

A *bet* involves two parties, A and B, over an outcome p. A wagers S_A *on* p being true; B wagers S_B *against* p being true (or on $\neg p$). The *stake* $S = S_A + S_B$. If p turns out true, A wins the stake (i.e., they take home their own and the other bettor's wagers); otherwise B does. The loser takes home nothing. The *odds* against p are written $S_Y : S_X$. The payoffs can be anything, but let's assume now they are small monetary amounts. If A bets S_A on p, her *betting rate* on p is $B(p) = S_A / S$.

Definition 12 (Fair bet). A bet on p with stake $S = S_1 + S_2$ is *fair* for A iff A is *indifferent* between the two options of

(i)   Betting on p with wager S_1; or
(ii) Betting against p with wager S_2.

The idea here is that, given a pre-established bet, A thinks the bet is fair if (when forced to choose) she doesn't care which side of the bet she ends up on. In other words, it is a bet where her betting rates for and against p are such that she wouldn't *prefer* either side of the bet at those rates. A fair bet is *not* one we would be keen to take: in betting we usually wish to win, and hence to bet at *unfair* rates—unfair in our favour! So here we measure our dispositions to bet, not bets we actually would take. Supposing that small quantities of money have value that tracks utility perfectly, it is easy to see that if b is a fair bet, then the bet b' which involves multiplying the stake by a constant n will also be fair, so all fair bets give rise to the same betting rates. The notion of *preferring* that enters into the definition of a fair bet is one Ramsey discusses extensively. He sets down axioms (pp. 59–60) that are supposed to govern preference between any options at all; in section 1.5 we will return to them. In the case of bets, preferences are simple: you prefer winning money to losing it, and if the stakes are small enough, the more the better.

Ramsey's key insight concerning bets is this: an agent

> will take a bet at any better odds than those corresponding to his state of belief; in fact his state of belief is measured by the odds he will just take. (p. 58)[2]

That is, the bets an agent takes to be fair are those that measure their degrees of belief, so that A's credence $C_A(p)$ is measured reliably by A's betting rate in any fair bet on p (with low enough stakes).[3]

Ramsey says we can measure the degree of belief directly in terms of our expectations for these bets. Let **Pay** be a random variable that takes on the values of the possible payoffs from the bet b (i.e., takes value S if p and 0 otherwise). A's subjective

29

expectation for **Pay**, $ex_A(\textbf{Pay})$, will represent her betting rates, since a fair bet on p for A is one where she would wager exactly her expectation for the payoff. Therefore one's subjective expectation is one's betting rate multiplied by the stake. The definition of expectation in the Primer (Definition 8) would show that subjective expectations are expectations *if* we can show that betting rates are probabilities. Having assigned numbers to partial beliefs, to this next task we now turn.

The Dutch book argument

We wish to show that, on pain of a certain type of inconsistency, we should have credences which are probabilities. Obviously, fully believing p and $\neg p$ is inconsistent, but having degrees of belief where $C(p) \neq 1 - C(p)$ doesn't necessarily give rise to that kind of inconsistency. Ramsey says that a set of credences that violate the laws of probability

> would be inconsistent in the sense that it violated the laws of preference between options ... If anyone's mental condition violated these laws, his choice would depend on the precise form in which the options were offered him, which would be absurd. He could have a book made against him by a cunning better and would then stand to lose in any event. (p. 61)

A *Dutch book* is a set of bets such that, if the agent takes them all, they are guaranteed a sure loss. While it is difficult to give a general account of rational action, any agent who thought it was subjectively fair (fair 'by their own lights') to accept such a book of bets would thereby accept a sure loss, and be irrational. What Ramsey gestures to in this passage is that an agent who assigned credences to outcomes in a way that violates the laws of probability would be susceptible to a Dutch book and hence irrational—the so-called *Dutch book theorem*:

Theorem 21 (Dutch book). *If an agent has credences which are not probabilities ('incoherent' credences), then there is a book of bets the agent judges to be subjectively fair, but which (if all taken) would lead to a guaranteed sure loss.*

Proof. The proof consists in showing that, for each axiom of probability, an agent who had credences which violated that axiom would regard a sure loss as fair.

Normality If $C_A(\top) = \alpha/\beta < 1$, then A is indifferent between: (i) betting α on $\top$ to win β; and (ii) betting $\beta - \alpha$ against $\top$ to win β. If $\alpha < \beta$, A would think it fair to pay a positive amount $\beta - \alpha$ for a bet that is guaranteed to lose, thus ensuring a loss of $\beta - \alpha$ no matter what. If $\beta < \alpha$, A would think it fair to pay α for a bet which is guaranteed to pay β, ensuring a profit of $\beta - \alpha$, which is negative. Either way, A is open to exploitation which A will subjectively regard as fair.

Non-negativity Suppose $C_A(p) = \alpha/\beta < 0$. Then either (but not both) α or β is negative. If the former, A will think it fair to wager $\beta - \alpha$ against p for a possible payoff of β; since $\beta - \alpha > \beta$, A is guaranteed a loss. If β is negative, A will think it fair to wager α for a payoff of β; but since $\alpha > \beta$, A will again be guaranteed a loss.

swoop addresses them all. While we're at it, the same theory also undergirds our best account of rational decision-making. These very successes, in turn, provide us with an argument for probabilism: our best theory of rational credences says that they obey the probability calculus, and that is a reason to think that they do.

Their argument is basically that believing in degrees of belief does have philosophical benefits, particularly if they are probabilities. And the recent upwelling of 'non-pragmatic' justifications of coherent credences—arguments that degrees of belief must be probabilities for distinctively epistemic reasons—supports this view by directly showing the epistemic usefulness of degrees of belief. So Joyce (Chapter 4, and the section on epistemic theories of credence below) argues that if your degrees of belief are probabilities, you are best placed to track the truth values of various outcomes you are interested in, where tracking truth values is seen to be a task of fundamental epistemic interest. Or perhaps degrees of belief should track frequencies, or chances (see Parts V and VI). In any case, there are putative norms that directly involve degrees of belief in crucial epistemic tasks without reducing them to anything like betting behaviour.

A final line of worry implicit in some of what Kyburg argues is that, as the psychological results show, human agents do not obey the probability calculus. It is not an empirically successful theory of human reasoning or action to suppose that our partial beliefs are probabilities. The results of Tversky and Kahneman discussed in the Primer show this quite well. It may be thought that if the normative theory is so distant from what actually happens, we should question whether it is achievable for creatures like us to have coherent credences, and thus whether it can really reflect a genuine obligation. Yet, for all that, the responses of the subjects in Tversky and Kahneman's studies do suggest that people think they have made a mistake; and that they do take probability to be an ideal to which they should aspire; and that, in many circumstances, they can in fact avoid the probabilistic fallacies of heuristic reasoning.

Representation theorems

Ramsey, while he hinted at the Dutch book theorem, actually proved something more general. This more general claim doesn't just concern people's rational attitudes to small bets, but their rational attitudes to potential actions in general. Ramsey considers an agent's *preferences* among options that are offered to them, and argues that we can measure the agent's credence in p by use of very special options. If an agent's credences were not probabilities, this would manifest in irrational preferences:

> Any definite set of degrees of belief which broke [the laws of probability] would be inconsistent in the sense that it violated the laws of preference between options, such as that preferability is a transitive asymmetrical relation, and that if α is preferable to β, β for certain cannot be preferable to α if p, β if not-p. (p. 61)

The *representation theorem* Ramsey proves is that if an agent's preferences are rational in his sense, then that agent can be represented as having rational degrees of belief, as follows. Suppose that the agent evaluates various outcomes by assigning some numbers, the values, to those outcomes. This will yield a value function, which is a random variable (pp. 15–9) on the space of outcomes. Ramsey shows that if an agent has a rational preference ranking on all outcomes, then there exists a probability function P such that ranking the outcomes in descending order of the expectations of the values of those outcomes (according to P) produces the same ranking as the agent's preferences. The agent thus can be *represented* as if the probability function P represented their beliefs, and the values represented the agent's desires, and the agent preferred to all others those outcomes which maximised their subjective expected Value. All representation theorems have a similar form: to show that natural constraints on preferences result in agents acting just as if they had probabilistically coherent credences guiding those preferences (at least insofar as those preferences are revealed in behaviour).

Ramsey's representation theorem has various odd features; it requires as an axiom the existence of an 'ethically neutral' proposition (one the agent does not care about the truth of), and it requires preferences amongst a specific class of options which the agent is offered, rather than amongst ordinary acts the agent may perform. Later representation theorems (proved by, among others, Savage, Jeffrey, and Maher) liberalise these requirements, but still share the basic idea: agents whose preferences are reasonable can be represented as subjective expected value maximisers.

Ramsey himself thinks the representation theorems simply allow us to measure degrees of belief through an agent's revealed preferences, in a way more reliable than their observed betting behaviour (because it does not rely on controversial assumptions about the value an agent assigns to money). Interpreted this way, preference is explained by degrees of belief; incoherent degrees of belief will (or could) produce unreasonable preferences. The uses of degrees of belief will be much as they were described in the previous section, and though our degrees of belief might not reveal themselves directly in our preferences, they will do so well enough for us to have reasonable views about what our and others' degrees of belief are.

Some have argued for a stronger position: that the representation theorem shows an equivalence between talking about an agent's preferences, and talking about their subjective values and degrees of belief. These people might take preference to be conceptually fundamental, and attempt to identify degrees of a belief with a construction out of preferences. They might even take preference to be the fundamental psychological phenomenon, and degree of belief as merely a way of representing a psychological reality in which nothing actually corresponds to probabilities in the head. For both of these projects, significant difficulties arise.

Kyburg worries first of all that our preferences aren't at all well behaved: they 'may be partly unknown and partly incoherent'. No irrationality arises thereby—it will simply be that the agent is unable to discern in their behaviour a preference between some options, or may not have a preference at all.[6] But in attempting to convert this partial ordering of options into a simple order, violations of one or more of the principles of reasonable preference will occur. But this doesn't show that the *original* preferences were unreasonable: 'It is precisely in the attempt to make one's preferences conform to the theory ... that one stumbles upon violations of the theory' (p. 80). The theory must then be normative: it tells us that we should aspire to a simple ordering of preferences, among other things. It does not provide much guidance on how to get to such an ordering if we don't have it already; but suppose we construct one. Then we can apply the representation theorem. The representation theorem will then tell us that, to maximise our expected value, we should choose a certain option. But of course we already knew that, for it is the option we most prefer! Kyburg objects:

> [I]f we've got a coherent preference ranking, we don't have to make any computations. On the other hand, if we don't have a coherent preference ranking, the theory won't tell us *how* to make it coherent. (p. 81)

He concludes that degrees of belief are 'either philosophically vacuous or impotent'.

Kyburg's argument for this conclusion is problematic—simply observing that if we have coherent preferences we don't need credences is hardly an objection to those who think that coherent preference is precisely what licenses the introduction of credences (if so, we have them whether we need them or not). However, a similar conclusion can be reached by other means, since the representation theorems can be adapted to show how reasonable preferences can be modelled as maximising non-expected value, according to non-probabilities. If preference is primary, there is no unique role for coherent credences, as the same work could be done by another non-probabilistic construct. Moreover, there has even been doubt raised about requiring the preference relation to be transitive and asymmetric, with some philosophers arguing that, sometimes, cyclic preferences may be rational. If acyclicity turns out not to be a structural feature of rational preference, probabilism cannot be a constraint on all rational agents. Altogether this suggests that, if degree of belief has a role at all, it is a fundamental one.

Epistemic theories of credence

The Dutch book argument offers a *practical* reason to have probabilistic credences. Joyce (Chapter 4) suggests this is to blame for the relatively minor impact that probabilism has had on mainstream epistemology, because the role of belief in action is traditionally subsidiary to the role of belief in 'representing the world's state' (p. 90). Moreover, such prudential arguments always involve the agent's desires; any overall irrationality is thus hard to pin precisely on the incoherent credences alone. So a purely epistemic defence of probabilism would be desirable, one that made incoherent credences a purely epistemic failing. The idea would be to show that incoherent credences are necessary and sufficient for a violation of norms on belief (just as Dutch book arguments intend to show that incoherent credences are necessary and sufficient for a violation of norms on rational betting preferences).

The simplest idea would be to adapt the Dutch book or representation theorem-based arguments to the case of specifically epistemic utilities. These arguments already show that rational preferences amongst outcomes lead rational agents to adopt probabilistic credences, and if the utilities of those outcomes are epistemic, rational agents adopt probabilistic credences to avoid a surely unpreferred epistemic outcome. Yet it remains an open question whether there are any specially epistemic utilities. They would have to be values assigned to outcomes involving beliefs, and one might wonder if there is any value to a belief beyond its role in action, or if beliefs are under enough voluntary control to be subject to rational preference at all. Even if epistemic utilities do exist, it is not clear if there is a non-circular reason to think they have the features needed for Dutch book-style arguments to get started.

A better developed argument is that it is epistemically good to be *well-calibrated*. An agent is well-calibrated just in case, of all the propositions they assign credence p to, proportion p are true, and this holds for every p between 0 and 1 inclusive. Well-calibrated agents assign homogenous credences to a set of propositions in line with the proportion of those propositions which are true. (The idea was introduced in connection with weather forecasting, where a well-calibrated forecaster estimates a probability p for rain on a given day if on proportion p of similar days it does in fact rain.) It can be shown that if an agent's credences aren't probabilities, there is a better calibrated credence function which is a probability function (and for which there is no non-probability credence function that is better calibrated than it). Calibration, however, only goes so far: it evaluates credences only insofar as they fit to the frequencies of truths in a set of propositions, but is indifferent as to which of the propositions in the set are in fact true. The epistemic goal of accurate representation of the state of world is only partly satisfied by being well-calibrated.

In Chapter 4, Joyce offers a purely epistemic defence of probabilism, offering an argument that if credences are to meet the epistemic norm of accurately representing the world (a stronger norm than merely being well-calibrated), they should be probabilities. Accuracy of a set of credences is measured by how close those credences come to an ideal credence function, one which assigns credence 1 to any actually true proposition and credence 0 to every actual falsehood. Other things being equal, a set of credences that assigns higher (respectively, lower) credence to truths (respectively, falsehoods) will be closer to this ideal than a rival set of credences. Accuracy in this *gradational* sense is a norm for partial beliefs, since epistemic agents *should*, on pain of purely epistemic irrationality, prefer more accurate credences to less accurate ones.

The bulk of Joyce's paper is an argument for his 'main theorem' (p. 105—7) that *any* appropriate measure of gradational accuracy that fits the norm just sketched, which he explicates as involving satisfaction of his six axioms, has the property that, for every set of credences which isn't a probability function, there is a more accurate set of credences which is a probability function, no matter how things actually turn out to be (so there is a single probability function which would improve your satisfaction of the epistemic norms in every possible state of affairs if you were to move to it). Joyce concludes 'To the extent that one accepts the axioms, this shows that the demand for probabilistic consistency follows from the purely epistemic requirement to hold beliefs that accurately represent the world' (Joyce, 2004: 143).

Joyce's result, and the argument for probabilism he gives using it, have been the subject of much recent discussion. Some worry that the axioms he gives, while they are sufficient to show that the best-scoring credence functions are probabilities, are too strong: that there are other 'scoring rules' for credences which are equally plausible ways of evaluating the accuracy of a representation and yet are ruled out by Joyce's axioms. Others have questioned the norm of gradational accuracy, wondering whether the aim of belief is merely to be as close to the truth as possible. Yet Joyce's argument remains the state of the art for those who think the thesis that rational credences are probabilities can be argued for directly, and not merely via the fact that probabilism has been a fruitful theoretical posit.

What makes credences reasonable?

If the credences of a reasonable person must be probabilities, we should also ask: are there any other constraints they must satisfy? Constraints between credences at different times have already been mentioned in passing, and are the main topic of Part II.

As a preview: nearly everyone who thinks credences must be probabilities also thinks that an agent's new credences after receiving evidence e should be their old conditional credences on e, and hence that agents update by *conditionalising* on new evidence. But are there any more conditions that an agent's credences at a single time have to meet in order to count as reasonable?

Regularity, sometimes known as strict coherence, has been proposed as one such condition: never assign a non-trivial credence (0 or 1) to a non-trivial proposition (not a contradiction or a tautology). Lewis (Chapter 27, p. 461) notes that regularity requires a revision to orthodox probability; but, as discussed in the Primer, the revision he proposes (to infinitesimals) doesn't seem to do the job, and no other plausible candidate presents itself. So regularity doesn't seem an appropriate constraint.

Regularity would be an a priori constraint, like coherence. More interesting are constraints on your belief state provided by the content of other contingent beliefs you have. A trivial example may be provided by credences about credence: if the betting behaviour interpretation of credences is right, then perhaps the fact that you believe that your credence in p is 0.5 is enough to make you indifferent between bets for and against p with the same stakes, and hence sufficient to make you really have credence 0.5 in p. Even if the identification of credences with ideal betting rates fails, if we are introspectively reliable then our credences will have the values we believe them to have. This version of the principle ensures that we do know our credences, and this is problematic on any externalist epistemology. But everyone can agree that if you knew your credence in p to be x, your credence in p conditional on that knowledge should be x. Letting $C_{p,x}$ be the proposition 'my credence in p is x', we should all endorse: $C_A(p|C_{p,x}) = x$. Of course this is not a particularly useful principle: as a norm of rationality, it tells you what your credences should be, conditional on what they are. We could argue that anyone whose credences violated this principle would be irrational, as they would have differing fair prices for bets on their own credences when they are presented in different ways. But even this is debatable—if an agent were deferential to another epistemic authority, they may reasonably violate this principle because they adopt the norm that their credence should match the authority's credence, not their own.

This principle still concerns only 'internal' constraints on credences. Everyone agrees that if there are credences at all, there are such constraints, and almost everyone agrees that there are credences. This much is uncontroversial about subjective probability. A much more controversial position also goes by that name, and it is the target of most of the ire about degrees of belief in the literature—the position that there are no other constraints on rational belief beyond coherence (and these other internal constraints). This is the perspective defended by de Finetti, and is sometimes known as *Subjective Bayesianism*: any coherent assignment of credences is rational.[7]

This view obviously conflicts with some of our views about rationality. Someone who has coherent degrees of belief that assign probability 1 to being a brain in a vat might be rational in de Finetti's sense, but is hardly rational. To ameliorate this worry, many Bayesians follow Ramsey's lead, and say that any *initial* credences are rational iff coherent:[8] 'we do not regard it as belonging to formal logic to say what should be a man's expectation of drawing a white or a black ball from an urn; his *original* expectations may within the limits of consistency be any he likes' (p. 64, my emphasis). Some of these Bayesians will then appeal to so-called *convergence of opinion* theorems, which say that two agents with divergent coherent initial credences will, if they update by conditionalising on the same evidence (Part II), eventually converge on the same opinions about further evidence in almost all cases. There are also *convergence to the truth* theorems, which state that almost all coherent initial credences will, if updated suitably on the evidence, come to assign credence 1 to the true hypothesis describing that evidence and 0 to rival false hypotheses. Yet these results don't provide much reassurance: the convergence is not guaranteed to take place within any reasonable amount of time (the theorems hold in the limit of an infinite data stream), the agents may still disagree on theoretical propositions not directly given in the evidence, and (in the case of convergence of opinion) the agents can't have been too far apart to begin with—in particular, they must agree on which outcomes deserve zero credence.[9] And since the claims hold only in almost all cases, there will also exist pairs of agents who do not converge, and indeed there exist agents who get further from the truth as they update on evidence. So the usefulness of these elegant theorems is limited.

Reacting against these difficulties, we may impose further constraints on initial credences. In his urn case, Ramsey permits any coherent assignment of credences whatsoever. But this will include some highly opinionated assignments—that all the balls are black—and some will think it unreasonable to permit such opinions prior to receiving any evidence in their favour. *Objective Bayesians* permit only 'unopinionated' prior credences. In this case, they would say that only the view which assigns probability 0.5 to black, and probability 0.5 to white, is a reasonable prior opinion. Objective Bayesians end up adopting something like a 'principle of indifference', a view that symmetry considerations on the space of outcomes help determine reasonable assignments of credence. The usual kind of constraint is that initial credences should maximise *entropy*, which is a measure of the disorderliness of a probability distribution (the thought being that ordered distributions show a bias toward certain hypotheses at the expense of others with equal claim to truth). This kind of principle is also advocated by adherents to the logical conception of probability, and is discussed in Part IV of this book, particularly in connection with the many paradoxes to which the principle gives rise. To foreshadow: the main problem is that one needs to know with respect to what feature we should prefer symmetrical or entropic distributions, and any such feature will involve privileging some family of hypotheses over others. There is no such thing as a genuinely informationless initial credence.

Deference

Some agents are very confident that their own credences represent the best opinion to be had, but most of us recognise that on most subjects others are more expert than we are. If we recognise someone else as an expert, it seems that we should rationally defer to their opinion. If this is indeed rational, then the theory of rational credence should be able to accommodate the existence of experts.

There seem to be two kinds of potential experts: those who are expert in virtue of having evidence you lack, and those who are expert in virtue of being better at analysing the evidence. These may be known as 'database experts' and 'analyst experts', respectively (Hall, 2004), or as 'experts' and 'gurus' (Elga, 2007). The first systematic exploration of deference to experts, in Gaifman (1988), gave the following characterisation of a database expert: if Q is the probability function representing the credences of your chosen expert, then you defer to the expert on p just in case $P(p|\ulcorner Q(p) = x \urcorner) = x$.[10] That is, your credence in p conditional on your expert's credence in p being x, is also x.

If there is a partition of propositions $Q(p) = x_i$, ... that express the different credences your expert might have, then $P(p) = \Sigma_i\, x_i P(\ulcorner Q(p) = x_i \urcorner)$—your credence in p now is the weighted average of your expert's possible credences, weighted by how probable you think it is that the expert has the credence in question. In the special case where you know the expert's credence with certainty, then you defer to your expert just in case your credence just is theirs.

Sometimes—in fact, frequently—you will be in a better epistemic position than an expert (you may have relevant evidence they lack, for example, that trumps their opinion). In that case you wouldn't adopt their credences. But you might adopt the credences they would have, were they also in possession of that same evidence—if they are an analyst expert, they are better at forming credences on the basis of the same evidence than you are. In that case, you defer to the *conditional* credences of the expert, conditional on the evidence e in your possession: $P(p \mid \ulcorner Q(p|e) = x \urcorner) = x$. Again, the theorem of total probability (in conjunction with the theorem that conditional probabilities are probabilities) will show that your current credence in p ought to be the weighted average of your advisor's credences conditional on your current evidence.

Even deference to analyst experts will be rare. The kind of epistemic trust involved in adopting another's credences wholesale is not often rational. As Elga (2007: 483) puts it, 'not even a perfect advisor deserves absolute trust, since one should be less than certain of one's own ability to identify good advisors.' There is thus considerable interest in 'partial' deference: how and to what extent is it rational to defer to the opinions of less than perfect advisors? With respect to the question of how much to defer, there is little in general to be said about how to judge the domain-specific abilities of a wide variety of different epistemic agents who all have opinions on subject matters that interest you. But the question of how to defer, given a fixed assessment of an advisor's level of competence, has received more attention. In particular, the case of what to do with the opinions of persons who are roughly one's epistemic *peers* has received much attention, with views ranging from Elga (2007)'s view that one should (at least sometimes) adopt the equally weighted average of your old opinion and the opinion of your advisor, to the idea that you should favour your own opinion, or favour whichever opinion has been arrived at for the right reasons. This is an active area of research, having important bearing on the epistemic role of testimony among other central topics in epistemology.

So far I've discussed deference to those probability functions that are the current credences of potential expert advisors. But there are two other central kinds of deference:

1   Deference to expert probability functions which are not the credences of any expert at all, but rather are *objective probabilities*. We've encountered one example of such deference already, in the case of the extreme objective Bayesian who requires deference to an objective logical probability function (and this will be discussed further in Part IV). But there are other potential objective expert probabilities. The most prominent is the idea that rational agents should defer to the *chances*, as captured by Lewis's 'principal principle' (Chapter 27). The principal principle says that chance is a database expert; the so-called 'new principle' is the variant that results if chance is treated as an analyst expert. There is also the principle of 'direct inference', that one should defer to the observed *frequencies*. If frequencies are chances, as frequentists argue (Part V), this is just the principal principle. But if not, as the other views of chance discussed in Part VI maintain, then we have two

41

apparent experts, frequency and chance, and we need to come to a decision about how and whether to defer to them.

2   Other people may be experts, but so can you. For example, you might think that it is reasonable to defer to a more knowledgeable future version of yourself; this is the 'reflection' principle of van Fraassen (Chapter 8). To deal with problem cases, Elga (2007) offers the variant principle that one should treat one's future self as an analyst expert, not simply a database expert as the original version of reflection has it. Closely connected with reflection is the principle that connects an agent's present credences to that agent's future credences once they have learned new evidence, namely that one should adopt one's old conditional credence on the new evidence e as one's new credence. (In effect, when one learns new evidence e, one simply takes one's past self as an analyst expert and adopts one's past conditional credences in e as one's new unconditional credences.[11]) Both reflection and this second principle of updating by *conditionalisation* are discussed in Part II.

As can be seen by the flurry of references to other parts of this volume, the constraints placed on credences by various proposed expert functions is a central (if somewhat hidden) theme in the philosophy of probability. Taking the notion of credence as central provides an illuminating perspective on the remainder of the philosophical literature on probability theory.

Further reading

The notion of a degree of belief is discussed in Eriksson and Hájek (2007), where the authors argue that credences exist and should be taken as a primitive notion not standing in need of any reductive analysis. Understanding the way that degrees of belief mesh with desires (or the more general notion of utilities) to explain decision is the province of *decision theory*; good philosophical discussions of the field include Jeffrey (1983), Lewis (1981) and Joyce (1999). The conjunction problem for threshold views of belief is discussed in Kyburg (1970); the decision-theoretic account of belief is due to Kaplan (1996). Christensen (2004) argues that degrees of belief have many roles outside of preference. Williamson (2000) offers a subtle account of the connections between knowledge and credences.

de Finetti's account of subjective probability can be found in his 1964 contribution. It includes the first explicit presentation of the Dutch book argument, the Dutch book argument for conditional probability, as well as introducing the notion of exchangeability as a surrogate for objective probability. Dutch book arguments for primitive conditional probability are offered by Shimony (1955) and Kemeny (1955); a critical discussion of such arguments, and a defence of the claim that they involve the assumption of regularity, which is in severe tension with the philosophical rationale for primitive conditional probability, is Döring (2000). Dutch book arguments for countable additivity are given by Adams (1962) and Williamson (1999). Objections to it are raised by de Finetti (1964) and by Savage (1954). One of Kolmogorov's original reasons for requiring countable additivity was expediency, as it allows, for example, the full power of measure theory to be used in probability. But denying it also leads to what have been seen as bad consequences; for example, finitely additive probability permits failures of conglomerability.[12] Non-conglomerable credences, in a decision-theoretic context, turn out to permit an infinite Dutch book. Even coherent agents with only finitely additive subjective probabilities are thus sometimes bound to make a loss—the (somewhat involved) details can be found in Seidenfeld and Schervish (1983). However, as Arntzenius *et al.* (2004: §4) point out, even requiring countable additivity isn't sufficient for conglomerability and avoiding potential Dutch books. See also the discussion of the de Finetti lottery in Chapter 17.

A good discussion of the Dutch book argument is Hájek (2008b). The objection to assumption (A), using the package principle, is due to Schick (1986). The package principle is particularly problematic in the infinite books used in the justification of countable additivity (Arntzenius *et al.*, 2004). Ramsey's 'inconsistency of valuation' interpretation is also defended by Skyrms (1984). The problem of 'logical omniscience' for Bayesianism has been discussed extensively in the literature on confirmation, and will come up again in Part III; Hacking (1967) gives a purely epistemic argument for permitting agents to assign different probabilities to the same proposition when expressed differently, so long as the cost of discovering the equivalence of the two expressions is non-trivial. The 'converse Dutch book theorem' was proved independently by Lehman (1955) and Kemeny (1955). Earlier I mentioned that these proofs require certain non-trivial assumptions. One such assumption is exposed by McGee (1999: 262), who argues that even coherent agents whose utility function is unbounded might be subject to a certain kind of infinite Dutch book. The converse Dutch book theorem thus requires the imposition of a bounded utility function in addition to coherence. However, Arntzenius *et al.* (2004) argue that susceptibility to an infinite Dutch book of this sort is not necessarily a symptom of irrationality, so it may be, on their view, that coherence is sufficient for avoiding irrationality (though for them stronger conditions are needed to ensure that one avoids a sure loss). A more controversial case of coherent susceptibility to Dutch book arises in Sleeping Beauty-type cases, discussed extensively in Part II; Hitchcock (2004: 418) argues that the structure of that case allows a coherent agent to be Dutch booked (though with a diachronic, not synchronic, Dutch book—see sect. 5.3) unless they meet a certain symmetry requirement in their credences. Another theoretically interesting case where fair betting prices and credences diverge is described by Seidenfeld *et al.* (1990).

Other representation theorems are proved by Savage (1954), Jeffrey (1983) and Maher (1993). An argument that reasonable preferences represent non-probabilities is by Zynda (2000); a related argument is offered by Hájek (2008a). Horowitz (2006) tentatively defends the rationality of cyclic preference, and a decision theory which still allows for reasonable decisions with such preferences.

Epistemic utility theory is discussed by Greaves and Wallace (2006) and Percival (2002). Other kinds of 'de-pragmatised' Dutch book arguments are discussed in Maher (1997). The calibration argument is developed by van Fraassen (1983) and Shimony (1988) (see also van Fraassen's Chapter 8), and criticised by Joyce (Chapter 4), Seidenfeld (1985) and Hájek (2008a: §4). Some of Joyce's axioms are criticised in Maher (2002), who also worries about the norm of gradational accuracy. Further worries about the norm (concerning whether epistemic rationality has anything to do with wanting to believe the truth for its own sake), and the permissibility of different scoring rules, are posed by Gibbard (2008), even while Gibbard remains broadly sympathetic to Joyce's project. Hájek (2008a: §5) raises some potential difficulties for Joyce's argument. Joyce (2009) develops the argument further. A sophisticated recent defence of probabilism, broadly along Joyce's inaccuracy-minimising lines, is given by Leitgeb and Pettigrew (2010a; b).

Strict coherence is defended by a Dutch book argument in Shimony (1955). The first convergence of opinion theorems were proved by Savage (1954); other similar theorems are proved by Doob (1971) and Blackwell and Dubins (1962); convergence to the truth theorems are proved by Halmos (1974) and Gaifman and Snir (1982). The philosophical significance of these theorems is questioned by Glymour (Chapter 15) as well as by Earman (1992), Hájek and Hartmann (2010: §5), Hesse (1975) and Howson (2000: 208–12). Hawthorne (1994) offers an overview and partial defence of some of the results in the area. An accessible discussion is Strevens (2006: §9.2).

Objective Bayesianism is discussed further in Ch. 17; an overview is Williamson (2009); general criticisms of symmetry principles in probability assignments are raised by van Fraassen's chapter in Part IV (Chapter 18). The particular case of simplicity constraints on priors is critically discussed by Glymour, Ch. 15.

The general theory of expert functions (and what are known as 'higher-order probabilities' more generally) is developed by Gaifman (1988); see also van Fraassen (1989: 198). In addition to Elga (2007), the debate over how and whether to defer to disagreeing peers is discussed in Kelly (2005) and Christensen (2009), and in further references therein. The debate over the old and new principles will be discussed further in Part VI, Chapter 26; a useful guide in the present context is Hall (2004). Principles of direct inference are articulated by Hacking (1965). Conditionalisation and reflection are covered in Part II.

Notes

1 Another notion which doesn't seem to have an analysis in terms of degree of belief is *suspension of judgement* about p, which is not equivalent to having a middling confidence in p.

2 We might quibble: since a fair bet is one in which the agent sees no potential gain in either side, it may be that no agent would volunteer to engage in a fair bet, in which case it would be better to say that one's state of belief is measured by the odds one would just refuse.

3 There may be very few fair bets, because as they are defined here a fair bet has a single precise betting rate. It may be that agents who will refuse a bet will generally also refuse similar bets too. If this is insisted upon, we will end up saying that there are many bets an agent sees no potential gain in, and thus regards as fair; the agent will thus have many credences in a single outcome. A realistic account of these matters would not neglect this, but I will from now on.

4 The theorem establishes the existence of a set of bets such that, if they were all taken, the agent would be guaranteed a loss; we need an additional assumption that the agent would take the bets to ensure that they are in fact susceptible to the loss.

5 I owe this point to John Cusbert.

6 It is obvious that the lack of a preference at all between A and B will lead to problems in generating a total order, but Kyburg thinks that unknown preferences also pose a problem. This is presumably because unknown preferences are at best theoretical posits, like unknown degrees of belief, and this undermines the apparently closer connection to the empirical that representation theorems aim to provide in connecting degrees of belief with revealed preference.

7 A somewhat weaker view would restrict this to *initial* credences, credences we adopt as a starting point before updating our credences in line with new empirical evidence, or credences it would be rational to have in the absence of empirical information—see Parts II and VI.

8 Or, as Lewis suggests in Ch. 27, credences are rational iff they are coherent *and* satisfy regularity.

9 The 'almost all' phrase in these results indicates that these claims hold with probability one— and the probability function in question is usually a subjective credence! This shows just that the agents must have prior credential certainty in their convergence to the truth or to each other, a rather different claim than an objective guarantee of convergence that we might have expected to justify subjective Bayesianism. (It should also be pointed out that these theorems require countable additivity, a controversial assumption for subjective Bayesians, and particularly for de Finetti.)

10 The device $\ulcorner p \urcorner$ is used to show that p is a proposition about which you have credences, and that, in particular, x as it occurs in $\ulcorner Q(p) = x \urcorner$ is not a free variable.

11 There are differences between these formulations: conditionalisation is a diachronic (at different times) connection between old and new credences, whereas treating one's past self as an analyst expert is a synchronic (at the same time) constraint between your current credences and *what you now think* your past credences were.

12 Conglomerability is the condition that for each proposition p, if π_i form a partition, and for each π_i, $k_1 \leq P(p|\pi_i) \leq k_2$, then $k_1 \leq P(p) \leq k_2$—if the conditional probabilities in p over a partition are bounded, so is the unconditional probability.

Bibliography

Adams, Ernest (1962), 'On Rational Betting Systems'. *Archive für Mathematische Logik und Grundlagenforschung*, vol. 6: pp. 7–29, 112–28.

Arntzenius, Frank, Elga, Adam and Hawthorne, John (2004), 'Bayesianism, Infinite Decisions and Binding'. *Mind*, vol. 113: pp. 251–83.

Blackwell, David and Dubins, Lester (1962), 'Merging of Opinions with Increasing Information'. *Annals of Mathematical Statistics*, vol. 33: pp. 882–6.

Christensen, David (2004), *Putting Logic in its Place*. Oxford: Oxford University Press.

—— (2009), 'Disagreement as Evidence: The Epistemology of Controversy'. *Philosophy Compass*, vol. 4: pp. 756–67.

de Finetti, Bruno (1964), 'Foresight: Its Logical Laws, Its Subjective Sources'. In Henry E. Kyburg, Jr. and Howard E. Smokler (eds.), *Studies in Subjective Probability*, New York: Wiley, pp. 93–158.

Doob, J. L. (1971), 'What is a Martingale?' *American Mathematical Monthly*, vol. 78: pp. 451–62.

Döring, Frank (2000), 'Conditional Probability and Dutch Books'. *Philosophy of Science*, vol. 67: pp. 391–409.

Earman, John (1992), *Bayes or Bust?*. Cambridge, MA: MIT Press.

Elga, Adam (2007), 'Reflection and Disagreement'. *Noûs*, vol. 41: pp. 478–502.

Eriksson, Lina and Hájek, Alan (2007), 'What Are Degrees of Belief?' *Studia Logica*, vol. 86: pp. 183–213.

Gaifman, Haim (1988), 'A Theory of Higher Order Probabilities'. In Brian Skyrms and William Harper (eds.), *Causation, Chance and Credence*, vol. 1, Dordrecht: Kluwer, pp. 191–219.

Gaifman, Haim and Snir, Marc (1982), 'Probabilities Over Rich Languages, Testing and Randomness'. *Journal of Symbolic Logic*, vol. 47: pp. 495–548.

Gibbard, Allan (2008), 'Rational Credence and the Value of Truth'. *Oxford Studies in Epistemology*, vol. 2: pp. 143–64.

Greaves, Hilary and Wallace, David (2006), 'Justifying conditionalization: Conditionalization maximizes expected epistemic utility'. *Mind*, vol. 115: pp. 607–32.

Hacking, Ian (1965), *The Logic of Statistical Inference*. Cambridge: Cambridge University Press.

—— (1967), 'Slightly More Realistic Personal Probability'. *Philosophy of Science*, vol. 34: pp. 311–25.

Hájek, Alan (2008), 'Arguments for—or against—Probabilism?' *British Journal for the Philosophy of Science*, vol. 59: pp. 793–819.

Hájek, Alan (2008), 'Dutch Book Arguments'. In Paul Anand, Prasanta Pattanaik and Clemens Puppe (eds.), *Oxford Handbook of Rational and Social Choice*, Oxford: Oxford University Press.

Hájek, Alan and Hartmann, Stephan (2010), 'Bayesian Epistemology'. In Matthias Steup (ed.), *Blackwell Companion to Epistemology*, Oxford: Blackwell.

Hall, Ned (2004), 'Two Mistakes About Credence and Chance'. In Frank Jackson and Graham Priest (eds.), *Lewisian Themes*, Oxford: Oxford University Press, pp. 94–112.

Halmos, Paul R. (1974), *Measure Theory*. New York: Springer.

Hawthorne, James (1994), 'On the Nature of Bayesian Convergence'. *PSA: Proceedings of the Biennial Meeting of the Philosophy of Science Association*, vol. 1: pp. 241–9.

Hesse, Mary (1975), 'Bayesian Methods and the Initial Probability of Theories'. In G. Maxwell and R. Anderson (eds.), *Induction, Probability, and Confirmation*, vol. 6 of *Minnesota Studies in the Philosophy of Science*, Minneapolis: University of Minnesota Press, pp. 50–105.

Hitchcock, Christopher (2004), 'Beauty and the Bets'. *Synthese*, vol. 139: pp. 405–20.

Horowitz, Tamara (2006), 'Making Rational Choices when Preferences Cycle'. In *The Epistemology of A Priori Knowledge*, Oxford: Oxford University Press, pp. 103–22.

Howson, Colin (2000), *Hume's Problem: Induction and the Justification of Belief*. Oxford: Oxford University Press.

Jeffrey, Richard C. (1983), *The Logic of Decision*. Chicago: University of Chicago Press, 2 ed.

—— (1992), 'Probability and the Art of Judgment'. In *Probability and the Art of Judgment*, Cambridge: Cambridge University Press, pp. 44–76.

Joyce, James M. (1999), *The Foundations of Causal Decision Theory*. Cambridge: Cambridge University Press.

—— (2004), 'Bayesianism'. In A. R. Mele and P. Rawlings (eds.), *The Oxford Handbook of Rationality*, Oxford: Oxford University Press, pp. 132–55.

—— (2009), 'Accuracy and Coherence: Prospects for an Alethic Epistemology of Partial Belief'. In Franz Hüber and Christof Schmidt-Petri (eds.), *Degrees of Belief*, Berlin: Springer.

Kaplan, Mark (1996), *Decision Theory as Philosophy*. Cambridge: Cambridge University Press.

Kelly, Thomas (2005), 'The Epistemic Significance of Disagreement'. *Oxford Studies in Epistemology*, vol. 1: pp. 167–96.

Kemeny, J. (1955), 'Fair Bets and Inductive Probabilities'. *Journal of Symbolic Logic*, vol. 20: pp. 263–73.

Kripke, Saul (1980), *Naming and Necessity*. Cambridge, MA: Harvard University Press.

Kyburg, Jr., Henry E. (1970), 'Conjunctivitis'. In Marshall Swain (ed.), *Induction, Acceptance and Rational Belief*, Dordrecht: D. Reidel, pp. 55–82.

Lehman, R. Sherman (1955), 'On Confirmation and Rational Betting'. *Journal of Symbolic Logic*, vol. 20: pp. 251–62.

Leitgeb, Hannes and Pettigrew, Richard (2010a), 'An Objective Justification of Bayesianism I: Measuring Inaccuracy'. *Philosophy of Science*, vol. 77: pp. 201–35.

—— (2010b), 'An Objective Justification of Bayesianism II: The Consequences of Minimizing Inaccuracy'. *Philosophy of Science*, vol. 77: pp. 236–72.

Lewis, David (1981), 'Causal Decision Theory'. *Australasian Journal of Philosophy*, vol. 59: pp. 5–30.

McGee, Vann (1999), 'An Airtight Dutch Book'. *Analysis*, vol. 59: pp. 257–65.

Maher, Patrick (1993), *Betting on Theories*. Cambridge: Cambridge University Press.

—— (1997), 'Depragmatized Dutch book arguments'. *Philosophy of Science*, vol. 64: pp. 291–305.

—— (2002), 'Joyce's Argument for Probabilism'. *Philosophy of Science*, vol. 69: pp. 73–81.

Percival, Philip (2002), 'Epistemic Consequentialism'. *Proceedings of the Aristotelian Society, Supplementary Volume*, vol. 76: pp. 121–51.

Savage, Leonard J. (1954), *The Foundations of Statistics*. New York: Wiley.

Schick, Frederic (1986), 'Dutch Bookies and Money Pumps'. *Journal of Philosophy*, vol. 83: pp. 112–19.

Seidenfeld, Teddy (1985), 'Calibration, Coherence, and Scoring Rules'. *Philosophy of Science*, vol. 52: pp. 274–94.

Seidenfeld, Teddy and Schervish, Mark J. (1983), 'A Conflict between Finite Additivity and Avoiding Dutch Book'. *Philosophy of Science*, vol. 50: pp. 398–412.

Seidenfeld, T., Schervish, M. J. and Kadane, J. B. (1990), 'When Fair Betting Odds Are Not Degrees of Belief'. *PSA: Proceedings of the Biennial Meeting of the Philosophy of Science Association*, vol. 1: pp. 517–24.

Shimony, Abner (1955), 'Coherence and the Axioms of Confirmation'. *Journal of Symbolic Logic*, vol. 20: pp. 1–28.

—— (1988), 'An Adamite Derivation of the Calculus of Probability'. In J. H. Fetzer (ed.), *Probability and Causality*, Dordrecht: D. Reidel, pp. 151–61.

Skyrms, Brian (1984), *Pragmatics and Empiricism*. New Haven, CT: Yale University Press.

Strevens, Michael (2006), 'Notes on Bayesian Confirmation Theory', URL http://www.nyu.edu/classes/strevens/BCT/BCT.pdf. Unpublished manuscript.

van Fraassen, Bas C. (1983), 'Calibration: A Frequency Justification for Personal Probability'. In R. S. Cohen and L. Laudan (eds.), *Physics, Philosophy and Psychoanalysis*, Dordrecht: D. Reidel, pp. 295–319.

—— (1989), *Laws and Symmetry*. Oxford: Oxford University Press.

Williamson, Jon (1999), 'Countable Additivity and Subjective Probability'. *British Journal for the Philosophy of Science*, vol. 50: pp. 401–16.

—— (2009), 'Philosophies of Probability'. In Andrew D. Irvine (ed.), *Philosophy of Mathematics (Handbook of the Philosophy of Science)*, Amsterdam: North-Holland, pp. 493-533.

Williamson, Timothy (2000), *Knowledge and its Limits*. Oxford: Oxford University Press.

Zynda, Lyle (2000), 'Representation Theorems and Realism about Degrees of Belief'. *Philosophy of Science*, vol. 67: pp. 45–69.

2

TRUTH AND PROBABILITY*

F. P. Ramsey

To say of what is that it is not, or of what is not that it is, is false, while to say of what is that it is and of what is not that it is not is true.
—Aristotle

When several hypotheses are presented to our mind which we believe to be mutually exclusive and exhaustive, but about which we know nothing further, we distribute our belief equally among them. ... This being admitted as an account of the way in which we *actually do* distribute our belief in simple cases, the whole of the subsequent theory follows as a deduction of the way in which we must distribute it in complex cases *if we would be consistent.*
—W. F. Donkin

The object of reasoning is to find out, from the consideration of what we already know, something else which we do not know. Consequently, reasoning is good if it be such as to give a true conclusion from true premises, and not otherwise.
—C. S. Peirce

Truth can never be told so as to be understood, and not be believed.
—W. Blake

Foreword

In this essay the Theory of Probability is taken as a branch of logic, the logic of partial belief and inconclusive argument; but there is no intention of implying that this is the only or even the most important aspect of the subject. Probability is of fundamental importance not only in logic but also in statistical and physical science, and we cannot be sure beforehand that the most useful interpretation of it in logic will be appropriate in physics also. Indeed the general difference of opinion between statisticians who for the most part adopt the frequency theory of probability and logicians who mostly reject it renders it likely that the two schools are really discussing different things, and that the word 'probability' is used by logicians in one sense and by statisticians in another. The conclusions we shall come to as to the meaning of probability in logic must not, therefore, be taken as prejudging its meaning in physics.

The frequency theory

In the hope of avoiding some purely verbal controversies, I propose to begin by making some admissions in favour of the frequency theory. In the first place this theory must be conceded to have a firm basis in ordinary language, which often uses 'probability' practically as a synonym for proportion; for example, if we say that the probability of recovery from smallpox is three-quarters, we mean, I think, simply that that is the proportion of smallpox cases which recover. Secondly, if we start with what is called the calculus of probabilities, regarding it first as a branch of pure mathematics, and then looking round for some interpretation of the formulae which shall show that our axioms are consistent and our subject not entirely useless, then much the simplest and least controversial interpretation of the calculus is one in terms of frequencies. This is true not only of the ordinary mathematics of probability, but also of the symbolic calculus developed by Mr. Keynes; for if in his *a/h*, *a* and *h* are taken to be not propositions but propositional functions or class-concepts which define finite classes, and *a/h* is taken to mean the proportion of members of *h* which are also members of *a*, then all his propositions become arithmetical truisms.

Besides these two inevitable admissions, there is a third and more important one, which I am prepared to make temporarily although it does not express my real opinion. It is this. Suppose we start with the mathematical calculus, and ask, not as before what interpretation of it is most convenient to the pure mathematicism, but what interpretation gives results of greatest value to science in general, then it may be that the answer is again an interpretation in terms of frequency; that probability as it is used in statistical theories, especially in statistical mechanics—the kind of probability whose logarithm is the entropy—is really a ratio between the numbers of two classes, or the limit of such a ratio. I do not myself believe this, but I am willing for the present to concede to the frequency theory that probability as used in modern science is really the same as frequency.

But, supposing all this admitted, it still remains the case that we have the authority both of ordinary language and of many great thinkers for discussing under the heading of probability what appears to be quite a different subject, the logic of partial belief. It may be that as some supporters of the frequency theory have maintained, the logic of partial belief will be found in the end to be merely the study of frequencies, either because partial belief is definable as, or by reference to, some sort of frequency, or because it can only be the subject of logical treatment when it is grounded on experienced frequencies. Whether these contentions are valid can, however, only be decided as a result of our investigation into partial belief, so that I propose to ignore the frequency theory for the present and begin an inquiry into the logic of partial belief. In this, I think, it will be most convenient if, instead of straight away developing my own theory, I begin by examining the views of Mr. Keynes, which are so well known and in essentials so widely accepted that readers probably feel that there is no ground for re-opening the subject *de novo* until they have been disposed of.

Mr. Keynes' theory

Mr. Keynes[1] starts from the supposition that we make probable inferences for which we claim objective validity; we proceed from full belief in one proposition to partial belief in another, and we claim that this procedure is objectively right, so that if another man in similar circumstances entertained a different degree of belief, he would be wrong in doing so. Mr. Keynes accounts for this by supposing that between any two propositions, taken as premiss and conclusion, there holds one and only one relation of a certain sort called probability relations; and that if, in any given case, the relation is that of degree α, from full belief in the premiss, we should, if we were rational, proceed to a belief of degree α in the conclusion.

Before criticising this view, I may perhaps be allowed to point out an obvious and easily corrected defect in the statement of it. When it is said that the degree of the probability relation is the same as the degree of belief which it justifies, it seems to be presupposed that both probability relations, on the one hand, and degrees of belief on the other can be naturally expressed in terms of numbers, and then that the number expressing or measuring the probability relation is the same as that expressing the appropriate degree of belief. But if, as Mr. Keynes holds, these things are not always expressible by numbers, then we cannot give his statement that the degree of the one is the same as the degree of the other such a simple interpretation, but must suppose him to mean only that there is a one-one correspondence between probability relations and the degrees of belief which they justify. This correspondence must clearly preserve the relations of greater and less, and so make the manifold of probability relations and that of degrees of belief similar in Mr. Russell's sense. I think it is a pity that Mr. Keynes did not see this clearly, because the exactitude of this correspondence would have provided quite as worthy material for his scepticism as did the numerical measurement of probability relations. Indeed some of his arguments against their numerical measurement appear to apply quite equally well against their exact correspondence with degrees of belief; for instance, he argues that if rates of insurance correspond to subjective, i.e. actual, degrees of belief, these are not rationally determined, and we cannot infer that probability relations can be similarly measured. It might be argued that the true conclusion in such a case was not that, as Mr. Keynes thinks, to the non-numerical probability relation corresponds a non-numerical degree of rational belief, but that degrees of belief, which were always numerical, did not correspond one to one with the probability relations justifying them. For it is, I suppose, conceivable that degrees of belief could be measured by a psychogalvanometer or some such instrument, and Mr. Keynes would hardly wish it to follow that probability relations could all be derivatively measured with the measures of the beliefs which they justify.

But let us now return to a more fundamental criticism of Mr. Keynes' views, which is the obvious one that there really do not seem to be any such things as the probability relations he describes. He supposes that, at any rate in certain cases, they can be perceived; but speaking for myself I feel confident that this is not true. I do not perceive them, and if I am to be persuaded that they exist it must be by argument; moreover I shrewdly suspect that others do not perceive them either, because they are able to come to so very little agreement as to which of them relates any two given propositions. All we appear to know about them are certain general propositions, the laws of addition and multiplication; it is as if everyone knew the laws of geometry but no one could tell whether any given object were round or square; and I find it hard to imagine how so large a body of general knowledge can be combined with so slender a stock of particular facts. It is true that about some particular cases there is agreement, but these somehow paradoxically are always immensely complicated; we all agree that the probability of a coin coming down heads is 1/2, but we can none of us say exactly what is the evidence which forms the other term for the probability relation about which we are then judging. If, on the other hand, we take the simplest possible pairs of propositions such as 'This is red' and 'That is blue' or 'This is red' and 'That is red', whose logical relations should surely be easiest to see, no one, I think, pretends to be sure what is the probability relation which connects them. Or, perhaps, they may claim to see the relation but they will not be able to say anything about it with certainty, to state if it is more or less than 1/3, or so on. They may, of course, say that it is incomparable with any numerical relation, but a relation about which so little can be truly said will be of little scientific use and it will be hard to convince a sceptic of its existence. Besides this view is really rather paradoxical; for any believer in induction must admit that between 'This is red' as conclusion and 'This is round', together with a billion propositions of the form 'a is round and red' as evidence, there is a finite probability relation; and it is hard to suppose that as we accumulate instances there is suddenly a point, say after 233 instances, at which the probability relation becomes finite and so comparable with some numerical relations.

It seems to me that if we take the two propositions 'a is red', 'b is red', we cannot really discern more than four simple logical relations between them; namely identity of form, identity of predicate, diversity of subject, and logical independence of import. If anyone were to ask me what probability one gave to the other, I should not try to answer by contemplating the propositions and trying to discern a logical relation between them, I should, rather, try to imagine that one of them was all that I knew, and to guess what degree of confidence I should then have in the other. If I were able to do this, I might no doubt still not be content with it but might say 'This is what I should think, but, of course, I am only a fool' and proceed to consider what a wise man would think and call that the degree of probability. This kind of self-criticism I shall discuss later when developing my own theory; all that I want to remark here is that no one estimating a degree of probability simply contemplates the two propositions supposed to be related by it; he always considers *inter alia* his own actual or hypothetical degree of belief. This remark seems to me to be borne out by observation of my own behaviour; and to be the only way of accounting for the fact that we can all give estimates of probability in cases taken from actual life, but are quite unable to do so in the logically simplest cases in which, were probability a logical relation, it would be easiest to discern.

Another argument against Mr. Keynes' theory can, I think. be drawn from his inability to adhere to it consistently even in discussing first principles. There is a passage in his chapter on the measurement of probabilities which reads as follows:—

> Probability is, *vide* Chapter II (§12), relative in a sense to the principles of *human* reason. The degree of probability, which it is rational for *us* to entertain, does not presume perfect logical insight, and is relative in part to the secondary propositions which we in fact know; and it is not dependent upon whether more perfect logical insight is or is not conceivable. It is the degree of probability to which those logical processes lead, of which our minds are capable; or, in the language of Chapter II, which those secondary propositions justify, which we in fact know. If we do not take this view of probability, if we do not limit it in this way and make it, to this extent, relative to human powers, we are

altogether adrift in the unknown; for we cannot ever know what degree of probability would be justified by the perception of logical relations which we are, and must always be, incapable of comprehending.[2]

This passage seems to me quite unreconcilable with the view which Mr. Keynes adopts everywhere except in this and another similar passage. For he generally holds that the degree of belief which we are justified in placing in the conclusion of an argument is determined by what relation of probability unites that conclusion to our premisses. There is only one such relation and consequently only one relevant true secondary proposition, which, of course, we may or may not know, but which is necessarily independent of the human mind. If we do not know it, we do not know it and cannot tell how far we ought to believe the conclusion. But often, he supposes, we do know it; probability relations are not ones which we are incapable of comprehending. But on this view of the matter the passage quoted above has no meaning: the relations which justify probable beliefs are probability relations, and it is nonsense to speak of them being justified by logical relations which we are, and must always be, incapable of comprehending.

The significance of the passage for our present purpose lies in the fact that it seems to presuppose a different view of probability, in which indefinable probability relations play no part, but in which the degree of rational belief depends on a variety of logical relations. For instance, there might be between the premiss and conclusion the relation that the premiss was the logical product of a thousand instances of a generalization of which the conclusion was one other instance, and this relation, which is not an indefinable probability relation but definable in terms of ordinary logic and so easily recognizable, might justify a certain degree of belief in the conclusion on the part of one who believed the premiss. We should thus have a variety of ordinary logical relations justifying the same or different degrees of belief. To say that the probability of a given h was such-and-such would mean that between a and h was some relation justifying such-and-such a degree of belief. And on this view it would be a real point that the relation in question must not be one which the human mind is incapable of comprehending.

This second view of probability as depending on logical relations but not itself a new logical relation seems to me more plausible than Mr. Keynes' usual theory; but this does not mean that I feel at all inclined to agree with it. It requires the somewhat obscure idea of a logical relation justifying a degree of belief, which I should not like to accept as indefinable because it does not seem to be at all a clear or simple notion. Also it is hard to say what logical relations justify what degrees of belief, and why; any decision as to this would be arbitrary, and would lead to a logic of probability consisting of a host of so-called 'necessary' facts, like formal logic on Mr. Chadwick's view of logical constants.[3] Whereas I think it far better to seek an explanation of this 'necessity' after the model of the work of Mr. Wittgenstein, which enables us to see clearly in what precise sense and why logical propositions are necessary, and in a general way why the system of formal logic consists of the propositions it does consist of, and what is their common characteristic. Just as natural science tries to explain and account for the facts of nature, so philosophy should try, in a sense, to explain and account for the facts of logic; a task ignored by the philosophy which dismisses these facts as being unaccountably and in an indefinable sense 'necessary'.

Here I propose to conclude this criticism of Mr. Keynes' theory, not because there are not other respects in which it seems open to objection, but because I hope that what

I have already said is enough to show that it is not so completely satisfactory as to render futile any attempt to treat the subject from a rather different point of view.

Degrees of belief

The subject of our inquiry is the logic of partial belief, and I do not think we can carry it far unless we have at least an approximate notion of what partial belief is, and how, if at all, it can be measured. It will not be very enlightening to be told that in such circumstances it would be rational to believe a proposition to the extent of 2/3, unless we know what sort of a belief in it that means. We must therefore try to develop a purely psychological method of measuring belief. It is not enough to measure probability; in order to apportion correctly our belief to the probability we must also be able to measure our belief.

It is a common view that belief and other psychological variables are not measurable, and if this is true our inquiry will be vain; and so will the whole theory of probability conceived as a logic of partial belief; for if the phrase 'a belief two-thirds of certainty' is meaningless, a calculus whose sole object is to enjoin such beliefs will be meaningless also. Therefore unless we are prepared to give up the whole thing as a bad job we are bound to hold that beliefs can to some extent be measured. If we were to follow the analogy of Mr. Keynes' treatment of probabilities we should say that some beliefs were measurable and some not; but this does not seem to me likely to be a correct account of the matter: I do not see how we can sharply divide beliefs into those which have a position in the numerical scale and those which have not. But I think beliefs do differ in measurability in the following two ways. First, some beliefs can be measured more accurately than others; and, secondly, the measurement of beliefs is almost certainly an ambiguous process leading to a variable answer depending on how exactly the measurement is conducted. The degree of a belief is in this respect like the time interval between two events; before Einstein it was supposed that all the ordinary ways of measuring a time interval would lead to the same result if properly performed. Einstein showed that this was not the case; and time interval can no longer be regarded as an exact notion, but must be discarded in all precise investigations. Nevertheless, time interval and the Newtonian system are sufficiently accurate for many purposes and easier to apply.

I shall try to argue later that the degree of a belief is just like a time interval; it has no precise meaning unless we specify more exactly how it is to be measured. But for many purposes we can assume that the alternative ways of measuring it lead to the same result, although this is only approximately true. The resulting discrepancies are more glaring in connection with some beliefs than with others, and these therefore appear less measurable. Both these types of deficiency in measurability, due respectively to the difficulty in getting an exact enough measurement and to an important ambiguity in the definition of the measurement process, occur also in physics and so are not difficulties peculiar to our problem; what is peculiar is that it is difficult to form any idea of how the measurement is to be conducted, how a unit is to be obtained, and so on.

Let us then consider what is implied in the measurement of beliefs. A satisfactory system must in the first place assign to any belief a magnitude or degree having a definite position in an order of magnitudes; beliefs which are of the same degree as the same belief must be of the same degree as one another, and so on. Of course this cannot be accomplished without introducing a certain amount of hypothesis or fiction. Even in physics we cannot maintain that things that are equal to the same thing are equal to one another unless we take 'equal' not as meaning 'sensibly equal' but a fictitious or hypothetical relation. I do not want to discuss the metaphysics or epistemology of this process, but merely to remark that if it is allowable in physics it is allowable in psychology also. The logical simplicity characteristic of the relations dealt with in a science is never attained by nature alone without any admixture of fiction.

But to construct such an ordered series of degrees is not the whole of our task; we have also to assign numbers to these degrees in some intelligible manner. We can of course easily explain that we denote full belief by 1, full belief in the contradictory by 0, and equal beliefs in the proposition and its contradictory by 1/2. But it is not so easy to say what is meant by a belief 2/3 of certainty, or a belief in the proposition being twice as strong as that in its contradictory. This is the harder part of the task, but it is absolutely necessary; for we do calculate numerical probabilities, and if they are to correspond to degrees of belief we must discover some definite way of attaching numbers to degrees of belief. In physics we often attach numbers by discovering a physical process of addition[4]: the measure-numbers of lengths are not assigned arbitrarily subject only to the proviso that the greater length shall have the greater measure; we determine them further by deciding on a physical meaning for addition; the length got by putting together two given lengths must have for its measure the sum of their measures. A system of measurement in which there is nothing corresponding to this is immediately recognized as arbitrary, for instance Mohs' scale of hardness[5] in which 10 is arbitrarily assigned to diamond, the hardest known material, 9 to the next hardest, and so on. We have therefore to find a process of addition for degrees of belief, or some substitute for this which will be equally adequate to determine a numerical scale.

Such is our problem; how are we to solve it? There are, I think, two ways in which we can begin. We can, in the first place, suppose that the degree of a belief is something perceptible by its owner; for instance that beliefs differ in the intensity of a feeling by which they are accompanied, which might be called a belief-feeling or feeling of conviction, and that by the degree of belief we mean the intensity of this feeling. This view would be very inconvenient, for it is not easy to ascribe numbers to the intensities of feelings; but apart from this it seems to me observably false, for the beliefs which we hold most strongly are often accompanied by practically no feeling at all; no one feels strongly about things he takes for granted.

We are driven therefore to the second supposition that the degree of a belief is a causal property of it, which we can express vaguely as the extent to which we are prepared to act on it. This is a generalization of the well-known view, that the differentia of belief lies in its causal efficacy, which is discussed by Mr. Russell in his *Analysis of Mind*. He there dismisses it for two reasons, one of which seems entirely to miss the point. He argues that in the course of trains of thought we believe many things which do not lead to action. This objection is however beside the mark, because it is not asserted that a belief is an idea which does actually lead to action, but one which would lead to action in suitable circumstances; just as a lump of arsenic is called poisonous not because it actually has killed or will kill anyone, but because it would kill anyone if he ate it. Mr. Russell's second argument is, however, more formidable. He points out that it is not possible to suppose that beliefs differ from other ideas only in their effects, for if they were otherwise identical their effects would be identical also.

This is perfectly true, but it may still remain the case that the nature of the difference between the causes is entirely unknown or very vaguely known, and that what we want to talk about is the difference between the effects, which is readily observable and important.

As soon as we regard belief quantatively, this seems to me the only view we can take of it. It could well be held that the difference between believing and not believing lies in the presence or absence of introspectible feelings. But when we seek to know what is the difference between believing more firmly and believing less firmly, we can no longer regard it as consisting in having more or less of certain observable feelings; at least I personally cannot recognize any such feelings. The difference seems to me to lie in how far we should act on these beliefs: this may depend on the degree of some feeling or feelings, but I do not know exactly what feelings and I do not see that it is indispensable that we should know. Just the same thing is found in physics; men found that a wire connecting plates of zinc and copper standing in acid deflected a magnetic needle in its neighbourhood. Accordingly as the needle was more or less deflected the wire was said to carry a larger or a smaller current. The nature of this 'current' could only be conjectured: what were observed and measured were simply its effects.

It will no doubt be objected that we know how strongly we believe things, and that we can only know this if we can measure our belief by introspection. This does not seem to me necessarily true; in many cases, I think, our judgment about the strength of our belief is really about how we should act in hypothetical circumstances. It will be answered that we can only tell how we should act by observing the present belief-feeling which determines how we should act; but again I doubt the cogency of the argument. It is possible that what determines how we should act determines us also directly or indirectly to have a correct opinion as to how we should act, without its ever coming into consciousness.

Suppose, however, I am wrong about this and that we can decide by introspection the nature of belief, and measure its degree; still, I shall argue, the kind of measurement of belief with which probability is concerned is not this kind but is a measurement of belief *qua* basis of action. This can I think be shown in two ways. First, by considering the scale of probabilities between 0 and 1, and the sort of way we use it, we shall find that it is very appropriate to the measurement of belief as a basis of action, but in no way related to the measurement of an introspected feeling. For the units in terms of which such feelings or sensations are measured are always, I think, differences which are just perceptible: there is no other way of obtaining units. But I see no ground for supposing that the interval between a belief of degree 1/3 and one of degree 1/2 consists of as many just perceptible changes as does that between one of 2/3 and one of 5/6, or that a scale based on just perceptible differences would have any simple relation to the theory of probability. On the other hand the probability of 1/3 is clearly related to the kind of belief which would lead to a bet of 2 to 1, and it will be shown below how to generalize this relation so as to apply to action in general. Secondly, the quantitative aspects of beliefs as the basis of action are evidently more important than the intensities of belief-feelings. The latter are no doubt interesting, but may be very variable from individual to individual, and their practical interest is entirely due to their position as the hypothetical causes of beliefs *qua* bases of action.

It is possible that some one will say that the extent to which we should act on a belief in suitable circumstances is a hypothetical thing, and therefore not capable of measurement. But to say this is merely to reveal ignorance of the physical sciences which constantly deal with and measure hypothetical quantities; for instance, the electric intensity at a given point is the force which would act on a unit charge if it were placed at the point.

Let us now try to find a method of measuring beliefs as bases of possible actions. It is clear that we are concerned with dispositional rather than with actualized beliefs; that is to say, not with beliefs at the moment when we are thinking of them, but with beliefs like my belief that the earth is round, which I rarely think of, but which would guide my action in any case to which it was relevant.

The old-established way of measuring a person's belief is to propose a bet, and see what are the lowest odds which he will accept. This method I regard as fundamentally sound; but it suffers from being insufficiently general, and from being necessarily inexact. It is inexact partly because of the diminishing marginal utility of money, partly because the person may have a special eagerness or reluctance to bet, because he either enjoys or dislikes excitement or for any other reason, e.g. to make a book. The difficulty is like that of separating two different co-operating forces. Besides, the proposal of a bet may inevitably alter his state of opinion; just as we could not always measure electric intensity by actually introducing a charge and seeing what force it was subject to, because the introduction of the charge would change the distribution to be measured.

In order therefore to construct a theory of quantities of belief which shall be both general and more exact, I propose to take as a basis a general psychological theory, which is now universally discarded, but nevertheless comes, I think, fairly close to the truth in the sort of cases with which we are most concerned. I mean the theory that we act in the way we think most likely to realize the objects of our desires, so that a person's actions are completely determined by his desires and opinions. This theory cannot be made adequate to all the facts, but it seems to me a useful approximation to the truth particularly in the case of our self-conscious or professional life, and it is presupposed in a great deal of our thought. It is a simple theory and one which many psychologists would obviously like to preserve by introducing unconscious desires and unconscious opinions in order to bring it more into harmony with the facts. How far such fictions can achieve the required result I do not attempt to judge: I only claim for what follows approximate truth, or truth in relation to this artificial system of psychology, which like Newtonian mechanics can, I think, still be profitably used even though it is known to be false.

It must be observed that this theory is not to be identified with the psychology of the Utilitarians, in which pleasure had a dominating position. The theory I propose to adopt is that we seek things which we want, which may be our own or other people's pleasure, or anything else whatever, and our actions are such as we think most likely to realize these goods. But this is not a precise statement, for a precise statement of the theory can only be made after we have introduced the notion of quantity of belief.

Let us call the things a person ultimately desires 'goods', and let us at first assume that they are numerically measurable and additive. That is to say that if he prefers for its own sake an hour's swimming to an hour's reading, he will prefer two hours' swimming to one hour's swimming and one hour's reading. This is of course absurd in the given case but this may only be because swimming and reading are not ultimate goods, and because we cannot imagine a second hour's swimming precisely similar to the first, owing to fatigue, etc.

Let us begin by supposing that our subject has no doubts about anything, but certain opinions about all propositions. Then we can say that he will always choose the course of action which will lead in his opinion to the greatest sum of good.

It should be emphasized that in this essay good and bad are never to be understood in any ethical sense but simply as denoting that to which a given person feels desire and aversion.

The question then arises how we are to modify this simple system to take account of varying degrees of certainty in his beliefs. I suggest that we introduce as a law of psychology that his behaviour is governed by what is called the mathematical expectation; that is to say that, if p is a proposition about which he is doubtful, any goods or bads for whose realization p is in his view a necessary and sufficient condition enter into his calculations multiplied by the same fraction, which is called the 'degree of his belief in p'. We thus define degree of belief in a way which presupposes the use of the mathematical expectation.

We can put this in a different way. Suppose his degree of belief in p is m/n; then his action is such as he would choose it to be if he had to repeat it exactly n times, in m of which p was true, and in the others false. [Here it may be necessary to suppose that in each of the n times he had no memory of the previous ones.]

This can also be taken as a definition of the degree of belief, and can easily be seen to be equivalent to the previous definition. Let us give an instance of the sort of case which might occur. I am at a cross-roads and do not know the way; but I rather think one of the two ways is right. I propose therefore to go that way but keep my eyes open for someone to ask; if now I see someone half a mile away over the fields, whether I turn aside to ask him will depend on the relative inconvenience of going out of my way to cross the fields or of continuing on the wrong road if it is the wrong road. But it will also depend on how confident I am that I am right; and clearly the more confident I am of this the less distance I should be willing to go from the road to check my opinion. I propose therefore to use the distance I would be prepared to go to ask, as a measure of the confidence of my opinion; and what I have said above explains how this is to be done. We can set it out as follows: suppose the disadvantage of going x yards to ask is $f(x)$, the advantage of arriving at the right destination is r, that of arriving at the wrong one w. Then if I should just be willing to go a distance d to ask, the degree of my belief that I am on the right road is given by

$$p = 1 - \frac{f(d)}{r - w}$$

For such an action is one it would just pay me to take, if I had to act in the same way n times, in np of which I was on the right way but in the others not.

For the total good resulting from not asking each time

$$= npr + n(1 - p)w$$
$$= nw + np(r - w),$$

that resulting from asking at distance x each time

$$= nr - nf(x). \qquad \text{[I now always go right.]}$$

57

F. P. RAMSEY

This is greater than the preceding expression, provided

$$f(x) < (r - w)(1 - p),$$

∴ the critical distance d is connected with p, the degree of belief, by the relation $f(d) = (r - w)(1 - p)$

$$\text{or } p = 1 - \frac{f(d)}{r - w} \qquad \text{as asserted above.}$$

It is easy to see that this way of measuring beliefs gives results agreeing with ordinary ideas; at any rate to the extent that full belief is denoted by 1, full belief in the contradictory by 0, and equal belief in the two by 1/2. Further, it allows validity to betting as means of measuring beliefs. By proposing a bet on p we give the subject a possible course of action from which so much extra good will result to him if p is true and so much extra bad if p is false. Supposing the bet to be in goods and bads instead of in money, he will take a bet at any better odds than those corresponding to his state of belief; in fact his state of belief is measured by the odds he will just take; but this is vitiated, as already explained, by love or hatred of excitement, and by the fact that the bet is in money and not in goods and bads. Since it is universally agreed that money has a diminishing marginal utility, if money bets are to be used, it is evident that they should be for as small stakes as possible. But then again the measurement is spoiled by introducing the new factor of reluctance to bother about trifles.

Let us now discard the assumption that goods are additive and immediately measurable, and try to work out a system with as few assumptions as possible. To begin with we shall suppose, as before, that our subject has certain beliefs about everything; then he will act so that what he believes to be the total consequences of his action will be the best possible. If then we had the power of the Almighty, and could persuade our subject of our power, we could, by offering him options, discover how he placed in order of merit all possible courses of the world. In this way all possible worlds would be put in an order of value, but we should have no definite way of representing them by numbers. There would be no meaning in the assertion that the difference in value between α and β was equal to that between γ and δ. [Here and elsewhere we use Greek letters to represent the different possible totalities of events between which our subject chooses—the ultimate organic unities.]

Suppose next that the subject is capable of doubt; then we could test his degree of belief in different propositions by making him offers of the following kind. Would you rather have world α in any event; or world β if p is true, and world γ if p is false? If, then, he were certain that p was true, he would simply compare α and β and choose between them as if no conditions were attached; but if he were doubtful his choice would not be decided so simply. I propose to lay down axioms and definitions concerning the principles governing choices of this kind. This is, of course, a very schematic version of the situation in real life, but it is, I think, easier to consider it in this form.

There is first a difficulty which must be dealt with; the propositions like p in the above case which are used as conditions in the options offered may be such that their truth or falsity is an object of desire to the subject. This will be found to complicate the problem, and we have to assume that there are propositions for which this is not the case, which

58

we shall call ethically neutral. More precisely an atomic proposition p is called ethically neutral if two possible worlds differing only in regard to the truth of p are always of equal value; and a non-atomic proposition p is called ethically neutral if all its atomic truth-arguments[6] are ethically neutral.

We begin by defining belief of degree 1/2 in an ethically neutral proposition. The subject is said to have belief of degree 1/2 in such a proposition p if he has no preference between the options (1) α if p is true, β if p is false, and (2) α if p is false, β if p is true, but has a preference between α and β simply. We suppose by an axiom that if this is true of any one pair α, β it is true of all such pairs.[7] This comes roughly to defining belief of degree 1/2 as such a degree of belief as leads to indifference between betting one way and betting the other for the same stakes.

Belief of degree 1/2 as thus defined can be used to measure values numerically in the following way. We have to explain what is meant by the difference in value between α and β being equal to that between γ and δ; and we define this to mean that, if p is an ethically neutral proposition believed to degree 1/2, the subject has no preference between the options (1) α if p is true, δ if p is false, and (2) β if p is true, γ if p is false.

This definition can form the basis of a system of measuring values in the following way:—

Let us call any set of all worlds equally preferable to a given world a value: we suppose that if world α is preferable to β any world with the same value as α is preferable to any world with the same value as β and shall say that the value of α is greater than that of β. This relation 'greater than' orders values in a series. We shall use α henceforth both for the world and its value.

Axioms

(1) There is an ethically neutral proposition p believed to degree 1/2.

(2) If p, q are such propositions and the option

$$\alpha \text{ if } p, \delta \text{ if not-}p \text{ is equivalent to } \beta \text{ if } p, \gamma \text{ if not-}p$$

then $$\alpha \text{ if } q, \delta \text{ if not-}q \text{ is equivalent to } \beta \text{ if } q, \gamma \text{ if not-}q.$$

Def. In the above case we say $\alpha\beta = \gamma\delta$.

Theorems. If $\alpha\beta = \gamma\delta$,

then $\beta\alpha = \delta\gamma, \alpha\gamma = \beta\delta, \gamma\alpha = \delta\beta$.

(2a) If $\alpha\beta = \gamma\delta$, then $\alpha > \beta$ is equivalent to $\gamma > \delta$

and $\alpha = \beta$ is equivalent to $\gamma = \delta$.

(3) If option A is equivalent to option B and B to C then A to C.

Theorem. If $\alpha\beta = \gamma\delta$ and $\beta\eta = \zeta\gamma$,

then $\alpha\eta = \zeta\delta$.

(4) If $\alpha\beta = \gamma\delta$, $\gamma\delta = \eta\zeta$, then $\alpha\beta = \eta\zeta$.

(5) (α, β, γ). E! $(\iota x)\,(\alpha x = \beta\gamma)$.

(6) (α, β). E! $(\iota x)\,(\alpha x = x\beta)$.

(7) Axiom of continuity :—Any progression has a limit (ordinal).

(8) Axiom of Archimedes.

These axioms enable the values to be correlated one-one with real numbers so that if α^1 corresponds to α, etc.

$$\alpha\beta = \gamma\delta \cdot \equiv \cdot \alpha^1 - \beta^1 = \gamma^1 - \delta^1.$$

Henceforth we use α for the correlated real number α^1 also.

Having thus defined a way of measuring value we can now derive a way of measuring belief in general. If the option of α for certain is indifferent with that of β if p is true and γ if p is false,[8] we can define the subject's degree of belief in p as the ratio of the difference between α and γ to that between β and γ; which we must suppose the same for all α's, β's and γ's that satisfy the conditions. This amounts roughly to defining the degree of belief in p by the odds at which the subject would bet on p, the bet being conducted in terms of differences of value as defined. The definition only applies to partial belief and does not include certain beliefs; for belief of degree 1 in p, α for certain is indifferent with α if p and any β if not-p.

We are also able to define a very useful new idea—'the degree of belief in p given q'. This does not mean the degree of belief in 'If p then q', or that in 'p entails q', or that which the subject would have in p if he knew q, or that which he ought to have. It roughly expresses the odds at which he would now bet on p, the bet only to be valid if q is true. Such conditional bets were often made in the eighteenth century.

The degree of belief in p given q is measured thus. Suppose the subject indifferent between the options (1) α if q true, β if q false, (2) γ if p true and q true, δ if p false and q true, β if q false. Then the degree of his belief in p given q is the ratio of the difference between α and δ to that between γ and δ, which we must suppose the same for any α, β, γ, δ, which satisfy the given conditions. This is not the same as the degree to which he would believe p, if he believed q for certain; for knowledge of q might for psychological reasons profoundly alter his whole system of beliefs.

Each of our definitions has been accompanied by an axiom of consistency, and in so far as this is false, the notion of the corresponding degree of belief becomes invalid. This bears some analogy to the situation in regard to simultaneity discussed above.

I have not worked out the mathematical logic of this in detail, because this would, I think, be rather like working out to seven places of decimals a result only valid to two. My logic cannot be regarded as giving more than the sort of way it might work.

From these definitions and axioms it is possible to prove the fundamental laws of probable belief (degrees of belief lie between 0 and 1):

(1) Degree of belief in p + degree of belief in $\bar{p} = 1$.

(2) Degree of belief in p given q + degree of belief in $\bar{p}$ given $q = 1$.

(3) Degree of belief in (p and q) = degree of belief in $p \times$ degree of belief in q given p.

(4) Degree of belief in (p and q) + degree of belief in (p and $\bar{q}$) = degree of belief in p.

The first two are immediate. (3) is proved as follows.

Let degree of belief in $p = x$, that in q given $p = y$.

Then ξ for certain $\equiv \xi + (1-x)t$ if p true, $\xi - xt$ if p false, for any t.

$$\xi + (1-x)t \text{ if } p \text{ true} \equiv$$
$$\begin{cases} \xi + (1-x)t + (1-y)u \text{ if '}p \text{ and } q\text{' true,} \\ \xi + (1-x)t - yu \text{ if } p \text{ true } q \text{ false;} \quad \text{for any } u. \end{cases}$$

Choose u so that $\xi + (1-x)t - yu = \xi - xt$,

i.e. let $u = t/y \, (y \neq 0)$

Then ξ for certain $\equiv$

$$\begin{cases} \xi + (1-x)t + (1-y)t/y \text{ if } p \text{ and } q \text{ true} \\ \xi - xt \text{ otherwise,} \end{cases}$$

$\therefore$ degree of belief in 'p and q' $= \dfrac{xt}{t+(1-y)t/y} = xy. \ (t \neq 0)$

If $y = 0$, take $t = 0$.

Then ξ for certain $\equiv \xi$ if p true, ξ if p false

$\equiv \xi + u$ if p true, q true; ξ if p false, q false; ξ if p false

$\equiv \xi + u, pq$ true; ξ, pq false

$\therefore$ degree of belief in $pq = 0$.

(4) follows from (2), (3) as follows:—

Degree of belief in $pq =$ that in $p \times$ that in q given p, by (3). Similarly degree of belief in $p\bar{q} =$ that in $p \times$ that in $\bar{q}$ given p $\therefore$ sum $=$ degree of belief in p, by (2).

These are the laws of probability, which we have proved to be necessarily true of any consistent set of degrees of belief. Any definite set of degrees of belief which broke them would be inconsistent in the sense that it violated the laws of preference between options, such as that preferability is a transitive asymmetrical relation, and that if α is preferable to β, β for certain cannot be preferable to α if p, β if not-p. If anyone's mental condition violated these laws, his choice would depend on the precise form in which the options were offered him, which would be absurd. He could have a book made against him by a cunning better and would then stand to lose in any event.

We find, therefore, that a precise account of the nature of partial belief reveals that the laws of probability are laws of consistency, an extension to partial beliefs of formal logic, the logic of consistency. They do not depend for their meaning on any degree of belief in a proposition being uniquely determined as the rational one; they merely distinguish those sets of beliefs which obey them as consistent ones.

Having any definite degree of belief implies a certain measure of consistency, namely willingness to bet on a given proposition at the same odds for any stake, the stakes being measured in terms of ultimate values. Having degrees of belief obeying the laws of probability implies a further measure of consistency, namely such a consistency between the odds acceptable on different propositions as shall prevent a book being made against you.

Some concluding remarks on this section may not be out of place. First, it is based fundamentally on betting, but this will not seem unreasonable when it is seen that all our lives we are in a sense betting. Whenever we go to the station we are betting that a train will really run, and if we had not a sufficient degree of belief in this we should decline the bet and stay at home. The options God gives us are always conditional on our guessing whether a certain proposition is true. Secondly, it is based throughout on the idea of mathematical expectation; the dissatisfaction often felt with this idea is due mainly to the inaccurate measurement of goods. Clearly mathematical expectations in terms of money are not proper guides to conduct. It should be remembered, in judging my system, that in it value actually defined by means of mathematical expectation in the case of beliefs of degree $1/2$, and so may be expected to be scaled suitably for the valid application of the mathematical expectation in the case of other degrees of belief also.

Thirdly, nothing has been said about degrees of belief when the number of alternatives is infinite. About this I have nothing useful to say, except that I doubt if the mind is capable of contemplating more than a finite number of alternatives. It can consider questions to which an infinite number of answers are possible, but in order to consider the answers it must lump them into a finite number of groups. The difficulty becomes practically relevant when discussing induction, but even then there seems to me no need to introduce it. We can discuss whether past experience gives a high probability to the sun's rising to-morrow without bothering about what probability it gives to the sun's rising each morning for evermore. For this reason I cannot but feel that Mr. Ritchie's discussion of the problem[9] is unsatisfactory; it is true that we can agree that inductive generalizations need have no finite probability, but particular expectations entertained on inductive grounds undoubtedly do have a high numerical probability in the minds of all of us. We all are more certain that the sun will rise to-morrow than that I shall not throw 12 with two dice first time, i.e. we have a belief of higher degree than 35/36 in it. If induction ever needs a logical justification it is in connection with the probability of an event like this.

The logic of consistency

We may agree that in some sense it is the business of logic to tell us what we ought to think; but the interpretation of this statement raises considerable difficulties. It may be said that we ought to think what is true, but in that sense we are told what to think by the whole of science and not merely by logic. Nor, in this sense, can any justification be found for partial belief; the ideally best thing is that we should have beliefs of degree 1 in all true propositions and beliefs of degree 0 in all false propositions. But this is too high a standard to expect of mortal men, and we must agree that some degree of doubt or even of error may be humanly speaking justified.

Many logicians, I suppose, would accept as an account of their science the opening words of Mr. Keynes' *Treatise on Probability*: "Part of our knowledge we obtain direct; and part by argument. The Theory of Probability is concerned with that part which we obtain by argument, and it treats of the different degrees in which the results so obtained are conclusive or inconclusive." Where Mr. Keynes says 'the Theory of Probability',

62

others would say Logic. It is held, that is to say, that our opinions can be divided into those we hold immediately as a result of perception or memory, and those which we derive from the former by argument. It is the business of Logic to accept the former class and criticize merely the derivation of the second class from them.

Logic as the science of argument and inference is traditionally and rightly divided into deductive and inductive; but the difference and relation between these two divisions of the subject can be conceived in extremely different ways. According to Mr. Keynes valid deductive and inductive arguments are fundamentally alike; both are justified by logical relations between premiss and conclusion which differ only in degree. This position, as I have already explained, I cannot accept. I do not see what these inconclusive logical relations can be or how they can justify partial beliefs. In the case of conclusive logical arguments I can accept the account of their validity which has been given by many authorities, and can be found substantially the same in Kant, De Morgan, Peirce and Wittgenstein. All these authors agree that the conclusion of a formally valid argument is contained in its premisses; that to deny the conclusion while accepting the premisses would be self-contradictory; that a formal deduction does not increase our knowledge, but only brings out clearly what we already know in another form; and that we are bound to accept its validity on pain of being inconsistent with ourselves. The logical relation which justifies the inference is that the sense or import of the conclusion is contained in that of the premisses.

But in the case of an inductive argument this does not happen in the least; it is impossible to represent it as resembling a deductive argument and merely weaker in degree; it is absurd to say that the sense of the conclusion is partially contained in that of the premisses. We could accept the premisses and utterly reject the conclusion without any sort of inconsistency or contradiction.

It seems to me, therefore, that we can divide arguments into two radically different kinds, which we can distinguish in the words of Peirce as (1) 'explicative, analytic, or deductive' and (2) 'amplifiative, synthetic, or (loosely speaking) inductive'.[10] Arguments of the second type are from an important point of view much closer to memories and perceptions than to deductive arguments. We can regard perception, memory and induction as the three fundamental ways of acquiring knowledge; deduction on the other hand is merely a method of arranging our knowledge and eliminating inconsistencies or contradictions.

Logic must then fall very definitely into two parts: (excluding analytic logic, the theory of terms and propositions) we have the lesser logic, which is the logic of consistency, or formal logic; and the larger logic, which is the logic of discovery, or inductive logic.

What we have now to observe is that this distinction in no way coincides with the distinction between certain and partial beliefs; we have seen that there is a theory of consistency in partial beliefs just as much as of consistency in certain beliefs, although for various reasons the former is not so important as the latter. The theory of probability is in fact a generalization of formal logic; but in the process of generalization one of the most important aspects of formal logic is destroyed. If p and $\bar{q}$ are inconsistent so that q follows logically from p, that p implies q is what is called by Wittgenstein a 'tautology' and can be regarded as a degenerate case of a true proposition not involving the idea of consistency. This enables us to regard (not altogether correctly) formal logic including mathematics as an objective science consisting of objectively necessary propositions. It thus gives us not merely the $\dot{\alpha}\nu\dot{\alpha}\gamma\kappa\eta$ $\lambda\dot{\varepsilon}\gamma\varepsilon\iota\nu$, that if we assert p we are bound in consistency to assert q also, but also the $\dot{\alpha}\nu\dot{\alpha}\gamma\kappa\eta$ $\varepsilon\tilde{\iota}\nu\alpha\iota$, that if p is true, so must q be. But when we extend formal logic to include partial beliefs this direct objective interpetation is lost; if we believe pq to the extent of 1/3, and $p\bar{q}$ to the extent of 1/3, we are bound in consistency to believe $\bar{p}$ also to the extent of 1/3. This is the $\grave{\alpha}\nu\acute{\alpha}\gamma\kappa\eta\ \lambda\acute{\varepsilon}\gamma\varepsilon\iota\nu$; but we cannot say that if pq is 1/3 true and $p\bar{q}$ 1/3 true, $\bar{p}$ also must be 1/3 true, for such a statement would be sheer nonsense. There is no corresponding $\grave{\alpha}\nu\acute{\alpha}\gamma\kappa\eta\ \varepsilon\hat{\iota}\nu\alpha\iota$. Hence, unlike the calculus of consistent full belief, the calculus of objective partial belief cannot be immediately interpreted as a body of objective tautology.

This is, however, possible in a roundabout way; we saw at the beginning of this essay that the calculus of probabilities could be interpreted in terms of class-ratios; we have now found that it can also be interpreted as a calculus of consistent partial belief. It is natural, therefore, that we should expect some intimate connection between these two interpretations, some explanation of the possibility of applying the same mathematical calculus to two such different sets of phenomena. Nor is an explanation difficult to find; there are many connections between partial beliefs and frequencies. For instance, experienced frequencies often lead to corresponding partial beliefs, and partial beliefs lead to the expectation of corresponding frequencies in accordance with Bernouilli's Theorem. But neither of these is exactly the connection we want; a partial belief cannot in general be connected uniquely with any actual frequency, for the connection is always made by taking the proposition in question as an instance of a propositional function. What propositional function we choose is to some extent arbitrary and the corresponding frequency will vary considerably with our choice. The pretensions of some exponents of the frequency theory that partial belief means full belief in a frequency proposition cannot be sustained. But we found that the very idea of partial belief involves reference to a hypothetical or ideal frequency; supposing goods to be additive, belief of degree m/n is the sort of belief which leads to the action which would be best if repeated n times in m of which the proposition is true; or we can say more briefly that it is the kind of belief most appropriate to a number of hypothetical occasions otherwise identical in a proportion m/n of which the proposition in question is true. It is this connection between partial belief and frequency which enables us to use the calculus of frequencies as a calculus of consistent partial belief. And in a sense we may say that the two interpretations are the objective and subjective aspects of the same inner meaning, just as formal logic can be interpreted objectively as a body of tautology and subjectively as the laws of consistent thought.

We shall, I think, find that this view of the calculus of probability removes various difficulties that have hitherto been found perplexing. In the first place it gives us a clear justification for the axioms of the calculus, which on such a system as Mr. Keynes' is entirely wanting. For now it is easily seen that if partial beliefs are consistent they will obey these axioms, but it is utterly obscure why Mr. Keynes' mysterious logical relations should obey them.[11] We should be so curiously ignorant of the instances of these relations, and so curiously knowledgeable about their general laws.

Secondly, the Principle of Indifference can now be altogether dispensed with; we do not regard it as belonging to formal logic to say what should be a man's expectation of drawing a white or a black ball from an urn; his original expectations may within the limits of consistency be any he likes; all we have to point out is that if he has certain expectations he is bound in consistency to have certain others. This is simply bringing probability into line with ordinary formal logic, which does not criticize premises but merely declares that certain conclusions are the only ones consistent with them. To be able to turn the Principle of Indifference out of formal logic is a great advantage; for it is fairly clearly impossible to lay down purely logical conditions for its validity, as is attempted by Mr. Keynes. I do not want to discuss this question in detail, because it leads to hair-splitting and arbitrary distinctions which could be discussed for ever. But anyone who tries to decide by Mr. Keynes' methods what are the proper alternatives to regard as equally probable in molecular mechanics, e.g. in Gibbs' phase-space, will soon be convinced that it is a matter of physics rather than pure logic. By using the multiplication formula, as it is used in inverse probability, we can on Mr. Keynes' theory reduce all probabilities to quotients of *a priori* probabilities; it is therefore in regard to these latter that the Principle of Indifference is of primary importance; but here the question is obviously not one of formal logic. How can we on merely logical grounds divide the spectrum into equally probable bands?

A third difficulty which is removed by our theory is the one which is presented to Mr. Keynes' theory by the following case. I think I perceive or remember something but am not sure; this would seem to give me some ground for believing it, contrary to Mr. Keynes' theory, by which the degree of belief in it which it would be rational for me to have is that given by the probability relation between the proposition in question and the things I know for certain. He cannot justify a probable belief founded not on argument but on direct inspection. In our view there would be nothing contrary to formal logic in such a belief; whether it would be reasonable would depend on what I have called the larger logic which will be the subject of the next section; we shall there see that there is no objection to such a possibility, with which Mr. Keynes' method of justifying probable belief solely by relation to certain knowledge is quite unable to cope.

The logic of truth

The validity of the distinction between the logic of consistency and the logic of truth has been often disputed; it has been contended on the one hand that logical consistency is only a kind of factual consistency; that if a belief in p is inconsistent with one in q, that simply means that p and q are not both true, and that this is a necessary or logical fact. I believe myself that this difficulty can be met by Wittgenstein's theory of tautology, according to which if a belief in p is inconsistent with one in q, that p and q are not both true is not a fact but a tautology. But I do not propose to discuss this question further here.

From the other side it is contended that formal logic or the logic of consistency is the whole of logic, and inductive logic either nonsense or part of natural science. This contention, which would I suppose be made by Wittgenstein, I feel more difficulty in meeting. But I think it would be a pity, out of deference to authority, to give up trying to say anything useful about induction.

Let us therefore go back to the general conception of logic as the science of rational thought. We found that the most generally accepted parts of logic, namely, formal logic, mathematics and the calculus of probabilities, are all concerned simply to ensure that our beliefs are not self-contradictory. We put before ourselves the standard of consistency and construct these elaborate rules to ensure its observance. But this is obviously not enough; we want our beliefs to be consistent not merely with one another but also with the facts[12]: nor is it even clear that consistency is always advantageous; it may well be better to be sometimes right than never right. Nor when we wish to be consistent are we always able to be: there are mathematical propositions whose truth or falsity cannot as yet be decided. Yet it may humanly speaking be right to entertain a certain degree of belief in them on inductive or other grounds: a logic which proposes to justify such a degree of belief must be prepared actually to go against formal logic; for to a formal truth formal logic can only assign a belief of degree 1. We could prove in Mr. Keynes' system that its probability is 1 on any evidence. This point seems to me to show particularly clearly that human logic or the logic of truth, which tells men how they should think, is not merely independent of but sometimes actually incompatible with formal logic.

In spite of this nearly all philosophical thought about human logic and especially induction has tried to reduce it in some way to formal logic. Not that it is supposed, except by a very few, that consistency will of itself lead to truth; but consistency combined with observation and memory is frequently credited with this power.

Since an observation changes (in degree at least) my opinion about the fact observed, some of my degrees of belief after the observation are necessarily inconsistent with those I had before. We have therefore to explain how exactly the observation should modify my degrees of belief; obviously if p is the fact observed, my degree of belief in q after the observation should be equal to my degree of belief in q given p before, or by the multiplication law to the quotient of my degree of belief in pq by my degree of belief in p. When my degrees of belief change in this way we can say that they have been changed consistently by my observation.

By using this definition, or on Mr. Keynes' system simply by using the multiplication law, we can take my present degrees of belief, and by considering the totality of my observations, discover from what initial degrees of belief my present ones would have arisen by this process of consistent change. My present degrees of belief can then be considered logically justified if the corresponding initial degrees of belief are logically justified. But to ask what initial degrees of belief are justified, or in Mr. Keynes' system what are the absolutely *a priori* probabilities, seems to me a meaningless question; and even if it had a meaning I do not see how it could be answered.

If we actually applied this process to a human being, found out, that is to say, on what *a priori* probabilities his present opinions could be based, we should obviously find them to be ones determined by natural selection, with a general tendency to give a higher probability to the simpler alternatives. But, as I say, I cannot see what could be meant by asking whether these degrees of belief were logically justified. Obviously the best thing would be to know for certain in advance what was true and what false, and therefore if any one system of initial beliefs is to receive the philosopher's approbation it should be this one. But clearly this would not be accepted by thinkers of the school I am criticising. Another alternative is to apportion initial probabilities on the purely formal system expounded by Wittgenstein, but as this gives no justification for induction it cannot give us the human logic which we are looking for.

Let us therefore try to get an idea of a human logic which shall not attempt to be reducible to formal logic. Logic, we may agree, is concerned not with what men actually believe, but what they ought to believe, or what it would be reasonable to believe. What then, we must ask, is meant by saying that it is reasonable for a man to have such and such a degree of belief in a proposition? Let us consider possible alternatives.

First, it sometimes means something explicable in terms of formal logic: this possibility for reasons already explained we may dismiss. Secondly, it sometimes means simply that were I in his place (and not e.g. drunk) I should have such a degree of belief. Thirdly, it sometimes means that if his mind worked according to certain rules, which we may roughly call 'scientific method', he would have such a degree of belief. But fourthly it need mean none of these things; for men have not always believed in scientific method, and just as we ask 'But am I necessarily reasonable', we can also ask 'But is the scientist necessarily reasonable?' In this ultimate meaning it seems to me that we can identify reasonable opinion with the opinion of an ideal person in similar circumstances. What, however, would this ideal person's opinion be? As has previously been remarked, the highest ideal would be always to have a true opinion and be certain of it; but this ideal is more suited to God than to man.[13]

We have therefore to consider the human mind and what is the most we can ask of it.[14] The human mind works essentially according to general rules or habits; a process of thought not proceeding according to some rule would simply be a random sequence of ideas; whenever we infer A from B we do so in virtue of some relation between them. We can therefore state the problem of the ideal as "What habits in a general sense would it be best for the human mind to have?" This is a large and vague question which could hardly be answered unless the possibilities were first limited by a fairly definite conception of human nature. We could imagine some very useful habits unlike those possessed by any men. [It must be explained that I use habit in the most general possible sense to mean simply rule or law of behaviour, including instinct: I do not wish to distinguish acquired rules or habits in the narrow sense from innate rules or instincts, but propose to call them all habits alike.] A completely general criticism of the human mind is therefore bound to be vague and futile, but something useful can be said if we limit the subject in the following way.

Let us take a habit of forming opinion in a certain way; e.g. the habit of proceeding from the opinion that a toadstool is yellow to the opinion that it is unwholesome. Then we can accept the fact that the person has a habit of this sort, and ask merely what degree of opinion that the toadstool is unwholesome it would be best for him to entertain when he sees it; i.e. granting that he is going to think always in the same way about all yellow toadstools, we can ask what degree of confidence it would be best for him to have that they are unwholesome. And the answer is that it will in general be best for his degree of belief that a yellow toadstool is unwholesome to be equal to the proportion of yellow toadstools which are in fact unwholesome (This follows from the meaning of degree of belief.) This conclusion is necessarily vague in regard to the spatio-temporal range of toadstools which it includes, but hardly vaguer than the question which it answers. (Cf. density at a point of gas composed of molecules.)

Let us put it in another way: whenever I make an inference, I do so according to some rule or habit. An inference is not completely given when we are given the premiss and conclusion; we require also to be given the relation between them in virtue of which the inference is made. The mind works by general laws; therefore if it infers q from p, this will generally be because q is an instance of a function ϕx and p the corresponding instance of a function ψx such that the mind would always infer ϕx from ψx. When therefore we criticize not opinions but the processes by which they are formed, the rule of the inference determines for us a range to which the frequency theory can be applied. The rule of the inference may be narrow, as when seeing lightning I expect thunder, or wide, as when considering 99 instances of a generalization which I have observed to be true I conclude that the 100th is true also. In the first case the habit which determines the process is 'After lightning expect thunder'; the degree of expectation which it would be best for this habit to produce is equal to the proportion of cases of lightning which are actually followed by thunder. In the second case the habit is the more general one of inferring from 99 observed instances of a certain sort of generalization that the 100th instance is true also; the degree of belief it would be best for this habit to produce is equal to the proportion of all cases of 99 instances of a generalization being true, in which the 100th is true also.

Thus given a single opinion, we can only praise or blame it on the ground of truth or falsity: given a habit of a certain form, we can praise or blame it accordingly as the degree of belief it produces is near or far from the actual proportion in which the habit leads to truth. We can then praise or blame opinions derivatively from our praise or blame of the habits that produce them.

This account can be applied not only to habits of inference but also to habits of observation and memory; when we have a certain feeling in connection with an image we think the image represents something which actually happened to us, but we may not be sure about it; the degree of direct confidence in our memory varies. If we ask what is the best degree of confidence to place in a certain specific memory feeling, the answer must depend on how often when that feeling occurs the event whose image it attaches to has actually taken place.

Among the habits of the human mind a position of peculiar importance is occupied by induction. Since the time of Hume a great deal has been written about the justification for inductive inference. Hume showed that it could not be reduced to deductive inference or justified by formal logic. So far as it goes his demonstration seems to me final; and the suggestion of Mr. Keynes that it can be got round by regarding induction as a form of probable inference cannot in my view be maintained. But to suppose that the situation which results from this is a scandal to philosophy is, I think, a mistake.

We are all convinced by inductive arguments, and our conviction is reasonable because the world is so constituted that inductive arguments lead on the whole to true opinions. We are not, therefore, able to help trusting induction, nor if we could help it do we see any reason why we should, because we believe it to be a reliable process. It is true that if any one has not the habit of induction, we cannot prove to him that he is wrong; but there is nothing peculiar in that. If a man doubts his memory or his perception we cannot prove to him that they are trustworthy; to ask for such a thing to be proved is to cry for the moon, and the same is true of induction. It is one of the ultimate sources of knowledge just as memory is: no one regards it as a scandal to philosophy that there is no proof that the world did not begin two minutes ago and that all our memories are not illusory.

We all agree that a man who did not make inductions would be unreasonable: the question is only what this means. In my view it does not mean that the man would in any way sin against formal logic or formal probability; but that he had not got a very useful habit, without which he would be very much worse off, in the sense of being much less likely[15] to have true opinions.

This is a kind of pragmatism: we judge mental habits by whether they work, i.e. whether the opinions they lead to are for the most part true, or more often true than those which alternative habits would lead to.

Induction is such a useful habit, and so to adopt it is reasonable. All that philosophy can do is to analyse it, determine the degree of its utility, and find on what characteristics of nature this depends. An indispensable means for investigating these problems is induction itself, without which we should be helpless. In this circle lies nothing vicious. It is only through memory that we can determine the degree of accuracy of memory; for if we make experiments to determine this effect, they will be useless unless we remember them.

Let us consider in the light of the preceding discussion what sort of subject is inductive or human logic—the logic of truth. Its business is to consider methods of thought, and discover what degree of confidence should be placed in them, i.e. in what proportion of cases they lead to truth. In this investigation it can only be distinguished from the natural sciences by the greater generality of its problems. It has to consider the relative validity of different types of scientific procedure, such as the search for a causal law by Mill's Methods, and the modern mathematical methods like the *a priori* arguments used in discovering the Theory of Relativity. The proper plan of such a subject is to be found in Mill[16]; I do not mean the details of his Methods or even his use of the Law of Causality. But his way of treating the subject as a body of inductions about inductions, the Law of Causality governing lesser laws and being itself proved by induction by simple enumeration. The different scientific methods that can be used are in the last resort judged by induction by simple enumeration; we choose the simplest law that fits the facts, but unless we found that laws so obtained also fitted facts other than those they were made to fit, we should discard this procedure for some other.

Probability and partial belief (1929)

The defect of my paper on probability was that it took partial belief as a psychological phenomenon to be defined and measured by a psychologist. But this sort of psychology goes a very little way and would be quite unacceptable in a developed science. In fact the notion of a belief of degree 2/3 is useless to an outside observer, except when it is used by the thinker himself who says 'Well, I believe it to an extent 2/3', i.e. (this at least is the most natural interpretation) 'I have the same degree of belief in it as in $p \vee q$ when I think p, q, r equally likely and know that exactly one of them is true.' Now what is the point of this numerical comparison? how is the number used? In a great many cases it is used simply as a basis for getting further numbers of the same sort issuing finally in one so near 0 or 1 that it is taken to be 0 or 1 and the partial belief to be full belief. But sometimes the number is used itself in making a practical decision. How? I want to say in accordance with the law of mathematical expectation; but I cannot do this, for we could only use that rule if we had measured goods and bads. But perhaps in some sort of way we approximate to it, as we are supposed in economics to maximize an unmeasured utility. The question also arises why just this law of mathematical expectation. The answer to this is that if we use probability to measure utility, as explained in my paper, then consistency requires just this law. Of course if utility were measured in any other way, e.g. in money, we should not use mathematical expectation.

If there is no meaning in equal differences of utility, then money is as good a way as any of measuring them. A meaning may, however, be given by our probability method, or by means of time: i.e. $x - y = y - z$ if x for 1 day and z for 1 day $= y$ for 2 days. But the periods must be long or associated with different lives or people to prevent mutual influence. Do these two methods come to the same thing? Could we prove it by Bernoulli? Obviously not; Bernoulli only evaluates chances. A man might regard 1 good and 1 bad as equal to 2 neutral; but regard 2 bad as simply awful, not worth taking any chance of. (But it could be made up! No, there would be a chance of its not being.) I think this shows my method of measuring to be the sounder; it alone goes for *wholes*.

All this is just an idea; what sense is there really in it? We can, I think, say this:—
A *theory* is a set of propositions which contains (p and q) whenever it contains p and q, and if it contains any p contains all its logical consequences. The *interest* of such sets comes from the possibility of our adopting one of them as all we believe.

A *probability-theory* is a set of numbers associated with pairs of propositions obeying the calculus of probabilities. The *interest* of such a set comes from the possibility of acting on it consistently.

Of course, the mathematician is only concerned with the form of probability; it is quite true that he only deals in certainties.

Notes

* Originally published in F. P. Ramsey, *The Foundations of Mathematics and Other Logical Essays*, ed. R. B. Braithwaite, Routledge and Kegan Paul: London, 1931, pp. 156–98.
1 J. M. Keynes, *A Treatise on Probability* (1921).
2 p. 32, his italics.
3 J. A. Chadwick, "Logical Constants," *Mind*, Volume 36, 1927, pp. 1—11.
4 See N. Campbell, *Physics The Elements* (1920), p. 277.
5 Ibid., p. 271.
6 I assume here Wittgenstein's theory of propositions; it would probably be possible to give an equivalent definition in terms of any other theory.
7 α and β must be supposed so far undefined as to be compatible with both p and not-p.
8 Here β must include the truth of p, γ its falsity; p need no longer be ethically neutral. But we have to assume that there is a world with any assigned value in which p is true, and one in which p is false.
9 A. D. Ritchie, "Induction and Probability," *Mind*, Volume 35, 1926, pp. 301—18, at p. 318. 'The conclusion of the foregoing discussion may be simply put. If the problem of induction be stated to be "How can inductive generalizations acquire a large numerical probability?" then this is a pseudo-problem, because the answer is "They cannot". This answer is not, however, a denial of the validity of induction but is a direct consequence of the nature of probability. It still leaves untouched the real problem of induction which is "How can the probability of an induction be increased?" and it leaves standing the whole of Keynes' discussion on this point.'
10 C. S. Peirce, *Chance Love and Logic*, p. 92.
11 It appears in Mr. Keynes' system as if the principal axioms—the laws of addition and multiplication—were nothing but definitions. This is merely a logical mistake; his definitions are formally invalid unless corresponding axioms are presupposed. Thus his definition of multiplication presupposes the law that if the probability of a given bh is equal to that of c given dk, and the probability of b given h is equal to that of d given k, then will the probabilities of ab given h and of cd given k be equal.
12 Cf. Kant: 'Denn obgleich eine Erkenntnis der logischen Form völlig gemäss sein möchte, dass ist sich selbst nicht widerspräche, so kann sie doch noch immer dem Gegenstande widersprechen.' *Kritik der reinen Vernunft*, First Edition, p. 59.
13 [Earlier draft of matter of preceding paragraph in some ways better.—F.P.R.]
   What is meant by saying that a degree of belief is reasonable? First and often that it is what I should entertain if I had the opinions of the person in question at the time but was otherwise as I am now, e.g. not drunk. But sometimes we go beyond this and ask: 'Am I reasonable?' This may mean, do I conform to certain enumerable standards which we call scientific method, and which we value on account of those who practise them and the success they achieve. In this sense to be reasonable means to think like a scientist, or to be guided only be ratiocination and induction or something of the sort (i.e. reasonable means reflective). Thirdly, we may go to the root of why we admire the scientist and criticize not primarily an individual opinion but a mental habit as being conducive or otherwise to the discovery of truth or to entertaining such degrees of belief as will be most useful. (To include habits of doubt or partial belief.) Then we can criticize an opinion according to the habit which produced it. This is clearly right because it all depends on this habit; it would not be reasonable to get the right conclusion to a syllogism by remembering vaguely that you leave out a term which is common to both premisses.

We use reasonable in sense 1 when we say of an argument of a scientist this does not seem to me reasonable; in sense 2 when we *contrast* reason and superstition or instinct; in sense 3 when we *estimate* the value of new methods of thought such as soothsaying.]

14 What follows to the end of the section is almost entirely based on the writings of C. S. Peirce. [Especially his "Illustrations of the Logic of Science", *Popular Science Monthly*, 1877 and 1878, reprinted in *Chance Love and Logic* (1923).]

15 'Likely' here simply means that I am not sure of this, but only have a certain degree of belief in it.

16 Cf. also the account of 'general rules' in the Chapter 'Of Unphilosophical Probability' in Hume's *Treatise*.

3

SUBJECTIVE PROBABILITY
Criticisms, reflections and problems*

Henry E. Kyburg, Jr.

Introduction

The theory of subjective probability is certainly one of the most pervasively influential theories of anything to have arisen in many decades. It was developed first by probability theorists and philosophers (Koopman and Ramsey, primarily); then by a few somewhat unconventional statisticians (De Finetti and Savage). Growth in interest in the topic among statisticians was slow at first, but turned out to be (it seems) exponential in character. From statistics it spread to economics, political science, and the social sciences in general. From philosophy it spread to psychology and decision theory, and thence again to economics and political science. Although one could not say that it was dominant in any of these fields, it occupies a respectable place, either as subject matter or as methodological doctrine, in each of them.

One reason for this spread is both cultural and practical. The theory of subjective probability is undogmatic and anti-authoritarian: one man's opinion is as good as another's. It imposes only relatively weak constraints on the beliefs that a man has; if two people disagree, their disagreement can be treated merely as a datum, rather than as a cause of conflict. The theory embodies a modern spirit of tolerance and democracy. At the same time, in many areas people's degrees of belief are in relatively close agreement. The theory can also simply accept this agreement as a datum, and go on from there.[0] There is no need to justify that agreement, or even to look into its source. We need not get hung up on deep and abstract (and possibly artificial) issues in order to proceed to use this theory of probability in testing hypotheses, in making statistical inferences, in formulating theories of rational decision, in describing choice behavior under uncertainty, and so on.

The reason for the philosophical popularity of the doctrine is that it appears to be minimally committal – that is, it is easy to say that whatever the true doctrine of probability may be, *at least* it requires that the ordinary of the probability calculus hold of it; and since it is just these axioms that are required by the subjective theory, anything we can establish using the subjective theory will, *a fortiori*, be established for a more demanding theory. The theory provides a good working basis for philosophical investigation because it is maximally tolerant and minimally restrictive.

In the pages that follow, I shall argue that although the theory appears to be all things to all people, in fact it is a snare and a delusion and is either vacuous and without systematic usefulness, or is simply false. Before charging off into the brush, however, let us get straight about the animal we are after. By 'the' theory of subjective probability, I mean any of quite a large group of interpretations of the probability calculus which lead to the assignment of a numerical probability to each sentence or proposition of a language (or event of a field of events), and in which these assignments do not reflect any known or hypothetical frequencies.

The language in question may be restricted to the part of a natural language in which sentences relevant to a given problem or decision may be formulated, or it may be a larger or smaller fragment of an explicitly formalized language. Sometimes (particularly in statistical applications) the propositions or sentences are parametrized, and we consider, not the assignment of probabilities to specific propositions, but rather the assignment of probability densities to the parameters.

What do the numbers represent? This depends on the way in which the theory is construed. It may be construed as a descriptive theory or as a normative theory; and it may be construed as a theory of decision under uncertainty, or as a theory concerned with degrees of belief. The interpretations offered by various authors may not always fall cleanly into one of the resulting four classifications, but if the theory does not work under any of the four pure interpretations, it is unlikely that it can be saved by ambiguity.

If the theory is construed as a descriptive theory of decision-making under uncertainty, the numbers represent theoretical psychological characteristics (conveniently, if loosely, referred to as degrees of belief) which enter into a general descriptive theory of actual behavior under uncertainty. If the theory is construed as a descriptive theory of degrees of belief, the numbers represent actual degrees of belief, which we may attempt to measure by examining behavior under uncertainty. If the theory is construed as a normative theory of decision, the numbers represent parameters which *ought* to satisfy certain constraints. If the theory is construed as a normative theory of degrees of belief, then the numbers represent the measures assigned to sentences of a language, and *ought* to satisfy at least the constraints of the probability calculus. I include among the latter theories such 'logical' theories as that sought by the early Carnap, according to which on logical grounds alone we should be able to assign a probability measure to every sentence of the language, those discussed by the later Carnap, in which the probability measures of the sentences of the language are determined by a few parameters that represent personal or subjective commitment, and those proposed by Hintikka, Tuomela, Niiniluoto and others in which the probability measures of the sentences are determined by a few parameters which reflect *empirical* 'judgments' about the actual nature of the world.

All of these interpretations impute the same structure to probabilities (relevant exceptions will be noted in due course):

$p(h)$ is a real number lying between 0 and 1
$p(e \wedge h) = p(e) \cdot p(h/e)$, where $p(h/e)$ is the conditional probability of h, *given e*.
If h and g are logically exclusive, $p(h \vee g) = p(h) + p(g)$.

The Dutch book argument

In subjectivistic interpretations of probability, there is a fundamental nexus in which logic and behavior meet. It is the betting situation, first described with the intent of clarifying the relation between probability and belief by F.P. Ramsey [20]. Basically, the connection is this:

Step I: The more convinced I am that something is going to happen, the higher the odds I am willing to offer in a bet that it will occur. Ramsey's idea was to take the *least odds* at which an individual would accept a gamble on the occurrence of E to indicate his degree of belief in E. We assume that these least odds are well defined: that is, we assume that if the agent is willing to accept a gamble at $P{:}S$, then he will accept a gamble at $P'{:}S$ for any P' less than P. This can be made more precise and more plausible as follows:[1] Consider a gamble for a fixed stake S where a price P is charged. The least odds at which the agent is willing to accept such a gamble is the least upper bound of the ratios $P/(S - P)$ representing the gambles the agent is willing to accept. We also assume that these least odds are independent of the size of the stake. We do not assume, yet, that the least odds will remain unchanged for a negative stake – i.e., for bets on the non-occurrence of E. We do assume, however, that the individual has least odds for a whole algebra of events (or propositions), i.e., that if his least odds are well defined for E and F, they are well defined for $\sim E$ and for $E \wedge F$.

Step II: We regard it as irrational for a person to have a book made against him – i.e., to accept a sequence of bets such that, no matter how events turn out, he loses.

Step III: We conclude that it is irrational for a person's beliefs to be represented by least odds such that the person can be the victim of a Dutch Book concocted by an unscrupulous bettor. (I don't know who first used the word 'unscrupulous' in this context, but it does create a persuasive image of the virtuous Rational Man protecting himself against the Forces of Evil.)[2] From this, in turn, it follows that those odds must be related in just the way that probabilities are related in the standard probability calculus. Whatever else is true about rational beliefs, then, (we might, for example, demand with Carnap that they reflect certain linguistic symmetries) they must at least satisfy the core axioms of the probability calculus. We have thus found, in the Dutch Book Argument, a justification for the demand that rational degrees of belief satisfy these axioms. (If we are construing the subjectivistic interpretation of probability empirically, we have found in the Dutch Book Argument *prima facie* warrant for taking the probability calculus as a plausible empirical hypothesis.)

Or have we? It is noteworthy that Carnap, in *The Logical Foundations of Probability* [1], does *not* employ these arguments to justify the axioms he lays down for degree of confirmation. He was perfectly aware of Ramsey's work, and devotes several pages to defending Ramsey against the charge of 'subjectivism', there construed as the denial that there is a difference between merely coherent degrees of belief and *rational* degrees of belief. Ramsey himself writes, "It is not enough to measure probability; in order to apportion correctly our belief to the probability, we must also be able to measure our belief." (Quoted by Carnap [1], p. 16.) Of course we know that Carnap was later persuaded that the Dutch Book Argument was sound, and on a subjectivistic view it may very well turn out to make no sense to attempt to measure probability and belief independently. Nevertheless, let us begin by taking a close look at the argument.

We first note that Step II has nothing to do with degrees of belief or with probabilities. No rational person, whatever his degrees of belief, would accept a sequence of bets under which he would be bound to lose no matter what happens. No rational person will in fact have a book made against him. If we consider a sequence of bets, then quite independently of the odds at which the person is willing to bet, he will decline any bet that converts the sequence into a Dutch Book. His least odds on E, for example, may be 2:1, while his least odds on E and F may be 4:1; this violates the calculus, but is no Dutch Book. His least odds on E may be 2:1, and his least odds on $\sim E$ may be 2:1; there is not even a Dutch Book here, unless he accepts each bet – and, of course, being rational, he will accept no more than one bet, for otherwise, at the same amount on each bet, he would be bound to lose.

According to the subjectivistic theory, it is irrational to offer 2:1 odds that a certain toss of a coin will land heads and to offer 1:1 odds that it will land tails. But it is *not* unreasonable, on this view, to offer 2:1 odds to A that the toss will land tails, and then to offer 2:1 odds to B that the following toss will land heads. Nor is it irrational to make the following bet: I agree to draw a card from an ordinary deck, and if it is red offer you 2:1 odds on heads, and if it is black, offer you 2:1 odds on tails. In fact, however, so far as the Dutch Book argument goes, it would be perfectly rational for me to offer you 2:1 odds on heads *and* 2:1 odds on tails, provided I make it clear that I am offering only one bet. Note that this has nothing to do with my placing a value on gambling: If I *accepted* both bets, it would imply that I valued the gamble in itself; but my refusal to accept more than one bet precludes warrant for the assertion that I am assigning a high value to the utility of gambling.

The rational man will not actually have a book made against him; but this is a matter of deductive logic, and not of probability; a matter of certainties and not a matter of degrees of belief. Step II then is a heuristic device, or, to put it less charitably, a red herring.

The conclusion that a rational man's degrees of belief, as reflected in his least odds, must satisfy the axioms of the probability calculus does not follow from the assumptions thus far made.

What we require in order to capture the intent of the Dutch Book Argument is an intermediate step:

Step I-A: We assume that the individual is willing to take any combination of bets, for any stakes, at the least odds that characterize his degrees of belief.

In effect, this step amounts to the demand that the individual post odds on a field of events or statements, and then *make book* according to the odds he has posted. Note how different this is from Step II: Step II points out that a rational man will not *actually* have a book made against him. But we already know that, and that has nothing to do with the 'least odds' at which he would bet on an event, or even on each event in a field of events. This consideration imposes no constraints on the numbers we assign to statements or events. Step I-A, on the other hand, imposes a constraint on the posted odds concerning a whole field of events, when the individual is required to accept all bets offered to him at those posted odds. The constraint here concerns *potential* sets of bets, not actual ones. The rational man, in posting his odds, protects himself against all possibilities; he must make book with all comers, as an equal opportunity bookie, according to the odds he has posted. Thus we must replace the assumption of Step II by the following assumption:

Step II-A: The rational man will not put himself in a position in which he can *potentially* have a book made against him.

Note, however, that the conclusion that these posted least odds can be converted into a set of numbers satisfying the axioms of the probability calculus still does not follow. The least odds the agent offers on E may be 2:5, and the least odds he offers on $\sim E$ may also be 2:5. In fact, if he is a professional gambler, the sum of the odds he offers on any two complementary bets will of course add up to less than 1; this is how he makes his money. And there is hardly anything irrational about this!

We may, however, arrive at the following conclusion: with every event or proposition we may associate two numbers, one representing the least odds at which the agent will bet *on* the event, the other representing the least odds at which the agent will bet *against* the event. We can now show that there exists a function *P*, satisfying the axioms of the probability calculus, such that for every event in our field of events the value of that function will belong to the closed interval determined by the corresponding numbers.

A number (a relatively small number) of writers follow the Dutch Book Argument only this far; C. A. B. Smith [25], I. J. Good [7], P. Suppes [26], I. Levi [15], A. Dempster [4] are among them. It is possible then to take the set of functions *P* satisfying the posted odds to characterize an individual's degrees of belief. Note that in so doing we are abandoning the notion that there is a single real-valued degree of belief associated with each proposition in our algebra, determined by the least odds at which an individual will bet *on* that proposition.

What we require in order to obtain the conclusion of the Dutch Book Argument is a stronger assumption by far than any we have made so far. It may be stated thus:

Step I-B: We assume that the individual is willing to take any combination of bets, for any stakes, *positive or negative*, at the least odds that characterize his degrees of belief.

To stipulate that the odds may be positive or negative has the effect of requiring that the agent be willing to take either side of a bet at his posted odds. Now, at last, the conclusion of Step III will follow from the assumptions of Steps I, I-B, and II-A. The posted odds can now be translated into numbers, associated with each member of the field in question, which satisfy the probability calculus. There are other ways to obtain such numbers which eliminate the need to be sloppy about the marginal utility of money and the desirability of gambling: for example we may force (or bribe) an individual to express a preference between acts that depend on the states of nature (the field of events). The best known approach along these lines is that of Savage [20].

What is noteworthy is that we obtain a set of numbers satisfying the probability calculus only by *compelling* the individual to do something: to post odds on *E* and odds on $\sim E$ and then to accept any bets, with positive or negative stakes, at these odds; or to express a preference between receiving a prize if it rains on March 3, 1986, and receiving a prize if between 1,456 and 1,603 heads appear on 3,341 tosses of a specific coin. It is only through this sort of compulsion that we can obtain a full set of numbers satisfying the probability calculus.

But now we see that the argument from Step I, Step I-B, and Step II-A, to Step III, while valid, is no longer sound: we have no reason to suppose that an individual would be willing to post odds under these conditions, or to take the time and effort to express a serious set of preferences. We must replace I-B by:

Step I-C: The individual can be *made* to post odds on which he will take any combination of bets, for any stakes, positive or negative.

It will follow that these odds will conform to the probability calculus. But now the connection between these odds and degrees of belief has become attenuated to the point of obscurity. However irrational and strange my degrees of belief, I will, under compulsion, post odds that are coherent (or publish a coherent preference ranking).

As I look out the window, it occurs to me that the least odds I would be comfortable about offering on rain today are about 3:7, and the least odds I would be comfortable about offering against rain are about 3:7. If I am forced, in accordance with Step I-C, to post odds and make book, I will pick a number between 0.3 and 0.7 to determine those odds. But I will be no more comfortable with 0.5 than with 0.4 or 0.6. The number I pick will depend on my mood and my circumstances. But it does not seem to me that my 'degree of belief' in rain is varying correspondingly according to my mood and circumstances.

There may indeed be a rough intuitive connection between my degree of belief in an even E and the least odds I am willing to offer in a bet on E. But this connection is much too loose to generate by itself a set of numbers conforming to the probability calculus. The Dutch Book Argument gives excellent reasons for adopting a table of odds or publishing a list of preferences which conform to the basic core of the probability calculus, but it does so at the cost of severing the immediate and intuitive connection between odds and degrees of belief that the argument originally depended on. In fact, at this point, we may find ourselves wondering if there *is* any such thing as 'degree of belief'.

There are a number of directions we can go from here, and various theories of subjective probability have explored these various directions. We can regard 'degree of belief' as a kind of intervening variable in an empirical decision theory: that is, a psychological theory that accounts for the decisions that people actually make. The theory would assert that people act as if they had degrees of belief conforming to the probability calculus, and so acted as to maximize their expected utilities. Or we can regard 'degree of belief' as a kind of intervening variable in a normative decision theory: people *ought* to act as if they had degrees of belief conforming to the probability calculus, and were maximizing their expected utility. Or we can suppose that decisions and preferences just constitute a way of *getting at* degrees of belief (or that there is some other way of getting at degrees of belief), and construe the probability calculus as a theory of people's actual beliefs. Or, finally, we can suppose that decisions and preferences are just ways of getting at degrees of belief (or that there is some other way of getting at degrees of belief) and construe the theory of subjective probability as a normative theory of degrees of belief. In the sections that follow, we shall explore each of these four alternatives in turn.

Empirical decision theory

A number of investigators have taken subjectivistic probability as an ingredient in an empirical theory of how people actually make decisions. People's decisions, of course, are highly complex, and involve a number of factors that are extremely hard to evaluate. The theory is tested, therefore, under relatively simple and artificial circumstances. For example, subjects are presented with a board containing a large number of red and white thumbtacks. Although the subject is not given enough time to count the thumbtacks, it is found that usually his judgment of the proportion of red thumbtacks is quite accurate. The subject is offered a pair of bets on red against white. He chooses a bet. A row and column of the thumbtack display are selected by a device which insures that each thumbtack will be selected equally often (and the subject knows this). The bet is then settled. The bet is sometimes a matter of real money; sometimes a matter of hypothetical real money bets; sometimes a matter of chips or counters [5].

There are a number of things to be noted about such experiments. First, subjective factors that might be regarded as extraneous to the probability–utility framework are excluded as rigorously as possible. Second, the 'amounts' involved in the bets are arranged so that they are quite strictly linear in utility. Third, although the probabilities involved are 'subjective', they very closely reflect the frequencies of the various outcomes. Thus these experiments constitute a simple and direct test of the SEU (subjective expected utility) theory of decision under circumstances highly favorable to the theory. As Edwards remarks, if the theory is going to work for subjective probabilities in general, it should certainly work for subjective probabilities which simply reflect objective frequencies [5].

It turns out that while the theory predicts reasonably well for probabilities in the middle range, it goes awry for large or small probabilities, despite the fact that the utilities involved are well within the linear range. Furthermore, it goes awry in different ways for positive expected utilities and for negative expected utilities.

Even in these highly artificial and simple situations, people do not act in ways that are consonant with the assumption that their degrees of belief, as reflected in their choices between bets, satisfy the axioms of the probability calculus.

From a psychological point of view, one is interested in developing a theory of choice behavior under uncertainty which will enable one to predict and understand people's choices, not in devising a theory of belief that embodies certain a priori constraints. Psychologists therefore seem to have largely moved away from the SEU model. Much of the recent literature relevant to this development is cited in [24], especially pp. 9–11.

That psychologists are abandoning the SEU model does not mean in itself that subjective probability is being abandoned. One possibility is that 'subjective probability' – i.e., degree of belief – may no longer be required to satisfy the axioms of the probability Calculus. Edwards [5] suggests the possibility that the additive property be abandoned. The abandonment of any such property entails the rejection of the Dutch Book Argument as yielding a description of choice behavior even under ideal circumstances. It strongly suggests that it is inappropriate to call the 'subjective probabilities' that enter into such a revised empirical theory 'probabilities' at all.

Another possibility that is being actively pursued is that an accurate descriptive decision theory will involve not only expected gain, but other moments of the gain as well. Thus people might be concerned not only with their *expectation* in a gamble, but with the *variance* of the outcome, preferring, say, gambles with modest expectation and small variance to gambles with larger expectations but much larger variance. Here again, however, we find problems for the conventional subjectivistic interpretation of probability. The conventional interpretation supposes (as in the Dutch Book Argument) that we can get at subjective probabilities in a straightforward way through compulsorily posted betting odds, or through the analysis of forced choices among alternatives. But this approach takes the SEU model for granted, and applies it inside out, so to speak, to determine subjective degrees of belief. If we suppose that preferences are not determined by subjective expected utility, but in some other more complicated way, it may be difficult to measure 'degrees of belief'.

In any event, the neat relations among 'degree of belief', 'utility', and 'expected utility' that underlie the Dutch Book Argument are not reflected in people's actual choice behavior.

Normative decision theory

One response to this situation (I think it would have been Savage's, and it would certainly be that of a large number of philosophers and economists) is to say that the subjective expected utility model of decision was never intended to be an empirical description of how people actually make decisions, even under 'ideal' circumstances, but rather a normative prescription of how people ought, rationally, to make decisions. Of course we suppose that people by and large are relatively rational – and the evidence of the psychological experiments for the midrange of probabilities provides gratifying confirmation of the general rationality of people. But the fact that when the probabilities become (according to the theory) large or small people cease somewhat to be rational should not be construed as *undermining* the normative theory.

Let us, then, confront this normative theory in its own terms, ignoring the fact that people are not always rational in their actual behavior. Indeed, were people always rational in their decisions, we would hardly be motivated (except perhaps as metaphysicians) to develop an elaborate theory of rationality. In point of fact, the main use of normative decision theory is in providing guidance under circumstances of uncertainty. Savage himself remarks that "... the main use I would make [of the axioms] is normative ..." ([23], p. 20).

There are a number of ways of formalizing normative decision theory in a subjectivistic framework. The following, adapted from Savage [23], will suffice for our purposes. We need to get at both utilities and probabilities; the mechanism for doing so is to look at preference rankings. Preference rankings of what? Of *acts*, construed as functions from states of affairs to consequences. We can choose our acts – that is what decision theory is all about – but we cannot choose the state of the world, nor can we choose the consequences of our acts. Normative decision theory is designed to guide our choices among acts.

The subjective approach supposes that on the basis of an individual's ranking of acts (functions, remember) we may infer both his probabilities and his utilities. It must be supposed that probabilities and utilities cannot be evaluated independently of the ranking of acts – else the agent might be in the position of ranking most highly an act whose mathematical expectation is not the highest, and this blatantly violates the basic thrust of the subjectivistic approach. On the other hand, if we begin with a complete preference ranking among acts, what is the point of the analysis into utilities and probabilities? The process seems obviously circular: we start with a preference ranking among acts, and by dint of careful analysis arrive at probabilities and utilities, and by computing mathematical expectations arrive at a ranking which (unless something has gone wrong) precisely matches the original one!

The point, however, is that the individual's initial preferences may be partly unknown and partly incoherent. For example, he may prefer act A to act B; act B to act C; and act C to act A. This is clearly irrational: preference should be transitive, and nothing should be preferred to itself. His preference ranking may be incoherent in a more sophisticated way: for example, he may prefer A if state X obtains and B if state not-X obtains to A if X, and he may prefer A if X to B if not-X. This set of preferences is incoherent because there is no assignment of probabilities and desirabilities that will lead to mathematical expectations that conform to this ranking. (Suppose that the probability of X is p; then the value of the first ranked alternative is p times the value of the second ranked alternative plus $(1 - p)$ times the value of the third ranked alternative; the value of the mixed alternative must be between the values of the pure alternatives, since $0 < p < 1$; this contradicts our original stipulation.)

If such an incoherence is pointed out to a rational individual, he will presumably alter his preference ranking. Savage says that to be in this state is to be 'uncomfortable' in the same sense as to find oneself committed to a logical inconsistency. But to be 'in this state' is to presuppose that one's preferences form a simple order, and as Savage himself recognizes, actual preferences form at best a partial ordering [23, p. 21]. It is precisely in the attempt to make one's preferences conform to the theory – that is, in the attempt to produce a simple order of preferences from one's actual partial order – that one stumbles on violations of the theory. Unlike logical consistency, coherence hangs on a doctrine that is admittedly unrealistic; without the doctrine we might not find anything uncomfortable about failures of the transitivity of indifference, for example.

The normative force of the theory, then, is that it says that the preference ranking of an individual *should* be such that there exists a probability function and a utility function for which the mathematical expectations computed in accordance with those functions agree with the preference ranking.

Axiomatizations of subjective theories generally require an assumption even stronger than that of simple order among preferences. Savage [23, p. 6, p. 39] requires that there are states of the world with arbitrarily small probabilities. He is able to show that a preference ranking satisfying his postulates can be decomposed into a unique probability function and a unique desirability function. The desirability of an act can then be represented as its mathematical expectation.

Jeffrey [11] imposes a condition that is somewhat weaker on preference rankings: the 'splitting condition' requires that any (non-neutral) element of the preference ranking can be expressed as the disjunction of two equiprobable incompatible elements that are ranked together [11, p. 104]. Jeffrey's system does not entail that there are *unique* probability and desirability functions that expresses the preference ranking; it merely entails that there is a family of pairs of probability and desirability functions which will *fit* the preference ranking, in the sense that mathematical expectations computed in accord with any of them will yield rankings among elements that conform to the original rankings.

Now how do we use this normative decision theory? We begin with a partial preference ranking. The axioms of the theory help us to make our preference ranking more complete. That this sort of exercise can be very useful is clear; subjectivist decision theory has become entrenched in business schools precisely because of this usefulness. It is most useful when there are relatively standard measures of desirabilities (dollars) or of probabilities (frequencies) or both. There are often a fairly large number of fixed points in a preference ranking that can be established by such considerations; these can give some indication of how 'inconsistencies' are to be resolved. But the axioms cannot do the whole job; if we start with a partial ranking, there may well be acts whose relative positions in the preference ranking are not determined by the initial partial ranking and the axioms of the theory. We must then consult our intuitions to decide how those alternatives are to be ranked.

It may be the case that our initial partial preference ranking is incoherent – even though it is only partial, it may conflict with the axioms of the normative theory. As Savage points out on numerous occasions, the theory cannot tell us how to resolve that conflict. Again we must consult our intuitions. The theory tells us that some change must be made in our preference ranking, but it does not tell us what change. It will generally be the case that our preference ranking is incomplete in the sense that, given our initial preferences, there will be alternatives whose location is not determined by those preferences together with the axioms of the theory. Again, we must call on intuition to complete the preference ranking, to the extent that it needs to be completed.

(In order to use the theory we need not always have a preference ranking complete in all detail.)

Once we have a preference ranking that satisfies the axioms of the theory, we can crank out at least one probability and desirability function, and perhaps a family of them. We can now use these probability and desirability functions to compute mathematical expectations. And we are then directed to perform that act with the greatest mathematical expectation. But of course that act is the act at the head of this coherent preference ranking. So if we've got a coherent preference ranking, we don't have to make any computations. On the other hand, if we don't have a coherent preference ranking, the theory won't tell us *how* to make it coherent. If we have a coherent but partial preference ranking, the theory may allow us to make it more complete. The theory thus functions as a heuristic device enabling us to specify our preference ranking in an organized way, and revealing incoherencies that require resolution.

We must now ask, however, how important the role of subjective probability is in enabling normative decision theory to perform its function. Our suspicions may be aroused by two facts: First, Jeffrey's form of the theory allows the derivation from the preference ranking of not one, but of a whole family of probability functions. If these functions are construed as yielding subjective probabilities – i.e., degrees of belief – this means that the preference ranking does not either yield or require a *unique* degree-of-belief function. Second, the most clear-cut and persuasive applications of the theory are those in which the subjective probability function simply mirrors well established statistical frequencies. In these applications, then, we can construe the function whose combination with a utility function is to yield the coherent preference ranking as a perfectly straightforward frequency function, having no psychological import whatever. (It *may* be the case that there are such things as degrees of belief, and it *may* be that in certain situations these degrees of belief have the same magnitudes as certain relative frequencies, but in the applications we are discussing both of these assumptions are gratuitous and irrelevant.)

Many of the most interesting of the applications of the normative decision theory, however, are applications that do *not* involve well-tested roulette wheels or other apparatus yielding alternatives with well-known frequencies. The question now is whether or not the probability numbers that emerge from the analysis of the preference ranking can nevertheless be construed as known (or reasonably believed) frequencies. Certainly in many of the instances in which the normative decision theory is applied – in business decisions, for example – it is not hard to imagine that the probability numbers can plausibly be construed as estimates of the relative frequency with which a given sort of thing happens in given circumstances. Again, to the extent that this is plausible, there is no need to construe these numbers as reflecting subjective degrees of belief.

It may be questioned whether or not this is always the case. There are certainly applications of Normative Bayesian Decision Theory in which the probability numbers emerge from a dialogue between the decision theorist and the executive decision maker, rather than from any recorded tables of statistical data. But this does not settle the question of what the numbers that thus emerge represent. On the subjectivistic interpretation of probability, they represent degrees of belief; but we may also suppose that these numbers represent the executive's (possibly "subjective") estimates of *objective* frequencies. We might be hard put, on occasion, to formalize these intuitive judgments: it can be far from obvious what frequency in what reference class is being intuitively estimated when the decision maker says that he would just bet even money that the sales of product X in 1979 will exceed 145,500 units. Nevertheless, it is not implausible to suppose that there is some estimate of an objective frequency underlying such judgments.

It is worth remarking that the specification of a reference class is not a trivial problem even in the case of probabilities that are quite clearly related to frequencies: probabilities that arise in weather forecasting, in insurance, and the like. For formal languages there is a mechanism that will yield a correct reference class, given a body of knowledge – see [13]. The extent to which this mechanism can be valuable heuristically in relatively informal contexts remains to be seen.

To sum up: If we suppose we begin with a full preference ranking among acts, there are two possibilities. Either the preference ranking is coherent, or it is not. If it is coherent, we are all set – we merely follow the dictates of our preference ranking with no further analysis. If it is not, then something must be changed; but as Savage never tired of pointing out, the subjectivistic theory will not tell you what to change. Subjectivistically interpreted, Normative Bayesian Decision Theory, whatever its heuristic virtues, is either philosophically vacuous or impotent. What has made the theory attractive to non-philosophers – to psychologists and economists and businessmen – is of course precisely its heuristic virtues. But as I have tried to point out, *these* virtues are preserved – and quite possible enhanced – by adopting a point of view in which probabilities are given an interpretation which rests ultimately of frequencies rather than on degree's of belief. Finally, since Jeffrey can achieve a representation of coherent preferences through the use of a whole family of pairs of utility and probability functions, it seems clear that it is unnecessary and perhaps ill advised to hypostatize these probabilities as 'degrees of belief' in even an idealized psychological sense.

Empirical theory of degrees of belief

Can we construe the subjectivistic theory of probability as an empirical theory of degrees of belief? We note that the failure of the theory as an empirical theory of decision does not entail its failure as a theory of degrees of belief. The subjectivistic theory construed as a theory of decision making involves two other ingredients besides degrees of belief: it involves utilities, and it involves the acceptance by the individual of the principle of maximizing mathematical expectation. Thus the kinds of experiments that psychologists have performed to test the subjectivistic theory of decision are not really decisive with regard to a subjectivistic theory of degrees of belief. But then in order to test the latter theory we must find some way – preferably more direct – to measure degrees of belief than that to which we are led by the full blown subjective expected utility theory.

One way would be to inquire of people what their degrees of belief in various propositions are. This is a very unlikely approach: people will often say they don't know, and they will often announce numbers that do not fit into the calculus of probability. We must assume – if the theory is to have a chance at all – that people have no very clear access to their degrees of belief.

Furthermore, it is not altogether clear that there are degrees of belief. We can introspectively distinguish a number of qualities of our beliefs: confidence, enthusiasm, intensity; but it is not so easy to sort our beliefs out along the linear array that we want to think of as representing degrees of belief. It is particularly difficult to do this introspectively.

Savage has suggested a number of ingenious ways to get at degrees of belief which do not involve the entire subjectivistic theory of decision. For example, one could discover the maximum amount that a person would pay for a ticket that would return him a dollar if S is true; that amount would represent his degree of belief in S. But this will not do for several reasons. First of all, the prices a person offers for tickets on a number of related propositions may well not satisfy the axioms of the probability calculus. In fact this will quite generally be the case, since there are traditional probability calculations (the birthday problem, for example) that most people find surprising. Second, on the subjectivistic view, a person may change his opinions at any time, for good reason or for no reason. To discover whether or not a person's degrees of belief satisfied the axioms of the probability calculus would require that we test all of his beliefs – or a large set of them – simultaneously. But of course we can't actually do this. Finally, it is difficult to see how in *this* program of measurement we can eliminate the influence of risk: a conservative sort would, I imagine, discount his tickets (say, offering $p - \epsilon$ for a dollar ticket on S, and $1 - p - \epsilon$ for a dollar ticket on $\sim S$), and an enthusiastic gambler might well offer a little extra for the fun of gambling. The same sorts of problems arise here as arise in the general attempt to assess probabilities by gambling behavior discussed in the section on the Dutch book argument.

Another device proposed by Savage, and endorsed by a number of writers on subjective probability, is the forced choice: the subject is asked to choose between receiving a substantial prize if it rains in Los Angeles three weeks from today, and receiving the same prize if a sequence of fifteen coin tosses contains 12 heads. Although no finite number of such forced choices can show that his degrees of belief *do* obey the probability calculus, a finite number of them can show that they don't. If the forced choices yield an ordering of propositions that can be explained by a set of degrees of belief satisfying the calculus, that is certainly evidence that the theory has something to it.

But we have every reason to expect that such a test would fail to support the theory. Just as the degrees of belief that people claim will not satisfy the probability calculus (else they would not be surprised by probability calculations), so their choices, which no doubt come close to reflecting the degrees of belief they would claim, will not be consistent with the probability calculus. And we have the same temporal problem as before: since on the subjective view, degrees of belief may change freely, we must measure a number of related degrees of belief simultaneously, and the proposed technique does not allow us to do that.

Finally, we may suppose that someone invents an epistemeter, which will measure a thousand degrees of belief simultaneously through electrodes wired to the head of an individual. If there were such a device, it could put our theory to relatively direct test. The device would have to be tuned and standardized, of course, but that could perhaps be done by means of some of the techniques mentioned earlier. Now if we had such a machine, it is conceivable that then we could discover something much like degrees of belief that characterizes people's brains, and which does indeed satisfy the axioms of the probability calculus. But I wouldn't bet on it. At any rate, so far as *present* evidence is concerned, we have no evidence that people's degrees of belief satisfy the probability calculus, and considerable evidence to the effect that they do not.

Normative theory of degrees of belief

Relatively few people, I assume, have seriously proposed that the subjective theory of probability be construed as an empirical theory of degrees of actual belief. They have said, rather, that the subjective theory is ideal or normative: should an individual discover that his degrees of belief do not conform to the probability calculus, he will just by that very fact be motivated to change them in such a way that they do conform. When someone shows me the calculation which establishes that the odds are better than even that that two people in a room of twenty-one people will have the same birthday, I revise my degree of belief accordingly. According to the introspective testimony of some, the feeling is much like that of being caught in a logical contradiction.

It is difficult to make much out of this introspective feeling; not all individuals testify to having felt it, and it hardly seems a firm enough foundation to build a normative theory of degrees of belief on. Ramsey [20] pointed out long ago that there was no point in a normative theory of belief if there were to be no way of measuring beliefs.

If we had an epistemeter, of course, we could apply the normative theory: we could take an individual, wire him up, and see whether or not his momentary degrees of belief conformed to the probability calculus; if they did, we could give him a gold star. Science fiction aside, however, there seems to be no behavioral way to get at degrees of belief. Even in the most persuasive case, when we demand that an individual post odds representing his degrees of belief, and take all bets offered, we have no assurance whatever that his degrees of belief will conform to the probability calculus, precisely because of the fact that if he is *deductively* rational, he will not post incoherent odds, however incoherent his degrees of belief may be.

At the moment, then, there is no way of getting at a person's degrees of belief which is dependable enough that it could serve as a ground for asserting that he is or is not rational in his degrees of belief. But we may nevertheless consider the subjectivistic theory as a standard of rationality that we are simply not in a position to *apply* practically at the moment. It may still be important theoretically and philosophically, and it may in fact turn out to be feasible to apply it practically some day. Indeed, this is the way in which most philosophers who take the subjectivistic theory of probability as a standard of rationality, more or less without argument, seem to look on it. It is simply assumed that whatever else may be said about rationality, at any rate one's degrees of belief should conform to the probability calculus.

There are several things to be said about this. The first and most obvious is that it is not at all clear that there *are* degrees of belief in the sense required by the demand that they conform to the probability calculus. The calculus requires that with each proposition there be associated a real number, and that these real numbers be related in certain ways. But there may be nothing that corresponds to the term 'degree of belief'; or if there is it may need to be measured by an interval, or by an n-dimensional vector. It seems reasonable to suppose that 'degree of belief' is a psychological concept which depends for its usefulness on the psychological theory in which it appears. But at the moment, there is no such psychological theory.

Second, this construal of the subjective theory entails that one should be very certain indeed of propositions that seem both very powerful and empirical. Thus if one has a degree of belief equal to p in a certain relatively rare kind of event (e.g., that the next ball drawn from an urn will be purple), and if one supposes that one's degree of belief that the second ball is purple, given that the first one is purple is no more than $2p$, and if one regards the draws as exchangeable in the subjectivist's sense, then one should be 99% sure that p plus or minus 0.01 of the draws, in the long run, will yield purple balls. (For details of such arguments, see [12].)

This is, indeed, what one's initial beliefs commit one to, if they conform to the probability calculus. On the other hand, most of us would regard the consequence as unintuitive. The moral, I believe, is that there is no way to make one's beliefs conform to the probability calculus – on the assumption that they are real numbers – without doing violence to some rational intuitions. To reject the consequence requires – essentially – rejecting the supposition that there are any exchangeable sequences of events, which would undermine the usefulness of the subjectivistic theory.

Finally, we may ask what functions this normative theory of degrees of belief performs. It is clear that it serves no function for non-philosophers. But is it possible that it performs a function for philosophers – can we get some mileage out of a theory which supposes that there are degrees of belief, and demands that they conform to the usual probability axioms?

We consider two cases. First, suppose that these are all the constraints there are on rational belief. Then any distribution of degrees of belief over the propositions of a language is as good as – as rational as – any other, provided the axioms of the probability calculus are satisfied. But the axioms are compatible with any degree of belief in any individual (non-logical) statement. No degree of belief in any non-logical proposition can, by itself, be ruled irrational. The set of degrees of belief in a number of related propositions are constrained, on this view, by the requirements of rationality. But what does this constraint tell us? It does not tell us that the rational individual will not in fact have a book made against him, for if we grant him deductive rationality we already know that he won't actually allow a book to be made against him, regardless of what his degrees of belief are.

It might be maintained, and would be by anyone who regarded the theory of subjective probability as providing insights into scientific inference, that its main function is dynamic: it is the changes in the probability function that are wrought by empirical evidence, through the mediation of Bayes' theorem (or a generalization thereof) that give the theory its philosophical importance. The most frequently cited examples are the convergence theorems: Given that two people have degrees of belief that satisfy the probability calculus, and given that their degrees of belief satisfy some relatively mild constraints in addition to the coherence constraints, then, as empirical evidence accumulates, their distributions of beliefs will become more and more nearly the same. Of course there is nothing *in the theory* that requires that even the mild constraints will be satisfied for a rational person. But the really serious problem is that there is nothing in the theory that says that a person should *change* his beliefs in response to evidence in accordance with Bayes' theorem. On the contrary, the whole thrust of the subjectivistic theory is to claim that the history of the individual's beliefs is irrelevant to their rationality: all that counts at a given time is that they conform to the requirements of coherence. It is certainly not required that the person got to the state that he is in by applying Bayes' theorem to the coherent degrees of belief he had in some previous state. No more, then, is it required that a rational individual pass from his present coherent state to a new coherent state by conditionalisation. Just as he may have got to his original coherent state by intuition, whimsy, imagination, evidence processed through Bayes' theorem, or any combination thereof, so he may with perfect rationality pass from his present coherent state to a future coherent state through any of these mechanisms. If he depends on Bayes' theorem, it is a matter of predilection, not of rationality. For all the subjectivistic theory has to say, he may with equal justification pass from one coherent state to another by free association, reading tea-leaves, or consulting his parrot.

This leads us to the second and more interesting case, in which the subjectivistic theory of degrees of belief embodies more than the constraint of coherence. The most obvious addition will be a principle that directs us to change our beliefs in accordance with Bayes' theorem: When we pass from one coherent epistemic state to another, as a result of acquiring evidence *e*, the probability function that describes our new state should be the conditional-on-*e* probability function of the old state. This is the principle of epistemic conditionalization, and is accepted, at least implicitly, by almost all writers who employ the subjectivistic theory.

The principle of conditionalization puts the theory in a new light. Thus supplemented, the theory makes the rationality of my beliefs at a future time depend not only on their coherence, but on their history. My beliefs at that time will be rational only if they are derived from my present beliefs by conditionalizing on the evidence that becomes available to me between now and then.

But if the rationality of my beliefs tomorrow depends on my having rational beliefs today, and conditionalizing to reach tomorrow's beliefs, it follows by the Relativity of Time that the rationality of my beliefs today depends on my have had rational beliefs yesterday, and having conditionalized on them to reach today's beliefs, or else that I can start being rational at any time – in particular, tomorrow, so that tomorrow's beliefs need not, after all, be based on applying conditionalization to today's beliefs. In the latter case we are back to pure subjectivism. But in the former case we are in Carnap's old position – the one he occupied before being seduced by the siren song of subjectivism: in theory and in principle a rational being would have beliefs that are precisely determined by his total body of evidental knowledge as accumulated from time zero to the present, and by the language he uses. Probabilities – degrees of belief – are logically determinate, and quite independent of what degrees of belief any actual person happens to have. The problem, then, as Carnap saw, is to determine the values of the absolutely prior probabilities – the probabilities that should be assigned to the statements of the language prior to any experience at all. We should assign these probabilities on the basis of *rational intuition*. It turned out that this was extremely difficult to do, and even Carnap, in his later years, began to doubt its possibility. The demands such a program imposes on rational intuition are simply too great.

A middle position is defended by Hintikka and some members of his school [9, 17, 18]. We define a logical probability measure on the sentences of a language, and assert conditionally that *if* this measure represents our prior belief, and *if* the principle of epistemic conditionalization is accepted, *then* such and such interesting results follow. But no attempt is made either to defend the prior measure assignment as demanded by rational intuition or to defend it as corresponding to anybody's actual beliefs. It is sometimes said that (if it did represent someone's beliefs) it would represent a 'presupposition' about the nature of the universe. Since no attempt is made to defend these presuppositions as rational, we would seem to be back in the realm of purely subjective theory; and since it is not argued that the measures in fact represent anyone's beliefs, we seem to be in a realm both hypothetical and subjective, from which we can learn little of either philosophical or practical import.[3]

Conclusion

Despite the fact that subjectivistic probability is highly fashionable both in statistics and in philosophy, it appears to have serious shortcomings. We may account for its popularity in statistics by its heuristic role in teasing out the commitments that are implicit in an agent's preference ranking; but its role there is purely heuristic, and we need not assume that there is anything psychological that corresponds to the 'degrees of belief' that emerge from certain of those analyses. And note that in some analyses – Jeffrey's for example – a unique probability function doesn't even emerge as an auxilliary notion from the analysis. We may account for the popularity of subjective probability in philosophy in part by fashion, in part by laziness (it is easy to manipulate), and in part by the fact that it has few viable competitors. Nevertheless it is poor philosophy to adopt a false theory to achieve a certain end just because one doesn't know of a true theory that will achieve that end.

I conclude that the theory of subjective probability is psychologically false, decision-theoretically vacuous, and philosophically bankrupt: its account is overdrawn.

Notes

* Originally published in *Journal of Philosophical Logic*, 7 (1978), pp. 157–80. Copyright © 1978 D. Reidel Publishing Company, Dordrecht, Holland. Reprinted by permission of Springer Science+Business Media.
0 In some cases this agreement can be explained by convergence theorems.
1 This formulation is due to Levi, "On Indeterminate Probabilities", [15], p. 413–14.
2 It is interesting to note, as pointed out to me by Teddy Seidenfeld, that the Dutch Book against the irrational agent can only be constructed by an irrational (whether unscrupulous or not) opponent. Suppose that the Agent offers odds of 2 : 1 on heads and odds of 2 : 1 on tails on the toss of a coin. If the opponent is rational, according to the theory under examination, there will be a number p that represents his degree of belief in the occurrence of heads. If p is less than a half, the opponent will maximize his expectation by staking his entire stake on tails in accordance with the first odds posted by the Agent. But then the Agent need not lose. Similarly, if p is greater than a half. But if p is exactly a half, then the rational opponent should be indifferent between dividing his stake (to make the Dutch Book) and putting his entire stake on one outcome: the expectation in any case will be the same.
3 It is worth noting, however, that Levi's proposals in [14] and [15] escape these criticisms, and most of those that follow. He supposes that the epistemic state of the agent is represented by a convex set of coherent probability functions, thus escaping criticism based on the alleged exactness of so-called "degrees of belief". More important, as a good pragmatist he does not demand that the rationality of an epistemic state depend on its history; he is concerned mainly with the rationality of changes from one epistemic state to another, and while he takes some of these changes to depend on conditionalization, he also admits changes that do not depend on conditionalization.

Bibliography

[1] Carnap, Rudolf, 1950, *Logical Foundations of Probability*, The University of Chicago Press, Chicago.
[2] Carnap, Rudolf, 1968, 'Inductive Logic and Inductive Intuition', in Lakatos (ed.), *The Problem of Inductive Logic*, North Holland, Amsterdam, pp. 258–267.
[3] Carnap, Rudolf, 1961, 'Inductive Logic and Rational Decisions', *Studies in Inductive Logic and Probability I*, Carnap and Jeffrey (eds.), pp. 5–31.
[4] Dempster, A., 1961, 'Upper and Lower Probabilities induced by a Multivalued Mapping', *Annals of Mathematical Statistics* 38, 325–339.
[5] Edwards, Ward, 1960, 'Measurement of Utility and Subjective Probability', in Gulliksen & Messick (eds.), *Psychological Scaling: Theory and Applications*, John Wiley & Sons, New York, pp. 109–128.
[6] Edwards, Ward, 1962, 'Subjective Probabilities Inferred from Decisions', *Psychological Review* 69, 109–135.

[7] Good, I. J., 1962, 'Subjective Probability as a Measure of a Non-Measurable Set', in Nagel, Suppes and Tarski, *Logic, Methodology and Philosophy of Science*, Stanford University Press, pp. 319–329.

[8] Harper, William L., 1975, 'Rational Belief Change, Popper Functions, and Counterfactuals', *Synthese* 30, 221–262.

[9] Hintikka, Jaakko, 1971, 'Unknown Probabilities, Bayesianism and De Finetti's Representation Theorem', *Boston Studies in the Philosophy of Science* VIII, Buck and Cohen (eds.), D. Reidel, Dordrecht.

[10] Holstein, C. Stael von, 1973, 'The Concept of Probability in Psychological Experiments', *Logic, Methodology and Philosophy of Science IV*, Suppes *et al.* (eds.), pp. 451–466.

[11] Jeffrey, Richard C., 1965, *The Logic of Decision*, McGraw-Hill Book Co., New York.

[12] Kyburg, H. E., 1968, 'Bets and Beliefs', *American Philosophical Quarterly* 5, 54–63.

[13] Kyburg, H. E., 1974, *The Logical Foundations of Statistical Inference*, Reidel, Dordrecht and Boston.

[14] Levi, Isaac, 1977, 'Direct Inference', *Journal of Philosophy* 74, 5–29.

[15] Levi, Isaac, 1974, 'On Indeterminate Probabilities', *Journal of Philosophy* 71, 391–418.

[16] Niiniluoto, Ilkka, 1972–73, 'Inductive Systematization: Definition and a Critical Survey', *Synthese* 25, 25–81.

[17] Nijniluoto, Ilkka, and Raimo Tuomela, 1973, *Theoretical Concepts and Hypothetical-Inductive Inference*, Reidel, Dordrecht.

[18] Pietarinen, Juhani, 1972, *Lawlikeness, Analogy, and Inductive Logic*, North Holland, Amsterdam.

[19] Popper, Karl R., 1955–56, 'Two Autonomous Axiom Systems for the Calculus of Probabilities', *British Journal for the Philosophy of Science* 6, 51–57.

[20] Ramsey, Frank P., 'Probability and Partial Belief', in Ramsey, *The Foundations of Mathematics*, pp. 256–257, reprinted in this volume, pp. 69—70.

[21] Ramsey, Frank P., 1950, *The Foundations of Mathematics*, Braithwaite (ed.), Routledge & Kegan Paul Ltd., London.

[22] Salmon, Wesley C., 1970, 'Partial Entailment as a Basis for Inductive Logic', *Essays in Honor of Carl G. Hempel, Rescher* (ed.), pp. 47–82.

[23] Savage, Leonard J., 1954, *Foundations of Statistics*, John Wiley, New York.

[24] Slovic, Paul, Fischhoff, Baruch, and Lichtenstein, Sarah, 1977, 'Behavioral Decision Theory', *Annual Review of Psychology* 28, 1–39.

[25] Smith, Cedric A. B., 1961, 'Consistency in Statistical Inference and Decision', *The Journal of the Royal Statistical Society*, Series B (Methodological), Vol. 23, No. 1, pp. 1–37.

[26] Suppes, Patrick, 1974, 'The Measurement of Belief', *Journal of the Royal Statistical Society*, Series B (Methodological), Vol. 36, pp. 160–191.

4

A NON-PRAGMATIC VINDICATION OF PROBABILISM*†

James M. Joyce

The pragmatic character of the Dutch book argument makes it unsuitable as an "epistemic" justification for the fundamental probabilist dogma that rational partial beliefs must conform to the axioms of probability. To secure an appropriately epistemic justification for this conclusion, one must explain what it means for a system of partial beliefs to accurately represent the state of the world, and then show that partial beliefs that violate the laws of probability are invariably less accurate than they could be otherwise. The first task can be accomplished once we realize that the accuracy of systems of partial beliefs can be measured on a *gradational* scale that satisfies a small set of formal constraints, each of which has a sound epistemic motivation. When accuracy is measured in this way it can be shown that any system of degrees of belief that violates the axioms of probability can be replaced by an alternative system that obeys the axioms and yet is more accurate *in every possible world*. Since epistemically rational agents must strive to hold accurate beliefs, this establishes conformity with the axioms of probability as a norm of *epistemic* rationality whatever its prudential merits or defects might be.

Introduction

According to the doctrine of *probabilism* (Jeffrey 1992, 44) any adequate epistemology must recognize that opinions come in varying gradations of strength and must make conformity to the axioms of probability a fundamental requirement of rationality for these *graded* or *partial* beliefs.[1] While probabilism has long played a central role in statistics, decision theory, and, more recently, the philosophy of science, its impact on the traditional theory of knowledge has been surprisingly modest. Most epistemologists remain committed to a *dogmatist* paradigm that takes *full belief*–the unqualified acceptance of some proposition as true–as the fundamental doxastic attitude. Partial beliefs, when considered at all, are assigned a subsidiary role in contemporary epistemological theories.

Probabilism's supporters deserve part of the blame for this unhappy state of affairs. We probabilists typically explicate the concept of partial belief in pragmatic terms, often quoting Frank Ramsey's dictum that, "the degree of a belief is a causal property of it, which we can express vaguely as the extent to which we are prepared to act on it"

(1931, 166). Moreover, when called upon to defend the claim that rational degrees of belief must obey the laws of probability we generally present some version of the *Dutch Book Argument* (Ramsey 1931, de Finetti 1964), which establishes conformity to the laws of probability as a norm of *prudential* rationality by showing that expected utility maximizers whose partial beliefs violate these laws can be induced to behave in ways that are sure to leave them less well off than they could otherwise be. This overemphasis on the pragmatic dimension of partial beliefs tends to obscure the fact that they have properties that can be understood independently of their role in the production of action. Indeed, probabilists have tended to pay little heed to the one aspect of partial beliefs that would be of most interest to epistemologists: namely, their role in representing the world's state. My strong hunch is that this neglect is a large part of what has led so many epistemologists to relegate partial beliefs to a second-class status.

I mean to alter this situation by first giving an account of what it means for a system of partial beliefs to accurately represent the world, and then explaining why having beliefs that obey the laws of probability contributes to the basic epistemic goal of accuracy. This strategy is not new. Roger Rosenkrantz (1981) has taken a similar approach, arguing that if the accuracy of degrees of belief is measured by a quantity called the *Brier score*, then systems of degrees of belief that violate the laws of probability are necessarily less accurate than they need to be. In a similar vein, Bas van Fraassen (1983) and Abner Shimony (1988) have maintained that accuracy can be measured using a quantity called the *calibration index*, and they have argued, in slightly different ways, that any system of degrees of belief that violates the probability axioms can be replaced by a better calibrated system that satisfies them. While both these approaches are on the right track, we shall see below that neither ultimately succeeds. The van Fraassen/Shimony strategy fails because calibration is not a reasonable measure of accuracy for partial beliefs, and Rosenkrantz ends up begging the question (albeit in a subtle and interesting way).

To secure my non-pragmatic vindication of probabilism I will need to clarify the appropriate *criterion of epistemic success* for partial beliefs. The relevant success criterion for full beliefs is well-known and uncontroversial.

> **The Norm of Truth (NT):**[2] An epistemically rational agent must strive to hold a system of full beliefs that strikes the best attainable overall balance between the epistemic good of fully believing truths and the epistemic evil of fully believing falsehoods (where fully believing a truth is better than having no opinion about it, and having no opinion about a falsehood is better than fully believing it).[3]

This principle underlies much of dogmatic epistemology. It implies that we should aim to accept truths and reject falsehoods whenever we have a choice in the matter, that we should evaluate our full beliefs, even those we cannot help holding, on the basis of their truth-values, and that we should treat evidence for the truth of some proposition as a prima facie reason for believing it. Probabilism's main shortcoming has been its inability to articulate any similarly compelling criterion of epistemic success to serve as the normative focus for an epistemology of partial belief. I shall formulate and defend such a criterion, and prove that holding degrees of belief that obey the laws of probability is an essential prerequisite to its satisfaction. This will establish the requirement of probabilistic consistency for partial beliefs as a norm of *epistemic* rationality, whatever its prudential costs or benefits might be.

My argument will be based on a new way of drawing the distinction between full and partial beliefs. The difference between these two sorts of attitudes, I claim, has to do with the appropriate *standard of accuracy* relative to which they are evaluated. While both "aim at the truth," they do so in quite different ways. Full beliefs answer to a *categorical*, "miss is as good as a mile," standard of accuracy that recognizes only two ways of "fitting the facts": getting them exactly right or having them wrong, where no distinctions are made among different ways of being wrong. This is reflected in the Norm of Truth, which is really nothing more than the prescription to maximize the categorical accuracy of one's full beliefs.

A simple accurate/inaccurate dichotomy does not work for partial beliefs because their accuracy is ultimately a matter of degree. As I shall argue, partial beliefs are appropriately evaluated on a *gradational*, or "closeness counts," scale that assigns true beliefs higher *degrees of accuracy* the more strongly they are held, and false beliefs lower *degrees of accuracy* the more strongly they are held. My position is that a rational partial believer must aim not simply to accept truths and reject falsehoods, but to hold partial beliefs that are gradationally accurate by adjusting the strengths of her opinions in a way that best maximizes her degree of confidence in truths while minimizing her degree of confidence in falsehoods. For the same reasons[4] that a person should aim to hold full beliefs that are categorically accurate, so too should she aim to hold partial beliefs that are gradationally accurate. We thus are lead to the following analogue of the Norm of Truth:

> **The Norm of Gradational Accuracy (NGA):** An epistemically rational agent must evaluate partial beliefs on the basis of their gradational accuracy, and she must strive to hold a system of partial beliefs that, in her best judgment, is likely to have an overall level of gradational accuracy at least as high as that of any alternative system she might adopt.

The system of partial beliefs with the highest attainable level of gradational accuracy will, of course, always be the one in which all truths are believed to the maximum degree and all falsehoods are believed to the minimum degree. This does not, however, imply that an epistemically rational agent must hold partial beliefs of only these two extreme types. Indeed, she should rarely do so. Unlike full believers, partial believers must worry about the epistemic costs associated with different ways of being wrong. Since the worst way of being wrong is to be maximally confident in a falsehood, there is a significant epistemic disincentive associated with the holding of extreme beliefs. Indeed, I shall argue that on any reasonable measure of gradational accuracy the incentive structure will force a rational agent to "hedge her epistemic bets" by adopting degrees of belief that are indeterminate between certainty of truth and certainty of falsehood for most contingent propositions.

The Norm of Gradational Accuracy will be the cornerstone of my non-pragmatic vindication of probabilism. To show that epistemically rational partial beliefs must obey the laws of probability, I will first impose a set of abstract constraints on measures of gradational accuracy, then argue that these constraints are requirements of epistemic rationality, and finally explain why conformity to the laws of probability improves accuracy relative to any measure that satisfies them. It will then follow from NGA that it is irrational, from the purely epistemic perspective, to hold partial beliefs that violate the laws of probability.

There are five sections to come. Section 2 ('The Dutch book argument and its short-comings') sketches a version of the Dutch book argument and explains why it does not provide an appropriately "epistemic" rationale for conforming one's degrees of belief to the axioms of probability. Section 3 ('The Concept of Gradational Accuracy') introduces the notion of gradational accuracy and explains why it is the appropriate standard of evaluation for degrees of belief. Section 4 ('Measures of Gradational Accuracy') criticizes rival accounts of accuracy for partial beliefs, and presents a formal theory of gradational accuracy. Section 5 ('Vindicating the Fundamental Dogma') shows that degrees of belief which violate the axioms of probability are less accurate than they otherwise could be relative to *any* reasonable measure of accuracy. Section 6 ('Some loose ends') explains how these results can be applied to more realistic cases in which agents are not assumed to have precise numerical degrees of belief.

The Dutch book argument and its shortcomings

To specify a partial belief one must indicate a *proposition* X and the *strength* with which it is held to be true. We will imagine that the propositions about which our subject has beliefs are included in a σ-*complete Boolean algebra* Ω, i.e., a non-empty set of propositions that is closed under negation and countable disjunction. The strength of the person's belief in X is a matter of how confident she is in its truth. For the moment, we will engage in the useful fiction that our agent's opinions are so definite and precise that their strengths can be measured by a real-valued *credence function b* that assigns every proposition $X \in \Omega$ a unique *degree of belief* $b(X)$. This is absurd, of course; in any realistic case there will be many propositions for which a rational agent need have no definite *degree* of belief. We discuss these imprecise beliefs in the last section of the essay.

According to probabilism, a rational believer's credence function must obey the laws of probability:

Normalization: $b(X \vee \neg X) = 1$.

Non-negativity: $b(X) \geq 0$ for all $X \in \Omega$.

Additivity: If $\{X_1, X_2, X_3, ...\}$ is a finite, or denumerably infinite, *partition* of the proposition X into pairwise incompatible disjuncts, so that $X = (X_1 \vee X_2 \vee X_3 \vee ...)$ where X_j and X_k are incompatible for all j and k, then $b(X) = b(X_1) + b(X_2) + b(X_3) ... $.

The principal aim of this essay is to provide a justification of the probabilist's "fundamental dogma" that rational agents must have degrees of belief that obey these three laws.

To understand the justification I am going to give, it will be useful to begin by considering a particularly revealing version of the Dutch book argument due to Bruno de Finetti (1974) and Leonard Savage (1971). Even though this argument ultimately fails to provide an acceptable epistemic rationale for the fundamental dogma it does suggest a fruitful way of approaching the problem. De Finetti and Savage developed an ingenious piece of psychometrics, which I call the *prevision game*, that was designed to reveal the strengths of a person's partial beliefs. To simplify things they assumed they were dealing with a *miser* who desires only money, and whose love of it remains fixed no matter how rich or poor she might become.[5] This miser is presented with a list of propositions $X = (X_1, X_2, ..., X_n)$ and is offered a dollar to designate a corresponding sequence of real numbers $p = (p_1, p_2, ..., p_n)$. The catch is that she must repay a portion of her dollar once the truth-values of the X_i have been revealed. The size of her loss is fixed by the game's *scoring rule*, a function $S(p, \omega)$ that assigns a penalty of up to \$1 to each pair consisting of a joint truth-value assignment ω for the propositions in Ω (hereafter a "possible world"), and a sequence of numbers p. For reasons that will be made clear shortly, de Finetti and Savage focused their attention on games scored using *quadratic-loss* rules that have the form $S(p,\omega) = \Sigma_i \lambda_i [\omega(X_i) - p_i]^2$ where $\lambda_1, ..., \lambda_n$ are non-negative real numbers that sum to one and $\omega(X_i)$ is the truth-value (either 0 or 1) that X_i has at world ω. An illuminating example is provided by the rule that weights each X_i equally, so that $\lambda_1 = \lambda_2 = ... = \lambda_n = 1/n$. This is called the *Brier score* in honor of the meteorologist George Brier (1950), who proposed that it be used to measure the accuracy of probabilistic weather forecasts (as in, "the chance of rain is 30%"). Following de Finetti, let us call the numbers that an agent reports in a game scored using a quadratic-loss function her *previsions* for the various X_i.

De Finetti and Savage used quadratic-loss functions to score prevision games because these rules have two properties that make them uniquely suited to the task. First, they force any minimally rational miser to report previsions that obey the laws of probability. Second, they reveal the beliefs of expected utility maximizers because a miser who aims to maximize her *expected* payoff will invariably report a prevision for each proposition that coincides with her degree of belief for it. The fact that there exist scoring rules with these two properties is supposed to show that it is irrational to hold partial beliefs that violate the laws of probability.

Quadratic-loss functions ensure that rational previsions will be probabilities in virtue of

> **De Finetti's Lemma:** In a prevision game scored by a quadratic-loss rule S, every prevision sequence p that violates the axioms of probability can be canonically associated with a sequence p^* that obeys the probability axioms and which *dominates* p in the sense that $S(p, \omega) > S(p^*, \omega)$ for all worlds ω.

In other words, for every sequence of previsions that violates the laws of probability there is a sequence that obeys them whose penalty is strictly smaller *in every possible world*. No rational miser would ever choose to report previsions that are dominated in this way, since doing so would be tantamount to throwing away money.

I shall leave it to the reader to work out why the quadratic-loss rules penalize violations of Normalization and Non-negativity. For Additivity, imagine a person who reports previsions (0.6, 0.2) for $(X, \neg X)$ when losses are given by the Brier score. This agent will incur a 10¢ penalty if X is true, and a 50¢ penalty if X is false. Figure 1 shows how she could have saved a sure penny by reporting the previsions (0.7, 0.3).

This example mirrors the general case. If X is a finite sequence of propositions, then its consistent truth-value assignments form a family of binary sequences

$$V = \big\{ \langle \omega(X_1), \omega(X_2), ..., \omega(X_n) \rangle : \omega \text{ a possible world} \big\}$$

within real n-dimensional space $\mathfrak{R}^n$. The *convex hull* of V is the subset V^+ of $\mathfrak{R}^n$ whose points can be expressed as *weighted averages* of V's elements. De Finetti showed that V^+

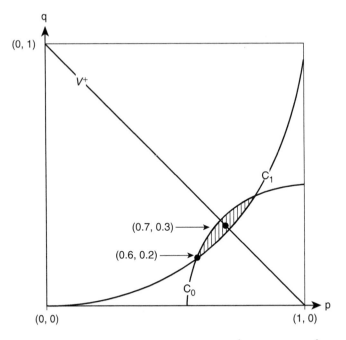

Figure 1 De Finetti's Lemma for $S((p, q), \omega) = 1/2[(\omega(X) - p)^2 + (\omega(\neg X) - q)^2]$. Previsions for $(X, \neg X)$ appear as points in the (p, q)-plane. $V = \{(1,0), (0,1)\}$ is the set of all consistent truth-value assignments for X and $\neg X$. The line segment V^+ is V's *convex hull*. It contains all (p, q) pairs with $p + q = 1$. Arc $C_1 = \{(p, q): S((p, q), 1) = 0.5\}$ is made up of points whose penalty is the same as that of $(0.6, 0.2)$ when X is true. $C_0 = \{(p, q): S((p, q), 0) = 0.1\}$ contains all points whose penalty is the same as that of $(0.6, 0.2)$ when X is false. The shaded *region of dominance* is the set of (p, q) pairs that have a smaller penalty than $(0.6, 0.2)$ *whether X is true or false*. This region always intersects V^+ at (p^*, q^*) where $p^* = [p + (1 - q)]/2$ and $q^* = [p + (1 - q)]/2$. The Lemma says that one only has $(p, q) = (p^*, q^*)$ when $p + q = 1$.

is the set of all prevision assignments for elements of X that obey the laws of probability. He then used the convexity of V^+ (the fact that it contains the line segment between any two of its points) to show that, for any quadratic-loss rule $S(p, \omega) = \Sigma_i \lambda_i(\omega(X_i) - p_i)^2$ and any $p \notin V^+$, there is a unique $p^* \in V^+$ that minimizes $d(q) = \Sigma_i \lambda_i[q_i - p_i]^2$ on V^+ and that this function has a lower S-score than p does relative to *every* truth-value assignment in V.[6]

De Finetti's Lemma shows that a rational miser will always report previsions that obey the laws of probability when playing a prevision game scored by a quadratic-loss rule. But why think these previsions to have anything special to do with her degrees of belief? De Finetti often spoke as if there were no meaningful question to be asked here. A person's degrees of belief, he suggested, are *operationally defined* as *whatever previsions she would report in a game scored with a quadratic-loss rule*. This cannot be right. Aside from familiar difficulties with behaviorist interpretations of mental states, this view actually undermines itself. The problem is that it always makes sense to ask why a quadratic-loss function, rather than some other scoring rule, should be used to define degrees of belief. And, even if it is granted that a quadratic-loss rule should be used, one can still wonder whether all such rules will lead a rational miser to report the same previsions. After all, what prevents previsions from varying with changes in the weighting constants $\lambda_1, \ldots, \lambda_n$? The point here is a general one. In the same way that it makes no sense to define "temperature" as "the quantity measured by thermometers" because it is impossible to know a priori either that such a quantity tracks any important physical property or that different thermometers will always assign similar values in similar circumstances, so too it makes no sense to define "degree of belief" as "the prevision reported in a quadratic-loss game" because it is impossible to know a priori either that previsions measure anything interesting or that different scoring rules elicit similar previsions in similar circumstances. It cannot be a definition which establishes that previsions reveal degrees of belief; it takes an argument.

As it turns out, de Finetti did not really need to rely on his operationism since he already had the required argument on hand (and indeed gave it). The reasoning turns on a substantive claim about the nature of practical rationality: viz., that a rational miser will always report previsions that maximize her *subjective expected utility*. She will, that is, always choose a prevision p_x for X that minimizes her *expected penalty* $Exp(p) = b(X) \, S\,(p, 1) + (1 - b(X)) \, S\,(p, 0)$ where $b(X)$ is her degree of belief for X. It is not difficult to show that this function is uniquely minimized at $p_x = b(X)$ when S is any quadratic-loss function. This means that the previsions of *expected utility maximizers* do indeed reveal their degrees of belief. Since de Finetti's Lemma shows that these previsions must obey the laws of probability, we are thus led to

> **The Dutch Book Theorem:** If prudential rationality requires expected utility maximization, then any prudentially rational agent must have degrees of belief that conform to the laws of probability.

There are two main reasons why the Dutch book argument fails to convince people. First, there are some who reject the idea that prudential rationality requires expected utility maximization.[7] I think these people are wrong, but will not argue the point here since for my purposes it is best to concede that the thesis is controversial so as to advertise the advantages of a defense of probabilism that does not presuppose it. A more significant problem has to do with the *pragmatic* character of the Dutch book argument. There is a distinction to be drawn between *prudential* reasons for believing, which have to do with the ways in which holding certain opinions can affect one's happiness, and epistemic reasons for believing, which concern the *accuracy* of the opinions as representations of the world's state. Since the Dutch book argument provides only a prudential rationale for conforming one's partial beliefs to the laws of probability, it is an open question whether it holds any interest for epistemology. There are some who think it does not. Ralph Kennedy and Charles Chihara have written that:

> The factors that are supposed to make it irrational to have a [probabilistically inconsistent] set of beliefs ... are irrelevant, epistemologically, to the truth of the propositions in question. The fact (if it is a fact) that one will be bound to lose money unless one's degrees of belief [obey the laws of probability] just isn't epistemologically relevant to the *truth* of those beliefs. (1979, 30).

Roger Rosenkrantz has expressed similar sentiments, writing that the Dutch book theorem is a

> roundabout way of exposing the irrationality of incoherent beliefs. What we need is an approach that ... [shows] why incoherent beliefs are irrational from the perspective of the agent's purely *cognitive* goals. (1981, 214).

If this is right, then the pragmatic character of the Dutch book argument may well make it irrelevant to probabilism construed as a thesis in epistemology.

Proponents of the Dutch book argument might try to parry this objection by going pragmatist and denying that there is any sense in which the *epistemic* merits of a set of beliefs can outrun its prudential merits. Some old-line probabilists took this position, but it is unlikely to move anyone who feels the force of the Kennedy/Chihara/Rosenkrantz objection. There does seem to be a clear difference between appraising a system of beliefs in terms of the behavior it generates or in terms of its agreement with the facts. Unless the pragmatists can convincingly explain this intuition away it is hard to see how their view amounts to more than the bald assertion that there is no such subject as traditional epistemology. Probabilism is not worth that price.

More sophisticated probabilist responses acknowledge that partial beliefs can be criticized on nonpragmatic grounds, but they go on to suggest that imprudence, while not *constitutive* of epistemic failings, often *reliably indicates* them. People who choose means insufficient to their ends frequently do so because they weigh evidence incorrectly, draw hasty conclusions, engage in wishful thinking, or have beliefs that do not square with the facts. While this last flaw is no defect in rationality, it is reasonable to think that *systematic* deficiencies in practical reasoning *that do not depend on the truth or falsity of the reasoner's beliefs*, like the tendency of probabilistically inconsistent misers to throw away money, are symptoms of deeper flaws. If this is so, then the Dutch book argument can be read as what Brian Skyrms (1984, 21–22) calls a "dramatic device" that provides a vivid pragmatic illustration of an essentially epistemic form of irrationality.

The kind of irrationality Skyrms has in mind is that of making *inconsistent value judgments*. As Ramsey first observed, an expected utility maximizer whose degrees of belief violate the axioms of probability cannot avoid assigning a utility to some prospect that is higher than the sum of the utilities she assigns to two others that together produce the same payoff as the first in *every* possible world. Her violations of the laws of probability thus leads her to commit both the prudential sin of squandering happiness and the epistemic sin of valuing prospects differently depending upon how they happen to be described. I want to agree that this is surely the right way to read the Dutch book argument: what the argument ultimately shows is that probabilistically inconsistent beliefs breed logically inconsistent preferences. The willingness to squander money is a side-effect of the more fundamental defect of having inconsistent desires. Still, even if we grant this point, it remains unclear why this should be counted an *epistemic* defect given that the inconsistency in question attaches to preferences or value judgments. It would be one thing if a Dutch book argument could show that the strengths of an agent's *beliefs* vary with changes in the ways propositions happen to be expressed when she violates the laws of probability, but it cannot be made to show any such thing unless degrees of belief are assumed to obey the Additivity axiom from the start. The sort of inconsistency-in-valuing Skyrms decries is undeniably a serious shortcoming, but it remains unclear precisely what clearly irrational property of *beliefs* underlies it.[8] In the end, the only way to answer the Chihara/Kennedy/Rosenkrantz objection is by presenting an argument that shows how having degrees of belief that violate the laws of probability engenders *epistemic* failings that go beyond their effects on an agent's preferences.

The concept of gradational accuracy

The main obstacle to such an argument is the lack of any compelling criterion of *epistemic success* for partial beliefs. Such a criterion has eluded probabilists because they have been slow to realize that full and partial beliefs "fit the facts" in different ways. The accuracies of full beliefs are evaluated on a *categorical* scale. The extent to which a full belief about X fits the facts is a matter of its "valence" (accept-X, reject-X, suspend belief), and X's truth-value. Maximum (minimum) accuracy is attained when X is true (false) and accepted or when X is false (true) and rejected, and an intermediate value is obtained when belief is suspended. The "fit" between partial beliefs and the world is determined in a similar way except that, being attitudes that can come in a continuum of "valences," their appropriate standard of accuracy must be a *gradational* one on which accuracy increases with the agent's degrees of confidence in truths and decreases with her degrees of confidence in falsehoods.

To see what I have in mind, it is useful to consider Richard Jeffrey's distinction between *guesses* and *estimates* of numerical quantities (Jeffrey 1986). When one tries to guess, say, the number of hits that a baseball player will get in his next ten at-bats, one aims to get the value exactly right. Guessing two hits when the batter gets three is just as wrong as guessing two hits when he gets ten. In guessing, closeness does not count. Not so for estimation. If the player gets five hits, it is better to have estimated that he would get three than to have estimated two or nine. Notice that, whereas it makes no sense to guess that a quantity will have a value that it cannot possibly have, it *can* make sense to estimate it to have such a value. One might, e.g., use a hitter's batting average to estimate that he will get 3.27 hits in his next ten at-bats. Such an estimate can never be exactly right of course, but in estimation there is no special advantage to being *exactly* right; the goal is to get as *close* as possible to the value of the estimated quantity. In conditions of uncertainty it is often wise to "hedge one's bets" by choosing a estimate that is sure to be off the mark by a little so as to avoid being off by a lot.

Following de Finetti, Jeffrey assumes that estimates must conform to the *laws of mathematical expectation*, and he identifies degrees of belief with *estimates of truth-values*. He is entirely right about the second point, but a bit too hasty with the first. When restricted to estimates of truth-values, the laws of mathematical expectation just are the laws of probability. Jeffrey takes this to provide a *justification* for requiring partial beliefs to satisfy the latter laws because he takes the former to be "as obvious as the laws of logic" (1986, 52). This, of course, is unlikely to convince anyone not already well disposed toward probabilism. The basic law of expectation is an additivity principle that requires a person's expectation for a quantity to be the sum of her expectations of its summands, so that $Exp(F) = \Sigma_i Exp (F_i)$ when $F = \Sigma_i F_i$. No one who has qualms about additivity as it applies to degrees of belief is going to accept this stronger constraint without seeing a substantive argument.

The way to give a substantive argument, I believe, is to (a) grant Jeffrey's basic point that an agent's degree of belief for a proposition X is that number $b(X)$ that she is committed to using as her estimate of X's truth-value when she recognizes that she will be evaluated for accuracy on a gradational standard appropriate for partial beliefs, and (b) argue that degrees of belief that obey the laws of probability are more accurate than those which do not when measured against this standard. What I have in mind here is a kind of "epistemic Dutch book argument" in which the relevant scoring rule assigns each credence function b and possible world ω a penalty $I(b, \omega)$ assessed in units of gradational inaccuracy. The rule I will gauge the extent to which the truth-value estimates sanctioned by b diverge from the truth-values that propositions would have were ω actual. My claim is going to be that, once we appreciate what I must look like, we will see that violations of the laws of probability always decrease the accuracy of partial beliefs.

Lest the reader think that I merely plan to restate the Dutch book argument and call it epistemology, let me highlight a crucial difference between my approach and that of de Finetti and Savage. Since a miser always aims to increase her fortune, de Finetti and Savage were at liberty to choose any scoring rule they wanted without having to worry about whether their subject would seek to minimize the penalties it assessed. This was advantageous for them because once they had discovered that the quadratic-loss rules rewarded the reporting of previsions that obey the laws of probability they could count on their subject to *want* to report such previsions. De Finetti and Savage did, of course, have to worry about whether their rules would induce a miser to report previsions that reveal her partial beliefs, which is why they needed to appeal to the principle of expected utility maximization. My problem is a mirror image of this. I cannot simply assume that my subjects will seek to minimize their penalties relative to any scoring rule I might choose. The Norm of Gradational Accuracy portrays an epistemically rational agent is a kind of "accuracy miser." So, if a rule I does not measure gradational inaccuracy, then there is no good reason to think that such an agent will aim to minimize it. On the other hand, if I does measure gradational inaccuracy, then we can be sure that she will strive to have a system b of degrees of belief that minimizes $I(b, \omega_0)$ with respect to the actual world ω_0. So, unless I can establish that my "scoring rule" really does measure inaccuracy in the epistemically relevant sense, I will have no grounds for concluding that we should care about its penalties. On the bright side, once I do find such a rule I can be sure that every epistemically rational agent will aim to have degrees of belief, not merely previsions, that minimize its values. This makes part of my task easier than the one that faced de Finetti and Savage since I will not need to invoke any analogue of expected utility maximization.

To see why this is an advantage, consider a justification for probabilism offered by Roger Rosenkrantz (1981). While he does not invoke the distinction between categorical and gradational accuracy, it is not too much of a stretch to see Rosenkrantz asking the question that concerns us: assuming that the gradational *in*accuracy of a system of degrees of belief can be measured by a function $I(b, \omega)$, what properties must I have if it is going to be the sort of thing epistemically rational agents will seek to minimize. Rosenkrantz answers by introducing axioms that are meant to pick out the quadratic-loss rules as the only candidates for I. Among them we find:

> Expected Accuracy Maximization: A rational agent should aim to hold a set of partial beliefs b that minimizes her *expected inaccuracy*, i.e., for any partition $X_1, X_2, ..., X_n$ it must be true that $Exp(I(b, \omega)) = \Sigma_i b(X_i)I(b, X_i) \geq Exp(I(b^*, \omega)) = \Sigma_i b(X_i)I(b^*, X_i)$ for any alternative sets of degrees of belief b^*.

Non-distortion: The function $Exp(I(b^*, \omega))$ attains a minimum at $b(X_j) = b^*(X_j) / \Sigma_i b^*(X_i)$.

The quadratic-loss rules satisfy these conditions, and Rosenkrantz conjectures that they do so uniquely. While this may be so, the point is moot unless some non-circular rationale can be given for Expected Accuracy Maximization and Non-distortion. Rosenkrantz does not offer any. Though I am happy to grant that both principles hold for partial beliefs that obey the axioms of probability, the problem is that they must also hold when the axioms are violated if they are to serve as premises in a justification for the fundamental dogma of probabilism. Here is a simple (but generalizable) example that shows why this cannot work. Let $\{X_1, X_2, X_3\}$ be a partition, and imagine someone with the probabilistcially inconsistent beliefs $b(X_1) = b(X_2) = b(X_3) = 1/3$ and $b(X_2 \vee X_3) = 3/4$. If Rosenkrantz was right, this person would have to think that the most accurate degree of belief for X_1 is simultaneously $1/3 = b(X_1)/[b(X_1) + b(X_2) + b(X_3)]$ and $4/10 = b(X_1)/[b(X_1) + b(X_2 \vee X_3)]$ because these are the answers that Non-distortion and Expected Accuracy Maximization sanction when applied to the partitions $\{X_1, X_2, X_3\}$ and $\{X_1, (X_2 \vee X_3)\}$ respectively. Perhaps Rosenkrantz would want to construe this inconsistency as an indication of irrationality, but unless he can offer us some independent rationale for his two principles we can just as well take the inconsistency to invalidate them as norms of epistemic rationality. The point here is basically the same as the one raised in connection with Jeffrey's identification of estimates and expectations: we cannot hope to justify probabilism by assuming that rational agents should maximize the *expected* accuracy of their opinions because the concept of an expectation really only makes sense for agents whose partial beliefs already obey the laws of probability.

Measures of gradational accuracy

Despite this flaw in his argument, Rosenkrantz was right to think that a defense of the fundamental dogma should start from an analysis of inaccuracy measures, and that it should show that agents whose partial beliefs violate the axioms of probability are always less accurate than they need to be. I will provide a defense along these lines by formulating and justifying a set of constraints on measures of gradational *in*accuracy, and then showing that any function that meets these constraints will encourage conformity to the laws of probability in the strongest possible manner. It will turn out that, relative to any such measure, a system of partial beliefs that violates the axioms of probability can always be replaced by a system that both obeys the axioms and better fits the facts no matter what the facts turn out to be.

In developing these ideas, I will speak as if gradational accuracy can be precisely quantified. This may be unrealistic since the concept of accuracy for partial beliefs may simply be too *vague* to admit of sharp numerical quantification. Even if this is so, however, it is still useful to pretend that it can be so characterized since this lets us take a "supervaluationist" approach to its vagueness. The supervaluationist idea is that one can understand a vague concept by looking at all the ways in which it can be made precise, and treating facts about the properties that all its "precisifications" share as facts about the concept itself. In this context a "precisification" is a real function that assigns a definite inaccuracy score $I(b, \omega)$ to each set of degrees of belief b and world ω. In what follows, I am going to be interested not so much in what the function I is, but in the properties that all reasonable "precisified" measures of gradational inaccuracy must share.

Let me begin by codifying the notation. The measure I is defined over pairs in $B \times V$, where B is the family of all credence functions defined on a countable[9] Boolean algebra of propositions Ω and V is the subset of B containing all consistent truth-value assignments to members of Ω. We will continue referring to these truth-value assignments as "possible worlds" and using "ω" as a generic symbol for them. The collection of all probability functions in B is V's convex hull V^+. $B \sim V^+$ is thus the set of all assignments of degrees of belief to the propositions in Ω that violate the laws of probability. The set B is endowed with a great deal of geometrical structure. It always contains a unique "line" $L = \{\lambda b + (1 - \lambda) \, b^*: \lambda \subset \Re\}$ that passes through any two of its "points" b and b^*. The *line segment* from b to b^*, hereafter bb^*, is the subset of L for which λ falls between zero and one. A function $[\lambda b + (1 - \lambda) \, b^*]$ that falls on this segment is called a *mixture* of b and b^* since it assigns each $X \in \Omega$ a "mixed" value of $\lambda b(X) + (1 - \lambda)b^*(X)$. This *mixture* effects a kind of compromise between b and b^* when the two differ. If $\lambda > 1/2$ the compromise favors the b beliefs since $\lambda \, b(X) + (1 - \lambda)b^*(X)$ is always closer to $b(X)$ than to $b^*(X)$. The reverse occurs when $\lambda < 1/2$. The *even* mixture ($\lambda = 1/2$) is a "fair" compromise that sets X's degree of belief exactly halfway between $b(X)$ and $b^*(X)$. A number of the constraints to be imposed below will exploit this geometry of lines and segments.

Our first axiom says that inaccuracy should be non-negative, that small changes in degrees of belief should not engender large changes in accuracy, and that inaccuracy should increase without limit as degrees of belief move further and further from the truth-values of the propositions believed.

> **Structure:** For each $\omega \in V$, $I(b, \omega)$ is a non-negative, *continuous* function of b that goes to infinity in the limit as $b(X)$ goes to infinity for any $X \in \Omega$.

This weak requirement should be uncontroversial given that gradational accuracy is supposed to be a matter of "closeness to the truth."

Our next constraint stipulates that the "facts" which a person's partial beliefs must "fit" are exhausted by the truth-values of the propositions believed, and that the only aspect of her opinions that matter is their strengths.

> **Extensionality:** At each possible world ω, $I(b, \omega)$ is a function of nothing other than the truth-values that ω assigns to propositions in Ω and the degrees of confidence that b assigns these propositions.

Most objections to Extensionality conflate the task of finding a measure of accuracy for partial beliefs with the more ambitious project of defining an *epistemic utility* function that gauges the overall goodness of a system of partial beliefs in all epistemologically relevant respects.[10] Accuracy is only one virtue among many that we want our opinions to possess. Ideally, a person will hold beliefs that are informative, simple, internally coherent, well-justified, and connected by secure causal links to the world. A notion of epistemic utility will balance off all these competing desiderata to provide an "all-in" measure of doxastic quality. While accuracy will be a strongly-weighted factor in any such measure, it will not be the only factor. Since properties like the informativeness of a belief or its degree of justification are not extensional, epistemic utility cannot be either. Extensionality does make sense for gradational accuracy, however, since gradational accuracy is supposed to be the analogue of *truth* for partial beliefs. Just as the accuracy of a full belief is a function of its attitudinal "valence" (accept/reject/suspend judgment) and its truth-value, so too the accuracy of a partial belief should be a function of its "valence" (degree) and truth-value.

A second objection to Extensionality is that it does not take *verisimilitude* into account.[11] Here is how the complaint might go:

> Copernicus (let us suppose) was exactly as confident that the earth's orbit is circular as Kepler was that it is elliptical. However, both were wrong since the gravitational attraction of the moon and the other planets causes the earth to deviate slightly from its largely elliptical path. Extensionality rates the two thinkers as *equally* inaccurate since both believed a falsehood to the same high degree. Still Kepler was obviously nearer the mark, which suggests that evaluations of accuracy must be sensitive not only to the truth-values of the propositions involved, but also to how *close* false propositions come to being true.

I am happy to admit that Kepler held more accurate beliefs than Copernicus did, but I think the sense in which they were more accurate is best captured by an extensional notion. While Extensionality rates Kepler and Copernicus as equally inaccurate when their false beliefs about the earth's orbit are considered *apart from their effects on other beliefs*, the advantage of Kepler's belief has to do with the other opinions it supports. An agent who strongly believes that the earth's orbit is elliptical will also strongly believe many more *truths* than a person who believes that it is circular (e.g., that the average distance from the earth to the sun is different in different seasons). This means that the overall effect of Kepler's inaccurate belief was to improve the *extensional* accuracy of his system of beliefs as a whole. Indeed, this is why his theory won the day. I suspect that most intuitions about falsehoods being "close to the truth" can be explained in this way, and that they therefore pose no real threat to Extensionality.

Our third axiom requires the accuracy of a system of degrees of belief to be an *increasing* function of the believer's degree of confidence in any truth and a decreasing function of her degree of confidence in any falsehood.

Dominance: If $b(Y) = b^*(Y)$ for every $Y \in \Omega$ other than X, then $I(b, \omega) > I(b^*, \omega)$ if and only if $|\omega(X) - b(X)| > |\omega(X) - b^*(X)|$.

This principle really says two things. First, it lets us speak of the accuracy of each *individual* degree of belief taken in isolation from the belief system as a whole. Second, it says that the accuracy of $b(X)$ always increases as it approaches $\omega(X)$. Thus, moving one's degree of belief for X closer to X's truth-value improves accuracy *no matter what one's other degrees of belief might be*. Were this not the case one could have a perverse incentive to *lower* one's degree of belief in a proposition for whose truth one has strong evidence because doing so would increase overall accuracy.

To see how bizarre these incentives can be, consider the *calibration index*, a measure of accuracy for degrees of belief that Bas van Fraassen and Abner Shimony have each tried to use in a vindication of probabilism similar to the one sought here.

As Wesley Salmon (1988) noted, many probabilists are attracted to *frequency driven* accounts of subjective probability. The *truth-frequency* of a family of propositions $X = \{X_1, X_2, ..., X_n\}$ at a world ω is the proportion of the X_i that hold in ω, so that $Freq(X, \omega) = [\omega(X_1) + \omega(X_n) + ... + \omega(X_n)]/n$. It is easy to show that an agent who has well-defined degrees of belief for all X's elements can only satisfy the axioms of probability if her *expected* frequency of truths in X is equal to her *average* degree of belief for the various X_i, so that $Exp(Freq(X)) = [b(X_1) + ... + b(X_n)]/n$. A special case of this is

> **The Calibration Theorem:** If an agent assigns the same degree of belief x to every proposition in X, then a necessary condition for her degrees of belief to satisfy the axioms of probability is that her expectation for the frequency of truths in X must be x.

This seems to get at something deep about partial beliefs. What can it mean, after all, to assign degree of belief x to X if not to think something like, "Propositions like X are true about x proportion of the time"? Moreover, unlike the principle of mathematical expectation from which it follows, the Calibration Theorem does not presuppose probabilism in any obvious way. Perhaps the thing to do is to replace "satisfy the axioms of probability" by "be rational" and "expectation" by "estimate," and to treat the Calibration Theorem as a conceptual truth about degrees of belief. And, if one does so, the accuracy of a set of degrees of belief can be analyzed as a function of the discrepancy between the relative frequency estimates it sanctions and the actual relative frequencies.

The meteorologist A. Murphy found a way to measure this discrepancy (Murphy 1973). For any credence function b defined over a *finite* family of propositions X, one can always subdivide X into disjoint *reference classes* $X_j = \{X \in X: b(X) = b_j\}$, where $\{b_1, ..., b_n\}$ lists all the values that b assumes on X. The Calibration Theorem tells us that b_j is the only estimate for $Freq(X_j)$ that b can sanction. Murphy characterized the divergence of these estimates from the actual frequencies at world ω using a quantity called the *calibration index* $Cal(b, X, \omega) = \Sigma_j(n_j/n)[Freq(\omega(X_j)) - b_j]^2$ where n is the number of propositions in X and n_j is the number of propositions in X_j. The function b is *perfectly calibrated* when $Cal(b, X, \omega) = 0$. In this case, half the elements of X assigned value 1/2 are true, two-fifths of those assigned value 2/5 are true, three-fourths of those assigned value 3/4 are true, and so on.

Some have championed calibration as the best measure of "fit" between partial beliefs and the world. Van Fraassen, for example, has written that calibration "plays the conceptual role that truth ... has in other contexts" (1983, 301), and has suggested that the appropriate analogue of consistency for degrees of belief is *calibrability*, the ability to be embedded within ever richer systems of beliefs whose calibration scores can be made arbitrarily small. He and Abner Shimony (1988) have even sought to vindicate probabilism by arguing, in different ways, that the only way to achieve calibrability with respect to finite sets of propositions is by having degrees of belief that conform to the laws of probability. If either of these arguments had succeeded we would have had our nonpragmatic vindication of probabilism.

They fail for two reasons. First, van Fraassen and Shimony need to employ very strong structural assumptions that are not well motivated as requirements of rationality. While the two assumptions are similar, van Fraassen's is easier to state because he deals only with propositions of the monadic form "x is A." He requires that for any assignment

b of degrees of belief to the elements of a set X of such propositions it should be possible to extend b to a function b^* defined on a superset X^* of X in such a way that each proposition "x is A" in X can be associated with a subset in X^* of the form

$$X(x, A) = \{x \text{ is } A, x_1 \text{ is } A, x_2 \text{ is } A, \ldots, x_k \text{ is } A\}$$

where (a) k may be any positive integer, (b) $b^*(x_j \text{ is } A) = b(x \text{ is } A)$ for every j, and (c) the propositions in $X(x, A)$ are *logically independent* of one another. In effect, van Fraassen is introducing dummy propositions to ensure that each element of X can be embedded in a probabilistically homogenous reference class of any chosen truth-frequency. Shimony uses a somewhat more general condition, his E_1 (1988, 156–157), to achieve substantially the same end. These are extremely strong, and rather ad hoc, assumptions, and it is not at all surprising that grand conclusions can be deduced from them. What remains unclear, however, is why rational degrees of belief should be required to satisfy any such conditions.

But, even supposing that it is possible to show that they should, a more substantive problem with the van Fraassen/Shimony approach is that calibration is simply not a reasonable measure of accuracy for partial beliefs.[12] Consider the following table, which gives four sets of degrees of belief for propositions in $X = \{X_1, X_2, X_3, X_4\}$ and their calibration scores at a world ω in which X_1 and X_2 are true and X_3 and X_4 are false:

	b_1	b_2	b_3	$X_j(\omega)$
X_1	1/2	1	9/10	1
X_2	1/2	1	9/10	1
X_3	1/2	1/10	1/2	0
X_4	1/2	0	1/2	0
Cal	0	1/400	13/100	0

Figure 2 Calibration scores.

Notice that b_1 is *better* calibrated than b_2 even though *all* of b_2's values are *closer* to the actual truth-values than those of b_1. This happens because each individual degree of belief can affect the overall calibration of its credence function not only by being closer to the truth-value of the proposition believed, but by manipulating the family of subsets relative to which calibration is calculated. To see why this is a problem imagine that an agent with degrees of belief b_3 who has strong evidence for X_1 and X_2, somehow learns that exactly two of the X_j hold, without being told which ones. What should he do with this information? One might think that a rational believer would lower his estimates for X_3 and X_4 to nearly zero and keep his estimates for X_1 and X_2 close to one. If we equate accuracy with good calibration, however, this is wrong! The best way for our agent to improve his calibration score (indeed to ensure that it will be zero) is to keep his estimates for X_3 and X_4 fixed, ignore all his evidence, and lower his estimates for X_1 and X_2 to 1/2. The Dominance requirement rules out this sort of absurdity.

Our fourth axiom says that differences among possible worlds that are not reflected in differences among truth-values of proposition that the agent believes should have no effect on the way in which accuracy is measured.

Normality: If $|\omega(X) - b(X)| = |\omega^*(X) - b^*(X)|$ for all $X \in \Omega$, then $I(b, \omega) = I(b^*, \omega^*)$.

In the presence of the other conditions, this merely says that the standard of gradational accuracy must not vary with changes in the world's state that do not effect the truth-values of believed propositions. Were this not so there would be no uniform notion of "what it takes" for a system of partial beliefs to fit the facts.

Our final two constraints concern mixtures of credence functions.

Weak Convexity: Let $m = (1/2b + 1/2b^*)$ be the midpoint of the line segment between b and b^*. If $I(b, \omega) = I(b^*, \omega)$, then it will always be the case that $I(b, \omega) \geq I(m, \omega)$ with identity only if $b = b^*$.

Symmetry: If $I(b, \omega) = I(b^*, \omega)$, then for any $\lambda \in [0, 1]$ one has $I(\lambda b + (1 - \lambda) b^*, \omega) = I((1 - \lambda) b + \lambda b^*, \omega)$.

To see why Weak Convexity is a reasonable constraint on gradational inaccuracy notice that in moving from b to m an agent would alter each of degree of belief $b(X)$ by adding an increment of $k(X) = 1/2[b^*(X) - b(X)]$. She would add the same increment of $k(X)$ to each $m(X)$ in moving from m to b^*. To put it in geometrical terms, the "vector" k that she must add to b to get m is the same as the vector she must add to m to get b^*. Furthermore, since $b^* = b + 2k$ the change in belief involved in going from b to b^* has the *same direction* but a *doubly greater magnitude* than change involved in going from b to m. This means that the former change is more *extreme* than the latter in the sense that, for *every* proposition X, both changes alter the agent's degree of belief for X in the same direction, either by moving it closer to one or closer to zero, but the b to b^* change will always move $b(X)$ twice as far as the b to m change moves it. Weak Convexity is motivated by the intuition that extremism in the pursuit of accuracy is no virtue. It says that if a certain change in a person's degrees of belief does not improve accuracy then a more radical change in the same direction and of the same magnitude should not improve accuracy either. Indeed, this is just what the principle says. If it did not hold, one could have absurdities like this: "I raised my confidence levels in X and Y and my beliefs became less accurate overall, so I raised my confidence levels in X and Y again, by exactly the same amounts, and the initial accuracy was restored."

To understand the rationale for Symmetry observe first that, when b and b^* are equally accurate at ω, Weak Convexity entails that there will always be a unique point on the interior of the line segment between them that minimizes inaccuracy over the segment, i.e., there will be a $c = \mu b + (1 - \mu) b^*$ with $0 < \mu < 1$ such that $I(\lambda b + (1 - \lambda)b^*, \omega) \geq I(c, \omega)$ for all λ with $0 \leq \lambda \leq 1$.[13] If c were not the midpoint of bb^*, then it would have to be closer to b or to b^*. Given the initial symmetry of the situation this would amount to an unmotivated bias in favor of one set of beliefs or the other. If $c = \frac{1}{4}b + 3/4b^*$, for example, then c would lie between b^* and the midpoint of bb^*. This would mean that a person who held the b beliefs would need to alter her opinions more radically than a person who held the b^* beliefs in order to attain the maximum accuracy along bb^*.

The reverse would be true if $c = 3/4b + \frac{1}{4}b^*$. Symmetry rules this sort of thing out. It says that when b and b^* are equally accurate there can be no grounds, based on considerations of accuracy alone, for preferring a "compromise" that favors b to a symmetrical compromise that favors b^*. It does this by requiring that the change in belief that moves an agent a proportion λ along the line segment from b toward b^* has the same overall effect on her accuracy as a "mirror image" change that moves her the same proportion λ along the line segment from b^* toward b.

Structure, Extensionality, Normality, Dominance, Weak Convexity, and Symmetry are the only constraints on measures of gradational accuracy we need to vindicate the fundamental dogma of probabilism. Those who find these conditions compelling, and who agree with my analysis of partial beliefs as estimates of truth-value, are thereby committed to thinking that epistemically rational degrees of belief must obey the laws of probability. Those who deny this will either need to explain where my conditions go wrong or will have to dispute my analysis of partial beliefs. For the reasons presented, I do not believe either line of attack will succeed.

Vindicating the "fundamental dogma"

In this section we will see how any system of degrees of belief that violates the axioms of probability can be replaced by a system that both obeys these axioms and is more accurate relative any assignment of truth-values to the propositions believed. The aim is to prove the

> Main Theorem: If gradational inaccuracy is measured by a function I that satisfies Structure, Extensionality, Normality, Dominance, Weak Convexity, and Symmetry, then for each $c \in B \sim V^+$ there is a $c^* \in V^+$ such that $I(c, \omega) > I(c^*, \omega)$ for *every* $\omega \in V$.

Begin the proof by defining a map $D(b, c) = I(\omega + (b - c), \omega)$ where $\omega + (b - c)$ is defined by $(\omega + b - c)(X) = \omega(X) + b(X) - c(X)$. (I have chosen the symbol "D" here to suggest the notion of a distance function.)

The following facts are simple consequences of the conditions we have imposed on I: (Proofs are left to interested readers, but the axioms needed for each case are given.)

I. $D(\bullet, c)$ is continuous for each $c \in B$. [Structure]
II. D's value does not depend on the choice of $\omega \in V$. [Structure]
III. $D(b, c)$ goes to infinity as $b(X)$ goes to infinity for any $X \in \Omega$. [Structure]
IV. $D(b, c) \geq D(b^*, c^*)$ if $|b(X) - c(X)| \geq |b^*(X) - c^*(X)|$ holds for all $X \in \Omega$, and the former inequality is strict if the latter is strict for some X. [Dominance]
V. If c^* lies on the line segment bc and if $c^* \neq b$, then $D(b, c) > D(c^*, c)$. [via IV]
VI. $D(b, c) = D(b^*, c)$ if and only if $D(\bullet, c)$ has a unique minimum along the line segment bb^* at its midpoint $1/2b + 1/2b^*$. [Symmetry, Weak Convexity]

We will use these facts to prove a series of lemmas that establish the Main Theorem.

Let c be any fixed element of $B \sim V^+$. Our first lemma shows how to select c^*, the point in V^+ that is "closer to the truth" than c is no matter what the truth turns out to be.

LEMMA-1: There is a point $c^* \in V^+$ such that the function $D(\bullet, c)$ attains its *unique* minimum on V^+ at c^*.

PROOF: A classic result from point-set topology says that a continuous, real-valued function defined on a closed, bounded region always attains a minimum on that region. Since V^+ is closed and bounded it follows from (I) that there is a point $c^* \in V^+$ with $D(c^*, c) \leq D(b, c)$ for all $b \in V^+$. To see why this minimum is unique, suppose it is attained by another $b^* \in V^+$. Since $D(b^*, c) = D(c^*, c)$, fact (VI) entails that $D(\bullet, c)$ assumes a unique minimum on the line segment c^*b^* at its midpoint $1/2c^* + 1/2b^*$. Since V^+ is convex it will contain this midpoint, which contradicts the hypothesis that c^* minimizes $D(\bullet, c)$ on V^+. Q.E.D.

Given Lemma-1, we can prove Main Theorem by showing that $I(c, \omega) > I(c^*, \omega)$ for all $\omega \in V$. Start by selecting an arbitrary ω. We may assume that c^* and ω are distinct, and thus that $D(c^*, c) < D(\omega, c)$, since the desired inequality follows trivially from (IV) if they are identical. Let $L = \{\lambda c^* + (1 - \lambda)\omega : \lambda \in \Re\}$ be the line in B that contains c^* and ω, and let $R = \{\lambda c^* + (1 - \lambda)\omega : \lambda \geq 1\}$ be the ray of L that begins at c^* but does not contain ω.

LEMMA-2: There is a point m on R such that (a) m uniquely minimizes $D(\bullet, c)$ on R, (b) c^* is an element of the segment of L that runs between m and ω, and (c) $I(m, \omega) \geq I(c^*, \omega)$.

PROOF: Fact (III) entails that $D(\bullet, c)$ goes to infinity on R as λ does. Given that $D(c^*, c) < D(\omega, c)$ it follows from (I), and the Intermediate Value Theorem, that there is a point k on R such that $D(k, c) = D(\omega, c)$. Let $m = 1/2k + 1/2\omega$ be the midpoint of the line segment $k\omega$. By (VI), m is the unique minimum of $D(\bullet, c)$ on this segment. m cannot lie strictly between c^* and ω on L because it would then be contained in V^+, which would entail that c^* does not minimize $D(\bullet, c)$ on V^+. Thus, c^* must be on segment $m\omega$, and (V) entails that $I(m, \omega) \geq I(c^*, \omega)$, with the equality strict if $c^* \neq m$. Q.E.D.

Given these two Lemmas, the Main Theorem follows if it can be shown that $I(c, \omega) > I(m, \omega)$. This is one of those cases where a picture is worth a thousand words.

LEMMA-3: $I(c, \omega) > I(m, \omega)$.

PROOF: By the construction of Lemma-2 we know that $D(k, c) = D(\omega, c)$. Since c minimizes $D(\bullet, c)$ on the line segment from k to $2c - k$, (VI) entails that $D(k, c) =$

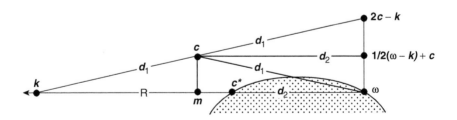

Figure 3 The key lemma in the proof of the main theorem: $d_1 > d_2$.

106

$D(2c - k, c)$. Together these identities yield

$$D(\omega, c) = D(2c - k, c). \tag{A}$$

Given (A), fact (VI) entails that $D(\bullet, c)$ attains a unique minimum on line segment between ω and $2c - k$ at $[1/2\,(\omega - k) + c]$. It follows that

$$D(\omega, c) > D(1/2(\omega - k) + c, c). \tag{B}$$

Since D is a symmetric function of its two arguments this means that

$$D(c, \omega) > D(c, 1/2(\omega - k) + c). \tag{C}$$

We can now use the definition of D to obtain

$$\begin{aligned}
I(c, \omega) = D(c,\omega) &> D(c,1/2(\omega - k) + c) \\
&= I(\omega + (c - [1/2(\omega - k) + c)], \omega) \\
&= I(1/2\omega + 1/2k, \omega) \\
&= I(m, \omega).
\end{aligned}$$

So, we have shown that $I(c, \omega) > I(m, \omega)$. Q.E.D.

Since we already know from Lemma-2 that $I(m, \omega) \geq I(c^*, \omega)$, we obtain the inequality $I(c, \omega) > I(c^*, \omega)$ from Lemma-3. This completes the proof of the Main Theorem. It is thus established that degrees of belief that violate the laws of probability are invariably less accurate than they could be. Given that an epistemically rational agent will always strive to hold partial beliefs that are as accurate as possible, this vindicates the fundamental dogma of probabilism.

Some loose ends

The foregoing results suggests two further lines of investigation. First, it would be useful to know what functions obey the constraints imposed on I. Second, to apply the Main Theorem in realistic cases we need to understand how it applies to partial beliefs that do not admit of measurement in precise numerical degrees.

I cannot now specify the class of functions that satisfy my axioms, but I do know it is not empty. The quadratic-loss rules are among its elements, as is any map $I(b, \omega) = F(\Sigma_{X \in \Omega}\, \lambda_X\, [\omega(X) - b(X)]^2)$ where F is a continuous, strictly increasing real function. The proofs of these claims are, however, beyond the scope of this paper. I am not certain whether there are other functions that meet the requirements,[14] but I suspect there are.

Turning to the second issue, the Main Theorem tells us that partial beliefs whose strengths can be measured in precise numerical degrees must conform to the laws of probability, but its import is less clear for partial beliefs specified in more realistic ways. Most probabilists recognize that opinions are often too vague to be pinned down in numerical terms, and it has therefore become standard to represent a person's partial beliefs not by some single credence function but by the class of all credence functions consistent with her opinions. One then thinks of a doxastic state not as a single element of B but as one of its subsets B^*.

The most minimal probabilistic consistency requirement for partial beliefs that are modeled in this way is that there should be *at least one* probability among the elements of B^*. In other words, an epistemically rational agent's partial beliefs should always be *extendible* to some system of degrees of belief that satisfy the axioms of probability. The Main Theorem provides a compelling rationale for this requirement because if B^* contained no probabilities then *every* way of making the agent's opinions precise would result in a system of degrees of belief that are less accurate than they could otherwise be. It would then be determinately the case that the agent's partial beliefs are not as accurate as they could be because every precisification of them would yield a credence function that is less accurate than it could be.

One of the best things about looking at matters in this way is that it helps to make sense of some old results pertaining to the probabilistic representation of ordinal confidence rankings. In a seminal paper, Kraft, et al. (1959) presented a set of necessary and sufficient conditions for a *comparative probability ranking* to be represented by a probability. We may think of such a ranking as a pair of relations (.>., .≥.) defined on Ω, where X .>. Y and X .≥. Y mean, respectively, that the agent is more confident in X than in Y, or as confident in X as in Y. The conditions Kraft *et al.* laid down can be expressed in a variety of ways, but the most tractable formulation is due to Dana Scott (1964). Say that two *ordered sequences* of (not necessarily distinct) propositions $(X_1, X_2, ..., X_n)$ and $(Y_1, Y_2, ..., Y_m)$ drawn from Ω are *isovalent* (my term) when the number of truths that appear in the first is necessarily identical to the number that appear in the second, so that $\omega(X_1) + \omega(X_2) + ... + \omega(X_n) = \omega(Y_1) + \omega(Y_2) + ... + \omega(Y_m)$ holds at *every* world ω. The important thing about isovalence is that a probability function β will always be additive over isovalent sequences, so that $\Sigma_i \beta(X_i) = \Sigma_i \beta(Y_i)$ when $(X_1, X_2, ..., X_n)$ and $(Y_1, Y_2, ..., Y_m)$ are isovalent. Scott introduced the following constraint on confidence rankings to ensure that all their representations would have this generalized additive property:

> **Scott's Axiom:** If $(X_1, X_2, ..., X_n)$ and $(Y_1, Y_2, ..., Y_m)$ are isovalent, it should never be the case that X_i .≥. Y_i for every i = 1, 2, ..., n where X_j .>. Y_j for some j.

He then proved that, for finite Ω, Scott's Axiom (plus a nontriviality requirement) is necessary and sufficient for the existence of a probability representation for (.>., .≥.).

Commentators have not known what to make of Scott's condition. Scott himself worried about its "non-Boolean" nature. Terrence Fine points out, quite rightly, that it makes essential reference to *sums* of propositions which generally will not be propositions themselves. A reasonable theory of comparative probability, he writes, should be, "concerned only with [propositions]. Why should we be concerned about objects that have no reasonable interpretation in terms of random phenomena?" (1973, 24) Peter Forrest, commenting on a condition of his own that is equivalent to Scott's Axiom, writes:

> My results are largely negative, I motivate the search for a certain kind of representation and I provide a condition which, given various intuitive rationality constraints, is necessary, sufficient and non-redundant. Unfortunately, this

condition is not itself an intuitive rationality constraint. That is why my results are negative. Their chief purpose is to throw out a challenge. Is it possible to provide an intuitive rationality constraint that implies [Scott's Axiom]? (1989, 280)

Fortunately, we already have one! Scott's Axiom is just the requirement one would impose if one wanted partial beliefs to be gradationally accurate. If $(X_1, X_2, ..., X_n)$ and $(Y_1, Y_2, ..., Y_m)$ are isovalent, then every logically consistent set of truth-value assignments ω will be found somewhere in the bounded, closed, convex set

$$U = \{b \in B: b(X_1) + ... + b(X_n) = b(Y_1) + ... + b(Y_n), \text{ for } 0 \le b(X_i), b(Y_i) \le 1\}.$$

If $X_i \gt Y_i$ for all i with $X_j \ge Y_j$ for some j, then any credence function c that represents these beliefs will satisfy $[c(X_1) + ... + c(X_n)] > [c(Y_1) + ... + c(Y_n)]$, which means that c will lie *outside* U. By recapitulating our argument for the Main Theorem we can find a point $c^* \in U$ such that $I(c, \omega) > I(c^*, \omega)$ for *every* world ω. Thus, once we start thinking in terms of gradational accuracy, Scott's Axiom can be interpreted as a constraint that prevents people from having partial beliefs that are less accurate than they need to be. This, as we have seen, is something to be avoided on pain of *epistemic* irrationality.

Notes

* Originally published in *Philosophy of Science*, 65 (1998), pp. 575–603. Copyright © 1998 Philosophy of Science Association. Reprinted by permission of University of Chicago Press.

† I have been helped and encouraged in the development of these ideas by Brad Armendt, Robert Batterman, Alan Code, David Christensen, Dan Farrell, Allan Gibbard, Alan Hajek, William Harper, Sally Haslanger, Mark Kaplan, Jeff Kasser, Louis Loeb, Gerhard Nuffer, Peter Railton, Gideon Rosen, Larry Sklar, Brian Skyrms, Bas van Fraassen, David Velleman, Peter Vranas, Nick White, Mark Wilson, Steve Yablo, and Lyle Zynda. Richard Jeffrey's influence on my thinking will be clear to anyone who knows his writings. Special thanks are also due to two anonymous referees from *Philosophy of Science*, whose splendidly detailed comments greatly improved the final version of this paper.

1 A further tenet of the view is that *Bayesian conditioning* is the only legitimate method for revising beliefs in light of new evidence. This aspect of probabilism, which remains an active topic of debate in philosophical circles, will not be our concern here.

2 Even though the Norm of Truth is widely accepted, there is no consensus about the basis of its prescriptive force. Some read it as expressing a prima facie intellectual obligation that is binding on all believers (Chisholm 1977, 7). Others portray it as an "internal" norm that is partially constitutive of what it is to *be* a believer, so that an attitude toward X cannot even be counted as a full belief (as opposed to a supposition or wish that X) unless its holder is committed to regarding the attitude as successful iff X is true. See, e.g., Anscombe 1957, Smith 1987, and Velleman 1996. A third view, which has been championed by Richard Foley (1987, 66), sees the Norm as being grounded in our practices of epistemic evaluation; terms like "justified" or "epistemically rational" can only be meaningfully applied to individuals who regard their full beliefs as successful iff they are true. For present purposes, it does not matter which of these rationales for the Norm of Truth one adopts. The important point is that there is little real dispute about its status as a basic criterion of epistemic success for full beliefs.

3 Mark Kaplan has observed that the Norm of Truth is not a pure accuracy principle since it places a premium on believing truths as against suspending judgment. He suggests, however, that none of my arguments rely upon this aspect of Norm, and that I could have just as easily made accuracy for systems of full belief a matter or the their truth-to-falsehood *ratio*. While I think this is right, I have decided to stick with NT as my official "success condition" for full beliefs because doing so helps make sense of some important debates in the epistemology of full belief.

Notice that NT does not say *how much* better (worse) it is to believe a truth (falsehood) than it is to have no opinion about it, nor does it give any hint about what the best overall balance of truths to falsehoods might be. The way we decide these issues will greatly effect the form of dogmatic epistemology. For example, those who tend to put great emphasis on the avoidance of error may see only a small difference between believing truly and suspending belief whereas the difference between suspending belief and believing falsely may loom quite large. Conversely, Popperians who want to encourage "bold conjecturing" will emphasize the "believe the truth" aspect of the Norm of Truth and downplay its prescription to avoid the false.

4 The options here are roughly the same as those listed in note 2.

5 In saying that a miser loves only money we imply that (a) all her desires are directed toward propositions that specify her net worth under various contingencies, and (b) that money has *constant marginal utility* for her, so that giving her an extra dollar always increases her happiness by the same amount no matter how large her fortune might be. Proponents of the Dutch book do of course realize that no misers actually exist, but they use them as a useful *idealization*. Insofar as a person is rational, it is claimed, she will pursue an abstract measure of overall satisfaction, *utility*, in the same way that a miser seeks wealth. The miser's craving for money is thus meant to mirror the universal desire for happiness.

6 Strictly speaking, this only establishes Additivity in the *finite* case. De Finetti did not go on to argue that the quadratic-loss rules enforce *countable* additivity because he felt a reasonable person should be able to assign the same, non-zero probability of winning to each ticket in a countably infinite lottery. As a number of authors have noted, however, de Finetti's argument for finite additivity extends easily to the infinite case. I have never seen a proof of this for the version of the Dutch book argument considered here. There are proofs for other versions (see Skyrms 1984, 21–23). Here is an (incomplete) sketch of how the proof would go: Normality and finite Additivity imply that any assignment p of previsions to a countably infinite set of pairwise incompatible propositions $X = (X_1, X_2, X_3, ...)$ is *square-convergent*, i.e. $\Sigma_i\ p_i^2$ is finite. V and $V+$ are subsets of the space of square-convergent sequences. V^+ contains the countably additive prevision assignments for X. If we imagine previsions scored using a rule the quadratic $S(p, \omega) = \Sigma_i\lambda_i(\omega(X_i) - p_i)^2$, then for any $\rho \notin V^+$ and q $\in V^+$ we can set $D(q) = (\Sigma_i\lambda_i(q_i - p_i)^2)^{1/2}$ and minimize to find p* $\notin V^+$. Calculation then shows that $S(p^*, \omega) > S(p, \omega)$ for all ω.

7 The references here are too numerous to list. See Gardenfors and Shalin 1988.

8 One might be tempted here to say that it is the agent's beliefs *about what is desirable* that are inconsistent. Aside from the fact that this would locate the epistemic flaw associated with my strongly believing both that it will be hot and that it will be cold tomorrow not in my beliefs about the weather but in my beliefs about the values of wagers, the underlying view that a desire can be understood as a kind of belief has serious difficulties. See Lewis 1988 and 1996 for relevant discussion.

9 It does no harm to assume that Ω is *countable* since violations of the laws of probability always occur in countable sets. On an uncountable algebra of propositions the probabilist requirement is that degrees of belief should obey the probability axioms on *every countable subalgebra*.

10 For an excellent recent discussion of epistemic utility, see Maher 1993.

11 Thanks to Bob Batterman for helping me think this issue through.

12 My discussion here is indebted to Seidenfeld 1985.

13 The proof of this fact is essentially the same as the proof of Lemma-1, below.

14 One large class of functions that do not satisfy them (because they violate Symmetry) are the $\mathcal{L}_p$-norms: $I(b, \omega) = (\Sigma_{x\in\Omega}\lambda_x\ [\omega(X_i) - b(X_i)]^p)^{1/p}$, for p $\geq$ 1 other than p $=$ 2.

Bibliography

Anscombe, G. E. M. (1957), *Intention*. Oxford: Basil Blackwell.

Brier, G. (1950) "Verification of Forecasts Expressed in Terms of Probability", *Monthly Weather Review* 78: 1–3.

Chisholm, R. (1977), *Theory of Knowledge*, 2nd ed. New York: Prentice Hall.

de Finetti, B. (1974), *Theory of Probability*, vol. 1. New York: John Wiley and Sons.

Fine, T. (1973), *Theories of Probability*. New York: Academic Press.

Foley, R. (1987), *The Theory of Epistemic Rationality*. Cambridge, MA: Harvard University Press.

Forrest, P. (1989), "The Problem of Representing Incompletely Ordered Doxastic Systems", *Synthese* 79: 18–33.

Gardenfors, P. and P. Shalin (1988), *Decision, Probability, and Utility*. Cambridge: Cambridge University Press.

Jeffrey, R. (1986), "Probabilism and Induction", *Topoi* 5: 51–58.

——. (1992), "Probability and the Art of Judgment", in *Probability and the Art of Judgment*. Cambridge: Cambridge University Press, 44–76.

Kennedy, R. and C. Chihara (1979) "The Dutch Book Argument: its Logical Flaws, its Subjective Sources", *Philosophical Studies* 36: 19–33.

Kraft, C., J. Pratt, and A. Seidenberg (1959), "Intuitive Probability on Finite Sets", *Annals of Mathematical Statistics* 30: 408–419.

Lewis, David (1988), "Desire as Belief", *Mind* 97: 323–332.

——. (1996), "Desire as Belief II", *Mind* 105: 303–313.

Maher, P. (1993), *Betting on Theories*. Cambridge: Cambridge University Press.

Murphy, A. (1973), "A New Vector Partition of the Probability Score", *Journal of Applied Meteorology* 12: 595–600.

Ramsey, F. P. (1931), "Truth and Probability", in R. B. Braithwaite (ed.), *The Foundations of Mathematics*. London: Routledge and Kegan Paul, 156–198, reprinted as Chapter 2 in this volume.

Rosenkrantz, R. (1981), *Foundations and Applications of Inductive Probability*. Atascadero, CA: Ridgeview Press.

Salmon, W. (1988), "Dynamic Rationality: Propensity, Probability and Credence", in J. H. Fetzer (ed.), *Probability and Causality*. Dordrecht: D. Reidel, 3–40.

Savage, L. (1971), "Elicitation of Personal Probabilities", *Journal of the American Statistical Association* 66: 783–801.

Scott, D. (1964), "Measurement Structures and Linear Inequalities", *Journal of Mathematical Psychology* 1: 233–247.

Seidenfeld. T. (1985), "Calibration, Coherence, and Scoring Rules", *Philosophy of Science* 52: 274–294.

Shimony, A. (1988), "An Adamite Derivation of the Calculus of Probability", in J. H. Fetzer (ed.), *Probability and Causality*. Dordrecht: D. Reidel, 151–161.

Skyrms, B. (1984), *Pragmatics and Empiricism*. New Haven: Yale University Press.

Smith, M. (1987), "The Humean Theory of Motivation", *Mind* 96: 36–61.

van Fraassen, B. (1983), "Calibration: A Frequency Justification for Personal Probability", in R. Cohen and L. Laudan (eds.), *Physics Philosophy and Psychoanalysis*. Dordrecht: D. Reidel, 295–319.

Velleman, J. D. (1996), "The Possibility of Practical Reason," *Ethics* 106: 694–726.

Part II

UPDATING DEGREES OF BELIEF

Conditionalisation and Reflection

5

INTRODUCTION

Suppose we accept the arguments offered in Part I that a rational agent's belief state can be modelled by a probability function. The Dutch book and other arguments offered to this conclusion require that, at each time, the agent's beliefs are probabilistically coherent. But this *synchronic* requirement of coherence at a particular time says nothing about how an agent should shift their belief over time in light of new evidence, and how different coherent credence functions of a rational agent might be *diachronically* related over time. But there do seem to be reasonable and unreasonable ways of adjusting and updating one's beliefs and commitments when new evidence arrives.

Updating full belief

In the epistemology of full belief, the belief state at a time of an agent is sometimes modelled by the set of propositions they believe. If the new evidence consists in a proposition e that can be consistently added to that set of propositions, then this kind of epistemology proposes the simplest rule of rational updating: simply come to believe the new evidence too. That is, if B is the agent's old set of beliefs, and B^+ the new set of beliefs, then $B^+ = B \cup \{e\}$. The agent will typically come to be committed to other things when they come to believe e: most importantly, they seem to be committed to logical consequences of e and their old beliefs, which we can model by taking the deductive closure of B^+, which is standardly taken to model the (perhaps implicit) epistemic commitments of the agent.

This presupposes that there is a proposition e which encapsulates the evidence you receive, or what you come to learn. Standardly, this proposition is taken to be the logically strongest proposition that comes to be fully believed after a learning experience. This functional specification of the evidence proposition means that the account of updating is only really useful in hindsight, for only then can it be seen what the evidence turned out to be for this agent.

One feature of full belief updating is of special interest. Suppose you believe $p \rightarrow q$, and then you come to believe evidence p. In the simple model, you are then committed to q—you've updated your beliefs to hold as true all things that formerly you held true conditional on p. This fits well with Ramsey's 'test' for the truth of a conditional:

> If two people are arguing 'If p will q?' and are both in doubt as to p, they are adding p hypothetically to their stock of knowledge and arguing on that basis about q ....

> (Ramsey, 1990: 155)

115

In this case, receiving the evidence that p allows you to non-hypothetically add p to your stock of knowledge and discharge the conditional knowledge you obtained in something like the way Ramsey suggests.

Two difficulties are worth noting:

1   Unless an agent is very timid in forming prior beliefs, they will often believe things that turn out inconsistent with e. This generates a commitment to everything, and perhaps an explicitly inconsistent belief set. There are answers as to what agents should do to revise their beliefs on receiving an inconsistent piece of new evidence. Usually the advice is to make the most minimal change to regain consistency, but how this can be measured is one difficulty. (Suppose you believe only $(p \land q) \rightarrow r, p$ and q, and then receive $\neg r$ as new evidence—clearly you are now committed to an inconsistency, but rejecting which of your three initial beliefs is the most minimal change?) Why minimal change is important is another difficulty—maybe making the most minimal change to a set of beliefs that led you into an inconsistency is only setting yourself up for another inconsistency soon.

2   But the main problem is that sometimes it is reasonable to revise beliefs even when the new evidence is consistent with your prior beliefs. Anyone who draws conclusions from their evidence will have beliefs that, even if they are consistent with the new evidence, aren't supported by it. When the new evidence comes along it might be reasonable to give up on an old belief and adopt a new one, even if adding the evidence to your prior beliefs yields a consistent set. But on this simple model, the only incentive one has to change beliefs is if there is an inconsistency in the set of beliefs; and, in particular, if the person lacks certain conditional beliefs on the evidence, then they will be able to retain all of their old beliefs, no matter how implausible they are in light of the evidence, since no inconsistency will be derivable.

Both of these problems emerge because a set of full beliefs has very little structure to guide revision, too little to facilitate the kinds of revisions we often have to make to our commitments in light of new evidence. If we model a belief state by a credence function, we have additional structure that might be able to avoid these difficulties while retaining some of the general spirit of these ideas about belief revision.

Introducing conditionalisation

The Ramsey test says: belief in a conditional contains information that would permit you to come to believe the consequent if you learned that the antecedent is true. Ramsey himself generalised this idea to the credential context, going on to say that the people in his case 'are fixing their degrees of belief in q given p' (Ramsey 1990: 155). Ramsey here has clearly in mind the idea that conditional degrees of belief are important; and again, if the agents find out that p is true, it seems they should adopt not necessarily the full belief in q, but exactly that degree of belief in q given p they have previously fixed.

There is an ambiguity here, however: does Ramsey mean by 'degree of belief in q given p' the conditional credence $C(q|p)$, or the credence in a conditional $C(p \rightarrow q)$? Since the triviality results of Lewis (1986) (discussed on p. 13ff), we know that these two notions come apart in general. The standard answer is that the role of conditionals in the epistemology of full belief is played by conditional probabilities.

Conditional probabilities seem to be well behaved; for example, it follows straight from the ratio rule that the conditional probability of rolling a six with a fair die, given that you rolled an even number, is 1/3. By contrast, it is difficult to assign a useful credence to the conditional 'If I roll an even number, it comes up six'; if anything it presents itself to the ear as straightforwardly false, not something which should get credence 1/3. And if we consider how we would evaluate the proposition 'the die comes up six', if we were to learn that an even number has been rolled, it seems plausible that the credence we assign to this is one in line with the conditional probability.[1]

So philosophers have proposed this updating rule, similarly inspired by Ramsey, for credences: If your old credence function is C, and you come to learn a proposition e which captures your new strongest evidence, then your updated credence function $C^+ = C(\bullet|e)$. This is the rule known as *conditionalisation* or *conditioning*. (Because conditional probabilities are probabilities, C^+ is a credence function.) An agent whose belief state is modelled by a probability function has already, in line with the ratio account of conditional probability, a well-defined conditional probability on every hypothesis to which they assign a non-zero credence. The reasoning is intuitive: if the probability of q conditional on p is x, then you assign a probability of x to q on the hypothetical assumption that p is true. Supposing now that you receive p as evidence, you non-hypothetically accept p and accept that the (now unconditional) probability of q is x.[2] Again, as before, the evidence e is functionally identified—it is the logically strongest proposition that, after a learning experience, comes to have credence 1. The proposal is, therefore, that someone undergoes a learning experience; they come to assign credence 1 to some propositions; they then update the remainder of their beliefs by exchanging the old credences for new credences, equal to their old conditional credences on the proposition which newly has credence 1 and which entails every other proposition that newly has credence 1.[3]

This updating scheme largely avoids the two problems mentioned above with non-probabilistic updating. Firstly, inconsistency is rarer: even arbitrarily low probabilities for e aren't inconsistent with the truth of e. Agents will be able to update even on very surprising evidence. It is only when an agent receives evidence to which they assign zero credence that the updating scheme fails; and if their credences broadly track how things are, such evidence will be extremely rare. Secondly, conditionalisation permits revision of credences in many propositions on receipt of new evidence, because all credence functions come already endowed with a full set of conditional credences. We don't need an explicit conditional belief, as was needed in the full belief case, for some new evidence to have an impact on all of the propositions to which it is probabilistically relevant. This allows the agent to change their credence in p in more subtle ways to reflect the evidence that tells for or against it, given the rest of the agent's beliefs.

Justifying conditionalisation

Conditionalisation is intuitively appealing. Hacking (1967) calls it 'the dynamic assumption', and takes it to be an implicit and needed assumption in all theories of credence up until that time. But others have offered arguments to the effect that not only is conditionalisation a plausible updating rule, but in fact it is the only sensible rule. The first such argument was Lewis's, presented in Chapter 6.

Lewis offers a Dutch book argument for conditionalisation, matching the Dutch book arguments discussed in Part I for the synchronic requirement for credences to be coherent. As such, it is of course subject to the worries raised there about Dutch books (the contingent existence of the bookie, worries about the converse theorem, and concerns about whether the guaranteed sure loss might be offset by the equal guarantee of sure gain from another subjectively fair bet). Nevertheless, it provides some motivation for conditionalisation.

Lewis's argument runs like this. Suppose you update in some other way than conditionalisation. Without loss of generality, suppose that $C^+(p) < C(p|e) = x$. Then the bookie can exploit this. He begins, at t, by selling you two bets: one that pays \$1 if $p \wedge e$, and nothing otherwise; and one that pays \$$x$ if $\neg e$, nothing otherwise. You will pay at most $C(p \wedge e) + xC(\neg e)$, which a bit of simple rearranging shows to be equal to $C(p|e)$. The bookie waits to see whether e turns out true, as do you. If e turns out false, you gain and lose nothing. If e is true, the bookie offers to buy from you a bet paying \$1 if p, and nothing otherwise, for your minimum price; this will of course be $C^+(p)$. But then, when e is true, you pay $C(p|e)$ for subjectively fair bets, and receive $C^+(p)$ for subjectively fair bets; since the former is greater than the latter, you are guaranteed a loss.

> As a result of your failure to conditionalise, I can inflict on you a risk of loss uncompensated by any chance of gain; and I can do this without at any point using knowledge that you do not have. ... If you can be thus exploited you are irrational; so you are rational only if you conditionalize.
>
> (Lewis, p. 134)

As in the static case (sect. 1.4), the Dutch book argument needs to be supplemented by a *converse* theorem, stating that if you do conditionalise, modulo certain tacit assumptions, you are not vulnerable to a Dutch book. One such converse theorem is proved in Skyrms (1987: 15–16).

This all sounds convincing, at least as convincing as the parallel argument for synchronic coherence. But the temporal aspect of conditionalisation adds new difficulties. As we saw, some follow Ramsey in characterising the lesson of the Dutch book argument as showing that incoherent credences display the irrationality of evaluating the same option differently when described differently. That sounds unreasonable at a single moment. But why should it be irrational over time? People can change their mind without being irrational, and that will undermine the argument. To adapt an example from Maher (p. 166), suppose the bookie sells you a bet on rain this afternoon. After consulting the weather charts, you realise that it will be increasingly cloudy in the afternoon, and you think those clouds will portend rain. So you assign a high conditional credence to rain given clouds. As the day progresses, you see the clouds, which are not looking threatening, and you come in the afternoon to have a low credence in rain. This violates conditionalisation, for $C_{afternoon}(\text{rain}) \neq C_{morning}(\text{rain}|\text{clouds})$. But this is because you changed your mind about what the experience of clouds suggested about the rain; a change of mind but not one that is unreasonable. Moreover, having taken the bets in the morning you will now foresee that you will lose money when they are called in, so you have no reason to avoid purchasing the last bet the bookie offers you—you think it might offset the loss you are already expecting to suffer. This is a case where one changes one's mind, and comes to regret decisions made by your earlier self, but without wishing to characterise those earlier decisions as irrational (even though you wouldn't make them now).

In general, conditionalising involves an update in which the bearing of what you learn on various propositions, as represented by your conditional credences, is held fixed. So it cannot readily accommodate cases where someone changes their mind, not about what they have learned, but about how what they've learned supports or undermines other claims they are considering. If the agent proposes a rule to govern this circumstance—a rule that tells them how to revise their opinions about conditional probabilities, given certain propositions as evidence—then, if it is not conditionalisation, the bookie will be able to exploit them. But an agent who changes their mind in a less predictable way, having had some unexpected insight or shift in perspective, will not conform to an alternative rule for updating than conditionalisation, and yet may be rational. Van Fraassen expresses this kind of view, when he considers

> the assertion that a rational person is committed beforehand to a recipe for belief-revision. ... But must we accept this assertion about the rational person? What of the person who says 'I can envisage all of these possible episodes, one and only one of which will come to pass—I do not know now exactly what opinions and expectations I will form in response, I shall in most respects make up my mind then and there ...'—is he not rational? ... I conclude that rationality does not require conditionalization ...
>
> (van Fraassen, 1989: 174)

Van Fraassen is concerned here with revolutionary insights and other exceptional cases, where no rule for updating one might commit to in advance can be relied upon. Yet he thinks that in most ordinary episodes of learning from experience one can commit to an updating rule in advance, and that if you are to rationally follow any such rule, it must be conditionalisation—and he offers something much like Lewis's Dutch book argument to support this view.

But just as with the Dutch book argument for coherence, many philosophers have been unhappy with the pragmatic character of the argument. Just as Joyce (p. 89) offered a non-pragmatic vindication of synchronic coherence, so others have offered non-pragmatic arguments for conditionalisation. A generalisation of the Joyce-style approach is the argument from epistemic utility theory offered by Greaves and Wallace (2006). They argue that there is sense to be made of 'cognitive utility', the assignment of values to epistemic states according to the state of the non-epistemic world, where those epistemic states are represented by synchronically coherent credence functions. The existence of such cognitive utilities is supported by the fact that it seems we can evaluate or score probability functions; Greaves and Wallace offer as an example an evaluation function which rewards a probability function for being close to the truth and far from falsehood (and is, as in Joyce's case, a proper scoring rule). The crux of their argument is a proof that, if an agent announces in advance an updating function, then (treating epistemic utility as a random variable) the updating strategy that gives the maximum expected epistemic utility is conditionalisation, at least in cases where the available credence functions are stable in a certain sense ('strongly self-recommending', in their terminology).

If epistemic utility exists and is distinct from the practical utility of adopting certain epistemic states, then the Greaves and Wallace argument provides a non-pragmatic justification of conditionalisation. It is important to know that their argument settles on conditionalisation as the optimal updating rule only in a case where the updating rule is

119

announced in advance, and when all the potential credence functions are strongly self-recommending. It is not clear whether it is a requirement of rationality that the potential credence functions of a rational agent have this feature. It is also worth considering that the epistemic utility theory they propose is the epistemic analogue of Savage-style decision theory, and the same kinds of cases that prompted that theory to be largely rejected by philosophers (namely, the existence of cases in which act-outcome independence fails) can apparently also be constructed for epistemic utility theory.

Another argument in support of conditionalisation is offered by Joyce (2008: sect. 3.4), drawing on links between conditionalisation and confirmation theory that we will explore more fully in Part III. Joyce's argument makes two assumptions: (i) the *Weak Likelihood Principle* (that a proposition e provides incremental evidence for a proposition h iff $P(e|h) > P(e|\neg h)$—that is, if e is more likely given h than not, then an observation of e is some (rarely conclusive) evidence that h is true), and (ii) the *Weak Evidence Principle*: 'If, relative to a prior P, e provides at least as much incremental evidence for h as for h', and if h is antecedently more probable than h', then h should remain more probable than h' after any learning experience whose sole immediate effect is to increase the probability of e.' Joyce then shows that the only strategy for changing from a prior credence P to an updated credence P' that can meet both these conditions, for every credence function P, is conditionalisation. Any other updating rule gives rise to cases where, even though all one learned was e, which supports h more than h', one might nevertheless end up believing h' more than h. It is suggested that this is an irrational response to evidence, and hence that rationality requires conditionalisation. This argument depends on whether we believe that the probabilistic account of evidence, involving likelihoods, is the correct approach to evidential support. As we will see, there is considerable dispute over this, so it is controversial whether it offers convincing considerations in favour of conditionalisation.

Generalised conditionalisation

To adopt conditionalisation as one's only updating rule supposes that one always will become certain of new evidence: when you get new evidence, its content is whichever is the strongest proposition to which you now assign credence 1. But, as Jeffrey points out (p. 135), there seem to be cases where one gets some evidence, but which proposition that evidence amounts to is not clear to you. So you might learn something, but be unable to articulate what you learn, and so be unable to fix on a proposition that you have now learned and must conditionalise on (even if there is one). The content of the evidence may, however, be able to be captured indirectly by its effects on other propositions you can articulate, if the articulable propositions form a partition:

> The agent inspects a piece of cloth by candlelight, and gets the impression that it is green, although he concedes that it might be blue, or even (but very improbably) violet. If G, B, and V are the propositions that the cloth is green, blue, and violet, respectively, then the outcome of the observation might be that, whereas originally his degrees of belief in G, B, and V were .30, .30, and .40, his degrees of belief in those same propositions after the observation are .70, .25, and .05. If there was a proposition e in his preference ranking that described the precise quality of his visual experience in looking at the cloth, one would say that what the agent learned from the observation was that e is

true. ... But there need be no such proposition *e* in his preference ranking; nor need any such proposition be expressible in the English language. ... It seems that the best we can do is to describe, not the quality of the visual experience itself, but rather its effects on the observer, by saying, 'After the observation, the agent's degrees of belief in *G*, *B*, and *V* were .70, .25, and .05.'

(Jeffrey, Chapter 7: 135–49)

Jeffrey's proposal for dealing with cases like this is, conceptually at least, a generalisation of simple conditionalisation. In the special case where we uncertainly receive evidence that bears on the two-cell partition {*e*, ¬*e*}, Jeffrey conditioning is:

$$C^+(p) = C^+(e)C(p|e) + C^+(\neg e)C(p|\neg e). \quad \text{(Jeffrey)}$$

In this, Jeffrey's model presupposes that the deliverances of the senses do immediately give a new credence in *e*; this was also tacitly assumed in the original presentation of conditionalisation. Jeffrey conditioning generalises the idea behind simple conditionalisation, because as $C^+(e)$ tends to 1, $C^+(p)$ tends to $C(p|e)$.[4] Jeffrey, in his chapter, extends his account to deal with any finite partition of the possible evidence, leaving simple conditionalisation behind, and begins to deal with the infinite case. This full account has now become known as *Jeffrey conditionalisation*, or *probability kinematics*.

As an updating rule, Jeffrey conditionalisation has considerable attraction as a psychologically more realistic account of taking evidence into consideration. It closely matches ordinary conditionalisation when *e* is learned certainly. And it can be defended by a Dutch book argument. But it does have some puzzling features. For example, Jeffrey conditionalisation is *non-commutative*—if one uncertainly gets evidence *e* and then uncertainly gets evidence *f*, the resulting credence will in general not be the same as if one had first got *f* and then *e*, even if the intrinsic character of the two *e* experiences is identical (and same for the *f*-experiences). This has been thought to be a problem:

> Two persons, who have the same relevant experiences on the same day, but in a different order, will [according to Jeffrey conditionalisation] not agree in the evening even if they had exactly the same opinions in the morning. Does this not make nonsense of the idea of learning from experience?
>
> (van Fraassen, 1989: 338)

But others have argued that this is no problem; rather, what this shows is either (i) precisely how people in different epistemic states respond differently to the same evidence; or (ii) that the order of one's experiences is part of one's evidence too, so that agents who have experiences in a different order have different evidence.

Jeffrey conditionalisation can be used to talk about uncertain evidence generally, if our learning experiences don't deliver certainties. Jeffrey thinks that only in such a framework can the promise of subjective probability in epistemology be fulfilled, by permitting cases where any trace of full belief, in the guise of certain evidence, disappears. As he puts it elsewhere, '[N]or am I disturbed by the fact that our ordinary notion of belief is only vestigially present in the notion of degree of belief. I am inclined to think Ramsey

sucked the marrow out of the ordinary notion, and used it to nourish a more adequate view' (Jeffrey 1970). The 'more adequate' view is his *radical probabilism*—a kind
of anti-foundationalist epistemology, in which certain evidence plays no role without
giving rise to scepticism.

Yet there is reason for doubt about whether it can play this role. In conditionalisation, we identified the proposition to be updated upon as the strongest one which was
learned. But there is no such proposition in general in Jeffrey conditionalisation, so it
is difficult to identify, even retrospectively, which proposition is *e* in (Jeffrey). And an
inappropriate choice of evidence partition in generalised Jeffrey conditionalisation can
trivialise the process (Williamson 2000: 216–7). And while Jeffrey conditionalisation
may seem anti-foundationalist in that it doesn't require one to become certain of any
proposition, the certainty of which is not required by coherence, it remains true that the
deliverances of the senses—in this case, in the guise of the new unconditional credences
in *e*—play an infallible role, as they are not themselves any more open to rational evaluation than the certain evidence conditioned on in ordinary conditionalisation. Finally,
one might be sceptical about the need for Jeffrey conditionalisation in the first place.
Even though the agent is unable to articulate it, there is some proposition *e* which precisely captures their evidence. So long as conditionalisation only requires that *e* be the
strongest proposition of which one is newly certain, without requiring any certainty
that *e* *is* the evidence, then the fact that the agent is unable to articulate their evidence
is unimportant; for they only need to articulate their evidence if they need to be certain of some proposition about their evidence. (An analogy: knowing that *p* doesn't
require knowing that one knows that *p*, so, similarly, conditionalising on *p* doesn't
require being certain that one is conditionalising on *p*.) Moreover, if we allow the agent
ordinary demonstratives, the ordinary sentence 'The tablecloth is *that* colour' may well
express the proposition that the agent learned.

Reflection

Conditionalisation provides one kind of connection between credences at different times,
but there are others. Van Fraassen (p. 150) offers the *Reflection* principle:

$$C(p|\ulcorner C^+(p) = x\urcorner) = x. \quad \text{(Reflection)}$$

Informally: your credence in *p*, given that your future credence in *p* will be *x*, should
now be *x*. If you became certain that your future credence in *p* will be *x*, perhaps because
you came to know what evidence you will get in the interim, then you should now have
that credence already, since you already know what the evidence you will get will be.
In this principle, the term '$C^+(p)$' can be treated as a random variable that can take
various values *x*. If one accepts the Reflection principle, and one now has credences in
all of one's possible future credences (say, one envisages all the possible future courses
of experience, and figures out what one's credences would be, were those courses of
experience to be actualised), this will constrain one's current credences. For, by the
theorem of total probability (Theorem 12 in the Primer), $C(p) = \Sigma_i C(\ulcorner C^+(p) = x_i\urcorner)$
$C(p|\ulcorner C^+(p) = x_i\urcorner)$; and by Reflection therefore, $C(p) = \Sigma_i C(\ulcorner C^+(p) = x_i\urcorner)x_i$. That is,
if Reflection is true, your current credence in *p* is your subjective expectation of your
future credences in *p* (p. 15).

Van Fraassen adopts Reflection to defend against a puzzle posed by the apparent rationality of someone's holding a belief while simultaneously being open to doubt about the truth of the belief (in the sense that they think it quite plausible that in the future they will think it false). Van Fraassen constructs a Dutch book argument to the effect that someone who is in this state is susceptible to sure loss; the upshot, he thinks, is that we must adopt a principle of Reflection—ensuring that future confidence that a hypothesis is false will be reflected in current credence—to avoid the Dutch book. He goes on to give further considerations to explain why the original puzzle is no puzzle, and to mitigate the apparent consequences of denying the rationality of the situation described.

The Dutch book he constructs is akin to Lewis's Dutch book for conditionalisation. Indeed, van Fraassen (1995) argues that conditionalisation entails (a generalised version of) Reflection. The argument he offers is a curious one (as Weisberg (2007) emphasises). Suppose an agent is *certain* they will conditionalise. Then their credence $C(p|\ulcorner C^+(p) = x\urcorner) = C(p|\ulcorner C(p|e) = x\urcorner \wedge e)$, because they know their credence will be x if they do come to conditionalise on e. If the agent knows what their conditional probabilities are, this reduces to $C(p|e)$, which is x, yielding Reflection. But since an agent could fail to conditionalise while being certain that they will, and vice versa, this only shows that agents who think they will conditionalise will obey Reflection. Note also that the assumption that agents have perfect introspective access to their own credences is also highly controversial, but necessary. This assumption also entails that an agent who knowingly violates Reflection cannot believe they will update by conditionalisation, and if the agent is correct, they will violate conditionalisation, and thus be irrational by the earlier arguments in favour of conditionalisation.

Van Fraassen (1999) also offers an argument that Reflection entails conditionalisation—but again, this argument involves the claim that if agents are certain they will obey Reflection, then they will be certain that they will conditionalise. If their certainty is well placed, they will conditionalise; but of course they might be wrong that they will obey Reflection. So there is a close connection between how agents think they will update, whether by conditionalisation or not, and whether they obey Reflection. In good cases, when agents are right to be certain about their updating strategy, and have introspective access to their credences, conditionalisation and Reflection stand or fall together—but such good cases may be rare.

Problems with conditionalisation and Reflection

There are a number of cases, however, where Reflection has struck philosophers as problematic. Given the connection between reflection and known conditionalisation, these cases also raise difficulties for conditionalisation.

One example involves *memory loss* (see also Arntzenius, p. 163). If an agent forgets something they used to know, they will clearly violate both regular conditionalisation and Jeffrey conditionalisation. For if what they knew had credence 1, and since no conditionalising update will ever reduce the credence in any proposition which has credence 1, then agents who update only by conditionalisation never forget. One case, due to Talbott, involves my forgetting what I had for dinner a year ago today. Though presumably I was, then, certain of what I had for dinner, I am now no longer certain. In this case there is no illegitimate interference in my epistemic state, just the natural passing of time, and apparently in virtue of that no departure from rationality—especially if the forgetting is unavoidable, for then it can't be a norm for me that I should not forget (at least if what I ought epistemically to do must be something I can do). While it may be in some sense undesirable for agents to forget, and it is unfortunate when they do, it is debatable whether it is irrational. It is implausible that each case of forgetting exemplifies irrationality; to make the constraints on updating so psychologically unrealistic tends to undermine the normative force of the Dutch book argument. If we accept that there might be rational forgetting, then there are some rational agents who are subject to a Dutch book, because they have (without becoming irrational) forgotten something, such that a cunning bettor who recalls it (or even a lucky bettor who does not) can exploit the information loss. If the agent in a forgetting case knows they will likely forget something—and induction from past experience suggests they should— they will also foresee a violation of conditionalisation, and in so doing fail to obey Reflection. For in such a case they should stick with their current credence in the thing they suspect they might forget. They shouldn't forget that they know the proposition now in order to satisfy Reflection. Indeed, even if the agent does not forget, and does in fact always conditionalise, the mere possibility of forgetting leads to violations of conditionalisation.

There are also cases where future experience can undermine presently known evidence without memory loss (Williamson 2000). Suppose I know that a coin is fair, but I happen to see it tossed numerous times and see that it lands heads each time. These observations are consistent with what I know; nevertheless, if the unbroken series of heads continues for long enough, I should come to lower my credence in the fairness of the coin, without forgetting that I was certain of it. The standard account of this case has it that I should never have assigned credence 1 to the hypothesis that the coin was fair in the first place; but the claim that I should not do that is rarely defended, except by question-begging appeal to conditionalisation.

Maher, in Chapter 9, offers further examples of rational violations of conditionalisation and Reflection. In one of his cases, you are sure that you will become impaired by alcohol; Reflection then seems to suggest that you should, while now sober, adopt the unreasonable credences you foresee that your future drunk self will have. Because the case involves an irrational future self (unlike the forgetting case) it is easier to resist; perhaps a codicil to the effect that Reflection should only hold concerning your future *rational* credences. But this appears to trivialise the principle, for the arguments in favour of Reflection were supposed to show that violations of Reflection were automatically irrational; if it only holds for rational credences in the first place, then one might wonder what the argument shows. And, in any case, the examples of forgetting and uncertain evidence (as also exhibited in Maher's second case of the coin toss) seem to provide impeccably rational foreseeable violations of conditionalisation and hence violations of Reflection.

Maher has a more positive proposal, however, for on pp. 173–5 he offers a decision-theoretic rationale for Reflection under certain precisely specified conditions. He concludes that, while violating Reflection is not irrational, often *choosing* a course of action that would ensure a violation of Reflection is irrational, at least in the sense that the chosen Reflection-violating course of action never has higher expected utility than the Reflection-endorsing course of action. But these conditions are not always satisfied. Even if they were, a purely prudential justification of Reflection like that which Maher offers might be thought to be problematic, just as Joyce argued in Chapter 4 that prudential Dutch book justifications of synchronic coherence are problematic. Maher also takes his proof to indicate the circumstances under which conditionalisation is (prudentially) rational: namely, those where it is (prudentially) rational to obey Reflection, and you are certain of what your possible evidence is. But since it may be rational to be uncertain of the possible future evidence, it is not obvious that Maher's defence of Reflection does extend to conditionalisation.

Self-locating belief and sleeping beauty

Another kind of problem case for Reflection is offered by Elga. In Chapter 10 he describes the case of Sleeping Beauty, who undergoes a certain type of forgetting—not forgetting any impersonal fact about the world, but forgetting her own location in the world. The examples of self-locating belief have provided a rich seam of problem cases for updating principles, and for the representation of epistemic states by means of probabilities more generally, as the chapters of Elga and Arntzenius (p. 163) show.

The Sleeping Beauty case is this:

> On Sunday she learns for certain that she is to be the subject of an experiment. The experimenters will wake her up on Monday morning, and tell her some time later that it is Monday. When she goes back to sleep, they will toss a fair coin. If the outcome of the toss is Heads, they will do nothing. If the outcome is Tails, they will administer a drug whose effect is to destroy all memories from the previous day, so that when she wakes up on Tuesday, she will be unable to tell that it is not Monday.
>
> (Dorr, 2002: 292)

When Beauty is awakened on Monday, and asked what her credence in the proposition ('Heads') that the coin landed heads is, what should she say? As Elga points out, Beauty seems to be pulled in two different directions. On the one hand, she gets no new information upon wakening that she did not already anticipate, and should retain her prior degree of belief in the fairness of the coin, so should on Monday assign Heads a credence of 1/2. But on the other hand, if she believes that the coin is fair, she should expect that about 1/3 of all possible awakenings, in the long run, occur in cases where the coin lands heads (for there are twice as many awakenings if the coin lands tails than if it lands heads). So on awakening she should believe that this awakening, drawn from the class of all awakenings, is 1/3 likely to be a heads-awakening—so her credence in Heads on Monday should be 1/3.

Elga develops this second line of reasoning for the 1/3 ('thirder') conclusion. He argues that there are three scenarios: *Heads and it's Monday, Tails and it's Monday,* and *Tails and it's Tuesday.* Elga argues first, that if Beauty learned Tails, she should have equal credence in it's being Monday or Tuesday; so conditional on the proposition Tails, the second and third scenarios have the same credence, and hence she assigns them the same unconditional credence. Similarly, if she was to learn that it was Monday, she should have equal credence in Heads and Tails conditional on that assumption, and hence unconditionally. The only way to satisfy both these lines of reasoning is to conclude that each scenario has equal credence, and therefore that Beauty should have credence 1/3 in Heads.

As Elga notes, this provides a new route to counterexamples to conditionalisation and reflection. Beauty forgets nothing, nor does she learn anything she didn't already know (she was certain on Sunday night that she would be awakened, and awakened on Monday) nor does she undergo any problematic cognitive interference between Sunday evening and Monday morning. Nevertheless, she changes her opinion about the proposition that the coin landed Heads. Moreover, Beauty knows all of this about herself; so she is not certain that she will update by conditionalisation, and so, as Elga points out, she violates Reflection. And yet she seems perfectly rational to do so.

Replies to Elga's argument come from several directions. One reply is to conclude that Beauty really does receive new information; that receiving the self-locating evidence that she is now awake, when she awakens on Monday morning, produces a conditionalising update of her credence. The problems with this seem to be that there seems no good reason why she is not already certain of her receipt of this evidence on Sunday night; and that it seems to be irrelevant to the question of Heads or Tails, so it is not clear why conditionalising on it would induce the relevant update.

Lewis (2001) offers a different reply, defending the 1/2 ('Halfer') position and therefore defending conditionalisation. Lewis agrees that there is no relevant evidence that Beauty receives on Monday morning, and thus insists that Beauty, if rational, didn't update her credences then. The further consequence, then, is that one of Elga's assumptions is incorrect. Lewis agrees with the assumption that the second and third scenarios get the same credence; but since the credence in Heads is just the credence in the scenario *Heads and it's Monday*, that scenario gets credence 1/2, and the other two scenarios therefore get credence 1/4 each. But then it cannot be maintained that the conditional credence in Heads, given that it is Monday, is 1/2; that conditional credence must be 2/3. So, once Beauty is told that it is now Monday, she then raises her credence in Heads. This does look like a new piece of information that she didn't already possess on awakening; the problem remains that—particularly in the case where the coin hasn't yet been flipped until Monday afternoon—she then seems to have credence 2/3 in Heads on a future fair coin toss! And this conflicts with a principle Lewis himself defends (see p. 434), that one's credence in p conditional on the chance of p and nothing inadmissible should be equal to the chance. Lewis offers a response that aims to satisfy both principles, to the effect that learning it is Monday does provide Beauty with inadmissible information about the future outcome of the coin toss—namely, the self-locating information that she is not in that future (something that was consistent with all she knew on awakening). But, it is fair to say, most philosophers have not been convinced that this really is inadmissible information that should warp Beauty's credences in Heads. The existence of further arguments for the thirder position, such as that offered by Dorr (2002) or by Arntzenius in sect. IV of Chapter 11, has pushed many into the thirder camp.

Regardless of the final result of the dispute over the Sleeping Beauty case, it is clear that the introduction of self-locating belief creates new difficulties for conditionalisation and Reflection. Many interesting examples are discussed by Arntzenius in Chapter 11. Self-locating propositions spawn cases where a rational agent's credences 'shift'. If there is no self-locating belief—if, that is, all the propositions you entertain are third-personal propositions about the world you inhabit—then all information you get will serve, at best, to narrow down the field of possibilities. But if self-locating propositions are included, then even third-personally omniscient agents can learn facts about their own location (for example, someone who knew the entire history of the world could come to know the self-locating fact about what time in that history is *now*), and this can shift their entire credence (so a historically omniscient agent could move from having all of their credence on the proposition 'the history is *h* and the time is 23.58' to having all of their credence on the proposition 'the history is *h* and the time is 23.59'). Such a shift violates conditionalisation because it is not a narrowing down of possibilities.

The other kind of case Arntzenius discusses is a credential 'spread', when—even without memory loss—an agent comes to be in a future state in which it is subjectively possible for them that there was memory loss (as in Arntzenius' Shangri La case). Unlike the first type of case, this case doesn't seem to involve self-locating belief; but it still involves a violation of conditionalisation, as the agent moves from a state of certainty to one of uncertainty. In contrast to the earlier cases of misleading evidence or genuine memory loss, nothing happens to the agent's epistemic state that is at all unexpected or problematic; what causes the spread of belief is their becoming aware of various relevant unelimineated possibilities. But, given that the agent was rational, and it is rational to assign some credence to these unelimineated possibilities, it is even more plausible in Arntzenius' cases that the agent is rational despite knowingly violating conditionalisation and also therefore violating reflection. Such cases thus circumscribe ever more tightly the realm where conditionalisation and reflection can be unproblematically applied—though it remains true, despite all the counterexamples, that there are many ordinary circumstances where both principles apply.

Sleeping beauty and Dutch book arguments

The last chapter in this part, Bradley and Leitgeb (Chapter 12), uses the Sleeping Beauty example to a different end. The Thirder argument offered by Hitchcock (2004) shows that, unless Beauty has a betting rate on Heads of 1/3, a Dutch book can be made against her. The response that Bradley and Leitgeb develop is that this kind of construction only shows that Beauty should *act as if* her credence in Heads was 1/3; and it is consistent with that action, and the consequent betting behaviour, that her credence in Heads remains 1/2. They construct other cases where the odds revealed by betting behaviour and an agent's real credences arguably come apart; and, in showing how these cases are analogous to the Sleeping Beauty case in the relevant respects, show that the existence of a Dutch book for 1/3 does not necessarily support the thirder position. Of course, the other arguments for the thirder position might still go through, for all they say; the key fact to note is that this is yet another kind of difficulty for the idea that Dutch book arguments serve to uniquely constrain rational credences, and therefore contributes further to the discussion in Part I concerning the viability of such arguments.

Further reading

The standard framework for treating belief update and revision in the context of sets of full beliefs is the AGM framework, developed by Alchourrón *et al.* (1985)—see also Hansson (Spring 2009). This is the source of the advice to make the most minimal change regaining consistency.

More details on the Stalnaker conditional and the connection with conditional probabilities, discussed in note 1, can be found in Stalnaker (1970).

The dynamic Dutch book argument was originally due to Lewis (p. 132), but received its first popular presentation by Paul Teller (1973). Another argument for conditionalisation is offered by Howson and Urbach (1993: 67). A nice discussion of the problem that, in conditionalisation, the conditional probabilities are always fixed and 'incorrigible' is Lange (1999); he also offers a calibration-style argument for conditionalisation in the context of justification, rather than shifts of opinion. The practical decision theory that inspired Greaves and Wallace's epistemic version is that of Savage (1954); the further evolution of decision theory is covered by Jeffrey (1983) and Joyce (1999), and may provide useful models for the future evolution of epistemic utility theory.

Dutch book arguments for Jeffrey conditionalisation are offered by Armendt (1980) and Skyrms (1987); van Fraassen (1989: Ch. 13) uses considerations of symmetry to defend it. A mathematically sophisticated treatment of Jeffrey conditionalisation is Diaconis and Zabell (1982), who pay considerable attention to the problem of non-commutativity. Domotor (1980) argues that successive updating should be commutative; (Lange, 2000) argues it need not be. Field (1978) discusses how to decide which sentences are to be taken as evidence under Jeffrey conditionalisation; a reply to Field is offered by Garber (1980). Leitgeb and Pettigrew (2010) cast doubt on Jeffrey conditionalisation in the context of inaccuracy-minimising justifications of Bayesianism, and offer an alternative rule.

The reflection principle was independently defended by Goldstein (1983); a further defence is offered by van Fraassen (1995). Evnine (2007) defends a similar principle. Weisberg (2007) offers a clear discussion of the connections between Reflection and conditionalisation. An evaluation of the role of Reflection in van Fraassen's philosophy of science is provided by Green and Hitchcock (1994).

The example of memory loss is clearly introduced in Talbott (1991); van Fraassen (1995) responds. Further relevant discussions of the desirability or otherwise of its being a principle of rationality that maximum credence is always retained are by Levi (1967), Skyrms (1987) and Williamson (2000: sect. 10.2). Levi and Williamson both offer alternative accounts of updating that do not involve constant evidence. Christensen (1991) discusses failures of Reflection rather like Maher's, and also argues that while these count against the diachronic Dutch book argument, the synchronic Dutch book argument remains powerful. A recent argument characterising the circumstances under which Reflection holds, though not with the pragmatic rationale given by Maher, is offered by Briggs (2009)—her principle of 'Qualified Reflection' is that reflection holds when one is certain one's conditional credences remain constant, and one is certain one will update on veridical evidence (as well as further idealisations). Briggs (p. 66) also offers a kind of counterexample to reflection not considered above, involving a change in epistemic standards.

Sleeping Beauty type examples were introduced to the literature by Stalnaker; his most recent treatment of them, and of self-locating belief, is Stalnaker (2008). Self-locating belief was brought to philosophical prominence by Lewis (1983). The Sleeping Beauty problem itself spawned a vast literature; in addition to those cited above, discussions include those of Halpern (2005), Hitchcock (2004), Meacham (2008), Titelbaum (2008) and White (2006). Elga (2007) follows up his discussion of reflection.

Notes

1 Though there is an approach to conditional probability which does hew closer to modern theories of conditionals, especially the theory of Stalnaker (1968). This is the *imaging* approach. On Stalnaker's approach, the indicative conditional 'If p, q', symbolised $p > q$, is true at a possible world w iff q is true at the possible world w_p, which is the closest world to w at which p

is true (by 'closest' is meant: the world that is most similar to w). The set of possible worlds W forms the basis for a σ-algebra; let us denote the proposition true only at world w by w. Let a probability function P_p be the *image* of P on proposition p iff, for each world-proposition w,

$$P_p(w) = \sum_{w' \in W} \left(P(w') \cdot \begin{cases} 1 & \text{if } w \text{ is } w_p \\ 0 & \text{otherwise} \end{cases} \right)$$

Informally, the image of a probability function 'is formed by shifting the original probability of each world w over to ... the closest p-world to w' (Lewis 1986: 147). Lewis shows in that paper that $P(p > q) = P_p(q)$—i.e., that the probability of the Stalnaker conditional is the imaged probability of q under p. Insofar as imaging is a way of updating belief, then, we could endorse the Ramsey test for credences and accept the original connection with conditionals. However, imaging and conditionalisation are not the same updating process; and insofar as there are reasons to believe conditionalisation is the right way to model coming to believe p, as we will see below, those reasons will show that imaging is not the right way to model coming to believe p. But there is more room for debate here.

2 As van Fraassen points (p. 158), this can't be used to explain or analyse conditional probability, for there are well-defined conditional probabilities, conditional on propositions that we cannot come non-hypothetically to accept.

3 This description presents the agent as consciously updating on the evidence, and requires them to be aware of what their evidence is, but this is an inessential feature of the description. Really, the principle only says that rational agents turn out to have updated credences that are related to their prior credences by conditionalisation, however they get there—it requires agents to update on their evidence e, and become certain in e, but does not require introspective certainty in the proposition 'e is my evidence'.

4 If we adopt a theory of probability according to which $C(p|\neg e)$ can be defined even if $C(\neg e) = 0$, we can say more straightforwardly that Jeffrey conditioning over a two-element partition reduces to conditionalisation in the special case where $C^+(e) = 1$.

Bibliography

Alchourrón, Carlos E., Gärdenfors, Peter and Makinson, David (1985), 'On the logic of theory change: Partial meet contraction and revision functions'. *Journal of Symbolic Logic*, vol. 50: pp. 510–530.

Armendt, Brad (1980), 'Is there a Dutch Book Argument for Probability Kinematics?' *Philosophy of Science*, vol. 47: pp. 583–589.

Briggs, Rachael (2009), 'Distorted Reflection'. *Philosophical Review*, vol. 118: pp. 59–85.

Christensen, David (1991), 'Clever Bookies and Coherent Beliefs'. *Philosophical Review*, vol. 100: pp. 229–247.

Diaconis, Persi and Zabell, Sandy (1982), 'Updating Subjective Probability'. *Journal of the American Statistical Association*, vol. 77: pp. 822–830.

Domotor, Zoltan (1980), 'Probability Kinematics and Representation of Belief Change'. *Philosophy of Science*, vol. 47: pp. 384–403.

Dorr, Cian (2002), 'Sleeping Beauty: in defence of Elga'. *Analysis*, vol. 62.

Elga, Adam (2007), 'Reflection and Disagreement'. *Noûs*, vol. 41: pp. 478–502.

Evnine, Simon J. (2007), 'Personhood and future belief: two arguments for something like Reflection'. *Erkenntnis*, vol. 67: pp. 91–110.

Field, Hartry (1978), 'A Note on Jeffrey Conditionalization'. *Philosophy of Science*, vol. 45: pp. 361–367.

Garber, Daniel (1980), 'Discussion: Field and Jeffrey Conditionalization'. *Philosophy of Science*, vol. 47: pp. 142–145.

Goldstein, Michael (1983), 'The Prevision of a Prevision'. *Journal of the American Statistical Association*, vol. 78: pp. 817–819.

Greaves, Hilary and Wallace, David (2006), 'Justifying conditionalization: Conditionalization maximizes expected epistemic utility'. *Mind*, vol. 115: pp. 607–32.

Green, Mitchell S. and Hitchcock, Christopher R. (1994), 'Reflections on Reflection'. *Synthese*, vol. 98: pp. 297–324.

Hacking, Ian (1967), 'Slightly More Realistic Personal Probability'. *Philosophy of Science*, vol. 34: pp. 311–325.

Halpern, Joseph Y. (2005), 'Sleeping Beauty Reconsidered: Conditioning and Reflection in Asynchronous Systems'. *Oxford Studies in Epistemology*, vol. 1: pp. 114–142.

Hansson, Sven Ove (Spring 2009), 'Logic of Belief Revision'. In Edward N. Zalta (ed.), *The Stanford Encyclopedia of Philosophy*, URL http://plato.stanford.edu/archives/spr2009/entries/logic-belief-revision/.

Hitchcock, Christopher (2004), 'Beauty and the Bets'. *Synthese*, vol. 139: pp. 405–420.

Howson, Colin and Urbach, Peter (1993), *Scientific Reasoning: the Bayesian Approach*. Chicago: Open Court, 2 ed.

Jeffrey, Richard C. (1970), 'Dracula Meets Wolfman: Acceptance vs. Partial Belief'. In Marshall Swain (ed.), *Induction, Acceptance and Rational Belief*, Dordrecht: D. Reidel, pp. 157–185.

—— (1983), *The Logic of Decision*. Chicago: University of Chicago Press, 2 ed.

Joyce, James M. (1999), *The Foundations of Causal Decision Theory*. Cambridge: Cambridge University Press.

—— (2008), 'Bayes' Theorem'. In Edward N. Zalta (ed.), *The Stanford Encyclopedia of Philosophy*, fall 2008 ed.

Lange, Marc (1999), 'Calibration and the Epistemological Role of Bayesian Conditionalization'. *Journal of Philosophy*, vol. 96: pp. 294–324.

—— (2000), 'Is Jeffrey Conditionalization Defective by Virtue of Being Non-Commutative? Remarks on the Sameness of Sensory Experiences'. *Synthese*, vol. 123: pp. 393–403.

Leitgeb, Hannes and Pettigrew, Richard (2010), 'An Objective Justification of Bayesianism II: The Consequences of Minimizing Inaccuracy'. *Philosophy of Science*, vol. 77: pp. 236–272.

Levi, Isaac (1967), 'Probability Kinematics'. *British Journal for the Philosophy of Science*, vol. 18: pp. 197–209.

Lewis, David (1983), 'Attitudes *De Dicto* and *De Se*'. In *Philosophical Papers*, vol. 1, Oxford: Oxford University Press, pp. 133–159.

—— (1986), 'Probabilities of Conditionals and Conditional Probabilities'. In *Philosophical Papers*, vol. 2, Oxford: Oxford University Press, pp. 133–152.

—— (2001), 'Sleeping Beauty: Reply to Elga'. *Analysis*, vol. 61: pp. 171–176.

Meacham, Christopher J. G. (2008), 'Sleeping Beauty and the Dynamics of *De Se* Beliefs'. *Philosophical Studies*, vol. 138: pp. 245–270.

Ramsey, F. P. (1990), 'General Propositions and Causality'. In *Philosophical Papers*, Cambridge, UK: Cambridge University Press, pp. 145–163.

Savage, Leonard J. (1954), *The Foundations of Statistics*. New York: Wiley.

Skyrms, Brian (1987), 'Dynamic Coherence and Probability Kinematics'. *Philosophy of Science*, vol. 54: pp. 1–20.

Stalnaker, Robert C. (1968), 'A Theory of Conditionals'. In Nicholas Rescher (ed.), *Studies in Logical Theory*, Oxford: Blackwell, pp. 98–112.

—— (1970), 'Probability and Conditionals'. *Philosophy of Science*, vol. 37: pp. 64–80.

—— (2008), *Our Knowledge of the Internal World*. Oxford: Oxford University Press.

Talbott, W. J. (1991), 'Two Principles of Bayesian Epistemology'. *Philosophical Studies*, vol. 62: pp. 135–150.

Teller, Paul (1973), 'Conditionalisation and Observation'. *Synthese*, vol. 26: pp. 218–258.

Titelbaum, Mike (2008), 'The Relevance of Self-Locating Beliefs'. *Philosophical Review*, vol. 117: pp. 555–605.

van Fraassen, Bas C. (1989), *Laws and Symmetry*. Oxford: Oxford University Press.

—— (1995), 'Belief and the Problem of Ulysses and the Sirens'. *Philosophical Studies*, vol. 77: pp. 7–37.

—— (1999), 'Conditionalization, A New Argument for'. *Topoi*, vol. 18: pp. 93–96.

Weisberg, Jonathan (2007), 'Conditionalization, Reflection, and Self-Knowledge'. *Philosophical Studies*, vol. 135: pp. 179–197.

White, Roger (2006), 'The generalized Sleeping Beauty problem: a challenge for thirders'. *Analysis*, vol. 66: pp. 114–119.

Williamson, Timothy (2000), *Knowledge and its Limits*. Oxford: Oxford University Press.

6

WHY CONDITIONALIZE?*

David Lewis

Introduction (1997)

This paper presents what is nowadays called the 'diachronic Dutch book argument'. I wrote it in 1972 as a handout for a course, with no thought of publication. I thought then that the argument was well-known.[1] Yet I could not find it presented in print, so I had to reconstruct it for myself. I showed my handout to Paul Teller; he presented the argument, with my permission and with full acknowledgement, in his article 'Conditionalization and Observation'.[2] Teller's article has become the standard source for the argument. But it seems to leave a question in some readers' minds: why does the argument call for conditionalizing on the subject's total increment of experiential evidence, no more and no less? Since my handout had addressed just that question, I decided there was some reason to publish it after all. Apart from a little editing to simplify notation, it appears here in its original form.

The diachronic Dutch book argument can be broken into two halves. Consider a conditional bet: that is, a bet that will be null and void unless its condition is met. We note, first, that the conditional bet is equivalent in its outcome, come what may, to a certain pair of unconditional bets. We note, second, that the conditional bet is also equivalent in its outcome, come what may, to a certain contingency plan whereby one's future betting transactions are made to depend on the arrival of new evidence. The first equivalence yields a well-known synchronic argument relating the prices of conditional and unconditional bets. The second equivalence yields a diachronic argument relating the present prices of conditional bets to the future prices, after various increments of evidence, of unconditional bets. We can stitch both halves together and leave the conditional bet unmentioned; and that is the argument presented here.

Richard Jeffrey (Chapter 7 of this volume) has suggested that we should respond to experiential evidence not by conditionalizing, but rather by a less extreme redistribution of degrees of belief. Despite appearances, I do not disagree. He and I are considering different cases. My advice is addressed to a severely idealized, superhuman subject who runs no risk of mistaking his evidence, and who therefore can only lose if he hedges against that risk. Jeffrey's advice is addressed to a less idealized, fallible subject who has no business heeding counsels of perfection that he is unable to follow.

Similarly, it seems that we should sometimes respond to conceptual discoveries by revising our beliefs. If first you divide your belief between hypotheses H_1, H_2, H_3, and 'none of the above', and then you discover that 'none of the above' includes a hitherto unnoticed H_4 that is far nicer than the other three, you would be wise to shift some of your belief to H_4, even though you would not be conditionalizing on experiential evidence. Our ideal subject, who never changes his belief except by con-ditionalizing, will never do that. Is he pig-headed? No — being ideal, he has left no conceptual discoveries unmade. He made them all in his cradle. So he has no occasion to respond to new conceptual discoveries. But we, who are not so smart, would be unwise to emulate him. Some of our departures from ideal rationality are just what we need to compensate for other departures.

Note also that the point of any Dutch book argument is not that it would be impru-dent to run the risk that some sneaky Dutchman will come and drain your pockets. After all, there aren't so many sneaky Dutchmen around; and anyway, if ever you see one coming, you can refuse to do business with him. Rather, the point is that if you are vulnerable to a Dutch book, whether synchronic or diachronic, that means that you have two contradictory opinions about the expected value of the very same trans-action. To hold contradictory opinions may or may not be risky, but it is in any case irrational.

*   *   *

Suppose that at time 0, you have a coherent belief function M. Let E_1, ..., E_n be mutually exclusive and jointly exhaustive propositions that specify, in full detail, all the alternative courses of experience you might undergo between time 0 and time 1. For each i from 1 to n, let M_i be the belief function you would have at time 1 if you had the experience specified by E_i – that is, if E_i were the true one of E_1, ..., E_n. You would *conditionalize* if, for any proposition P (in the domain of M),

$$M_i(P) = C(P/E_i) =^{\text{df}} M(PE_i)/M(E_i)$$

Why would it be irrational to respond to experience in any other way?

Assume that your belief functions both at times 0 and 1 can be measured by your betting behavior, as follows: your degree of belief that P is the price at which you would be willing either to buy or to sell the bet [$1 if P, 0 otherwise]. Assume also that if any betting transactions are acceptable to you, so are any sums or multiples thereof.

Suppose $M_i(P)$ is less than $C(P/E_i)$. Then I can follow this three-step plan to exploit the fact.

(1) Sell you the two bets

[$1 if PE_i, $0 otherwise]
[$x if not-$E_i$, $0 otherwise]

where $x = C(P/E_i)$, for the maximum price you will pay: *viz.* $M(PE_i) + xM (not-E_i) = $C(P/E_i)$.

(2) Wait and see whether E_i is true. (Thus I need to have as much knowledge as you, but no more; for you also will know by time 1 whether E_i is true.)

(3) If E_i is true, buy from you at time 1 the bet

[$1 if P, $0 otherwise]

for the minimum price you will accept: *viz.* $M_i(P)$.

133

If E_i is false, your net loss will be \$0. If E_i is true (regardless of P) your net loss will be \$$C(P/E_i)$ – \$$M_i(P)$, which by hypothesis is positive. As a result of your failure to conditionalize, I can inflict on you a risk of loss uncompensated by any chance of gain; and I can do this without at any point using knowledge that you do not have.

Likewise if $M_i(P)$ is greater than $C(P/E_i)$ I can exploit that by the opposite plan: buy at step (1), sell at step (3).

If you can be thus exploited you are irrational; so you are rational only if you conditionalize.

Why doesn't a parallel argument work for *any* set D_1, ..., D_n of mutually exclusive and jointly exhaustive propositions, showing that your belief function ought to evolve by conditionalization on the true one of *this* set? If $M_j(P)$ is less than $C(P/D_j)$, why can't I take advantage of this?

(1) Suppose D_j is wholly contained in (implies) some E_i, but $D_j \neq E_i$. Then to carry out my plan of exploitation, I must learn that D_j while you learn only that E_i. It proves nothing derogatory about your rationality that I can exploit you by taking advantage of my greater knowledge.

(2) If $D_j = E_i$, I can take advantage of you, but this adds nothing to the argument that you should conditionalize on the true one of E_1, ..., E_n.

(3) Otherwise D_j overlaps two or more distinct E's; thus you can distinguish two or more ways for D_j to come true, and it is not legitimate to assume that there is a *unique* new belief function M_j that you will end up with if D_j is true. We should consider separately the various belief functions determined by the different distinguishable ways for D_j to be true; we thus revert to cases (1) and (2).

It has been pointed out[3] that if you fail to conditionalize, I still have no safe strategy for exploiting you unless I *know* in advance what you do instead of conditionalizing. That is: I must know whether $M_i(P)$ is less than or greater than $C(P/E_i)$. But suppose you don't know this yourself. Then I can reliably exploit you only with the aid of superior knowledge, which establishes nothing derogatory about your rationality. – Granted. But I reply that if you can't tell in advance how your beliefs would be modified by a certain course of experience, that also is a kind – a different kind – of irrationality on your part.

Notes

* Originally published in *Papers in Metaphysics and Epistemology*, Cambridge University Press: Cambridge, 1999, pp. 403–407. Copyright © David Lewis 1999. Reproduced by permission of Cambridge University Press.

1 Hilary Putnam alludes to, but does not state, a diachronic Dutch book argument in his 'Probability and Confirmation' in *Philosophy of Science Today*, ed. by Sidney Morgenbesser (Basic Books, 1967), p. 113. He says that if one follows a certain learning rule, it can be shown 'that even if one's bets at any one time are coherent, one's total betting strategy through time will not be coherent'.

2 *Synthese* 26 (1973), pp. 218–258.

3 By D. Kaplan, a student at Princeton in 1972; and by Gilbert Harman.

7

PROBABILITY KINEMATICS*

Richard C. Jeffrey

So far, we have considered probability and desirability statically: we have used the functions *prob* and *des* to describe the agent's attitudes either at a single moment, or during a period within which they do not change. But an adequate account must include changes in the agent's probability and desirability assignments.

Conditionalization and its limits

The beginnings of such an account have already been given in Jeffrey (1983: section 5.10, problem 13). There we considered the case in which the agent becomes certain of the truth of a proposition B in which he had formerly had some positive degree of belief short of 1. If the original desirability and probability of a proposition A were

$$des\ A,\ prob\ A,$$

what should the new desirability and probability be after the agent changes his degree of belief in B from *prob* B to 1? The assumption (5–7) was that the new desirability of A should be identical with the old desirability of AB; and it was indicated how, from that assumption, one could deduce that the new probability of A ought to be the ratio of the old probability of AB to the old probability of B. Then the new desirability and probability of A should be

$$des\ AB \quad \frac{prob\ AB}{prob\ B}$$

The second of these numbers is called the *conditional probability* of A on the evidence B, and will be written either as

$$prob\ (A/B)$$

or as

$$prob_B A$$

The process of *conditionalization*—of the agent's changing his subjective probability assignment from *prob* to $prob_E$ upon learning that the evidence-proposition E is true— is thus justified when it is applicable. However, there are cases in which a change in the

135

probability assignment is clearly called for, but where the device of conditionalization cannot be applied because the change is not occasioned simply by learning of the truth of some proposition E. In particular, the change might be occasioned by an observation, but there might be no proposition E in the agent's preference ranking of which it can correctly be said that what the agent learned from his observation is that E is true.

Example 1: Observation by candlelight

The agent inspects a piece of cloth by candlelight, and gets the impression that it is green, although he concedes that it might be blue or even (but very improbably) violet. If G, B, and V are the propositions that the cloth is green, blue, and violet, respectively, then the outcome of the observation might be that, whereas originally his degrees of belief in G, B, and V were .30, .30, and .40, his degrees of belief in those same propositions after the observation are .70, .25, and .05. If there were a proposition E in his preference ranking which described the precise quality of his visual experience in looking at the cloth, one would say that what the agent learned from the observation was that E is true. If his original subjective probability assignment was *prob*, his new assignment should then be $prob_E$, and we would have

$$prob\ G = .30\quad prob\ B = .30\quad prob\ V = .40$$

representing his opinions about the color of the cloth before the observation, but would have

$$prob\ (G/E) = .70\quad prob\ (B/E) = .25\quad prob\ (V/E) = .05$$

representing his opinions about the color of the cloth after the observation. But there need be no such proposition E in his preference ranking; nor need any such proposition be expressible in the English language. Thus, the description "The cloth looked green or possibly blue or conceivably violet," would be too vague to convey the precise quality of the experience. Certainly, it would be too vague to support such precise conditional probability ascriptions as those noted above. It seems that the best we can do is to describe, not the quality of the visual experience itself, but rather its effects on the observer, by saying, "After the observation, the agent's degrees of belief in G, B, and V were .70, .25, and .05."

The problem

It is easy enough to cite examples like 1 for the other senses. Transcribing a lecture in a noisy auditorium, the agent might think he had heard the word "red," but still think it possible that the word was actually "led." He might be unsure about whether the meat he is tasting is pork or veal, or about whether the cheese he is smelling is Camembert or Brie. In all such cases there is some definite quality of his sensuous experience which leads the agent to have various degrees of belief in the various relevant propositions; but there is no reason to suppose that the language he speaks provides the means for him to describe that experience in the relevant respects. Or to put the matter in physical terms: in example 1 when the agent looks at the piece of cloth by candlelight there is a particular complex pattern of physical stimulation of his retina, on the basis of which his beliefs about the possible colors of the cloth change in the indicated ways. However, the pattern of stimulation need not be describable in the language he speaks; and even if it is, there is every reason to suppose that the agent is quite unaware of what that pattern is and is quite incapable of uttering or identifying a correct description of it. Thus, a complete description of the pattern of stimulation includes a record of the firing times of all the rods and cones in the outer layer of retinal neurons during the period of the observation. Even if the agent is an expert physiologist, he will be unable to produce or recognize a correct record of this sort on the basis of his experience during the observation.

The remark made at the end of Jeffrey 1983 (section 4.7) remains true: the theory of preference is ours, but not necessarily the agent's. The theory can be true of an agent even if he is quite ignorant of the theory, and in particular, the language in which we express the propositions in his preference ranking need not be a language that the agent understands. Then, in principle, it is conceivable that we might use propositions about firing patterns of the agent's retinal neurons to record the effects of his visual experience.

All this would be relevant if we were using the theory of preference to describe and interpret the behavior of de facto Bayesians: of agents who in fact behave as if they had preference rankings that satisfy the hypotheses of the uniqueness theorem, although they need not speak of themselves as acting in that way, and perhaps do not use the notions of subjective probability and desirability in discussing their actions. One day Bayesian robots may be built; but at present there are no such creatures, and in particular, human beings are not de facto Bayesians. Bayesian decision theory provides a set of norms for human decision making; but it is far from being a true description of our behavior. Similarly, deductive logic provides a set of norms for human deductive reasoning, but can not usefully be reinterpreted as a description of human reasoning (unless we define reasoning so as to exclude everything that violates the rules of deductive logic, in which case the description becomes true but fragmentary and uninteresting). Indeed, it is because logic and decision theory are woefully inadequate as descriptions that they are of interest as norms. "To stay alive, you must keep inhaling and exhaling" is of little interest as a bit of advice precisely because it is so generally and effortlessly followed by those who can. To serve its normative function, the theory of decision making must be used by the agent, who must therefore be able to formulate and understand the relevant propositions. When Bayesian robots are built, they will conform to Bayesian principles in the way in which steam engines conform to the principles of thermodynamics; but human conformity to Bayesian principles is based on conscious use of them.

Lack of an adequate account of the way in which uncertain evidence can be assimilated into one's beliefs makes for philosophical as well as practical difficulties. C. I. Lewis, taking conditionalization to be the only way of assimilating evidence, concludes that there must exist an "expressive" use of language, by means of which the observer can infallibly record the content of his experience:

> If anything is to be probable, then something must be certain. The data which themselves support a genuine probability, must themselves be certainties. We do have such absolute certainties, in the sense data initiating belief and in those passages of experience which later may confirm it. But neither such initial data nor such later verifying passages of experience can be phrased in the language of objective statement—because what can be so phrased is never more than probable. Our sense certainties can only be formulated by the expressive use

137

of language, in which what is signified is a content of experience and what is asserted is the givenness of this content.

[C. I. Lewis (1946), p. 186]

Now it may be that no objective statement can be rendered more than probable by experience. This position is less startling than it might appear at first, if we reflect that .999999 is a probability and that it is short of 1. Then the kind of "practical certainty" that leisurely observation of a bit of cloth in sunlight can lend to the proposition G that the cloth is green can be represented by setting the subjective probability of G after the observation equal to .999999; and this is as close to certainty as makes no odds, practically speaking. But it is quite another matter to conclude from this that there must be a proposition E that can be formulated by an expressive use of language, which has the characteristics that $prob\ (G/E) = .999999$ and that the observer's degree of belief in E after the observation is 1.

To solve the philosophical problem posed by Lewis's argument, and the practical problems illustrated by example 1, it is necessary to give a positive account of how the agent is to assimilate uncertain evidence into his beliefs. It will not do, in example 1, simply to change the degrees of belief in G, B, and V from .30, .30, and .40, to the new values .70, .25, and .05 without making any further changes in the belief function, for we should then have a belief function which violated the probability axioms. Thus, if $prob\ V$ is .40, $prob\ \overline{V}$ must be .60. If we change $prob\ V$ from the value .40 to the new value .05 without making a compensating change in $prob\ \overline{V}$, we shall have $prob(V \vee \overline{V}) = .65$, which contradicts the requirement that the probability of the necessary proposition be 1.

Then the problem is this. Given that a passage of experience has led the agent to change his degrees of belief in certain propositions $B_1, B_2, ..., B_n$ from their original values,

$$prob\ B_1,\ prob\ B_2,\ ...,\ prob\ B_n$$

to new values,

$$PROB\ B_1,\ PROB\ B_2,\ ...,\ PROB\ B_n$$

how should these changes be propagated over the rest of the structure of his beliefs? If the original probability measure was $prob$, and the new one is $PROB$, and if A is a proposition in the agent's preference ranking but is not one of the n propositions whose probabilities were directly affected by the passage of experience, how shall $PROB\ A$ be determined?

Solution for $n = 2$

As a first step toward answering this question, we consider the important special case in which $n = 2$, and where the pair B_1, B_2 has the form $B, \overline{B}$, so that we would be willing to describe the result of the observation simply by saying that it led the agent to change his degree of belief in some one proposition B, from $prob\ B$ to a new value $PROB\ B$. (It then goes without saying that degree of belief in $\overline{B}$ changes from $prob\ \overline{B} = 1 - prob\ B$ to $PROB\ \overline{B} = 1 - PROB\ B$.) This does not mean that the only difference between the old and new belief functions lies in the values they assign to the argument B; but it does mean that the values of $PROB$ for all arguments ought to be deducible from a knowledge of (a) the values of $prob$ for all arguments, (b) the value of $PROB$ for the argument B, and the fact that (c) the change from $prob$ to $PROB$ *originated* in B in the sense that for every proposition A in the preference ranking we have

$$(7\text{--}1) \quad \text{(a) } PROB\,(A/B) = prob\,(A/B)$$
$$\text{(b) } PROB\,(A/\overline{B}) = prob\,(A/\overline{B}).$$

Then while the observation changed the agent's degree of belief in B and in certain other propositions, it did not change the conditional degrees of belief in any propositions on the evidence B or on the evidence $\overline{B}$.

Example 2: The mudrunner

A racehorse performs exceptionally well on muddy courses. A gambler's degree of belief in the proposition A that the horse will win a certain race should change if a fresh weather forecast leads him to change his degree of belief in the proposition B that the course will be muddy. However, the forecast should have no effect on his degrees of belief in the proposition that the horse will win conditionally on the course being muddy, or on its not being muddy.

Now suppose that neither $prob\ B$ nor $PROB\ B$ has either of the extreme values, 0 and 1; suppose that $prob$ and $PROB$ satisfy the probability axioms (Jeffrey 1983, 5–1); and define conditional probability in the usual way,

$$prob\,(A/B) = \frac{prob\ AB}{prob\ B}$$
$$PROB\,(A/B) = \frac{PROB\ AB}{PROB\ B}$$

Then it is straightforward to show that condition (7–1) is equivalent to the condition that for all propositions A in the preference ranking we have

$$(7\text{--}2) \quad PROB\ A = prob\,(A/B)\ PROB\ B + prob\,(A/\overline{B})\ PROB\ \overline{B}.$$

Now (7–2) is a formula of the required sort. It determines all values of $PROB$ in terms of knowledge of all values of $prob$ and a knowledge of the value that $PROB$ assigns to the argument B; and it is applicable in exactly the case where the change from $prob$ to $PROB$ originates in B in the sense that (7–1) holds for all A in the preference ranking.

Example 3: The mudrunner, continued

In example 2, suppose that the gambler's degree of belief in the proposition A that the horse will win conditionally on the proposition B that the track will be muddy is .8, but that his degree of belief in A conditionally on $\overline{B}$ is only .1; and suppose that a fresh weather forecast leads him to change his degree of belief in B from .3 to a new value .6. Then by (7–2) his degree of belief in A should assume the new value

$$(.8)(.6) + (.1)(.4) = .52.$$

Notice that by (7–3) (a) below, his original degree of belief in A must have been

$$(.8)(.3) + (.1)(.7) = .31.$$

Relevance

The probability axioms, together with the definition of conditional probability, imply that if neither *prob B* nor *PROB B* is 0 or 1 we have

(7–3) (a) $prob\ A = prob\ (A/B)\ prob\ B + prob\ (A/\overline{B})\ prob\ \overline{B}$

  (b) $PROB\ A = PROB\ (A/B) PROB\ B + PROB\ (A/\overline{B})\ PROB\ \overline{B}.$

Thus, (7–2) is derived from (7–3) (b) in conjunction with (7–1). Now we can get some further insight into the effects of the change from *prob* to *PROB* by subtracting equation (7–3) (a) termwise from equation (7–2) and using the facts that

$$prob\ \overline{B} = 1 - prob\ B \quad PROB\ \overline{B} = 1 - PROB\ B$$

to obtain

$$PROB\ A - prob\ A = (PROB\ B - prob\ B)[prob\ (A/B) - prob\ (A/\overline{B})]$$

This last equation holds whenever the change from *prob* to *PROB* is governed by (7–2), and expresses the change in the probability of an arbitrary proposition A as the result of multiplying the original change, in the probability of B, by the factor

(7–4) $rel\ (A/B) = prob\ (A/B) - prob\ (A/\overline{B})$

which we may call the *relevance to A of B* (relative to *prob*). Then the relationship between the changes in probability of A and of B is

(7–5) $PROB\ A - prob\ A = (PROB\ B - prob\ B)rel\ (A/B).$

Example 4: The mudrunner, concluded

In example 3, *rel (A/B)* is $.8 - .1$, so that the increase $.52 - .31 = .21$ in the gambler's degree of belief in A must be seven tenths of the increase $.6 - .3 = .3$ in his degree of belief in the proposition B in which the change originated.

It is evident from equation (7–5) that when the change from *prob* to *PROB* originates in an increase in the agent's degree of belief in B, then the probability of a proposition A increases, decreases, or remains the same accordingly as the relevance of B to A is positive, negative, or zero; and it is evident that the effect on A is opposite if the change originates in a decrease in the agent's degree of belief on B. This is as it should be if positive, negative, and null values of *rel* in (7–4) correspond to what we would ordinarily mean by "positive relevance," "negative relevance," and "irrelevance." It appears that

140

this is so. Certainly, the sign of *rel* (*A/B*) will always agree with that of the measure of relevance that Carnap has proposed.

$$prob\ AB - prob\ A\ prob\ B,$$

for it is straightforward to verify that we have

$$rel(A/B) = \frac{prob\ AB - prob\ A\ prob\ B}{prob\ B\ prob\overline{B}}$$

as long as *prob B* is neither 0 nor 1.

Comparison with conditionalization

It is plain that when *PROB B* is close to 1, equation (7–2) determines *PROB A* as approximately *prob* (*A/B*) for each proposition *A*, and thus determines *PROB* as approximately the same assignment as $prob_B$. Then conditionalization is a limiting case of the present more general method of assimilating uncertain evidence, and the case of conditionalization is approximated more and more closely as the probability of the evidence *B*, approaches 1. It would make no detectable difference if we adhered to C. I. Lewis's line and refused ever to assign subjective probability 1 to an objective proposition other than T, provided we were willing to assign such propositions values that are "practically" 1, e.g., .999999. And there would be a certain advantage in taking this line, for as long as *PROB B* is neither 0 nor 1, the change from *prob* to *PROB* is reversible in a way in which the change from *prob* to $prob_B$ is not.

To see that the change from *prob* to $prob_B$ is irreversible by conditionalization, suppose that the agent uses conditionalization to change from the belief function *prob* to a new belief function *PROB* in response to an observation, the effect of which is to convince him of the truth of *B*; but suppose that a further observation convinces him that he completely misconstrued the first observation, which in fact yielded no information. Then he would like to change from the belief function *PROB* back to his original belief function *prob*. However, he cannot do this by conditionalization: There is no proposition *C* which has the characteristic that $PROB_c$ is identical with the original assignment *prob*, except in the trivial case where *prob B* = 1, in which case, he was sure of the truth of *B* even before the first observation. To see that no such *C* exists, note that $PROB_c B$ must equal *prob B* if the reversal is to take place, and that for any *A* we have *PROB A* = *prob* (*A/B*). Then we must have $PROB_c B$ = *prob* (*B/BC*) = 1, so that if $PROB_c B$ is to be the same number as *prob B*, that number must have been 1.

On the other hand the change from *prob* to *PROB* via (7–2) is reversible by another application of (7–2) as long as neither *prob B* nor *PROB B* has either of the extreme values, 0 and 1. In particular, suppose that the agent makes an observation of which the effect is to change his degree of belief in *B* from *prob B* to a new value *p*. Then by (7–2), his degree of belief in an arbitrary proposition *A* will change from *prob A* to

$$PROB\ A = prob\ (A/B)p + prob\ (A/\overline{B})(1-p).$$

Suppose that a further observation has as its effect a change in his degree of belief in B from p back to *prob* B. Applying (7–2) again, his degree of belief in an arbitrary proposition A will become

$$PROB\ (A/B)prob\ B + PROB\ (A/\overline{B})prob\ \overline{B}$$

or, by (7–1) and (7–3) (a),

$$prob\ A.$$

Then the method of changing belief that is given by (7–2) has the advantage of reversibility: mistakes can be erased.

Solution for finite n

Now what of the general case where the effect of the observation is to simultaneously change the agent's degrees of belief in two or more propositions? In the case of conditionalization, there is no separate difficulty here, because the result of conditionalizing relative to B is to change *prob* (...) to *prob* (.../B), and the result of then conditionalizing relative to C is to change *prob* (.../B) to *prob* (.../BC); and this is exactly what the result would have been if the agent had straightway conditionalized relative to BC. Then the effect of first changing the probability of B to 1, and then changing the probability of C to 1 can be achieved by immediately changing the probability of a single proposition BC to 1. It is not so for the more general technique of assimilating changes in belief via (7–2). There the effect of first changing the probability of B to p and then changing the probability of C to q cannot generally be produced by changing the probability of some one proposition to some new value r. Nor need it always be the case that the result of two applications of (7–2) is independent of the order: the belief function obtained from *prob* by first changing the probability of B to p and then changing the probability of C to q need not be the same as the belief function that would have been obtained if first the probability of C had been changed to q, and then the probability of B had been changed to p. But in the case of conditionalization, order is irrelevant: $prob_{BC}$ is always the same assignment as $prob_{CB}$ because BC is always the same proposition as CB.

In generalizing (7–2) to cover the general case in which the change in belief originates in a set of n propositions

$$(7–6)\quad B_1, B_2, \ldots, B_n$$

it will be necessary to consider not the B's themselves, but rather the collection of all conjunctions of form

$$C_1 C_2 \ldots C_n$$

where each of the C's is identical either with the corresponding B or with its denial, and where the whole conjunction is not identical with the impossible proposition F. Each such conjunction will be called an *atom* of the set (7–6). There may be as many as 2^n distinct atoms of such a set.

Example 5: Observation by candlelight, continued

In example 1, n is 3 and B_1, B_2, B_3 are the propositions G, B, V. There are $2^3 = 8$ expressions of form $C_1 C_2\, C_3$:

$$GBV, GB\overline{V},\ G\overline{B}V, G\overline{B}\,\overline{V}, \overline{G}BV, \overline{G}B\overline{V}, \overline{G}\,\overline{B}V, \overline{G}\,\overline{B}\,\overline{V}$$

However, if we interpret G as meaning that the cloth is green *all over*, and, similarly, for B and V, and if we suppose that for some reason it is impossible that the cloth have any color other than these three, the eight expressions denote (with repetitions) only four distinct propositions,

$$F, F, F, G, F, B, V, F$$

Thus, the first of the eight conjunctions asserts that the cloth is at once green, blue, and violet all over, and is therefore impossible; the fourth of them asserts that the cloth is green all over and then redundantly denies that it is blue all over and that it is violet all over; and the last of them is impossible because we have assumed that $G \vee B \vee V$ is necessary. Then the atoms of the set G, B, V are those three propositions themselves.

Origination, closure

Suppose that the distinct atoms of the set (7–6) are the propositions

$$A_1, A_2, \ldots, A_m$$

Then the appropriate generalization of the formula (7–2) will prove to be

$$(7\text{–}7) \quad PROB\ A = prob\ (A/A_1)PROB\ A_1 + prob\ (A/A_2)PROB\ A_2$$
$$+\ \ldots\ + prob\ (A/A_m)PROB\ A_m$$

and the appropriate generalization of formulas (7–1) will prove to be

$$(7\text{–}8) \quad PROB\ (A/A_i) = prob\ (A/A_i)\ \text{ for each }\ i = 1, 2,\ \ldots,\ m$$

which defines what we shall mean by saying that the change from *prob* to *PROB* *originated* in the set (7–6). It is straightforward to show that conditions (7–7) and (7–8) are equivalent if both *prob* and *PROB* satisfy the probability axioms and none of the m numbers *prob* A_i is either 0 or 1.

Example 6: Observation by candlelight, concluded

If the observation described in example 1 changes the probabilities of G, B, and V from .30, .30, and .40 to .70, .25, and .05, but does not change the probabilities of any propositions conditionally on G, or on B, or on V, then the change from *prob* to *PROB* does originate in the set G, B, V, and the atoms of that set are those three propositions themselves. Then by (7–7) we have

$$PROB\ A = .70\ prob\ (A/G) + .25\ prob\ (A/B) + .05\ prob\ (A/V).$$

143

Note that since distinct sets of propositions can have the same set of atoms, there is a certain latitude in the choice of a set (7–6) in which the change from *prob* to *PROB* is viewed as originating.

Example 7: Observation by candlelight, reviewed

The change described in example 6 as originating in the set G, B, V might equally well be regarded as originating in the set

$$B_1 = G \vee B \quad B_2 = G$$

for the four conjunctions of form $C_1 C_2$ would then be

$$(G \vee B)G = G \quad (G \vee B)\overline{G} = B \quad (\overline{G \vee B})G = F \quad (\overline{G \vee B})\overline{G} = V$$

so that we have the same set of atoms as before, and formula (7–7) will yield the same function *PROB* as before.

Let us speak of a set of propositions as being *closed* if it is closed under the operations of conjunction, disjunction, and denial, in the sense that whenever A and B are members of the set, so are

$$\overline{A}, \overline{B}, AB, A \vee B.$$

Thus, the set consisting of F together with all of the propositions in the agent's preference ranking is a closed set. And let us speak of the *closure* of a set B of propositions as being the least inclusive closed set to which every member of B belongs. If B is finite, its closure will consist of F, together with the atoms of B, together with all disjunctions of two or more atoms of B. Then if B has m atoms, the closure of B will consist of 2^m propositions.

If the members of B are $G \vee B$ and G, as in example 7, and if $V = \overline{G \vee B}$, then the atoms of B are G, V, and B, and its closure will consist of the eight propositions

$$F, G, B, V, G, \vee B, G \vee V, B \vee V, T.$$

The simplest cases of change from *prob* to *PROB* are those for which we can find a proposition B such that (7–1) holds for every proposition A in the agent's preference ranking. The change is then said to originate in the proposition B or, alternatively, in the set consisting of the two propositions B, $\overline{B}$. This notion of origination was then generalized to cover cases where the change is said to originate in a finite set (7–6) of propositions: these are the cases where (7–8) holds for every proposition A in the agent's preference ranking. It only remains to generalize the notion of origination to cover cases where the change would properly be said to originate in an infinite set B.

The continuous case

Example 8: Observation by candlelight, generalized

The possible hues of a piece of cloth of uniform hue form a continuum which can be described conveniently in terms of the wavelength of reflected sunlight, measured in millimicrons (mμ). The range from green to violet falls within the interval from 550 to 350 on this scale, and it is conceivable that the observer thinks of hues in terms of wavelengths instead of (or, in addition to) thinking of them in terms of color words in English. His beliefs about the hue of the cloth before and after the observation might then be represented by two probability distributions as illustrated in figure 7.1, where B_x is the proposition that the average wavelength of the light that would be reflected from the cloth in sunlight is between 350 mμ and x mμ. Presumably, the probabilities of all propositions of form $B_y\overline{B_x}$ where y is greater than x approach 0 as y approaches x: such propositions say that the wavelength is between x and y mμ, and as the interval shrinks to 0, so does the probability that the average wavelength is in that precise interval. In particular, for any x, the probability of the proposition that the wavelength is exactly x is 0, both before and after the observation. In terms of wavelengths, the propositions V, B, and G of example 1 are $B_{425}\overline{B_{375}}$, $B_{475}\overline{B_{425}}$, and $B_{525}\overline{B_{475}}$; according to figure 7.1 (a), the probabilities of these propositions before the observation are .40, .30, and .30; and according to figure 7.1 (b), the probabilities of the same propositions after the observation are .05, .25, and .70. Thus, $prob\ B$ is $prob\ B_{475}\overline{B_{425}}$ or $prob\ B_{475}$ − $prob\ B_{425}$, and by figure 7.1 (a) we have $prob\ B_{475} = .70$ and $prob\ B_{425} = .40$, so that indeed $prob\ B = .30$.

In cases of the sort considered in example 8, the set B in which the change is taken to originate would be infinite; thus, in Example 8, B might be taken to be the set of

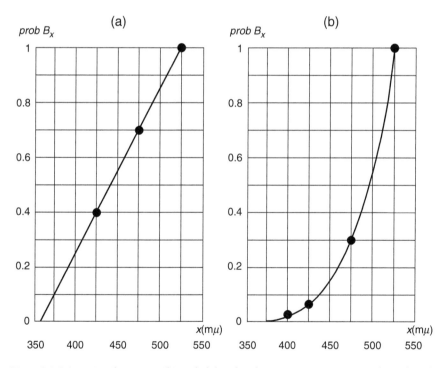

Figure 7.1 Prior (a) and posterior (b) probability distributions over propositions about the color of reflected light.

all propositions of form B_x where x lies between 350 and 550. Formula (7–7) can be applied approximately, in such cases.

$$A_1 = B_{375}\overline{B_{350}} \quad A_2 = B_{400}\overline{B_{375}} \quad \ldots A_8 = B_{550}\overline{B_{525}}$$

These eight A's behave like atoms in that they are incompatible and together exhaust the range within which x must lie; and they satisfy conditions (7–8) approximately, in the sense that for any proposition A in the preference ranking the numbers $prob\ (A/A_1)$ and $PROB\ (A/A_1)$ will be approximately the same, for each $i = 1, 2, \ldots, 8$. (The approximation would be even better if we were to divide the interval into sixteen equal subintervals, obtaining sixteen such A's.) Now equation (7–7) can be used to get approximate values of $PROB\ A$ for any proposition A in the preference ranking.

Example 9

Divide the interval from 350 to 550 into eight equal subintervals, and define eight propositions which behave approximately like atoms

$$PROB\ A \approx prob\ (A/A_1)PROB\ A_1 + prob\ (A/A_2)\ PROB\ A_2$$
$$+ \ldots + prob\ (A/A_8)\ PROB\ A_8$$
$$= prob\ (A/A_1)(0) + prob\ (A/A_2)(.01) + \ldots + prob\ (A/A_8)(0)$$

To obtain more accurate values of $PROB\ A$, use sixteen (or 32, or 64) pseudoatoms.

In such cases as these, we may think of the agent's change in belief as originating in the closure of the set $\mathcal{B}$, and as being propagated over the remainder of the structure of his beliefs by the method illustrated in example 9. To discuss the matter more rigorously and generally, it is necessary to use the notion of integration over abstract spaces; but the essential ideas are illustrated in example 9, since the integrals in question would be defined by exactly the sort of process of successive approximation that was indicated there.

Probabilistic acts; trying

The situation that we have been studying in relation to probabilistic observations has its parallel in the case of probabilistic acts. It may be that the agent decides to perform an act which is not simply describable as *making the proposition B true*, but must be described as changing the probabilities of two or more propositions (7–6) from

$$prob\ B_1, prob\ B_2, \ldots, prob\ B_n$$

to a new set of values,

$$PROB\ B_1, PROB\ B_2, \ldots, PROB\ B_n.$$

In the simplest cases, where $n = 2$, where B_1 is some good proposition B, and where B_2 is the bad proposition $\overline{B}$, we speak of the agent as *trying to make B true*; and where $PROB\ B$, the probability that B would have if the agent decided to perform the act, is very close to 1, we may speak of the agent as believing it to be in his power to make *B* happen if he chooses. Here *PROB* reflects the agent's belief, before seeing the act's outcome, in his ability to make *B* true by the act in question. (Then the change in the agent's degree of belief from *prob B* to *PROB B* is what Anscombe calls "knowledge without observation.") But where we and the agent are willing to speak of him as trying to make *B* true, there need be no corresponding proposition in the agent's preference ranking, just as in example 1 there need be no such proposition as the cloth's looking green. There, the situation that we and the agent might describe as the cloth's looking green is represented as a change in the agent's degree of belief in the proposition *G* that the cloth *is* green from .30 to .70, rather than by a change in the agent's degree of belief in some corresponding expressive proposition *E* (that the cloth looks green) from some value *prob E* to 1. We do not assume that propositions like *E* occur in the agent's preference ranking. Here the "trying" idiom has the same sort of function in connection with acting that the "looking" idiom has in connection with observing. We do not suppose that where we and the agent are willing to speak of him as trying to make *B* true, his preference ranking must contain a proposition

$$E = \text{ that the agent tries to make } B \text{ true.}$$

Rather, to speak of the agent's trying to make *B* true is to speak of his performing an act of which he takes the net effect to be an increase in the probability of *B*. We or the agent may speak in this way without thereby assuming the existence of a proposition *E* in his preference ranking for which we have

$$(7\text{--}9) \quad PROB\ E = 1\ PROB\ B = prob\ (B/E)$$

where *PROB* is the agent's belief function after he decides to perform the act. Thus, trying to hit the bullseye may be an act without there being any proposition that plays *E* in hitting the *B* bullseye, above.

Example 10: The comforter

The agent is trying to comfort a lady whose cat has been killed. This may consist in any of a variety of acts, such as giving her another cat, holding her hand, or saying "He was getting old and stiff, anyway." And there are many ways of performing the last-mentioned act, of saying the words, some of which would be more likely to produce comfort than others: variations in volume of voice, proximity of speaker to hearer, and facial expression might all be important. The agent might have an accurate sense of how he is speaking the comforting words in each of these respects without being able to verbalize it. Thus, he might be tacitly aware that saying the words in a loud voice from across a room with his facial muscles relaxed might have a disturbing effect; and he might be able to control his distance, volume, and facial expression in the relevant ways; and he might nevertheless be unable to produce or recognize a true description of what he is doing, in terms of distance, volume, and facial expression. The overall effect of his tacit awareness of what he is doing might well be that he takes his act of speaking the comforting words to impart a certain high probability *PROB B* to the woman's being comforted, without his being able to characterize the act by means of a proposition *E* in his preference ranking for which (7–9) holds. (The importance of such tacit knowledge in epistemology—knowledge *how*, unaccompanied by knowledge *that*—has been stressed by Michael Polanyi.)

Observation; meaning

It has been held by many empiricists that the propositions expressible in the agent's language can usefully be classified as *observational* or not, and that the nonobservational propositions derive their significance from their logical relationships with the observational ones, in virtue of which nonobservational propositions can be confirmed or disconfirmed to various degrees on the basis of the agent's observations. (Something like this position was maintained by Carnap, e.g., in "Testability and Meaning," *Philosophy of Science* 3 [1936]: 419–71 and 4 [1937]: 1–40.) In view of what we have said here it seems unpromising to construe the observational propositions as the ones whose truth or falsehood can be ascertained with certainty by making suitable observations; but the notion might still be defined in terms of changes that originate in sets (7–6) of propositions in the sense that (7–8) holds for all propositions *A* that are expressible in the language. The *observational basis* of a certain language for a certain agent might then be taken to be the smallest set of propositions expressible in the language which has the characteristic that any possible change in the agent's belief function which is occasioned by an observation can be described as originating in some set (7–6) of propositions, all of which belong to the observational basis.

Similarly, there will be an *actual basis* for a given agent and a given language, consisting in the smallest set of propositions expressible in the language which has the characteristic that the effect of any possible act on the agent's belief function can be described as a change which originates in a set (7–6) of propositions, all of which belong to the actual basis. It is to be expected that the actual basis will be a proper subset of the observational basis, which will be in turn a proper subset of the collection of all propositions that are expressible in the language. Roughly speaking, the actual basis is the set of propositions whose truth values the agent thinks he can directly influence by his acts, and the observational basis is the set of propositions whose truth values the agent thinks capable of having a direct influence on his belief function via observations.

No doubt, paradigm cases play an important role in discussions of meaning. To know the proper use of the English color words "green," "blue," and "violet" is in no small part to be able to apply them correctly to objects observed in sunlight whose colors fall well within the ranges of hues that are covered by the three words; and in such cases it would be grotesque to balk at describing the agent as having seen that the objects were green, blue, and violet, and as having seen that the corresponding propositions are true. But often enough the agent will have to deal with unparadigmatic cases, in which (say) the light conditions or the actual hues are such as to make it clearly inappropriate for him or us to describe his observation in such simple terms. Here it becomes necessary to recognize the components of meaning that must be described in terms of degrees of belief short of certainty. Thus, suppose that the light is dim and that the hue of the object being observed is between violet and blue: the wavelength of reflected midday sunlight would be 425 mµ, let us say. Then doubt might be cast on the agent's mastery of the English color words if he responded to the observation by changing the probabilities of the propositions $V, B,$ and G from .4, .4, and .2, to .2, .2, and .6. It seems fair to put the matter in this way: mastery of the English color words involves a working knowledge—tacit or otherwise—of the fact that blue comes between violet and greet on the color spectrum. And more generally, mastery of a language involves an accurate sense of the *confirmational proximity* of propositions, in the light of which certain changes in belief would be viewed as inappropriate to the observation in question.

It is true that such a sense of confirmational proximity would be acquired through experience, but this need not count against its status as a condition for mastery of the language, and as an ingredient in a grasp of the meanings of the relevant words. In "logical reconstruction" of language as in actual construction of a robot, one might draw a sharp line between aspects of the agent's belief function that are built into the semantics of his language and those which arise in response to experience. But by and large, we speak unreconstructed languages and are never done with the business of learning them; and it is some part of the business of epistemology to treat of human beings as they are.

Note

* Originally published as Chapter 11 of *The Logic of Decision*, 2nd ed., University of Chicago Press: Chicago, 1983, pp. 165–80. Copyright © 1965, 1983 The University of Chicago. Reprinted by permission of The University of Chicago Press.

Bibliography

Carnap, R. (1962) *The Logical Foundations of Probability*, 2 ed., University of Chicago Press: Chicago.

Jeffrey, Richard (1983) *The Logic of Decision*, 2 ed., University of Chicago Press: Chicago.

Lewis, C.I. (1946) *An Analysis of Knowledge and Valuation*, Open Court: LaSalle, IL.

8

BELIEF AND THE WILL*†

Bas C. van Fraassen

Can we rationally come to believe a proposition that is entailed neither by those we have believed heretofore nor by our previous opinions conjoined to the evidence before us? Discussing this question, William James quoted W. K. Clifford's statement (in "Ethics of Belief") that it is wrong always, everywhere, and for everyone to believe anything on insufficient evidence.[1] Arguing against this, James claimed that, in forming beliefs, we pursue two aims: to believe truth and to avoid error, and argued that the extent to which we pursue either at the cost of the other is a matter of choice: "he who says 'Better go without belief forever than believe a lie!' merely shows his own preponderant private horror of becoming a dupe. He may be critical of many of his desires and fears, but this fear he slavishly obeys ... a certain lightness of heart seems healthier than this excessive nervousness [about error]. At any rate, it seems the fittest thing for the empirialist philosopher."[2]

In philosophy of science, until recently, something of this sort was regarded as part of the received view: general theories, such as Darwin's Einstein's, or Bohr's, cannot be established on the basis of the evidence, but we may rationally come to believe that they are true. In addition, what we take as evidence itself is not indubitable, and we may later come to regard it as having been false. We regard ourselves as infallible neither with respect to what we take as evidence nor with respect to our extrapolation beyond the evidence, but neither do we think ourselves irrational for engaging in this cognitive enterprise.

The situation is prima facie not affected by the replacement of undogmatic full belief by gradations of partial belief. Perhaps when I profess belief or acceptance, I merely indicate that the proposition seems highly likely to me. But the evidence at hand, especially if itself not fully believed, plus our opinions heretofore, generally do not entail a high probability of truth for general hypotheses or theories—especially not for the sort studied by scientists, which have empirical consequences for all past and future. Only recently have these views come under attack, by writers inspired by Bayesian foundations of statistics.

My strategy in this paper will be first to submit the traditional epistemological views to a critique along Bayesian lines (without claiming to be a Bayesian of any sort). Then I shall show the implications of that critique for those ways of changing one's opinions which Bayesians have generally admitted as rational. The result will be, I think, a puzzle for all concerned. Indeed, this puzzle suggests that we must obey a principle (which I shall call *Reflection*), going beyond the simple laws of probability, which looks prima facie quite unacceptable. I selected James's essay to introduce the topic because I wish to propose a solution to the puzzle along the broadly voluntarist lines of the views he defended. I hope that by consistently carrying through the voluntarist point of view we can, without sacrificing the theory of personal probability as a logic of epistemic judgment, nevertheless maintain the traditional epistemology.[3]

To believe a theory

Imagine that today I do not profess total certainty about whether the basic theory of evolution is true nor about whether I shall be sure of its truth next year. It does seem quite possible to me that I shall become sure of its truth, but also, unfortunately, some-what possible that I shall form this belief although it is in fact false. Does the state of opinion I have just described seem totally absurd or irrational to you? If not, this section may convince you otherwise.

The critique I am about to offer is along Bayesian lines, though not exactly standard ones, nor perhaps uncontroversial. I request the reader to bear with my rather informal and naive presentation here; in the next section I shall make the argument at once more general and more precise. As described, my present state of opinion is one of uncertainty. The degrees of uncertainty about the different propositions are not the same; it is common today to describe them in terms of subjective or personal probability.[4] In Bayesian eyes, personal probability is the guide to life. The simplest cases we find are in buying contracts, insurance policies, and wagers. Without going into the details, I shall take the following as paradigm: if a contract is worth 1 to me if A be the case, and nothing otherwise, then its present value for me equals my personal probability for A. More generally,

> if it is worth z to me if A and nothing otherwise and if my personal probability that A is the case equals $P(A)$, then the value of this contract for me (fair in buying or selling) equals $zP(A)$.

That is all we shall need for our discussion.

So let H be the hypothesis under discussion—say, the theory of evolution—and let E be the proposition that Bas van Fraassen will fully believe that H (say, one year from today). For definiteness, suppose that $P(E)$—my degree of belief that E will be the case—equals 0.4 and $P(\sim H \& E)$—my degree of belief that I will mistakenly come to bestow full belief on H—equals 0.2. For now I shall assume that full belief entails personal probability equal to 1. The argument would go through for a degree very close to 1 as well, but I shall in any case consider more explicitly the case of non-full-belief formation below.

At this point we may introduce into the story a Dutch bookie.[5] He elicits all the above information from me, and he decides on a secret strategy for betting with me. As a first step, he offers me three bets. I call him Dutch, because what he has offered me is what is called a *Dutch book*, a set of bets such that, no matter what happens, I will lose money. And the unfortunate fact is that each of the bets is fair, according to my own state of opinion.

Because I will describe his betting scheme in full generality in the next section, I ask the reader to consider the present figures only cursorily. The trick up his sleeve is that (a) if I do not come to fully believe H, I win only the second bet, and (b) if I do come to fully believe H, then I lose the second bet, but I also tell the bookie myself that I have lost the first bet as well. At this point he takes the second step in his strategy, which is in

151

effect to buy back the ticket for the first bet, for a pittance. (He can do this by formally offering to buy from me a bet that H is false; since I am sure that H is true, any price at all for that new bet will be more than fair in my opinion.) In either case I will have a net loss.

Here are the bets: the first pays 1 if I come to believe H and H is really false—he asks 0.2 for it. The second will pay 0.5 if I do not come to believe H, and he asks me 0.3 for that one. The third pays 0.5 if I really do come to believe H; that one costs 0.2. All these prices are fair, given my state of opinion. (I leave out units of value; so they can be adjusted for inflation and the like.) None of the bets pay anything if they are not won. My total cost is 0.7 for all three.

On one scenario I do not embrace H; I win the second bet and lose the other two. On the other scenario I do embrace the hypothesis; now I lose the second bet, tell him myself that H is true, so I get nothing for the first bet (though I receive a pittance when I sell him back a bet on $\sim H$ for next to nothing), and I win the third. On either scenario I get at most a little more than 0.5, and I have a net loss. This bookie had a strategy which he knew beforehand would allow him to offer me only bets that would be fair by my lights, and yet necessarily give him a net profit. He devised this strategy without any special knowledge either of whether Darwin was right or of whether I would come to believe that hypothesis.

All this may look like so much *léger-de-main* at this point. Suppose for a moment, however, that I have not pulled any tricks. In that case whoever is as I described myself, hypothetically, at the beginning of this section, is in a state of opinion which the Bayesian calls incoherent (a polite word for irrational). Whether or not I actually bought the bets does not matter, of course: my incoherence consists in regarding them as fair.

Unhappy mortal! I found myself in this incoherence merely by contemplating that I could do what James said I could—without even actually deciding to believe Darwin's theories, or anything like it. Not only people so rash as actually to come to believe theories on less than totally compelling evidence, but anyone who does not, with Clifford, reject such a new belief as utterly irrational, is caught in the trap. Who, upon seeing this Bayesian refutation, does not immediately find himself in full flight from voluntarism and pragmatism, toward the imitation of Carnap's robot?

To raise one's opinion of a matter of fact

The preceding argument gives rise to three initial suspicions. The first is that bets cannot sensibly be made on propositions, like Darwin's hypothesis, which cannot be verified or falsified in a finite amount of time. The second is that it is irrational to become fully certain of any propositions except tautologies. The third suspicion one may have is that it is irrational to change one's mind in any way except by what the Bayesians call "conditionalization on one's evidence." [Roughly speaking, this means that one becomes fully certain of the proposition(s) one takes as evidence, and makes only the minimal adjustments to the rest of one's opinions needed to accommodate this new certainty. We may think of this as Clifford's position, updated to accommodate degrees of belief.] Note well that the second and third suspicion cannot be jointly entertained unless evidence is always tautological. So we must confront the second and third separately, but I think we can show the irrelevance of the first along the way. Later on we shall turn to still further suspicions, for example, about the suitability of one's own future opinions as a subject for prevision.

BELIEF AND THE WILL

Before going on to examples, we should look at what exactly is involved in Dutch book arguments. In the simple or *synchronic* case, the bookie is able (without having knowledge superior to the agent's) to offer the agent several bets, which demonstrably have the following features: (a) each bet taken individually looks fair to the agent at this time, and (b) taken together the bets are such that, no matter what happens, the agent will suffer a net loss. The expression 'looks fair' is explicated by the Bayesians in terms of the agent's personal probability P and utility evaluations, following the paradigm that $zP(A)$ is the exact value of a bet on proposition A with payoff z. In the case described, the bets in question constitute a Dutch book, and the agent's vulnerability brands his state of opinion as *incoherent* (and indeed, it can be deduced that P violates the probability calculus).

In the *diachronic* case we should speak of a *Dutch strategy* rather than a Dutch book. The bookie is able (without superior knowledge of present or later circumstances) to devise a strategy for offering bets to the agent which is demonstrably to the agent's disadvantage. This strategy is demonstrably such that, under all eventualities, the agent will be offered bets with two features: (a) individually, each bet will look fair to the agent at the time of the offer, and (b) taken together, the bets offered will be such that, whatever happens, the agent will suffer a net loss. Let us emphasize especially that these features are demonstrable *beforehand*, without appeal to any but logical considerations, and the strategy's implementation requires no information inaccessible to the agent himself. The general conclusion must be that an agent vulnerable to such a Dutch strategy has an initial state of opinion or practice of changing his opinion, which together constitute a demonstrably bad guide to life. In this paper, success of the strategies discussed will be independent of the agent's practices for changing opinion, and hence any blame must attach to his initial state of opinion—his vulnerability reveals an initial incoherence.

It is now time to describe the exact betting strategy used by our Dutch bookie. We have two propositions, H (the hypothesis) and E, a proposition about the customer's future attitude to the hypothesis. The customer has degrees of belief $P(E)$ and $P(\sim H \& E)$, neither of which is 0 or 1. The three bets are:

(I) The bet which pays 1 if $(\sim H \& E)$ and which costs $P(\sim H \& E)$
(II) The bet which pays x if $\sim E$ and which costs $xP(\sim E)$
(III) The bet which pays y if E and which costs $yP(E)$

Here the probability of $\sim E$ equals 1 minus the probability of E. The number x is the usual conditional probability of $\sim H$ given E; that is, $P(\sim H \& E) \div P(E)$. And finally y is x minus the subjective probability the customer will have for the hypothesis, when and if E becomes true. It helps to observe that I and II together form in effect a *conditional bet* on $\sim H$ on the supposition that E, which bears the cost x and has prize 1, with the guarantee of your money back should the supposition turn out to be false.[6] So the total cost of all the bets together must equal $x + yP(E)$.

Let us now consider an example in which all propositions will have their truth value settled by a certain definite time and in which it is not strictly implied that anyone is fully certain of the truth of any nontautology. Since we are now on the attack, the example should be made as simple and hygienic as possible. Let it be a race, at Hollywood Park, tomorrow at noon. The proposition H is that the horse Table Hands will run in that race and win it. The bookie now asks me seriously to consider the possibility that

153

tomorrow morning, at 8 A.M., I shall consider fair a bet on this proposition at odds 2 to 1. I say I do not know if that will happen—my personal probability for that eventuality, call it E, is $P(E) = 0.4$. Next he elicits my opinion about how reliable I think I am as a handicapper of horses. What is my subjective probability that E will indeed be true but that the hypothesis that Table Hands will win, is false? Suppose I answer that this degree of belief of mine, $P(\sim H \& E)$, equals 0.3. The exact numbers do not matter here too much, except that they indicate a certain lack of confidence in my own handicapping skill. In this case they entail that my present conditional probability for Table Hands' winning, on the supposition that tomorrow morning I will have subjective probability 1/3 for it, is only 1/4. The calculation is simple.[7]

What the bookie does now, if I buy the bets, is also simple. He approaches me at 8 A.M. the next morning. If I do not consider odds of 2 to 1 on Table Hands fair, he pays me off on the second bet, but he has won (I) and (III). On the other hand, if I do call those odds fair, he first of all pays me for bet (III). But then he buys from me a bet, with prize 1, against Table Hands' winning, at my newly announced odds. The result of this is, of course, that whether or not Table Hands wins at noon, no money need change hands between us—he has, so to say, bought (I) back from me. So we can now tally up our prospective losses and gains, and again it turns out that I shall have been the loser come what may.[8]

I chose this example to disarm both the first two initial suppositions at once. For there is no implication, in the description of this case, that anyone ever raises the probability of any nontautology to *one* (though in that case the bookie is being quite agreeable about paying me off before he is totally certain that he has heard me correctly). On the other hand, every proposition becomes settled in a certain finite amount of time. The disaster—which consists of course in my present vulnerability to his strategy, not in any actual bets made or lost—happened again because I profess some doubts today about my judgment of tomorrow.

Let us therefore not think about gambling anymore, and turn to the scientist in his lair, Clifford's ideal who (according to James's quotation) "will guard the purity of his belief with a very fanaticism of jealous care, lest at any time it should rest on an unworthy object, and catch a stain which can never be wiped away" and who, therefore, never believes anything upon insufficient evidence (James, *op. cit.*, p. 92). He is then just like Carnap's robot: his senses bring him propositions that he takes as evidence, and his total response to this consists in *conditionalizing* his present state of opinion on these propositions.[9] To conditionalize on a proposition X taken as evidence means this: your odds for various eventualities on the supposition that X are still the same, but that supposition you now regard as certainly true.

Well suppose that e is the sort of proposition that I typically do take as evidence. We need not decide here exactly what sort that is. Perhaps it is the sort of report that comes from Mount Wilson observatory, after having been checked and verified numerous times. Or perhaps it is simple everyday propositions like "That rose is red" or "That is a rose." In any of these cases, the example is decided on the basis of perception. Now let me give the reins over to you, reader: do you think that I am infallible when it comes to perception? Do you think that I shall certainly not take a rose to be red if it is not? Or that a needle will never turn out to have been to the left of the number 7 on a dial, when I said it was to the right? All right, you have convinced me: my subjective probability that e is false, on the supposition that I shall take it as evidence, is not zero.

154

It is not difficult to see that, formally speaking, I am now in exactly the same position as I was when I thought that I might come to believe a false hypothesis of Darwin's. (Let E be the proposition that I shall take e as evidence, and H the hypothesis that e is true.) Merely by contemplating this eventuality and admitting that I am not sure it cannot happen, I imply that I regard as fair each of three bets which together form the basis for a Dutch strategy. Even if I insist that my epistemic life is lived in the Imitation of Carnap's Robot, mere admission of my fallibility, it seems, makes me diachronically incoherent.

Prevision of our own previsions

When we begin to think about the laws and sources of our own epistemic judgments and states of opinion, we are automatically led to deal with them as facts in the world and to consider them in general: that is, with no regard to persons, treating others' no differently from our own. Yet a closer reading of the preceding arguments, once the initial suspicions have been disarmed, presents us with only two possible ways out. The first is that we should have no opinion at all concerning the reliability of our own future judgments; the second, to form as a matter of principle an exceptionally high opinion of their reliability in our own case.[10]

The first may claim precedent in the discussions of de Finetti and Savage themselves, rejecting the intelligibility of higher-order degrees of belief. Their reasons have been incisively criticized by Brian Skyrms.[11] As I shall explain later, I think there is something to the view that the statement that my opinion is such and such "is not a proposition." But we can, I think, quickly dismiss the simpler objections along this line. First of all, whatever is done by the person who says "It seems as likely to me as not that today will be rainy," we do have a proposition that is true if and only if he is at the moment in the psychological state of considering rain as likely as not, being as willing to bet on rain as on the toss of a coin, and so forth. Psychological studies of this subject are well known and we do not think them, surely, to be of an illusory or nonexistent phenomenon.

More important is the worry that, in asking us to consider our own states of opinion, we may be led into the vagaries and paradoxes of self-reference. It would be no surprise if the attempt to assign degrees of credence or credibility to self-referential statements generally were as beset with paradox as the attempt to assign them all truth values. But actually the puzzles or arguments I have presented do not presuppose that degrees of belief are accorded to self-referential statements at all. Suppose that "Cicero" and "D-Day" are context-independent rigid designators referring to a person and a time, respectively, and that p is a function defined on some set of propositions such that $p(A) = r$ if and only if Cicero has on D-Day subjective probability r for proposition A. For definiteness, suppose that the domain of p contains only propositions of an extremely simple sort, such as that Table Hands wins the race or that a certain coin lands heads up or that a certain rose is red. There can surely be no difficulty in anyone's having at any time a degree of belief for the proposition that $p(A) = r$. Hence Cicero may have exactly that the day before D-Day. In addition, there is (independent of these considerations) surely no problem about Cicero's being able to know that he is Cicero or to know that the day in question is in fact the day before D-Day. If there are difficulties with any of these suppositions, they must be deep skeptical problems concerning the very coherence (in the nontechnical sense) of the concept of subjective probability and the concept of knowledge about who we are and what time it is. This coherence is all our arguments required. At no point did we need to assume that anyone's degrees of belief were accorded to any but time- and context-independent propositions.

We come therefore finally to the last way out, which is to say that all three examples were cases in which I made the agent out to be genuinely irrational. This could only be because in each case his degree of belief about what would happen, on the supposition that he would have a certain opinion about that in the future, differed from *that* opinion. The principle we are thereby led to postulate as a new requirement of rationality, in addition to the usual laws of probability calculation is this:

$$\text{(Reflection)} \quad P_t^a \, (A|p_{t+x}^a(A) = r) = r$$

Here P_t^a is the agent a's credence function at time t, x is any non-negative number, and $(p_{t+x}^a(A) = r)$ is the proposition that at time $t + x$, the agent a will bestow degree r of credence on the proposition A. To satisfy the principle, the agent's present subjective probability for proposition A, on the supposition that his subjective probability for this proposition will equal r at some later time, must equal this same number r. It is tempting to call this principle of reflection by some more memorable name, such as 'Self-confidence', 'Optimism', or perhaps 'EST', or even 'Self-deception', but I have chosen a more neutral name because I propose to examine, and indeed advocate, serious attempts to defend the principle.[12]

Since none of us is willing to adopt a similar principle governing our own opinion concerning the reliability of others' opinions—or the corollary that they will never take as evidence something that is in fact false—justification of this principle can follow no ordinary route! Indeed, it would seem that we already believe that most people whose credence function obeys this principle of Reflection are by that very fact mistaken about themselves.

At the same time we can give independent or indirect reasons to think that criteria of coherence, concerning degrees of belief that are guides for action, will require this Reflection principle for their satisfaction. To show this I must first briefly outline another justification for the additivity of synchronic degrees of belief, a sort of dual to the Dutch book argument.[13]

To explain the idea of *calibration*, consider a weather forecaster who says in the morning that the probability of rain equals 0.8. That day it either rains or does not. How good a forecaster is he? Clearly to evaluate him we must look at his performance over a longer period of time. Calibration is a measure of agreement between judgments and actual frequencies. Without going into detail, it is still easy to explain perfect calibration. This forecaster was perfectly calibrated over the past year, for example, if, for every number r, the proportion of rainy days among those days on which he announced probability r for rain, equalled r.

Although perfect calibration may not be a reasonable aim by itself, and hardly to be expected at the best of times, it certainly looks like a virtue. It would seem to be irrational to organize your degrees of belief in such a way as to ruin, a priori, the possibility of perfect calibration. A few qualifications must at once be introduced: this forecaster would not have been perfectly calibrated over the past year if he had announced irrational numbers, or even numbers not equal to some fraction of form $x/365$. So the only possibility that we should require him not to ruin beforehand is that of arbitrarily close approximation to perfect calibration if he were asked sufficiently often about events that he considers exactly similar to those he was actually asked about during the evaluation period. It can now be proved that satisfaction of this criterion of potential perfect calibration is exactly equivalent to satisfaction of the probability calculus (in exactly the same sense that this equivalence can be claimed for the criterion of invulnerability to Dutch books).

But it is easy to see what will happen if the evaluation is extended to the forecaster's opinions concerning the calibration of his own judgments. For suppose that he is actually perfectly calibrated in his judgments concerning rain over the next year. Then if he has made judgments to the effect that there will be a discrepancy between the actual frequencies and his announced probabilities, *those* judgements will not be perfectly calibrated. Hence by adding such a judgment as "The probability of rain on days on which I announce the probability of rain to be 0.8, equals 0.7" he would automatically ensure that the class of all his judgments was not perfectly calibrated on any possible scenario. Our criterion accordingly appears to require him to express perfect confidence in the calibration of his own judgments.

Dutch book considerations are of course more familiar; it is interesting to see that the principle of Reflection follows as an immediate corollary to this equivalent, less familiar criterion of coherence. It helps to dispel as vain the small hope that criteria of rationality of this general sort could be satisfied by anyone with doubts that violate Reflection. Yet—and here is the puzzle—we all begin with the intuition that such doubts are not of the radically skeptical kind, but reasonable and rightly common.

Circumventing Moore's paradox

The main purpose of this section will be to show that certain attempts to defend the principle of Reflection do not work. But at the same time I will attempt to show that even an agent adhering to that principle may have some way to express doubt about the reliability of his own future opinions. Hence the discussion will at least undermine one objection to the principle, even if it does not yet issue in a good defense.

The first proposal to defend (Reflection) is this: to announce my subjective conditional probability for X, on the supposition that Y, is simply to announce what my opinion concerning X would be, should I learn that Y. This thesis implies (Reflection) at once, but the thesis is quite untenable. Richmond Thomason once objected to a similar theory of what it was to believe a conditional, that he believed to be true the proposition that, if his wife were not faithful to him (she being so clever), he would believe that she was. If I go on to reflect on other examples, it is only because I wish to do more than defeat the proposal.[14]

Are there propositions that we must admit to be possibly true but could never believe? Hilary Putnam has argued this status for the proposition that we are brains in a vat, and Donald Davidson for the proposition that most of our beliefs are false. These are forms of general and radical skepticism. An older and simpler case is Moore's paradox: "There is a goldfinch in the garden and I do not believe that there is." This statement could of course be true (at the moment I do not believe that there is, yet there might be one) but I could not very well assert it, for this is not a proposition that I can believe. Note, however, that I have just stated parenthetically that, for all I know or believe, it may be true; so I clearly do not *dis*believe it. It is also to be remarked that Moore's paradox does not presuppose that belief is a propositional attitude that we can have toward self-referential propositions. For if Cicero knows himself to be Cicero, he cannot believe that (there is a goldfinch and Cicero does not believe that there is). To consider a somewhat more general version, we must introduce the distinction between probabilities as gradations of belief and as degrees of objective chance.

This distinction is now commonly made, and several recent papers have been devoted to the principles governing their combination.[15] The minimal such principle looks formally similar to the synchronic version of (Reflection):

$$\text{(Miller) } P_t(A| \text{ ch}_t(A) = r) = r$$

so called because of its role in the (famous but fallacious) argument known as Miller's paradox.[16] To satisfy this principle, the agent's subjective probability for a proposition A, on the supposition that the objective chance that A equals r, must be equal to that same number r. Justification of this principle certainly rests on nontrivial assumptions about what we are like—namely, that we are temporal and finite beings, aware of our temporality and finitude. To see this we deduce that, for an agent whose epistemic history satisfies (Miller), perfect foreknowledge is incompatible with indeterminism. For suppose that such an agent had subjective probability P equalling 1 or 0 for every factual proposition, and indeed, 1 exactly if the proposition is true. Then there is, for each factual proposition A, a number r such that $\text{ch}_t(A) = r$ and $P_t (\text{ch}_t(A) = r) = 1$. Hence also $P_t(A) = r$, by (Miller); but then it follows that r is 0 or 1; so whether or not A will be the case is already determined with certainty by the facts at this time.[17]

If we add to (Miller) the synchronic—I should think, uncontroversial—part of (Reflection) we can now find a proposition which I can admit to be quite possibly true but which I know I could never fully believe. Suppose I have a coin in my hand which I am about to toss and I have picked it at random from a box that contained one fair coin and one magician's coin, the latter having a two-to-one chance of landing heads up. My present subjective probability for the coin in my hand to land heads up is, accordingly, the average of the two objective chances, $1/2(1/2 + 2/3) = 7/12$. So my present subjective probability for the proposition (the chance of heads equals 1/2 and my personal probability for it equals 7/12) equals 1/2. But of course I could never fully believe that conjunction; for, by (Miller), if I fully believed the first conjunct, my personal probability would automatically equal 1/2 too. [More rigorously: (Miller) and the synchronic ($x = 0$) part of (Reflection) together entail that if $P_t(\text{ch}_t(A) = r \ \& \ p_t(A) = s) = 1$ then $r = s$.]

So now we have found a proposition Y to which we can indeed assign a positive subjective probability, but which we cannot conditionalize on. Hence it is clear that $P(X|Y)$ is not to be thought of as the probability we would accord X should we learn that Y. The proposal for defending (Reflection) made at the beginning of this section has failed. But we have learned something useful. Even while adhering to (Reflection) we can to some extent express doubts about the correctness or reliability of our future opinions. For example, without violating (Reflection) I can say: "It does not seem unlikely to me that Table Hands' objective chance of winning tomorrow will be considerably less than my subjective probability for that event tomorrow morning."

Those who believe that we conditionalize on—hence raise to subjective certainty— propositions that we take as evidence, do not have this sort of consolation. For presumably we mean to take as evidence at $t + x$ only propositions A whose truth value becomes settled at or by that time, which implies that A is equivalent to $\text{ch}_{t+x}(A) = 1$. To say, therefore, that it is not totally unlikely that tomorrow morning I shall take A as evidence even though its chance is less than 1 is to violate (Reflection) by implication. A simple one-place probability function will never allow us to characterize the epistemic state of someone who says that he may become certain of a proposition but will not reject as absurd the possibility that future evidence will prove him wrong.[18] But it remains that in the preceding paragraphs we have seen considerable leeway for the person who wishes to be diachronically coherent and yet express doubt about the reliability of his future opinions considered as indicators of what will happen.

Leaving this (at least somewhat) happy digression, let us turn to another proposal to defend (Reflection). Could it not be entailed by some more general principle about conveyance of factual information? Perhaps it would not be rational to have a state of opinion that it was not rational to convey, in so many words, to a suitable audience. But suppose I were to tell you: "If I say tomorrow morning that it will rain, there will still be a 50/50 chance that it will not." You would certainly look at me askance and reply that, in that case, you might as well not listen to me tomorrow morning. But then my assertion just now has taken away all value from my words of tomorrow morning about rain. We can see this as pathological if we take the following point of view: my expressions of opinion make statements about my mental state and, more particularly, about the aspect of my mental state which is meant to be a reliable indicator of relevant facts outside it. The value of these descriptions of my mental state—whether in the terminology of belief or of subjective probability—to my audience lies exactly in the information thus conveyed indirectly about what it is meant to be a reliable indicator of. Hence I have made a statement that cancels the normal conversational force of my statements of that sort.

I do not think that these reflections are entirely without force or relevance to (Reflection), but, as they stand, the rationale is quite wrong, and they do not constitute a defense. There is some ambiguity in the common use of both 'say' and 'there is a chance'. The first can be used to mean "assert" in a sense that implies belief, or requires in some other way that the assertor believes what he asserts; and the terminology of chance is sometimes used simply to express degrees of credence. If we adopt these interpretations when reading the example, it certainly has something putatively wrong with it, but that something is exactly that it implies a violation of (Reflection). Hence it does not manage to point to a more general principle to help us. If on the other hand we understand 'say' as "utter the words" or 'chance' as "objective chance," we have merely a statement that expresses doubt about the reliability of either my mental states or feelings or my words as indicators of rain. Although it is true that the audience is thereafter well advised not to take my words or opinion into account when deciding about the need for umbrellas, no principles or conversational maxims have been contravened. Such statements about my reliability as indicator of rain, need no more be logically odd or conversationally pathological than similar statements about the reliability of my watch. The audience is simply, in strict accordance with our conventions of conversational cooperation, advised to listen to the radio weather report (respectively, time signal) rather than to my guesses about this particular topic.

Voluntarism as solution

"for what else is it to believe but to assent to the truth of what is propounded? Consent being a matter of the will ..."
(St. Augustine, *On the Spirit and the Letter*, 54)

159

The problem raised by the apparent need for principle of Reflection is, it seems to me, one of interpretation. A tenable interpretation of personal probability must either sever the link between rationality and coherence or else entail that Reflection is a form of epistemic judgment to which we must assent. It seems to me that among the debris in the preceding section there are some usable materials for the construction of an interpretation of the latter sort. The interpretation will first of all consider how the probability calculus can be viewed as a logic of epistemic judgments, and then consider exactly what such judgments are.

Let us begin with two challenges, one very familiar, the other due to Gilbert Harman. The first is that we simply do not have such a finely graded state of opinion as numerically precise subjective probabilities require. This challenge is answered by the admission that our personal probabilities are to some extent vague. Rain tomorrow seems no less likely to me than a tossed coin's coming up heads four times in a row, no more likely than at least one of four tossed coins' coming up heads. My state of opinion is no more precise than this. Harman's challenge goes deeper. Since probabilities, unlike truth values, are not functional—$P(A\&B)$ is not a function of $P(A)$ and $P(B)$—, storing the information contained in an assignment of probabilities to sentences of even a "small" simple language quickly gets beyond the storage capacity of the mind. With vague probabilities the information storage problem gets worse, because each sentence now has two numbers assigned—a lower and upper probability. To circumvent this information explosion we must characterize a person's opinions as consisting of some which are more or less directly accessible plus all those to which the former commit him, on pain of violation of some higher criteria of rationality to which he subscribes.

No one, we say, has numerically precise degrees of belief. But at a given time I may, more or less consciously or overtly, make or be committed to a number of judgments of such forms as: it seems likely to rain, it seems as likely as not to snow, it seems likely to me—supposing it rains—that it will be cold, and so forth. These judgments express my opinions on various matters of fact; let us call them *epistemic judgments*. A certain family of these, accordingly, characterize my present state of opinion; they are *mine*. Unless I am very opinionated, they are not many, and they leave gaps: they may for instance not include, either directly or by implication, any judgment nontrivially comparing in such terms as the above, rain and newspaper reports of murder, or Darwin's theories and Einstein's.

It will be clear how an assignment of numbers to propositions could in principle reflect these judgments, because we are all familiar with their counterparts in the terminology of subjective probability. A person has, in the technical sense, a *coherent* state of opinion only if there exists at least one probability function P such that $P(A) > P(B)$ if it seems more likely to him that A than that B, $P(A) \geq P(B)$ if it seems no less likely to him that A than that B, $P(A|C) > P(B|C)$ if on the supposition that C it seems more likely to him that A than that B, and so forth. Let us say that such a function P *satisfies* his judgments. The lack of precision and other gaps in his judgments entail now that, if any one probability function P satisfies his judgments, then so do a number of others. The class of all that do, we may call the *representor* for his state of opinion. Unless that representation contains only a single function, we also say that his degrees of belief, or subjective probabilities, are to some extent vague or indeterminate.[19]

We can now introduce a quite exact concept of implication among epistemic judgments for coherent states of opinion: if all probability functions satisfying each of a class X of judgments also satisfy judgment J, then (and only then) does X *coherently entail J*. It is exactly in such a case, when a person overtly makes all the judgments in X, which we say that he is also committed to J, on pain of incoherence.

Obviously a coherent state of opinion can be re-expressed in judgments formulated in the language of vague probability theory. "My subjective probability for A is no less than x, no greater than y" characterizes my state of opinion correctly if and only if, for every member P of my representor, $x \leq P(A) \leq y$. Similarly for subjective conditional probability, subjective odds, and subjective expectation. We see, therefore, that subjective-probability talk is merely the formulation, in sophisticated and flexible language, of judgments that have exactly the same status as, and indeed are entailed by, the epistemic judgments with which we began our discussion—for coherent states of opinion.

Therefore, we must now look closely at exactly what an epistemic judgment is. Suppose I express my opinion as follows: "It seems more likely to me—supposing that it stays this cold—that it will snow than that it will rain." What exactly have I just done? One answer, the answer I wish to dispute, is that I have just made an autobiographical statement, describing my own psychological state.[20] Certainly, if you hear me say the above, you will be able to infer something about my psychological state, and perhaps this fact even provided the motive for my utterance. But that is very different from saying that what I did was to make an autobiographical statement of fact. (I belabor the point only because John Austin is not generally discussed in writings on subjective probability.) Consider this story: yesterday morning I said to you "I promise you a horse by nightfall." This morning you point out that I have not got you a horse, and you accuse me of the heinous immorality of breaking my promise. Not at all, I say, I am guilty only of the lesser sin of lying; what I said yesterday morning was only a false autobiographical statement, for I was not in fact promising you a horse.

The sentence "I promised you a horse yesterday" is clearly a statement of fact, the fact that became true yesterday when I made the promise (perhaps by saying "I promise you a horse"). I wish to make the same sort of distinction with respect to the terminology of personal probability. In the preceding sections I already introduced a symbolic distinction, with the capital and lower-case distinction in $P(p_t(A) = r) = s$. If I were to say that, I would be expressing my opinion concerning a factual proposition about what my opinion was (is, will be) at time t. As analogue, consider "I promise you that I will not make you any promises concerning future dividends until I have carefully looked into the chances of success."

I do not mean that to express an opinion is to make a promise. The latter is a sort of ceremony in which I take upon myself, bring into being, an obligation to someone else. Two other alternatives suggest themselves: to express my opinion is to express my feelings, or it is to express an intention or commitment. There is something to be said for the first. A promise properly made will *follow* the agent's realization that he is willing, and able, to enter the corresponding contract or obligation. But expressing one's feelings generally involves, and may be the only means for, exploration of those feelings—I know that I feel strongly about this subject, but I don't know what I feel until I begin to talk or act or paint or write, and I discover almost as much about what I feel as the onlooker does. In this respect expressing one's opinions is often less like promising and more like emotive expression. But in this respect, expression of intentions is often the same. A difference is that, both in the case of opinion and of intention, and not in the case of feeling, the act of expression does not typically turn from genuine expression into something else, if one deliberately repeats the act.

Suppose, for example, that I have looked at my calibration score, found that I have generally overestimated the chances of rain, and now have exactly the same feelings on the question of rain as I did yesterday. Then my judgment about rain will now be different from what it was yesterday, for this judgment does not have the function of merely expressing my feelings—properly made, formulating my judgment follows deliberation.

It seems then that, of the alternatives examined, epistemic judgments are most like expressions of intention. I may express an intention either by simply stating the outcome of what I have decided upon ("You will be my successor") or by choosing a form of words traditionally suited to such expression ("You shall be my successor"). In either case, it is conveyed that I have made a decision, have formed an intention, am committed to a certain stance or program or course of action. There is no direct obligation to anyone else to fulfill this intention, but I have, as it were, entered a contract with myself. If I express this intention to an audience, then, just as in the case of a promise, I invite them to rely on my integrity and to feel assured that they now have knowledge of a major consideration in all my subsequent deliberation and courses of action. In this respect, expressing a considered judgment is similar.

Returning now to the principle (Reflection), consider the following analogies. I say, "I promise you a horse," and you ask, "And what are the chances that you'll get me one"? I say, "I am starting a diet today," and you ask, "And how likely is it that you won't overeat tomorrow"? In both cases, the *first* reply I must give is "You heard me"! To express anything but a full commitment to stand behind my promises and intentions, is to undermine my own status as a person of integrity and, hence, my entire activity of avowal. This applies equally in the case of conditional questions. "If you promise to marry me, will you actually do it"? "If you decide to join our crusade, will you really participate"? In the first instance these questions are not invitations to an academic discussion of the objective chances, but challenges or probes of one's avowed intentions and commitments. It is confusing that the same words can be used for either purpose—not confusing in actual dialogue where contextual factors disambiguate, but confusing in written discussion.

Avowal, qua avowal, has its own constraints, which affect the logic of expressions of avowal. In none of the above cases do we have a simple way of characterizing what it is to be "false" to one's commitment. Having made a promise, I also have some obligation to prevent circumstances that would make it impossible to keep the promise. Having decided on a program of regular exercise, I have obliged myself to some extent to prevent travel arrangements, hangovers, lack of proper clothes and shoes, and so forth, that would interfere. It may not be easy for the onlooker, or even for me, to allocate blame or to decide whether I was false to myself or merely a victim of circumstances. In the same way, if I express my opinion, I invite the world to rely on my integrity and to infer from this what advice to myself and anyone else in like circumstances, concerning the carrying of umbrellas, purchase of insurance policies, entering wagers, I would presently consider the best. Only in clinically hygienic cases would it be uncontroversially clear whether or not I really stood behind my expressed opinion. But that is so in the case of any expression of commitment or intention.

I conclude that my integrity, qua judging agent, requires that, if I am presently asked to express my opinion about whether A will come true, on the supposition that

I will think it likely tomorrow morning, I must stand by my own cognitive *engagement* as much as I must stand by my own expressions of commitment of any sort. I can rationally and objectively discuss the possibility of a discrepancy between objective chance and my previsions. But I can no more say that I regard *A* as unlikely on the supposition that tomorrow morning I shall express my high expectation of *A*, than I can today make the same statement on the supposition that tomorrow morning I shall promise to bring it about that *A*. To do so would mean that I am now less than fully committed (a) to giving due regard to the felicity conditions for this act, or (b) to standing by the commitments I shall overtly enter.

Traditional epistemology revisited

This paper began with a statement of what I regard as a traditional epistemological view in philosophy of science: that we may rationally decide or come to believe propositions, hypotheses, theories which are not entailed (and which we ourselves do not regard as being made certain by) the evidence at hand. In addition—still spelling out this view—evidence itself is only the body of propositions that we have taken as evidence, and what we take to be evidence on a particular occasion may in fact be false. The refutation, along familiar Bayesian lines, was quick and sure and deadly: anyone who even regards himself as not totally unlikely to do what this view calls rational, is diachronically incoherent: vulnerable in that he implicitly regards as fair, disastrous combinations of wagers.

But then we also saw that the refutation is blocked by adherence to a principle, which goes well beyond the probability calculus, but which is equally required for the diachronic coherence of agents that Bayesian writers regard as rational. So the refutation is no refutation: we need not stop at conditionalization on the evidence on pain of incoherence, as long as we adhere to this principle, which even the strict conditionalizer himself (and also the less committal observer described by Jeffrey) needs equally badly. Of course, the more improbable the proposition we decide to believe, or equivalently, the more we raise our credence in an uncertain proposition, the more risk we take. But that is merely a matter of degree, and there is no violation of coherence or any other criterion of rationality. Any accusation of epistemic extravagance is in any case to be met, by Jamesian and Bayesian alike, with the cool judgment "My credence that *A* is true, on the supposition that tomorrow I shall accord it credence to degree *r*, equals *r*." We can put the matter in either of two ways, depending on how we value the epithet of "Bayesian". Either that non-Bayesian epistemic behavior is defensible by exactly the same defense needed for Bayesian behavior; or, if you like, that apparently non-Bayesian behavior described by James and other traditional epistemologists, turns out to be, after all, entirely acceptable as far as Bayesian standards go. It may be a bit scary to think that such leaps of faith as James described in "The Will to Believe" or St. Augustine in "On Belief in Things Unseen"—he included his own belief in the existence of the Ocean—are not ruled out by the Bayesian's standards of coherence. But it is also a welcome thought, if we regard considerations of coherence as eminently rational, yet hope to find room for independence and enterprise in forming our world picture.

But then there is still the matter of the defense of the defence. I have argued that it is in fact indefensible if we regard the epistemic judgment—whether formulated in probabilistic or more qualitative terms—as a statement of autobiographical fact. The principle (Reflection) can be defended, namely as a form of commitment to stand behind

163

one's own commitments, if we give a different, voluntarist interpretation of epistemic judgment. I call it "voluntarist," because it makes judgment in general, and subjective probability in particular, a matter of cognitive commitment, intention, *engagement*. Belief is a matter of the will.

Notes

* Originally published in *Journal of Philosophy*, 81 (1984), pp. 235–56. Copyright © 1984 The Journal of Philosophy, Inc. Reprinted by permission of The Journal of Philosophy and Bas C. van Fraassen.

† The author wishes to thank the National Science Foundation and Princeton University for support of his research and sabbatical leave, and the participants of Richard Jeffrey's seminar (especially David Lewis) for much helpful discussion of a preliminary draft of sections II and III [8.2 AND 8.3], circulated under the title "A Puzzle for Both True and Partial Believers" in November, 1982. Thanks is also due for help to improve this paper, to Nancy Cartwright, Roger Cooke, Paul Fitzgerald, William Harper, and Zeno Swijtinga, and especially to Isaac Levi and Brian Skyrms who prepared detailed commentaries.

1 "The Will to Believe." Page references will be to his *Essays in Pragmatism* (New York: Hafner, 1948).

2 *Op. cit.* p. 100. Note that on the next page James grants that scientists doing science proceed as Clifford has it. This concession may have been for the sake of argument (for compare the skepticism about the reach of science on pages 23, 25, and 38), rather than a genuine subscription to the objectivity of strict induction from the evidence. Recent philosophy of science has in any case not been so sanguine.

3 James's view may be attacked on the flank by arguing that belief is not a matter of the will at all, not under voluntary control. Voluntarism with respect to belief is usually attacked in its naive versions and defended in its sophisticated formulation; I will of course not suggest that we can believe just any proposition at will. Cf. James, *op. cit.* p. 90; Barbara Winters, "Believing at Will," *Journal of Philosophy*, LXXVI, 5 (May 1979): 243–256; and Robert Holyer, "Belief and Will Revisited," *Dialogue*, XXII, 2 (June 1983): 273–290.

4 Some common objections, such as that we do not have numerically precise degrees of certainty and uncertainty, are, I think, easily met (see, further, section V [8.5] below). But if the reader is willing to conclude that it is the idea of subjective probability that is at fault, he does not need my present defense of traditional epistemology.

5 This term is a reference to the so-called "Dutch book theorem." The usual or synchronic Dutch book argument establishes the obedience of degrees of belief to the probability calculus as a criterion of rationality ("coherence") for one's state of opinion at a single time. The betting scheme I am about to describe is part of David Lewis's diachronic Dutch book argument to justify conditionalization as the correct rule for transforming prior into posterior degrees of belief [see P. Teller, "Conditionalization, Observation, and Change of Preference" in W. L. Harper and C. A. Hooker, *Foundations of Probability Theory*, vol. 1 (Boston: Reidel, 1976); Lewis (Chapter 6 in this volume)]. Bayes himself had given a similar argument, and a more sophisticated theorem has been proved by Glen Shafer; see his "Bayes' Two Arguments for Conditioning," *Annals of Statistics*, X (1982): 1075–1089, and "A Subjective Approach to Conditional Probability" *Journal of Philosophical Logic*, XII, 3 (November 1983): 453–466.

6 To see what the total cost is of I and II together, calculate

$$P(\sim H \& E) + xP(\sim E) = P(\sim H|E)P(E) + xP(\sim E) = x(P(E) + P(\sim E)) = x$$

7 E implies that my probability for H tomorrow morning will be 1/3, and so my probability for $\sim H$ then is 2/3. We have $x = 0.3 \div 0.4 = 3/4$ and $y = x - 2/3 = 1/12$. The costs of the bets are 0.3 for (I), $x(1 - P(E)) = (3/4)(0.6) = 0.45$ for bet (II), and $yP(E) = (1/12)(0.4) = (1/30)$ for (III), for a total cost of $(3/4) + (1/30)$.

8 From footnote 7 we know that the initial total cost was $(3/4) + (1/30)$. If E is false, I collect only $x = (3/4)$. If E is true, I collect 1/12 on the third bet, but then I receive in addition only what I then consider a fair price for the bet against Table Hands' winning, namely 2/3; so my total return equals 3/4 again.

9 When conditionalized on A, the function P becomes the function P' such that $P'(X) = P(X|A)$ $= P(X \& A) \div P(A)$ for all propositions X. This can be done only if $P(A)$ is not zero.

10 A third possibility was advocated in discussion by David Lewis: that the standard of rationality exemplified by Dutch-book Invulnerability applies to a certain sort of ideally rational agent, who not only believes himself to be, but is, infallible with respect to perception, and which we explicitly realize ourselves not to be. But this leaves us still with the task of constructing an epistemological theory that does apply to our own case.

11 "Higher Order Degrees of Belief" in D. H. Mellor, ed. *Prospects for Pragmatism: Essays in Honour of F. P. Ramsey* (New York: Cambridge, 1980), pp. 109–137, and Appendix 2 of his *Causal Necessity* (New Haven, Conn.: Yale, 1980).

12 In Skyrms' article the synchronic form $(x = 0)$ is advocated; the discussion contains diachronic examples as well, but they concern the supposition that the agent *learns* his posterior credence, whereupon the synchronic form applies.

13 See my "Calibration: A Frequentist Justification of Personal Probability," in L. Laudan and R. Cohen, eds., *Philosophy, Physics, Psychoanalysis* (Boston: Reidel, 1983). Please note well that calibration by itself is not a good scoring rule, and the criterion explained below does not entail that better calibration is always better *tout court*.

14 It would not help to say that $P(A|B)$ is the probability that A would have for me if B were to become my total new evidence, just because that would tell us nothing about what $P(A|B)$ is when B is not the sort of proposition that could be one's total new evidence. Instead I interpret conditional probability in a way that has no logical connection with learning. To say that $P(A) = 2/3$ is to say that, to me, A is twice as likely to be the case as not—this re-expresses the opinion in terms of personal odds for A as against $\sim A$. Similarly, $P(A|B) = 2/3$ expresses my personal odds for $(A \& B)$ as against $(\sim A \& B)$.

15 See my "A Temporal Framework for Conditionals and Chance," *Philosophical Review*, LXXXIX, 1 (January 1980), 91–108, and reprinted in W. L. Harper, *Ifs* (Boston: Reidel, 1981); and David Lewis, "A Subjectivist's Guide to Objective Chance," *ibid.*, pp. 267–298 (reprinted as Chapter 27 in this volume).

16 See Richard Jeffrey's review of articles by David Miller *et al., Journal of Symbolic Logic*, XXXV, 1 (March 1970): 124–127.

17 If we generalize (Miller) to $P_t(A| \text{ch}_{t+x}(A) = r) = r$, then we can derive the stronger result that if the truth value of A becomes settled at time $t + x$ [this truth value then equals $\text{ch}_{t+x}(A)$, and must be 0 or 1], the agent cannot at t believe with certainty that the present chance of A is something different from 0 or 1 if he also believes that A will be true (respectively false) at its settling time ("there are no crystal balls").

18 This is not meant as an argument against conditionalization as a rational procedure; more sophisticated machinery than single one-place probability functions can be explored. This problem of how to represent certainty without dogmatism, which I shall not go into further here, is broached in Isaac Levi, *The Enterprise of Knowledge* (Cambridge, Mass.: MIT Press, 1980). It is not a problem if full certainty is not rational.

19 This emphasis on vagueness, and this sort of way to represent it, is especially to be found in Isaac Levi's and Richard Jeffrey's writings. For more technical details see also my "Rational Belief and Probability Kinematics," *Philosophy of Science*, XLVII, 2 (June 1980): 165–187.

20 It is never easy to gauge one's agreement with other writers, but I think that in this I side with de Finetti—see p. 189 of his *Probability, Induction and Statistics* (New York: Wiley, 1972)—against Ramsey—see "Truth and Probability" in his *Foundations of Mathematics and Other Essays* (New York: Humanities Press, 1950) (reprinted as Chapter 2 in this volume). I would also like to refer to Stuart Hampshire's discussions of the connections between intention and knowledge or belief, in his *Freedom of the Individual* (Princeton, N.J.: University Press, 1975). Let me emphasize, however, with reference to the examples used here, that I regard acceptance of scientific theories as involving both more and less than belief; see my *The Scientific Image* (New York: Oxford, 1980), pp. 12/3, 80–83, 198–200.

9

DIACHRONIC RATIONALITY*

Patrick Maher

We have seen that Bayesian confirmation theory rests on two assumptions: (1) That rational scientists have probabilities for scientific hypotheses, and (2) the principle of conditionalization. The latter is a *diachronic* principle of rationality, because it concerns how probabilities at one time should be related to probabilities at a later time.

Chapters 1–4 [of *Betting on Theories*] gave an extended argument in support of (1). This chapter will examine what can be said on behalf of (2). I will reject the common Bayesian view that conditionalization is a universal requirement of rationality, but argue that nevertheless it should hold in normal scientific contexts.

I begin by discussing a putative principle of rationality known as Reflection. A correct understanding of the status of this principle will be the key to my account of the status of conditionalization.

Reflection

Suppose you currently have a (personal) probability function p, and let R_q denote that at some future time $t + x$ you will have probability function q. Goldstein (1983) and van Fraassen (1984) have claimed that the following identity is a requirement of rationality:[1]

$$p(\cdot | R_q) = q(\cdot).$$

Following van Fraassen (1984), I will refer to this identity as *Reflection*.

As an example of what Reflection requires, suppose you are sure that you cannot drive safely after having ten drinks. Suppose further that you are sure that after ten drinks, you would be sure (wrongly, as you now think) that you could drive safely. Then you violate Reflection. For if p is your current probability function, q the one you would have after ten drinks, and D the proposition that you can drive safely after having ten drinks, we have

$$p(D | R_q) \approx 0 < 1 \approx q(D).$$

Reflection requires $p(D | R_q) = q(D) \approx 1$. Thus you should now be sure that you would not be in error, if in the future you become sure that you can drive safely after having ten drinks.

The Dutch book argument

Why should we think Reflection is a requirement of rationality? According to Goldstein and van Fraassen, this conclusion is established by a diachronic Dutch book argument. A diachronic Dutch book argument differs from a regular Dutch book argument in that the bets are not all offered at the same time. But like a regular Dutch book argument, it purports to show that anyone who violates the condition is willing to accept bets that together produce a sure loss, and hence is irrational.

Since the diachronic Dutch book argument for Reflection has been stated in full generality elsewhere (Goldstein 1983, van Fraassen 1984, Skyrms 1987b), I will here merely illustrate how it works. Suppose, then, that you violate Reflection with respect to drinking and driving, in the way indicated above. For ease of computation, I will assume that $p(D) = 0$ and $q(D) = 1$. (Using less extreme values would not change the overall conclusion.) Let us further assume that your probability that you will have ten drinks tonight is 1/2. The Dutch bookie tries to make a sure profit from you by first offering a bet b_1 whose payoff in units of utility is[2]

$$-2 \text{ if } DR_q; \quad 2 \text{ if } \overline{D}R_q; \quad -1 \text{ if } \overline{R}_q.$$

For you at this time, $p(DR_q) = 0$, and $p(\overline{D}R_q) = p(\overline{R}_q) = 1/2$. Thus the expected utility of b_1 is 1/2. We are taking the utility of the status quo to be 0, and so the bookie figures that you will accept this bet. If you accept the bet and do not get drunk (R_q is false), you lose one unit of utility. If you accept and do get drunk (R_q is true), the bookie offers you b_2, whose payoff in units of utility is

$$1 \text{ if } D; \quad -3 \text{ if } \overline{D}.$$

Since you are now certain D is true, accepting b_2 increases your expected utility, and so the bookie figures you will accept it. But now, if D is true, you gain 1 from b_2 but lose 2 from b_1, for an overall loss of 1. And if D is false, you gain 2 from b_1 but lose 3 from b_2, again losing 1 overall. Thus no matter what happens, you lose.[3]

Counter examples

Despite this argument, there are compelling prima facie counterexamples to Reflection. Indeed, the drinking/driving example is already a prima facie counterexample; it seems that you would be right to now discount any future opinions you might form while intoxicated – contrary to what Reflection requires. But we can make the counterexample even more compelling by supposing you are *sure* that tonight you will have ten drinks. It then follows from Reflection that you should *now* be sure that you can drive safely after having ten drinks.

> **Proof.** $p(D) = p(D|R_q)$, since $p(R_q) = 1$
> $= q(D)$, by Reflection
> $= 1$.

This result seems plainly wrong. Nor does it help to say that a rational person should not drink so much; for it may be that the drinking you know you will do tonight will not be voluntary.

A defender of Reflection might try responding to such counterexamples by claiming that the person you would be when drunk is not the same person who is now sober. If you were absolutely sure of this, then for you $p(R_q) = 0$, since R_q asserts that *you* will come to have probability function q.[4] In that case, $p(\cdot|R_q)$ may be undefined and the counterexample thereby avoided. But this is a desperate move. Nobody I know gives any real credence to the claim that having ten drinks, and as a result thinking he or she can drive safely, would destroy his or her personal identity. They are certainly not sure that this is true.

Alternatively, defenders of Reflection may bite the bullet, and declare that even when it is anticipated that one's probabilities will be influenced by drugs, Reflection should be satisfied. Perhaps nothing is too bizarre for such a die-hard defender of Reflection to accept. But it may be worth pointing out a peculiar implication of the position here being embraced: It entails that rationality requires taking mind-altering drugs, in circumstances where that position seems plainly false. I will now show how that conclusion follows.

It is well known that under suitable conditions, gathering evidence increases the expected utility of subsequent choices, if it has any effect at all. The following conditions are sufficient:[5]

1 The evidence is "cost free"; that is, gathering it does not alter what acts are subsequently available, nor is any penalty incurred merely by gathering the evidence.
2 Reflection is satisfied for the shifts in probability that could result from gathering the evidence. That is to say, if p is your current probability function, then for any probability function q you could come to have as a result of gathering the evidence, $p(\cdot|R_q) = q(\cdot)$.
3 The decision to gather the evidence is not "symptomatic"; that is, it is not probabilistically relevant to states it does not cause.
4 Probabilities satisfy the axioms of probability, and choices maximize expected utility at the time they are made.

Now suppose you have the opportunity of taking a drug that will influence your probabilities in some way that is not completely predictable. The drug is cost free (in particular, it has no direct effect on your health or wealth), and the decision to take the drug is not symptomatic. Assume also that rationality requires condition 4 above to be satisfied. If Reflection is a general requirement of rationality, condition 2 should also be satisfied for the drug-induced shifts. Hence all four conditions are satisfied, and it follows that you cannot reduce your expected utility by taking this drug; and you may increase it.

For example, suppose a bookie is willing to bet with you on the outcome of a coin toss. You have the option of betting on heads or tails; you receive US$1 if you are right and lose US$2 if you are wrong. Currently your probability that the coin will land heads is 1/2, and so you now think the best thing to do is not bet. (I assume that your utility function is roughly linear for such small amounts of money.) But suppose you can take a drug that will make you certain of what the coin toss will be; you do not know in advance whether it will make you sure of heads or tails, and you antecedently think both results equally likely.[6] The drug is cost free, and you satisfy condition 4. Then if Reflection should hold with regard to the drug-induced shifts, you think you can make money by taking the drug. For after you take the drug, you will bet on the outcome you are then certain will result; and if you satisfy Reflection, you are now certain that bet will be successful. By contrast, if you do not take the drug, you do not expect to make a profit betting on this coin toss. Thus the principle of maximizing expected utility requires you to take the drug.

But in fact, it is clear that taking the drug need not be rational. You could perfectly rationally think that the bet you would make after taking the drug has only a 50–50 chance of winning, and hence that taking the drug is equivalent to choosing randomly to bet on heads or tails. Since thinking that violates Reflection, we have another reason to deny that Reflection is a requirement of rationality.

The fallacy

We now face a dilemma. On the one hand, we have a diachronic Dutch book argument to show that Reflection is a requirement of rationality. And on the other hand, we have strong reasons for saying that Reflection is *not* a requirement of rationality. There must be a mistake here somewhere.

In (Maher 1992), following Levi (1987), I argued that a sophisticated bettor who looks ahead will not accept the bets offered in the Dutch book argument for Reflection. The thought was that if you look ahead, you will see that accepting b_1 inevitably leads to a sure loss, and hence will refuse to take the first step down the primrose path. This diagnosis assumed that if you do not accept b_1, you will not be offered b_2. However, Skyrms (1993) points out that the bookie could offer b_2 if R_q obtains, regardless of whether b_1 has been accepted. Faced with this strategy, you do best (maximize expected utility) to accept b_1 as well, and thus ensure a sure loss.

So with Skyrms' emendation, the diachronic Dutch book argument does show that if you violate Reflection, you can be made to suffer a sure loss. Yet as Skyrms himself agrees, it is not necessarily rational to conform to Reflection. Thus we have to say that *susceptibility to a sure loss does not prove irrationality*. This conclusion may appear counterintuitive; but that appearance is an illusion, I will now argue.

We say that act *a dominates* act *b* if, in every state, the consequence of *a* is better than that of *b*. It is uncontroversial that it is irrational to choose an act that is dominated by some other available act. Call such an act *dominated*. One might naturally suppose that accepting a sure loss is a dominated act, and thereby irrational.

But consider this case: I have bet that it will not rain today. The deal, let us say, is that I lose US$1 if it rains and win US$1 otherwise. How I came to make this bet does not matter – perhaps it looked attractive to me at the time; perhaps I made it under duress. In any case, storm clouds are now gathering and I think I will lose the bet. I would now gladly accept a bet that pays me US$0.50 if it rains and in which I pay US$1.50 otherwise. If I did accept such a new bet, then together with the one I already have, I would be certain to lose US$0.50. So I am willing to accept a sure loss. But I am not thereby irrational. The sure loss of US$0.50 is better than a high probability of losing US$1. Note also that although I am willing to accept a sure loss, I am *not* willing to accept a dominated option. My options are shown in Figure 9.1. The first option, which gives the sure loss, is not dominated by the only other available act.

So we see that acceptance of a sure loss is not always a dominated act; and when it is not, acceptance of a sure loss can be rational. I suggest that the intuitive irrationality of accepting (or being willing to accept) a sure loss results from the false supposition that acceptance of a sure loss is always a dominated option, combined with the correct principle that it is irrational to accept (or be willing to accept) a dominated option.

	No rain	Rain
Accept 2nd bet	–$0.50	–$0.50
Don't accept	$1	–$1

Figure 9.1 Available options after accepting bet against rain.

Let us apply this to the Dutch book argument for Reflection. In the example of 'The Dutch book argument', you are now certain that accepting b_2 would result in a loss, and hence you prefer that you not accept it. However, you also know that you will accept it if you get drunk. This indicates that your willingness to accept b_2 when drunk is not something you are now able to reverse (for if you could, you would). Thus you are in effect now stuck with the fact that you will accept b_2 if you get drunk, that is, if R_q is true. Hence you are in effect now saddled with the bet

$$1 \text{ if } DR_q; \quad -3 \text{ if } \overline{D} \, R_q,$$

though it looks unattractive to you now. (This is analogous to the first bet in the rain example.) But you do have a choice about whether or not to accept b_1. Since b_1 pays

$$-2 \text{ if } DR_q; \quad 2 \text{ if } \overline{D}R_q; \quad -1 \text{ if } \overline{R}_q$$

your options and their payoffs are as in Figure 9.2. Accepting b_1 ensures that you suffer a sure loss; but it is not a dominated option. In fact, since $p(D) = 0$ and $p(R_q) = 1/2$, accepting b_1 reduced your expected loss from -1.5 to -1. So in this case, as in the rain example, the willingness to accept a sure loss does not involve willingness to accept a dominated option, and does not imply irrationality.

If there is any irrationality in this case, it lies in the potential future acceptance of b_2. But because that future acceptance is outside your present control, it is no reason to say that you are now irrational. Perhaps your future self would be irrational when drunk, but that is not our concern. Reflection is a condition on your present probabilities only, and what we have seen is that you are not irrational to now have the probabilities you do, even though having these probabilities means you are willing to accept a sure loss.

Let us say that a Dutch book *theorem* asserts that violation of some condition leaves one susceptible to a sure loss, while a Dutch book *argument* infers from the theorem that violation of the condition is irrational. In Section 4.6 [of *Betting on Theories*], the condition in question was satisfaction of the axioms of probability, and my claim in effect was that the argument fails because the theorem is false. In the present section, the condition in question has been Reflection, and my claim has been that here the Dutch

	DR_q	$\overline{D}R_q$	$\overline{R}_q$
Accept b_1	–1	–1	–1
Reject b_1	1	–3	0

Figure 9.2 Available options for Reflection violator.

book theorem is correct but the argument based on it is fallacious. Consequently, this argument provides no reason not to draw the obvious conclusion from the counter-examples in the preceding section: Reflection is not a requirement of rationality. (Christensen [1991] and Talbott [1991] arrive at the same conclusion by different reasoning.)

Integrity

Recognizing the implausibility of saying Reflection is a requirement of rationality, van Fraassen (1984, pp. 250–5) tried to bolster its plausibility with a voluntarist conception of personal probability judgments. He claimed that personal probability judgments express a kind of commitment; and he averred that integrity requires you to stand behind your commitments, including conditional ones. For example, he says your integrity would be undermined if you allowed that were you to promise to marry me, you still might not do it. And by analogy, he concludes that your integrity would be undermined if you said that your probability for A, given that tomorrow you give it probability r, is something other than r.

I agree that a personal probability judgment involves a kind of commitment; to make such a judgment is to accept a constraint on your choices between uncertain prospects. For example, if you judge A to be more probable than B, and if you prefer V\$1 to nothing, then faced with a choice between

(i)   V\$1 if A, nothing otherwise

and

(ii)   nothing if A, V\$1 otherwise,

you are committed to choosing (i). But of course, you are not thereby committed to making this choice at all times in the future; you can revise your probabilities without violating your commitment. The commitment is to make that choice *now*, if *now* presented with those options. But this being so, a violation of Reflection is not analogous to thinking you might break a marriage vow. To think you might break a marriage vow is to think you might break a commitment. To violate Reflection is to not *now* be committed to acting in accord with a future commitment, on the assumption that you will in the future have that commitment. The difference is that in violating Reflection, you are not thereby conceding that you might ever act in a way that is contrary to your commitments at the time of action. A better analogy for violations of Reflection would be saying that you now think you would be making a foolish choice, if you were to decide to marry me. In this case, as in the case of Reflection, you are not saying you could violate your commitments; you are merely saying you do not now endorse certain commitments, even on the supposition that you were to make them. Saying this does not undermine your status as a person of integrity.

Reflection and learning

In the typical case of taking a mind-altering drug, Reflection is violated, and we also feel that while the drug would shift our probabilities, we would not have *learned* anything in the process. For instance, if a drug will make you certain of the outcome of a coin toss, then under typical conditions the shift produced by the drug does not satisfy Reflection, and one also does not regard taking the drug as a way of *learning* the outcome of the coin toss.

Conversely, in typical cases where Reflection is satisfied, we do feel that the shift in probabilities would involve learning something. For example, suppose Persi is about to toss a coin, and suppose you know that Persi can (and will) toss the coin so that it lands how he wants, and that he will tell you what the outcome will be if you ask. Then asking Persi about the coin toss will, like taking the mind-altering drug, make you certain of the outcome of the toss. But in this case, Reflection will be satisfied, and we can say that by asking Persi you will *learn* how the coin is going to land.

What makes the difference between these cases is not that a drug is involved in one and testimony in the other. This can be seen by varying the examples. Suppose you think Persi really has no idea how the coin will land but has such a golden tongue that if you talked to him you would come to believe him; in this case, a shift caused by talking to Persi will not satisfy Reflection, and you will not think that by talking to him you will learn the outcome of the coin toss (even though you will become sure of some outcome). Conversely, you might think that if you take the drug, a benevolent genie will influence the coin toss so that it agrees with what the drug would make you believe; in this case, the shift in probabilities caused by taking the drug will satisfy Reflection, and you will think that by taking the drug you will learn the outcome of the coin toss.

These considerations lead me to suggest that regarding a potential shift in probability as a learning experience is the same thing as satisfying Reflection in regard to that shift. Symbolically: You regard the shift from p to q as a learning experience just in case $p(\cdot|R_q) = q(\cdot)$.[7]

Shifts that do not satisfy Reflection, though not learning experiences in the sense just defined, may still involve some learning. For example, if q is the probability function you would have after taking the drug that makes you sure of the outcome of the coin toss, you may think that in shifting to q you would learn that you took the drug but not learn the outcome of the coin toss. In general, what you think you would learn in shifting from p to q is represented by the difference between p and $(\cdot|R_q)$.[8] When Reflection is satisfied, what is learned is represented by the difference between p and q, and we call the whole shift a learning experience.

Learning, so construed, is not limited to cases in which new empirical evidence is acquired. You may have no idea what is the square root of 289, but you may also think that if you pondered it long enough you would come to concentrate your probability on some particular number, and that potential shift may well satisfy Reflection. In this case, you would regard the potential shift as a learning experience, though no new empirical evidence has been acquired. On the other hand, any shift in probability that is thought to be due solely to the influence of evidence is necessarily regarded as a learning experience. Thus satisfaction of Reflection is necessary, but not sufficient, for regarding a shift in probability as due to empirical evidence.

A defender of Reflection might think of responding to the counterexamples by limiting the principle to shifts of a certain kind. But the observations made in this section show that such a response will not help. If Reflection were said to be a requirement of rationality only for shifts caused in a certain way (e.g., by testimony rather than drugs), then there would still be counterexamples to the principle. And if Reflection were said to be a requirement of rationality for shifts that are regarded as learning experiences, or as due to empirical evidence, then the principle would be one that it is impossible to violate, and hence vacuous as a principle of rationality.[9]

Reflection and rationality

Although there is nothing irrational about violating Reflection, it is often irrational to implement those potential shifts that violate Reflection. That is to say, while one can rationally have $p(\cdot|R_q) \neq q(\cdot)$, it will in such cases often be irrational to choose a course of action that might result in acquiring the probability function q. The coin-tossing example of the section entitled 'Counterexamples' provides an illustration of this. Let H denote that the coin lands heads, and let q be the probability function you would have if you took the drug, and it made you certain of H. Then if you think taking the drug gives you only a random chance of making a successful bet, $p(H|R_q) = .5 < q(H) = 1$, and you violate Reflection; but then you would be irrational to take the drug, since the expected return from doing so is $(1/2)(\$1) - (1/2)(\$2) < 0$.[10]

This observation can be generalized, and made more precise, as follows. Let d and d' be two acts; for example, d might be the act of taking the drug in the coin-tossing case, and d' the act of not taking the drug. Assume that

(i) Any shift in probability after choosing d' would satisfy Reflection.

In the coin-tossing case, this will presumably be satisfied; if q' is the probability function you would have if you decided not to take the drug, q' will not differ much from p, and in particular $p(H|R_{q'}) = q'(H) = p(H) = .5$.
Assume also that

(ii) d and d' influence expected utility only via their influence on what subsequent choices maximize expected utility.

More fully: Choosing d or d' may have an impact on your probability function, and thereby influence your subsequent choices; but (ii) requires that they not influence expected utility in any other way. So there must not be a reward or penalty attached directly to having any of the probability functions that could result from choosing d or d'; nor can the choice of d or d' alter what subsequent options are available. This condition will also hold in the coin-tossing example if the drug is free and has no deleterious effects on health and otherwise the situation is fairly normal.[11]
Assume further that

(iii) If anything would be learned about the states by choosing d, it would also be learned by choosing d'.

What I mean by (iii) is that the following four conditions are all satisfied. Here Q is the set of all probability functions that you could come to have if you chose d.

(a) You are sure there is a fact about what probability function you would have if you chose d; that is, you give probability 1 to the proposition that for some q, the counterfactual conditional $d \rightarrow R_q$ is true.
(b) For all $q \in Q$ there is a probability function q' such that $p(d' \rightarrow R_{q'}|d \rightarrow R_q) = 1$.

173

(c) There is a set S of states of nature that are suitable for calculating the expected utility of the acts that will be available after the choice between d and d' is made. (What this requires is explained in the first paragraph of the proof given in Appendix A of *Betting on Theories*.)

(d) For all $q \in Q$, and for q' related to q as in (b), and for all $s \in S$, $p(s|R_q) = p(s|R_{q'})$.

In the coin-tossing example, condition (a) can be assumed to hold: Presumably the drug is deterministic, so that there is a fact about what probability function you would have if you took the drug, though you do not know in advance what that fact is. Condition (b) holds trivially in the coin-tossing example, because not taking the drug would leave you with the same probability function q' regardless of what effect the drug would have. Condition (c) is satisfied by taking $S = \{H, \overline{H}\}$. And it is a trivial exercise to show that (d) holds, since

$$p(H|R_q) = p(H) = 1/2 = p(H|R_{q'}).$$

The coin-tossing example thus satisfies condition (iii). We could say that in this example, you learn nothing about the states whether you choose d or d'.

Also assume that

(iv) d and d' have no causal influence on the states S mentioned in (c).

In the coin-tossing example, neither taking the drug nor refusing it has any causal influence on how the coin lands; and so (iv) is satisfied.

Finally, assume that

(v) d and d' are not evidence for events they have no tendency to cause.

In the coin-tossing example, (iv) and (v) together entail that $p(H|d) = p(H|d') = 1/2$, which is what one would expect to have in this situation.

Theorem. *If conditions (i)–(v) are known to hold, then the expected utility of d' is not less than that of d, and may be greater.*

So it would always be rational to choose d', but it may be irrational to choose d. The proof is given in Appendix A.

The theorem can fail when the stated conditions do not hold. For one example of this, suppose you are convinced there is a superior being who gives eternal bliss to all and only those who are certain that pigs can fly. Suppose also that there is a drug that, if you take it, will make you certain that pigs can fly. If q is the probability function you would have after taking this drug, and F is the proposition that pigs can fly, then $q(F) = 1$. Presumably $p(F|R_q) = p(F) \approx 0$. So the shift resulting from taking this drug violates Reflection. On the other hand, not taking the drug would leave your current probability essentially unchanged. But in view of the reward attached to being certain pigs can fly, it would (or at least, could) be rational to take the drug and thus implement a violation of Reflection.[12] Here the result fails, because condition (ii) does not hold: Taking the drug influences your utility other than via its influence on your subsequent decisions.

174

To illustrate another way in which the result may fail, suppose you now think there is a 90 percent chance that Persi knows how the coin will land, but that after talking to him you would be certain that what he told you was true. Again letting H denote that the coin lands heads, and letting q_H be the probability function you would have if Persi told you the coin will land heads, we have $p(H|R_{q_H}) = 0.9$, while $q_H(H) = 1$. Similarly for $q_{\bar{H}}$. Thus talking to Persi implements a shift that violates Reflection. If you do not talk to Persi, you will have probability function q' which, so far as H is concerned, is identical to your current probability function p; so $p(H|R_{q'}) = q'(H) = .5$. Thus not talking to Persi avoids implementing a shift that violates Reflection. Your expected return from talking to Persi is

$$(0.9)(\$1) + (0.1)(-\$2) = \$0.70.$$

Since you will not bet if you do not talk to Persi, the expected return from not talking to him is zero. Hence talking to Persi maximizes your expected monetary return. And assuming your utility function is approximately linear for small amounts of money, it follows that talking to Persi maximizes expected utility. Here the theorem fails because condition (iii) fails. By talking to Persi, you do learn something about how the coin will land; and you learn nothing about this if you do not talk to him. The theorem I stated implies that the expected utility of talking to Persi is no higher than that of learning what you would learn from him, without violating Reflection; but in the problem I have described, the latter option is not available.

I will summarize the foregoing theorem by saying that, other things being equal, implementing a shift that violates Reflection cannot have greater expected utility than implementing a shift that satisfies Reflection. Conditions (i)–(v) specify what is meant here by "other things being equal." This, not the claim that a rational person must satisfy Reflection, gives the true connection between Reflection and rationality.

Conditionalization

In Chapter 4 of *Betting on Theories*, I noted that Bayesian confirmation theory makes use of a principle of conditionalization. The principle, as I formulated it there, was:

Conditionalization. *If your current probability function is p, and if q is the probability function you would have if you learned E and nothing else, then q(·) should be identical to p(·|E).*

An alternative formulation, couched in terms of evidence rather than learning, will be discussed in the section entitled 'Van Fraassen on conditionalization' below.

Paul Teller (1973, 1976) reports a Dutch book argument due to David Lewis, which purports to show that conditionalization is a requirement of rationality. The argument is essentially the same as the Dutch book argument for Reflection,[13] and is fallacious for the same reason.

Conditionalization, reflection, and rationality

In this section, I will argue that conditionalization is not a universal requirement of rationality, and will explain what I take to be its true normative status.

Recall what the conditionalization principle says: If you learn E, and nothing else, then your posterior probability should equal your prior probability conditioned on E. But what does it mean to "learn E, and nothing else"? In the section entitled 'Reflection and learning' above, I suggested that what you think you would learn in shifting from p to q is represented by the difference between p and $p(\cdot|R_q)$. From this perspective, we can say that you think you would learn E and nothing else, in shifting from p to q, just in case $p(\cdot|R_q) = p(\cdot|E)$.

This is only a subjective account of learning; it gives an interpretation of what it means to *think* E would be learned, not what it means to *really* learn E. But conditionalization is plausible only if your prior probabilities are rational; and then the subjective and objective notions of learning presumably coincide. So we can take the "learning" referred to in the principle of conditionalization to be learning as judged by you. In what follows, I use the term 'learning' in this way.

So if you learned E and nothing else, and if your probabilities shifted from p to q, then $p(\cdot|R_q) = p(\cdot|E)$. If you also satisfy Reflection in regard to this shift, then $p(\cdot|R_q) = q(\cdot)$, and so $q(\cdot) = p(\cdot|E)$, as conditionalization requires. This simple inference shows that Reflection entails conditionalization.

It is also easy to see that if you learn E, and nothing else, and if your probabilities shift in a way that violates Reflection, then your probability distribution is not updated by conditioning on E. For since you learned E, and nothing else, $p(\cdot|R_q) = p(\cdot|E)$; and since Reflection is not satisfied in this shift, $q(\cdot) \neq p(\cdot|R_q)$, whence $q(\cdot) \neq p(\cdot|E)$.

These results together show that conditionalization is equivalent to the following principle: When you learn E and nothing else, do not implement a shift that violates Reflection. But we saw, in the section entitled 'Reflection and rationality', that there are cases in which it is rational to implement a shift that violates Reflection. I will now show that some of these cases are ones in which you learn E, and nothing else. This suffices to show that it can be rational to violate conditionalization.

Consider again the situation in which you are sure there is a superior being who will give you eternal bliss, if and only if you are certain that pigs can fly; and there is a drug available that will make you certain of this. Let d be the act of taking the drug, and q the probability function you would have after taking the drug. Then we can plausibly suppose that $p(\cdot|R_q) = p(\cdot|d)$, and hence that in taking the drug you learn d, and nothing else. Consequently, conditionalization requires that your probability function after taking the drug be $p(\cdot|d)$, which it will not be. (With F denoting that pigs can fly, $p(F|d) = p(F) \approx 0$, while $q(F) = 1$.) Hence taking the drug implements a violation of conditionalization. Nevertheless, it is rational to take the drug in this case, and hence to violate conditionalization.

Similarly for the other example of that section. Here you think there is a 90 percent chance that Persi knows how the coin will land, but you know that after talking to him, you would become certain that what he told you was true. We can suppose that in talking to Persi, you think you will learn what he said, and nothing else. Then an analysis just like that given for the preceding example shows that talking to Persi implements a violation of conditionalization. Nevertheless, it is rational to talk to Persi, because (as we saw) this maximizes your expected utility.

It is true that in both these examples, there are what we might call "extraneous" factors that are responsible for the rationality of violating conditionalization. In the first example, the violation is the only available way to attain eternal bliss; and in the second example, it is the only way to acquire some useful information. Can we show that, putting aside such considerations, it is irrational to violate conditionalization? Yes, we have already proved that. For we saw that when other things are equal (in a sense made precise in the section entitled 'Reflection and rationality'), expected utility can always be maximized without implementing a violation of Reflection. As an immediate corollary, we have that when other things are equal, expected utility can always be maximized without violating conditionalization.[14]

To summarize: The principle of conditionalization is a special case of the principle that says not to implement shifts that violate Reflection. Like that more general principle, it is not a universal requirement of rationality; but it is a rationally acceptable principle in contexts where other things are equal, in the sense made precise in the section entitled 'Reflection and rationality'.

Other arguments for conditionalization

Lewis's Dutch book argument is not the only argument that has been advanced to show that conditionalization is a requirement of rationality. What I have said in the preceding section implies that these other arguments must also be incorrect. I will show that this is so for arguments offered by Teller, and by Howson.

After presenting Lewis's Dutch book argument, Teller (1973, 1976) proceeds to offer an argument of his own for conditionalization. The central assumption of this argument is that if you learn E and nothing else, then for all propositions A and B that entail E, if $p(A) = p(B)$, then it ought to be the case that $q(A) = q(B)$. (Here, as before, p and q are your prior and posterior probability functions, respectively.) Given this assumption, Teller is able to derive the principle of conditionalization. But the counterexamples that I have given to conditionalization are also counterexamples to Teller's assumption. To see this, consider the first counterexample, in which taking a drug will make you certain pigs can fly, and this will give you eternal bliss. Let F and d be as before, and let G denote that the moon is made of green cheese. We can suppose that in this example, $p(Fd) = p(Gd)$, and $q(Fd) = q(F) > q(G) = q(Gd)$. Assuming that d is all you learn from taking the drug, we have a violation of Teller's principle. But the shift from p to q involves no failure of rationality. You do not want $q(F)$ to stay small, or else you will forgo eternal bliss; nor is there any reason to become certain of G, and preserve Teller's principle that way. Thus Teller's principle is not a universal requirement of rationality, and hence his argument fails to show that conditionalization is such a requirement. (My second counterexample to conditionalization could be used to give a parallel argument for this conclusion.)

Perhaps Teller did not intend his principle to apply to the sorts of cases considered in my counterexamples. If so, there may be no dispute between us, since I have agreed that conditionalization is rational when other things are equal. But then I would say that Teller's defense of conditionalization is incomplete, because he gives no method for distinguishing the circumstances in which his principle applies. By contrast, the decision-theoretic approach I have used makes it a straightforward matter of calculation to determine under what circumstances rationality requires conditionalization.

I turn now to Howson's argument for conditionalization (Howson and Urbach 1989, p. 67f.). Howson interprets $p(H)$ as the betting quotient on H that you now regard as fair, $p(H|E)$ as the betting quotient that you now think would be fair were you to learn E (and nothing else), and $q(H)$ as the betting quotient that you will in fact regard as fair after learning E (and nothing else). His argument is the following. (I have changed the notation.)

> $p(H|E)$ is, as far as you are concerned, just what the fair betting-quotient would be on H were E to be accepted as true. Hence from the knowledge that E is true you should infer (and it is an inference endorsed by the standard analyses of subjunctive conditionals) that the fair betting quotient on H is equal to $p(H|E)$. But the fair betting quotient on H after E is known is by definition $q(H)$.

I would not endorse Howson's conception of conditional probability. But even granting Howson this conception, his argument is fallacious. Howson's argument rests on an assumption of the following form: People who accept "If A then B" are obliged by logic to accept B if they learn A. But this is a mistake; on learning A you might well decide to abandon the conditional "If A then B," thereby preserving logical consistency in a different way.

In the case at hand, Howson's conception of conditional probability says that you accept the conditional "If I were to learn E and nothing else, then the fair betting quotient for H would be $p(H|E)$." Howson wants to conclude from this that if you do learn E and nothing else, then logic obliges you to accept that the fair betting quotient for H is $p(H|E)$. But as we have seen, this does not follow; for you may reject the conditional. In fact, if you adopt a posterior probability function q, then your conditional probability for H becomes $q(H|E) = q(H)$; and according to Howson, this means you now accept the conditional "If I were to learn E and nothing else, then the fair betting quotient for H would be $q(H)$." In cases where conditionalization is violated, $q(H) \neq p(H|E)$, and so the conditional you now accept differs from the one you accepted before learning E.

Thus neither Teller's argument nor Howson's refutes my claim that it is sometimes rational to violate conditionalization. And neither is a substitute for my argument that, when other things are equal, rationality never requires violating conditionalization.

Van Fraassen on conditionalization

In a recent article, van Fraassen (1993) argues that conditionalization is not a requirement of rationality. From the perspective of this chapter, that looks at first sight to be a paradoxical position for him to take. I have argued that conditionalization is a special case of the principle not to implement shifts that violate Reflection. If this is accepted, then van Fraassen's claim that Reflection is a requirement of rationality implies that conditionalization is also a requirement of rationality.

I think the contradiction here is merely apparent. Van Fraassen's idea of how you could rationally violate conditionalization is that you might think that when you get some evidence and deliberate about it, you could have some unpredictable insight that will cause your posterior probability to differ from your prior conditioned on the evidence. Now I would say that if you satisfy Reflection, your unpredictable insight will be part of what you learned from this experience, and there is no violation of conditionalization. But there is a violation of what we could call

Evidence-conditionalization. *If your current probability function is p, and if q is the probability function you would have if you acquired evidence E and no other evidence, then $q(\cdot)$ should be identical to $p(\cdot|E)$.*

This principle differs from conditionalization as I defined it, in having E be the total *evidence* acquired, rather than the totality of what was *learned*. These are different things because, as argued in the section entitled 'Reflection and learning', not all learning involves getting evidence. Where ambiguity might otherwise arise, we could call conditionalization as I defined it *learning-conditionalization*.

These two senses of conditionalization are not usually distinguished in discussions of Bayesian learning theory, presumably because those discussions tend to focus on situations in which it is assumed that the only learning that will occur is due to acquisition of evidence. But once we consider the possibility of learning without acquisition of evidence, evidence-conditionalization becomes a very implausible principle. For example, suppose you were to think about the value of $\sqrt{289}$, and that as a result you substantially increase your probability that it is 17. We can suppose that you acquired no evidence over this time, in which case evidence-conditionalization would require your probability function to remain unchanged. Hence if evidence-conditionalization were a correct principle, you would have been irrational to engage in this ratiocination. This is a plainly false conclusion. (On the other hand, there need be no violation of learning-conditionalization; you may think you *learned* that $\sqrt{289}$ is 17.)

So van Fraassen is right to reject evidence-conditionalization, and doing so is not inconsistent with his endorsement of Reflection. But that endorsement of Reflection does commit him to learning-conditionalization; and I have urged that this principle should also be rejected.

The rationality of arbitrary shifts

Speaking of the theory of subjective probability, Henry Kyburg writes:

> But the really serious problem is that there is nothing in the theory that says that a person should *change* his beliefs in response to evidence in accordance with Bayes' theorem. On the contrary, the whole thrust of the subjectivist theory is to claim that the history of the individual's beliefs is irrelevant to their rationality: all that counts at a given time is that they conform to the requirements of coherence. It is certainly not required that the person got to the state he is in by applying Bayes' theorem to the coherent degrees of belief he had in some previous state. No more, then, is it required that a rational individual pass from his present coherent state to a new coherent state by conditionalization. ... For all the subjectivist theory has to say, he may with equal justification pass from one coherent state to another by free association, reading tea-leaves, or consulting his parrot.
>
> (Kyburg 1978, pp. 176–7)

The standard Bayesian response to this objection is to claim that conditionalization has been shown to be a requirement of rationality, for example, by the diachronic Dutch book argument (Skyrms 1990b, Ch. 5). But I have shown that the arguments for conditionalization are fallacious and that the principle is not a general requirement of rationality. Nevertheless, Kyburg's objection is still mistaken.

If you think there is something wrong with revising your probabilities by free association, reading tea-leaves, or consulting your parrot, then presumably shifts in probability induced by these means do not satisfy Reflection for you. If that is so, then the theorem of the section entitled 'Reflection and rationality' shows that if these shifts would make any difference at all to your expected utility, then implementing them would not maximize expected utility, other things being equal. Thus under fairly weak conditions, Bayesian theory does imply that it is irrational for you to revise your beliefs by free association, and so forth.

Probability kinematics

It is possible for the shift from p to q to satisfy Reflection without it being the case that there is a proposition E such that $q(\cdot) = p(\cdot|E)$. When this happens, you think you have learned something, but there is no proposition E that expresses what you learned. The principle of conditionalization is then not applicable.

Jeffrey (1965, Ch. 11) proposed a generalization of conditionalization, called probability kinematics, that applies in such cases. Jeffrey supposed that what was learned can be represented as a shift in the probability of the elements of some partition $\{E_i\}$. The rule of probability kinematics then specifies that the posterior probability function q be related to the prior probability p by the condition.

$$q(\cdot) = \sum_i p(\cdot|E_i)q(E_i)$$

Armendt (1980) has given a Dutch book argument to show that the rule of probability kinematics is a requirement of rationality. But this argument has the same fallacy as the Dutch book arguments for Reflection and conditionalization. Furthermore, my account of the true status of conditionalization also extends immediately to probability kinematics.

A natural interpretation of what it means for you to think what you learned is represented by a shift from p to q' on the E_i would be that the shift is to q, and

$$p(\cdot|R_q) = \sum_i p(\cdot|E_i)q'(E_i)$$

But then it follows that the requirement to update your beliefs by probability kinematics is equivalent to the requirement not to implement any shifts that violate Reflection. Hence updating by probability kinematics is not in general a requirement of rationality, though it is a rational principle when other things are equal, in the sense of the section entitled 'Reflection and rationality'.

Conclusion

If diachronic Dutch book arguments were sound, then Reflection, conditionalization, and probability kinematics would all be requirements of rationality. But these arguments are fallacious, and in fact none of these three principles is a general requirement of rationality. Nevertheless, there is some truth to the idea that these three principles are requirements of rationality. Bayesian decision theory entails that when other things are equal, rationality never requires implementing a shift in probability that violates Reflection. Conditionalization and probability kinematics are special cases of the principle not to implement shifts that violate Reflection. Hence we also have that when other things are equal, it is always rationally permissible, and may be obligatory, to conform to conditionalization and probability kinematics.

Notes

* Originally published as Chapter 5 of *Betting on Theories*, Cambridge University Press: Cambridge, 1993, pp. 105–29. Copyright © 1993 Cambridge University Press. Reproduced with permission.

1 Goldstein actually defends a stronger condition; but the argument for his stronger condition is the same as for the weaker one stated here.

2 Conjunction is represented by concatenation, and negation by overbars. For example, $\overline{D}\,R_q$ is the proposition that D is false and R_q is true.

3 In presentations of this argument, it is usual to have two bets, where I have the single bet b_1. Those two bets would be a bet on R_q, and a bet on $\overline{D}$ which is called off if R_q is false. By using a single bet instead, I show that the argument does not here require the assumption that bets that are separately acceptable are also jointly acceptable.

4 I assume that you are sure you cannot come to have q other than by drinking. This is a plausible assumption if (as we can suppose) q also assigns an extremely high probability to the proposition that you have been drinking.

5 I assume causal decision theory. For a discussion of this theory, and a proof that the stated conditions are indeed sufficient in this theory, see (Maher 1990b). In that work, I referred to Reflection as *Miller's principle*.

6 This condition is necessary in order to ensure that your decision to take the drug is not symptomatic. If you thought the drug was likely to make you sure the coin will land heads (say), and if Reflection is satisfied, then the probability of the coin landing heads, given that you take the drug, would also be high. Since taking the drug has no causal influence on the outcome of the toss, and since the unconditional probability of heads is 1/2, taking the drug would then be a symptomatic act.

7 This proposal was suggested to me by Skyrms (1990a), who assumes that what is thought to be a learning experience will satisfy Reflection. (He calls Reflection "Principle (M)".)

8 This assumes that q records everything relevant about the shift. Otherwise, it would be possible to shift from p to q in different ways (e.g., by acquiring evidence or taking drugs), some of which would involve more learning than others. This assumption could fail, e.g., if after making the shift, you would forget some relevant information about the shift. Such cases could be dealt with by replacing R_q with a proposition that specifies your probability distribution at every instant between t and $t+x$.

9 Jeffrey (1988, p. 233) proposed to restrict Reflection to shifts that are "reasonable," without saying what that means. His proposal faces precisely the dilemma I have just outlined. If a "reasonable" shift is defined by its causal origin, Jeffrey's principle is not a requirement of rationality. If a "reasonable" shift is defined to be a learning experience, Jeffrey's principle is vacuous. In the next section, we will see that if a "reasonable" shift is a shift that it would be rational to implement, Jeffrey's principle is again not a requirement of rationality.

10 Here and in what follows, I assume that the proviso of Section 1.9 [of *Betting on Theories*] holds. That is, I assume your probabilities and utilities are themselves rational, so that rationality requires maximizing expected utility.

11 According to an idea floated in Section 1.8 [of *Betting on Theories*], satisfaction of (ii) ensures that the subjective probabilities that it is rational to have are also justified.

12 If eternal bliss includes epistemic bliss, taking the drug could even be rational from a purely epistemic point of view. Nevertheless, your certainty that pigs can fly would not be justified (see Section 1.8 [of *Betting on Theories*]).

13 But this way of putting the matter reverses the chronological order, since Lewis formulated the argument for conditionalization before the argument for Reflection was advanced.

14 Brown (1976) gives a direct proof of a less general version of this result. What makes his result less general is that it applies only to cases where for each E you might learn, there is a probability function q such that you are sure q would be your probability function if you learned E, and nothing else. This means that Brown's result is not applicable to the coin-tossing

example of the section entitled 'Counterexamples', for example. (In this example, your posterior probability, on learning that you took the drug, could give probability 1 to either heads or tails.) Another difference between Brown's proof and mine is that his does not apply to probability kinematics (cf. Section 5.3 [of *Betting on Theories*]).

Bibliography

Armendt, B. (1980), 'Is there a Dutch Book Argument for Probability Kinematics?', *Philosophy of Science* 47: 583–588.

Brown, P. M. (1976), 'Discussion: Conditionalization and Expected Utility', *Philosophy of Science* 43: 415–419.

Christensen, D. (1991), 'Clever Bookies and Coherent Beliefs', *Philosophical Review* 50: 229–247.

Goldstein, M. (1983), 'The Prevision of a Prevision', *Journal of the American Statistical Association* 78: 817–819.

Howson, C. and Urbach, P. (1989), *Scientific Reasoning: The Bayesian Approach*. La Salle, IL: Open Court.

Jeffrey, R. C. (1983), *The Logic of Decision*. 2d ed. Chicago: University of Chicago Press. (Relevant chapter is Jeffrey, Chapter 7 in this volume.)

—— (1988), 'Conditioning, Kinematics, and Exchangeability', in B. Skyrms and W. L. Harper (eds.), *Causation, Chance, and Credence*, vol. 1. Dordrecht: Kluwer, pp. 221–255.

Levi, I. (1987), 'The Demons of Decision', *The Monist* 70: 193–211.

Maher, P. (1987), 'Causality in the Logic of Decision', Theory and Decision 22: 155–172.

—— (1990), 'Symptomatic Acts and the Value of Evidence in Causal Decision Theory', *Philosophy of Science* 57: 479–498.

—— (1992), 'Diachronic Rationality', *Philosophy of Science*, 59: 120–141.

Ramsey, F. P. (1926), 'Truth and Probability', reprinted as Chapter 2 in this volume.

Savage, L. J. (1954), *The Foundations of Statistics*. New York: Wiley.

Skyrms, B. (1987), 'Dynamic Coherence and Probability Kinematics', *Philosophy of Science* 54: 1–20.

—— (1990), 'The Value of Knowledge', in C. W. Savage (ed.), *Minnesota Studies in the Philosophy of Science. Vol. 14, Scientific Theories*. Minneapolis: University of Minnesota Press, pp. 245–266.

—— (1993) 'A Mistake in Dynamic Coherence Arguments?', *Philosophy of Science* 60 (2): 320–328.

Teller, P. (1973), 'Conditionalization and Observation', *Synthese* 26: 218–258.

—— (1976), 'Conditionalization, Observation, and Change of Preference', in W. Harper and C. Hooker (eds.), *Foundations of Probability Theory, Statistical Inference, and Statistical Theories of Science*, vol. 1. Dordrecht: Reidel, pp. 205–253.

van Fraassen, B. C. (1984), 'Belief and the Will', reprinted as Chapter 8 in this volume.

—— (1993), 'Rationality Does Not Require Conditionalization', in E. Ullmann–Margalit (ed.), The Israel Colloquium Studies in the History, Philosophy, and Sociology of Science, vol. 5. Dordrecht: Kluwer.

10

SELF-LOCATING BELIEF AND THE SLEEPING BEAUTY PROBLEM*

Adam Elga

In addition to being uncertain about what the world is like, one can also be uncertain about one's own spatial or temporal location in the world. My aim is to pose a problem arising from the interaction between these two sorts of uncertainty, solve the problem, and draw two lessons from the solution.

The Sleeping Beauty problem[1]

Some researchers are going to put you to sleep. During the two days that your sleep will last, they will briefly wake you up either once or twice, depending on the toss of a fair coin (Heads: once; Tails: twice). After each waking, they will put you to back to sleep with a drug that makes you forget that waking.[2]

When you are first awakened, to what degree ought you believe that the outcome of the coin toss is Heads?

First answer: 1/2, of course! Initially you were certain that the coin was fair, and so initially your credence in the coin's landing Heads was 1/2. Upon being awakened, you receive no new information (you knew all along that you would be awakened). So your credence in the coin's landing Heads ought to remain 1/2.

Second answer: 1/3, of course! Imagine the experiment repeated many times. Then in the long run, about 1/3 of the wakings would be Heads-wakings – wakings that happen on trials in which the coin lands Heads. So on any particular waking, you should have credence 1/3 that that waking is a Heads-waking, and hence have credence 1/3 in the coin's landing Heads on that trial. This consideration remains in force in the present circumstance, in which the experiment is performed just once.

I will argue that the correct answer is 1/3.

[The argument]

Suppose that the first waking happens on Monday, and that the second waking (if there is one) happens on Tuesday. Then when you wake up, you're certain that you're in one of three 'predicaments':

H_1 HEADS and it is Monday.

T_1 TAILS and it is Monday.

T_2 TAILS and it is Tuesday.

Notice that the difference between your being in T_1 and your being in T_2 is not a difference in which possible world is actual, but rather a difference in your temporal location within the world. (In a more technical treatment we might adopt a framework similar to the one suggested in Lewis 1983, according to which the elementary alternatives over which your credence is divided are not possible worlds, but rather centred possible worlds: possible worlds each of which is equipped with a designated individual and time. In such a framework, H_1, T_1, and T_2 would be represented by appropriate sets of centred worlds.)

Let P be the credence function you ought to have upon first awakening. Upon first awakening, you are certain of the following: you are in predicament H_1 if and only if the outcome of the coin toss is Heads. Therefore, calculating $P(H_1)$ is sufficient to solve the Sleeping Beauty problem. I will argue first that $P(T_1) = P(T_2)$, and then that $P(H_1) = P(T_1)$.

If (upon first awakening) you were to learn that the toss outcome is Tails, that would amount to your learning that you are in either T_1 or T_2. Since being in T_1 is subjectively just like being in T_2, and since exactly the same propositions are true whether you are in T_1 or T_2, even a highly restricted principle of indifference yields that you ought then to have equal credence in each. But your credence that you are in T_1, after learning that the toss outcome is tails, ought to be the same as the conditional credence $P(T_1 | T_1$ or $T_2)$, and likewise for T_2. So $P(T_1 | T_1$ or $T_2) = P(T_2 | T_1$ or $T_2)$, and hence $P(T_1) = P(T_2)$.

The researchers have the task of using a fair coin to determine whether to awaken you once or twice. They might accomplish their task by either

(1) *first* tossing the coin and then waking you up either once or twice depending on the outcome; or

(2) first waking you up once, *and* then tossing the coin to determine whether to wake you up a second time.

Your credence (upon awakening) in the coin's landing Heads ought to be the same regardless of whether the researchers use method (1) or (2). So without loss of generality suppose that they use – and you know that they use – method (2).

Now: if (upon awakening) you were to learn that it is Monday, that would amount to your learning that you are in either H_1 or T_1. Your credence that you are in H_1 would then be your credence that a fair coin, soon to be tossed, will land Heads. It is irrelevant that you will be awakened on the following day if and only if the coin lands Tails – in this circumstance, your credence that the coin will land Heads ought to be 1/2. But your credence that the coin will land Heads (after learning that it is Monday) ought to be the same as the conditional credence $P(H_1 | H_1$ or $T_1)$. So $P(H_1 | H_1$ or $T_1) = 1/2$, and hence $P(H_1) = P(T_1)$.

Combining results, we have that $P(H_1) = P(T_1) = P(T_2)$. Since these credences sum to 1, $P(H_1) = 1/3$.

[The lessons of self-locating belief]

Let H be the proposition that the outcome of the coin toss is Heads. Before being put to sleep, your credence in H was 1/2. I've just argued that when you are awakened on

Monday, that credence ought to change to 1/3. This belief change is unusual. It is not the result of your receiving new information – you were already certain that you would be awakened on Monday.[3] (We may even suppose that you knew at the start of the experiment exactly what sensory experiences you would have upon being awakened on Monday.) Neither is this belief change the result of your suffering any cognitive mishaps during the intervening time – recall that the forgetting drug isn't administered until well after you are first awakened. So what justifies it?

The answer is that you have gone from a situation in which you count your own temporal location as irrelevant to the truth of H, to one in which you count your own temporal location as relevant to the truth of H.[4] Suppose, for example, that at the start of the experiment, you weren't sure whether it was 1:01 or 1:02. At that time, you counted your temporal location as irrelevant to the truth of H: your credence in H, conditional on its being 1:01, was 1/2, and your credence in H, conditional on its being 1:02, was also 1/2.

In contrast (assuming that you update your beliefs rationally), when you are awakened on Monday you count your current temporal location as relevant to the truth of H: your credence in H, conditional on its being Monday, is 1/2, but your credence in H, conditional on its being Tuesday, is 0. On Monday, your unconditional credence in H differs from 1/2 because it is a weighted average of these two conditional credences – that is, a weighted average of 1/2 and 0.

It is no surprise that the manner in which an agent counts her own temporal location as relevant to the truth of some proposition can change over time. What is surprising – and this is the first lesson – is that this sort of change can happen to a perfectly rational agent during a period in which that agent neither receives new information nor suffers a cognitive mishap.

At the start of the experiment, you had credence 1/2 in H. But you were also certain that upon being awakened on Monday you would have credence 1/3 in H – even though you were certain that you would receive no new information and suffer no cognitive mishaps during the intervening time. Thus the Sleeping Beauty example provides a new variety of counter-example to Bas Van Fraassen's 'Reflection Principle' (1984: 244, 1995: 19), even an extremely qualified version of which entails the following:

> Any agent who is certain that she will tomorrow have credence x in proposition R (though she will neither receive new information nor suffer any cognitive mishaps in the intervening time) ought *now* to have credence x in R.[5]

David Lewis once asked 'what happens to decision theory if we [replace the space of possible worlds by the space of centred possible worlds]?' and answered 'Not much'. (Lewis 1983: 149) A second lesson of the Sleeping Beauty problem is that something does happen: a new question arises about how a rational agent ought to update her beliefs over time.[6]

Notes

* Originally published in *Analysis*, 60 (2000), pp. 143–7. Copyright © 2000 Adam Elga. Reprinted with permission.
1 So named by Robert Stalnaker (who first learned of examples of this kind in unpublished work by Arnold Zuboff). This problem appears as Example 5 of Piccione 1997, which motivates two distinct answers but suspends judgment as to which answer is correct (1997: 12–14).

Aumann 1997 uses a fair lottery approach to analyse a similar problem. Adapted to the Sleeping Beauty problem, that analysis yields the same answer as the one I will defend. However, unlike the argument in Aumann 1997, my argument does not depend on betting considerations.

2   The precise effect of the drug is to reset your belief-state to what it was just before you were put to sleep at the beginning of the experiment. If the existence of such a drug seems fanciful, note that it is possible to pose the problem without it – all that matters is that the person put to sleep believes that the setup is as I have described it.

3   To say that an agent receives new information (as I shall use that expression) is to say that the agent receives evidence that rules out possible worlds not already ruled out by her previous evidence. Put another way, an agent receives new information when she learns the truth of a proposition expressible by an eternal sentence (Quine 1960: 191) of some appropriately rich language.

4   To say that an agent counts her temporal location as relevant to the truth of a certain proposition is to say that there is a time t such that the agent's beliefs are compatible with her being located at t, and her credence in the proposition, conditional on her being located at t, differs from her unconditional credence in the proposition.

5   I am indebted to Ned Hall for pointing out that an answer of 1/3 conflicts with the Reflection Principle.

6   Many thanks to Jamie Dreier, Gary Gates, Ned Hall, Vann McGee, Robert Stalnaker, Roger White, Sarah Wright, the participants in a 1999 conference at Brown University (at which an earlier version of this paper was presented), and an anonymous referee.

Bibliography

Aumann, R. J., S. Hart, and M. Perry. 1997. The forgetful passenger. *Games and Economic Behavior* 20: 117–120.

Lewis, D. 1983. Attitudes *de dicto* and *de se*. In his *Philosophical Papers, Volume I*, 133–159. New York: Oxford University Press.

Piccione, M. and A. Rubenstein. 1997. On the interpretation of decision problems with imperfect recall. *Games and Economic Behavior* 20: 3–24.

Quine, W. V. 1960. *Word and Object*. Cambridge, Mass.: The MIT Press.

van Fraassen, B. C. 1984. Belief and the will. *Journal of Philosophy* 81: 235–256, reprinted as Chapter 8 in this volume.

van Fraassen, B. C. 1995. Belief and the problem of Ulysses and the sirens. *Philosophical Studies* 77: 7–37.

11

SOME PROBLEMS FOR CONDITIONALIZATION AND REFLECTION*†

Frank Arntzenius

I will present five puzzles that show that rational people can update their degrees of belief in manners that violate Bayesian conditionalization and Bas van Fraassen's reflection principle. I will then argue that these violations of conditionalization and reflection are due to the fact that there are two as yet unrecognized ways in which the degrees of belief of rational people can develop.

Two roads to Shangri La

Every now and then, the guardians to Shangri La will allow a mere mortal to enter that hallowed ground. You have been chosen because you are a fan of the Los Angeles Clippers. But there is an ancient law about entry into Shangri La: you are only allowed to enter, if, once you have entered, you no longer know by what path you entered. Together with the guardians, you have devised a plan that satisfies this law. There are two paths to Shangri La, the Path by the Mountains, and the Path by the Sea. A fair coin will be tossed by the guardians to determine which path you will take: if heads you go by the Mountains, if tails you go by the Sea. If you go by the Mountains, nothing strange will happen: while traveling you will see the glorious Mountains, and even after you enter Shangri La, you will forever retain your memories of that Magnificent Journey. If you go by the Sea, you will revel in the Beauty of the Misty Ocean. But, just as you enter Shangri La, your memory of this Beauteous Journey will be erased and be replaced by a memory of the Journey by the Mountains.

Suppose that in fact you travel by the Mountains. How will your degrees of belief develop? Before you set out your degree of belief in heads will be 1/2. Then, as you travel along the Mountains and you gaze upon them, your degree of belief in heads will be one. But then, once you have arrived, you will revert to having degree of belief 1/2 in heads. For you will know that you would have had the memories that you have either way, and hence you know that the only relevant information that you have is that the coin was fair.

This seems a bizarre development of degrees of belief. For as you are traveling along the Mountains, you know that your degree of belief in heads is going to go down from one to 1/2. You do not have the least inclination to trust those future degrees of belief.

187

Those future degrees of belief will not arise because you will acquire any evidence, at least not in any straightforward sense of "acquiring evidence." Nonetheless, you think you will behave in a fully rational manner when you acquire those future degree of belief. Moreover, you know that the development of your memorise will be completely normal. It is only because something strange would have happened to your memories had the coin landed tails that you are compelled to change your degree of belief to 1/2 when that counterfactual possibility would have occurred.

The prisoner

You have just been returned to your cell on death row, after your last supper. You are to be executed tomorrow. You have made a last minute appeal to President George W. Bush for clemency. Since Dick Cheney is in the hospital and cannot be consulted, George W. will decide by flipping a coin: heads you die, tails you live. His decision will be made known to the prison staff before midnight. You are friends with the prison officer who will take over the guard of your cell at midnight. He is not allowed to talk to you, but he will tell you of Bush's decision by switching the light in your cell off at the stroke of midnight if it was heads. He will leave it on if it was tails. Unfortunately you do not have a clock or a watch. All you know is that it is now 6 PM since that is when prisoners are returned to their cells after supper. You start to reminisce and think fondly of your previous career as a Bayesian. You suddenly get excited when you notice that there is going to be something funny about the development of your degrees of belief. Like anybody else, you do not have a perfect internal clock. At the moment you are certain that it is 6 PM, but as time passes your degrees of belief are going to be spread out over a range of times. What rules should such developments satisfy?

Let us start on this problem by focusing on one particularly puzzling feature of such developments. When in fact it is just before midnight, say 11:59 PM, you are going to have a certain, nonzero, degree of belief that it is now later than midnight. Of course, at 11:59 PM the light in your cell is still going to be on. Given that at this time you will have a nonzero degree of belief that it is after midnight, and given that in fact you will see that the light is still on, you will presumably take it that the light provides some evidence that the outcome was tails. Indeed, it seems clear that as it gets closer to midnight, you will monotonically increase your degree of belief in tails. Moreover you know in advance that this will happen. This seems puzzling. Of course, after midnight, your degree of belief in tails will either keep on increasing, or it will flip to zero at midnight and stay there after midnight. But that does not diminish the puzzlement about the predictable and inevitable increase in your degree of belief in tails prior to midnight. In fact, it seems that this increase is not merely puzzling, it seems patently irrational. For since this increase is entirely predictable, surely you could be made to lose money in a sequence of bets. At 6 PM you will be willing to accept a bet on heads at even odds, and at 11:59 PM you will, almost certainly, be willing to accept a bet on tails at worse than even odds. And that adds up to a sure loss. And surely that means you are irrational.

Now, one might think that this last argument shows that your degree of belief in tails in fact should not go up prior to midnight. One might indeed claim that since your degree of belief in heads should remain 1/2 until midnight, you should adjust your idea of what time it is when you see that the light is still on, rather than adjust your degree of belief in tails as time passes. But of course, this suggestion is impossible to carry out. Armed with an imperfect internal clock, you simply cannot make sure that your degree of belief in heads stays 1/2 until midnight, while allowing it to go down after midnight. So how should they develop?

Let us start with a much simpler case. Let us suppose that there is no coin toss and no light switching (and that you know this). You go into your cell at 6 PM. As time goes by there will be some development of your degrees of belief as to what time it is. Let us suppose that your degrees of belief in possible times develop as pictured in the top half of Figure 1.

Next, let us ask how your degrees of belief should develop were you to know with certainty that the guard will switch the light off at midnight, 12 PM. It should be clear then that at 11:59 PM your degree of belief distribution should be entirely confined to the left of midnight, as depicted in the bottom half of Figure 1. For at 11:59 PM the light will still be on, so that you know that it must be before 12 PM. But other than that it should be entirely confined to the left of 12 PM, it is not immediately clear exactly what your degree of belief distribution should be at 11:59 PM. It is not even obvious that there should be a unique answer to this question. A very simple consideration, however, leads to a unique answer.

Suppose that, even though the guard is going to switch the light off at 12 PM, you were not told that the guard is going to switch the light off at 12 PM. Then the development of your degree of belief would be as pictured in the top half of Figure 1. Next, suppose that at 11:59 PM you are told that the guard will switch the light off at 12 PM, but you are not told that it is now 11:59 PM. Obviously, since the light is still on you can infer that it is prior to 12 PM. Surely you should update your degrees of belief by conditionalization: you should erase that part of your degree of belief distribution that is to the right of 12 PM, and renormalize the remaining part (increase the remaining part proportionally). Now it is clear that this is also the degree of belief distribution that you should have

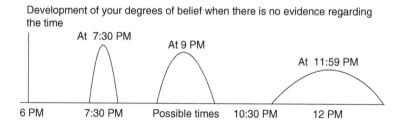

Development of your degrees of belief when there is no evidence regarding the time

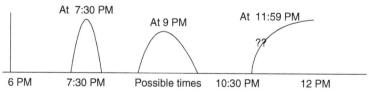

Development of your degrees of belief when you know the light will be turned off at 12 PM

Figure 1

189

arrived at had you known all along that the guard would turn the light off at 12 PM. For either way you have accumulated exactly the same relevant information and experience by 11:59 PM. This uniquely determines how your degree of belief distribution should develop when you know all along that the guard will turn the light off at 12 PM. At any time this (constrained) distribution should be the distribution that you arrive at by conditionalizing the distribution that you have if you have no evidence regarding the time, on the fact that it is now before 12 PM. One can picture this development in the following way. One takes the development of the top part of Figure 1. As this distribution starts to pass through the 12 PM boundary, the part that passes through this boundary gets erased, and, in a continuous manner, it gets proportionally added to the part that is to the left of the 12 PM boundary.

Now we are ready to solve the original puzzle. Your degrees of belief in that case can be pictured as being distributed over possible times in two possible worlds: see Figure 2. The development is now such that when the bottom part of the degree of belief distribution hits midnight, it gets snuffed out to the right of midnight, and the rest of the degree of belief distribution is continuously renormalized, that is, the top part of the degree of belief distribution and the remaining bottom part are continuously proportionally increased as time passes. Note that Figure 2 is essentially different from Figure 1. In Figure 2, the top distribution starts to increase its absolute size once the leading edge of the bottom distribution hits midnight. This does not happen in Figure 1, since there the degree of belief distributions each were total degree of belief distributions in separate scenarios. Also, in Figure 2, the bottom distribution starts to increase in size once its leading edge hits midnight, but it only increases half as much as it does in Figure 1, since half of the "gains" is being diverted to the top degree of belief distribution.

Thus, at the very least, until it actually is midnight, the top and the bottom degrees of belief distribution will always be identical to each other, in terms of shape and size, to the

The development of your degrees of belief within the tails world

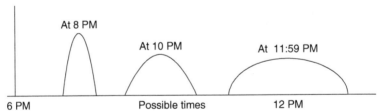

The development of your degrees of belief within the heads world

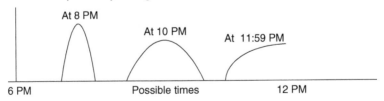

Figure 2

190

left of midnight. Prior to midnight, your degrees of belief will be such that conditional upon it being prior to midnight, it is equally likely to be heads as tails. Your unconditional degree of belief in tails, however, will increase monotonically as you approach midnight.

After midnight there are two possible ways in which your degree of belief distribution can develop. If the light is switched off, your degree of belief distribution collapses completely onto midnight and onto the heads world. If in fact it is not switched off, your degree of belief distribution continues to move to the right in both worlds, and it continues to be snuffed out in the heads world to the right of midnight, and the remaining degrees of belief keep being proportionally increased.[1]

Now I can answer the questions that I started with. It is true, as I surmised, that your degree of belief in tails will have increased by 11:59 PM. You will take your internal sense of the passing of time, and combine it with the fact that the light is still on, and you will take this as providing some evidence that the outcome is tails. It is also true, as I surmised, that the light still being on will be taken by you as providing some evidence that it is not yet midnight. For at 11:59 PM your degree of belief distribution over possible times (averaged over the heads and tails worlds) will be further to the left than it would have been had you believed that the light would stay on no matter what. More generally, we have found a unique solution to the puzzle of how a rational person's sense of time must interact with evidence, given how that person's sense of time works in the absence of evidence.

Rather surprisingly, this interaction can be such that, as it is in my example, you know in advance that at some specified later time you will, almost certainly, have increased your degree of belief in tails, and that you could not possibly have decreased your degree of belief in tails.[2] It is also interesting to note that nothing essential changes in this example if one assumes that the coin toss will take place exactly at midnight. Thus it can be the case that one knows in advance that one will increase one's degrees of belief that a coin toss, *which is yet to occur*, will land tails. Of course, at the time that one has this increased degree of belief one does not know that this coin toss is yet to occur. Nonetheless, such predictable increases in degrees of belief seem very strange.

John Collins's prisoner

John Collins has come up with the following variation of the case of the prisoner that was described in the previous section. In Collins's variation, the prisoner has two clocks in his cell, both of which run perfectly accurately. However, clock A initially reads 6 PM, clock B initially reads 7 PM. The prisoner knows that one of the clocks is set accurately, the other one is one hour off. The prisoner has no idea which one is set accurately; indeed, he initially has degree of belief 1/2 that A is set accurately, and degree of belief 1/2 that B is set accurately. As in the original case, if the coin lands heads the light in his cell will be turned off at midnight, and it will stay on if it lands tails. So initially the prisoner has degree of belief 1/2 in each of the following four possible worlds:

W_1: heads and clock A is correct
W_2: heads and clock B is correct
W_3: tails and clock A is correct
W_4: tails and clock B is correct

When in fact it is 11:30 PM the light, for sure, will still be on. What will the prisoner's degrees of belief then be? Well, if the actual world is W_1, then, when it actually is 11:30 PM clock A will read 11:30 PM and clock B will read 12:30 AM. In that case, since the prisoner sees that the light is still on, he will know that it cannot be that the coin landed heads and clock B is correct. That is to say, his degree of belief in W_2 will be 0, and his degrees of belief in the three remaining options will be 1/3 each. Similarly if the actual world is W_3 then at 11:30 PM the prisoner will have degree of belief 0 in W_2 and degree of belief 1/3 in each of the remaining options. On the other hand, if the actual world is W_2 or W_4, then when it is actually 11:30 PM, the clock readings will be 10:30 PM and 11:30 PM, and the prisoner will still have the degrees of belief that he started with, namely 1/4 in each of the four possibilities. The prisoner, moreover, knows all of this in advance.

This is rather bizarre, to say the least. For, in the first place, at 6 PM the prisoner knows that at 11:30 PM his degrees of belief in heads will be less or equal to what they now are, and cannot be greater. So his current expectation of what his degrees of belief in heads will be at 11:30 PM is less than his current degree of belief in heads. Second, there is a clear sense in which he does not trust his future degrees of belief, even though he does not think that he is, or will be, irrational, and even though he can acquire new evidence (the light being on or off). Let D_t denote the prisoner's degrees of belief at time t. Then, for example, $D_{6:00}$ (clock B is correct/$D_{11:30}$ (clock B is correct) = 1/3) = 0. For $D_{11:30}$ (clock B is correct) = 1/3 only occurs in worlds W_1 and W_3, and in each of those worlds clock B is not correct, and the prisoner knows this. Thus his current degrees of belief conditional upon his future degrees of belief do not equal those future degrees of belief. So he systematically distrusts his future degrees of belief. Strange indeed.

Sleeping Beauty

Some researchers are going to put Sleeping Beauty to sleep on Sunday night. During the two days that her sleep will last the researchers will wake her up either once, on Monday morning, or twice, on both Monday and Tuesday morning. They will toss a fair coin Sunday night in order to determine whether she will be woken up once or twice: if it lands heads she will be woken upon Monday only, if it lands tails she will be woken up on Monday and Tuesday. After each waking, she will be asked what her degree of belief is that the outcome of the coin toss is heads. After she has given her answer she will be given a drug that erases her memory of the waking up; indeed it resets her mental state to the state that it was on Sunday just before she was put to sleep. Then she is put to sleep again. The question now is: When she wakes up, what should her degree of belief be that the outcome was heads?

> *Answer 1*: Her degree of belief in heads should be 1/2. It was a fair coin and she learned nothing relevant by waking up.

> *Answer 2*: Her degree of belief in heads should be 1/3. If this experiment is repeated many times, approximately 1/3 of the awakenings will be heads-awakenings—that is, awakenings that happen on trials in which the coin landed heads.

Adam Elga[3] has argued for the second answer. I agree with him, and I agree with his argument. But let me amplify this view by giving a different argument for the same conclusion. Suppose that Sleeping Beauty is a frequent and rational dreamer. Suppose in fact that every morning if Sleeping Beauty is not woken up at 9 AM, she dreams at 9 AM that she is woken up at 9 AM. Suppose that the dream and reality are indistinguishable in terms of her experience, except that if Sleeping Beauty pinches herself and she is dreaming, it does not hurt (and she does not wake up), while if she does this while she is awake it does hurt. And let us suppose that Sleeping Beauty always remembers to pinch herself a few minutes after she experiences waking up (whether for real, or in a dream.) What should her degrees of belief be when she experiences waking up? It seems obvious she should consider the four possibilities equally likely (the four possibilities being – Monday & Tails & Awake, Monday & Heads & Awake, Tuesday & Tails & Awake, Tuesday & Heads & Dreaming). If Sleeping Beauty then pinches herself and finds herself to be awake, she should conditionalize and then have degree of belief 1/3 in each of the remaining three possibilities (Monday & Tails & Awake, Monday & Heads & Awake, Tuesday & Tails & Awake). Suppose now that at some point in her life Sleeping Beauty loses the habit of dreaming. She no longer needs to pinch herself; directly upon waking she knows that she is not asleep. It seems clear, however, that this lack of dreaming should make no difference as to her degrees of belief upon realizing that she is awake. The process now occurs immediately, without the need for a pinch, but the end result ought to be the same.

Here again, the crucial assumption is commutativity: if the relevant evidence and experience collected is the same, then the order of collection should not matter for the final degrees of belief.[4] But there is clearly something very puzzling about such foreseeable changes in degrees of belief.

Duplication

Scenario 1: While you are at the beach, Vishnu tells you that, contrary to appearances, you have existed only for one month: Brahma created you one month ago, complete with all your memories, habits, bad back, and everything. What is more, says Vishnu, one month ago Brahma in fact created two human beings like you (you are one of them), in exactly the same environment, at two different ends of the universe: one on earth, one on twin earth. Unfortunately, Vishnu has a further surprise for you: one month ago Shiva tossed a coin. If it landed heads, Shiva will destroy the human being that is on twin earth one month from now. If it landed tails, Shiva will do nothing. Vishnu does not tell you whether you are to be destroyed, but recommends that if you want to know, you should go check your mail at home. If there is a letter from President Bush for you, then you will be destroyed. Before running home, what degree of belief should you have in the four possibilities (Earth & Heads, Earth & Tails, Twin Earth & Heads, Twin Earth & Tails)? It seems clear that you should have degree of belief 1/4 in each, or at the very least, that it is not irrational to have degree of belief 1/4 in each. You run home, and find no letter from Bush. What should your degrees of belief now be? Well, by conditionalization, they should now be 1/3 in each of the remaining possibilities (Earth & Tails, Twin Earth & Heads, Twin Earth & Tails). Consequently you should now have degree of belief 1/3 that the toss landed heads and 2/3 that it landed tails.

Scenario 2: same as Scenario 1, except that Vishnu tells you that if the toss came heads, your identical twin was destroyed by Shiva one week ago. Since you were obviously not destroyed, you do not need to rush home to look for a letter from Bush. In essence, you have learned the same as you learned in the previous scenario when you found you had no letter from Bush, and hence you should now have degree of belief 1/3 that the toss landed heads.

Scenario 3: same as Scenario 2, except that Vishnu tells you that rather than that two beings were created one month ago by Brahma, one of them already existed and had exactly the life you remember having had. This makes no relevant difference and you should now have degree of belief 1/3 that the coin landed heads.

Scenario 4: same as Scenario 3, except that Vishnu tells you that if the coin landed heads one month ago, Shiva immediately prevented Brahma from creating the additional human being one month ago. The upshot is that only if the coin landed tails will Brahma have created the additional human being. Since the timing of the destruction/prevention makes no relevant difference, you should again have degree of belief 1/3 that the coin landed heads.

Scenario 5:[5] you are on earth, and you know it. Vishnu tells you that one month from now Brahma will toss a coin. If it lands tails, Brahma will create, at the other end of the universe, another human being identical to you, in the same state as you will then be, and in an identical environment as you will then be. What do you now think that your degrees of belief should be in one month's time? The answer is that they should be the same as they are in Scenario 5, since in one month's time you will be in exactly the epistemic situation that is described in Scenario 5. Of course, it is plausible to claim that your future self will actually be on earth, since it is only your future continuation on earth that can plausibly be called "your future self." That does not mean, however, that your future self can be sure that he is on earth. For your future self will know that he will have the same experiences and memories, whether or not he is on earth or on twin earth, and thus he will not know whether he can trust his memories. Thus you now have degree of belief 1/2 in heads, and yet you know that in one month's time, you will have degree of belief 1/3. This is bizarre, to say the least.

Yet again, the crucial assumption in this reasoning is commutativity: your final degrees of belief should not depend on the order in which you receive all the relevant experience and evidence. You should end up with the same degree of belief—namely, degree of belief 1/2 in heads, whether you all along knew you were on earth, or whether you only later found out that you were on earth. But that can only be so if you had degree of belief 1/3 in heads prior to discovering that you were on earth.

Diagnosis

van Fraassen's reflection principle[6] says that one should trust one's future degrees of belief in the sense that one's current degree of belief D_0 in any proposition X, given that one's future degree of belief D_t in X equals p, should be p: $D_0(X/D_t(X) = p) = p$. Given that one is sure that one will have precise degrees of belief at time t, the reflection principle entails that one's current degrees of belief equal the expectations of one's future degrees of belief: $D_0(X) = \Sigma\ pD_0(D_t(X) = p)$. The reflection principle is violated in each of the five puzzles that I have presented, for in each case there is a time at which one's expectation of one's future degree of belief in heads differs from one's current degree of belief in heads. This is presumably why we find these cases, prima facie, so worrying and strange.

194

The source of the problem, I claim, is that the degrees of belief of perfectly rational people, people who are not subject to memory loss or any other cognitive defect, can develop in ways that are as yet unrecognized, and indeed are not allowed according to standard Bayesian lore. Standard Bayesian lore has it that rational people satisfy the principle of conditionalization: rational people alter their degrees of belief only by strict conditionalization on the evidence that they acquire.[7] Strict conditionalization of one's degrees of belief upon proposition X can be pictured in the following manner. One's degrees of belief are a function on the set of possibilities that one entertains. Since this function satisfies the axioms of probability theory it is normalized: it integrates (over all possibilities) to one. Conditionalizing such a function on proposition X then amounts to the following: the function is set to zero over those possibilities that are inconsistent with X, while the remaining nonzero part of the function is boosted (by the same factor) everywhere so that it integrates to one once again. Thus, without being too rigorous about it, it is clear that conditionalization can only serve to "narrow down" one's degree of belief distribution (one really *learns* by conditionalization). In particular a degree of belief distribution that becomes more "spread out" as time passes cannot be developing by conditionalization, and a degree of belief distribution that exactly retains its shape, but is shifted as a whole over the space of possibilities, cannot be developing by conditionalization. Such spreading out and shifting, however, is exactly what occurs in the five puzzles that I presented.

The reasons for such spreading and shifting are very simple. First, let us consider shifting. Suppose that one knows exactly what the history of the world that one inhabits is like. And suppose that one is constantly looking at a clock one knows to be perfect. One's degrees of belief will then be entirely concentrated on one possible world, and at any given moment one's degrees of belief within that world will be entirely concentrated on one temporal location, namely, the one that corresponds to the clock reading that one is then seeing. And that of course means that the location where one's degree of belief distribution is concentrated is constantly moving. That is to say, one's degree of belief distribution is constantly shifting, and such a constant shifting is simply not a case of conditionalization. Self-locating beliefs will therefore generically develop in ways that violate conditionalization. Collins's prisoner case involves exactly such a shifting of one's self-locating degrees of belief. The only difference is that, in his case, one additionally has an initial uncertainty as to which clock is accurate, that is, one is initially uncertain whether one is in a world in which clock A is correct or one in which clock B is correct. It is somewhat surprising that this kind of violation of conditionalization can be parlayed into a violation of reflection. But Collin's prisoner case shows exactly how one can do this.

Next, let us consider spreading. The simplest case of spreading is the case of the traveler who takes the path by the Mountains to Shangri La. His degrees of belief become more spread out when he arrives in Shangri La: at that time he goes from degrees of belief one in heads and zero in tails, to degrees of belief 1/2 in heads and 1/2 in tails.[8] The reason why this happens is that there are two distinct possible experiential paths that end up in the same experiential state. That is to say, the traveler's experiences earlier on determine whether possibility A is the case (Path by the Mountain), or whether possibility B is the case (Path by the Ocean). But because of the memory replacement that occurs if possibility B is the case, those different experiential paths merge into the same experience, so that that experience is not sufficient to tell which path was taken. Our traveler therefore has an unfortunate loss of information, due to the loss of the

195

discriminating power of his experience. What is somewhat surprising is that this loss of discriminating power is not due to any loss of memory or any cognitive defect on his part: it is due to the fact that something strange would have happened to him had he taken the other path! This loss of discriminatory power of experience, and consequent spreading out of degrees of belief here does not involve self-locating degrees of belief. Suppose, for example, that our traveler is the only person ever to travel along either path. Then our traveler initially is unsure whether he is in a world in which path A is never taken or whether he is in a world in which path B is never taken. He then becomes sure that he is in a world in which path B is never taken. Even later, upon arrival, he again becomes unsure as to which world he is in. None of this has anything to do with self-locating beliefs.[9]

The source of the Sleeping Beauty and Duplication problems is exactly the same. In the case of Sleeping Beauty, the possibility of memory erasure ensures that the self-locating degrees of belief of Sleeping Beauty, even on Monday when she has suffered no memory erasure, become spread out over two days. In the Duplication case, yet again, the possible duplication of experiences forces one to become uncertain as to where (or who) one is. The cause of the spreading of degrees of belief in both cases is "experience duplication," and has nothing to do with the self-locating nature of these beliefs.[10]

It is not very surprising that the spreading of degrees of belief can bring about a violation of reflection. For instance, in the non-self-locating case a predictable reduction from degree of belief one in some proposition X to anything less than one will immediately violate reflection: now you know it, now you do not. The argument is slightly less straightforward in the self-locating case. Consider, for example, a case in which one is on Earth and one knows that at midnight a duplicate of oneself will be created on Mars. One might claim that since one now is certain that one is on Earth, and at midnight one will be uncertain as to whether one is on Earth, thus one has a clear violation of reflection. This is too quick, however. To have a clear violation of reflection it has to be the very same "content of belief" such that one's current degree of belief differs from one's expectation of one's future degree of belief. Depending on what one takes to be the contents of belief when it concerns self-locating beliefs (propositions? maps from locations to propositions? ...), one might argue that the contents of belief are not the same at the two different times, and hence there is no violation of reflection. The arguments in the sections on Sleeping Beauty and on Duplication, however, show that one can in any case parlay such spreading of self-locating degrees of belief into violations of reflection concerning such ordinary beliefs as to whether a coin lands heads or tails. So reflection is suckered anyhow.

Finally, the original case of the prisoner involves both a spreading of degrees of belief and a shifting of degrees of belief. The shifting is due simply to the passage of time and the self-locating nature of the beliefs. The spreading is due to the fact that our prisoner does not have experiences that are discriminating enough to pick out a unique location in time.[11] The analysis on pages 188–191 shows, yet again, that such a spreading and shifting of self-locating degrees of belief can be parlayed into a violation of reflection concerning such ordinary beliefs as to whether a coin lands heads or tails.

Conclusions

The degrees of belief of rational people can undergo two as yet unrecognized types of development. Such degrees of belief can become more spread out due to the duplication of experiences, or more generally, due to the loss of discriminating power of experiences, and thereby violate conditionalization. In addition, self-locating degrees of belief will generically be shifted over the space of possible locations, due to the passage of time, and thereby violate conditionalization. Such violations of conditionalization can be parlayed into violations of reflection, and lead to a distrust of one's future degrees of belief. Strange, but not irrational.

Notes

* Originally published in *Journal of Philosophy*, 100 (2003), pp. 356–70. Copyright © 2003 The Journal of Philosophy, Inc. Reprinted by permission of The Journal of Philosophy and Frank Arntzenius.

† I would like to thank John Collins, Adam Elga, John Hawthorne, Isaac Levi, Barry Loewer, and Tim Maudlin for extensive and crucial comments and discussions on earlier versions of this article.

1 Thus, for instance, if the light is not switched off, there must be a moment (which could be before or after midnight) such that you have an equal degree of belief in each of the three possibilities: heads and it is before midnight, tails and it is before midnight, tails and it is after midnight.

2 One might wonder why I inserted the phrase 'almost certainly' in this sentence. The reason for this is that there is a subtlety as to whether you know at 6 PM that you will have an increased degree of belief in tails at 11:59 PM. There is an incoherence in assuming that at 6 PM you know with certainty what your degree of belief distribution over possible times will be at 11:59 PM. For if you knew that, you could simply wait until your degree of belief distribution was exactly like that. (You can presumably establish by introspection what your degree of belief distribution is.) And when you reach that distribution, you would know that it has to be 11:59 PM. So when that happens you should then collapse your degree of belief distribution completely on it being 11:59 PM. But this is incoherent. Thus, the fact that you do not have a perfect internal clock also implies that you cannot know in advance what your degree of belief distribution is going to look like after it has developed (guided only by your internal clock). Thus you cannot in advance be certain how your degree of belief distribution over possible times will develop. Nonetheless, you can be certain at 6 PM that your degree of belief in tails will not decrease prior to midnight, and that it is extremely likely to have increased by 11:59 PM. At 6 PM your expectation for your degree of belief in tails at 11:59 PM will be substantially greater than 1/2.

3 "Self-Locating Belief and the Sleeping Beauty Problem," *Analysis*, LX (2000): 143–47; reprinted as Chapter 10 in this volume.

4 Cian Dorr has independently arrived at the idea of using commutativity in order to argue for the degrees of belief that Elga advocates in the Sleeping Beauty case—see Dorr, "Sleeping Beauty: In Defense of Elga," *Analysis* 62 (2002): 292–295.

5 This scenario is similar to the "Dr. Evil scenario" in Elga, "Defeating Dr. Evil with Self-Locating Belief" *Philosophy and Phenomenological Research* 69 (2004): 383–96.

6 See van Fraassen, "Belief and the Problem of Ulysses and the Sirens," *Philosophical Studies*, LXXVII (1995): 7–37.

7 Strict conditionalization: when one learns proposition X at t, one's new degree of belief D_t equals one's old degree of belief D_0 conditional upon X: $D_t(Y) = D_0(Y/X)$. One might also allow Jeffrey conditionalization. It matters not for our purposes.

8 van Fraassen, in conversation with me, has suggested that in such situations conditionalization indeed should be violated, but reflection should not. In particular, he suggested that the degrees of belief of the traveler should become *completely vague*, upon arrival in Shangri La. This does not strike me as plausible. Surely upon arrival in Shangri La our traveler is effectively in the same epistemic situation as someone who simply knows that a fair coin has been tossed. One can make this vivid by considering two travelers, A and B. Traveler A never looks out of the window of the car, and hence maintains degree of belief 1/2 in heads all the way. (The memory replacement device does not operate on travelers who never look out of the window.) Traveler A, even by van Frassen's lights, upon arrival in Shangri La, should still have degree of belief 1/2 in heads. Traveler B, however, does look out of the window during the trip. Upon arrival, by van Frassen's lights, B's degrees of belief should become completely vague. But it seems odd to me that

traveler B is epistemically penalized, that is, is forced to acquire completely vague degrees of belief, just because he looked out of the window during the trip, when it seems clear that he ends up in exactly the same epistemic position as his companion, who did not look out of the window.

9 It is obvious how to generalize this case to a case in which there are memory replacement devices at the end of both roads, where these memory replacement devices are indeterministic, that is, when it is the case that for each possible path there are certain objective chances for certain memories upon arrival in Shangri La. For, given such chances (and the principal principle), one can easily calculate the degrees of belief that one should have (in heads and tails) given the memory state that one ends up with. And, generically, one will still violate conditionalization and reflection.

10 Some people will balk at some of the degrees of belief that I have argued for in this paper, in particular in the self-locating cases. For instance, some people will insist that tomorrow one should still be certain that one is on Earth, even when one now knows (for sure) that a perfect duplicate of oneself will be created on Mars at midnight tonight. I beg to differ. Even if in this case, and other cases, however, one disagrees with me as to which degrees of belief are rationally mandated, the main claim of this paper still stands. The main claim is that in such cases of possible experience duplication, it is at the very least *rationally permissible* that one's degrees of belief become more spread out as time progresses, and hence rational people can violate conditionalization and reflection.

11 One might model the prisoner here as having unique distinct experiences at each distinct, external clock, time, and as initially having precise degrees of belief over the possible ways in which those experiences could correlate to the actual, external clock, time. If one were to do so, then the prisoner would merely be initially uncertain as to which world he was in (where worlds are distinguished by how his experiences line up with the actual, external clock, time), but for each such possible world would be always certain as to where he was located in it. And, if one were to do so, then the original prisoner case would be essentially the same case as Collins's prisoner case: no uncertainty of location in any given world, merely an initial uncertainty as to which world one is in, and a subsequent shifting of the locally concentrated degrees of belief within each of the possible worlds. There is no need, however, to represent the original prisoner case that way. Indeed, it seems psychologically somewhat implausible to do so. More importantly, the arguments and conclusions here do not depend on how one models this case.

12

WHEN BETTING ODDS AND CREDENCES COME APART

More worries for Dutch book arguments*

Darren Bradley and Hannes Leitgeb

If an agent believes that the probability of E being true is 1/2, should she accept a bet on E at even odds or better? Yes, but only given certain conditions. This paper is about what those conditions are. In particular, we think that there is a condition that has been overlooked so far in the literature. We discovered it in response to a paper by Hitchcock (2004) in which he argues for the 1/3 answer to the Sleeping Beauty problem. Hitchcock argues that this credence follows from calculating her fair betting odds, plus the assumption that Sleeping Beauty's credences should track her fair betting odds. We will show that this last assumption is false. Sleeping Beauty's credences should not follow her fair betting odds owing to a peculiar feature of her epistemic situation.

Dutch books

Suppose that rational agents bet in line with their beliefs. This means that if an agent believes proposition E with certainty, he will bet in favour of the truth of E at any odds, no matter how long. If he believes E with 50% certainty, he will accept a bet on E that pays twice the stake (or more). If he believes E with 33% certainty, he will accept a bet on E that pays 3 times the stake (or more). Some writers *defined* partial beliefs in terms of betting behaviour, making the link constitutive. We have no need for such a strong link. All we need is for there to be a normative link between the belief and the bet. Something like 'Other things being equal (risk-neutral, utility linear with money, ...), an agent who accepts E with 50% certainty is rationally permitted to accept a bet on E that pays twice the stake or better'. This link is broadly accepted, and will be all we need. The issue that we are interested in within this paper is the 'other things'.

Assuming agents bet in line with their beliefs, can we say anything about the beliefs an agent may rationally have by looking at the bets they will make? Dutch book arguments say that we can. A Dutch book is a series of bets such that anyone who accepts the bets will end up losing money however the world turns out. A Dutch book argument says that any set of beliefs that justifies an agent's accepting a Dutch book is irrational. The beliefs lead to the bets; the bets leads to a guaranteed loss; therefore the beliefs were irrational. Dutch book arguments have been the main arguments given for probabilism – the doctrine that one's beliefs should conform to the probability calculus (Ramsey 1927; cf. Skyrms 1987). Given the importance of this idea, the argument deserves careful scrutiny.

A Dutch book argument is also used by Chris Hitchcock (2004); not for probabilism, but in arguing that an agent should have a *particular* set of beliefs. In the Sleeping Beauty problem (as explained below), the disagreement is about the degree of belief Sleeping Beauty should have that a coin landed Heads. Some argue for 1/3, others for 1/2. Hitchcock points out that 1/3 is the only degree of belief that avoids a Dutch book. We agree with him on this point. Hitchcock concludes that 1/3 is the only rationally permissible belief. We disagree. Various examples have already been given in the literature where correct betting behaviour comes apart from rational degree of belief. Hitchcock is careful to make sure that his example avoids being like any of these cases. But we think he has highlighted a new case, not previously noticed, where betting behaviour should come apart from rational degrees of belief. Thus betting considerations in Sleeping Beauty, as in other cases, are inconclusive.

Sleeping Beauty

Sleeping Beauty is about to be put to sleep. She will be woken on Monday then put back to sleep. If a fair coin lands Heads, she will not be awoken again. If it lands Tails, she will also be woken on Tuesday. But the drug is such that on Tuesday she will have no memory of the Monday awakening. So she will not know, when awoken, whether it is Monday or Tuesday. And of course this will be true of the Monday awakening as well, as she is not told how the coin lands. When Beauty finds herself awake, what credence should she have in the proposition that the coin landed Heads?

There are two compelling, mutually exclusive arguments:

Half: Her credence should be 1/2, because she has learnt no new evidence that is relevant to the coin landing Heads.

Third: Her credence should be 1/3, because if the experiment is repeated there will be twice as many awakenings due to Tails.

Admittedly this last one is not a very good argument. Hitchcock has a better one. He imagines a bookie who offers Sleeping Beauty various bets, but each on the outcomes of the single coin toss that was described in the story above. The bookie has no more information than Sleeping Beauty (otherwise Dutch books are not a sign of irrationality), so we can imagine him being subject to the same druggings and awakenings as Beauty. Nevertheless, Hitchcock shows that Beauty can avoid being Dutch booked if and only if she assigns Tails a credence of 1/3 on being awoken. Let us review the betting situations that occur in the 1/2 and in the 1/3 case:

$$P(E) = \tfrac{1}{2}:$$

Suppose Beauty refuses to follow Hitchcock's advice, and stubbornly assigns $P(E) = 1/2$ on being awoken. The bookie then offers the following set of bets: On Sunday, Beauty is offered a bet of £15 that wins £15 if Tails lands; on each awakening, Beauty is offered a bet of £10 that wins £10 if Heads lands; i.e.:

	Sunday	Monday	Tuesday	Net
Heads	−15	10		−5
Tails	15	−10	−10	−5

Suppose the coin lands Heads. The first bet loses £15. The second bet, on Monday, wins £10. Beauty and the bookie sleep through Tuesday. Overall, Beauty loses £5. Suppose the coin lands Tails. The first bet wins £15. The second bet, on Monday, loses £10. The third bet, on Tuesday, loses £10. Overall, Beauty loses £5. Either way, Beauty loses £5. She has accepted a Dutch book. She did so because she bet in accordance with her 50% credence that the coin landed Heads.

$$P(E) = \tfrac{1}{3}:$$

Disaster can be avoided if Beauty follows Hitchcock's advice: while she first assigns $P(E) = 1/2$ on Sunday, she changes her assignment to $P(E) = 1/3$ when awoken. She will not accept the evens bet on Heads when awoken. The deal would have to be sweetened. A layout of £10 would have to be rewarded with winnings of £20 (instead of £10), as Heads has fallen in probability:

	Sunday	Monday	Tuesday	Net
Heads	−15	20		5
Tails	15	−10	−10	−5

Now the bet looks as it should. She loses £5 if Tails, and wins £5 if Heads. It can be shown that no Dutch book can be made against Beauty in this new setting. In order to see this, note that the bookie is not able to distinguish the Monday awakening from the Tuesday awakening himself – otherwise he would have more background information than Beauty has, which we want to avoid – so he is not able to come up with two distinct bets on Monday and Tuesday in any systematic manner. Thus, we may assume that he actually offers the same bet twice: now let the money which Beauty would lose on Monday and Tuesday given Tails, respectively, be of amount x, and let what she would win on Monday given Heads be of amount $2x$ or more; if y is what she would lose on Sunday given Heads while winning y or more given Tails, then it is impossible that both the total Heads outcome $-y + 2x$ and the total Tails outcome $y - 2x$ are negative, so there is no way Beauty is bound to lose. We can also see that 1/3 is the only probability that leads to 'fair bets' on awakening, in the sense that Beauty is equally happy to take either side of the bet. Each waking bet costs x, so $2x$ is lost if Tails. Whence the fair payoff given Heads must be $2x$. This bet will be considered fair if and only if Beauty's credence in Heads on waking is 1/3.

Hitchcock concludes that $P(E) = 1/3$ is the rationally required answer, which tells us Beauty really ought to believe with 1/3 probability that the coin landed Tails. We think this is incorrect. It is true that 1/3 is the only credence that avoids a Dutch book, but we think the example is one in which the agent should not bet in line with her credences. The only way to avoid a Dutch book is to bet *as if* one believed Heads landed with 1/3 certainty. But from this it does not follow that the agent really is rationally required nor even permitted to believe that Heads landed with 1/3 probability. Let us take a look at a similar example, where betting *as if* one believed a proposition to 1/3 certainty will avoid a Dutch book.

Separating credences from betting odds

What we need is a case where it is clear that the probability of a coin landing Heads is 1/2, but nevertheless, one should bet as if the probability were something other than 1/2. This would happen if the bet were only 'actually' offered if the coin landed Tails. We propose two ways of getting this result.

Forgery. Imagine that you knew a fair coin was about to be flipped. If the coin lands Heads, no bet will be made. If the coin lands Tails, you are offered a bet on Heads, but not Heads of a new coin flip but of the flip that has just taken place. Should you accept this bet? Of course not. You should not take a bet, no matter how generous the odds, on the proposition that the coin landed Heads. So perhaps we have a case where your betting odds have come apart from your credences? Not yet; this is no good as it stands, because the fact that you have been offered the bet might tell you that the coin landed Tails. You have received extra information that shifts your credences. So in fact your credence in Tails is close to 1. And it is therefore in line with your credences not to accept bets on Heads. Credences and betting odds are still aligned.

What we need is a way of making sure that offering the bet does not inform the agent that the coin landed Tails. And we can do that by offering a fake bet. Imagine that instead of no bet being offered if the coin lands Heads, a bet will indeed be offered, except with fake money. Your notes, and the bookie's, have been switched for excellent, but worthless, forgeries. Neither you nor the bookie can tell the difference. If the coin lands Tails, you will be offered a bet (on Heads) with real money. If it lands Heads, you will be offered a bet (on Heads) with fake money. Should you take the bet? Of course not. Either the coin lands Tails and you lose real money, or it lands Heads and you win fake money. You are much better off holding on to your real money. Nevertheless, your credence that the coin landed Heads should remain at 1/2. Why should your subjective degree of belief in the outcome of the coin landing event be affected by the existence of a fake bet that you are not even aware of as being fake? So we have a case where your credence that the (fair) coin landed Heads (1/2) should not guide your betting behaviour.

Hallucination. The point can be made even more vividly by making the example such that the fake bet does not exist at all; it will just be in your head. As in the Sleeping Beauty case, we also add a second time period. Suppose that if the coin lands Tails, you will be offered two real bets on Heads (of the same flip), one after the other. There is no funny business here. But if the coin lands Heads, you will be offered a real bet on Heads and you will also hallucinate being offered a bet on Heads. You won't know whether the hallucination occurs at the first stage or the second stage. You do know that one of the bets will be real and one will be a hallucination. Whether or not you accept the hallucinatory bet, you will later wake up and find your wallet untouched. So we have:

	Stage 1	Stage 2
Tails	Real Bet	Real Bet
Heads	Real Bet or Hallucinatory Bet	Real if the first bet was hallucinatory, hallucinatory if the first bet was real

Should you accept any of these bets? No. Your credence in Tails should remain at 50%, but you should not accept either (evens) bet on Heads. Again, we have found a case where your credences and betting odds come apart. Hopefully this is already intuitively correct, but let us go carefully through the reasoning: It is straightforward why the credence should stay the same. You have the same experiences given either Heads or Tails, so you have learnt nothing that could give you relevant information. What about the bets? We can sum over the possible bets to find the expected utility is negative. There are 4 possible bets:

(a) Tails and Real (first bet)
(b) Tails and Real (second bet)
(c) Heads and Real (first or second bet)
(d) Heads and Hallucinatory (first or second bet, in any case not real)

Head and Tails still have a 50% probability. How do we divide these probabilities up further between (a) and (b) (and (c) and (d))? Using Elga's (2004) Restricted Principle of Indifference, accepted by all concerned including Hitchcock (and implicitly used earlier), each of these 4 possibilities gets a probability of 25%. What is the expected value of each one? Let s be the stake. a has a value of $-s$, and c has a value of s (the bet is even), so these cancel. d has a value of 0 as no bet is made. The net effect comes from b, which has a value of $-s$. So the expected utility is:

$$\tfrac{1}{4}^*(-s) + \tfrac{1}{4}^*(-s) + \tfrac{1}{4}^*s + \tfrac{1}{4}^*0 = \tfrac{1}{4}^*(-s)$$

We get negative expected utility, but credence in Tails stays at 50%. If you take a bet with negative expected utility, a Dutch book can be made against you, as shown by Hitchcock. The reason for the negative utility is that one of the bets only exists for real if you are going to lose it. Normally the existence of such an unfair bet would tell the agent what the result is. But the agent's unfortunate epistemic state (hallucinating a bet) prevents him from learning this piece of information. However, this does not stop him from losing money if he takes the bet. So we have a case where credences come apart from betting odds.

Sleeping Beauty revisited

It is a small step from this example to Sleeping Beauty. All we need to do is change the hallucination to a state where the agent is not conscious at all; in either case there is no real bet. And to stop Beauty learning from the offer of a second bet, we need to give her amnesia so she does not know whether it is the first or second bet. These are the only two changes needed to turn the example into Sleeping Beauty.

In the Hallucination case, if the first bet was real, then the second bet should not be accepted because it is only offered for real if it is a losing bet. That is, there is only a second real bet if the coin landed Tails, in which case the bet offered on Heads will lose.

In Sleeping Beauty, the Tuesday bet (if there is one) should not be accepted because it is only offered if it is a losing bet. That is, it only exists if the coin landed Tails, so the bet on Heads will lose. Beauty does not know if the bet offered to her is the Monday bet (fair) or the Tuesday bet (unfair). So she simply sums the expected utility. She adds the expected utility of the Monday bet (0) to the expected utility of the Tuesday bet (negative). The result is negative. So neither waking bet should be accepted. We can see that the key move in Hitchcock's argument is not the Dutch book as a package, but his claim that the waking bets should be accepted. We have shown that the waking bets should not be accepted as they have negative utility, so the Dutch book is avoided.

In Hallucination, we think the fact that the agent only avoids a Dutch book by betting *as if* her credence in Heads is 1/3 gives her no reason to actually *believe* that the probability of Heads is 1/3. Similarly, we think that in Sleeping Beauty the fact that the agent only avoids a Dutch book by betting *as if* her credence in Heads is 1/3 gives her no reason to actually *believe* that the probability of Heads is 1/3. Hitchcock must show why the agent's credence in Heads (in Hallucination) should be 1/3, or show that Sleeping Beauty has received some extra piece of information that is omitted from Hallucination. We think neither move is plausible.

What is the reason that in all these cases a subject's credences should differ from his betting rates? Forgery, Hallucination, and Sleeping Beauty have a key feature in common. The trick being played on the agent is that the size or the very existence of a bet on event E is correlated with the outcome of E. In Forgery, the agent is offered a large bet if they are betting on the wrong result, i.e. on what has *not* happened, and a small bet (of value zero) if they are betting on the correct result. In Hallucination, we also get a correlation between the size of a bet and the outcome of the corresponding event. This is because one of the bets is only *actually* made if the agent is betting on the wrong result – another way of getting a bet of size zero in the winning situation. There are various other examples in the literature of cases where an agent should not make bets in accordance with her credences. One example is Talbott's (1991) where the agent has less information than the bookie. Further ones are Maher's (1993) and Seidenfeld et al. (1990) where utilities are not linear in money. Another is that the agent is irrational at a future time (Christensen 1991). Hitchcock avoids these problems, but we think he has not noticed the one we point out – where the size of a bet on an event is correlated with the outcome of the event. It is not surprising this has not been noticed before. It is a very peculiar epistemic state to be in, such that you are only offered a bet given a certain condition, but nevertheless the offer of the bet does not tell you that the condition is satisfied.

Hitchcock has attempted to give a Dutch book argument to the conclusion that only particular credences are rationally acceptable. This result assumes that if only particular betting odds will avoid a Dutch book, these odds should guide our credences. We have attempted to show that Sleeping Beauty is (yet another) case where credence and betting odds diverge. If either the size or the existence of a bet on E is correlated with the result of E and the agent is at the same time unaware of the size or existence of the bet, a Dutch book can be constructed. But the Dutch book argument does not help us figure out what sleeping Beauty should believe. If there is a normative link between beliefs and bets, then the corresponding norm should include the proviso: 'Other things being equal (risk-neutral, utility linear with money, ..., and: *the agent believes that neither the size nor the existence of the bet is correlated with the outcome of the event that the bet is on*) ...'.[1]

Notes

* Originally published in *Analysis*, **66** (2006), pp. 119–27. Copyright © 2006 Darren Bradley and Hannes Leitgeb. Reprinted with permission.
1 We want to thank Christopher Hitchcock for various very helpful discussions on a preliminary draft of the paper.

Bibliography

Christensen, D. 1991. Clever bookies and coherent beliefs. *Philosophical Review* 100: 229–247.

Elga, A. 2004. Defeating Dr. Evil with self-locating belief. *Philosophy and Phenomenological Research* 69: 383–396.

Hitchcock, C. 2004. Beauty and the bets. *Synthese* 139: 405–420.

Maher, P. 1993. *Betting on Theories*. Cambridge: Cambridge University Press.

Ramsey. 1927. Truth and probability. In *Philosophical Papers*, ed. D. H. Mellor. Cambridge: Cambridge University Press, reprinted as Chapter 2 in this volume.

Seidenfeld, T., M. Schervish and J. Kadane. 1990. When fair betting odds are not degrees of belief. *PSA* (proceedings of the Philosophy of Science Association) 1: 517–524.

Skyrms, B. 1987. Coherence. In *Scientific Inquiry in Philosophical Perspective*, ed. N. Rescher. Pittsburgh, PA: University of Pittsburgh Press.

Talbott, W. 1991. Two principles of Bayesian epistemology. *Philosophical Studies* 62: 135–150.

Part III

EVIDENCE AND PROBABILITY

Bayesian confirmation theory

13

INTRODUCTION

Science is founded on the supposition that the evidence makes some theories reasonable to accept, and others unreasonable. Some hypotheses, that is, are supported by the evidence, but not all. Moreover, we have a pretty good idea of which hypotheses those are: for example, evolution, plate tectonics, the theory of relativity. And we have a pretty good idea of how to subject new hypotheses to evidential test. We have a broad competence, that is, with the scientific method, and reasonable agreement between scientists about how to deploy it and interpret its results.

On the other hand, there are famous philosophical arguments to the effect that observational evidence will never support any particular beliefs about the future, or any theoretical hypothesis about the unobserved more generally, and that inductive or ampliative inference is not rational (Hume, 1748). So, if there is no reasonable inference from evidence to hypothesis, how can it be that science is successful and there is a broad agreement on its methods? To explain this, we need to develop some understanding of evidential support that either goes beyond or evades Hume's arguments.

Famously, Popper (1959) agreed with Hume and concluded that there could be no reasonable grounds to accept a theory on the basis of evidence. Rather, we could at best *reject* theories that turned out to be inconsistent with the evidence (where inconsistency is the ordinary logical notion). This doctrine of *falsificationism* is still a dominant trope in scientists' own conception of the scientific method; unfortunately it fits very poorly with scientific practice—often it poorly fits the practice even of those who espouse it. For most scientists do think that past evidence and the success of science in predicting new evidence provides excellent reason to believe a scientific theory, not just good reason to refrain from rejecting it, as Popper would have it. So our delicate position continues: science is manifestly successful, vindicating scientific inference; but we have philosophical reason to suspect that there are no good theories of rational inference that would validate scientific reasoning.

The views on credence and updating we have explored in the previous two parts suggest a way out of this Humean impasse. As we saw, there is a sense in which our credences represent our confidence in particular propositions; and there is a good sense in which updating our credences on the basis of new evidence represents our subsequent confidence in those propositions. What if, by updating on new evidence, we become more confident in a proposition than we were previously? In that case, it seems, the evidence we have received has supported the proposition in question. Hume's arguments—if they succeed—would show that there is no rationally required inductive response to evidence. The *Bayesian* alternative, where 'Bayesian' is intended to capture broadly probabilist views on credence and updating, is to say that the rational updating of coherent credences on receipt of new evidence is rational. But how one responds to evidence depends on one's prior conditional credences, which may vary from person to person, and those priors are not in any sense rationally mandated. We shall look more closely at these kinds of Humean arguments in Part IV, where views that dispute Hume's contention that there is no a priori support for inductive reasoning will be discussed.

Confirmation

The Bayesian account of confirmation focuses on the inferences of individual scientists when confronted with evidence. As suggested above, the proposal is that, if C is the scientist's prior credence, and C^+ their posterior credence, then an experience provides evidence that *confirms* a hypothesis h, for that scientist, if $C^+(h) > C(h)$. If the posterior credence is assumed to obey conditionalisation on the evidence proposition e, as discussed in Part II, this is equivalent to $C(h|e) > C(h)$. This evidence 'boosts' the scientist's credence in the hypothesis.

It might initially be suspected that, while this might explain the inferences of an individual scientist, the variety of permissible degrees of belief that the subjective probability framework permits will undermine any attempt to explain general community-wide patterns of scientific inference—the patterns which have collectively been called the 'scientific method'. But, in fact, from what seem like relatively minimal and uncontroversial assumptions on prior credences, many of the accepted canons of scientific inference can be given a reconstruction within the Bayesian framework. Insofar as those constraints on priors are widely followed, there is therefore a reason for most to follow the scientific method, which is thereby given a justification. Of course, the justification here is that the scientific method encapsulates in simple heuristics the inferences which could have been directly established by conditionalising on the evidence, so it is hardly independent reason for anyone to adopt prior credences which obey the required constraints. (If (i) agents are not perfectly introspective and cannot tell whether or not they satisfy the constraints, and (ii) there is advantage to being in line with community standards with respect to confirmation, as it seems there might well be in actual scientific communities, then acting so as to follow the rules, and thereby ensure that one acts as if one's credences are of the appropriate sort, might be prudentially justified.) The justification on offer, then, is dependent on the fact that—as things actually stand—we do tend to have credences with the right kind of structure.

This has seemed like grounds for imposing additional constraints on prior credence. So Williamson, in arguing for a kind of objective Bayesianism, in which there is a unique rational initial credence distribution which 'measures something like the intrinsic plausibility of hypotheses prior to investigation' (the kind of view we will consider in Part IV), writes that 'successful [subjective] Bayesian treatments of specific epistemological problems ... assume that subjects have "reasonable" prior distributions. We judge a prior distribution reasonable if it complies with our intuitions about the intrinsic plausibility of hypothesis. This is the same sort of vagueness as infects the present approach, if slightly better hidden' (Williamson, 2000: 211–12). The successes of Bayesianism, in effect, are claimed to be by-products of the prior and have little to do with the minimal requirement of coherence. (A similar observation is made by Glymour, Chapter 15, p. 256, where he argues that an *ad hoc* assignment of priors can be constructed that will ratify any particular canons of scientific inference. But we didn't want to show that the scientific method was *consistently implementable* in the Bayesian framework—we wanted to show that it followed from all (or most) reasonable credences that these inferences were good ones.)

Yet it is arguably not reasonable to expect something as strong as a unique prior assignment of intrinsic plausibility, as it seems manifestly plausible that people can reasonably disagree over the prior plausibility of a hypothesis. What matters more, surely, is posterior agreement, or at least agreement on what confirms what. The examples developed by Howson and Urbach in Chapter 14 seem to show that the goal of explaining the substantive agreement on confirmation amongst scientists can be met by subjective Bayesians who appeal to the *de facto* structural similarity between scientists' priors. But this goal is equally satisfied by the theories of evidential probability discussed in Chapter 17, particularly the strand that takes the existence of strong constraints on prior conditional probabilities as a starting point. And note, moreover, that whether the agreement on the prior conditional probabilities is given by a rationality constraint or just what is institutionally or congenitally true of us, the same patterns of explanation of the maxims in the examples below will obtain.

Before developing some of those examples, I will mention an argument some Bayesians offer that the subjectivity of the priors doesn't matter. This argument points to the existence of 'convergence of opinion' theorems (discussed by Glymour in Chapter 15; also mentioned in Chapter 1), to the effect that two Bayesian agents who start off with regular priors (more generally, who assign credences of 1 and 0 to the same propositions as each other), and who successively update by conditionalisation on the same sequence of evidence propositions will, in the limit with probability 1, come to have posterior credences that are arbitrarily close to one another, no matter where they started out. The differences in the priors are swamped by the agreement on the evidence. It can also be shown that, if the evidence sequences are relatively simple, and the hypotheses under consideration similarly simple (perhaps just being hypotheses about the total evidence sequence), these agents will converge not just on each other, but will both converge on the true hypothesis in the limit, with probability 1. So in this case it seems that the subjectivity of the priors doesn't matter, because these two agents will come to agree in their final judgements about which hypotheses are most plausible in light of the evidence. But we never have infinite sequences of data, so there seems no guarantee from these theorems that actual people will come to agree. It is an equally false idealisation to assume that two agents might have the same evidence—even ideal agents will differ at least in their *de se* (self-locating) evidence. Whatever explains our actual general agreement, it can't be anything like what is involved in the conditions for the convergence of opinion theorems to hold, and so appeal to those theorems seems unlikely to provide a justification for the methodology actually employed in scientific inference. Finally, a point that Glymour makes is worth noting: the relevant convergence theorem

> does not tell us that in the limit any rational Bayesian will assign probability 1 to the true hypothesis and probability 0 to the rest; it only tells us that rational Bayesians are certain that he will. It may reassure those who are already Bayesians, but it is hardly grounds for conversion.
>
> (Chapter 15: 255)

Even if it is thereby rational to expect convergence and that differences in the priors don't matter, that doesn't yet show that these rational expectations will be fulfilled.

Successes of the Bayesian approach to confirmation

A 'success' for Bayesian confirmation theory is a case where, if the pre-theoretical notion of evidential support is analysed in Bayesian terms, the apparently rational responses to evidence that are licensed by the informal notion can be motivated and reconstructed in the Bayesian framework. There can generally be two types of such cases: *assumption-free* cases where the reconstruction succeeds regardless of the prior credences involved, and *assumption-laden* cases where the reconstruction requires some assumptions about the priors. The latter cases will also permit the Bayesian to construct circumstances where agents have coherent prior credences that diverge from those needed to reconstruct the target inference. Such cases will provide another direction of support for the Bayesian analysis of confirmation if it can be shown that, in these cases where the Bayesian predicts it is not necessarily rational to respond to evidence in a certain familiar way, our intuitive judgements also make the same prediction. (This latter kind of case is arguably what has happened with the Bayesian response to Hempel's paradox of confirmation, where Good (1961) gave a case that persuaded many that a prima facie plausible attempt to capture in a maxim some of the intuitive features of confirmation by instances had an unexpected counterexample, the existence of which is revealed by a Bayesian approach.)

The approach of Howson and Urbach in Chapter 14 is to offer Bayesian reconstructions and explanations of a number of widely accepted doctrines about evidence in science. For example, they show how Bayesians can explain the following familiar maxims of scientific interference:

> **Surprising evidence.** Surprising evidence *e* supports a hypothesis *h* which predicts it—that is, assigns it a high *likelihood* $C(e|h)$—over those which do not predict it. Moreover, the more surprising *e* is, other things being equal, the higher the posterior credence in *h* will be (pp. 226–230).

> **Paradox of Confirmation.** It seems that generalisations are confirmed by their instances ('Nicod's condition'), and logically equivalent propositions are each confirmed by the same evidence. But it follows from this that the observation of a white shoe, confirming as it does the generalisation 'All non-black things are non-ravens', should thereby confirm the logically equivalent generalisation 'all ravens are black'. Yet it does not seem to. On pages 204–6, Howson and Urbach argue, following Hosiasson-Lindenbaum (1940), that in the Bayesian framework the paradoxical conclusion does not follow (for Nicod's condition is not generally satisfied). Even under those circumstances when Nicod's condition is satisfied, and the observation of a white shoe does confirm the hypothesis that all ravens are black, it will typically (i.e., given ordinary background assumptions) only raise the posterior probability by a negligible amount, and much less than the boost offered by the observation of a black raven. They take the comparatively weak evidential support offered by the observation of a white shoe to explain our ordinary judgements about the problem cases; we fail to distinguish negligible support from no support at all.

> **Duhem's problem.** Duhem and Quine argued that a hypothesis can be brought into contact with evidence only with the aid of auxiliary claims (so, for example, a theory of the motion of the planets can only make predictions about what we observe through the telescope with the aid of an auxiliary theory

of how telescopes work). *Duhem's problem* is to rationalise our rejection (in most cases) of the hypothesis rather than the auxiliary; on pages 230–236, Howson and Urbach, following the work of Dorling (1979), provide a Bayesian rationale.

Ad hoc **hypotheses.** It is often maintained that *ad hoc* theories constructed to fit the data are less believable than independently motivated theories; relatedly, that predicting a piece of evidence provides more support for a theory than being constructed so as to accommodate a piece of evidence. The discussion on pages 238–245 summarises the Bayesian rationale for these practices.

Some of these cases, like the case of surprising evidence, are assumption-free; the treatment of *ad hoc* theories, on the other hand, is assumption-laden. Even so, the fact that Bayesianism can provide a plausible theoretical framework in which all of these various canons of scientific inference can be argued for is already a mark in its favour. Certainly there is no current alternative general theory of what confirmation consists in that can explain them, which is (at least by the Bayesian's own lights) some support for the Bayesian analysis of confirmation. Rather than go through the details of these examples, which are clearly laid out in Chapter 14 and dealt with more fully in the items cited in Further Reading below, I will illustrate the kind of reconstruction on offer from Bayesianism with reference to another example: the evidential value of diverse evidence (see also Chapter 14, pp. 244–5).

Imagine we are considering a hypothesis h. The likelihood of the evidence is the conditional credences assigned to evidence, conditional on the hypotheses $C(e|h)$. The *Bayes factor* of $\neg h$ against h is defined as this ratio:

$$\beta(\neg h : h) = \frac{C(e|\neg h)}{C(e|h)}.$$

It can be shown that we can rewrite Bayes' theorem (Probability Primer, theorem 13) in terms of the Bayes factor and the prior probability of h (the prior probability of e going unmentioned):[1]

$$C(h|e) = \frac{C(h)}{C(h) + \beta(\neg h : h)C(\neg h)}. \qquad \text{(Useful)}$$

This form is useful, at least, because many have thought that the likelihoods are less 'subjective' than the other credences (it is commonly thought that the likelihood of evidence conditional on a theory is something that is determined by the content of the theory, and what evidence it predicts); this form shows where the updated credence ends up in terms of the prior of the hypothesis and these less subjective likelihoods. (Of course, since the likelihoods replace an expression referring to the prior credence in the evidence, which is supposed to be subjective, perhaps this claim about the objectivity of likelihoods is not sustainable.)

It appears to be a methodological rule that, other things being equal, the more diverse the sources of evidence for one's theory, the more strongly confirmed that theory is. This can be captured in this maxim: *A theory which makes predictions in a number of disparate and seemingly unconnected areas is more confirmed by that evidence than is a theory which is confirmed by predictions only about a narrow and circumscribed range.* The Bayesian insight is that diverse evidence is not internally correlated (Earman, 1992: Sect. 3.5). If the evidence is diverse, it consists of at least two propositions, e_1 and e_2, such that truth of one is not positively relevant to the truth of the other if the hypothesis in question is false. So e_1 and e_2 are diverse relative to h iff the likelihood $C(e_1 \wedge e_2 | \neg h)$ is low, or at least if it is not greater than the product of the individual credences $C(e_1 | \neg h)C(e_2 | \neg h)$. If, for example, the hypothesis is that all swans are white, then swans collected from different countries would, if white, provide better evidence for the hypothesis than swans collected from the same pond, as we know that if one swan on a pond is white, it is much more likely to be related to other swans in its pond, and those are more likely therefore to be white.

If the hypothesis h predicts both e_1 and e_2, then the likelihood $C(e_1 \wedge e_2 | h)$ is high (close to one). So the Bayes' factor is approximately equal to its numerator, $C(e_1 \wedge e_2 | \neg h)$. Substituting this into (Useful), we get

$$C(h|e) \approx \frac{C(h)}{C(h) + C(e_1 \wedge e_2 | \neg h)C(\neg h)}$$
$$\geq \frac{C(h)}{C(h) + (C(e_1 | \neg h)C(e_2 | \neg h))C(\neg h)}.$$

The second line follows from the diversity of the evidence. Thus far, we are only drawing out consequences of the probability calculus. In practical cases, we are interested in evidence that is diverse in such a way as to ensure that, if the hypothesis is false, at least one of the pieces of evidence is unlikely. It would be surprising, given that not all swans are white, if arbitrary swans taken from diverse locations were all likely to be white. There is an additional assumption on the priors in this case: that at least one of $C(e_1 | \neg h)$ and $C(e_2 | \neg h)$ is low, and perhaps both are low. Given that, $C(h) + (C(e_1 | \neg h)C(e_2 | \neg h))C(\neg h)$ may be approximately $C(h)$ and therefore $C(h|e)$ may be close to 1. If h was not antecedently plausible, diverse evidence of this form has strongly confirmed it. (A similar rationale exists for the practice of *random sampling*, if the idea is to ensure pieces of evidence that are uncorrelated with one another.)

Problems for Bayesianism

The picture for Bayesianism is bright, but far from unalloyed. Glymour in Chapter 15 proffers a number of difficulties for Bayesianism, additional to those already raised above. The first part of his chapter primarily concerns the assignment of degrees of belief and the implementation of respect for simplicity in priors; but the final part of his chapter concerns the Bayesian account of evidence.

Glymour raises a number of problems for that account. One interesting puzzle (at p. 271) for the understanding of science more generally is that, if we can (even in a rough and ready way) separate propositions into those directly about observation, and those which are theoretical, then we can construct a 'rival' h' to any theory h, which is just the conjunction of the observational consequences of h. These two theories are equally confirmed by the evidence, since they predict the same appearances; but since $h \rightarrow h'$, the posterior credence in h' cannot be lower than the posterior in h, and hence h' is at least as credible. But this doesn't seem right: this kind of rival is never seriously considered in science, and the theoretical virtues of simplicity, explanatory power, etc., which h' lacks and h may possess, do play a role in scientific inference. The Bayesian, at least in this respect, seems to flout standard scientific practice.

But it is another worry—the problem of *old evidence*—which has been a major stumbling block for Bayesianism. This is the simple observation that, while 'scientists commonly argue for their theories from evidence known long before the theories were introduced' (p. 262), and that even in these cases there can be striking confirmation of a new theory because it explains some well-known anomalous piece of evidence, the Bayesian framework doesn't seem to permit this. For if e is old evidence, then one's credence function at the time the new theory h is proposed, C_t, has come from conditionalising on e at some stage. But then $C_t(h|e) = C_t(h)$, so that the posterior credence in h on e is equal to the prior; h is not confirmed.

Glymour's own diagnosis of the problem is that Bayesianism is (at best) a theory of *learning*, of how to represent your credence at a time and how to update your credence when you learn something new. Sometimes our evidence is something we learn; but sometimes, as in these cases, we have already learned our evidence. The relation of evidential support between evidence and hypotheses seems as though it should be indifferent to whether we know the evidence before or after considering the theory; by elevating the accidental fact that sometimes we learn our evidence into an account of evidence, Bayesianism is unable to accommodate this.

One response is to go on the offensive: if the evidence really is old, then all the scientists already believe it, and have already updated their credences in the hypothesis in question. If there seems to be additional confirmation in these cases, it is because those scientists have imperfect access to their own credences; or are incoherent, since (despite already knowing e) they are more confident in h after noticing e, even though no new evidence has arrived. These Bayesians say: if confirmation doesn't have a close connection with learning, that only undermines its importance—for the main aim of scientific inference isn't to see what confirms what for its own sake, but to discover what we should believe, and what we believe is constrained by the theory of subjective probability.

There are a variety of Bayesian responses which are more concessive than this. Two responses share the idea that, while the old evidence doesn't support the hypothesis given the agent's current credences, there are other credences which are appropriate in some way and on which the evidence does confirm the hypothesis, because it is learned. One response appeals to counterfactual credences—what our credences would have been, had we not learned e. The other appeals to past credences—what our credences were, before we learned e. And the claim is that h is confirmed by e against the background of these counterfactual or historical credences. Both responses seem to run into difficulty from the same kind of case. Take a very old piece of evidence, well-known and very familiar, which, in conjunction with some auxiliary claim a that we learned much more recently, turn out to support a new hypothesis. But if we return to our credence before we learned e, we abandon not only e but also a; and it needn't be that h is confirmed by e without a. (Consider: we've known that the earth was round since classical times, but that doesn't mean that the way in which that fact supports hypotheses must involve only auxiliaries also known since classical times.) If, furthermore, a was only learned because e was learned (e is a striking fact about some subject matter, which prompted further investigation of that area and related areas, which led to the discovery of a), then our counterfactual credence again needn't confirm h because a is not known. (The nearest possibility in which we hadn't learned e is also one where we hadn't learned a either.)

An alternative approach (favourably discussed by Glymour at pp. 265–6) is to say that, while *e* is already certain, what is learned is that *h* entails *e*. Garber (1983) argues that this is best considered a failure of logical omniscience, and that it is possible that Bayesian agents who fail to be certain of all logical truths can, when they learn such a truth, come to be aware of new confirmation relations. But liberalising knowledge of logic threatens to undermine the whole Bayesian approach (since, for example, those who are not logically omniscient can be Dutch booked), quite apart from the difficulties involved in trying to construct a theory that permits logically equivalent propositions to have different credences.

Old evidence remains a live problem for Bayesianism. But other problems have been raised too. The problem of *new theories* arises when a well-confirmed theory is undermined by the postulation of a new hypothesis, even though no new evidence has been received and no credential update has occurred. Again, this kind of case could be solved by appeal to (logical or introspective) ignorance, since a new theory in this sense should still be one which is a proposition over which the credence function is defined, and its novelty must derive from its being unrecognised. A more radical proposal is that this might be a case in which an new algebra of propositions must be considered; it is fair to say that changing the algebra of outcomes is a non-conditionalising update which Bayesians have no account of, though it is equally unclear whether anyone else does either.

Various alternative theories of confirmation also pose challenges for the Bayesian. The main one is the classical theory of statistical testing, developing from the work of Fisher (and ultimately representing the application of Popperian ideas to probabilistic hypotheses); a good recent account of how this project bears on confirmation theory is offered by Mayo (1996). The computational epistemology defended by Kelly (2003) does away with the idea that evidence justifies hypotheses, replacing it with the notion of a reliable procedure for accommodating evidence to converge on the truth. The goodness of such a procedure is evaluated on the externalist criterion of whether or not it leads to the truth. This is a radical alternative to internalist conceptions of rationality, as captured by Bayesianism's emphasis on explaining scientific inferences from within the framework of one's own priors. Once there are other options on the table, it may be that there are better justifications for the scientific method than just that our priors happen to have the right form. Finally, Norton (forthcoming) provides a useful compendium of problems for the Bayesian approach to confirmation.

Measures of confirmation

So far the focus has been on the qualitative relation of confirmation, whether *e* confirms *h*. But there is a follow-up question: *how much* does *e* confirm *h*? Does *e* confirm *h more than* it confirms *h'*? Many of the maxims of scientific inference involve implicit appeal to notions like this. In the case of diverse evidence, what really seems to matter is that diverse evidence confirms a theory more than narrow evidence does. Another example is provided by Howson and Urbach's attempt to explain away our intuition that a non-black non-raven does not confirm the hypothesis that all ravens are black. They claim that, while there is confirmation in some cases like Hempel's,

> Once it is recognised that confirmation is a matter of degree, the conclusion
> is no longer so counter-intuitive, because it is compatible with [a non-black

non-raven] confirming 'All ravens are black', but to a minuscule and negligible degree.

(Chapter 14, page 228)

Hopefully, any plausible measure of confirmation will agree with their assessment of the degree of confirmation in these cases, but it is important to recognise that an adequate Bayesian response to the paradox will require some account of degree of confirmation that will yield this result.

Moreover, if degree of confirmation could be accounted for in the Bayesian framework, it would provide another answer to the subjectivity of the priors—for it could perhaps be argued that, if *e* supports *h* much more than it supports *h'*, there is a reason to believe *h* independently of the prior probability of these hypotheses.

Eells and Fitelson (Chapter 16) address both the issue of how to define the *degree of confirmation* and the role that notion plays in Bayesian reconstructions of the scientific method. They proceed by noting three symmetry constraints on degree of confirmation, intuitively motivated by consideration of the examples they describe in Sect. 3 of their chapter. Our intuitions about strength of evidence are, as seen in many cases, quite as strong as our intuitions about qualitative confirmation. So the failure or holding of these symmetry constraints provides natural and intuitive support for those measures of confirmation that agree with those judgements. Eells and Fitelson argue that, of the natural measures that have been proposed in the literature, only the difference measure *d* (that *e* confirms *h* to the degree that the posterior exceeds the prior) and the log-likelihood measure *l* (that *e* confirms *h* to a degree measured by the log of the ratio of the likelihood of *e* on *h* to the likelihood of *e* on ¬*h*) satisfy all three of their symmetry constraints. Insofar as these symmetry constraints are motivated by the counterexamples, the field is narrowed to those two measures. (Note that their positive argument for the symmetry condition HS is not strictly needed, as the other measures are ruled out by their satisfaction of other intuitively violated symmetry constraints.)

These observations are not unimportant. As Fitelson (1999) points out, several Bayesian treatments of issues of interest, including the problem of diverse evidence, seem to depend on properties of the measure of confirmation, and the success of these treatments then depends on the measure of confirmation having the right form.

Those who favour other measures can either try to respond to the cases on offer (and those on offer in Fitelson 1999), or argue that since there are intuitive considerations in favour of their preferred measures too, there is no univocal notion of degree of support here to be explicated. This approach has bold and reasonable varieties. The bold variety would be to argue that the intuitive notion of degree of support is inconsistent, supporting many constraints that cannot be jointly sustained. (It would be analogous to the way in which, it might be argued, natural language seems to support the T-schema and the existence of names for arbitrary sentences of the language, giving rise to the inconsistencies involved in the Liar paradox.) The more reasonable variety is *pluralist* about degree of confirmation; there are many overlapping but distinct notions of evidence and support in play, all of which have a home in the Bayesian framework, and each of which has a role to play in coming to understand the complexities of pre-theoretical intuitions about confirmation. Again, the debate over which, if any, measure of confirmation is 'the' right one is far from settled.

217

Further reading

The idea that Bayesian confirmation theory provides a concessive way out of Hume's problem of induction is clearly presented in Howson (2000). A recent discussion of the connection between confirmation theory and induction, with reference to Howson's book, is Strevens (2004). Accounts of how Bayesian confirmation theory bears on the so-called 'new riddle' of induction (Goodman 1954) include those of Sober (1994) and Fitelson (2008).

The further reading in Chapter 1 contains details of convergence of opinion theorems.

Perhaps in 1980 it was fair of Glymour to complain that 'There is very little Bayesian literature about the hotchpotch of claims and notions that are usually canonised as scientific method' (Chapter 15, p. 256), but the picture has changed dramatically in the interim. General discussions of Bayesian confirmation theory are provided by Earman (1992), Fitelson (2001), Horwich (1982), Jeffrey (2004: Ch. 2), Talbott (2008: Sect. 4), Rosenkrantz (1977), Sober (2002), and Strevens (2006). A broader discussion of the consequences of Bayesian principles in epistemology is Bovens and Hartmann (2003).

The paradox of confirmation arises obviously in logical theories of confirmation, like that of Hempel (1945). (A useful recent discussion of such theories, aimed at rehabilitating something in the neighbourhood of what Hempel wanted, is Huber (2008a)). The Bayesian counterexample to the principles involved was offered by Good (1967). Vranas (2004) provides a thorough account of the standard Bayesian solutions, like that of Horwich (1982: 54–63), and notes an apparent gap. Fitelson (2006) gives an accessible recent overview, containing (as does the article by Vranas) extensive references to the literature, and offering at the end a patch for the gap identified by Vranas. Maher (1999) provides an account of the paradox from a Carnapian/logical probability perspective.

The orthodox Bayesian solution to Duhem's problem is by Dorling (1979); a recent account, under some conditions, is Bovens and Hartmann (2003: Sect. 4.5). A revised version of the Bayesian account is proposed by Strevens (2001), which is disputed by Fitelson and Waterman (2005).

Regarding *ad hoc* hypotheses, the example of Neptune is discussed by Jeffrey (2004: Sect. 2.3). Two disagreeing but nevertheless orthodox Bayesian treatments of prediction versus accommodation are by Horwich (1982: 108–18) and Maher (1988). A clear recent discussion of the methodological precept that Bayesians are supposedly capturing is White (2003).

Horwich (1982: 118–22) offers a more general account of the value of diverse evidence, predicated upon the ability of diverse evidence to rule out competitors to a hypothesis that agree with the hypothesis on some narrower body of evidence. The standard Bayesian solution is criticised by Wayne (1995); replies are offered by Fitelson (1996) and Steel (1996).

The Bayesian difficulty with confirmation of theories, as opposed to summaries of their observational consequences, is turned into an argument for anti-realism about scientific theories by van Fraassen (1980), who appeals to the same fact that theories are conjunctions of their observational content and theoretical content. Van Fraassen (1989: Ch. 7) offers a Dutch book argument against inference to the best explanation, and other realist patterns of scientific inference. There is a huge literature on this kind of argument for anti-realism about science; some pertinent discussions are offered by Douven (1999), Lipton (1991) and Milne (2003).

The historical or counterfactual credences approach to the problem of old evidence is discussed by Jeffrey (2004: Sect. 2.5), drawing on a series of papers by Wagner that culminate in Wagner (2001). Lange (1999) argues that a 'rational reconstruction' of the ur-credence function can permit a Bayesian account of old evidence. The relaxation of the logical omniscience condition advocated by Garber is also advocated by Niiniluoto (1983) and further discussed by Jeffrey (1983); a critical evaluation is Earman (1992: Ch. 5). A useful account of different threads in the discussion of old evidence is in Joyce (1999). The problem of new hypotheses was raised by Chihara (1987); a Bayesian response is provided by Otte (1994). The relation between old evidence and new theories is discussed by Zynda (1995).

The computational learning theory alternative to Bayesianism is put forward and used to argue that Bayesianism can't capture all of scientific methodology by Kelly and Glymour (2004).

Eells' treatment of the grue paradox where d plays some role is to be found in Eells (1982). Fitelson (2001) offers considerations in favour of the log-likelihood measure l. Eells and Fitelson have extensive references to the literature on measures of confirmation in their chapter. The pluralist approach is defended in a paper by Joyce (2003); his 2008 contribution (Sect. 3) contains further hints of his pluralism. Milne (1996) defends an explicitly non-pluralist account of degree of support, though Huber (2008b) shows that a minor variation of Milne's argument supports an alternative measure of confirmation. Further useful discussions are by Christensen (1999) and Eells and Fitelson (2000). The psychology of judgements of degree of confirmation, looking at how a real subject's judgements conform to the measures proposed, is explored by Tentori *et al.* (2007).

Note

1 Proof:

$$C(h|e) = \frac{C(e|h)C(h)}{C(e)} = \frac{C(h)}{\left(\frac{C(e)}{C(e|h)}\right)} = \frac{C(h)}{\left(\frac{C(e|h)C(h)+C(e|\neg h)C(\neg h)}{C(e|h)}\right)}$$

$$= \frac{C(h)}{C(h) + \left(\frac{C(e|\neg h)}{C(e|h)}C(\neg h)\right)} = \frac{C(h)}{C(h) + \beta(\neg h : h)C(\neg h)}$$

Bibliography

Bovens, Luc and Hartmann, Stephan (2003), *Bayesian Epistemology*. Oxford: Oxford University Press.

Chihara, Charles (1987), 'Some Problems for Bayesian Confirmation Theory'. *British Journal for the Philosophy of Science*, vol. 38: pp. 551–560.

Christensen, David (1999), 'Measuring Confirmation'. *Journal of Philosophy*, vol. 96: pp. 437–461.

Dorling, Jon (1979), 'Bayesian Personalism, the Methodology of Scientific Research Programmes, and Duhem's Problem'. *Studies in History and Philosophy of Science*, vol. 10: pp. 177–187.

Douven, Igor (1999), 'Inference to the Best Explanation Made Coherent'. *Philosophy of Science*, vol. 66 (Proceedings): pp. S424–S435.

Earman, John (1992), *Bayes or Bust?*. Cambridge, MA: MIT Press.

Eells, Ellery (1982), *Rational Decision and Causality*. Cambridge: Cambridge University Press.

Eells, Ellery and Fitelson, Branden (2000), 'Measuring Confirmation and Evidence'. *Journal of Philosophy*, vol. 97: pp. 663–672.

Fitelson, Branden (1996), 'Wayne, Horwich, and Evidential Diversity'. *Philosophy of Science*, vol. 63: pp. 652–660.

—— (1999), 'The Plurality of Bayesian Measures of Confirmation and the Problem of Measure Sensitivity'. *Philosophy of Science*, vol. 66 (Proceedings): pp. S362–S378.

—— (2001), *Studies in Bayesian Confirmation Theory*. PhD thesis, University of Wisconsin, Madison, URL http://fitelson.org/thesis.pdf.

—— (2006), 'The Paradox of Confirmation'. *Philosophy Compass*, vol. 1: pp. 95–113.

—— (2008), 'Goodman's "New Riddle"'. *Journal of Philosophical Logic*, vol. 37: pp. 613–643.

Fitelson, Branden and Waterman, Andrew (2005), 'Bayesian Confirmation and Auxiliary Hypotheses Revisited: A Reply to Strevens'. *British Journal for the Philosophy of Science*, vol. 56: pp. 293–302.

Garber, Daniel (1983), 'Old Evidence and Logical Omniscience in Bayesian Confirmation Theory'. In John Earman (ed.), *Testing Scientific Theories*, Minneapolis: University of Minnesota Press.

Good, I. J. (1961), 'The Paradox of Confirmation (III)'. *British Journal for the Philosophy of Science*, vol. 11: pp. 63–64.

—— (1967), 'The White Shoe is a Red Herring'. *British Journal for the Philosophy of Science*, vol. 17: p. 322.

Goodman, Nelson (1954), *Fact, Fiction and Forecast*. Cambridge, MA: Harvard University Press.

Hempel, Carl (1945), 'Studies in the Logic of Confirmation'. *Mind*, vol. 54: pp. 1–26, 97–121.

Horwich, Paul (1982), *Probability and Evidence*. Cambridge: Cambridge University Press.

Hosiasson-Lindenbaum, Janina (1940), 'On Confirmation'. *Journal of Symbolic Logic*, vol. 5: pp. 133–148.

Howson, Colin (2000), *Hume's Problem: Induction and the Justification of Belief*. Oxford: Oxford University Press.

Huber, Franz (2008a), 'Hempel's Logic of Confirmation'. *Philosophical Studies*, vol. 139: pp. 181–189.

—— (2008b), 'Milne's Argument for the Log-Ratio Measure'. *Philosophy of Science*, vol. 75: pp. 413–420.

Hume, David (1748 [1999]), *An Enquiry Concerning Human Understanding*. Oxford Philosophical Texts, Oxford: Oxford University Press. Edited by Tom L. Beauchamp.

Jeffrey, Richard C. (1983), 'Bayesianism with a Human Face'. In John Earman (ed.), *Testing Scientific Theories*, vol. X of *Minnesota Studies in the Philosophy of Science*, Minneapolis: University of Minnesota Press, pp. 133–156.

—— (2004), *Subjective Probability (The Real Thing)*. Cambridge: Cambridge University Press.

Joyce, James M. (1999), *The Foundations of Causal Decision Theory*. Cambridge: Cambridge University Press.

—— (2003), 'On the Plurality of Probabilist Measures of Evidential Relevance', URL http://www.uni-konstanz.de/ppm/kirchberg/Joyce_1.pdf. Unpublished manuscript, presented at the Bayesian Epistemology workshop at the 26th International Wittgenstein Symposium, Kirchberg, Austria, 5 August 2003.

—— (2008), 'Bayes' Theorem'. In Edward N. Zalta (ed.), *The Stanford Encyclopedia of Philosophy*, Fall 2008 ed.

Kelly, Kevin T. (2003), 'The Logic of Success'. In Peter Clark and Katherine Hawley (eds.), *Philosophy of Science Today*, Oxford: Oxford University Press, pp. 11–38.

Kelly, Kevin T. and Glymour, Clark (2004), 'Why Probability does not Capture the Logic of Scientific Justification'. In Christopher Hitchcock (ed.), *Contemporary Debates in Philosophy of Science*, Oxford: Blackwell, pp. 94–114.

Lange, Marc (1999), 'Calibration and the Epistemological Role of Bayesian Conditionalization'. *Journal of Philosophy*, vol. 96: pp. 294–324.

Lipton, Peter (1991), *Inference to the Best Explanation*. London: Routledge.

Maher, Patrick (1988), 'Prediction, Accommodation, and the Logic of Discovery'. *PSA: Proceedings of the Biennial Meeting of the Philosophy of Science Association*, vol. 1: pp. 273–285.

—— (1999), 'Inductive Logic and the Ravens Paradox'. *Philosophy of Science*, vol. 66: pp. 50–70.

Mayo, Deborah (1996), *Error and the Growth of Experimental Knowledge*. Chicago: University of Chicago Press.

Milne, Peter (1996), 'log[$P(h|eb)/P(h|b)$] is the One True Measure of Confirmation'. *Philosophy of Science*, vol. 63: pp. 21–26.

—— (2003), 'Bayesianism v. Scientific Realism'. *Analysis*, vol. 63: pp. 281–288.

Niiniluoto, I. (1983), 'Novel Facts and Bayesianism'. *British Journal for the Philosophy of Science*, vol. 34: pp. 375–379.

Norton, John D. (forthcoming), 'Challenges to Bayesian Confirmation Theory'. In Prasanta Bandyopadhyay and Malcolm Forster (eds.), *Handbook of the Philosophy of Science, vol. 7: Philosophy of Statistics*, Amsterdam: Elsevier. URL: http://www.pitt.edu/~jdnorton/papers/Challenges.pdf

Otte, Richard (1994), 'A Solution to a Problem for Bayesian Confirmation Theory'. *British Journal for the Philosophy of Science*, vol. 45: pp. 764–769.

Popper, Karl (1959), *The Logic of Scientific Discovery*. London: Hutchinson.

Rosenkrantz, R. D. (1977), *Inference, Method and Decision: Towards a Bayesian Philosophy of Science*. Dordrecht: D. Reidel.

Sober, Elliott (1994), 'No Model, No Inference: A Bayesian Primer on the Grue Problem'. In Douglas Stalker (ed.), *GRUE! The new riddle of induction*, Chicago: Open Court, pp. 225–240.

—— (2002), 'Bayesianism: its Scope and Limits'. In Richard Swinburne (ed.), *Bayes' Theorem*, Oxford: Oxford University Press.

Steel, Daniel (1996), 'Bayesianism and the Value of Diverse Evidence'. *Philosophy of Science*, vol. 63: pp. 666–674.

Strevens, Michael (2001), 'The Bayesian Treatment of Auxiliary Hypotheses'. *British Journal for the Philosophy of Science*, vol. 52: pp. 515–537.

—— (2004), 'Bayesian Confirmation Theory: Inductive Logic or Mere Inductive Framework?' *Synthese*, vol. 141: pp. 365–379.

—— (2006), 'Notes on Bayesian Confirmation Theory', http://www.nyu.edu/classes/strevens/BCT/BCT.pdf. Unpublished manuscript.

Talbott, William (2008), 'Bayesian Epistemology'. In Edward N. Zalta (ed.), *The Stanford Encyclopedia of Philosophy*, Fall 2008 ed., http://plato.stanford.edu/archives/fall2008/entries/epistemology-bayesian/

Tentori, Katya, Crupi, Vincenzo, Bonini, Nicolao and Osherson, Daniel (2007), 'Comparison of Confirmation Measures'. *Cognition*, vol. 103: pp. 107–119.

van Fraassen, Bas C. (1980), *The Scientific Image*. Oxford: Oxford University Press.

—— (1989), *Laws and Symmetry*. Oxford: Oxford University Press.

Vranas, Peter (2004), 'Hempel's Raven Paradox: a Lacuna in the Standard Bayesian Solution'. *British Journal for the Philosophy of Science*, vol. 55: pp. 545–560.

Wagner, Carl (2001), 'Old Evidence and New Explanation III'. *Philosophy of Science*, vol. 68 (Proceedings): pp. S165–S175.

Wayne, Andrew (1995), 'Bayesianism and Diverse Evidence'. *Philosophy of Science*, vol. 62: pp. 111–121.

White, Roger (2003), 'The Epistemic Advantage of Prediction over Accomodation'. *Mind*, vol. 112: pp. 653–683.

Williamson, Timothy (2000), *Knowledge and its Limits*. Oxford: Oxford University Press.

Zynda, Lyle (1995), 'Old Evidence and New Theories'. *Philosophical Studies*, vol. 77: pp. 67–95.

14

BAYESIAN VERSUS NON-BAYESIAN APPROACHES TO CONFIRMATION*

Colin Howson and Peter Urbach

The Bayesian notion of confirmation

Information gathered in the course of observation is often considered to have a bearing on the acceptability of a theory or hypothesis (we use the terms interchangeably), either by confirming it or by disconfirming it. Such information may either derive from casual observation or, more commonly, from experiments deliberately contrived in the hope of obtaining relevant evidence. The idea that evidence may count for or against a theory, or be neutral towards it, is a central feature of scientific inference, and the Bayesian account will clearly need to start with a suitable interpretation of these concepts.

Fortunately, there is a suitable and very natural interpretation, for if $P(h)$ measures your belief in a hypothesis when you do not know the evidence e, and $P(h|e)$ is the corresponding measure when you do, e surely confirms h when the latter exceeds the former. So we shall adopt the following as our definitions:

e **confirms or supports** h when $P(h|e) > P(h)$

e **disconfirms or undermines** h when $P(h|e) < P(h)$

e **is neutral with respect to** h when $P(h|e) = P(h)$

One might reasonably take $P(h|e) - P(h)$ as measuring the degree of e's support for h, though other measures have been suggested (e.g., Good, 1950); disagreements on this score will not need to be settled in this book. We shall refer, in the usual way, to $P(h)$ as 'the prior probability of h' and to $P(h|e)$ as h's 'posterior probability' relative to, or in the light of, e. The reasons for this terminology are obvious, but it ought to be noted that the terms have a meaning only in relation to evidence: as Lindley (1970, p. 38) put it, "[t]oday's posterior distribution is tomorrow's prior". It should be remembered too that all the probabilities are evaluated in relation to accepted background knowledge.

The application of Bayes's Theorem

Bayes's Theorem relates the posterior probability of a hypothesis, $P(h|e)$, to the terms $P(h)$, $P(e|h)$, and $P(e)$. Hence, knowing the values of these last three terms, it is possible to determine whether e confirms h, and, more importantly, to calculate $P(h|e)$. In practice, of course, the various probabilities may only be known rather imprecisely; we shall have more to say about this practical aspect of the question later.

The dependence of the posterior probability on the three terms referred to above is reflected in three striking phenomena of scientific inference. First, other things being equal, the extent to which evidence e confirms a hypothesis h increases with the likelihood of h on e, that is to say, with $P(e|h)$. At one extreme, where e refutes h, $P(e|h) = 0$; hence, disconfirmation is at a maximum. The greatest confirmation is produced, for a given $P(e)$, when $P(e|h) = 1$, which will be met in practice when h logically entails e. Statistical hypotheses are more substantially confirmed the higher the value of $P(e|h)$.

Secondly, the posterior probability of a hypothesis depends on its prior probability, a dependence sometimes discernible in scientific attitudes to ad hoc hypotheses and in frequently expressed preferences for the simpler of two hypotheses. As we shall see, scientists always discriminate, in advance of any experimentation, between theories they regard as more-or-less credible (and, so, worthy of attention) and others.

Thirdly, the power of e to confirm h depends on $P(e)$, that is to say, on the probability of e when it is not assumed that h is true (which, of course, is not the same as assuming h to be false). This dependence is reflected in the scientific intuition that the more surprising the evidence, the greater its confirming power. However, $P(e) = P(e|h)P(h) + P(e|\sim h)P(\sim h)$, so that really, the posterior probability of h depends on the three basic quantities $P(h)$, $P(e|h)$, and $P(e|\sim h)$.

We shall deal in greater detail with each of these facets of inductive reasoning in the course of this chapter.

Falsifying hypotheses

A characteristic pattern of scientific inference is the refutation of a theory, when one of a theory's empirical consequences has been shown to be false in an experiment. This kind of reasoning, with its straightforward and unimpeachable logical structure, exercised such an influence on Popper that he made it the centrepiece of his scientific philosophy.

Although the Bayesian approach was not conceived specifically with this aspect of scientific reasoning in view, it has a ready explanation for it. The explanation relies on the fact that if, relative to background knowledge, a hypothesis h entails a consequence e, then (relative to the same background knowledge) $P(h|\sim e) = 0$. Interpreted in the Bayesian fashion, this means that h is maximally disconfirmed when it is refuted. Moreover, as we should expect, once a theory is refuted, no further evidence can ever confirm it, unless the refuting evidence or some portion of the background assumptions is revoked.

Checking a consequence

A standard method of investigating a deterministic hypothesis is to draw out some of its logical consequences, relative to a stock of background knowledge, and check whether they are true or not. For instance, the General Theory of Relativity was confirmed by establishing that light is deflected when it passes near the sun, as the theory predicts.

It is easy to show, by means of Bayes's Theorem, why and under what circumstances a theory is confirmed by its consequences.

If h entails e, then, as may be simply shown, $P(e|h) = 1$. Hence, from Bayes's Theorem: $P(e|h) = P(h)/P(e)$. Thus, if $0 < P(e) < 1$, and if $P(h) > 0$, then $P(h|e) > P(h)$. It follows that any evidence whose probability is neither of the extreme values must confirm every hypothesis with a non-zero probability of which it is a logical consequence.

Succeeding confirmations must eventually diminish in force, for the theory has an upper limit of probability beyond which no amount of evidence can push it. This too follows from Bayes's Theorem. Suppose $e_1, e_2, ..., e_n, ...$ are consequences of h. Then Bayes's Theorem asserts that

$$p(h|e_1 \& e_2 \& ... \& e_n) = \frac{P(h)}{p(h|e_1 \& e_2 \& ... \& e_n)}$$

Now

$$P(e_1 \& e_2 \& ... \& e_n) = P(e_1)P(e_2 \& ... \& e_n|e_1)$$

and

$$P(e_2 \& ... \& e_n|e_1) = P(e_2|e_1)P(e_3 \& ... \& e_n|e_1 \& e_2).$$

Thus, in general,

$$P(e_1 \& e_2 \& ... \& e_n) = P(e_1)P(e_2|e_1) ... P(e_n|e_1 \& ... \& e_{n-1}).$$

Hence

$$P(h|e_1 \& e_2 \& ... \& e_n) = \frac{P(h)}{P(e_1)P(e_2|e_1) ... P(e_n|e_1 \& ... \& e_{n-1})}$$

Provided $P(h) > 0$, the term $P(e_n|e_1 \& ... \& e_{n-1})$ must tend to 1 as n increases. If it did not, the posterior probability of h would at some point exceed 1, which is impossible (Jeffreys, 1961, pp. 43–4). This explains why it is not sensible to test a hypothesis indefinitely, though without more detailed information on the individual's belief-structure, in particular regarding the values of $P(e_n|e_1 \& ... \& e_{n-1})$, one could not know the precise point beyond which further predictions of the hypothesis were sufficiently probable not to be worth examining.

Specific categories of a theory's consequences also have a restricted capacity to confirm (Urbach, 1981). Suppose h is the theory under discussion and that h_r is a substantial restriction of that theory. A substantial restriction of Newton's theory might, for example, express the idea that freely falling bodies near the earth descend with a constant acceleration or that the period and length of a pendulum are related by the familiar formula. Since h entails h_r, $P(h) \leq P(h_r)$, and if h_r is much less speculative than its progenitor, it will often be significantly more probable.

Now consider a series of predictions derived from h, but which also follow from h_r. If the predictions are verified, they may confirm both theories, whose posterior probabilities are given by Bayes's Theorem, thus:

$$p(h|e_1 \& e_2 \& \ldots \& e_n) = \frac{P(h)}{p(e_1 \& e_2 \& \ldots \& e_n)}$$

and

$$p(h_r|e_1 \& e_2 \& \ldots \& e_n) = \frac{P(h_r)}{p(e_1 \& e_2 \& \ldots \& e_n)}.$$

Combining these two equations to eliminate the common denominator, one obtains

$$p(h|e_1 \& e_2 \& \ldots \& e_n) = \frac{P(h)}{P(h_r)} P(h_r|e_1 \& e_2 \& \ldots \& e_n).$$

Since the maximum value of the last probability term in this equation is 1, it follows that however many predictions of h_r have been verified, the main theory, h, can never acquire a posterior probability in excess of $P(h)/P(h_r)$. Hence, the type of evidence characterised by entailment from h_r may well be limited in its capacity to confirm h.

This result explains the familiar phenomenon that repetitions of a particular experiment often confirm a general theory only to a limited extent, for the predictions verified by means of a given kind of experiment (that is, an experiment designed to a specified pattern) do normally follow from and confirm a much-restricted version of the predicting theory. When an experiment's capacity to generate confirming evidence has been exhausted through repetition, further support for h would have to be sought from other experiments, experiments whose outcomes were predicted by different parts of h.

The arguments and explanations in this section rely on the possibility that evidence already accumulated from an experiment may increase the probability of further performances of the experiment producing similar results. Such a possibility is denied by Popperians on the grounds that the probabilities involved are subjective. How then do they explain the fact, attested by every scientist, that by repeating some experiment, one eventually (usually quickly) exhausts its capacity to confirm a given hypothesis? Alan Musgrave (1975) attempted an explanation designed on Popperian lines. He claimed that after a certain, unspecified number of repetitions of an experiment, the scientist would form a generalisation to the effect that whenever the experiment was performed, it would yield a similar result. Musgrave then proposed that the generalisation should be entered into 'background knowledge'. Relative to this newly augmented background knowledge, the experiment is certain to produce a similar result at its next performance. Musgrave then appealed to the principle that evidence confirms a hypothesis in proportion to the difference between its probability relative to the hypothesis together with background knowledge and its probability relative to background knowledge alone. That is, the degree to which e confirms h is proportional to $P(e|h \& b) - P(e|b)$, b being background knowledge. Musgrave then inferred that even if the experiment did produce the expected result when next performed, the hypothesis would receive no new confirmation. Watkins (1984, p. 297) has endorsed this account.

A number of decisive objections may be raised against it, though. First, as we shall show in the next section, although it seems to be a fact and is an essential constituent of Bayesian reasoning, there is no basis in Popperian methodology for confirmation to depend on the probability of the evidence; Popper simply invoked the principle ad hoc. Secondly, Musgrave's suggestion takes no account of the fact that particular experimental results may be generalised in infinitely many ways. This is a substantial objection, since different generalisations give rise to different expectations about the outcomes of future experiments. Musgrave's account is incomplete without a rule to specify in each case the appropriate generalisation that should be formulated and adopted, and it is hard to imagine how such a rule could be justified within the confines of Popperian philosophy. Finally, the decision to designate the generalisation background knowledge, with the consequent effect on our evaluation of other theories and on our future conduct regarding, for example, whether to repeat certain experiments, is comprehensible only if we have invested some confidence in the theory. But then Musgrave's account tacitly calls on the same kind of inductive considerations as it was designed to circumvent, so its aim is defeated.

The probability of the evidence

The degree to which h is confirmed by e depends, according to Bayesian theory, on the extent to which $P(e|h)$ exceeds $P(e)$. An equivalent way of putting this is to say that confirmation is correlated with the difference between $P(e|h)$ and $P(e|\sim h)$, that is, with how much more probable the evidence is if the hypothesis is true than if it is false. This is obvious from another form of Bayes's Theorem:

$$\frac{P(h|e)}{P(h)} = \frac{1}{P(h) + \dfrac{P(e|\sim h)}{P(e|h)}P(\sim h)}.$$

These facts are reflected in the everyday experience that information that is particularly unexpected or surprising, unless some hypothesis is assumed to be true, supports that hypothesis with particular force. Thus, if a soothsayer predicts that you will meet a dark stranger sometime and you do, your faith in his powers of precognition would not be much enhanced: you would probably continue to think his predictions were just the result of guesswork. However, if the prediction also gave the correct number of hairs on the head of that stranger, your previous scepticism would no doubt be severely shaken.

Cox (1961, p. 92) illustrated this point with an incident in *Macbeth*. The three witches, using their special brand of divination, predicted to Macbeth that he would soon become both Thane of Cawdor and King of Scotland. Macbeth finds both these prognostications almost impossible to believe:

By Sinel's death, I know I am Thane of Glamis,
But how of Cawdor?
The Thane of Cawdor lives, a prosperous gentleman,
And to be King stands not within the prospect of belief.
No more than to be Cawdor.

But a short time later he learns that the Thane of Cawdor prospered no longer, was in fact dead, and that he, Macbeth, has succeeded to the title. As a result, Macbeth's attitude to the witches' powers is entirely altered, and he comes to believe in their other predictions and in their ability to foresee the future.

The following, more scientific, example was used by Jevons (1874, vol. 1, pp. 278–79) to illustrate the dependence of confirmation on the improbability of the evidence. The distinguished scientist Charles Babbage examined numerous logarithmic tables published over two centuries in various parts of the world. He was interested in whether they derived from the same source or had been worked out independently. Babbage (1827) found the same six errors in all but two and drew the "irresistible" conclusion that, apart from these two, all the tables originated in a common source.

Babbage's reasoning was interpreted by Jevons roughly as follows. The theory t_1, which says of some pair of logarithmic tables that they shared a common origin, is moderately likely in view of the immense amount of labour needed to compile such tables *ab initio*, and for a number of other reasons. The alternative, independence theory might take a variety of forms, each attributing different probabilities to the occurrence of errors in various positions in the table. The only one of these which seems at all likely would assign each place an equal probability of exhibiting an error and would, moreover, regard those errors as more-or-less independent. Call this theory t_2 and let e^i be the evidence of i common errors in the tables. The posterior probability of t_1 is inversely proportional to $P(e^i)$, which, under the assumption of only two rival hypotheses, can be expressed as $P(e^i) = P(e^i|t_1)P(t_1) + P(e^i|t_2)P(t_2)$ (This is the theorem of total probability.). Since t_1 entails e^i, $P(e^i) = P(t_1) + P(e^i|t_2)P(t_2)$. The quantity $P(e^i|t_2)$ clearly decreases with increasing i. Hence $P(e^i)$ diminishes and approaches $P(t_1)$, as i increases; and so e^i becomes increasingly powerful evidence for t_1, a result which agrees with scientific intuition.

In fact, scientists seem to regard a few shared mistakes in different mathematical tables as so strongly indicative of a common source that at least one compiler of such tables attempted to protect his copyright by deliberately incorporating three minor errors "as a trap for would-be plagiarists" (L. J. Comrie, quoted by Bowden, 1953, p. 4).

The relationship between how surprising a piece of evidence is on background assumptions and its power to confirm a hypothesis is a natural consequence of Bayesian theory and was not deliberately built in. On the other hand, methodologies that eschew probabilistic assessments of hypotheses seem constitutionally incapable of accounting for the phenomenon. Such approaches would need to be able, first, to discriminate between items of evidence on grounds other than their deductive or probabilistic relation to a hypothesis. And having established such a basis for discriminating, they must show a connection with confirmation. The objectivist school has more-or-less dodged this challenge. An exception is Popper. In tackling the problem, he moved partway towards Bayesianism; however, the concessions he made were insufficient. Thus Popper conceded that, in regard to confirmation, the significant quantities are $P(e|h)$ and $P(e)$, and as we have already reported, he even measured the amount of confirmation (or "corroboration", to use Popper's preferred term) which e confers on h by the difference between these quantities (Popper, 1959, appendix *ix).

But Popper never stated explicitly what he meant by the probability of evidence. On the one hand, he would never have allowed it to have a subjective connotation, for that would have compromised the supposed objectivity of science; on the other hand, he never worked out what objective significance the term could have. His writings suggest that he had in mind some purely logical notion of probability, but there is no adequate account of logical probability. Popper also never explained satisfactorily why a hypothesis benefits from improbable evidence or, to put the objection another way, he failed to provide a foundation in non-Bayesian terms for the Bayesian confirmation function which he appropriated. (For a discussion and decisive criticism of Popper's account, see Grünbaum, 1976.)

The Bayesian position has recently been misunderstood to imply that if some evidence is known, then it cannot support any hypothesis, on the grounds that known evidence must have unit probability.

The Ravens Paradox

That evidence supports a hypothesis more the greater the ratio $P(e|h)/P(e)$ scotches a famous puzzle first posed by Hempel (1945) and known as the *Paradox of Confirmation* or sometimes as the *Ravens Paradox*. It was called a paradox because its premises were regarded as extremely plausible, despite their counter-intuitive, or in some versions contradictory, implications, and the reference to ravens stems from the paradigm hypothesis ('All ravens are black') which is frequently used to expound the problem. The difficulty arises from three assumptions about confirmation. They are as follows:

1 Hypotheses of the form 'All Rs are B' are confirmed by the evidence of something that is both R and B. For example, 'All ravens are black' is confirmed by the observation of a black raven. (Hempel called this Nicod's condition, after the philosopher Jean Nicod.)
2 Logically equivalent hypotheses are confirmed by the same evidence. (This is the Equivalence condition.)
3 Evidence of some object not being R does not confirm 'All Rs are B'.

We shall describe an object that is both black and a raven with the term RB. Similarly, a non-black, non-raven will be denoted $\overline{R}\,\overline{B}$. A contradiction arises for the following reasons: an RB confirms 'All Rs are B', on account of the Nicod condition. According to the Equivalence condition, it also confirms 'All non-Bs are non-Rs', since the two hypotheses are logically equivalent. But contradicting this, the third condition implies that RB does not confirm 'All non-Bs are non-Rs'.

The contradiction may be avoided by revoking the third condition, as is sometimes done. (We shall note later another reason for not holding on to it.) However, although the remaining conditions are compatible, they have a consequence which many philosophers have regarded as blatantly false, namely, that by observing a non-black, non-raven (say, a red herring or a white shoe) one confirms the hypothesis that all ravens are black. (The argument is this: 'All non-Bs are non-R' is equivalent to 'All Rs are B'; according to the Nicod condition, the first is confirmed by $\overline{R}\,\overline{B}$; hence, by the Equivalence condition, so is the second.)

If non-black, non-ravens support the raven hypothesis, this seems to imply the paradoxical result that one could investigate that and other generalisations of a similar form just as well by observing white paper and red ink from the comfort of one's writing desk as by studying ravens on the wing. However, this would be a non sequitur. For the fact that RB and $\overline{R}\,\overline{B}$ both confirm a hypothesis does not imply that they do so with equal force. Once it is recognised that confirmation is a matter of degree, the conclusion is no longer so counter-intuitive, because it is compatible with $\overline{R}\,\overline{B}$ confirming 'All Rs are B', but to a minuscule and negligible degree.

Indeed, most people do have a strong intuition that an RB confirms the ravens hypothesis (h) more than an $\overline{R}\,\overline{B}$. We can appreciate why that might be by consulting Bayes's Theorem as it applies to the two types of datum:

$$\frac{P(h|RB)}{P(h)} = \frac{P(RB|h)}{P(RB)} \quad \& \quad \frac{p(h|\overline{R}\,\overline{B})}{P(h)} = \frac{P(\overline{R}\,\overline{B}|h)}{P(\overline{R}\,\overline{B})}.$$

These expressions can be simplified. First, $P(RB|h) = P(B|h\,\&\,R)P(R|h) = P(R|h) = P(R)$. We arrived at the last equality by assuming that whether some arbitrary object is a raven is independent of the truth of h, which seems plausible to us, at any rate as a good approximation, though Horwich (1982, p. 59) thinks it has no plausibility. By similar reasoning, $P(\overline{R}\,\overline{B}\,|h) = P(\overline{B}\,|h) = P(\overline{B})$. Also $P(RB) = P(B|R)P(R)$, and $P(B|R) = \Sigma P(B|R\,\&\,\theta)P(\theta|R) =$ (assuming independence between θ and R) $\Sigma P(B|R\,\&\,\theta)P(\theta)$, where θ represents possible values of the percentage of ravens in the universe that are black (according to h, of course, $\theta = 1$). Finally, $P(B|R\,\&\,\theta) = \theta$, for if the percentage of black ravens in the universe is θ, the probability of an arbitrary raven being black is also θ. (This is intuitively correct and is formalised in the so-called Principal Principle.) Combining all these considerations with the above forms of Bayes's Theorem yields

$$\frac{P(h|RB)}{P(h)} = \frac{1}{\Sigma\theta P(\theta)} \quad \& \quad \frac{P(h|\overline{R}\,\overline{B})}{P(h)} = \frac{1}{P(\overline{R}|\overline{B})}.$$

Consider first the term $P(\overline{R}|\overline{B})$. Presumably there are vastly more non-black things in the universe than ravens. So even if no ravens are black, the probability of some object about which we know nothing, except that it is not black, being a non-raven must be very high, indeed, practically 1. Hence, $P(h|\overline{R}\,\overline{B}) \approx P(h)$, and, so, the observation that some object is neither a raven nor black provides very little confirmation for h.

According to the equation above, the degree to which RB confirms h is inversely proportional to $\Sigma\theta P(\theta)$. This means, for example, that if it is initially very probable that all or virtually all ravens are black, then $\Sigma\theta P(\theta)$ would be large and RB would confirm h rather little. While if it is initially relatively probable that most ravens are not black, confirmation could be substantial. Intermediate levels of uncertainty about the proportion of ravens that are black would bring their own levels of confirmation. By contrast, because the class of non-black objects is so much larger than the class of ravens, $\overline{R}\,\overline{B}$ confirms 'All ravens are black' to only a tiny extent, irrespective of $P(\theta)$. Mackie's well-known Bayesian solution to the ravens paradox, is similar and also depends on an assumed large disparity in the number of non-black objects and ravens.

Our Bayesian working of the raven example appears to support the Nicod condition, with the minor limitation that no confirmation is possible, even with positive instances, when the hypothesis has a prior probability of 1. But a Bayesian approach anticipates the violation of Nicod's condition in other circumstances too. And numerous examples have been suggested as plausible instances of such violations. The first of these seems to be due to Good (1961). We shall use an example that is taken, with some modification, from Swinburne (1971). The hypothesis under examination is 'All grasshoppers are located outside the County of Yorkshire'. The observation of a grasshopper just beyond the county border is an instance of this generalisation and, according to Nicod, confirms it. But it might be more reasonably argued that since there are no border controls or other obstacles restricting the movement of grasshoppers in that area, the observation of one on the edge of the county increases the probability that others have actually entered and hence undermines the hypothesis. In Bayesian terms, this is a case where, relative to background information, the probability of some datum is reduced by a hypothesis—that is, $P(e|h) < P(e)$—which is therefore disconfirmed—in other words, $P(h|e) < P(h)$.

A much more striking example where Nicod's conditions break down was invented by Rosenkrantz (1977, p. 35). Three people leave a party, each with a hat. The hypothesis that none of the three has his own hat is confirmed, according to Nicod, by the observation that person 1 has person 2's hat and by the observation that person 2 has person 1's hat. But since there are only three people, the second observation must *refute* the hypothesis, not confirm it.

Our grasshopper example provides an instance where a datum of the type $\overline{R}B$ confirms a generalisation of the form 'All Rs are B'. Imagine that an object which looked for all the world like a grasshopper had been found hopping about just outside Yorkshire and that it turned out to be some other sort of insect. The discovery that the object was not a grasshopper would be relatively unlikely unless the grasshopper hypothesis was true (hence, $P(e) < P(e|h)$); thus it would confirm that hypothesis. If the deceptively grasshopper-like object were within the county boundary, the same conclusion would follow, though the degree of confirmation would be greater. This shows that 'All Rs are B' may also be confirmed by a datum of the $\overline{R}\,\overline{B}$ type. Hence, the impression that non-Rs never confirm such hypotheses may be dispelled.

Horwich (1982) has argued that the raven hypothesis may be differently confirmed, depending on how the black raven was chosen, either by randomly selecting an object from the population of ravens or by making the selection from the population of black objects. (Horwich denotes the evidence that some object is a black raven as either R^*B or RB^*, depending on whether it was discovered by the first selection process or the second.) Prompted by a paper by Kevin Korb (1994), we agree with Horwich that this is so.

But Horwich offers another explanation, which fits poorly with his Bayesian one. For he claims that the datum R^*B is always more powerfully confirming than RB^*, because, he says, only it subjects the raven hypothesis to the risk of falsification. But this surely conflates the process of collecting evidence, which may indeed subject the hypothesis to different risks of refutation, with the evidence itself, which either refutes the hypothesis or does not refute it, and in the case of R^*B and RB^*, it does not.

Our conclusions are, first, that the supposedly paradoxical consequences of Nicod's condition and the Equivalence condition are not problematic, and, secondly, that there are separate reasons for rejecting Nicod's condition, which, moreover, conform to Bayesian principles.

The Duhem problem

The problem

The so-called Duhem (or Duhem-Quine) problem is a problem for theories of science of the type associated with Popper, which emphasise the power of certain evidence to refute a hypothesis. According to Popper's influential views, the characteristic of a theory which makes it 'scientific' is its falsifiability: "Statements or systems of statements, in order to be ranked as scientific, must be capable of conflicting with possible, or conceivable, observations" (Popper, 1963, p. 39). And, claiming to apply this criterion, Popper (1963, Ch. 1) judged Einstein's gravitational theory to be scientific and Freud's psychology, unscientific. There is a strong flavour of commendation about the term *scientific* which has proved extremely misleading. For a theory that is scientific in Popper's sense is not necessarily true, or even probably true or so much as close to the truth, nor can it be said definitely that it is likely to lead to the truth. In fact, there seems to be no conceptual connection between a theory's capacity to pass Popper's test of scientificness and its having any epistemic or inductive value. There is little alternative, then, so far as we can see, to regarding Popper's demarcation between scientific and unscientific statements as part of a theory about the content and character of what is usually termed science, not as having any normative significance.

Yet as an attempt at understanding the methods of science, Popper's ideas bear little fruit. His central claim was that scientific theories are falsifiable by "possible, or conceivable, observations". This poses a difficulty, for an observation can only falsify a theory (that is, conclusively demonstrate its falsity) if it is itself conclusively certain. But observations cannot be conclusively certain. Popper himself recognised this but seems not to have appreciated its incongruity with his falsificationist thesis. He held every observation report to be fallible; but, reluctant to admit degrees of fallibility or anything of the kind, he concluded that observation reports that are admitted as evidence "are accepted as the result of a decision or agreement; and to that extent they are *conventions*" (Popper, 1959, p. 106; our italics). It is unclear to us to what psychological attitude this sort of acceptance corresponds, but whatever it is, Popper's view of evidence statements seems to pull the rug from under falsificationism: it implies that no theory can really be falsified by evidence. The nearest thing to a refutation would occur when 'conventionally accepted' evidence was inconsistent with a theory, which could then, at best, be described as 'conventionally' rejected. Indeed, Popper conceded this much: "From a logical point of view, the testing of a theory depends upon basic statements whose acceptance or rejection, in its turn, depends upon our *decisions*. Thus it is *decisions* which settle the fate of theories" (Popper, 1959, p. 108).

Watkins is one of those who saw that falsificationism presupposes the existence of some infallibly true observation statements, and he attempted to restore the Popperian position by advancing the claim that such statements do in fact exist. He would agree that statements like 'The hand on this dial is pointing to the numeral 6' are fallible—it is unlikely, but possible, that the person reporting it missaw the position of the hand. But he claimed that introspective perceptual reports, such as 'In my visual field there is now a silvery crescent against a dark blue background', "may rightly be regarded by their authors when they make them as infallibly true" (Watkins, 1984, pp. 79 and 248). But in our view Watkins is wrong, and the statements he regards as infallible are open to exactly the same sceptical doubts as any other observation report. We can illustrate this through Watkins's example: clearly, it is possible, though admittedly not very probable, that the introspector has misremembered and mistaken the shape he usually describes as a crescent or the sensation he usually receives on reporting blue and silvery images. These and other sources of error ensure that introspective reports are not exempt from the rule that non-analytic statements are fallible.

Of course, the kinds of observation statements we have mentioned, if asserted under appropriate circumstances, would never be seriously doubted. That is, although they could be false, they have a force and immediacy that carries conviction; they are 'morally certain', to use the traditional phrase. But if observation statements are merely indubitable, then whether a theory is regarded as refuted by observational data or not must rest ultimately on a subjective feeling of certainty. The fact that such convictions are so strong and uncontroversial may disguise their fallibility, but cannot undo it. Hence, no theory is strictly falsifiable, for none could be conclusively shown to be false by empirical observations. In practice the closest one could get to a refutation would be arriving at the conclusion that a theory that clashes with almost certainly true observations is almost certainly false.

A second objection to Popper's falsifiability criterion, and the one upon which we shall focus for its more general interest, is that it describes as unscientific most of those theories which are usually deemed science's greatest achievements. This is the chief aspect of the well-known criticisms advanced by Polanyi (1962), Kuhn (1970), and Lakatos (1970), amongst others. They have pointed out that, as had already been established by Duhem (1905), many notable theories of science are not falsifiable by what would generally be regarded as observation statements, even if those statements were infallibly true. Predictions drawn from Newton's laws or from the Kinetic Theory of Gases turn out to depend not only on those theories but also on certain auxiliary hypotheses. Hence, if such predictions fail, one is not compelled by logic to infer that the main theory is false, for the fault may lie with one or more of the auxiliary assumptions. The history of science has many occasions when an important theory led to a false prediction and where that theory, nevertheless, was not blamed for the failure. In such cases we find that one or more of the auxiliary assumptions used to derive the prediction was taken to be the culprit. The problem that arose from Duhem's investigations was which of the several distinct theories involved in deriving a false prediction should be regarded as the false element or elements in the assumptions.

The Duhem problem solved by Bayesian means

This problem may be resolved with the help of Bayes's Theorem, as Dorling (1979) has shown, by considering how the individual probabilities of several theories are altered when, as a group, they have been refuted.

Suppose a theory, t, and an auxiliary hypothesis, a, together imply an empirical consequence which is shown to be false by the observation of the outcome e. Let us assume that while the combination of $t \& a$ is refuted by e, the two components taken individually are not refuted. We wish to consider the separate effects wrought on the probabilities of t and a by the adverse evidence e. The comparisons of interest here are between $P(t|e)$ and $P(t)$, and between $P(a|e)$ and $P(a)$. The conditional probabilities can be expressed using Bayes's Theorem, as follows:

$$P(t|e) = \frac{P(e|t)P(t)}{P(e)} \quad P(a|e) = \frac{P(e|a)P(a)}{P(e)}.$$

In order to evaluate the posterior probabilities of t and of a, one must first determine the values of the various terms on the right-hand sides of these equations. Before attempting this, it is worth noting that the equations convey no expectation that the refutation of $t \& a$ jointly considered will in general have a symmetrical effect on the separate probabilities of t and of a, nor any reason why the degree of asymmetry may not be considerable in some cases. It is evident that the probability of t changes very little if

$P(e|t) \approx P(e)$, while that of a is reduced substantially just in case $P(e|a)$ is substantially less than $P(e)$. The equations also allow us to discern the factors that determine which hypothesis suffers most in the refutation.

A historical example might best illustrate how a theory that produces a false prediction may still remain very probable; we shall, in fact, use an example that Lakatos (1970, pp. 138–40, and 1968, pp. 174–75) drew heavily on. In 1815, William Prout, a medical practitioner and chemist, advanced the hypothesis that the atomic weights of all the elements are whole number multiples of the atomic weight of hydrogen, the underlying assumption being that all matter is built out of different combinations of some basic element. Prout believed hydrogen to be that fundamental building-block, though the idea was entertained by others that a more primitive element might exist out of which hydrogen itself was composed. Now the atomic weights recorded at the time, though approximately integral when expressed as multiples of the atomic weight of hydrogen, did not match Prout's hypothesis exactly. Those deviations from a perfect fit failed to convince Prout that his hypothesis was wrong however; he instead took the view that there were faults in the methods that had been used to measure the relative weights of atoms. The noted chemist Thomas Thomson drew a similar conclusion. Indeed, both he and Prout went so far as to adjust several reported atomic weights in order to bring them into line with Prout's hypothesis. For instance, instead of accepting 0.829 as the atomic weight (expressed as a proportion of the weight of an atom of oxygen) of the element boron, which was the experimentally reported value, Thomson (1818, p. 340) preferred 0.875 "because it is a multiple of 0.125, which all the atoms seem to be". (Thomson erroneously took 0.125 as the atomic weight of hydrogen, relative to that of oxygen.) Similarly, Prout adjusted the measured atomic weight of chlorine (relative to hydrogen) from 35.83 to 36, the nearest whole number.

Thomson's and Prout's reasoning can be explained as follows: Prout's hypothesis t, together with an appropriate assumption a asserting the accuracy (within specified limits) of the measuring technique, the purity of the chemicals employed, and so forth, implies that the measured atomic weight of chlorine (relative to hydrogen) is a whole number. Suppose, as was the case in 1815, that chlorine's measured atomic weight was 35.83, and call this the evidence e. It seems that chemists of the early nineteenth century, such as Prout and Thomson, were fairly certain about the truth of t, but less so of a, though more sure that a is true than that it is false. Contemporary near-certainty about the truth of Prout's hypothesis is witnessed by the chemist J. S. Stas. He reported (1860, p. 42) that "In England the hypothesis of Dr Prout was almost universally accepted as absolute truth", and he confessed that when he started researching into the matter, he himself had "had an almost absolute confidence in the exactness of Prout's principle" (1860, p. 44). (Stas's confidence eventually faded after many years' experimental study, and by 1860 he had "reached the complete conviction, the entire certainty, as far as certainty can be attained on such a subject, that Prout's law ... is nothing but an illusion", 1860, p. 45.) It is less easy to ascertain how confident Prout and his contemporaries were in the methods by which atomic weights were measured, but it is unlikely that this confidence was very great, in view of the many clear sources of error and the failure of independent measurements generally to produce identical results. On the other hand, chemists of the time must have felt that their methods for determining atomic weights were more likely to be accurate than not, otherwise they would not have used them. For these reasons, we conjecture that $P(a)$ was of the order of 0.6 and that $P(t)$ was around 0.9, and these are the figures we shall work with. It should be stressed that these numbers and those we shall assign to other probabilities are intended chiefly to illustrate how Bayes's Theorem resolves Duhem's problem; nevertheless, we believe them to be sufficiently accurate to throw light on the progress of Prout's hypothesis. As will become apparent, the results we obtain are not very sensitive to variations in the assumed prior probabilities.

In order to evaluate the posterior probabilities of t and of a, one must fix the values of the terms $P(e|t)$, $P(e|a)$, and $P(e)$. These can be expressed, using the theorem on total probability, as follows:

$$P(e) = P(e|t)P(t) + P(e| \sim t)P(\sim t)$$
$$P(e|t) = P(e \& a|t) + P(e \& \sim a|t)$$
$$= P(e|t \& a)P(a|t) + P(e|t \& \sim a)P(\sim a|t)$$
$$= P(e|t \& a)P(a) + P(e|t \& \sim a)P(\sim a)$$

Since $t \& a$, in combination, is refuted by e, the term $P(e|t \& a)$ is zero. Hence:

$$P(e|t) = P(e|t \& \sim a)P(\sim a).$$

It should be noted that in deriving the last equation but one, we have followed Dorling in assuming that t and a are independent, that is, that $P(a|t) = P(a)$ and, hence, $P(\sim a|t) = P(\sim a)$. This seems to accord with many historical cases and is clearly right in the present case. By parallel reasoning to that employed above, we may derive the results:

$$P(e|a) = P(e| \sim t \& a)P(\sim t)$$
$$P(e| \sim t) = P(e| \sim t \& a)P(a) + P(e| \sim t \& \sim a)P(\sim a)$$

Provided the following terms are fixed, which we have done in a tentative way, to be justified presently, the posterior probabilities of t and of a can be determined:

$$P(e| \sim t \& a) = 0.01$$
$$P(e| \sim t \& \sim a) = 0.01$$
$$P(e|t \& \sim a) = 0.02$$

The first of these gives the probability of the evidence if Prout's hypothesis is not true but if the method of atomic weight measurement is accurate. Such probabilities were explicitly considered by some nineteenth-century chemists, and they typically took a theory of random assignment of atomic weights as the alternative to Prout's hypothesis (e.g., Mallet, 1880); we shall follow this. Suppose it had been established for certain that the atomic weight of chlorine lay between 35 and 36. (The final results we obtain respecting the posterior probabilities of t and a are, incidentally, not affected by the width of this interval.) The random-allocation theory would assign equal probabilities to the atomic weight of an element lying in any 0.01-wide band. Hence, on the assumption that a is true, but t false, the probability that the atomic weight of chlorine lies in the interval 35.825 to 35.835 is 0.01. We have assigned the same value to $P(e| \sim t \& \sim a)$

on the grounds that if *a* were false because, say, some of the chemicals were impure or the measuring techniques faulty, then, still assuming *t* to be false, one would not expect atomic weights to be biased towards any particular part of the interval between adjacent integers.

We have set the probability $P(e|t \,\&\, \sim a)$ rather higher, at 0.02. The reason for this is that although some impurities in the chemicals and some degree of inaccuracy in the method of measurement were moderately likely in the early nineteenth century, chemists would not have considered their techniques entirely haphazard. Thus if Prout's hypothesis were true, but the measuring technique imperfect, the measured atomic weights would have been likely to deviate somewhat from integral values; but the greater the deviation, the less likely, on these assumptions, so the probability of an atomic weight lying in any part of the 35–36 interval would not be distributed uniformly over the interval, but would be more concentrated around the whole numbers.

Let us proceed with the figures we have assumed for the crucial probabilities, noting however that the particular values of the three probability terms are unimportant, only their relative values need be taken into account in the calculation. Thus we would arrive at the same posterior probabilities for *a* and *t* with the weaker assumptions that $P(e| \sim t \,\&\, a) = P(e| \sim t \,\&\, \sim a) = 1/2 P(e|t \,\&\, \sim a)$. We thus obtain

$$P(e| \sim t) = 0.01 \times 0.6 + 0.01 \times 0.4 = 0.01$$
$$P(e|t) = 0.02 \times 0.4 = 0.008$$
$$P(e|a) = 0.01 \times 0.1 = 0.001$$
$$P(e) = 0.008 \times 0.9 + 0.01 \times 0.1 = 0.0082$$

Finally, Bayes's Theorem enables us to derive the posterior probabilities in which we were interested:

$$P(t|e) = 0.878 \text{ (Recall that } P(t) = 0.9.)$$
$$P(a|e) = 0.073 \text{ (Recall that } P(a) = 0.6.)$$

These striking results show that evidence of the kind we have-described may exert a sharply asymmetric effect on the probabilities of *t* and of *a*. The initial probabilities we assumed seem appropriate for chemists such as Prout and Thomson, and if they are correct, the results deduced from Bayes's Theorem explain why those chemists regarded Prout's hypothesis as being more-or-less undisturbed when certain atomic-weight measurements, diverged from integral values, and why they felt entitled to adjust those measurements to the nearest whole number. Fortunately, these results are relatively insensitive to changes in our assumptions, so the accuracy of those assumptions is not a vital matter as far as our explanation is concerned. For example, if one took the initial probability of Prout's hypothesis (*t*) to be 0.7, instead of 0.9, keeping the other assignments, we find that $P(e|t) = 0.65$, while $P(a|e) = 0.21$. Hence, as before, after the refutation, Prout's hypothesis is still more likely to be true than false, and the auxiliary assumptions are still much more likely to be false than true. Other substantial variations in the initial probabilities produce similar results, though with so many factors at work, it is difficult to state concisely the conditions upon which these results depend without just pointing to the equations above.

Thus Bayes's Theorem provides a model to account for the kind of scientific reasoning that gave rise to the Duhem problem. And the example of Prout's hypothesis, as well as

235

others that Dorling (1979 and 1982) has described, show, in our view, that the Bayesian model is essentially correct. By contrast, non-probabilistic theories seem to lack entirely the resources that could deal with Duhem's problem.

A fact that emerges when slightly different values are assumed for the various probabilities in the Prout's hypothesis example is that one or other of the theories may actually become more probable after the conjunction $t \& a$ has been refuted. For instance, when $P(e|t \& \sim a)$ equals 0.05, the other probabilities being assigned the same values as before, the posterior probability of t is 0.91, which exceeds its prior probability. This may seem bizarre, but, as Dorling (1982) has argued, it is not so odd when one bears in mind that the refuting evidence normally contains a good deal more information than is required merely to disprove $t \& a$ and that this extra information may be confirmatory. In general, such confirmation occurs when $P(e) < P(e|t)$, which is easily shown to be equivalent to the condition $P(e|t) > P(e| \sim t)$. In other words, when evidence is easier to explain (in the sense that it receives a higher probability) if a given hypothesis is true than if it is not, then that theory is confirmed by the evidence.

Bad data, and data too good to be true

Bad data. An interesting fact that emerges from the Bayesian analysis is that a successful prediction derived from a combination of two theories, say t and a, does not always redound to the credit of t, even if the prior probability of the evidence is small; indeed, it can even undermine it. We may illustrate this by referring again to the example of Prout's hypothesis.

Suppose the atomic weight of chlorine were 'measured', not in the old-fashioned chemical way, but by concentrating hard on the element in question and picking a number in some random fashion from a given range of numbers. And let us assume that this method assigns a whole-number value to the atomic weight of chlorine. This is just what one would predict on the basis of Prout's hypothesis, if the outlandish measuring technique were reliable. But reliability is obviously most unlikely, and it is equally obvious that, as a result, the measured atomic weight of chlorine adds practically nothing to the probability of Prout's hypothesis, notwithstanding its integral value. This intuition is upheld by Bayes's Theorem, as a simple calculation based on the above formulas shows. (As before, let t be Prout's hypothesis and a the assumption that the measuring technique is accurate. Then set $P(e|t \& \sim a) = P(e| \sim t \& \sim a) = P(e| \sim t \& a) = 0.01$, for reasons similar to those stated earlier, and let $P(a)$ be very small, say 0.0001, for obvious reasons. It then follows that $P(t)$ and $P(t|e)$ are equal to two decimal places.)

This example shows that Leibniz was wrong to declare as a general principle that "It is the greatest commendation of an hypothesis (next to truth) if by its help predictions can be made even about phenomena or experiments not tried". Leibniz and Lakatos, who quoted these words with approval (1970, p. 123), seem to have overlooked the fact that if a prediction can be deduced from a hypothesis only with the assistance of highly questionable auxiliary claims, then that hypothesis may accrue very little credit. This explains why the various sensational predictions which Velikovsky drew from his theory of planetary collisions failed to impress most serious astronomers, even when some of those predictions were to their amazement fulfilled. For instance, Velikovsky's prediction of the existence of large quantities of petroleum on the planet Venus relied not only on his pet theory that various natural disasters in the past had been caused by collisions between the earth and a comet, but also on a string of unsupported and not very plausible assumptions, such as that the comet in question originally carried hydrogen and carbon, that these had been converted to petroleum by electrical discharges supposedly created in the violent impact with the earth, that the comet had later evolved into the planet Venus, and some others (Velikovsky, 1950, p. 351). (More details of Velikovsky's theory are given in the next section.)

Data too good to be true. Data are sometimes said to be 'too good to be true' when they fit a favoured hypothesis more perfectly than seems reasonable to expect. For instance, suppose all the atomic weights listed in Prout's paper had been whole numbers, exactly. Such a result almost looks as if it was designed to impress, and it is just for this reason that it fails to.

We may analyse this response as follows. Let e be the evidence of, say, 20 atomic-weight measurements, each a perfect whole number. No one could have regarded precise atomic weights measured at the time as absolutely reliable. The most natural view would have been that such measurements are subject to experimental error and, hence, that they would give a certain spread of results about the true value. On this assumption, which we shall label a', it is extremely unlikely that numerous independent atomic-weight measurements would all produce whole numbers, even if Prout's hypothesis were true. So $P(e|t \& a')$ is extremely small and, clearly, $P(e| \sim t \& a')$ would be no larger. Now a' has many possible alternatives, one of the more plausible (though initially it might not be very plausible) being that the experiments were consciously or unconsciously rigged in favour of Prout's hypothesis. If this were the only significant alternative (and so, in effect, equivalent to $\sim a'$), $P(e|t \& \sim a')$ would be very high, as would $P(e| \sim t \& \sim a')$. It follows from the equations on page 234 above that

$$P(e|t) \approx P(e|t \& \sim a')P(\sim a') \text{ and}$$
$$P(e| \sim t) \approx P(e| \sim t \& \sim a')P(\sim a'),$$

and, hence,

$$P(e) \approx P(e|t \& \sim a')P(\sim a')P(t) + P(e| \sim t \& \sim a')P(\sim a')P(\sim t).$$

Now, presumably the rigging of the results to produce whole numbers, if it took place, would produce whole numbers equally effectively whether t was true or not; in other words,

$$P(e|t \& \sim a') = P(e| \sim t \& \sim a');$$

hence

$$P(e) \approx P(e|t \& \sim a')P(\sim a').$$

Therefore,

$$P(t|e) = \frac{P(e|t)P(t)}{P(e)} \approx \frac{P(e|t \& \sim a')P(\sim a')P(t)}{P(e|t \& \sim a')P(\sim a')} = P(t)$$

Thus *e* does not confirm *t* significantly, even though, in a misleading sense, it fits the theory perfectly. This is why it is said to be too good to be true. A similar calculation shows that the probability of *a'* is diminished and, on the assumptions that we made, this implies that the probability of the experiments having been fabricated is enhanced. (The above analysis is essentially the same as given in Dorling, 1982).

A famous case of data that were allegedly too good to be true is that of Mendel's plant-breeding results. Mendel's genetic theory of inheritance allows one to calculate the probabilities with which certain plants would produce specific kinds of offspring. For instance, under certain circumstances, pea plants of a particular strain may be calculated to yield round and wrinkled seeds with probabilities 0.75 and 0.25, respectively. Mendel obtained seed-frequencies that matched the corresponding probabilities in this and in similar cases remarkably well, suggesting (misleadingly, Fisher contended) substantial support for the genetic theory. Fisher did not believe that Mendel had deliberately falsified his results to appear in better accord with his theory than they really were. To do so, Fisher claimed, would "contravene the weight of the evidence supplied in detail by ... [Mendel's] paper as a whole". But Fisher thought it a "possibility among others that Mendel was deceived by some assistant who knew too well what was expected" (1936, p. 132), an explanation he backed up with some (rather meagre) evidence. Dobzhansky (1967, p. 1589), on the other hand, thought it "at least as plausible" that Mendel had himself discarded results that deviated much from his ideal, in the sincere belief that they were contaminated or that some other accident had befallen them. (For a comprehensive review see Edwards, 1986.)

The argument put forward earlier to show that too-exactly whole-number atomic-weight measurements would not have supported Prout's hypothesis depends on the existence of some sufficiently plausible alternative hypothesis that would explain the data better. We believe that, in general, data are too good to be true relative to one hypothesis only if there are such alternatives. This principle accords with intuition; for if the technique for eliciting atomic weights had long been established as precise and accurate, and if careful precautions had been taken against experimenter bias and deception, all the natural alternatives to Prout's hypothesis could be discounted and the data would no longer seem suspiciously good; they would be straightforwardly good. Fisher, however, did not subscribe to the principle, at least, not explicitly; he believed that Mendel's results told against the genetic theory whatever alternative explanations might suggest themselves. Nevertheless, as just indicated, the consideration of such alternatives played a part in his argument.

Ad hoc hypotheses

As we have seen, an important scientific theory which, in combination with other hypotheses, has made a false prediction may nevertheless emerge relatively unscathed, while one or more of the auxiliary hypotheses are largely discredited. (We are using such expressions in the normal way to describe how hypotheses are received, regarding them as harmless metaphors for obvious and more-or-less precise probabilistic notions. Thus, a hypothesis that is unscathed by negative evidence is one whose posterior and prior probabilities are similar. On the other hand, it is difficult to see what opponents of the Bayesian approach could have in mind when they talk of theories being 'accepted' or 'retained', or 'put forward' or 'saved' or 'vindicated'.) When a set of auxiliary assumptions is discredited in a test, scientists frequently think up new assumptions which assist the main theory to explain the previously anomalous data. Sometimes these new assumptions give the impression that their role is simply to 'patch up' the theory, and in such cases Francis Bacon called them "frivolous distinctions" (1620, Book I, aphorism xxv). More recently they have been tagged 'ad hoc hypotheses', presumably because they would not have been introduced if the need to bring theory and evidence into line had not arisen.

But although particular ad hoc theories are fairly easy to evaluate intuitively, there is controversy over what general criteria apply. We shall see that the Bayesian approach clarifies the question. First let us consider a few examples of ad hoc theories.

Some examples of ad hoc hypotheses

Velikovsky's theory of collective amnesia. Immanuel Velikovsky, in a daring book called *Worlds in Collision* that attracted a great deal of attention some years ago, put forward the theory that the earth has been subject, at various stages in its history, to cosmic disasters produced by near collisions with massive comets. One of these comets, which went on to make a distinguished career as the planet Venus, is supposed to have passed close by the earth during the Israelites' captivity in Egypt and to have caused many of the various remarkable events of the time, such as the ten plagues and the parting of the Red Sea, related in the Bible. One of the theory's predictions, apparently, is that since no group of people could have missed these tremendous goings-on, if they kept records at all, they would have recorded them. However, many communities failed to note in their writings anything out of the ordinary at that time. But Velikovsky, still convinced by his main theory, put this exceptional behaviour down to what he called a "collective amnesia". He argued that the cataclysms were so terrifying that whole peoples behaved "as if [they had] obliterated impressions that should be unforgettable". There was a need, Velikovsky said, to "uncover the vestiges" of these events, "a task not unlike that of overcoming amnesia in a single person" (1950, p. 288).

Individual amnesia is the issue in the next example.

Dianetics. Dianetics is a theory that purports to analyse the causes of insanity and mental stress, which it sees as the 'misfiling' of information in unsuitable locations in the brain. By refiling these 'engrams', it claims, sanity may be restored, composure enhanced, and, incidentally, the memory vastly improved. Not surprisingly, the therapy is long and expensive, and few people have been through it and borne out the theory's claims. However, one triumphant success, a young student, was announced by the inventor of Dianetics, L. Ron Hubbard, and in 1950 he exhibited this person to a large audience, claiming that she had a "full and perfect recall of every moment of her life". But questions from the floor ("What did you have for breakfast on October 3, 1942?"; "What colour is Mr. Hubbard's tie?", and the like) soon demonstrated that the hapless young woman had a most imperfect memory. Hubbard accounted for this to what remained of the assembly by saying that when the woman first appeared on the stage and was asked to come forward "now", the word "now" had frozen her in "present time" and paralysed her ability to recall the past. (An account of the incident and of the history of Dianetics is given by Miller, 1987.)

An example from psychology. Investigations into the IQs of different groups of people show that average levels of measured intelligence vary. Some environmentalists, so-called, attribute low scores primarily to poor social and educational conditions, an explanation that ran into trouble when it was discovered that a large group of Eskimos, leading a feckless, poor, and drunken existence, scored very highly on IQ tests. The distinguished biologist Peter Medawar (1974), in an effort to deflect the difficulty away from the environmentalist thesis, tried to explain this unexpected observation by saying that an "upbringing in an igloo gives just the right degree of coziness, security and mutual contact to conduce to a good performance in intelligence tests."

In each of these examples, the theory which was proposed in place of the refuted one seems rather unsatisfactory. It is not likely that they would have been put forward except in response to particular empirical anomalies, hence the label "ad hoc", which suggests that the theory was advanced for the specific purpose of evading a difficulty. However, some theories of this kind cannot be condemned so readily. For instance, an ad hoc alteration which rescued Newtonian theory from a difficulty led directly to the discovery of a new planet and was generally deemed a shining success.

The discovery of the planet Neptune. The planet Uranus was discovered by Sir William Herschel in 1781. Astronomers quickly sought to describe the orbit of the new planet, using Newtonian theory and taking account of the perturbing influence of other known planets, so that predictions could be made concerning its future positions. But discrepancies between predicted and observed positions of Uranus substantially exceeded the admitted limits of experimental error and grew year by year. The possibility that the fault lay with Newton's laws was mooted by a few astronomers, but the prevailing opinion was that there must be some unknown planet providing an extra source of gravitational attraction on Uranus, which ought to be included in the Newtonian calculations. Two astronomers in particular, John Couch Adams and U. J. J. Le Verrier, working independently, were convinced of this, and using all the known sightings of Uranus, they estimated where the hypothetical planet should be. This was a remarkable mathematical achievement, but more importantly, careful telescopic observations and studies of old astronomical charts revealed in 1846 the presence of a planet with the anticipated characteristics. The planet was later called Neptune. Newton's theory was saved, for the time being. (The fascinating story of this episode is told by W. M. Smart, 1947.)

A standard account of adhocness

The common features of the examples we are considering are that a theory t, which we can call the main theory, was combined with an auxiliary hypothesis a, to predict e, when in fact e' occurred, e' being incompatible with e. And in order to retain the main theory in its desired explanatory role, a new auxiliary, a', was proposed which, with t, implies e'. The new theories are ad hoc in the sense that they were advanced "for the sole purpose of saving a hypothesis seriously threatened by adverse evidence" (Hempel, 1966, p. 29). However, many philosophers have distinguished two kinds of ad hoc theory. Theory $t \& a'$ is of the first kind if it possesses no independent test implications— independent, that is, from the evidence that refuted its predecessor $t \& a$. It is ad hoc in the second sense if it does have such test implications but none has been verified. Lakatos (1970, p. 175) called the first kind of theory ad hoc$_1$, the second kind ad hoc$_2$. Often, the designation *ad hoc* is applied just to the new theory, a', rather than to its conjunction with t.

The term *ad hoc* for hypotheses that do not meet one or other of these conditions seems not to be an old one; its earliest occurrence in English that we know of was in 1936, in a critical review of a book of psychology. The reviewer, W. J. H. Sprott, commented on some explanations offered in the book of certain aspects of childish behaviour:

> There is a suspicion of '*ad-hoc*-ness' about the 'explanations'. The whole point is that such an account cannot be satisfactory until we can predict the child's movements from a knowledge of the tensions, vectors and valences which are operative, *independent of our knowledge of how the child actually behaved*. So far we seem reduced to inventing valences, vectors and tensions from a knowledge of the child's behaviour.
>
> (Sprott, 1936, p. 249; our emphasis)

Sprott clearly regarded ad hoc theories as unsatisfactory, a view which many philosophers nowadays share. For example, Popper states it as one of his 'requirements' that a theory should not be ad hoc$_1$:

> We require that the new theory should be *independently testable*. That is to say, apart from explaining all the *explicanda* which the new theory was designed to explain, it must have new and testable consequences (preferably consequences of a *new kind*).
>
> (Popper, 1963, p. 241)

A further requirement laid down by Popper is that the new theory "should pass the independent tests in question", that is, they should not be ad hoc$_2$. Lakatos (1970) agreed with Popper that a theory is unacceptable if it is ad hoc in either sense; others such as Hempel (1966, p. 29) emphasise only the first sense. Disapproval of ad hoc theories is not new; in the early seventeenth century, Bacon criticized as a "frivolous distinction" the type of hypothesis that is "framed to the measure of those particulars only from which it is derived" (i.e., ad hoc$_1$ hypotheses). Bacon argued that a hypothesis ought to be "larger and wider" than the observations that gave rise to it and, moreover, that "that largeness and wideness" should be confirmed "by leading us to new particulars" (i.e., the theory should not be ad hoc$_2$).

The theories advocated by Velikovsky, Medawar, and Hubbard in response to anomalous data are probably ad hoc$_1$, since they seem to make no independent predictions, though, of course, a closer study of those theories might reverse that judgment. According to the criteria we have discussed, the theories appear therefore to represent unsatisfactory scientific developments, which is intuitively right. The Adams–Le Verrier hypothesis, on the other hand, is not ad hoc in either sense, because it did make new predictions, some of which were verified by telescopic sightings of Neptune. Again, philosophical and intuitive judgment coincides.

Despite this seeming success, we believe the adhocness criterion to be misconceived and unfounded. In setting out our position, we shall show why the criterion must be wrong, and then we shall present the Bayesian view on ad hoc theories.

Why the standard account must be wrong

According to the standard account, all ad hoc hypotheses are unsatisfactory, though ad hoc$_1$, not surprisingly, is often regarded as worse than ad hoc$_2$. As we explained, we do not think any of the attempts to justify the adhocness criterion a priori have been successful. And we shall argue that this is to be expected, since there are positive reasons to reject the criterion, which we shall now set out. Our argument will appeal to counter-examples and to some more general considerations. An attraction of the adhocness criterion, no doubt, is its apparent objectivity and its avoidance of subjective probability, but, as we shall show, the non-Bayesian account has its own subjective aspect, one which, in our view, is very inappropriate.

Consider first some counter-examples to the standard account. Suppose one were examining the hypothesis that a particular urn contains only white counters. Next, imagine that a counter is withdrawn from the urn at random, that after its colour has been noted, it is replaced, and that this operation is repeated 10,000 times. If 4950, say, of the selected counters were red and the rest white, the initial hypothesis and the various necessary auxiliary assumptions, taken together, would be refuted; and it is then natural to conclude that, contrary to the original assumption, the urn contains both red and white counters in approximately equal numbers. This seems a perfectly reasonable inference, the revised hypothesis appears well justified by the evidence, yet there is no independent evidence for it. And if we complicate the example by letting the urn vapourise just after the last counter has been inspected, there will be no possibility of such independent evidence. So the hypothesis about the (late) urn's contents is ad hoc$_{1\&2}$; but for all that, it seems plausible and satisfactory (Howson, 1984; Urbach, 1991).

Speculating on the contents of an urn is but a humble form of enquiry, which we cite for the simple way it illustrates that a theory can be acceptable even when we have no evidence independent of the observations which caused the theory to be proposed, nor any possibility of such evidence. Hence, the two adhocness criteria are misguided. Examples from the higher sciences confirm this. Take the following case from the science of genetics: suppose it was initially assumed or believed that two characteristics of a certain plant are inherited in accordance with Mendel's principles through the agency of a pair of independently acting genes located on different chromosomes. Imagine now that plant-breeding experiments throw up a surprising number of plants carrying both characteristics, so that the original assumption that the genes act independently is revised in favour of a theory that they are linked on the same chromosome. Again, the revised theory would be strongly confirmed and established as acceptable merely on the evidence that stimulated its formulation and without the necessity of further, independent evidence. (An example of this sort is worked out by Fisher, 1970, Ch. IX.)

The discovery of the planet Neptune illustrates the same point. Adams arrived at what he regarded as the most likely mass and elements of the orbit of the hypothetical planet by the mathematical technique of least squares applied to all the observations that had hitherto been collected on the positions of Uranus. Adams's hypothesis fitted these observations so well that *even before Neptune had been seen through the telescope or detected on astronomical charts*, its existence was contemplated with the greatest confidence by the leading astronomers of the day. For instance, in his retirement address as president of the British Association, Sir John Herschel, after remarking that the previous year had seen the discovery of a new minor planet, went on: "It has done more. It has given us the probable prospect of the discovery of another. We see it as Columbus saw America from the shores of Spain. Its movements have been felt, trembling along the far-reaching line of our analysis, *with a certainty hardly inferior to that of ocular demonstration*" (quoted in Smart, 1947, p. 61; our italics). And the Astronomer Royal,

Sir George Airy, who was initially inclined to believe that the problem with *Uranus* would be resolved by introducing a slight adjustment to the inverse-square law, spoke of *"the extreme probability* of now discovering a new planet in a very short time" (also quoted in Smart, 1947, p. 61; our italics). Neptune was discovered a very short time later.

We turn now to a more general objection to the idea that hypotheses are acceptable only if corroborated by independent evidence. Imagine a scientist who is interested in the conjunction of hypotheses *t & a*, whose implication *e* can be checked in an experiment. The experiment is performed with the result *e'*, incompatible with *e*, and the scientist advances a new theory, *t & a'*, which is consistent with the observations but is ad hoc in one or other of the two senses, that is, there is either no fresh evidence for *a'* or no possibility of such evidence. The new theory therefore is unacceptable according to the view we are considering.

Suppose, next, that another scientist, working without knowledge of his colleague, also wished to test *t & a* but that he chose a different experiment for this purpose, one with only two possible outcomes: either *e* or ∼ *e*. Of course, he would obtain the latter, and having done so, he would be obliged to revise the refuted theory, to *t & a'*, say. This scientist now notices that *e'* follows from the new theory, and he performs the orthodox experiment to verify *e'*. The new theory can then count a successful prediction to its credit, and so is not ad hoc. Hence, according to the standard view, it is perfectly acceptable.

This is strange, to say the least, because we have arrived at opposite evaluations of the very same theory, breaching at the same time what we previously called the Equivalence condition and showing that the standard adhocness criterion is inconsistent. Whatever measures might be taken to resolve the inconsistency, it seems to us that one element of the criterion ought to be removed, namely, the significance it attaches to whether the theory concerned was thought up before or after the evidence was known. This introduces into the principles of theory-evaluation considerations concerning the state of the experimenters' minds, which are intuitively irrelevant and incongruous in a methodology with pretensions to objectivity. No such considerations enter the corresponding Bayesian evaluations.

The Bayesian view of ad hoc theories

We have argued, contrary to the standard view, that a theory could be scientific and plausible even if it is ad hoc. An acceptable ad hoc theory is a possibility allowed for by the Bayesian principle that theories should be evaluated according to their probabilities. To illustrate, consider the ad hoc theory *a'*, which we have supposed was put forward in response to some refuting evidence *e'*. The probability of this theory must be reckoned relative to *e'* and any other available relevant information, *b*. The probability calculus places no restrictions on the value of $P(a'|e' \& b)$; it might, for example, be below 0.5, so that *a'* would be more likely false than true, or greater than 0.5, when the reverse would be the case. Hence *a'* does not need the support of new independent predictions in order to be quite plausible and acceptable (Horwich, 1982, pp. 105–8).

Scientists are also interested in whether *t* in the presence of the newly thought-up *a'* provides a competent explanation of the previously anomalous *e'*. It would only do so if *t & a'* was sufficiently credible; since $P(t \& a'|e' \& b) \le P(a'|e' \& b)$, this would be the case only if *a'* was itself acceptable, in the sense indicated.

The Bayesian approach, incidentally, explains why people often respond immediately with incredulity, even derision, on first hearing certain ad hoc hypotheses. It is hardly likely that their amusement stems from perceiving, or even thinking that they perceive, that the hypothesis leads to no new predictions. Surely it is more likely that they are reacting to what they see as the utter implausibility of the hypothesis.

The notion of independent evidence

As we have explained, a standard non-Bayesian account of adhocness asserts that a theory consisting of the combination $t \& a$ is only replaced with $t \& a'$ in an acceptable, scientific fashion when a' is successfully tested by evidence independent of that which refuted the first theory. This thesis is often associated with another, rather similar view, namely, that no theory is acceptable unless it is supported by evidence independent of that which prompted its initial proposal, whether that evidence also refuted a predecessor or not. We have shown that these views are neither reasonable nor compatible with scientific practice and, moreover, that they fail to live up to the standards of objectivity to which they aspire. (Howson, 1984, addresses a number of other objections.) One problem with the non-Bayesian criterion of adhocness, which we have not needed to exploit in our criticisms, is that the notion of 'independence' with regard to evidence is left vague and intuitive. Moreover, it seems difficult to give it a satisfactory meaning, except in the context of Bayesian induction.

There is an established notion of probabilistic independence, which, however, is unable to supply a suitable interpretation. For suppose theory h was advanced in response to a refutation by e' and that h both explains the old e' and makes the novel prediction e''. It is the general opinion, certainly shared by Popperians, and a consequence of Bayes's Theorem, that e'' confirms h, provided it is sufficiently improbable relative to background information. As discussed earlier in this chapter (pp. 226–7), such confirmation is available, in particular, when $P(e''|h \& e') > P(e''|e')$. But this inequality is quite compatible with e'' and e' *not* being independent in the probabilistic sense.

Another possible way to interpret the independence notion is in terms of logical independence, so that e' and e'' would be said to be independent just in case neither entails the other. This would mean that if the two bits of evidence were trivially distinct in, say, relating to different times or slightly different places, then they would be independent in the sense employed in the adhocness criterion. But then practically no theory would be ad hoc. Take Medawar's peculiar theory about the Eskimo's cozy style of life, which was propounded in response to some surprising IQ measurements. Presumably, one could infer from the theory that tests applied during the following week to the same group of Eskimos would produce similarly high IQs. But although this prediction is logically independent of the earlier results, its success would not significantly improve the standing of Medawar's theory. Mere logical independence from the old results is clearly insufficient to ensure evidential support.

Intuitively, new evidence supports a theory only when it is substantially different from known results, not just trivially different in the logical sense described, and it is this intuition which, it seems to us, underlies the standard adhocness criterion. The idea that 'different' or 'varied' evidence gives more support to a hypothesis than a similar volume of homogeneous evidence is an old and widely held one. As Hempel put it, "the confirmation of a hypothesis depends not only on the quantity of the favorable evidence available, but also on its variety: the greater the variety, the stronger the resulting support" (1966, p. 34). So, for example, the report of the rate at which a stone falls to the ground from a given height on a Tuesday is similar to that relating to the stone's fall on a Thursday; it is very different, however, from a report of the trajectory of a planet or of how a given fluid rises in a particular capillary tube. But although the notions of similarity and diversity amongst evidence seem intuitively clear, it is not easy to give them a precise analysis, except, in our view, in probabilistic terms, in the context of Bayesian induction.

The similar instances in the above list have the characteristic that when one of them is known, any other would thereby be anticipated with relatively high probability. This recalls Bacon's characterisation of similarity in the context of inductive evidence. He spoke of observations "with a promiscuous resemblance one to another, insomuch that if you know one you know all" and was probably the first to point out that it would be superfluous to cite more than a small representative sample of such observations in evidence (see Urbach, 1987, pp. 160–64). This idea of similarity between items of evidence is expressed naturally in probabilistic terms by saying that e_1 and e_2 are similar provided $P(e_2|e_1)$ is higher than $P(e_2)$; and one might add that the more the first probability exceeds the second, the greater the similarity. This means that e_2 would provide less support if e_1 had already been cited as evidence than if it was cited by itself.

On the other hand, knowing that one of a pair of dissimilar instances has occurred gives little or no guidance as to whether the other will occur. For example, unless Newton's, or some comparable, theory had already been firmly established, a knowledge of the rate of fall of a given object on some specific occasion would not significantly affect one's confidence that the planet Venus, say, would appear in a particular position in the sky on a designated day. Different pieces of evidence may also have a mutually discrediting effect. An example of this might be the observations of the same constant acceleration of heavy bodies dropped at sea level and the unequal rates of fall of objects released on different mountain tops. Both sets of observations would confirm Newton's laws, but in circumstances where those laws are not already well established, the first set might suggest that all objects falling freely (whether on top of a mountain or not) do so with the same acceleration. In other words, with different instances, say e_3 and e_1, $P(e_3|e_1)$ is either close to or less than $P(e_3)$. Of course, e_3 merely differing from e_1 in this sense does not imply that it supports any hypothesis significantly; whether it does or not depends on its probability. The notion of similarity, as we have characterised it, is reflexive, as it should be; that is, if e_2 is (dis)similar to e_1, then e_1 is (dis)similar to e_2 (this follows directly from Bayes's Theorem).

To summarize, the non-Bayesian appraisal of hypotheses based on the notion of adhocness is ungrounded in epistemology, has highly counterintuitive consequences, and relies on a concept of independence among items of evidence which seems unanalysable except in Bayesian terms. In brief, it is not a success.

Infinitely many theories compatible with the data

The problem

Galileo carried out numerous experiments on freely falling bodies and on bodies rolling down inclined planes in which he examined how long they took to descend various distances. These experiments led him to formulate the well-known law to the effect that $s = ut + 1/2gt^2$, where s is the distance fallen by a freely falling body in time t, u is its initial downward velocity, and g is a constant. Jeffreys (1961, p. 3) pointed out that Galileo might also have advanced the following as his law:

$$s = ut + \frac{1}{2} gt^2 + f(T)(T - T_1)(T - T_2) \ldots (T - T_n),$$

where T represents the date of the experiment, which could for example be recorded as the number of minutes that have elapsed since the start of the year AD 1600; T_1, T_2, ..., T_n are the specific dates on which Galileo performed his experiments; and f can represent any function of T. Thus Jeffreys's modification stands for an infinite number of alternatives to Galileo's theory. Although all these theoretical alternatives contradict one another and make different predictions about future experiments, the interesting feature of Jeffrey's unorthodox laws of free fall is that they all imply Galileo's experimental data.

This is a particular problem for those non-probabilistic theories of scientific method which hold that the scientific value of a theory is determined just by $P(e|h)$ and, in some versions, by $P(e)$. These philosophical approaches, of which Popper's is one example and maximum-likelihood estimation another, would have to regard the standard law of free fall and those peculiar alternatives described by Jeffreys as equally good scientific theories relative to the evidence available to Galileo, although this is a judgment with which no scientist would agree.

The same point emerges from a well-known example due to Nelson Goodman (1954; for an amusing and illuminating discussion, see Jeffrey, 1983, pp. 187–90). Goodman noted that the evidence of very many and varied green emeralds would normally suggest that all emeralds are green. But he pointed out that that evidence bears the same relation to 'All emeralds are green' as it does to a type of hypothesis he formulated as 'All emeralds are grue'. According to Goodman's definition, something is grue if it was either observed before time t and was green, or was not observed before t and is blue. If t denotes some time after the emeralds described in the evidence were observed, then both the green- and the grue-hypotheses imply that the emeralds observed so far should be green. However, on the assumption that there are unobserved emeralds, the hypotheses are incompatible, differing in their predictions about the colours of emeralds looked at after the critical time. As with Jeffreys's variants of Galileo's theory, the grue-hypothesis represents an infinite number of alternatives to the more natural hypothesis, for t can assume any value, provided it is later than now.

Our examples illustrate a general problem for methodology: that a theory which explains (in the sense of implying or associating a certain probability with) some data is merely one out of an infinite set of rival theories, each of which does exactly the same. The existence of this infinite set of possible explanations, it will be remembered, spelled ruin for any attempt at a positive solution to the problem of induction. The problem with which we are concerned here arises because, in practice, scientists discriminate between possible explanations and typically pick out just one, or at any rate relatively few, as meriting serious attention. An account of scientific method ought to explain how and why they do this.

The Bayesian approach to the problem

This has not proved easy. For the Bayesian, the nature of the problem, at least, is straight-forward. Moreover, Bayesian theory does not imply that every hypothesis similarly related to the data is of equal merit. Suppose one were comparing two theories in the light of the same evidence. Their relative posterior probabilities are given by

$$\frac{P(h_1|e)}{P(h_2|e)} = \frac{P(e|h_1)P(h_1)}{P(e|h_2)P(h_2)}$$

If both theories imply the evidence, then $P(e|h_1) = P(e|h_2) = 1$. And if, in addition, $P(h_1|e)$ exceeds $P(h_2|e)$, then it follows that $P(h_1)$ is larger than $P(h_2)$. More generally, if two theories which explain the data equally well nevertheless have different posterior probabilities, then they must have had different priors too. So theories such as the contrived alternatives to Galileo's law and Goodman's grue-variants must, for some reason, have lower prior probabilities. Indeed, this is clearly reflected in most people finding such hypotheses quite unbelievable. The problem then is to discover the criteria and rationales by which theories assume particular prior probabilities.

Sometimes there is a clear reason why a theory is judged improbable. For instance, suppose the theory concerned a succession of events in the development of a human society; it might, for example, assert that the elasticity of demand for herring remains constant or that the surnames of all future British prime ministers and American presidents will start with the letter Z. These theories, which of course could be true, are however, monstrously improbable. And the reason for this is that the events they describe are influenced by numerous independent processes whose separate outcomes are improbable. The probability that all these processes will turn out to favour the hypotheses in question is therefore the product of many small probabilities, and so itself is very small indeed (Urbach, 1987b). The question of how the probabilities of the causal factors are estimated, of course, remains. This could be answered by reference to other probabilities, in which case the question is just pushed one stage back, or else by some different process that does not depend on probabilistic reasoning. For instance, the simplicity of a hypothesis has been thought to have an influence on its initial probability.

It is worth mentioning here that the equation given above, relating the posterior probabilities of two theories to their prior probabilities, explains an important feature of inductive reasoning. The scientist often prefers a theory which explains the data imperfectly, in that $P(e|h_1) < 1$, to an alternative, h_2, which predicts them with complete accuracy. Thus, even Galileo's data were not in precise conformity with his theory; nevertheless, he did not consider any more-complicated function of u and t to be a better theory of free fall than his own, even though it could have embraced the evidence he possessed more perfectly. According to the above equation, this is because the better explanatory power of the rival hypotheses was offset by their inferior prior probabilities (Jeffreys, 1961, p. 4).

Conclusion

Charles Darwin (1868, vol. 1, p. 8) said that "In scientific investigations it is permitted to invent any hypothesis, and if it explains various large and independent classes of facts it rises to the rank of a well-grounded theory". This is, perhaps, an exaggeration, for not any hypothesis would do; the hypothesis must not be refuted or substantially disconfirmed, nor should it be intrinsically too implausible. With these provisos, Bayesianism, we suggest, is just such a well-grounded hypothesis as Darwin referred to, it arises from natural and intuitively reasonable attitudes to risk and uncertainty. It is neither refuted nor undermined by any of the phenomena of scientific reasoning. On the contrary, as we have seen, it explains a wide variety of them.

Note

* Originally published as 'Bayesian versus non-Bayesian approaches', Chapter 7 of *Scientific Reasoning: The Bayesian Approach*, 2nd ed., Open Court: Chicago, 1993, pp. 117–64 (omitting sections g, h.2, part of i, j.3, and the exercises). Copyright © 1989, 1993 Open Court Publishing Company. Reprinted with permission.

Bibliography

Babbage, C. (1827), 'Notice Respecting Some Errors Common to Many Tables of Logarithms'. *Memoirs of the Astronomical Society*, **3**: 65–67.

Bacon, F. (1620), *Novum Organum*. In *The Works of Francis Bacon*, vol. 4, J. Spedding, R. L. Ellis, and D. D. Heath (eds), London: Longman and Company, 1857–1858.

Bowden, B. V. (1953), 'A Brief History of Computation', in *Faster than Thought*, B. V. Bowden (ed), London: Pitman Publishing.

Cox, R. T. (1961), *The Algebra of Probable Inference*, Baltimore: Johns Hopkins Press.

Darwin, C. (1868), *The Variation of Animals and Plants under Domestication*, 2 vols., London: John Murray.

Dobzhansky, T. (1967), 'Looking Back at Mendel's Discovery', *Science*, **156**: 1588–1589.

Dorling, J. (1979), 'Bayesian Personalism, the Methodology of Research Programmes, and Duhem's Problem', *Studies in History and Philosophy of Science*, **10**: 177–187.

—— (1982), 'Further illustrations of the Bayesian Solution of Duhem's Problem', unpublished.

Duhem, P. (1905), *The Aim and Structure of Physical Theory*, P. P. Weiner (trans.), Princeton: Princeton University Press, 1954.

Edwards, A. W. F. (1986), 'Are Mendel's Results Really Too Close?', *Biological Reviews of the Cambridge Philosophical Society*, **61**: 295–312.

Fisher, R. A. (1936), 'Has Mendel's Work Been Rediscovered?', *Annals of Science*, **1**: 115–137.

—— (1970), *Statistical Methods for Research Workers*, 14 ed., Edinburgh: Oliver and Boyd.

Good, I. J. (1950), *Probability and the Weighing of Evidence*, London: Griffin.

—— (1961), 'The Paradox of Confirmation', *British Journal for the Philosophy of Science*, **11**: 63–64.

Goodman, N. (1954), *Fact, Fiction, and Forecast*, London: Athlone Press.

Grünbaum, A. (1976), 'Is the Method of Bold Conjectures and Attempted Refutations *Justifiably* the Method of Science?', *British Journal for the Philosophy of Science*, **27**: 105–136.

Hempel, C. G. (1945), 'Studies in the Logic of Confirmation', *Mind*, **54**: 1–26 and 97–121.

—— (1966), *Philosophy of Natural Science*, Englewood Cliffs, NJ: Prentice-Hall.

Horwich, P. (1982), *Probability and Evidence*, Cambridge: Cambridge University Press.

Howson, C. (1984), 'Bayesianism and Support by Novel Facts', *British Journal for the Philosophy of Science*, **35**: 245–251.

Jeffrey, R. (1983), *The Logic of Decision*, 2 ed., Chicago: University of Chicago Press.

Jeffreys, H. (1961), *Theory of Probability*, 3 ed., Oxford: Clarendon Press.

Jevons, W. S. (1874), *The Principles of Science*, London: Macmillan and Co.

Korb, Kevin (1994), 'Infinitely many resolutions of Hempel's paradox', in *Theoretical aspects of reasoning about knowledge*, R. Fagin (ed.), Asilomar, California: V. Morgan Kaufmann, pp. 138–149.

Kuhn, T. S. (1970), *The Structure of Scientific Revolutions*, 2 ed., Chicago: University of Chicago Press.

Lakatos, I. (1970), 'Falsificationism and the Methodology of Scientific Research Programmes', in *Criticism and the Growth of Knowledge*, I. Lakatos and A. Musgrave (eds.), Cambridge: Cambridge University Press.

Lindley, D. V. (1970), 'Bayesian Analysis in Regression Problems', in *Bayesian Statistics*, D. L. Meyer and R. O. Collier (eds), Itasca, IL: F. E. Peacock.

Mallet, J. W. (1880), 'Revision of the Atomic Weight of Aluminium', *Philosophical Transactions*, **171**: 1003–1035.

Medawar, P. (1974) 'More Unequal Than Others', *New Statesman*, **87**: 50–51.

Miller, R. (1987) *Bare-faced Messiah*, London: Michael Joseph.

Musgrave, A. (1975), 'Popper and "Diminishing Returns From Repeated Tests" ', *Australasian Journal of Philosophy*, **53**: 248–253.

Polanyi, M. (1962), *Personal Knowledge*, 2 ed., London: Routledge and Kegan Paul.

Popper, K. R. (1959), *The Logic of Scientific Discovery*, London: Hutchinson.

—— (1963), *Conjectures and Refutations*, London: Routledge and Kegan Paul.

Rosenkrantz, R. D. (1977), *Inference, Method, and Decision: Towards a Bayesian Philosophy of Science*, Dordrecht: Reidel.

Smart, W. M. (1947), 'John Couch Adams and the Discovery of Neptune', *Occasional Notes of the Royal Astronomical Society*, number **11**.

Sproutt, W. J. H. (1936), 'Review of K. Lewin's *A Dynamical Theory of Personality*', *Mind*, **45**: 246–251.

Stas, J. S. (1860), 'Researches on the Mutual Relations of Atomic Weights', *Bulletin de l'Academie Royale de Belgigue*, 208–336.

Swinburne, R. G. (1971), 'The Paradoxes of Confirmation—A Survey', *American Philosophical Quarterly*, **8**: 318–329.

Thomson, T. (1818), 'Some Additional Observations of the Weights of the Atoms of Chemical Bodies', *Annals of Philosophy*, **12**: 338–350.

Urbach, P. (1981), 'On the Utility of Repeating the "Same" Experiment', *Australasian Journal of Philosophy*, **59**: 151–162.

—— (1987), *Francis Bacon's Philosophy of Science*, La Salle, IL: Open Court.

—— (1987b), 'The Scientific Standing of Evolutionary Theories of Society' *The LSE Quarterly*, **1**: 23–42.

—— (1991), 'Bayesian Methodology: Some Criticisms Answered', *Ratio (new series)*, **4**: 170–184.

Velikovsky, I. (1950) *Worlds in Collision*, London: Victor Gollancz. (Page references are to 1972 reprint, Sphere Books, Ltd.)

Watkins, J. W. N. (1984), *Science and Scepticism*, London: Hutchinson and Princeton: Princeton University Press.

15

WHY I AM NOT A BAYESIAN*†

Clark Glymour

The aim of confirmation theory is to provide a true account of the principles that guide scientific argument in so far as that argument is not, and does not purport to be, of a deductive kind. A confirmation theory should serve as a critical and explanatory instrument quite as much as do theories of deductive inference. Any successful confirmation theory should, for example, reveal the structure and fallacies, if any, in Newton's argument for universal gravitation, in nineteenth-century arguments for and against the atomic theory, in Freud's arguments for psychoanalytic generalizations. Where scientific judgements are widely shared, and sociological factors cannot explain their ubiquity, and analysis through the lens provided by confirmation theory reveals no good explicit arguments for the judgements, confirmation theory ought at least sometimes to suggest some good arguments that may have been lurking misperceived. Theories of deductive inference do that much for scientific reasoning in so far as that reasoning is supposed to be demonstrative. We can apply quantification theory to assess the validity of scientific arguments, and although we must almost always treat such arguments as enthymematic, the premises we interpolate are not arbitrary; in many cases, as when the same subject-matter is under discussion, there is a common set of suppressed premises. Again, there may be differences about the correct logical form of scientific claims; differences of this kind result in (or from) different formalizations, for example, of classical mechanics. But such differences often make no difference for the assessment of validity in actual arguments. Confirmation theory should do as well in its own domain. If it fails, then it may still be of interest for many purposes, but not for the purpose of understanding scientific reasoning.

The aim of confirmation theory ought not to be simply to provide precise replacements for informal methodological notions, that is, explications of them. It ought to do more; in particular, confirmation theory ought to *explain* both methodological truisms and particular judgements that have occurred within the history of science. By 'explain' I mean at least that confirmation theory ought to provide a rationale for methodological truisms, and ought to reveal some systematic connections among them and, further, ought, without arbitrary or question-begging assumptions, to reveal particular historical judgements as in conformity with its principles.

Almost everyone interested in confirmation theory today believes that confirmation relations ought to be analysed in terms of *probability* relations. Confirmation theory is the theory of probability plus introductions and appendices. Moreover, almost everyone believes that confirmation proceeds through the formation of conditional probabilities of hypotheses on evidence. The basic tasks facing confirmation theory are thus just those of explicating and showing how to determine the probabilities that confirmation involves, developing explications of such meta-scientific notions as 'confirmation', 'explanatory power', 'simplicity', and so on in terms of functions of probabilities and conditional probabilities, and showing that the canons and patterns of scientific inference result. It was not always so. Probabilistic accounts of confirmation really became dominant only after the publication of Carnap's *Logical Foundations of Probability* (1950), although of course many probabilistic accounts had preceded Carnap's. An eminent contemporary philosopher (Putnam 1967) has compared Carnap's achievement in inductive logic with Frege's in deductive logic: just as before Frege there was only a small and theoretically uninteresting collection of principles of deductive inference, but after him the foundation of a systematic and profound theory of demonstrative reasoning, so with Carnap and inductive reasoning. After Carnap's *Logical Foundations*, debates over confirmation theory seem to have focused chiefly on the interpretation of probability and on the appropriate probabilistic explications of various meta-scientific notions. The meta-scientific notions remain controversial, as does the interpretation of probability, although, increasingly, logical interpretations of probability are giving way to the doctrine that probability is degree of belief.[1] In very recent years a few philosophers have attempted to apply probabilistic analyses to derive and to explain particular methodological practices and precepts, and even to elucidate some historical cases.

I believe these efforts, ingenious and admirable as many of them are, are none the less misguided. For one thing, probabilistic analyses remain at too great a distance from the history of scientific practice to be really informative about that practice, and in part they do so exactly because they are probabilistic. Although considerations of probability have played an important part in the history of science, until very recently, explicit probabilistic arguments for the confirmation of various theories, or probabilistic analyses of data, have been great rarities in the history of science. In the physical sciences at any rate, probabilistic arguments have rarely occurred. Copernicus, Newton, Kepler, none of them give probabilistic arguments for their theories; nor does Maxwell or Kelvin or Lavoisier or Dalton or Einstein or Schrödinger or. ... There are exceptions. Jon Dorling has discussed a seventeenth-century Ptolemaic astronomer who apparently made an extended comparison of Ptolemaic and Copernican theories in probabilistic terms; Laplace, of course, gave Bayesian arguments for astronomical theories. And there are people—Maxwell, for example—who scarcely give a probabilistic argument when making a case for or against scientific hypotheses but who discuss *methodology* in probabilistic terms. This is not to deny that there are many areas of contemporary physical science where probability figures large in confirmation; regression analysis is not uncommon in discussion of the origins of cosmic rays, correlation and analysis of variance in experimental searches for gravitational waves, and so on. It *is* to say that, explicitly, probability is a distinctly minor note in the history of scientific argument.

The rarity of probability considerations in the history of science is more an embarrassment for some accounts of probability than for others. Logical theories, whether Carnap's or those developed by Hintikka and his students, seem to lie at a great distance from the history of science. Still, some of the people working in this tradition have made interesting steps towards accounting for methodological truisms. My own inclination is to believe that the interest such investigations have stems more from the insights they obtain into syntactic versions of structural connections among evidence and hypotheses than to the probability measures they mesh with these insights.

251

Frequency interpretations suppose that for each hypothesis to be assessed there is an appropriate reference class of hypotheses to which to assign it, and the prior probability of the hypothesis is the frequency of true hypotheses in this reference class. The same is true for statements of evidence, whether they be singular or general. The matter of how such reference classes are to be determined, and determined so that the frequencies involved do not come out to be zero, is a question that has only been touched upon by frequentist writers. More to the point, for many of the suggested features that might determine reference classes, we have no statistics, and cannot plausibly imagine those who figure in the history of our sciences to have had them. So conceived, the history of scientific argument must turn out to be largely a history of fanciful guesses. Further, some of the properties that seem natural candidates for determining reference classes for hypotheses—simplicity, for example—seem likely to give perverse results. We prefer hypotheses that posit simple relations among observed quantities, and so on a frequentist view should give them high prior probabilities. Yet simple hypotheses, although often very useful approximations, have most often turned out to be literally false.

At present, perhaps the most philosophically influential view of probability understands it to be degree of belief. The subjectivist Bayesian (hereafter, for brevity, simply Bayesian) view of probability has a growing number of advocates who understand it to provide a general framework for understanding scientific reasoning. They are singularly unembarrassed by the rarity of explicit probabilistic arguments in the history of science, for scientific reasoning need not be explicitly probabilistic in order to be probabilistic in the Bayesian sense. Indeed, a number of Bayesians have discussed historical cases within their framework. Because of its influence and its apparent applicability, in what follows it is to the subjective Bayesian account that I shall give my full attention.

My thesis is several-fold. First, there are a number of attempts to demonstrate a priori the rationality of the restrictions on belief and inference that Bayesians advocate. These arguments are altogether admirable, but ought, I shall maintain, to be unconvincing. My thesis in this instance is not a new one, and I think many Bayesians do regard these a priori arguments as insufficient. Second, there are a variety of methodological notions that an account of confirmation ought to explicate and methodological truisms involving these notions that a confirmation theory ought to explain: for example, variety of evidence and why we desire it, *ad hoc* hypotheses and why we eschew them, what separates a hypothesis integral to a theory from one 'tacked on' to the theory, simplicity and why it is so often admired, why 'de-Occamized' theories are so often disdained, what determines when a piece of evidence is relevant to a hypothesis, and what, if anything, makes the confirmation of one bit of theory by one bit of evidence stronger than the confirmation of another bit of theory (or possibly the same bit) by another (or possibly the same) bit of evidence. Although there are plausible Bayesian explications of some of these notions, there are not plausible Bayesian explications of others. Bayesian accounts of methodological truisms and of particular historical cases are of one of two kinds: either they depend on general principles restricting prior probabilities, or they don't. My claim is that many of the principles proposed by the first kind of Bayesian are either implausible or incoherent, and that, for want of such principles, the explanations the second kind of Bayesians provide for particular historical cases and for truisms of method are chimeras. Finally, I claim that there are elementary but perfectly common features of the relation of theory and evidence that the Bayesian scheme cannot capture at all without serious—and perhaps not very plausible—revision.

It is not that I think the Bayesian scheme or related probabilistic accounts capture nothing. On the contrary, they are clearly pertinent where the reasoning involved is explicitly statistical. Further, the accounts developed by Carnap, his predecessors, and his successors are impressive systematizations and generalizations, in a probabilistic framework, of certain principles of ordinary reasoning. But so far as understanding scientific reasoning goes, I think it is very wrong to consider our situation to be analogous to that of post-Fregean logicians, our subject-matter transformed from a hotchpotch of principles by a powerful theory whose outlines are clear. We flatter ourselves that we possess even the hotchpotch. My opinions are outlandish, I know; few of the arguments I shall present in their favour are new, and perhaps none of them is decisive. Even so, they seem sufficient to warrant taking seriously entirely different approaches to the analysis of scientific reasoning.

The theories I shall consider share the following framework, more or less. There is a class of sentences that express all hypotheses and all actual or possible evidence of interest; the class is closed under Boolean operations. For each ideally rational agent, there is a function defined on all sentences such that, under the relation of logical equivalence, the function is a probability measure on the collection of equivalence classes. The probability of any proposition represents the agent's degree of belief in that proposition. As new evidence accumulates, the probability of a proposition changes according to Bayes's rule: the posterior probability of a hypothesis on the new evidence is equal to the prior conditional probability of the hypothesis on the evidence. This is a scheme shared by diverse accounts of confirmation. I call such theories 'Bayesian', or sometimes 'personalist'.

We certainly have *grades* of belief. Some claims I more or less believe, some I find plausible and tend to believe, others I am agnostic about, some I find implausible and far-fetched, still others I regard as positively absurd. I think everyone admits some such gradations, although descriptions of them might be finer or cruder. The personalist school of probability theorists claim that we also have *degrees* of belief, degrees that can have any value between 0 and 1 and that ought, if we are rational, to be representable by a probability function. Presumably, the degrees of belief are to co-vary with everyday gradations of belief, so that one regards a proposition as preposterous and absurd just if his degree of belief in it is somewhere near zero, and he is agnostic just if his degree of belief is somewhere near a half, and so on. According to personalists, then, an ideally rational agent always has his degrees of belief distributed so as to satisfy the axioms of probability, and when he comes to accept a new belief, he also forms new *degrees* of belief by conditionalizing on the newly accepted belief. There are any number of refinements, of course; but that is the basic view.

Why should we think that we really do have *degrees* of belief? Personalists have an ingenious answer: people have them because we can measure the degrees of belief that people have. Assume that no one (rational) will accept a wager on which he expects a loss, but anyone (rational) will accept any wager on which he expects a gain. Then we can measure a person's degree of belief in proposition P by finding, for fixed amount v, the highest amount u such that the person will pay u in order to receive $u + v$ if P is true, but receive nothing if P is not true. If u is the greatest amount the agent is willing to pay for the wager, his expected gain on paying u must be zero. The agent's gain if P is the case is v; his gain if P is not the case is $-u$. Thus

$$v \cdot \text{prob}(P) + (-u) \cdot \text{prob}(\sim P) = 0.$$

Since $\text{prob}(\sim P) = 1 - \text{prob}(P)$, we have

$$\text{prob}(P) = u/(u+v).$$

The reasoning is clear: any sensible person will act so as to maximize his expected gain; thus, presented with a decision whether or not to purchase a bet, he will make the purchase just if his expected gain is greater than zero. So the betting odds he will accept determine his degree of belief.[2]

I think that this device really does provide evidence that we have, or can produce, degrees of belief, in at least some propositions, but at the same time it is evident that betting odds are not an unobjectionable device for the measurement of degrees of belief. Betting odds could fail to measure degrees of belief for a variety of reasons: the subject may not believe that the bet will be paid off if he wins, or he may doubt that it is clear what constitutes winning, even though it is clear what constitutes losing. Things he values other than monetary gain (or whatever) may enter into his determination of the expected utility of purchasing the bet: for example, he may place either a positive or a negative value on risk itself. And the very fact that he is offered a wager on P may somehow change his degree of belief in P.

Let us suppose, then, that we do have degrees of belief in at least some propositions, and that in some cases they can be at least approximately measured on an interval from 0 to 1. There are two questions: why should we think that, for rationality, one's degrees of belief must satisfy the axioms of probability, and why should we think that, again for rationality, changes in degrees of belief ought to proceed by conditionalization? One question at a time. In using betting quotients to measure degrees of belief, it was assumed that the subject would act so as to maximize *expected* gain. The betting quotient determined the degree of belief by determining the coefficient by which the gain is multiplied in case that P is true in the expression for the expected gain. So the betting quotient determines a degree of belief, as it were, in the *role* of a probability. But why should the things, degrees of belief, that play this role be probabilities? Supposing that we do choose those actions that maximize the sum of the product of our degrees of belief in each possible outcome of the action and the gain (or loss) to us of that outcome. Why must the degrees of belief that enter into this sum be probabilities? Again, there is an ingenious argument: if one acts so as to maximize his expected gain using a degree-of-belief function that is not a probability function, and if for every proposition there were a possible wager (which, if it is offered, one believes will be paid off if it is accepted and won), then there is a circumstance, a combination of wagers, that one would enter into if they were offered, and in which one would suffer a net loss whatever the outcome. That is what the Dutch-book argument shows; what it counsels is prudence.

Some of the reasons why it is not clear that betting quotients are accurate measures of degrees of belief are also reasons why the Dutch-book argument is not conclusive: there are many cases of propositions in which we may have degrees of belief, but on which, we may be sure, no acceptable wager will be offered us; again, we may have values other than the value we place on the stakes, and these other values may enter into our determination whether or not to gamble; and we may not have adopted the policy of acting so as to maximize our expected gain or our expected utility: that is, we may save ourselves from having book made against us by refusing to make certain wagers, or combinations of wagers, even though we judge the odds to be in our favour.

The Dutch-book argument does not succeed in showing that in order to avoid absurd commitments, or even the possibility of such commitments, one must have degrees of belief that are probabilities. But it does provide a kind of justification for the personalist viewpoint, for it shows that if one's degrees of belief are probabilities, then a certain kind of absurdity is avoided. There are other ways of avoiding that kind of absurdity, but at least the personalist way is one such.[3]

One of the common objections to Bayesian theory is that it fails to provide any connection between what is inferred and what is the case. The Bayesian reply is that the method guarantees that, in the long run, everyone will agree on the truth. Suppose that B_i are a set of mutually exclusive, jointly exhaustive hypotheses, each with probability $B(i)$. Let $\bar{x}_r$ be a sequence of random variables with a finite set of values and conditional distribution given by $P(\bar{x}_r = x_r | B_i) = \varepsilon(x_r | B_i)$; then we can think of the values x_r as the outcomes of experiments, each hypotheses determining a likelihood for each outcome. Suppose that no two hypotheses have the same likelihood distribution; that is, for $i \neq j$ it is not the case that for all values x_r of $\bar{x}_r$, $\varepsilon(x_r | B_i) = \varepsilon(x_r | B_j)$, where the ε's are defined as above. Let $\bar{x}$ denote the first n of these variables, where x is a value of $\bar{x}$. Now imagine an observation of these n random variables. In Savage's words:

> Before the observation, the probability that the probability given x of whichever element of the partition actually obtains will be greater than α is
>
> $$\sum_i B(i) P(P(B_i | x) > \alpha | B_i),$$
>
> where summation is confined to those i's for which $B(i) \neq 0$. (1972: 49)

In the limit as n approaches infinity, the probability that the probability given x of whichever element of the partition actually obtains is greater than α is 1. That is the theorem. What is its significance? According to Savage, 'With the observation of an abundance of relevant data, the person is almost certain to become highly convinced of the truth, and it has also been shown that he himself knows this to be the case' (p. 50). That is a little misleading. The result involves second-order probabilities, but these too, according to personalists, are degrees of belief. So what has been shown seems to be this: in the limit as n approaches infinity, an ideally rational Bayesian has degree of belief 1 that an ideally rational Bayesian (with degrees of belief as in the theorem) has degree of belief, given x, greater than α in whichever element of the partition actually obtains. The theorem does not tell us that in the limit any rational Bayesian will assign probability 1 to the true hypothesis and probability 0 to the rest; it only tells us that rational Bayesians are certain that he will. It may reassure those who are already Bayesians, but it is hardly grounds for conversion. Even the reassurance is slim. Mary Hesse points out (1974: 117–19), entirely correctly I believe, that the assumptions of the theorem do not seem to apply even approximately in actual scientific contexts. Finally, some of the assumptions of stable estimation theorems can be dispensed with if one assumes instead that all of the initial distributions considered must agree regarding which evidence is relevant to which hypotheses. But there is no evident a priori reason why there should be such agreement.

I think relatively few Bayesians are actually persuaded of the correctness of Bayesian doctrine by Dutch-book arguments, stable estimation theorems, or other a priori arguments. Their frailty is too palpable. I think that the appeal of Bayesian doctrine derives from two other features. First, with only very weak or very natural assumptions about prior probabilities, or none at all, the Bayesian scheme generates principles that seem to accord well with common sense. Thus, with minor restrictions, one obtains the principle that hypotheses are confirmed by positive instances of them; and, again, one obtains the result that if an event that actually occurs is, on some hypothesis, very unlikely to occur, then that occurrence renders the hypothesis less likely than it would otherwise have been. These principles, and others, can claim something like the authority of common sense, and Bayesian doctrine provides a systematic explication of them. Second, the restrictions placed a priori on rational degrees of belief are so mild, and the device of probability theory at once so precise and so flexible, that Bayesian philosopohers of science may reasonably hope to explain the subtleties and vagaries of scientific reasoning and inference by applying their scheme together with plausible assumptions about the distribution of degrees of belief. This seems, for instance, to be Professor Hesse's line of argument. After admitting the insufficiency of the standard arguments for Bayesianism, she sets out to show that the view can account for a host of alleged features of scientific reasoning and inference. My own view is different: particular *inferences* can almost always be brought into accord with the Bayesian scheme by assigning degrees of belief more or less *ad hoc*, but we learn nothing from this agreement. What we want is an explanation of scientific argument; what the Bayesians give us is a theory of learning—indeed, a theory of personal learning. But arguments are more or less impersonal; I make an argument to persuade anyone informed of the premises, and in doing so I am not reporting any bit of autobiography. To ascribe to me degrees of belief that make my slide from my premises to my conclusion a plausible one fails to explain anything, not only because the ascription may be arbitrary, but also because, even if it is a correct assignment of my degrees of belief, it does not explain why what I am doing is *arguing*—why, that is, what I say should have the least influence on others, or why I might hope that it should. Now, Bayesians might bridge the gap between personal inference and argument in either of two ways. In the first place, one might give arguments in order to change others' beliefs because of the respect they have for his opinion. This is not very plausible; if that were the point of giving arguments, one would not bother with them, but would simply state one's opinion. Alternatively, and more hopefully, Bayesians may suggest that we give arguments exactly because there are general principles restricting belief, principles that are widely subscribed to, and in giving arguments we are attempting to show that, supposing our audience has certain beliefs, they must in view of these principles have other beliefs, those we are trying to establish. There is nothing controversial about this suggestion, and I endorse it. What is controversial is that the general principles required for argument can best be understood as conditions restricting prior probabilities in a Bayesian framework. Sometimes they can, perhaps; but I think that when arguments turn on relating evidence to theory, it is very difficult to explicate them in a plausible way within the Bayesian framework. At any rate, it is worth seeing in more detail what the difficulties may be.

There is very little Bayesian literature about the hotchpotch of claims and notions that are usually canonized as scientific method; very little seems to have been written, from a Bayesian point of view, about what makes a hypothesis *ad hoc*, about what makes one body of evidence more various than another body of evidence, and why we should prefer a variety of evidence, about why, in some circumstances, we should prefer simpler theories, and what it is that we are preferring when we do. And so on. There is little to nothing of this in Carnap, and more recent, and more personalist, statements of the Bayesian position are almost as disappointing. In a lengthy discussion of what he calls 'tempered personalism', Abner Shimony (1970) discusses only how his version of Bayesianism generalizes and qualifies hypothetico-deductive arguments. (Shimony does discuss simplicity, but only to argue that it is overvalued.) Mary Hesse devotes the later chapters of her book to an attempt to show that certain features of scientific method do result when the Bayesian scheme is supplemented with a postulate that restricts assignments of prior probabilities. Unfortunately, as we shall see, her restrictive principle is incoherent.[4]

One aspect of the demand for a variety of evidence arises when there is some definite set of alternative hypotheses between which we are trying to decide. In such cases we naturally prefer the body of evidence that will be most helpful in eliminating false competitors. This aspect of variety is an easy and natural one for Bayesians to take account of, and within an account such as Shimony's it is taken care of so directly as hardly to require comment. But there is more to variety. In some situations we have some reason to suspect that if a theory is false, its falsity will show up when evidence of certain kinds is obtained and compared. For example, given the tradition of Aristotelian distinctions, there was some reason to demand both terrestrial and celestial evidence for seventeenth-century theories of motion that subjected all matter to the same dynamical laws. Once again, I see no special reason why this kind of demand for a variety of evidence cannot be fitted into the Bayesian scheme. But there is still more. A complex theory may contain a great many logically independent hypotheses, and particular bodies of evidence may provide grounds for some of those hypotheses but not for others. Surely part of the demand for a variety of evidence, and an important part, derives from a desire to see to it that the various independent parts of our theories are tested. Taking account of this aspect of the demand for a variety of evidence is just taking account of the relevance of evidence to pieces of theory. How Bayesians may do this we shall consider later.

Simplicity is another feature of scientific method for which some Bayesians have attempted to account. There is one aspect of the scientific preference for the simple that seems beyond Bayesian capacities, and that is the disdain for 'de-Occamized' hypotheses, for theories that postulate the operation of a number of properties, determinable only in combination, when a single property would do. Such theories can be generated by taking any ordinary theory and replacing some single quantity, wherever it occurs in the statement of the theory, by an algebraic combination of new quantities. If the original quantity was not one that occurs in the statement of some body of evidence for the theory, then the new, de-Occamized theory will have the same entailment relations with that body of evidence as did the original theory. If the old theory entailed the evidence, so will the new, de-Occamized one. Now, it follows from Bayesian principles that if two theories both entail e, then (provided the prior probability of each hypothesis is neither 1 nor 0), if e confirms one of them, it confirms the other. How then is the fact (for so I take it to be) that pieces of evidence just don't seem to *count* for de-Occamized theories to be explained? Not by supposing that de-Occamized theories have lower prior probabilities than un-de-Occamized theories, for being 'de-Occamized' is a feature that a theory has only with respect to a certain body of evidence, and it is not hard to imagine artificially restricted bodies of evidence with respect to which perfectly good theories might count as de-Occamized. Having extra wheels is a feature a theory has only in relation to a body of evidence; the only Bayesian relation that appears available and relevant to scientific preference is the likelihood of the evidence on the theory, and unfortunately the likelihood is the same for a theory and for its de-Occamized counterparts whenever the theory entails the evidence.

It is common practice in fitting curves to experimental data, in the absence of an established theory relating the quantities measured, to choose the 'simplest' curve that will fit the data. Thus linear relations are preferred to polynomial relations of higher degree, and exponential functions of measured quantities are preferred to exponential functions of algebraic combinations of measured quantities, and so on. The problem is to account for this preference. Harold Jeffreys, a Bayesian of sorts, offered an explanation (1979) along the following lines. Algebraic and differential equations may be ordered by simplicity; the simpler the hypothetical relation between two or more quantities, the greater is its prior probability. If measurement error has a known probability distribution, we can then compute the likelihood of any set of measurement results given an equation relating the measured quantities. It should be clear, then, that with these priors and likelihoods, ratios of posterior probabilities may be computed from measurement results. Jeffreys constructed a Bayesian significance test for the introduction of higher-degree terms in the equation relating the measured quantities. Roughly, if one's equation fits the data *too* well, then the equation has too many terms and too many arbitrary parameters; and if the equation does not fit the data well enough, then one has not included enough terms and parameters in the equation. The whole business depends, of course, entirely on the ordering of prior probabilities. In his *Theory of Probability* Jeffreys (1967) proposed that the prior probability of a hypothesis decreases as the number of arbitrary parameters increases, but hypotheses having the same number of arbitrary parameters have the same prior probability. This leads immediately to the conclusion that the prior probability of every hypothesis is zero. Earlier, Jeffreys proposed a slightly more complex assignment of priors that did not suffer from this difficulty. The problem is not really one of finding a way to assign finite probabilities to an infinite number of incompatible hypotheses, for there are plenty of ways to do that. The trouble is that it is just very implausible that scientists typically have their prior degrees of belief distributed according to any plausible simplicity ordering, and still less plausible that they would be rational to do so. I can think of very few simple relations between experimentally determined quantities that have withstood continued investigation, and often simple relations are replaced by relations that are infinitely complex: consider the fate of Kepler's laws. Surely it would be naïve for anyone to suppose that a set of newly measured quantities will truly stand in a simple relation, especially in the absence of a well-confirmed theory of the matter. Jeffreys' strategy requires that we proceed in ignorance of our scientific experience, and that can hardly be a rational requirement.

Consider another Bayesian attempt, this one due to Mary Hesse. Hesse puts a 'clustering' constraint on prior probabilities: for any positive r, the conjunction of $r + 1$ positive instances of a hypothesis is more probable than a conjunction of r positive instances with one negative instance. This postulate, she claims, will lead us to choose, *ceteris paribus*, the most economical, the simplest, hypotheses compatible with the evidence. Here is the argument:

> Consider first evidence consisting of individuals $a_1, a_2, ..., a_n$, all of which have properties P and Q. Now consider an individual a_{n+1} with property P. Does a_{n+1} have Q or not? If nothing else is known, the clustering postulate will direct us to predict Q_{n+1} since, *ceteris paribus*, the universe is to be postulated to be

as homogeneous as possible consistently with the data. ... But this is also the prediction that would be made by taking the most economical general law which is both confirmed by the data and of sufficient content to make a prediction about the application of Q to a_{n+1}. For h = 'All P are Q' is certainly more economical than the 'gruified' conflicting hypothesis of equal content h': 'All x up to a_n that are P and Q, and all other x that are P are $\sim Q$.'

If follows in the [case] considered that if a rule is adopted to choose the prediction resulting from the most probable hypothesis on grounds of content, or, in case of a tie in content, the most economical hypothesis on those of equal content, this rule will yield the same predictions as the clustering postulate.

Here is the argument applied to curve-fitting:

Let f be the assertion that two data points (x_1, y_1), (x_2, y_2) are obtained from experiments. ... The two points are consistent with the hypothesis $y = a + bx$, and also of course with an indefinite number of other hypotheses of the form $y = a_0 + a_1 + \ldots + a_n x$, where the values of $a_0, \ldots, a_n$ are not determined by (x_1, y_1), (x_2, y_2). What is the most economical prediction of the y-value of a further point g, where the x-value of g is x_3? Clearly it is the prediction which uses only the information already contained in f, that is, the calculable values of a, b rather than a prediction which assigns arbitrary values to the parameters of a higher-order hypothesis. Hence the most economical prediction is about the point $g = (x_3, a + bx_3)$, which is also the prediction given by the 'simplest' hypothesis on almost all accounts of the simplicity of curves. Translated into probabilistic language, this is to say that to conform to intuitions about economy we should assign higher initial probability to the assertion that points $(x_1, a + bx_1)$, $(x_2, a + bx_2)$, $(x_3, a + bx_3)$ are satisfied by the experiment than to that in which the third point is inexpressible in terms of a and b alone. In this formulation economy is a function of finite descriptive lists of points rather than general hypotheses, and the relevant initial probability is that of a universe containing these particular points rather than that of a universe in which the corresponding general law is true. ... Description in terms of a minimum number of parameters may therefore be regarded as another aspect of homogeneity or clustering of the universe.

(Hesse 1974: 230–2)

Hesse's clustering postulate applies directly to the curve-fitting case, for her clustering postulate then requires that if two paired values of x and y satisfy the predicate $y = ax + b$, then it is more probable than not that a third pair of values will satisfy the predicate. So the preference for the linear hypothesis in the next instance results from Hesse's clustering postulate and the probability axioms. Unfortunately, with trivial additional assumptions, everything results. For, surely, if $y = a + bx$ is a legitimate predicate, then so is $y = a_1 + b_1 x^2$, for any definite values of a_1 and b_1. Now Hesse's first two data points can be equally well described by $(x_1, a_1 + b_1 x_1^2)$ and $(x_2, a_1 + b_1 x_2^2)$, where

$$b_1 = \frac{y_1 - y_2}{x_1^2 - x_2^2} \qquad a_1 = y_1 - x_1^2 \left(\frac{y_1 - y_2}{x_1^2 - x_2^2} \right)$$

Hence her first two data points satisfy both the predicate $y = a + bx$ and the predicate $y = a_1 + b_1 x^2$. So, by the clustering postulate, the probability that the third point satisfies the quadratic expression must be greater than one-half, and the probability that the third point satisfies the linear expression must also be greater than one-half, which is impossible.

Another Bayesian account of our preference for simple theories has recently been offered by Roger Rosencrantz (1976). Suppose that we have some criterion for 'goodness of fit' of a hypothesis to data—for example, confidence regions based on the χ^2 distribution for categorical data, or in curve-fitting perhaps that the average sum of squared deviations is less than some figure. Where the number of possible outcomes is finite, we can compare the number of such possible outcomes that meet the goodness-of-fit criterion with the number that do not. This ratio Rosencrantz calls the 'observed sample coverage' of the hypothesis. Where the possible outcomes are infinite, if the region of possible outcomes meeting the goodness-of-fit criterion is always bounded for all relevant hypotheses, we can compare the volumes of such regions for different hypotheses, and thus obtain a measure of comparative sample coverage.

It seems plausible enough that the smaller the observed sample coverage of a hypothesis, the more severely it is tested by observing outcomes. Rosencrantz's first proposal is this: the smaller the observed sample coverage, the simpler the hypothesis. But further, he proves the following for hypotheses about categorical data: if H_1 and H_2 are hypotheses with parameters, and H_1 is a special case of H_2 obtained by letting a free parameter in H_2 take its maximum likelihood value, then if we average the likelihood of getting evidence that fits each hypothesis well enough over all the possible parameter values, the average likelihood of H_1 will be greater than the average likelihood of H_2. The conclusion Rosencrantz suggests is that the simpler the theory, the greater the average likelihood of data that fit it sufficiently well. Hence, even if a simple theory has a lower prior probability than more complex theories, because the average likelihood is higher for the simple theory, its posterior probability will increase more rapidly than that of more complex theories. When sufficient evidence has accumulated, the simple theory will be preferred. Rosencrantz proposes to identify average likelihood with support.

Rosencrantz's approach has many virtues; I shall concentrate on its vices. First, observed sample coverage does not correlate neatly with simplicity. If H is a hypothesis, T another utterly irrelevant to H and to the phenomena about which H makes predictions, then $H\&T$ will have the same observed sample coverage as does H. Further, if H^* is a de-occamization of H, then H^* and H will have the same observed sample coverage. Second, Rosencrantz's theorem does not establish nearly enough. It does not establish, for example, that in curve-fitting the average likelihood of a linear hypothesis is greater than the average likelihood of a quadratic or higher-degree hypothesis. We cannot explicate support in terms of average likelihood unless we are willing to allow that evidence supports a de-Occamized hypothesis as much as un-de-Occamized ones, and a hypothesis with tacked-on parts as much as one without such superfluous parts.

Finally, we come to the question of the relevance of evidence to theory. When does a piece of evidence confirm a hypothesis according to the Bayesian scheme of things? The natural answer is that it does so when the posterior probability of the hypothesis is greater than its prior probability, that is, if the conditional probability of the hypothesis on the evidence is greater than the probability of the hypothesis. That is what the condition of positive relevance requires, and that condition is the one most commonly advanced by philosophical Bayesians. The picture is a kinematic one: a Bayesian agent moves along in time having at each moment a coherent set of degrees of belief; at discrete intervals he learns new facts, and each time he learns a new fact, e, he revises his degrees of belief by conditionalizing on e. The discovery that e is the case has confirmed those hypotheses whose probability after the discovery is higher than their probability before. For several reasons, I think this account is unsatisfactory; moreover, I doubt that its difficulties are remediable without considerable changes in the theory.

The first difficulty is a familiar one. Let us suppose that we can divide the consequences of a theory into sentences consisting of reports of actual or possible observations, and simple generalizations of such observations, on the one hand; and on the other hand, sentences that are theoretical. Then the collection of 'observational' consequences of the theory will always be at least as probable as the theory itself; generally, the theory will be less probable than its observational consequences. A theory is never any better established than is the collection of its observational consequences. Why, then, should we entertain theories at all? On the probabilist view, it seems, they are a gratuitous risk. The natural answer is that theories have some special function that their collection of observational consequences cannot serve; the function most frequently suggested is explanation—theories explain; their collection of observational consequences do not. But however sage this suggestion may be, it only makes more vivid the difficulty of the Bayesian why of seeing things. For whatever explanatory power may be, we should certainly expect that goodness of explanation will go hand in hand with warrant for belief; yet, if theories explain, and their observational consequences do not, the Bayesian must deny the linkage. The difficulty has to do both with the assumption that rational degrees of belief are generated by probability measures and with the Bayesian account of evidential relevance. Making degrees of belief probability measures in the Bayesian way already guarantees that a theory can be no more credible than any collection of its consequences. The Bayesian account of confirmation makes it impossible for a piece of evidence to give us more total credence in a theory than in its observational consequences. The Bayesian way of setting things up is a natural one, but it is not inevitable, and wherever a distinction between theory and evidence is plausible, it leads to trouble.

A second difficulty has to do with how praise and blame are distributed among the hypotheses of a theory. Recall the case of Kepler's laws (discussed in Glymour 1981, Ch. 2). It seems that observations of a single planet (and, of course, the sun) might provide evidence for or against Kepler's first law (all planets move on ellipses) and for or against Kepler's second law (all planets move according to the area rule), but no observations of a single planet would constitute evidence for or against Kepler's third law (for any two planets, the ratio of their periods equals the 3/2 power of the ratio of their distances). Earlier [in Ch. 2 of Glymour's *Theory and Evidence*] we saw that hypothetico-deductive accounts of confirmation have great difficulty explaining this elementary judgement. Can the Bayesians do any better? One thing that Bayesians can say (and some have said) is that our degrees of belief are distributed—and historically were distributed—so that conditionalizing on evidence about one planet may change our degrees of belief in the first and second laws, but not our degree of belief in the third law.[5] I don't see that this is an explanation for our intuition at all; on the contrary, it seems merely to restate (with some additional claims) what it is that we want to be explained. Are there any reasons why people had their degrees of belief so distributed? If their beliefs had been different, would it have been equally rational for them to view observations of Mars as a test of the third law, but not of the first? It seems to me that we never succeed in explaining a widely shared judgement about the relevance or irrelevance of some piece of evidence merely by asserting that degrees of belief happened to be so distributed as to generate those judgements according to the Bayesian scheme. Bayesians may instead try to explain the case by appeal to some structural difference among the hypotheses; the only gadget that appears to be available is the likelihood of the evidence about a single planet on various combinations of hypotheses. If it is supposed that the observations are such that Kepler's first and second laws entail their description, but Kepler's third law does not, then it follows that the likelihood of the evidence on the first and second laws—that is, the conditional probability of the evidence given those hypotheses—is unity, but the likelihood of the evidence on the third law may be less than unity. But any attempt to found an account of the case on these facts alone is simply an attempt at a hypothetico-deductive account. The problem is reduced to one already unsolved. What is needed to provide a genuine Bayesian explanation of the case in question (as well as of many others that could be adduced) is a *general* principle restricting conditional probabilities and having the effect that the distinctions about the bearing of evidence that have been noted here do result. Presumably, any such principles will have to make use of relations of content or structure between evidence and hypothesis. The case does nothing to establish that no such principles exist; it does, I believe, make it plain that without them the Bayesian scheme does not *explain* even very elementary features of the bearing of evidence on theory.

A third difficulty has to do with Bayesian kinematics. Scientists commonly argue for their theories from evidence known long before the theories were introduced. Copernicus argued for his theory using observations made over the course of millennia, not on the basis of any startling new predictions derived from the theory, and presumably it was on the basis of such arguments that he won the adherence of his early disciples. Newton argued for universal gravitation using Kepler's second and third laws, established before the *Principia* was published. The argument that Einstein gave in 1915 for his gravitational field equations was that they explained the anomalous advance of the perihelion of Mercury, established more than half a century earlier. Other physicists found the argument enormously forceful, and it is a fair conjecture that without it the British would not have mounted the famous eclipse expedition of 1919. Old evidence can in fact confirm new theory, but according to Bayesian kinematics, it cannot. For let us suppose that evidence e is known before theory T is introduced at time t. Because e is known at t, $\text{prob}_t(e) = 1$. Further, because $\text{prob}_t(e) = 1$, the likelihood of e given T, $\text{prob}_t(e, T)$, is also 1. We then have

$$\text{prob}_t(T, e) = \frac{\text{prob}_t(T) \times \text{prob}_t(e, T)}{\text{prob}_t(e)} = \text{prob}_t(T).$$

The conditional probability of T on e is therefore the same as the prior probability of T: e cannot constitute evidence for T in virtue of the positive relevance condition nor in virtue of the likelihood of e on T. None of the Bayesian mechanisms apply, and if we are strictly limited to them, we have the absurdity that old evidence cannot confirm new theory. The result is fairly stable. If the probability of e is very high but not unity, $\text{prob}_t(e, T)$ will still be unity if T entails e, and so $\text{prob}_t(T, e)$ will be very close to $\text{prob}_t(T)$. How might Bayesians deal with the old evidence/new theory problem?[6]

Red herrings abound. The prior probability of the evidence, Bayesians may object, is not really unity; when the evidence is stated as measured or observed values, the theory does not really entail that those exact values obtain; an ideal Bayesian would never suffer the embarrassment of a novel theory. None of these replies will do: the acceptance of old evidence may make the degree of belief in it as close to unity as our degree of belief in some bit of evidence ever is; although the exact measured value (of, e.g., the perihelion advance) may not be entailed by the theory and known initial conditions, that the value of the measured quantity lies in a certain interval may very well be entailed, and that is what is believed anyway; and, finally, it is beside the point that an ideal Bayesian would never face a novel theory, for the idea of Bayesian confirmation theory is to explain scientific inference and argument by means of the assumption that good scientists are, about science at least, approximately ideal Bayesians, and we have before us a feature of scientific argument that seems incompatible with that assumption.

A natural line of defence lies through the introduction of counterfactual degrees of belief. When using Bayes's rule to determine the posterior probability of a new theory on old evidence, one ought not to use one's actual degree of belief in the old evidence, which is unity or nearly so; one ought instead to use the degree of belief one would have had in e if. ... The problem is to fill in the blanks in such a way that it is both plausible that we have the needed counterfactual degrees of belief, and that they do serve to determine how old evidence bears on new theory. I tend to doubt that there is such a completion. We cannot merely throw e and whatever entails e out of the body of accepted beliefs; we need some rule for determining a counterfactual degree of belief in e and a counterfactual likelihood of e on T. To simplify, let us suppose that T does logically entail e, so that the likelihood is fixed.

If one flips a coin three times and it turns up heads twice and tails once, in using this evidence to confirm hypotheses (e.g. of the fairness of the coin), one does not take the probability of two heads and one tail to be what it is after the flipping—namely, unity—but what it was before the flipping. In this case there is an immediate and natural counterfactual degree of belief that is used in conditionalizing by Bayes's rule. The trouble with the scientific cases is that no such immediate and natural alternative distribution of degree of belief is available. Consider someone trying, in a Bayesian way, to determine in 1915 how much Einstein's derivation of the perihelion advance confirmed general relativity. There is no single event, like the coin flipping, that makes the perihelion anomaly virtually certain. Rather, Leverrier first computed the anomaly in the middle of the nineteenth century; Simon Newcomb calculated it again around 1890, using Leverrier's method but new values for planetary masses, and obtained a substantially higher value than had Leverrier. Both Newcomb and Leverrier had, in their calculations, approximated an infinite series by its first terms without any proof of convergence, thus leaving open the possibility that the entire anomaly was the result of a mathematical error. In 1912 Eric Doolittle calculated the anomaly by a wholly different method, free of any such assumption, and obtained virtually the same value as had Newcomb.[7] For actual historical cases, unlike the coin-flipping case, there is no single counterfactual degree of belief in the evidence ready to hand, for belief in the evidence sentence may have grown gradually—in some cases, it may have even waxed, waned, and waxed again. So the old evidence/new theory problem cannot be assimilated to coin flipping.

The suggestion that what is required is a counterfactual degree of belief is tempting, none the less; but there are other problems with it besides the absence of any unique historical degree of belief. A chief one is that various ways of manufacturing counterfactual degrees of belief in the evidence threaten us with incoherence. One suggestion, for example, is the following, used implicitly by some Bayesian writers. At about the time T is introduced, there will be a number of alternative competing theories available; call them T_1, T_2, ..., T_k, and suppose that they are mutually exclusive of T and of each other. Then $P(e)$ is equal to

$$P(T_1)P(e, T_1) + P(T_2)P(e, T_2) + ... + P(T_k)P(e, T_k) + P(\sim(T_1 \vee ... \vee T_k))P(e, \sim(T_1 \vee ... \vee T_k)),$$

and we may try to use this formula to evaluate the counterfactual degree of belief in e. The problem is with the last term. Of course, one could suggest that this term just be ignored when evaluating $P(e)$, but it is difficult to see within a Bayesian framework any rationale at all for doing so. For if one does ignore this term, then the collection of prior probabilities used to evaluate the posterior probability of T will not be coherent unless either the likelihood of e on T is zero or the prior probability of T is zero. One could remedy this objection by replacing the last term by

$$P(T)P(e, T),$$

but this will not do either, for if one's degree of belief in

$$P(T_1 \vee T_2 \vee ... \vee T_k \vee T)$$

is not unity, then the set of prior degrees of belief will still be incoherent. Moreover, not only will it be the case that if the actual degree of belief in e is replaced by a counterfactual degree of belief in e according to either of these proposals, then the resulting set of priors will be incoherent, it will further be the case that if we conditionalize on e the resulting conditional probabilities will be incoherent. For example, if we simply delete the last term, one readily calculates that

$$P(T_1 \vee ... \vee T_k, e) = \frac{P(T_1 \vee ... \vee T_k)P(e, T_1 \vee ... \vee T_k)}{P(e, T_1 \vee ... \vee T_k)P(T_1 \vee ... \vee T_k)} = 1,$$

and further that

$$P(T, e) = \frac{P(T)P(e, T)}{P(e, T_1 \vee ... \vee T_k)P(T_1 \vee ... \vee T_k)}.$$

But because T is supposed inconsistent with $T_1 \vee ... \vee T_k$ and $P(T, e)$ is not zero, this is incoherent.

Let us return to the proposal that when new theory confronts old evidence, we should look backwards to the time when the old evidence e had not yet been established and use for the prior probability of e whatever degree of belief we would have had at that time. We cannot just stick in such a counterfactual value for the prior probability of e and change nothing else without, as before, often making both prior and conditionalized probabilities incoherent. If we give all of our sentences the degree of belief they would have had in the relevant historical period (supposing we somehow know what period that is) and then conditionalize on e, incoherence presumably will not arise; but it is not at all clear how to combine the resulting completely counterfactual conditional probabilities with our actual degrees of belief. It does seem to me that the following rather elaborate procedure will work when a new theory is introduced. Starting with your actual degree of belief function P, consider the degree of belief you would have had in e in the relevant historical period, call it $H(e)$. Now change P by regarding $H(e)$ as an arbitrary change in degree of belief in e and using Richard Jeffrey's (1965) rule,

$$P'(S) = H(e)P(S, e) + (1 - H(e))P(S, \sim e).$$

Jeffrey's rule guarantees that P' is a probability function. Finally, conditionalize on e:

$$P''(S) = P'(S, e),$$

and let P'' be your new actual degree of belief function. (Alternatively, P'' can be formed by using Jeffrey's rule a second time.)

There remain a number of objections to the historical proposal. It is not obvious that there are, for each of us, degrees of belief we personally would have had in some historical period. It is not at all clear which historical period is the relevant one. Suppose, for example, that the gravitational deflection of sunlight had been determined experimentally around 1900, well before the introduction of general relativity.[8] In trying to assess the confirmation of general relativity, how far back in time should a twentieth-century physicist go under this supposition? If only to the nineteenth, then if he would have shared the theoretical prejudices of the period, gravitational deflection of light would have seemed quite probable. Where ought he to stop, and why? But laying aside these difficulties, it is implausible indeed that such a historical Bayesianism, however intriguing a proposal, is an accurate account of the principles by which scientific judgements of confirmation are made. For if it were, then we should have to condemn a great mass of scientific judgements on the grounds that those making them had not studied the history of science with sufficient closeness to make a judgement as to what their degrees of belief would have been in relevant historical periods. Combined with the delicacy that is required to make counterfactual degrees of belief fit coherently with actual ones, these considerations make me doubt that we should look to counterfactual degrees of belief for a plausible Bayesian account of how old evidence bears on new theory.

Finally, consider a quite different Bayesian response to the old evidence/new theory problem. Whereas the ideal Bayesian agent is a perfect logician, none of us are, and there are always consequences of our hypotheses that we do not know to be consequences. In the situation in which old evidence is taken to confirm a new theory, it may be argued that there is *something* new that is learned, and typically, what is learned is that the old evidence is entailed by the new theory. Some old anomalous result is lying about, and it is not this old result that confirms a new theory, but rather the new discovery that the new theory entails (and thus explains) the old anomaly. If we suppose that semi-rational agents have degrees of belief about the entailment relations among sentences in their language, and that

$$P(h \vdash e) = 1 \text{ implies } P(e, h) = 1,$$

this makes a certain amount of sense. We imagine the semi-rational Bayesian changing his degree of belief in hypothesis h in light of his new discovery that h entails e by moving from his prior degree of belief in h to his conditional degree of belief in h given that e, that $h \vdash e$, and whatever background beliefs there may be. Old evidence can, in this vicarious way, confirm a new theory, then, provided that

$$P(h, b \& e \& (h \vdash e)) > P(h, b \& e).$$

Now, in a sense, I believe this solution to the old evidence/new theory problem to be the correct one; what matters is the discovery of a certain logical or structural connection between a piece of evidence and a piece of theory, and it is in virtue of that connection that the evidence, if believed to be true, is thought to be evidence for the bit of theory. What I do not believe is that the relation that matters is simply the entailment relation between the theory, on the one hand, and the evidence, on the other. The reasons that the relation cannot be simply that of entailment are exactly the reasons why the hypothetico-deductive account (see Glymour 1981, Ch. 2) is inaccurate; but the suggestion is at least correct in sensing that our judgement of the relevance of evidence to theory depends on the perception of a structural connection between the two, and that degree of belief is, at best, epiphenomenal. In the determination of the bearing of evidence on theory, there seem to be mechanisms and stratagems that have no apparent connection with degrees of belief, which are shared alike by people advocating different theories. Save for the most radical innovations, scientists seem to be in close agreement regarding what would or would not be evidence relevant to a novel theory; claims as to the relevance to some hypothesis of some observation or experiment are frequently buttressed by detailed calculations and arguments. All of these features of the determination of evidential relevance suggest that that relation depends somehow on structural, objective features connecting statements of evidence and statements of theory. But if that is correct, what is really important and really interesting is what these structural features may be. The condition of positive relevance, even if it were correct, would simply be the least interesting part of what makes evidence relevant to theory.

None of these arguments is decisive against the Bayesian scheme of things, nor should they be; for in important respects that scheme is undoubtedly correct. But taken together, I think they do at least strongly suggest that there must be relations between evidence and hypotheses that are important to scientific argument and to confirmation but to which the Bayesian scheme has not yet penetrated.

Notes

* Originally published as Chapter III of *Theory and Evidence*, Princeton University Press: Princeton, 1980, pp. 63–93. Copyright © Princeton University Press. Reprinted by permission of Princeton University Press.

† Who cares whether a pig-farmer is a Bayesian?—R. C. Jeffrey.

1 A third view, that probabilities are to be understood exclusively as frequencies, has been most ably defended by Wesley Salmon (1969).

2 More detailed accounts of means for determining degrees of belief may be found in Jeffrey 1965. It is a curious fact that the procedures that Bayesians use for determining subjective degrees of belief empirically are an instance of the general strategy described in Glymour 1981, Ch. 5. Indeed, the strategy typically used to determine whether or not actual people behave as rational Bayesians involves the bootstrap strategy described in that chapter.

3 For further criticisms of the Dutch-book argument see Kyburg, 1978.

4 Moreover, I believe that much of her discussion of methodological principles has only the loosest relation to Bayesian principles.

5 This is the account suggested by Horwich 1978.

6 All of the defences sketched below were suggested to me by one or another philosopher sympathetic to the Bayesian view; I have not attributed the arguments to anyone for fear of misrepresenting them. None the less, I thank Jon Dorling, Paul Teller, Daniel Garber, Ian Hacking, Patrick Suppes, Richard Jeffrey, and Roger Rosencrantz for valuable discussions and correspondence on the point at issue.

7 The actual history is still more complicated. Newcomb and Doolittle obtained values for the anomaly differing by about 2 seconds of arc per century. Early in the 1920s. Grossmann discovered that Newcomb had made an error in calculation of about that magnitude.

8 Around 1900 is fanciful, before general relativity is not. In 1914 E. Freundlich mounted an expedition to Russia to photograph the eclipse of that year in order to determine the gravitational deflection of starlight. At that time, Einstein had predicted an angular deflection for light passing near the limb of the sun that was equal in value to that derived from Newtonian principles by Soldner in 1801. Einstein did not obtain the field equations that imply a value for the deflection equal to twice the Newtonian value until late in 1915. Freundlich was caught in Russia by the outbreak of World War I, and was interned there. Measurement of the deflection had to wait until 1919.

Bibliography

Carnap, R. (1950). *The Logical Foundations of Probability*. Chicago: University of Chicago Press.
Glymour, C. (1981). *Theory and Evidence*. Chicago: University of Chicago Press.
Hesse, M. (1974). *The Structure of Scientific Inference*. Berkeley: University of California Press.
Horwich, P. (1978). 'An Appraisal of Glymour's Confirmation Theory.' *Journal of Philosophy*, 75: 98–113.
Jeffrey, R. (1965). *The Logic of Decision*. New York: McGraw-Hill; relevant sections are reprinted as Chapter 7 in this volume.
Jeffreys, H. (1967). *Theory of Probability*. Oxford: Clarendon Press.
——(1973). *Scientific Inference*. Cambridge: Cambridge University Press.
Kyburg, H. (1978). 'Subjective Probability: Criticisms, Reflections and Problems.' *Journal of Philosophical Logic*, 7: 157–180, reprinted as Chapter 3 in this volume.
Putnam, H. (1967). 'Probability and Confirmation.' In S. Morgenbesser (ed.), *Philosophy of Science Today*. New York: Basic Books.
Rosencrantz, R. (1976). 'Simplicity.' In W. Harper and C. Hooker (eds.), *Foundations and Philosophy of Statistical Inference*. Boston Reidel.
Salmon, W. C. (1969). *Foundations of Scientific Inference*. Pittsburgh: University of Pittsburgh Press.
Savage, L. (1972). *The Foundations of Statistics*. New York: Dover.
Shimony, A. (1970). 'Scientific Inference.' In R. G. Colodny (ed.), *The Nature and Function of Scientific Theories*, 79–179. Pittsburgh: University of Pittsburgh Press.

16

SYMMETRIES AND ASYMMETRIES IN EVIDENTIAL SUPPORT*†

Ellery Eells and Branden Fitelson

Introduction

A plethora of non-equivalent measures of evidential support (or confirmation)[1] have been proposed and defended in the philosophical literature.[2] This plurality of measures of support is problematic, since it affects a great many arguments surrounding Bayesian confirmation theory (and inductive logic, generally).[3] Unfortunately, only a few arguments have been proposed which can serve to significantly narrow the field of alternative measures of support.[4] Typically, these arguments are relatively complex, and they tend to involve rather sophisticated premises and presuppositions.[5] In the present paper, we will show that the field of competing measures of inductive support can be drastically narrowed by appealing to just a few simple, intuitive considerations of symmetry. In particular, we will show that, simply by thinking about the following three relatively easy questions, we can eliminate all but a very small number of the competing measures of support.

- Does a piece of evidence E support a hypothesis H equally well as E's negation ($\neg E$) undermines, or countersupports, the same hypothesis H?
- Does a piece of evidence E support a hypothesis H equally well as H supports E?
- Does a piece of evidence E support a hypothesis H equally well as E undermines, or countersupports, the negation of $H(\neg H)$?

These are, of course, three quite different questions, concerning different kinds of possible symmetry of evidential support. Presently, we show that the first two of these three kinds of symmetry do not hold in general. This will have implications for the adequacy of many measures of confirmation (or evidential support) that have been proposed in the recent and not so recent literature on inductive logic. We will first define, on pages 289–290, some of these measures of evidential support and, in terms of the idea of such quantitative measures, formulate the symmetry theses involved in the questions with which we began. Then, we will show (pages 270–271) – by way of some intuitive counterexamples – that the answers to the first two questions raised above are (clearly) both "No." The discussion there will not appeal to any of the measures of evidential support defined in the previous section, nor (at least this is our intent) the intuitions that lie behind them, the intent being to evaluate the symmetry theses independently of any such measure. Next (pages 271–2), we will discuss the third kind of symmetry mentioned above. We will provide some (less than definitive) reasons for thinking that the answer to our third question is "Yes." In the final section (and in the appendix), we detail the implications of these conclusions for the various standard measures of evidential support.

The measures and the symmetry theses

Measures of evidential support (that are our topic) are supposed to quantify the degree to which a piece of evidence E provides, intuitively speaking, "evidence for or against" or "support for or against" a hypothesis H – in an incremental as opposed to a final or absolute way. They are supposed to capture what would be the impact of, rather than the final result of, the "absorption" of a piece of evidence. (We will sometimes use the terms "confirmation" and "evidential support" generically, to include disconfirmation and evidential irrelevance; and for a given evidence/hypothesis pair, a measure's value's being positive, negative, or 0 is supposed to correspond specifically to confirmation, disconfirmation, and evidential irrelevance, respectively.) Here we define and label the pertinent measures of evidential support (with comments and some relevant references given in footnotes, and where "Pr" denotes probability, on some appropriate interpretation, usually a "subjective," or "logical" interpretation):

$$d(H, E) =_{df} \Pr(H|E) - \Pr(H).^{6}$$

$$s(H, E) =_{df} \Pr(H|E) - \Pr(H|\neg E).^{7}$$

$$r(H, E) =_{df} \log\left[\frac{\Pr(H|E)}{\Pr(H)}\right].^{8}$$

$$\mathfrak{r}(H, E) =_{df} \Pr(H \& E) - \Pr(H) \cdot \Pr(E).^{9}$$

$$l(H, E) =_{df} \log\left[\frac{\Pr(E|H)}{\Pr(E|\neg H)}\right].^{10}$$

Where "c" stands for a measure of support (e.g., d or s or r, etc., as above), the first symmetry thesis described at the outset can be formulated as follows, where "ES" stands for "Evidence Symmetry."[11]

$$c(H, E) = -c(H, \neg E) \qquad (ES)$$

The second symmetry thesis, which we call "Commutativity Symmetry" can be formulated as:

$$c(H, E) = c(E, H) \qquad (CS)$$

Finally, the third symmetry property, which we call "Hypothesis Symmetry," can be formulated as:

$$c(H, E) = -c(\neg H, E) \qquad (HS)$$

Of course, the difference between (ES) and (HS) is just in the placement of the logical negation symbol (in front of evidence E or in front of the hypothesis H, respectively, on

269

the right hand sides). (ES) says that a piece of evidence E would confirm (or disconfirm) a hypothesis to the same degree that E's negation would disconfirm (or confirm) the same hypothesis, while (HS) says that evidence E would confirm (or disconfirm) H equally well as the same evidence would disconfirm (or confirm) the negation of H. It is easy to show that (ES) and (HS) are equivalent, given the assumption of (CS).[12]

Just to round out the list of what may initially seem to be natural symmetry theses for measures of evidential support, we list here (what we call) Total Symmetry:

$$c(H, E) = c(\neg H, \neg E) \tag{TS}$$

It is easy to see that (TS) follows from the conjunction of (ES) and (HS).[13]

Definitive negative answers to our first two questions

Our first two questions can now be expressed as follows: "Do (ES) and (CS) hold in general?" The examples described in this section will show that the (intuitive) answer to both of these questions is "No."[14]

Suppose that after years of research – having carefully examined thousands and thousands of ravens, nonravens, black things, and nonblack things – we have become virtually convinced, but not absolutely certain, of the hypothesis, H^*, that all ravens are black. Suppose also, as is somewhat standard, that positive instances of the hypothesis – that is, black ravens – still confirm, though to a very small degree, the hypothesis, as do nonblack nonravens and black nonravens. Suppose even that, in accordance with Hempelian confirmation theory, the information about a newly found object, not previous tested for color or ravenhood, that it is not a nonblack raven would confirm H^*, though again of course only to a minute degree.[15] Call this evidence E^*. Since H^* is already so highly confirmed, evidence E^* should be no surprise and would seem to provide little evidence in favor of H^*. However, $\neg E^*$ (the information about that object that it is a nonblack raven) would seem to disconfirm H^* very strongly (and of course conclusively). $\neg E^*$ would be a surprise, and intuitively, to us at least, would seem to provide very strong evidence against H^*, and stronger evidence against H^* than E^* would provide in favor of H^*. That is, we should have: $c(H^*, E^*) \ll |c(H^*, \neg E^*)| = -c(H^*, \neg E^*)$, so that this is, we claim, a counterexample to Evidence Symmetry.

Here is a more quantifiable, and thus perhaps clearer, counterexample to Evidence Symmetry. A card is randomly drawn from a standard deck. Let E^{**} be the evidence that the card is the seven of spades, and let H^{**} be the hypothesis that the card is black. We take it to be intuitively clear that E^{**} is not only conclusive, but also strong, evidence in favor of H^{**}, whereas $\neg E^{**}$ (that the card drawn is not the seven of spades) is close to useless, or close to "informationless," with regard to the color of the card. Again we have an intuitive counterexample to Evidence Symmetry, and we should have: $c(H^{**}, E^{**}) \gg |c(H^{**}, \neg E^{**})| = -c(H^{**}, \neg E^{**})$.

We note that the first counterexample involves conclusive disconfirmation while the second involves conclusive confirmation. This of course is simply due to taking the "evidence" in the first example to be E^* rather than $\neg E^*$, and in the second example to be E^{**} rather than $\neg E^{**}$. We also note that the conclusiveness feature of the examples (that $\neg E^*$ logically implies $\neg H^*$, and E^{**} logically implies H^{**}) is not what is at the heart of the counterexamples. To see this, simply consider a modification of the examples where E^* and E^{**} are reports of color/ravenhood and suit/rank, respectively, of very reliable, but fallible, assistants.

Of course, these examples also tell intuitively against Total Symmetry (e.g., E^{**}, that the card is the seven of spades, is highly informative, confirmatory, and of course also conclusive for the card's being black, H^{**}, while on the other hand the card's not being the seven of spades is nearly silent on whether the card is nonblack).

Moreover, the very same examples can be used to show that Commutativity Symmetry (CS) is not generally true either. It seems clear from these examples that a piece of evidence E can confirm a hypothesis H to a much different degree than H confirms E. Consider for example whether the observation that a card is the seven of spades confirms the proposition that the card is black equally well as the proposition that the card is black confirms the proposition that the card is the seven of spades. With initial uncertainty about the value of the card, we consider the seven of spades, as evidence, to be more highly informative and confirmatory of the blackness of the card, as hypothesis, than the blackness of the card, as evidence, is for the card's being the seven of spades in particular. Other examples like this (against both (CS) and (ES)) can easily be multiplied, where X logically implies (or just confers probability 1 on) Y but not vice versa, though again the extremeness of logical implication of (or conferring probability 1 on) Y is not what is crucial to the examples for the purposes of evaluating (CS) (or (ES)). So, the examples in this section undergird firm, negative answers to both of our first two questions, about (ES) and (CS).

Toward an affirmative answer to our third question

Turning now to Hypothesis Symmetry, we cannot, of course, offer an argument for the thesis as concrete as the counterexamples offered against Evidence Symmetry and Commutativity Symmetry. We note first that we are comparing the evidential significance of E for H to the evidential significance of E for the negation of H, where H and $\neg H$ are mutually exclusive and collectively exhaustive competitors. So it is of course natural at least that the significance of E for H should be of the opposite sign $(+/-)$ as the significance of E for $\neg H$: when there are exactly two such competitors, it is natural to think of E's confirming or disconfirming one of them only "at the (positive or negative) expense of" its single competitor.[16] As to the magnitudes of degrees of support and countersupport, it would seem that, intuitively speaking (which, again, is the rule of this section), there is "only so much credence to pass around" – and a constant amount to be divided between exclusive and exhaustive hypotheses – so that whatever enhancement of credence one of the two such alternatives enjoys (from a particular piece of evidence E) should be exactly the amount that is taken away from the other (where else could it go, or be taken from?).[17] While we do not claim to have a definitive argument in favor of Hypothesis Symmetry, we do find (HS) appealing, and we have not been able to think of any intuitive counterexamples to it.[18]

Narrowing the field

The table below summarizes verdicts concerning each of the five measures of evidential support defined in Section 2. Each cell contains two answers: the answer on the left says whether (as a matter of mathematical/logical fact) the relevant (row) measure satisfies the relevant (column) symmetry thesis, and the answer on the right says whether, based on the considerations advanced above, we think the answer on the left is "good news" (☺) or "bad news" (☹) for the relevant measure.

Measure	(ES)	(HS)	(CS)	(TS)
d	No/☺	Yes/☺	No/☺	No/☺
s	Yes/☹	Yes/☺	No/☺	Yes/☹
r	No/☺	No/☹	Yes/☹	No/☺
τ	Yes/☹	Yes/☺	Yes/☹	Yes/☹
l	No/☺	Yes/☺	No/☺	No/☺

We have already argued for the ☺/☹ answers on the rights, and we have nothing further to add here in support of these verdicts. The yes/no answers on the lefts are verified in the appendix, where we credit others for having previously noted some of these facts (basically, the proofs of the "yes" answers rest on easy probabilistic considerations, and the "no" answers are verified by the cards counterexample described above).

We note that the measures d and l are the only ones with a perfect score (and that the violations of (ES) and (CS) by these measures for the examples of Section 3 are inequalities going in the correct directions urged in Section 3, as verified in the appendix, A.1, A.3, E.1, and E.3, for the cards example). In particular, s and τ are ruled-out because of their satisfaction of (ES), and r and τ are ruled-out because of their satisfaction of (CS).[19]

In closing, we point out that the measures $\Pr(E|H) - \Pr(E)$ (Mortimer, 1988) and $\Pr(E|H) - \Pr(E|\neg H)$ (Nozick, 1981) are both ruled-out by their satisfaction of (ES), and the measure $\Pr(E|H)/\Pr(E)$ (Kuipers, 2000) is ruled-out by its satisfaction of (CS) (proofs omitted). We suspect other measures of evidential support appearing in the literature will also be affected by the present symmetry considerations.

Appendix

There are twenty (5 × 4) theorems implicit in the table above. We address them in five parts below, one for each measure of confirmation, each part establishing four theorems.

A. Theorems pertaining to the difference measure d

A.1. d violates Evidence Symmetry (ES)

The cards example suffices to show this. In the cards example, we have (suppressing the**'s here and throughout the appendix) the following four atomic probabilities: $\Pr(H \& \neg E) = 25/52, \Pr(H \& E) = 1/52, \Pr(\neg H \& E) = 0, \Pr(\neg H \& \neg E) = 1/2$. Therefore, in the cards example, we have: $d(H, E) = 1/2 \gg 1/102 = -d(H, \neg E)$.

A.2. d satisfies Hypothesis Symmetry (HS)

$$Proof: \ d\,(\neg H, E) = (1 - \Pr(H|E)) - (1 - \Pr(H))$$
$$= -[\Pr(H|E) - \Pr(H)]$$
$$= -d(H, E).$$

A.3. d *violates Commutativity Symmetry (CS)*

In the cards example, we have: $d(H, E) = 1/2 \gg 1/52 = d(E, H)$.

A.4. d *violates Total Symmetry (TS)*

In the cards example, we have: $d(H, E) = 1/2 \neq 1/102 = d(\neg H, \neg E)$.

B. *Theorems pertaining to Christensen's measure* s

B.1. s *satisfies Evidence Symmetry (ES)*

$$\begin{aligned} \text{Proof: } s(H, E) &= \Pr(H|E) - \Pr(H|\neg E) \\ &= -[\Pr(H|\neg E) - \Pr(H|\neg\neg E)] \\ &= -s(H, \neg E). \end{aligned}$$

B.2. s *satisfies Hypothesis Symmetry (HS)*

$$\begin{aligned} \text{Proof: } s(\neg H, E) &= (1 - \Pr(H|E)) - (1 - \Pr(H|\neg E)) \\ &= -[\Pr(H|E) - \Pr(H|\neg E)] \\ &= -s(H, E). \end{aligned}$$

B.3. s *violates Commutativity Symmetry (CS)*

In the cards example, we have: $s(H, E) = 26/51 \gg 1/26 = s(E, H)$.

B.4. s *satisfies Total Symmetry (TS)*

Proof. This is an easy consequence of s's satisfaction of both (ES) and (HS) (see note 13 below).

C. *Theorems Pertaining to the Ratio Measure* r

C.1. r *violates Evidence Symmetry (ES)*

In the cards example, $r(H, E) = \log(2) \neq \log(51/50) = -r(H, \neg E)$.

C.2. r *violates Hypothesis Symmetry (HS)*

In the cards example, $r(H, E) = \log(2) \neq +\infty = -r(\neg H, E)$. Both Good (1987) and Fitelson (1999) mention that r has this undesirable property (in contrast to both d and l).

C.3. r *satisfies Commutativity Symmetry (CS)*

$$\begin{aligned} \text{Proof: } r(H, E) &= \log[\Pr(H|E)/\Pr(H)] \\ &= \log[\Pr(E|H)/\Pr(E)] \text{ (by Bayes' Theorem)} \\ &= r(E, H). \end{aligned}$$

273

C.4. r violates Total Symmetry (TS)

In the cards example, $r(H, E) = \log(2) \neq \log(52/51) = r(\neg H, \neg E)$.

D. Theorems Pertaining to Carnap's Relevance Measure r

Carnap (1962, §67) proves that his relevance measure r obeys all four of the symmetry properties discussed in this paper (he also seems to have been aware of the relevant theorems pertaining to the measures d and r). Carnap thinks this is a virtue of his measure. Apparently, Carnap likes all of this symmetry for two reasons: (1) he's concerned mainly with representing quantitatively a (completely symmetric) *qualitative* relevance relation, and (2) r is more "convenient" (mathematically, we suppose) because it exhibits such robust mathematical symmetry. It is worth nothing, however, that Carnap (1962, pp. xvi–xvii and 361) seems to think that the difference measure d agrees with intuitions in applications to *confirmation*, despite its lack of total and utter mathematical symmetry. Carnap seems to be less sympathetic to the ratio measure r (which he calls the "relevance quotient"), but he does not discuss either of the measures s or l.

E. Theorems Pertaining to the Likelihood-Ratio Measure l

E.1. l violates Evidence Symmetry (ES)

In the cards example, we have: $l(H, E) = +\infty \gg \log(26/25) = -l(H, \neg E)$.

E.2. l satisfies Hypothesis Symmetry (HS)

$$
\begin{aligned}
\textit{Proof: } l(H, E) &= \log[\Pr(E|H)/\Pr(E|\neg H)] \\
&= -\log[\Pr(E|\neg H)/\Pr(E|\neg\neg H)] \\
&= -l(\neg H, E).
\end{aligned}
$$

E.3. l violates Commutativity Symmetry (CS)

In the cards example, we have: $l(H, E) = +\infty \gg \log(51/25) = l(E, H)$.

E.4. l violates Total Symmetry (TS)

In the cards example, we have: $l(H, E) = +\infty \neq \log(26/25) = l(\neg H, \neg E)$.

Notes

* Originally published in *Philosophical Studies*, **107** (2002), pp. 129–42. Copyright © 2002 Kluwer Academic Publishers. Reprinted by permission of Springer Science+Business Media.

† We thank Alan Hájek, Dan Hausman, Patrick Maher, Elliott Sober, and an anonymous referee for useful comments on previous drafts of this paper.

1 See Eells (1985) and Eells and Fitelson (2000) on terminology: "evidence" vs. "confirmation". We suppose here that evidence E is not already known so that this terminology issue and "the problem of old evidence" are not issues here, and we will use "confirmation" and "evidence" interchangeably.

2 See Kyburg (1983) for a survey of the many measures of inductive support (or confirmation) that have been proposed and defended over the years.

3 See Festa (1999) and Fitelson (1999, 2001b) for discussions of the ramifications of the plurality of Bayesian measures of (incremental) confirmation.

4 See, for instance, Carnap, 1962, §67; Fitelson, 2001a, 2001b; Good, 1984; Heckerman, 1988; Kemeny and Oppenheim, 1952; Milne, 1996.

5 See Fitelson (2001b) for a critical discussion of several of these arguments.

6 Among those who have used or defended the difference measure d are Earman (1992), Eells (1982), and Gillies (1986; see also Chihara and Gillies 1988), where Gillies tries to defend his use of d), Jeffrey (1992), and Rosenkrantz (1994).

7 The name "s" is borrowed from Christensen (1999), where the measure s is applied to "the problem of old evidence." See also Joyce (1999).

8 We use the logarithm of the ratio $\Pr(H|E)/\Pr(H)$ to ensure that the ratio measure r is $+/-/0$ if and only if E confirms/disconfirms/is confirmationally irrelevant to H. Since logarithms are strictly monotonic increasing functions, this will not change the ordinal structure imposed by r. Among those who have used or defended r (or measures ordinally equivalent to r) are Horwich (1982), Keynes (1921), Mackie (1969), Milne (1995, 1996), Schlesinger (1995), and Pollard (1999).

9 The relevance measure $\mathfrak{r}$ is introduced by Carnap (1962, §67). It is unclear whether Carnap intended to argue that $\mathfrak{r}$ was a superior measure of *the degree to which E (incrementally) confirms H*. It seems that Carnap (1962, §67) was mainly using $\mathfrak{r}$ for the purpose of establishing certain *qualitative* results concerning probabilistic relevance. While Carnap (1962, p. 361) does suggest that he prefers $\mathfrak{r}$ over d and r, he seems to be thinking of $\mathfrak{r}$ as a measure of the *mutual dependence* between E and H. For *this* purpose, the kinds of symmetries exhibited by $\mathfrak{r}$ (which make $\mathfrak{r}$ a *poor* measure of *confirmation*) may be desirable. See appendix §D above.

10 As with r, we use the logarithm of the likelihood ratio $\Pr(E|H)/\Pr(E|\neg H)$ to ensure that the measure l is $+/-/0$ if and only if E confirms/disconfirms/is confirmationally irrelevant to H. Among those who have used or defended l (or measures ordinally equivalent to l) are Kemeny and Oppenheim (1952), Good (1984), Heckerman (1988), Pearl (1988), Schum (1994), and Fitelson (2001a, 2001b).

11 Each of these symmetry conditions is (implicitly) *universally quantified*.

12 *Proof*: Assuming (CS) and (HS), we have: $c(H, E) =_{\text{by (CS)}} c(E, H) =_{\text{by (HS)}} -c(\neg E, H) =_{\text{by (CS)}} -c(H, \neg E)$, showing that (ES) follows from (CS) and (HS). Assuming (CS) and (ES), we have: $c(H, E) =_{\text{by (CS)}} c(E, H) =_{\text{by (ES)}} -c(E, \neg H) =_{\text{by (CS)}} -c(\neg H, E)$, showing that (HS) follows from (CS) and (ES).

13 *Proof*: $c(H, E) =_{\text{by (HS)}} -c(\neg H, E) =_{\text{by (ES)}} - -c(\neg H, \neg E) = c(\neg H, \neg E)$.

14 Examples like these are described in Eells (2000) for the narrower purpose of comparing two specific measures of confirmation, namely d and s.

15 We do not mean to endorse Hempelian confirmation theory, the positive instance criterion, or any of the other standard assumptions underlying traditional discussions of the ravens paradox. We are simply using the ravens example to illustrate why (ES) is unintuitive. If the reader is uncomfortable with the Hempelian lore in this example, they may prefer the example below which does not appeal to anything of the kind.

16 We are not the first to have intuitions that accord with (HS). Kemeny and Oppenheim (1952, p. 309) impose (HS) as one of their (twelve) conditions of adequacy for measures of inductive support. Their reasons for requiring (HS) are quite similar to (and, we think, no more or less definitive than) ours.

17 We have heard of athletic coaches, and bosses, exhorting people to "give 110%," but this of course is beside the point. Also, we are ignoring here proposals of interval valued credences, on which both the formulation and the evaluation of (HS), as well as of (ES) and (CS), would be different.

18 If (CS) were generally true, then we could turn our intuitive (ES) counterexamples into (HS) counterexamples. However, as we have seen, both (ES) and (CS) seem to fall prey to the same kinds of intuitive counterexamples.

19 Although we have given ⊗'s to measures that violate (HS) (and ☺'s to those that satisfy it), we wish to stress that *we do not need* (HS) to rule-out s, r, or $\mathfrak{r}$. As we explained above, we do not

claim to have a knock-down argument in favor of (HS). But, so long as there is no knock-down argument *against* (HS), d and l will remain the only measures which pass through the present "symmetry filter."

References

Carnap, R. (1962): *Logical Foundations of Probability*, 2nd edn., Chicago: University of Chicago Press.

Chihara, C. and Gillies, D. (1988): 'An Interchange on the Popper-Miller Argument', *Philosophical Studies* 54, 1–8.

Christensen, D. (1999): 'Measuring Confirmation', *Journal of Philosophy* XCVI, 437–461.

Earman, J. (1992): *Bayes or Bust: A Critical Examination of Bayesian Confirmation Theory*, Cambridge: MIT Press.

Eells, E. (1982): *Rational Decision and Causality*, Cambridge: Cambridge University Press.

Eells, E. (1985): 'Problems of Old Evidence', *Pacific Philosophical Quarterly* 66, 283–302.

Eells, E. (2000): 'Review: *The Foundations of Causal Decision Theory*, by James M. Joyce', *The British Journal for the Philosophy of Science* 51, 893–900.

Eells, E. and Fitelson, B. (2000): 'Measuring Confirmation and Evidence', *Journal of Philosophy* XCVII(12), 663–672.

Festa, R. (1999): 'Bayesian Confirmation', in M. Galavotti and A. Pagnini (eds.), *Experience, Reality, and Scientific Explanation* (pp. 55–87), Dordrecht: Kluwer Academic Publishers.

Fitelson, B. (1999): 'The Plurality of Bayesian Measures of Confirmation and the Problem of Measure Sensitivity', *Philosophy of Science* 66, S362–S378.

Fitelson, B. (2001a): 'A Bayesian Account of Independent Evidence with Applications', *Philosophy of Science* (to appear).

Fitelson, B. (2001b): *Studies in Bayesian Confirmation Theory*. Ph.D. thesis, University of Wisconsin, Madison.

Gillies, D. (1986): 'In Defense of the Popper-Miller Argument', *Philosophy of Science* 53, 110–113.

Good, I. (1984): "The Best Explicatum for Weight of Evidence', *Journal of Statistical Computation and Simulation* 19, 294–299.

Good, I. (1987): 'A Reinstatement, in Response to Gillies, of Redhead's Argument in Support of Induction', *Philosophy of Science* 54, 470–472.

Heckerman, D. (1988): 'An Axiomatic Framework for Belief Updates', in L. Kanal and J. Lemmer (eds.), *Uncertainty in Artificial Intelligence* 2 (pp. 11–22), New York: Elsevier Science Publishers.

Horwich, P. (1982): *Probability and Evidence*, Cambridge: Cambridge University Press.

Jeffrey, R. (1992): *Probability and the Art of Judgment*, Cambridge: Cambridge University Press.

Joyce, J. (1999): *The Foundations of Causal Decision Theory*, Cambridge: Cambridge University Press.

Kemeny, J. and Oppenheim, P.: 1952, 'Degrees of Factual Support', *Philosophy of Science* 19, 307–324.

Keynes, J. (1921): *A Treatise on Probability*, London: Macmillan.

Kuipers, T. (2000): *From Instrumentalism to Constructive Realism*, Dordrecht: Kluwer.

Kyburg, H. (1983): 'Recent Work in Inductive Logic', in T. Machan and K. Lucey (eds.), *Recent Work in Philosophy* (pp. 87–150), Lanham: Rowman & Allanheld.

Mackie, J. (1969): 'The Relevance Criterion of Confirmation', *The British Journal for the Philosophy of Science* 20, 27–40.

Milne, P. (1995): 'A Bayesian Defence of Popperian Science?', *Analysis* 55, 213–215.

Milne, P. (1996): '$\log[P(h/eb)/P(h/b)]$ is the One True Measure of Confirmation', *Philosophy of Science* 63, 21–26.

Mortimer, H. (1988): *The Logic of Induction*, Paramus: Prentice Hall.

Nozick, R. (1981): *Philosophical Explanations*, Cambridge: Harvard University Press.

Pearl, J. (1988): *Probabilistic Reasoning in Intelligent Systems: Networks of Plausible Inference*, San Francisco: Morgan Kauffman.

Pollard, S. (1999): 'Milne's Measure of Confirmation', *Analysis* 59, 335–337.

Rosenkrantz, R. (1994): 'Bayesian Confirmation: Paradise Regained', *The British Journal for the Philosophy of Science* 45, 467–476.

Schlesinger, G. (1995): 'Measuring Degrees of Confirmation', *Analysis* 55, 208–212.

Schum, D. (1994): *The Evidential Foundations of Probabilistic Reasoning*, New York: John Wiley & Sons.

Part IV

EVIDENCE AND PROBABILITY

Evidential probability and principles
of indifference

17

INTRODUCTION

It is clear that some probability claims are related to *evidential support*—a measure of how good the reasons to believe a hypothesis provided by the evidence are. Natural language expressions like 'Given the evidence, the probability that the defendant is guilty is high' express judgements of how well the evidence supports the hypothesis. The Bayesian approach to confirmation, discussed in Part III, aims to give a theory of the support of hypotheses by evidence. The Bayesian takes the very natural idea that *e* confirms *h* just in case *e* makes *h* more probable, and interprets the word 'probable' as referring to credence. But, it was objected there, why think that whether *e* supports a theory should vary from individual to individual, as credences conditional on the evidence could? Because, it seems, agents can genuinely disagree, saying 'No; in light of that evidence, the probability is low', while two agents who were merely reporting their own degrees of belief would not be disagreeing, there is a prima facie case to be made that inductive probability judgements in ordinary language attempt to express objective judgements of evidential support.

Credences seem poorly suited to the role of evidential support in other ways too. A first example is that it seems to be paradigmatically reasonable to come to believe a theory on the basis of evidence that supports it; one would be justified in that belief, and justified by the evidence. But, it is said, the posterior credences are justified only if the prior credences were justified; so for the Bayesian to claim that a belief in theory on the basis of evidence for it is justified requires them to provide a justification for the priors, something that the orthodox view considered in Part III does not attempt. A second example is the way in which the Bayesian approach to confirmation is troubled by the problem of old evidence. For it seems that whether *e* is evidence for *h* doesn't depend on whether *e* has been learned or not, but, as Glymour pointed out in Chapter 15, the Bayesian cannot separate what is learnt (or what the agent thinks they learnt) from what is evidence.

These observations have motivated investigations into alternative views of what 'probable' might mean in the gloss on confirmation. Let us introduce *evidential probability* as a name for the kind of objective probability involved in confirmation. The idea is captured in this remark by Keynes:

> We are claiming, in fact, to cognise correctly a logical connection between one set of propositions which we call our evidence and which we suppose ourselves to know, and another set which we call our conclusions, and to which we attach more or less weight according to the grounds supplied by the first. ... It is not straining the use of words to speak of this as the relation of probability.
>
> (Keynes, 1921: 5–6)

It will be a fundamentally conditional notion, characterising the objective degree of support a body of evidence gives to a hypothesis: let $E(h|e)$ represent the evidential probability of h on e.

Objective probability is familiar from the *chances* that are involved in coin tosses, gambling games, statistical theories in physics and elsewhere, and in quantum mechanics, which seem to be objective—if they exist. But chances are not a good account of evidential probabilities, because in confirmation theory we are dealing with theories which aren't known to be true, but which are already either true or false, and it is a familiar thought that what is already true or false cannot have non-trivial chance. Yet evidential probabilities must be able to take intermediate values under these circumstances. Objective physical probabilities will be discussed in Parts V and VI.

One way in which we can figure out what evidential probabilities might be like is to think of what plays the parallel role in the case of conclusive evidence. In that case, when e is conclusive evidence for h, e eliminates all possibilities in which $\neg h$. In this case we begin with a space of possibilities and, by adding the constraint that e must hold, narrow to a smaller set of possibilities. The generalisation is clear: if e doesn't conclusively rule out $\neg h$, then some $\neg h$ possibilities will remain. But—and here's the key thought—there should be proportionally fewer $\neg h$ possibilities than there were, if e does in fact support h. This model is rather problematic, since the counting of possibilities required to make sense of this notion is poorly defined given the infinite cardinality of plausible possibility spaces.

It is a point recognised since Leibniz that probability is a kind of graded possibility (Chapter 18, p. 300). The fact that the Kolmogorov axiomatisation makes probability theory mathematically akin to abstract measure theory also suggests that probability might measure the possibility of some proposition. This leads to the following conception of evidential probability: there is an objective probability function which is the real measure of the space of possibilities; the conditional probabilities given by this probability function are the appropriate ones to use in the confirmation relation, because they measure objectively how likely it is that one possibility is true, given some evidence about what the true possibility is like. Because this probability distribution is over all possibilities for which hypotheses turn out true, it is itself necessary. Since this probability distribution is also an indicator of rational credence (someone who finds out e is justified in having a credence identical with the conditional evidential probability of h on e), it is also supposed to be a priori. The necessity and a priority of evidential probability, so conceived, as well as the way in which it generalises conclusive evidential support, have led many to characterise it as *logical* probability.

A quasi-logical evidential probability function would play some useful roles; for example, in the justification of belief. For if your belief in the evidence is justified, and you derive your posterior credence by conditionalising on total evidence (using the evidential probabilities as your conditional credences), then if those evidential probabilities are a priori justified (as the theory of logical probability proposes) your posterior credences will be justified too. Evidential probability might also be useful in answering the problem of old evidence, since $E(h|e)$ doesn't itself get updated by conditionalising on e. The idea that there should be an a priori constraint on the shape of rational probability functions is also involved in the project of objective Bayesianism (mentioned in Chapter 1, p. 27), which (in our terms) requires that a rational initial credence function be equal to the evidential probability function.[1]

Classical and evidential probability

The obvious question is: does evidential probability so described exist? A direct answer would be to construct the required probability function. There is a tradition which attempts to do just that, deriving from the *classical* theory of probability. In slogan form, the classical theory says that (i) 'equal possibilities' should be assigned equal probabilities; and (ii) that every probability is reducible to some combination of equal probabilities. Both of these ideas can be seen in a famous formulation of the theory due to Laplace:

> The theory of chance consists in reducing all the events of the same kind to a certain number of cases equally possible, that is to say, to such as we may be equally undecided about in regard to their existence, and in determining the number of cases favorable to the event whose probability is sought. The ratio of this number to that of all the cases possible is the measure of this probability, which is thus simply a fraction whose numerator is the number of favorable cases and whose denominator is the number of all the cases possible.
>
> (Laplace, 1951: 6–7)

Here Laplace suggests both that every chance is to be first reduced to a Boolean combination of some of the basic cases $c_1, \ldots, c_n$, and second, that a uniform distribution over the basic cases be obtained by simply assigning each case c_i a probability $P(c_i) = 1/n$.

There are many situations where this proposal seems to work out, and many textbook problems in probability theory implicitly involve an equiprobability assumption (in an urn-drawing case, the set-up implicitly involves the idea that because drawing any ball is possible, they are all equally probable). Yet as an account of chance, it leaves much to be desired. There are clearly cases of non-uniform chances, like biased coins and weighted dice (and their quantum analogues), where the space of possibilities is the same as in the uniform case and yet the probabilities differ. Since there can be a difference in the chances with no difference in the space of possibilities, chance cannot supervene on possibility in the way envisaged by the classical theory. In these cases, contingent empirical facts (e.g., about the mass distribution of a die) trump the uniform assignment suggested by the structure of the space of possibilities.

But while the classical theory looks bad as an account of empirical probabilities like chance, it holds promise in the case of logical evidential probability, where the probability distribution is supposed to be fixed entirely by a priori considerations independent of contingent empirical constraints. Laplace's somewhat cryptic formulation involving cases 'we may be equally undecided about in regard to their existence' can be read in an evidential way, for if it is (rationally) permissible that we be equally undecided in regard to which case is actual, then we can have no evidence that favours one case over another, and we take Laplace's suggested uniform distribution as reflecting that symmetrical prior evidential position. Indeed, to avoid vexing questions over just what 'equal' possibility might mean if not equally probable, the natural suggestion is to take logical probability, which reflects no empirical evidence about which possibility is actual, to involve a uniform distribution over the space of possibilities somehow characterised.

283

Principles of indifference

This idea is fundamental to all extant constructive theories of evidential probability. In Keynes (1921), this uniformity constraint is termed *the principle of indifference*, which he formulates as follows:

> The Principle of Indifference asserts that if there is no *known* reason for predicating of our subject one rather than another of several alternatives, then relatively to such knowledge the assertions of each of these alternatives have an *equal* probability.
>
> (Keynes, 1921: 42)

A little later Keynes clarifies that by 'known reason' he means that our evidence is 'symmetrical with regard to the alternatives' (Keynes, 1921: 53)—see also Carnap's remarks in Ch. 19, p. 317. Given that a priori we have no evidence that favours one empirical hypothesis over any other, the principle of indifference would require that all of the alternatives must have equal or at least symmetrical probability. This would indeed be an argument that there was a uniquely privileged prior probability which could play the evidential probability role. As van Fraassen argues (Chapter 18, Sect. 4, p. 296), there also seem to be cases where the principle gives testable predictions which have been borne out. And it does seem to be a rationality constraint:

> it would be arbitrary for [someone betting on dice not known to be biased] to have more confidence in the appearance of one face than in that of any other face and therefore it would be *unreasonable* for him to let his betting decisions be guided by such arbitrary expectations.
>
> (Carnap, p. 316; my emphasis)

Unfortunately for both the classical theory of probability and those who would ground evidential probability on indifference, the principle seems unworkable. There are some very obvious problems if indifference is to apply to situations with more than finitely many alternatives, for then the best equal assignment of probabilities to hypotheses will be to assign them all zero (we can't consistently assign them all non-zero standard probability, and even using infinitesimals, Williamson's case, discussed in the Primer, seems to need a uniform probability zero distribution over the individual infinite sequences). In the case of uncountably many hypotheses (for example, a uniform distribution over the [0, 1] interval), we can assign them all probability zero and still have the probability of the entire space adding up to probability 1—though how precisely to define uniformity in this case, where the probabilities of atomic outcomes don't determine the probabilities of finite-sized regions, is a trickier matter we return to below.[2] But even this cannot be done in the case where we have only countably many outcomes. For example, consider the de Finetti lottery, involving picking a natural number at random. If H_n is the hypothesis that n is picked, indifference would have us assign $P(H_n) = P(H_m)$ for all $m \neq n$. Suppose we let $P(H_n) = x > 0$. Then, by additivity and arithmetic, there is a j such that $P(\cup_{i=0}^{j} H_i) = \Sigma_{i=0}^{j} P(H_i) = jx > 1$. But this violates the normality axiom. So $P(H_n) = 0$. But then countable additivity entails that $P(\cup_{i=0}^{\infty} H_i) = 0$, because the sum of countably many zeros is still zero, violating normality again since $\cup_{i=0}^{\infty} H_i = \top$. So there is no uniform assignment of probabilities at all in this case. One could abandon countable additivity, as de Finetti himself advocated, but the existence of a Dutch book justification for it (as mentioned in Chapter 1, p. 27) means that, arguably, rejecting countable additivity means undermining the justification of the other axioms of probability.

But even in the simplest cases, as van Fraassen argues in Chapter 18, the principle goes wrong. If symmetry is the key to the principle of indifference, then deeper symmetries should be respected too: so if two cases are merely different descriptions of the same problem, the Indifferent probability distribution over hypotheses in those cases should also be the same. But the principle of indifference in its simple forms cannot meet this condition. Van Fraassen offers the case of the perfect cube factory to show this (p. 303). A factory produces cubes with a side length less than or equal to 2 cm. What are the probabilities of the hypotheses that a given cube has side length: (a) less than 1 cm; (b) greater than or equal to 1 cm? The indifference principle suggests $P(a) = P(b)$. What about the probabilities of the hypotheses that a given cube has face area: (c) less than 1 cm^2; (d) greater than or equal to 1 cm^2? Indifference in this case suggests at least that $P(c) \neq P(d)$, because the hypotheses take up unequal regions of the [0, 4] interval. But of course the proposition expressed by a is the same as the proposition expressed by c, and similarly for b and d, so these propositions should get the same probability. Indifference not only fails to give a sensible distribution, it gives conflicting distributions.

The problem arises because the transformation of one interval into another does not preserve the measures of regions which make true the same propositions. The natural suggestion is to propose a measure which is invariant under these transformations. As van Fraassen notes, the standard measure—the one that 'really' shows the essential structure of the problem—is the log uniform measure;[3] this one gives the right result in the perfect cube factory, and in other cases where the transformations on the description of the space of outcomes are equally simple (dilations and translations). In any case, the required application of the principle of indifference proceeds rather differently than does the classical case. Rather than take the outcome space as given and expect every transformation to preserve the probabilities given by indifference, one takes the problem, sees which transformations preserve the essential structure of the problem, and then fixes on the measure which is invariant under exactly those transformations. As Rosenkrantz puts it:

> The needed invariances, however, are not obtained by looking at parameter transformations *per se*, but at transformations of the problem itself into equivalent form. Given the statement of the problem, it may for example, be indifferent in what scale units the data are expressed. Such 'indifference between problems' determines what parameter transformations are admissible—not the other way around.
>
> (Rosenkrantz, 1977: 63)

This procedure requires prior knowledge of precisely how the problem is to be set up, and cannot be said to be truly a priori in virtue of that; but even this kind of principle of indifference will deliver non-trivial predictions of the probabilities from very general descriptions of what is essential and what is not essential in the statement of a problem.

But, van Fraassen argues, following Milne (1983), even this refined and circumscribed version of the principle won't work in every case, in particular in those cases where the essential structure is preserved by transformations which are not simple translations or dilations, etc. The von Mises water/wine problem—the problem of establishing the probability that at least half of a given mixture is water, given that it has a total volume of 1 litre and there is at least 100 ml each of water and wine (discussed by van Fraassen, Chapter 18, pages 304–5 and 311–3)—provides a case where the transformation of the space of outcomes is not so simple. A description of this problem in terms of the proportion of water to the total volume can be transformed to a description in terms of the proportion of water to wine, but only by using both dilation *and* translation; this transformation is not invariant under the log uniform measure. (As Milne notes, the transformation of temperature outcomes measured in Celsius and Fahrenheit also fails to be invariant, as the transformation between them is not a ratio-scale; but surely that notational difference does not make for a genuine difference in the underlying problem.) There simply is no measure which is invariant under an arbitrary transformation. To apply the principle of indifference without leading to contradiction, one must characterise the natural and allowable transformations of the problem. Different problems receive different characterisations. But to know which measure to use is certainly not an a priori matter. The a priori principle of indifference is either silent in these cases, refraining from assigning any probabilities at all, or it leads to inconsistent assignments.

The a posteriori principle of indifference used in these cases cannot be the simple equal assignment to evidentially symmetrical hypotheses envisaged by Keynes, for that principle says nothing at all in the cases at issue, which are those in which there is evidential asymmetry, because one knows something about the permissible invariances of the problem. The principle which can be used is the maximum entropy principle.[4] If the prior knowledge of the invariant transformations of the problem can be expressed as constraints $c_1, ..., c_n$, let the *allowable* distributions A be the set of all those P that meet the constraints. The space of outcomes is $x_1, ...,$ and each allowable distribution assigns some probability $p_1, ...$ to each outcome. The maximum entropy distribution is then that $P^* \in A$, for which the following quantity H is maximised:

$$H = -\sum_i p_i \log p_i \qquad \text{(Entropy)}$$

In cases without constraint, this gives the uniform distribution; but it can also give non-uniform distributions if the constraints demand that the invariant representations of the problem be of a certain sort that is different to the one over which the distribution is defined. But the mathematical complexities don't matter much; what is essential is that these constraints are crucial to getting the theory to avoid problem cases and cannot be generated a priori. They don't look, for example, like rationality constraints on prior credences—for is it irrational to not realise which of many possible transformations ensure that two descriptions are of 'essentially' the same problem? And in fact almost all contemporary defenders of maximum entropy prior probabilities admit that 'typically, there is plenty of background evidence, explicit or implicit' (Franklin, 2001: 286). Whatever the merits of this proposal, it will not help with the project of evidential probability—for that background evidence has apparently already had a bearing on the agent's beliefs about the situation, already confirming some hypotheses about the problem, and disconfirming others, before the maximum entropy principle has been applied![5]

So much for the principle of indifference in general. Before turning back to the project of evidential probability, it is worth considering the project that Jaynes himself, and many others, aimed to use maximum entropy distributions for: determining the rational objective priors for a Bayesian agent. One reason for deep suspicion about this use of maximum entropy to define rational prior distributions for a particular problem is brought out by this example. The (subjective) Bayesian says: given some evidence about a problem situation, update your credences by conditionalising on that evidence. The objective Bayesian says: given some evidence about a problem situation, codify it as a constraint and adopt the maximum entropy prior. But, as Seidenfeld (1979) shows, there are cases where conditionalisation and maximum entropy come apart. It cannot be that both are the unique rational assignment of credence in light of that evidence, and it doesn't seem that treating the evidence as a constraint versus a proposition to update on could possibly make a difference to whether the agent is rational. Objective Bayesianism seems to treat a case the subjective Bayesian can already handle, updating on evidence, and disagrees with them; it can be difficult to see, in light of that disagreement, how the objective Bayesian's attempt to secure the objectivity of the priors is supposed to help the Bayesian project more generally.

Carnap's logical probability

It is crucial, if evidential probability is to shed light on confirmation, that the evidential probability function could 'learn from experience'; the posterior probabilities, conditional on evidence, should be, at least in some cases, different from the prior probabilities. Suppose we use the principle of indifference or maximum entropy to give a distribution over a partition of the outcome space where each total way things could go falls into its own cell. (The partition plays the role of defining the admissible transformations, in Jaynes' sense, for those events which fall into the same cell will be those that are permissibly transformable into one another.) For example, suppose we are to toss a coin ten times. The outcome space consists of the 2^{10} distinct sequences of heads and tails that could result. The maximum entropy distribution is uniform over this partition, assigning each sequence a probability of $1/2^{10}$. Suppose we observe 9 heads in a row. This rules out many of the possible sequences, leaving only two: nine heads followed by a tail, and nine heads followed by a head. But these sequences have equal probability under the initial distribution, and updating on the observed evidence cannot do anything except uniformly increase the probability of all remaining hypotheses. This entails that heads and tails on the last toss are still assigned the same probability of 1/2. This probability function does not learn from experience, because the maximum entropy distribution renders all distinct events probabilistically independent (Earman, 1992: 17).

The problem, Carnap argues (Chapter 19), is that this partition of the outcome space into maximal 'ways things could go' distinguishes outcomes that are in fact just different ways of representing the very same state of affairs. In our example, we distinguished the event that began with a head and ended with nine tails from the one beginning with nine tails and ending with a head. But these are *structurally* alike; if we simply renamed the first toss '10th' and the last toss '1st' we would have the very same underlying structure. Carnap proposes then that structurally alike descriptions of a situation should be given the same probability, being the invariant transformations of the problem.

Carnap's key novel suggestion is that the property of being structurally alike was a purely *logical* one, definable using only syntactic resources. This would make the correct class of allowable transformations a logical matter too, and hence arguably a

priori. This, combined with a maximum entropy distribution over that logically determined space of outcomes, would yield an appropriately logical prior. His proposal, at
least for the elementary case he discusses in Chapter 19, is straightforward. A *state
description* is a complete description, in a simple logical language, of how some things
might be arranged. If we have one predicate P and three individual constants (a, b, c) in
our language, then a state s_1 would be something like $Pa \wedge Pb \wedge \neg Pc$. A *structure description* is a set of states each of which can result from any other in the set by permuting the
individual constants; so the state $s_2 = Pb \wedge Pc \wedge \neg Pa$ will be in the same structure as s_1 as
it results from 'relabelling' the individual constants. While a state description is specific
about which individuals are said to have which properties, a structure description simply
says: there are two things which are P, and one thing which is not. Carnap argues that
a structure description is the appropriate way to capture the essential structure of a situation, as state descriptions seem to give undue significance to the fact that we labelled
the individuals in a certain way.

Applying the principle of indifference to state descriptions gives a probability function
that does not learn from experience, like the one introduced in our discussion of the
sequence of ten coin tosses. But Carnap's 'Method II' of the use of the principle of
indifference is to assign probability uniformly to structure descriptions, and then to
subdivide that probability among the constituent state descriptions. (This extends to a
probability measure m^* on every possibility describable in a suitably restricted language,
since every such possibility is a disjunction of state descriptions of this simple form.)
As Carnap suggests, the confirmation function c^* induced by the uniform distribution
over structure descriptions m^* can learn from experience. Evidence from frequencies is
evidence that the possibility as a whole—which is individuated by the statistics—exhibits
those statistics.

While c^* is a simple function, for a simple language, there are many methods,
including many involving uniform distributions, which also learn positively from experience. Elsewhere, Carnap (1952) sets down general principles characterising acceptable
confirmation functions, which include both probabilistic principles and symmetry principles reminiscent of the principle of indifference, and the demand that confirmation
functions learn positively from experience. He shows that there is a general characterisation of the probability that the next individual will be F, given the frequency f of Fs
in the n individuals so far—that probability takes the value $(fn + \lambda/2)/n + \lambda$, where λ is
a positive real.[6] Various values of λ determine how quickly the confirmation function
learns from experience; the higher the value of λ, the more evidence is needed to shift
the probability of the proposition that the $n + 1$th individual will be F from its initial
value by a given amount (the higher λ, the less sensitive to evidence the confirmation
function is).[7]

Carnap's logical probabilities are defined over very restricted languages, without even
the resources of quantification theory. Attempts to extend Carnap's theory to richer languages were made by both Carnap and Hintikka. Yet even these theories have some odd
results: universally quantified claims *never* get any positive support from the evidence,
no matter how uniform, if the universe of possible individuals is infinite. And while
in some cases structure descriptions do seem to capture the structure of a situation, in
others they do not. The frequency of an attribute in a collection of entities is a structural
property of that collection; but if the collection is infinite, and the frequency can only be
defined as the limit of finite frequencies in longer and longer initial segments (as in for
example the hypothetical frequentist view of physical probability discussed in Part V),

288

the order of the outcomes in the collection is crucial (Hájek, Chapter 25, p. 410). So at least some structural properties require that permutations of order, as in the original coin tossing case, are not always structure-preserving, contrary to Carnap's contention. Whether some more general syntactic notion can cover all cases is not clear.

But the main worry is that Carnap's proposal doesn't really address the objections we've already seen to evidential probability based on indifference. One of those concerns was a worry about circularity: that it is possible to characterise a problem in terms of its admissible transformations (so that we can define a probability function over the alternative hypotheses about it) only if our prior knowledge already provides evidence in support of one such characterisation, which seems to presuppose that we already have an evidential probability function. Carnap proposes to eliminate this potential circularity by giving a purely syntactic and a priori characterisation of our prior knowledge about the problem. But this in fact leaves us worse off. For consider the language $\mathcal{L}_1$ containing the predicate 'green', and the different language $\mathcal{L}_2$ containing the predicate 'grue' (defined—in English, but not in $\mathcal{L}_1$—as 'green and observed, or blue and unobserved'). Carnap's confirmation functions over these languages give quite different predictions; in the first language, the observation of many green emeralds confirms the hypothesis that the next emerald will be green, while in the second language, the observation of many green emeralds confirms the hypothesis that the next emerald will be blue. To suppose that these are on a par is to abandon the idea that there is a logical notion of confirmation that helps with scientific inference at all; so we must give grounds for preferring 'green' language to 'grue' language. These grounds will *not* be syntactic; the most promising suggestion is that 'green' denotes a more natural property than 'grue', and that natural properties are the only ones which experience can teach us about. But this approach, however promising it may be, is in the same position as Jaynes'—we need some evidence prior to the setup of a problem for preferring one class of transformations (those that preserve the representation of natural properties) over other possible transformations.

Taking evidential probability as basic

The prospects for a purely logical and information-free evidential probability constructed from the principle of indifference seem dim. But perhaps the problem lies not in evidential probability, but in the idea that it can be given an a priori construction from more meagre resources. Perhaps we should simply take the existence of evidential probability as basic—it is whatever probability function reflects our judgements about the bearing of evidence on hypotheses, and facts about 'the intrinsic plausibility of hypotheses prior to investigation' (Williamson 2000: 211). If we want a reductive analysis of this probability function, then something like the principle of indifference is the natural place to look. But we can't, on pain of regress, offer reductive analyses of every concept we make use of; and the continuing failure of proposed reductive analyses of evidential probability, combined with the continuing existence of robust judgements about reasonable and unreasonable priors, gives a situation in which taking evidential probability as a new primitive is not implausible.

One version of a primitivist position is expressed by Stove in Chapter 20. He argues, with characteristic force, that the theory of evidential probability stands in as little need of external justification as the theory of deductive logic. He agrees that reasons can be given for particular assignments of evidential probability, just as reasons can be given for adopting particular deductive inferences; but the reasonableness of these reasons will presuppose the framework which is at issue. There is no 'anchorage for it outside logic'; that doesn't mean there is no anchorage for it at all. For the particular judgements of epistemic probability at issue are so obvious that their self-evidence obviates the need for, and undermines the existence of, reasons to believe them that are in a better epistemic condition.

Stove's trenchant insistence on the good standing of evidential probability, whether or not the form of the correct function can be defended by appeal to reasons, is clearly primitivist in our sense. There is the probability function which, in the relevant sense, is the one true generalisation of deductive logic to the more general case of non-conclusive evidential support. At least some statements about this function are obviously true, which is evidence that we have it and some data about its form; but it should not be expected to be defined in other terms. Similar remarks are made by White (2010), when he is considering the circumstances in which rationality requires us to respond indifferently to symmetrical credence.

White responds to two potential objections to primitivism about evidential probability. One is the argument that it is useless: if we can't give an explicit construction of the function, it can play no role in guiding our credence, and if it cannot guide credence it cannot govern how we respond to evidence. In van Fraassen's perfect cube case, what is the unique evidential probability? He replies:

> Yes, I suppose [evidential probability] is pretty useless when it comes to the mystery square [a simplification of van Fraassen's case] and other such cases. It by no means follows that it is always useless. There are Bayesian principles of coherence and conditionalization that I'm just too dense to apply to some cases, either because they are too complex or too confusing. But that doesn't stop me usefully applying them in easier cases. Perhaps in plenty of cases I can tell perfectly well that various possibilities are evidentially symmetric.
>
> (White, 2010: Sect. 3)

White claims that we can, and often do, get useful results out of evidential probability, even if there are well-known puzzle cases in which the evidential probabilities are very obscure. We have lots of evidence that, in particular cases, one assignment of symmetrical probabilities is right and others are wrong, and we are perfectly entitled to take this evidence at face value.

A second kind of objection is that such an entitlement does not exist: we must have reasons for our judgements. Stove's reply to this objection appeals to the internalist notion of self-evidence. Ramsey (Chapter 2, p. 48) offered a refined version of this kind of objection against Keynes's theory of evidential probability: people 'are able to come to so very little agreement' about it, which seems to suggest that it is not self-evident, but also suggests that there is no genuine reason to adopt one rather than another function. An answer to both strands of this objection draws on the externalist tradition in epistemology (Williamson 2000). This says that, while there should be reasons for our belief, those reasons cannot in general be transparently accessible to us. So it cannot be an objection to the primitivist view that the reasons for one judgement about evidential probability rather than another aren't accessible to us, unless that is an objection to almost all of our judgements which are based on evidence it is not known to us that we have.[8] (It might, of course, also be objected that Ramsey's contention is false—there is in fact wide agreement on many cases, as White suggests.)

White (2005) offers a different line of argument in favour of primitivism, by suggesting problems for one aspect of subjective Bayesian confirmation theory. Orthodox Bayesian confirmation theory says that any response to evidence can be rationalised by suitable priors, so there is no one uniquely rational set of attitudes to take to propositions in light of evidence. That is, Bayesians deny the uniqueness thesis on posterior credence, and thus subscribe to a 'permissive' epistemology. But, when generalised to the case of standard epistemology, White argues, there are costs to denying uniqueness. He puts the general challenge like this:

> If my current beliefs are not rationally obligatory for me, why should I take propositions that I *actually* believe as a basis for action and reasoning, rather than some others that I don't believe, but would be rational in believing? Why should *my* beliefs be privileged in my practical and theoretical deliberations, over equally rational alternative beliefs? Suppose that due to a bump on the head, I lose my belief in p and forget that I ever held it. The Epistemology Oracle informs me that believing p is just one of a range of epistemically permissible options for me given my evidence. In figuring out what to believe now, surely the fact that I *used to believe p* is entirely irrelevant; I might just as well start over again and form a new rational belief. Why then should it be any different if I still happen to believe p?

White's argument could be extended: if there are many credences it could now be rational to have (since they would have been rational if I had different priors), there is no rationale for privileging my current rational credences in deliberation and thought rather than some others I could equally have had. This argument can of course be resisted. That other credences are possibly rational (had my priors been different) doesn't obviously entail that adopting those alternative credences is actually rational. And one might reject the initial supposition that there must be a more substantive reason for me to base my deliberations on my current rational credences apart from the fact that they are mine. Nevertheless, this is a suggestive line for primitivists to take.

Other primitivists have offered a different conception of what a primitive evidential probability function might be. So Maher (2006b) argues that we have a widely agreed set of intuitions about what supports what. This is not directly an evidential probability function; that is proposed as an explication of the vague and informal judgements we are predisposed to make. Maher argues that many objections to evidential probability, particularly its apparent arbitrariness with respect to the evidence, are misplaced on this view. It would be an objection if our practices already encoded an arbitrary probability function; but it is not, if that probability function is merely a theoretical posit, giving a rational reconstruction of those practices. The conditions of adequacy are whether the probability function agrees with the judgements it explicates, and it is to be judged on the basis of its consequences, not on its intrinsic features. Of course, it should be noted that subjective Bayesianism is similarly a rational reconstruction; one must place a lot of weight on the idea that our shared judgements are explained by the rationality of those judgements, rather than by something more acceptable to Bayesians, to get evidential probability out of this framework.

The primitivist position is a new alternative in the debate over evidential probability; while the arguments for it are clearly not conclusive, they have revitalised a somewhat moribund area of debate. Particularly interesting are those arguments from broader epistemology against the permissive stance of orthodox Bayesianism; one more area in which Bayesian and traditional epistemology have many common tasks to address.

Further reading

The idea that subjective Bayesian confirmation theory cannot account for justification, and that it must, is developed in Mellor (2005). The argument that subjective Bayesianism, because of the problem of old evidence, cannot explain the notion of something's being evidence for a hypothesis, and that the modifications proposed to avoid this problem end up proposing versions of evidential probability, is due to Maher (1996). An argument that there is a genuine concept of inductive or evidential probability, not to be identified with degrees of belief, is given by Maher (2006a).

The idea that probability is a measure of possibility has been defended for various kinds of probability; so Mellor (2000) defends the connection between chance and objective possibility [as does Eagle (2010)]; some recent work by Swanson (2006) and Yalcin (1997) give accounts of epistemic modality ('it might be that ϕ') in terms of probability; and a very general possible worlds representation of probability is given by Bigelow (1976).

The principle of indifference has a venerable history, sometimes under the name 'The principle of insufficient reason'; Hacking (1971) discusses the history of the classical theory and other views which tie probabilities to equal possibilities. After Keynes, Jeffreys (1961) also used something like a principle of indifference to characterise evidential probability. The de Finetti lottery is introduced by de Finetti (1974), who used it—in conjunction with a symmetry argument intimately related to the principle of indifference—to argue against countable additivity. Kelly (1996) agrees that countable additivity is problematic, but offers a different kind of argument against it (that any assignment of probabilities to a countable hypothesis space must be biased towards the hypotheses coming earlier in the ordering we use to manage the assignment, and this seems to be irrational, so is certainly not required by rationality). Bartha (2004) offers a novel proposal that preserves countable additivity in a more general framework of relative betting quotients, allowing each outcome in the de Finetti lottery to be assigned an equal relative betting quotient, but not one that is equal to any probability (unrelativised betting quotient).

The log uniform measure was proposed by Jaynes (1973); as van Fraassen suggests, Jaynes is in fact fairly circumspect about its prospects for being a fully general representation of any transformable outcome space, saying that 'in practice we will always have some kind of prior knowledge' that restricts the permissible transformations (Jaynes 1968: 240). The maximum entropy generalisation of the principle of indifference draws on Shannon's work on informational entropy in communication theory (Shannon and Weaver 1949); the definition of entropy is very similar to that used in classical statistical mechanics, where the expression represents the 'disorderliness' of a physical system. The analogy is supposed to be that a very disorderly system has minimal additional constraints apart from those imposed by the definition of what kind of system it is; from this perspective Jaynes' use of the formalism is quite natural. Jaynes (1968) also offers a generalisation of maximum entropy methods to continuous outcome spaces. Other objective Bayesians who make use of maximum entropy as a constraint on rational priors include Rosenkrantz (1977) and Williamson (2009). Seidenfeld (1986) generalises his earlier negative results about objective Bayesianism;

Williams (1980) argues for the idea that, far from being in conflict, maximum entropy generalises conditionalisation. A contemporary defence of the principle of indifference that does not adopt the maximum entropy generalisation is Bartha and Johns (2001).

The siren song of rational constraints on priors continues to motivate attempts to defend indifference; see, for example, papers by Castell (1998), Norton (2008) and White (2010). Among those remaining sceptical of the principle, in addition to Seidenfeld, are Shackel (2007), Strevens (1998) and Uffink (1995). Strevens, while not defending a priori indifference, does think that the project of inferring physical probabilities from physical symmetries is a live one; and that the appeal of indifference principles can be largely traced to the success we can have in empirically inferring probabilities from symmetries. North (2010) argues for something similar.

Carnap's own major works are 1952, 1962, 1971 and 1980. Hintikka (1965) begins to extend Carnap's system to richer languages. An early precedent for requiring that inductive probabilities should 'learn from experience' was Laplace's additional imposition of his 'rule of succession' along with the principle of indifference (Zabell 1989). Williamson (2007) offers a response on the part of objective Bayesianism to the problem of learning from experience. Interesting recent work on symmetry arguments in inductive probability is collected in Zabell (2005). The problem of probability-zero universally quantified hypotheses is discussed further by Earman (1992). The problem of 'grue' and 'green' for syntactic conceptions of inductive inference is due to Goodman (1954). Sider (unpublished: Sect. 3.3) offers an argument that privileged metaphysical structure will yield a characterisation of a natural language, simplicity with respect to expressions of which constrains priors to yield an objective Bayesian prior that assigns, e.g., 'all emeralds are green' higher prior probability than 'all emeralds are grue'. An approach to the water/wine problem along similar lines—that volume of water and volume of wine are the natural properties in the vicinity—is offered by Mikkelson (2004).

White's uniqueness thesis is also defended by Feldman (2007); some arguments against uniqueness, which would of course also undermine the existence of a unique evidential probability function, are offered by Rosen (2001) and Kelly (2010).

Notes

1 This is perhaps too strong; for there remains room for an agent who sets their conditional initial credences equal to the evidential probabilities, but whose unconditional credences are relatively unconstrained. Of course, since (supposing the evidence forms a partition) $C(h) = \Sigma_i C(e_i)C(h|e_i)$, the unconditional credences will be a weighted average of the evidential probabilities. But if the unconditional probability of the evidence can be arbitrary, such an agent can have arbitrary prior credences in hypotheses. Upon receipt of evidence e, such an agent will update by conditionalisation to the justified credence in h, and so long as their credence in e is rational, their entire posterior distribution will be rational too. We may conclude that if objective Bayesianism is to be plausible, it should permit leeway in the assignment of unconditional priors, and impose the rationality constraint only that the conditional probabilities be such as to reflect the genuine objective relations of evidential support.

2 Note also that such probability distributions, where the basic equiprobable probability zero outcomes don't determine the probabilities of complex events, seem to undermine Laplace's idea that evaluations of probability involve the reduction of complex events to more basic ones.

3 This is the measure over the real line defined by assigning the measure $\log b - \log a$ to the basic intervals $[a, b]$, and extending it to a full measure over arbitrary sets of reals by decomposing those sets into non-overlapping basic intervals and adding the measures together. If we have, as in van Fraassen's example, a finite partition, we can normalise this measure and obtain a probability distribution over the partition.

4 I state the version for the discrete case—note that this includes countable spaces, where the principle doesn't of course yield a uniform distribution, but rather a distribution in the limit of a succession of flatter and flatter distributions.

5 One thing that might be going on concerning those who nevertheless say that the principle of indifference is a constraint on prior knowledge is that they are identifying strictly probabilistic information about the system with observed frequencies, as in the frequency interpretation of chance (Part V). The maximum entropy distribution can be applied without frequency constraints, and still (as Jaynes (1968: Sect. IV) is concerned to show) make predictions in agreement with the frequency data. So, on some crude empiricist model of posterior information about probability, the maximum entropy distribution doesn't involve any. But viable views of chance all end up saying that empirical symmetries, which do play a role in the constraints on maximum entropy, do provide genuinely empirical information about chances.

6 Assuming that the family of predicates possible for an individual is $\{F, \neg F\}$. Note that m^* satisfies this condition, as does Laplace's 'rule of succession'.

7 The 'preferred' value of λ is open to debate, and it seems difficult to give purely logical reasons for preferring one value to another—surely it is a contingent matter how much risk is reasonable when inferring to a hypothesis from some evidence.

8 Williamson's own view is that our evidence is what we know; since we don't always know what we know, we don't always know our evidence; yet that evidence is still a reason for belief.

Bibliography

Bartha, Paul (2004), 'Countable Additivity and the de Finetti Lottery'. *British Journal for the Philosophy of Science*, vol. 55: pp. 301–21.

Bartha, Paul and Johns, Richard (2001), 'Probability and Symmetry'. *Philosophy of Science*, vol. 68: pp. S109–S122.

Bigelow, John (1976), 'Possible Worlds Foundations for Probability'. *Journal of Philosophical Logic*, vol. 5: pp. 299–320.

Carnap, Rudolf (1952), *The Continuum of Inductive Methods*. Chicago: University of Chicago Press.

—— (1962), *Logical Foundations of Probability*. Chicago: University of Chicago Press, 2 ed.

—— (1971), 'A Basic System of Inductive Logic, Part 1'. In Rudolf Carnap and Richard C. Jeffrey (eds.), *Studies in Inductive Logic and Probability*, vol. 1, Berkeley: University of California Press, pp. 33–165.

—— (1980), 'A Basic System of Inductive Logic, Part 2'. In Richard C. Jeffrey (ed.), *Studies in Inductive Logic and Probability*, vol. 2, Berkeley: University of California Press, pp. 7–155.

Castell, P. (1998), 'A Consistent Restriction of the Principle of Indifference'. *British Journal for the Philosophy of Science*, vol. 49: pp. 387–95.

de Finetti, Bruno (1974), *Theory of Probability*. New York: Wiley.

Eagle, Antony (2010), 'Deterministic Chance'. *Noûs*, DOI 10.1111/j.1468-0068.2010.00771.

Earman, John (1992), *Bayes or Bust?*. Cambridge, MA: MIT Press.

Feldman, Richard (2007), 'Reasonable Religious Disagreements'. In Louise M. Antony (ed.), *Philosophers without Gods*, New York: Oxford University Press, pp. 194–214.

Franklin, J. (2001), 'Resurrecting Logical Probability'. *Erkenntnis*, vol. 55: pp. 277–305.

Goodman, Nelson (1954), *Fact, Fiction and Forecast*. Cambridge, MA: Harvard University Press.

Hacking, Ian (1971), 'Equipossibility Theories of Probability'. *British Journal for the Philosophy of Science*, vol. 22: pp. 339–355.

Hintikka, Jaakko (1965), 'A Two-Dimensional Continuum of Inductive Methods'. In Jaakko Hintikka and Patrick Suppes (eds.), *Aspects of Inductive Logic*, Amsterdam: North-Holland.

Jaynes, E. T. (1968), 'Prior Probabilities'. *IEEE Transactions on Systems Science and Cybernetics*, vol. 4: pp. 227–241.

—— (1973), 'The Well-Posed Problem'. *Foundations of Physics*, vol. 3: pp. 477–492.

Jeffreys, Harold (1961), *Theory of Probability*. Oxford: Oxford University Press, 2 ed.

Kelly, Kevin T. (1996), *The Logic of Reliable Inquiry*. Oxford: Oxford University Press.

Kelly, Thomas (2010), 'Peer Disagreement and Higher Order Evidence'. In Richard Feldman and Ted A. Warfield (eds.), *Disagreement*, Oxford: Oxford University Press.

Keynes, John Maynard (1921), *A Treatise on Probability*. London: Macmillan.

Laplace, Pierre-Simon (1951), *Philosophical Essay on Probabilities*. New York: Dover.

Maher, Patrick (1996), 'Subjective and Objective Confirmation'. *Philosophy of Science*, vol. 63: pp. 149–174.

—— (2006a), 'The Concept of Inductive Probability'. *Erkenntnis*, vol. 65: pp. 185–206.

—— (2006b), 'A Conception of Inductive Logic'. *Philosophy of Science*, vol. 73: pp. 513–523.

Mellor, D. H. (2000), 'Possibility, Chance and Necessity'. *Australasian Journal of Philosophy*, vol. 78: pp. 16–27.

—— (2005), *Probability: A Philosophical Introduction*. London: Routledge.

Mikkelson, J. M. (2004), 'Dissolving the Water/Wine Paradox'. *British Journal for the Philosophy of Science*, vol. 55: pp. 137–145.

Milne, Peter (1983), 'A Note on Scale Invariance'. *British Journal for the Philosophy of Science*, vol. 34: pp. 49–55.

North, Jill (2010), 'An empirical approach to symmetry and probability'. *Studies in History and Philosophy of Modern Physics*, Vol. 41: pp. 27–40.

Norton, John (2008), 'Ignorance and Indifference'. *Philosophy of Science*, vol. 75: pp. 45–68.

Rosen, Gideon (2001), 'Nominalism, Naturalism, Epistemic Relativism'. *Philosophical Perspectives*, vol. 15: pp. 60–91.

Rosenkrantz, R. D. (1977), *Inference, Method and Decision: Towards a Bayesian Philosophy of Science*. Dordrecht: D. Reidel.

Seidenfeld, Teddy (1979), 'Why I am Not an Objective Bayesian'. *Theory and Decision*, vol. 11: pp. 413–440.

—— (1986), 'Entropy and Uncertainty'. *Philosophy of Science*, vol. 53: pp. 467–491.

Shackel, Nicholas (2007), 'Bertrand's Paradox and the Principle of Indifference'. *Philosophy of Science*, vol. 74: pp. 150–175.

Shannon, Claude E. and Weaver, William (1949), *Mathematical Theory of Communication*. Urbana: University of Illinois Press.

Sider, Theodore (unpublished), *Writing the Book of the World*.

Strevens, Michael (1998), 'Inferring Probabilities from Symmetries'. *Noûs*, vol. 32: pp. 231–246.

Swanson, Eric (2006), *Interactions with Context*. PhD thesis, MIT, URL http://www-personal.umich.edu/~ericsw/Swanson,%20Interactions%20with%20Context.pdf.

Uffink, Jos (1995), 'Can the Maximum Entropy Principle be Explained as a Consistency Requirement?' *Studies in History and Philosophy of Modern Physics*, vol. 26: pp. 223–261.

White, Roger (2005), 'Epistemic Permissiveness'. *Philosophical Perspectives*, vol. 19: pp. 445–459.

—— (2010), 'Evidential Symmetry and Mushy Credence'. *Oxford Studies in Epistemology*, vol. 3: pp. 161–186.

Williams, P. M. (1980), 'Bayesian Conditionalisation and the Principle of Minimum Information'. *British Journal for the Philosophy of Science*, vol. 31: pp. 131–144.

Williamson, Jon (2007), 'Inductive Influence'. *British Journal for the Philosophy of Science*, vol. 58: pp. 689–708.

—— (2009), 'Philosophies of Probability'. In Andrew D. Irvine (ed.), *Philosophy of Mathematics (Handbook of the Philosophy of Science)*, Amsterdam: North-Holland, pp. 493–533.

Williamson, Timothy (2000), *Knowledge and its Limits*. Oxford: Oxford University Press.

Yalcin, Seth (1997), 'Epistemic Modals'. *Mind*, vol. 116: pp. 983–1026.

Zabell, Sandy L. (1989), 'The Rule of Succession'. *Erkenntnis*, vol. 31: pp. 283–321.

—— (2005), *Symmetry and Its Discontents*. Cambridge: Cambridge University Press.

18

INDIFFERENCE

The symmetries of probability*

Bas C. van Fraassen

On estime la probabilité d'un événement par le
nombre des cas favourables divisé par le nombre
des cas possibles. La difficulté ne consiste que
dans l'énumération des cas.

Lagrange, quoted as epigraph to Ch. 1 of J. Bertrand,
Calcul des probabilités.

Since its inception in the seventeenth century, probability theory has often been guided by the conviction that symmetry can dictate probability. The conviction is expressed in such slogan formulations as that equipossibility implies equal probability, and honoured by such terms as indifference and sufficient reason. As in science generally we can find here symmetry arguments proper that are truly a priori, as well as arguments that simply assume contingent symmetries, and 'arguments' that reflect the thirst for a hidden, determining reality. The great failure of symmetry thinking was found here, when indifference disintegrated into paradox; and great success as well, sometimes real, sometimes apparent. The story is especially important for philosophy, since it shows the impossibility of the ideal of logical probability.

Intuitive probability

A traveller approaches a river spanned by bridges that connect its shores and islands. There has been a great storm the night before, and each bridge was as likely as not to be washed away. How probable is it that the traveller can still cross? This puzzle, devised by Marcus Moore, clearly depends on the pattern of bridges represented in Figure 18.1.

It also depends on whether the survival of a bridge affects the survival of another. The traveller believes not. Thus for him each bridge had an independent 50 per cent probability of washing away.

There is a simple but plodding solution (see *Proofs and illustrations*). But there is a symmetry argument too. Imagine that besides the traveller, there is also a boat moving downstream. The boatman's problem is to get through, which is possible if sufficiently many bridges have been washed away. What is the probability he can get through? Our first observation is that he faces a problem with the same abstract structure. For the traveller, the *entries* are bridges 1 and 2, while for the boatman they are 1 and 4.

296

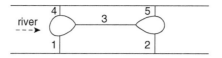

Figure 18.1 A symmetry argument for probabilities.

The *exits* are 4 and 5 for traveller, and are 2 and 5 for boatman. For both there is a *connector*, namely bridge 3. So each sees lying before him the 'maze'

entry	exit
connector	
entry	exit

Good and bad are reversed for traveller and boatman; but suppose that for each, the good state of a bridge has the same independent probability of 50 per cent. Now, by the great Symmetry Requirement, essentially similar problems must have the same solution. Hence:

1 Probability (traveller crosses) = Probability (boat gets through)

But the problems are not only similar; they are also related. For if the traveller has some unbroken path across, the boat cannot get through; and vice versa. Therefore:

2 Probability (boat gets through) = Probability (traveller does not cross)
3 [from 1 and 2] Probability (traveller crosses) = Probability (traveller does not cross)

So it is exactly as likely as not that the traveller will cross—the probability is 50 per cent.
   This is a remarkable example, not only as a pure instance of a symmetry argument, but because it introduces all the basic ingredients in the three centuries of controversy over the relation between symmetry and probability. In this problem, the *initial probabilities* are given: 50 per cent for any bridge that it will wash away. We are also given the crucial probability datum about how these eventualities are related: they are *independent*. That means that the collapse of one bridge is neither more nor less probable, on the supposition that some other bridge is washed away. (We are here distinguishing simple probability from *conditional* probability, marked by such terms as 'on the supposition that' or 'given that'.) Then, purely a priori reasoning gives us the probabilities for the events of interest.
   The great question for classical probability theory was: can the initial probabilities themselves be deduced too, on the basis of symmetry considerations? If we knew absolutely nothing about storms and bridges, except that one can wash away the other, would rationality not have required us to regard both possible outcomes as equally likely? Once the answer seemed to be obviously *Yes*, and now it seems self-evidently to be *No*, to many of us. But our century also saw the most sophisticated defences of the *yes* answer. And the history of the controversy spun off important and lasting insights.

297

Proofs and illustrations

In our example, the symmetry transformation used mapped bridge 2 into 4, and vice versa, leaving the others fixed. The *entry-connector-exit* structure is invariant, as is the probability of 'good' (i.e. *whole* for traveller and *broken* for boatman). The reader is invited to consider similar patterns with 1, 3, 4, 5 islands, and to generalize.

The single probability calculus principle that was utilized was—writing '*P*' for 'Probability':

$$P(A) = 1 - P(A)$$

which itself is an immediate corollary to the two axioms

I $0 = P(\text{contradiction}) \leq P(A) \leq P(\text{tautology}) = 1$
II $P(A) + P(B) = P(A \text{ or } B) + P(A \text{ and } B)$

which together exhaust the entire finitary probability theory. For our present purposes, it is not necessary to focus on this calculus, but the following notions will be relevant (and will be employed intuitively in this chapter):

The *conditional probability* $P(A|B)$ of *A given* that *B* equals $P(A \text{ and } B)/P(B)$
A and *B* are (*stochastically* or *statistically*) *independent* exactly if $P(A|B) = P(A)$

That conditional probability $P(A|B)$ is defined only if the *antecedent B* has probability $P(B) \neq 0$. The independence condition is equivalent to

$$P(B|A) = P(B)$$
$$P(A \text{ and } B) = P(A)P(B)$$

always provided the conditional probabilities are defined. The last equation shows clearly, of course, that the condition is symmetric in *A* and *B*.

Celestial prior probabilities

The modern history of probability began with the Pascal-Fermat correspondence of 1654. The problems they discussed concerned gambling, games of chance. If someone wanted to draw practical advantage from these studies, he would learn from them how to calculate probabilities of winning (or expectation of gain) from initial probabilities in the gambling set-up. But of course he would have to know those initial probabilities already. While we cannot attribute much sophistication here to the gambler, we may plausibly believe that he takes a hard-nosed empirical stance on this. He believes that the dice are fair exactly if all possible numerical combinations come up equally often— and that this assertion is readily testable even in a small number of tosses. Daggers and rapiers will be drawn if a challenged and tested die comes up even three sixes in a row. We know of course from the play *Rosencrantz and Guildenstern Are Dead* how inconclusive such tests must be on a more sophisticated understanding of probability. But the crucial role and status of initial probability hypotheses appears much more clearly in a different sort of problem.

298

The Academy of Sciences in Paris proposed a prize subject for 1732 and 1734: the configuration of planetary orbits in our solar system. This configuration may be described as follows: each planet orbits in a plane inclined no more than 7.5° to the sun's equator, and the orbits all have the same direction.[2]

The prize was divided between John Bernoulli and his son Daniel. The latter included three arguments that this configuration cannot be attributed to mere chance. Of these the third argument is a typical eighteenth-century 'calculation' of initial probabilities: 7.5° is 1/12 of 90° (possible maximum inclination of orbit to equator if we ignore direction); there are six (known) planets, so the probability of this configuration happening 'by chance' is $(1/12)^6$, which is negligibly small (*circa* 3 in 10 million).

Daniel Bernoulli has here made two assumptions: of a certain *uniformity* (the probability of at most 1/12 of the maximum, equals 1/12) and of *independence* (the joint probability of the six statements is the product of their individual probabilities). Before scrutinizing these assumptions, let us look at two more examples.

Buffon, in his *Historie naturelle* gives an argument similar to Daniel Bernoulli's.[3] Buffon says that the mutual inclination of any two planetary orbits is at most 7.5°. Taking direction into account, the maximum is 180°, so the chance of this equals 1/24. Taking now one planet as fixed, we have five others. The joint probability of all five orbits to be inclined no more than 7.5° is therefore $(1/24)^5$. This probability (*circa* 1 in 10 million) is approximately three times smaller than the one noted by Bernoulli. Independently Buffon notes that the probability that all six planets should move in the same west to east direction for us, equals $(1/2)^6$. It is clear that he is calculating initial probabilities by the same assumptions as Daniel Bernoulli.

In Laplace's writings on celestial mechanics we find another such example.[4] Bernoulli and Buffon argued for a common origin of the planets, that is, a common cause, on the basis of the improbability of mere chance or coincidence. Laplace argues conversely that a certain fact is not initially improbable, and therefore needs no common-cause explanation. The fact in question was that among the many observed comets, not a single hyperbolic trajectory has been reported.[5] Laplace demonstrates that the probability of a comet with hyperbolic orbit is exceedingly low. The demonstration is based on a uniform distribution of probability over the possible directions of motion of comets entering the sun's gravitational field at some large given distance from the sun.

Indifference and sufficient reason

It is clear that each of these authors is entertaining what we may call a chance hypothesis: that the phenomenon in question arises 'by mere chance', that is, without the presence of causal or other factors constraining the outcome. There is an ambiguity here: are the probabilities assigned the correct ones (*a*) given *no* hypotheses or assumptions about the physical situation, or (*b*) given a substantial, contingent hypothesis about the absence of certain physical features?

If the former is the case, we have here typical symmetry thinking: the fact that certain information is absent in the statement of the problem, is used as a constraint on the solution. If the latter, we are in the presence of a metaphysical assumption, which may have empirical import: that nature, when certain physical constraints are absent, is equally likely to produce any of the unconstrained possibilities, and therefore tends to produce each equally often.

Ian Hacking locates the first theoretical discussion of this topic in Leibniz's memorandum '*De incerti aestimatione*' (1678).[6] In this note Leibniz equates probability with gradations of possibility ('*probabilitas est gradus possibilitas*'). He states the Principle of Indifference, that equipossible cases have the same probability, and asserts that such a principle can be 'proved by metaphysics'.

We can only speculate what metaphysical proof Leibniz envisaged, but it must surely be based on his Principle of Sufficient Reason. Leibniz's programme set out in the *Discourse of Metaphysics* was to deduce the structure of reality from the nature of God. As a first step, this nature entails that God does, or creates, nothing without sufficient reason. In this marriage of metaphysics with divine epistemology, the difference between points (*a*) and (*b*) above vanishes. For Leibniz's God solves the problem of what nature shall do without contributing factors of his own to destroy the symmetries of the problem-as-stated.

This is how Leibniz must have derived symmetry principles governing nature—determining what the real, objective probabilities shall be in a physical situation. We cannot be sure on the basis of this brief note, but he must have given the principle of sufficient reason also this form: that a rational being should assign equal probabilities to distinct possibilities unless there be explicit reason to differentiate them. Since Leibniz clearly appreciated the great value of such an equation for metaphysics, he must have appreciated that strictly speaking, his new beginning for metaphysics effects a collapse of two logically distinct problems.

It was certainly in the terminology of sufficient reasons—perhaps always with an equivocation between (*we have reason*) and (*there is reason*)—that principles of indifference were formulated. There were two; we have seen both at work in the arguments of Bernoulli, Buffon, and Laplace.

The first is the *Principle of Uniform Distribution*. Suppose I shoot bullets at a target and am such a poor marksman that it makes no difference at which point of the target I am. Then any two equal areas on the target are equally likely to be hit. We call this a uniform distribution. The first indifference principle for assigning probabilities is *to assume a uniform distribution in the absence of reasons to the contrary*.

The second is the *Principle of Stochastic Independence*. I explained independence above; let me illustrate it here. Suppose we are told that 40 per cent of the population smokes and 10 per cent has lung cancer. This gives me the probability that a randomly chosen person is a smoker, or has lung cancer, but does not tell me the joint probability of these two characteristics. There are three cases (see Fig. 18.2). Each of the three lines *p*, *q*, *r* has 10 per cent of the area below it. In the case of the horizontal line *q*, the joint probability of lung cancer *and* smoking is 10 per cent of

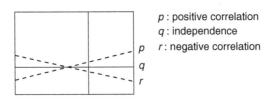

Figure 18.2 Cases illustrating the Principle of Stochastic Independence.

300

40 per cent, namely 4 per cent. For p it is larger and for r it is smaller. The second indifference principle is *to assume statistical independence, in the absence of reasons to the contrary*.

Are these two principles consistent with each other? The joint probability of two events is the same as the ordinary probability of a single complex event. It seems possible therefore that the two principles could be made to apply to the same example, and offer contradictory advice. In the *Proofs and illustrations* we will see that this is not so; the two are consistent with each other.

Proofs and illustrations

Let us consider two variables, say *height h* and *weight w*. Suppose height varies from zero to 10 and weight from zero to 100. Given no other information (hence no reasons to diverge from uniformity or independence), assign probabilities to all possibilities.

The first procedure is to choose uniform distributions for each:

1    $P(0 \leq h \leq a) = a/10$ $P(0 \leq w \leq b) = b/100$

Then calculate the joint probability by assuming independence:

2    $P(0 \leq h \leq a \text{ and } 0 \leq w \leq b) = (a/10)(b/100)$

The other procedure is to look at the complex variable hw which has pairs of numbers as values. A person with height 6 and weight 60 has hw equal to $\langle 6, 60 \rangle$. The big rectangle in Fig. 18.3 encompasses all possibilities ($0 \leq h \leq 10 \text{ and } 0 \leq w \leq 100$) while the smaller one describes the possibility of having hw fall between $\langle 0, 0 \rangle$ and $\langle a, b \rangle$ in the proper sense of 'between'. Uniformity alone applies now and demands a probability proportional to the area:

3    $P(\langle 0, 0 \rangle \leq hw \leq \langle a, b \rangle) = ab/1000$

But as we see, 2 and 3 agree. We have proved in effect that if variables h and w are uniformly distributed and independent, then the complex variable hw is uniformly distributed. Hence the two principles are mutually consistent and together constitute the great symmetry principle of classical probability theory—the *Principle of Indifference*.

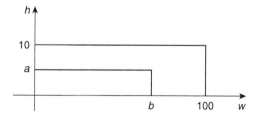

Figure 18.3 The distribution of height and weight.

Buffon's needle: empirical import of indifference

If we must assign initial probabilities, in the absence of relevant information, reason bids us be like Buridan's ass. Do not choose between $P(A) > P(\neg A)$ and $P(A) < P(\neg A)$, but set them equal. Similarly in such a case, do not choose between $P(A \text{ and } B) > P(A)$. $P(B)$ and $P(A \text{ and } B) < P(A)P(B)$, but set those equal as well. Very well; but will nature oblige us with frequencies to which these initial probabilities have a good fit? Is this dictate of reason one that will let reason unlock the mysteries of nature?

An empiricist will ask these questions with a distinct tinge of mockery to his voice. But here we should report a marvellous example in which calculation by the Principle of Indifference led to beautifully confirmed empirical results. This is Buffon's needle problem. It is much more probative than planetary orbit and comet examples, where one only finds *explanation*—that beautiful but airy creature of the fecund imagination— and not *prediction*.

Buffon's needle problem[7]

Given: a large number of parallel lines are drawn on the floor, and a needle is dropped. What is the probability that the needle cuts one of the lines?

To simplify the problem without loss of essential generality, let the lines be exactly two needle lengths apart. Touching will count as cutting, but clearly at most one line is cut. We may even speak sensibly of the line nearest the needle's point (choose either if the point is exactly halfway between). Then our question is equivalent to: what is the probability that the needle cuts this nearest line? In Fig. 18.4 the needle point is a distance $0 \leq d \leq 1$ away from line L, and its inclination to L is the angle θ. Thus we have:

favourable cases: the needle cuts L exactly if $d \leq y = \sin\theta$

This θ varies from zero to 2π ($= 360$ degrees), and so we can diagram the situation with an area of 1 (needle length) by 2π (radians) as in Fig. 18.5. To distinguish the favourable cases from the unfavourable ones, we draw in the sine curve and shade the area where $y \geq d$. Assuming independence and uniform distribution, the probability of the favourable cases must be proportional to the shaded area. Since a little calculus quickly demonstrates that this area equals 2, we arrive at the number $2/2\pi$.

The probability of a favourable case equals $1/\pi$, the solution Buffon himself found for his problem.

Since the experiment can be carried out, this is an empirical prediction. It has been carried out a number of times and the outcomes have been in excellent agreement with

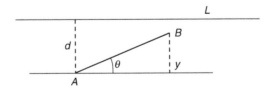

Figure 18.4 Buffon's needle.

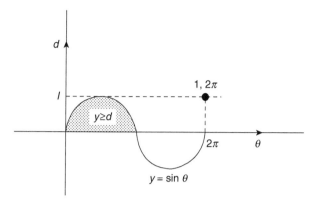

Figure 18.5 Buffon's probability calculation.

Buffon's prediction.[8] Now is this not marvellous and a result to make the rationalist metaphysician squeal with delight? For the assumption of symmetry in the probabilities of equipossible cases has here led to a true prediction made a priori.

The challenge: Bertrand's paradoxes

What I have so far recounted has been very favourable to the Principle of Indifference. Many readers, knowing of its later rejection, but perhaps less familiar with attempts to refine and save it, may already be a little impatient. I will argue for the rejection of its uncritical versions—the empirical phenomena cannot be predicted a priori—but this will be a rejection of naïve symmetry arguments in favour of deeper symmetries, with due respect for the insights that were gained along the way.

We have seen that the Principle has two parts, which are indeed consistent with each other. We have also seen the significant successes of explanations and predictions arrived at in the eighteenth century by means of this Principle. But the challenge to this attempt to calculate initial probabilities on the basis of physical symmetry came exactly from the fundamental principle of symmetry arguments. If two problems are essentially the same, they must receive essentially the same solution. So *a fortiori* if a situation can be equally described in terms of different parameters, we should arrive at the same probabilities if we apply the Principle of Indifference to these other parameters. There will be a logical difficulty—indeed, straightforward inconsistency—if different descriptions of the problem lead via Indifference to distinct solutions.

This logical difficulty with the idea was expounded systematically in a series of paradoxes by Joseph Bertrand at the end of the nineteenth century.[9] Leaving his rather complex geometric examples for *Proofs and Illustrations*, let us turn immediately to a paradigmatic but simple example: the perfect cube factory.[10]

A precision tool factory produces iron cubes with edge length ≤ 2 cm. What is the probability that a cube has length ≤ 1 cm, given that it was produced by that factory?

A naïve application of the Principle of Indifference consists in choosing length l as parameter and assuming a uniform distribution. The answer is then 1/2. But the problem could have been stated in different words, but logically equivalent form:

Possible cases	Favourable
edge length ≤ 2	length ≤ 1
area of side ≤ 4	area ≤ 1
volume ≤ 8	volume ≤ 1

Treating each statement of the problem naïvely we arrive at answers 1/2, 1/4, 1/3. These contradict each other.

> The correspondence $l^m \leftrightarrow l^n$, for a parameter l with range $(0, k)$ is one to one, but does not preserve equality of intervals.

Hence uniform distribution on l^m entails non-uniform distribution on l^n. Now sometimes the problem is indeed constrained by symmetries. The cubes example illustrates how these constraints may be so minimal as to leave the set of possible solutions unreduced. More information about the factory could improve the situation. But the Indifference Principle is supposed to fill the gap left by missing information!

Even taken by itself, the example is devastating. But since we shall discuss various attempts to salvage Indifference, it is important to assess two more examples, with somewhat different logical features.

Von Kries posed a problem which is like that of the perfect cube factory, in that several parameters are related by a simple logical transformation. Consider volume and density of a liquid. If mass is set equal to 1, then these parameters are related by:

$$\text{density} = 1/\text{volume}; \text{volume} = 1/\text{density}.$$

But a uniform distribution on parameter x is automatically non-uniform on $y = (1/x)$. For example,

x is between 1 and 2 exactly if y is between 1/2 and 1
x is between 2 and 3 exactly if y is between 1/3 and 1/2.

Here the two intervals for x are equal in length, but the corresponding ones for y are not. Thus Indifference appears to give us two conflicting probability assignments again.

Von Mises's example of a Bertrand-type paradox concerned a mixture of two liquids, wine and water. We have a glass container, with a mixture of water and wine. To remove division by zero from every inversion, let the following be data:

> the glass contains 10 cc of liquid, of which at least 1 cc is water and at least 1 cc is wine.

What is the probability that at least 5 cc is water? Let the parameters be:

$a = $ proportion of wine to total: $(1/10) \leq a \leq (9/10)$

b = proportion of water to total: $(1/10) \leq b \leq (9/10)$
x = proportion of wine to water: $(1/9) \leq x \leq 9$
y = proportion of water to wine: $(1/9) \leq y \leq 9$

Obviously $b = (1-a)$, $x = (a/b)$, $y = 1/x$, and $a = x/(1+x)$, so descriptions of the situation by means of any parameter can be completely translated into any other parameter. It is easy to see that the same problem recurs. Here are two equal intervals for the proportion of wine to total:

a = **Proportion of wine to total**	x = **Proportion of wine to water**
4/10	4/6 = 2/3
5/10	5/5 = 1
6/10	6/4 = 3/2

Since $1 - (2/3)$ is not equal to $(3/2) - 1$, it is clear that a uniform distribution on the proportion a entails a non-uniform proportion on proportion x.

In each case the Principle of Uniformity is applied to one perfectly adequate description of the problem. The statements of the problem, both as to sets of possible cases and set of favourable cases, differ only verbally. But the great underlying principle of symmetry thinking is that essentially similar problems must receive the same solution. Thus the attempt to assign uniform distribution on the basis of symmetries in these *statements* of the problem, is drastically misguided—it violates symmetry in a deeper sense.

Most writers commenting on Bertrand have described the problems set by his paradoxical examples as not well posed. In such a case, the problem as initially stated is really not one problem but many. To solve it we must be told *what* is random; which means, *which* events are equiprobable; which means, *which* parameter should be assumed to be uniformly distributed.

But that response asserts that in the absence of further information we have no way to determine the initial probabilities. In other words, this response rejects the Principle of Indifference altogether. After all, if we were told as part of the problem which parameter should receive a uniform distribution, no such Principle would be needed. It was exactly the function of the Principle to turn an incompletely described physical problem into a definite problem in the probability calculus.

There have been different reactions. We have to list Henri Poincaré, E. T. Jaynes, and Rudolph Carnap among the writers who believed that the Principle of Indifference could be refined and sophisticated, and thus saved from paradox.

Proofs and illustrations

The famous chord problem asks for the problem that a stick, tossed randomly on a circle, will mark out a chord of given length. For a definite standard of comparison we inscribe an equilateral triangle ABC in the circle (see Fig. 18.6). However we draw the triangle, it is clear that the separated arcs, like arc AEB, must each be 1/3 of the circumference. Thus the length of the side of any such triangle is the same. In fact it is $r\sqrt{3}$, where r is the radius, and the point D is exactly halfway along the radius OE.

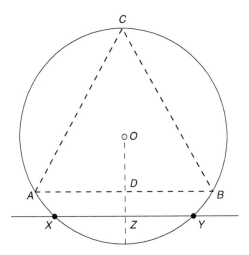

Figure 18.6 Bertrand's chord problem.

What is the probability that chord *XY* is greater than side *AB*? If we try to answer this question on the basis of the Principle of Indifference, we actually find three variables which might be asserted to have uniform distribution:

XY > AB exactly if any of the following holds:

(a) *OZ < r/2*
(b) *Y* is located between 1/3 and 2/3 of the circumference away from *X*, as measured along the circumference
(c) the point *Z* falls within the 'inner' circle with centre 0 and radius *r/2*.

This gives us three possible applications of the Principle of Uniformity.

Using description (*a*) we reason: *OZ* can be anything from 0 to *r*; the interval [0, *r/z*] of favourable cases has length 1/2 of the interval [0, *r*] of possible cases; hence the probability equals 1/2 (*Solution A*).

Using (*b*) we reason: each point of contact *X*, *Y* can be any point on the circle. So given the point *X*, we can find point *Y* at any fraction between 0 and 1 of the circumference, measuring counter-clockwise. Of these possible locations, 1/3 fall in the favourable interval [1/3, 2/3]; hence the probability equals 1/3 (*Solution B*).

Using (*c*) we note that the centre *Z* of the stick can fall anywhere in the whole circle. In the favourable cases it falls in the 'inner' circle with radius *r/2*—which has an area 1/4 that of the big circle. Hence the probability equals 1/4 (*Solution C*).

Symmetries to the rescue?

Henri Poincaré and E. T. Jaynes both argued that if we pay attention to the geometric symmetries in Bertrand's problem, we do arrive at a unique solution.[11] Their general idea applies to all apparent ambiguities in the Principle of Indifference: a careful consideration of the exact symmetries of the problem will remove the inconsistency, provided we focus on the symmetry transformations themselves, rather than on the objects transformed.

In order to show the logical structure very clearly I will concentrate on the simple examples of the perfect cubes, mass versus density, and water mixed with the wine. Let us begin by analysing the intuitive reaction to the cube factory, which led us into paradox. Focusing first on the parameter of length, we used the natural length measure for intervals:

$$m(a, b) = b - a$$

This is the *underlying measure*[12] that gave us our probabilities for cases inside the range $[0, 2]$:

$$P(a, b) = m(a, b)/m(\text{range}) \text{ for } a, b \text{ inside the range.}$$

Now this underlying measure has a very special feature, from the point of view of symmetry:

$$\text{Translation invariance}: \text{if } x' = x + k$$
$$\text{then } m(a, b) = m(a', b').$$

Up to multiplication by a scalar, m is the unique measure to have this feature. That is easy to see, because one interval can be moved into another by a translation exactly if they have the same length (and are of the same type: open, half-open, etc.).[13]

The number K represents the scale, if $m' = Km$, because for example the length in inches is numerically 12 times that in feet. It will not affect the probability at all, because it will cancel out (being present in both numerator and denominator in the equation for P in terms of m). We have therefore the following result:

> *Translation invariant measure.* The probability distribution on a real valued parameter x is uniquely determined, if we are given its range and the requirement that it derive from an underlying measure which is translation invariant.

In what sort of example would the given be exactly as required? Suppose I tell you that Peter is a marksman with no skill whatever, and an unknown target. Now I ask you the probability that his bullet will land between 10 and 20 feet from my heart, given that it lands within 20 feet. Treating this formally, I choose a line that falls on both my heart and the impact point of the bullet, coordinatize this line by choosing a point to call zero, and one foot away from it a point to call $+1$. I choose a measure m' on this line, call my heart's coordinate X, and calculate

$$m'(X + 10, X + 20)/m'(X, X + 20)$$

and give you the resulting number as answer. If my procedure was properly in tune with the problem, this answer should better not depend on how I chose the points to call zero and $+1$ (which two choices together determined the coordinate X). That entails that m' must be translation invariant, and is therefore now uniquely identified. We note with pleasure that the answer is also not affected by the choice of the foot as unit of measurement—as indeed it should not, because nothing in the problem hinged on its Anglo-Saxon peculiarities.

Now, in what sort of problem is the 'given' so different that this procedure is inappropriate? Obviously, when translation invariance is the wrong symmetry. This happens when the range of the physical quantity in question is not closed under addition and subtraction, for example, if the quantity has an infimum, which acts as natural zero point. For example, no classical object has negative or zero volume, mass, or absolute temperature.

In such a case, the scale or unit may still be irrelevant. For the transformation of the scaling unit consists simply in multiplication by a positive number, which operation does not take us out of this range. Consider now von Kries's problem, which concerns the positive quantities mass and density. With the units of measurement essentially irrelevant we look for an underlying measure

$$M(a, b) = M(ka, kb)$$

for any positive number k (invariance under *dilations*).

There is indeed such a measure, and it is unique in the same sense.[14] That is the *log uniform* distribution:

$$M(a, b) = \log b - \log a$$

where log is the natural logarithm. This function has the nice properties:

$\log(xy) = \log x + \log y$
$\log(x^n) = n \log x$
$\log(1) = 0$

but should be used only for positive quantities, because it moves zero to minus infinity. The first of these equations shows already that M is dilation invariant. The second shows us what is now regarded as equiprobable:

The intervals (b^n, b^{n+k}) all receive the same value $k \log b$, so if within the appropriate range, the following are series of equiprobable cases:

$$(0.1, 1), (1, 10), (10, 100), \ldots, (10^n, 10^{n+l}), \ldots$$
$$(0.2, 1), (1, 5), (5, 25), \ldots, (5^n, 5^{n+l}), \ldots$$

and so forth. A probability measure derived from the log uniform distribution will therefore always give higher probabilities 'closer' to zero, by our usual reckoning.

For example, in the case of temperature we have since Kelvin accepted that this is essentially a positive quantity. Of course we are at liberty to give the name -273 to absolute zero. But this does not remove the infimum; subtraction eventually takes one outside the range. The presence of this infimum creates, or rather is, an asymmetry: it obstructs translation invariance. But it is no obstacle to dilation invariance, so the log uniform distribution is right—it is dictated by the symmetries of the problem.

This reasoning, being rather abstract, may not get us over our initial feeling of surprise. But as Roger Rosencrantz pointed out, we can test all this on the von Kries problem.[15] Our argument implies that von Kries's puzzle is due to focusing on the wrong transformation group. Attention to the right one dictates use of the log uniform distribution. To our delight this removes the conflict:

$$M(1/b \leq 1/x \leq 1/a) = K(\log a^{-1} - \log b^{-1})$$
$$= K(\log b - \log a)$$
$$= M(a \leq x \leq b).$$

This is certainly a success for this approach to Indifference.

Consider next the perfect cube factory. Suppose that again we regard the unit of measurement as essentially irrelevant to this problem, conceived in true generality, but observe that length, area, volume are positive quantities. The uniqueness of the log uniform measure for dilation invariance, forces us then to use it as underlying the correct probabilities. This will not help us, unless we ask all our questions about intervals that exclude *zero*; but for them it works wonderfully well:

What is the probability that the length is ≤ 2, given that it is between 1 and 3 inclusive?
What is the probability that the area is ≤ 4, given that it is between 1 and 9 inclusive?
The probability that the length is ≤ 2, given that it is between 1 and 3 inclusive, equals
    $M(1, 2)/M(1, 3) = \log 2/\log 3 = 0.631$.
The probability that the area is ≤ 4, given that it is between 1 and 9 inclusive, equals
    $M(1, 4)/M(1, 9) = 2\log 2/2\log 3 = 0.631$.

Thus the two equivalent questions do receive the same answer. The point is perfectly general, because the exponent becomes a multiplier, which appears in both numerator and denominator, and so cancels out. This is again a real success. By showing us how to reformulate the problem, and then using its symmetries to determine a unique solution, this approach has as it were taught us how to understand our puzzled but insistent intuitions.

There is therefore good prima-facie reason to take this approach seriously. In the *Proofs and Illustrations* I shall show how this approach does give us a neat solution for the puzzle of Buffon's needle, construed as a Bertrand problem. But in subsequent sections we'll see that the approach does not generalize sufficiently to save the Principle of Indifference.

Proofs and illustrations

I shall here explain this rescue by geometric symmetries with another illustration. For this purpose I choose Buffon's needle problem again, for properly understood it can itself be described as a rudimentary Bertrand paradox.[16]

Buffon assumes no marksmanship—the location of the lines on the floor does not, as far as we know, affect the location of the fallen needle. So our description of the situation utilizes a frame of reference chosen for convenience, in which we treat as X-axis the line through needle point A which is parallel to the drawn lines, as in Fig. 18.4. Here d is the Y-coordinate of line L, θ the inclination of line AB to the X-axis, and y is Y-coordinate of B, and A is the origin.

309

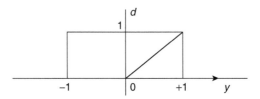

Figure 18.7 Possible and favourable cases in Buffon's needle.

Why not assume that y and d are independent and uniformly distributed? We must be careful to describe y so that it does not depend on d. But it is just sine 0, and 0 does not depend on d, so that is fine. Thus y ranges from -1 to $+1$ (being measured from the X-axis, chosen so that the line L has equation $Y = 1$). The possible and favourable cases are depicted in Fig. 18.7, and we see that the probability of $y \leq d$ equals 1/4. Hence by applying the Principle of Indifference to Buffon's problem *differently but equivalently described*, we have arrived at a different solution.

But our description—or rather the solution that utilizes this description in the Principle of Indifference—may itself be faulted for failing to respect geometric symmetry. Consider what happens if the axes are rotated through some angle around point A— that is, the orientation of the lines drawn on the floor is changed. Whatever method of solution we propose, should not make the answer—probability of a cut—depend on this orientation, for the problem remains essentially unchanged. (The aspect varied did not appear at all in the statement of the problem.) How do the two rival solutions vary with respect to this criterion?

Buffon's solution fares very well. For the initial parameter (angle which the needle makes with the X-axis) is changed by adding something (the angle of rotation), modulo $360°$. A uniform distribution on that initial parameter induces automatically a uniform distribution also on its transform—equal angular intervals continue to receive equal probability.

But, and here is the rub, if we assume that y is uniformly distributed, it follows that y' (the corresponding coordinate in the rotated frame) is not. The easy way to see this is to look at equal increments in y and notice that they do not correspond to equal increments in y'.

To see this it is necessary to use the formula that transforms coordinates, when the frame is rotated. If the original coordinates of a point are (x, y) they become, upon rotation through angle a around the origin

$$t(x) = x \cos a - y \sin a$$
$$t(y) = x \sin a + y \cos a$$

In our case, point B has coordinates (x, y) but because $AB = 1$ we know that $x^2 + y^2 = 1$. Hence $x = \sqrt{(1 - y^2)}$ and we have

$$t(y) = \sqrt{(1 - y^2)} \sin a + y \cos a$$

Let us now look at two events that have equal probability if y has uniform distribution:

$$[y \in (0, 1/2)] \quad [y \in (1/2, 1)]$$

310

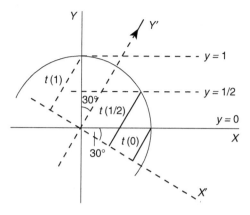

Figure 18.8 Illustration of different cases for counterexample in rotated Buffon's needle.

These are the same events as

$$[t(y) \in (t(0), t(1/2))] \quad [t(y) \in (t(1/2), t(1))]$$

If the variable $t(y)$ has uniform distribution, these events will have equal probabilities only if

$$t(1/2) - t(0) = t(1) - t(1/2)$$

so that is what we need to check. A single counter-example will do, so let us choose the angle of 30° (i.e. $\pi/6$ radians) which has sine 1/2 and cosine $(\sqrt{3})/2$. Therefore:

$$t(0) = \sin\left(\tfrac{1}{6}\pi\right) = \tfrac{1}{2}$$
$$t(\tfrac{1}{2}) = (\sqrt{3})/2 \sin \tfrac{1}{6}\pi + \tfrac{1}{2}\cos \tfrac{1}{6}\pi$$
$$= (\sqrt{3})/2(\tfrac{1}{2}) + \tfrac{1}{2}((\sqrt{3})/2) = (\sqrt{3})/2$$
$$t(1) = \cos \tfrac{1}{6}\pi = (\sqrt{3})/2$$

It is very obvious that our desired equation does not hold. Figure 18.8 shows the different cases.

Pyrrhic victory and ultimate defeat

The successes we found in the preceding section, even together with their more sophisticated variants (to be discussed in the *Proofs and Illustrations*), constitute only a Pyrrhic victory. Again we can see this in simple examples, just because of the power of the uniqueness results utilized. Recall that invariance under translations and invariance under dilations each dictate an essentially *unique* answer to all probability questions. What happens when the examples take on more structure?

Peter Milne, writing about Rosencrantz's solution to von Kries's problem, has shown exactly how things go wrong.[17] To show this, he asked how the above results are to be

311

applied to von Mises's water and wine problem. Let us again ask the same question in two different ways, referring back to the notation we had before.

What is the probability that at least 5 cc is water?
b = proportion of water to the total
x = proportion of wine to water.
$P(b \geq 0.5|0.1 \leq b \leq 0.9) = (\log 0.9 - \log 0.5)/(\log 0.9 - \log 0.1) = 0.267$
$P(x \leq 1|1/9 < x \leq 9) = (\log 1 - \log(1/9))/(\log 9 - \log(1/9)) = \log 9/2\log 9 = 0.5$

We have received two contradictory answers.

Were we justified in treating the problem in this way? Well, the problem specified cc as unit of measurement but we have just as much warrant to regard this as irrelevant as we had for cm in the cubes problem. If we focus on parameter x here, say, we must treat it in the same way, if we have indeed found the correct form of the Principle of Indifference. Restating the problem then in terms of b, we have not introduced any new information—so we must derive the answer from the probability distribution on x, plus the definition of b in terms of x. Exactly the same would apply if we had started with b, and then moved on to x. But the two end results are not the same, so we have our paradox back.

It is also rather easy to see the pattern that will produce such paradoxes. A translation invariant measure will be well behaved with respect to addition and multiplication, while a dilation invariant measure will be equally good with respect to multiplication and exponentiation. But the relation between b and x uses both sorts of operations:

b = water/(water + wine) = water/10
x = wine/water = (10 − water)/water
hence, water = $10b$ and $x = (100 - b)/b$.

Now neither sort of measure will do. If the required dilation invariance did not dictate an essentially unique measure, we would perhaps have had some leeway to look for something other than logarithms—but we do not.

The history of the Principle of Indifference is instructive. If its mention in scientific sermons serves to remind us to look for symmetries, then it serves well. But a rule to determine initial probabilities a priori it is not. It violates a higher symmetry requirement when it is conceived of in that way.

Even if the Principle were unambiguous, the question whether its results would be probability functions with a good fit to actual frequencies in nature, would anyway be a purely contingent one. To imagine that it would not be—that empirical predictions could be made a priori, by 'pure thought' analysis—is feasible only on the assumption of some metaphysical scheme such as Leibniz's, in which the symmetries of the problems which God selects for attention, determine the structure of reality.[18] But because it is not unambiguous, even that assumption would leave us stranded, unless we knew how God selected his problems.

When E. T. Jaynes[19] discussed Bertrand's chord paradox, although noting that most writers had regarded it as an ill-posed problem, he responded:

But do we really believe that it is beyond our power to predict by 'pure thought' the results of such a simple experiment? The point at issue is far more important than merely resolving a geometric puzzle; for ... applications of probability theory to physical experiments usually lead to problems of just this type. ... (p. 478)

Jaynes's analysis of the Bertrand chord problem is along the lines of the preceding section. He shows that there is only one solution which derives from a measure which is invariant under Euclidean transformations.

But when we look more carefully at other parts of Jaynes's paper we see that his more general conclusions nullify the radical tone. Jaynes says of von Mises's water and wine problem, that the fatal ambiguities of the Principle of Indifference remain. More important: the strongest conclusion Jaynes manages to reach is merely one of *advice*, to regard a problem as having a definite solution until the contrary has been proved. The method he advises us to follow is that of symmetry arguments:

> To summarize the above results: if we merely specify complete ignorance, we cannot hope to obtain any definite prior distribution, because such a statement is too vague to define any mathematically well-defined problem. We are defining what we mean by complete ignorance far more precisely if we can specify a set of operations which we recognize as transforming the problem into an equivalent one, and the desideratum of consistency then places non-trivial restrictions on the form of the prior.[20]

But as we know, this method always rests on assumptions which may or may not fit the physical situation in reality. Hence it cannot lead to a priori predictions. Success, when achieved, must be attributed to the good fortune that nature fits and continues to fit the general model with which the solution begins.

Proofs and illustrations

Harold Jeffreys introduced the search for invariant priors into the foundations of statistics; there has been much subsequent work along these lines by others.[21] We must conclude with Dawid, however, that the programme 'produces a whole range of choices in some problems, and no prior free from all objections in others' ('Invariant Prior Distributions', 235). I just wish to take up here the elegant logical analysis that Jaynes introduced to generalize the approach which we have been studying in these last two sections.[22]

Here some powerful mathematical theorems come to our aid. For under certain conditions, there exists indeed only one possible probability assignment to a group, so there is no ambiguity.

The general pattern of the approach I have been outlining is as follows. First one selects the correct group of transformations of our sets K which should leave the probability measure invariant. Call the group G. Then one finds the correct probability measure p on this group. Next define

(1) $P(A) = p(\{g \text{ in } G : g(x_0) \in A\})$

313

where x_0 is a chosen reference point in the set K on which we want our probability defined. If everything has gone well, P is the probability measure 'demanded' by the group.

What is required at the very least is that (*a*) p is a privileged measure on the group; (*b*) P is invariant under the action of the group; and (*c*) P is independent of the choice of x_0. Mathematics allows these desiderata to be satisfied: if the group G has some 'nice' properties, and we require p to be a left Haar measure (which means that $p(S) = p(\{gg' : g' \in S\})$ for any part S of G and any member g) then these desired consequences follow, and p, P are essentially unique.[23]

This is a very tight situation, and the required niceties can be expected in geometric models such as are used to define Bertrand's chord problem. But other sorts of models will not be equally nice; and even if they are, different models of the same situation could fairly bring us diverse answers. In any case there is a no a priori reason why all phenomena should fit models with such 'nice' properties only.

The ethics of ambiguity

From the initial example, of a traveller on a treacherous shore, to the partial but impressive successes in the search for invariant priors, I have tried to emphasize how much symmetry considerations tell us. That is the positive side of this definitive dissolution of the idea of unique logical probability. Yet the story is far from complete, and its tactical and strategic suggestions for model construction far from exhausted.

But throughout the history of this subject, there wafts the siren melody of empirical probabilities determined a priori on the basis of pure symmetry considerations. The correct appreciation leads us to exactly the same conclusion as in Chapter 10. Once a problem is modelled, the symmetry requirement may give it a unique, or at least greatly constrained solution. The modelling, however, involves substantive assumptions: an implicit selection of certain parameters as alone relevant, and a tacit assumption of structure in the parameter space. Whenever the consequent limitations are ignored, paradoxes bring us back to our senses—symmetries respected in one modelling of the problem *entail* symmetries broken in another model. As soon as we took the first step, symmetries swept us along in a powerful current—but nature might have demanded a different first step, or embarkation in a different stream.

Facts are ambiguous. It is vain to desire prescience: which resolution of the present ambiguities will later facts vindicate? Our models of the facts, on the other hand, are not ambiguous; they had better not be. To choose one, is therefore a risk. To eliminate the risk is to cease theorizing altogether. That is one message of these paradoxes.

Notes

* Originally published as Chapter 12 of Bas C. van Fraassen, *Laws and Symmetry*, Oxford University Press, Oxford, 1989, pp. 293–317. Copyright © 1989 Bas C. van Fraassen. Reprinted by permission of Oxford University Press.
1 I want to thank Mr. Moore for allowing use of this example, and Dorothy Edgington for telling me about it.
2 See I. Todhunter, *A History of the Mathematical Theory of Probability* (London, 1865), 222–3.
3 See L. E. Maistrov, *Probability Theory: A Historical Sketch* (New York, 1974), 118–19.
4 See I. Todhunter, op. cit., 491–4.

5 In the Euclidean plane, a hyperbola is described by an equation of form $(x^2/a^2) - (y^2/b^2) = 1$, an ellipse by $(x^2/a^2) + (y^2/b^2) = 1$, and a parabola by $y^2 = 2px$.

6 I. Hacking, 'Equipossibility Theories of Probability', *British Journal for the Philosophy of Science*, 22 (1971), 339–55; K.-R. Bierman and M. Falk, 'G. W. Leibniz' *De incerti aestimatione*', *Forschungen und Fortschritte*, 31 (1957), 168–73; Leibniz, *Opuscules et fragments inédits*, ed. L. Couturat (Paris, 1903), 569–71.

7 Buffon's needle problem is discussed in many probability texts (e.g. J. V. Uspensky, *Introduction to Mathematical Probability* (New York, 1937) and in the standard histories of probability. It appeared in G. Buffon's supplement to his Natural History, *Essai d'arithmétique morale*. See further E. F. Schuster, 'Buffon's Needle Experiment', *American Mathematical Monthly*, 81 (1974), 26–9 and for a survey, H. Solomon, *Geometric Probability* (Philadelphia, 1978), Ch. 1.

8 Results of the experiment are described in M. G. Kendall and P. A. P. Moran, *Geometrical Probability* (London, 1963). For serious doubts as to the reliability of the actual experiments, see N. T. Gridgeman, 'Geometric Probability and the Number π', *Scriptag Mathematica*, 25 (1960), 183–95. The number of trials required according to Gridgeman is of the order of 90.10^{2n} for precision to n decimal places.

9 *Calcul des probabilités* (Paris, 1889), 4–5; 2nd edn. 1907, 4–7 (reprinted as 3rd edn., New York, 1972). See further the discussion of Bertrand's book on pages 306–11 above.

10 Bertrand himself stated the problem in roughly this form: the problem of choosing a number at random from [0, 100] is the same as that of choosing its square (*Calcul des probabilités*, 2nd edn., 4). He adds that these contradictions can be multiplied to infinity. His own conclusion is that when the sample space is infinite, the notion of choosing at random '*n'est pas une indication suffisante*'—presumably not sufficient to create a well-posed problem.

11 See E. T. Jaynes, 'The Well-Posed Problem', *Foundations of Physics*, 3 (1973), 477–92, which has references to preceding discussions.

12 Note here that a measure assigns non-negative numbers and is additive.

13 See van Fraassen, *Laws and Symmetry*, Ch. 13, Sect. 3.

14 The probabilities must be the same for the events $(a \le x \le b)$ and $(ka \le y \le kb)$, so we deduce:

$$\int_0^b f(x)dx = \int_0^{kb} f(kx)\,\mathrm{d}(kx) \text{ for all } b$$

hence $f(x) = kf(kx)$, for any positive constant k. This equation has a unique solution up to a constant multiplier:

$$f(x) = (1/x)$$

This gives us the basic measure:

$$M(a \le x \le b) = K(\log b - \log a)$$

because $(1/x)$ is the derivative of $\log x$ (natural logarithm).

15 R. D. Rosenkranz, *Inference, Method and Decision* (Dordrecht, 1977), 63–8. See also R. D. Rosencrantz, *Foundations and Applications of Inductive Probability* (Atascadero, Calif., 1981), Sects. 4.2 and 4.1.

16 A discussion of Buffon's needle along these lines is provided by M. Kac, E. R. van Kampen, and A. Winter, 'On Buffon's Problem and its Generalizations', *American Journal of Mathematics*, 61 (1939), 672–4.

17 P. Milne, 'A Note on Scale Invariance', *British Journal for the Philosophy of Science*, 34 (1983), 49–55.

18 Despite some rhetoric that seems to express the wish it were not so, Jaynes's article really agrees. Specifically, he implies that to treat a problem as solvable by symmetry considerations is to assume—what might be empirically false—that all relevant factors have been indicated in the statement of the problem ('The Well-Posed Problem', 489). Thus to treat a specific problem that way can itself not be justified a priori; the solution is correct for reality only conditional on that substantial assumption.

19 Ibid. 477–92.
20 E. T. Jaynes, *Papers on Probability, Statistics and Statistical Physics*, ed. R. Rosencrantz (Dordrecht, 1983), 128.
21 See the concise, perspicuous exposition in A. P. Dawid, 'Invariant Prior Distributions', in S. Kotz and N. L. Johnson, *Encyclopedia of Statistical Sciences* (New York, 1983), 228–36. The main figures in the search for 'invariant priors' besides Jaynes were H. Jeffreys' classic text *Theory of Probability* (Oxford, 1939), and D. Fraser (see e.g. his 'The Fiducial Method and Invariance', *Biometrica*, 48 (1961), 261–80).
22 See E. T. Jaynes, 'Prior Probabilities', *IEEE Transactions of the Society of Systems Sciences Cybernetics* SSC–4 (1968), 227–41; C. Villegas, 'On Haar Priors', in V. P. Godambe *et al.* (eds.), *Foundations of Statistical Inference* (Toronto, 1971), 409–14; 'Inner Statistical Inference', *Journal of the American Statistical Association*, 72 (1977), 453–8 and *Annals of Statistics*, 9 (1981), 768–76. I want to thank Dr F. G. Perey, of the Oak Ridge National Laboratory, for letting me have a copy of his excellent and insightful presentation of this approach, 'Application of Group Theory to Data Reduction', Report ORNL-5908 (Sept. 1982).
23 The 'nice properties' referred to in the text are topological properties of the group; if it is locally compact and transitive (for any y and z in the set there is a member g of G such that $g(y) = z$) then the left Haar measure is unique up to a multiplicative constant. However, in order for P to be also independent of the choice of reference point x_0, the left and right Haar measure must be the same; this is guaranteed if the group is compact.

19

STATISTICAL AND INDUCTIVE PROBABILITY*

Rudolf Carnap

If you ask a scientist whether the term 'probability' as used in science has always the same meaning, you will find a curious situation. Practically everyone will say that there is only one scientific meaning; but when you ask that it be stated, two different answers will come forth. The majority will refer to the concept of probability used in mathematical statistics and its scientific applications. However, there is a minority of those who regard a certain non-statistical concept as the only scientific concept of probability. Since either side holds that its concept is the only correct one, neither seems willing to relinquish the term 'probability'. Finally, there are a few people – and among them this author – who believe that an unbiased examination must come to the conclusion that both concepts are necessary for science, though in different contexts.

I will now explain both concepts – distinguishing them as 'statistical probability' and 'inductive probability' – and indicate their different functions in science. We shall see, incidentally, that the inductive concept, now advocated by a heretic minority, is not a new invention of the 20th century, but was the prevailing one in an earlier period and only forgotten later on.

The *statistical concept of probability* is well known to all those who apply in their scientific work the customary methods of mathematical statistics. In this field, exact methods for calculations employing statistical probability are developed and rules for its application are given. In the simplest cases, probability in this sense means the relative frequency with which a certain kind of event occurs within a given reference class, customarily called the 'population'. Thus, the statement 'The probability that an inhabitant of the United States belongs to blood group A is p' means that a fraction p of the inhabitants belongs to this group. Sometimes a statement of statistical probability refers, not to an actually existing or observed frequency, but to a potential one, i.e. to a frequency that would occur under certain specifiable circumstances. Suppose, for example, a physicist carefully examines a newly made die and finds it is a geometrically perfect and materially homogeneous cube. He may then assert that the probability of obtaining an ace by a throw of this die is 1/6. This means that *if* a sufficiently long series of throws with this die were made, the relative frequency of aces would be 1/6. Thus, the probability statement here refers to a potential frequency rather than to an actual one. Indeed, if the die were destroyed before any throws were made, the assertion would still be valid. Exactly speaking, the statement refers to the physical microstate of the die; without specifying its details (which presumably are not known), it is characterized as being such that certain results would be obtained if the die were subjected to certain

317

experimental procedures. Thus the statistical concept of probability is not essentially different from other disposition concepts which characterize the objective state of a thing by describing reactions to experimental conditions, as, for example, the I.Q. of a person, the elasticity of a material object, etc.

Inductive probability occurs in contexts of another kind; it is ascribed to a hypothesis with respect to a body of evidence. The hypothesis may be any statement concerning unknown facts, say, a prediction of a future event, e.g., tomorrow's weather or the outcome of a planned experiment or of a presidential election, or a presumption concerning the unobserved cause of an observed event. Any set of known or assumed facts may serve as evidence; it consists usually in results of observations which have been made. To say that the hypothesis h has the probability p (say, 3/5) with respect to the evidence e, means that for anyone to whom this evidence but no other relevant knowledge is available, it would be reasonable to believe in h to the degree p or, more exactly, it would be unreasonable for him to bet on h at odds higher than $p : (1 - p)$ (in the example, 3:2). Thus inductive probability measures the strength of support given to h by e or the *degree of confirmation* of h on the basis of e. In most cases in ordinary discourse, even among scientists, inductive probability is not specified by a numerical value but merely as being high or low or, in a comparative judgment, as being higher than another probability. It is important to recognize that every inductive probability judgement is relative to some evidence. In many cases no explicit reference to evidence is made; it is then to be understood that the totality of relevant information available to the speaker is meant as evidence. If a member of a jury says that the defendant is very probably innocent or that, of two witnesses A and B who have made contradictory statements, it is more probable that A lied than that B did, he means it with respect to the evidence that was presented in the trial plus any psychological or other relevant knowledge of a general nature he may possess. Probability as understood in contexts of this kind is not frequency. Thus, in our example, the evidence concerning the defendant, which was presented in the trial, may be such that it cannot be ascribed to any other person; and if it could be ascribed to several people, the juror would not know the relative frequency of innocent persons among them. Thus the probability concept used here cannot be the statistical one. While a statement of statistical probability asserts a matter of fact, a statement of inductive probability is of a purely logical nature. If hypothesis and evidence are given, the probability can be determined by logical analysis and mathematical calculation.

One of the basic principles of the theory of inductive probability is the *principle of indifference*. It says that, if the evidence does not contain anything that would favor either of two or more possible events, in other words, if our knowledge situation is symmetrical with respect to these events, then they have equal probabilities relative to the evidence. For example, if the evidence e_1 available to an observer X_1 contains nothing else about a given die than the information that it is a regular cube, then the symmetry condition is fulfilled and therefore each of the six faces has the same probability 1/6 to appear uppermost at the next throw. This means that it would be unreasonable for X_1 to bet more than one to five on any one face. If X_2 is in possession of the evidence e_2 which, in addition to e_1, contains the knowledge that the die is heavily loaded in favor of one of the faces without specifying which one, the probabilities for X_2 are the same as for X_1. If, on the other hand, X_3 knows e_3 to the effect that the load favors the ace, then the probability of the ace on the basis of e_3 is higher than 1/6. Thus, inductive probability, in contradistinction to statistical probability, cannot be ascribed to a material object by itself, irrespective of an observer. This is obvious in our example; the die is the same for all three observers and hence cannot have different properties for them. Inductive probability characterizes a hypothesis relative to available information; this information may differ from person to person and vary for any person in the course of time.

A brief look at the historical development of the concept of probability will give us a better understanding of the present controversy. The mathematical study of problems of probability began when some mathematicians of the sixteenth and seventeenth centuries were asked by their gambler friends about the odds in various games of chance. They wished to learn about probabilities as a guidance for their betting decisions. In the beginning of its scientific career, the concept of probability appeared in the form of inductive probability. This is clearly reflected in the title of the first major treatise on probability, written by Jacob Bernoulli and published posthumously in 1713; it was called *Ars Conjectandi*, the art of conjecture, in other words, the art of judging hypotheses on the basis of evidence. This book may be regarded as marking the beginning of the so-called classical period of the theory of probability. This period culminated in the great systematic work by Laplace, *Theorie analytique des probabilities* (1812). According to Laplace, the purpose of the theory of probability is to guide our judgments and to protect us from illusions. His explanations show clearly that he is mostly concerned, not with actual frequencies, but with methods for judging the acceptability of assumptions, in other words, with inductive probability.

In the second half of the last century and still more in our century, the application of statistical methods gained more and more ground in science. Thus attention was increasingly focussed on the statistical concept of probability. However, there was no clear awareness of the fact that this development constituted a transition to a fundamentally different meaning of the word 'probability'. In the nineteen twenties the first probability theories based on the frequency interpretation were proposed by men like the statistician R. A. Fisher, the mathematician R. von Mises [see Chapter 22], and the physicist-philosopher H. Reichenbach. These authors and their followers did not explicitly suggest to abandon that concept of probability which had prevailed since the classical period, and to replace it by a new one. They rather believed that their concept was essentially the same as that of all earlier authors. They merely claimed that they had given a more exact definition for it and had developed more comprehensive theories on this improved foundation. Thus, they interpreted Laplace's word 'probability' not in his inductive sense, but in their own statistical sense. Since there is a strong, though by far not complete analogy between the two concepts, many mathematical theorems hold in both interpretations, but others do not. Therefore these authors could accept many of the classical theorems but had to reject others. In particular, they objected strongly to the principle of indifference. In the frequency interpretation, this principle is indeed absurd. In our earlier example with the observer X_1, who knows merely that the die has the form of a cube, it would be rather incautious for him to assert that the six faces will appear with equal frequency. And if the same assertion were made by X_2, who has information that the die is biased, although he does not know the direction of the bias, he would contradict his own knowledge. In the inductive interpretation, on the other hand, the principle is valid even in the case of X_2, since in this sense it does not predict frequencies but merely says in effect, that it would be arbitrary for X_2 to have more confidence in the appearance of one face than in that of any other face and therefore it would be unreasonable for him to let his betting decisions be guided by such

319

arbitrary expectations. Therefore it seems much more plausible to assume that Laplace meant the principle of indifference in the inductive sense rather than to assume that one of the greatest minds of the eighteenth century in mathematics, theoretical physics, astronomy, and philosophy chose an obvious absurdity as a basic principle.

The great economist John Maynard Keynes made the first attempt in our century to revive the old but almost forgotten inductive concept of probability. In his *Treatise on Probability* (1921) he made clear that the inductive concept is implicitly used in all our thinking on unknown events both in every-day life and in science. He showed that the classical theory of probability in its application to concrete problems was understandable only if it was interpreted in the inductive sense. However, he modified and restricted the classical theory in several important points. He rejected the principle of indifference in its classical form. And he did not share the view of the classical authors that it should be possible in principle to assign a numerical value to the probability of any hypothesis whatsoever. He believed that this could be done only under very special, rarely fulfilled conditions, as in games of chance where there is a well determined number of possible cases, all of them alike in their basic features, e.g., the six possible results of a throw of a die, the possible distributions of cards among the players, the possible final positions of the ball on a roulette table, and the like. He thought that in all other cases at best only comparative judgments of probability could be made, and even these only for hypotheses which belong, so to speak, to the same dimension. Thus one might come to the result that, on the basis of available knowledge, it is more probable that the next child of a specified couple will be male rather than female; but no comparison could be made between the probability of the birth of a male child and the probability of the stocks of General Electric going up tomorrow.

A much more comprehensive theory of inductive probability was constructed by the geophysicist Harold Jeffreys (*Theory of Probability*, 1939). He agreed with the classical view that probability can be expressed numerically in all cases. Furthermore, in view of the fact that science replaces statements in qualitative terms (e.g., 'the child to be born will be very heavy') more and more by those in terms of measurable quantities ('the weight of the child will be more than eight pounds'). Jeffreys wished to apply probability also to hypotheses of quantitative form. For this reason, he set up an axiom system for probability much stronger than that of Keynes. In spite of Keynes' warning, he accepted the principle of indifference in a form quite similar to the classical one: [If there is no reason to believe one hypothesis rather than another, the probabilities are equal]. However, it can easily be seen that the principle in this strong form leads to contradictions. Suppose, for example, that it is known that every ball in an urn is either blue or red or yellow but that nothing is known either of the color of any particular ball or of the numbers of blue, red, or yellow balls in the urn. Let B be the hypothesis that the first ball to be drawn from the urn will be blue, R, that it will be red, and Y, that it will be yellow. Now consider the hypotheses B and non-B. According to the principle of indifference as used by Laplace and again by Jeffreys, since nothing is known concerning B and non-B, these two hypotheses have equal probabilities, i.e., one half. Non-B means that the first ball is not blue, hence either red or yellow. Thus 'R or Y' has probability one half. Since nothing is known concerning R and Y, their probabilities are equal and hence must be one fourth each. On the other hand, if we start with the consideration of R and non-R, we obtain the result that the probability of R is one half and that of B one fourth, which is incompatible with the previous result. Thus Jeffreys' system as it stands is inconsistent. This defect cannot be eliminated by simply omitting the principle of indifference. It plays an essential role in the system; without it, many important results can no longer be derived. In spite of this defect, Jeffreys' book remains valuable for the new light it throws on many statistical problems by discussing them for the first time in terms of inductive probability.

Both Keynes and Jeffreys discussed also the statistical concept of probability, and both rejected it. They believed that all probability statements could be formulated in terms of inductive probability and that therefore there was no need for any probability concept interpreted in terms of frequency. I think that in this point they went too far. Today an increasing number of those who study both sides of the controversy which has been going on for thirty years, are coming to the conclusion that here, as often before in the history of scientific thinking, both sides are right in their positive theses, but wrong in their polemic remarks about the other side. The statistical concept, for which a very elaborate mathematical theory exists, and which has been fruitfully applied in many fields in science and industry, need not at all be abandoned in order to make room for the inductive concept. Both concepts are needed for science, but they fulfill quite different functions. Statistical probability characterizes an objective situation, e.g., a state of a physical, biological or social system. Therefore it is this concept which is used in statements concerning concrete situations or in laws expressing general regularities of such situations. On the other hand, inductive probability, as I see it, does not occur *in* scientific statements, concrete or general, but only in judgments *about* such statements; in particular, in judgments about the strength of support given by one statement, the evidence, to another, the hypothesis, and hence about the acceptability of the latter on the basis of the former. Thus, strictly speaking, inductive probability belongs not to science itself but to the methodology of science, i.e., the analysis of concepts, statements, theories, and methods of science.

The theories of both probability concepts must be further developed. Although a great deal of work has been done on statistical probability, even here some problems of its exact interpretation and its application, e.g., in methods of estimation, are still controversial. On inductive probability, on the other hand, most of the work remains still to be done. Utilizing results of Keynes and Jeffreys and employing the exact tools of modern symbolic logic, I have constructed the fundamental parts of a mathematical theory of inductive probability or inductive logic (*Logical Foundations of Probability*, 1950). The methods developed make it possible to calculate numerical values of inductive probability ('degree of confirmation') for hypotheses concerning either single events or frequencies of properties and to determine estimates of frequencies in a population on the basis of evidence about a sample of the population. A few steps have been made towards extending the theory to hypotheses involving measurable quantities such as mass, temperature, etc.

It is not possible to outline here the mathematical system itself. But I will explain some of the general problems that had to be solved before the system could be constructed and some of the basic conceptions underlying the construction. One of the fundamental questions to be decided by any theory of induction is, whether to accept a principle of indifference and, if so, in what form. It should be strong enough to allow the derivation of the desired theorems, but at the same time sufficiently restricted to avoid the contradictions resulting from the classical form.

The problem will become clearer if we use a few elementary concepts of inductive logic. They will now be explained with the help of the first two columns of the accompanying diagram. We consider a set of four individuals, say four balls drawn

321

Statistical distributions		Individual distributions	Method I	Method II	
Number of blue	Number of white		Initial probability of individual distributions	Initial probability of: Statistical distributions	Individual distributions
1. 4	0	1. ●●●●	1/16	1/5	1/5 = 12
2. 3	1	2. ●●●○	1/16	1/5	1/20 = 3
		3. ●●○●	1/16		1/20 = 3
		4. ●○●●	1/16		1/20 = 3
		5. ○●●●	1/16		1/20 = 3
3. 2	2	6. ●●○○	1/16	1/5	1/30 = 2
		7. ●○●○	1/16		1/30 = 2
		8. ●○○●	1/16		1/30 = 2
		9. ○●●○	1/16		1/30 = 2
		10. ○●○●	1/16		1/30 = 2
		11. ○○●●	1/16		1/30 = 2
4. 1	3	12. ●○○○	1/16	1/5	1/20 = 3
		13. ○●○○	1/16		1/20 = 3
		14. ○○●○	1/16		1/20 = 3
		15. ○○○●	1/16		1/20 = 3
5. 0	4	16. ○○○○	1/16	1/5	1/5 = 12

This diagram is reprinted here by permission of the Scientific American.

from an urn. The individuals are described with respect to a given division of mutually exclusive properties; in our example, the two properties black (B) and white (W). An *individual distribution* is specified by ascribing to each individual one property. In our example, there are sixteen individual distributions; they are pictured in the second column (e.g., in the individual distribution No. 3, the first, second, and fourth ball are black, the third is white). A *statistical distribution*, on the other hand, is characterized by merely stating the number of individuals for each property. In the example, we have five statistical distributions, listed in the first column (e.g., the statistical distribution No. 2 is described by saying that there are three B and one W, without specifying *which* individuals are B and which W).

By the *initial probability* of a hypothesis ('probability a priori' in traditional terminology) we understand its probability before any factual knowledge concerning the individuals is available. Now we shall see that, if any initial probabilities which sum up to one are assigned to the individual distributions, all other probability values are thereby fixed. To see how the procedure works, put a slip of paper on the diagram alongside the list of individual distributions and write down opposite each distribution a fraction as its initial probability; the sum of the sixteen fractions must be one, but otherwise you may choose them just as you like. We shall soon consider the question whether some choices might be preferable to others. But for the moment we are only concerned with the fact that any arbitrary choice constitutes one and only one *inductive method* in the sense that it leads to one and only one system of probability values which contain an initial probability for any hypothesis (concerning the given individuals and the given properties) and a relative probability for any hypothesis with respect to any evidence. The procedure is as follows. For any given statement we can, by perusing the list of individual distributions, determine those in which it holds (e.g., the statement 'among the first three balls there is exactly one *W*' holds in distributions No. 3, 4, 5, 6, 7, 9). Then we assign to it as initial probability the sum of the initial probabilities of the individual distributions in which it holds. Suppose that an evidence statement *e* (e.g., 'The first ball is *B*, the second *W*, the third *B*') and a hypothesis *h* (e.g., 'The fourth ball is *B*') are given. We ascertain first the individual distributions in which *e* holds (in the example, No. 4 and 7), and then those among them in which also *h* holds (only No. 4). The former ones determine the initial probability of *e*; the latter ones determine that of *e* and *h* together. Since the latter are among the former, the latter initial probability is a part (or the whole) of the former. We now divide the latter initial probability by the former and assign the resulting fraction to *h* as its relative probability with respect to *e*. (In our example, let us take the values of the initial probabilities of individual distributions given in the diagram for methods I and II, which will soon be explained. In method I the values for No. 4 and 7 – as for all other individual distributions – are 1/16; hence the initial probability of *e* is 2/16. That of *e* and *h* together is the value of No. 4 alone, hence 1/16. Dividing this by 2/16, we obtain 1/2 as the probability of *h* with respect to *e*. In method II, we find for No. 4 and 7 in the last column the values 3/60 and 2/60 respectively. Therefore the initial probability of *e* is here 5/60, that of *e* and *h* together 3/60; hence the probability of *h* with respect to *e* is 3/5.)

The problem of choosing an inductive method is closely connected with the problem of the principle of indifference. Most authors since the classical period have accepted some form of the principle and have thereby avoided the otherwise unlimited arbitrainess in the choice of a method. On the other hand, practically all authors in our century agree that the principle should be restricted to some well-defined class of hypotheses. But there is no agreement as to the class to be chosen. Many authors advocate either method I or method II, which are exemplified in our diagram. Method I consists in applying the principle of indifference to individual distributions, in other words, in assigning equal initial probabilities to individual distributions. In method II the principle is first applied to the statistical distributions and then, for each statistical distribution, to the corresponding individual distributions. Thus, in our example, equal initial probabilities are assigned in method II to the five statistical distributions, hence 1/5 to each; then this value 1/5 or 12/60 is distributed in equal parts among the corresponding individual distributions, as indicated in the last column.

If we examine more carefully the two ways of using the principle of indifference, we find that either of them leads to contradictions if applied without restriction to all divisions of properties. (The reader can easily check the following results by himself. We consider, as in the diagram, four individuals and a division D_2 into two properties;

blue (instead of black) and white. Let h be the statement that all four individuals are white. We consider, on the other hand, a division D_3 into three properties: dark blue, light blue, and white. For division D_2, as used in the diagram, we see that h is an individual distribution (No. 16) and also a statistical distribution (No. 5). The same holds for division D_3. By setting up the complete diagram for the latter division, one finds that there are fifteen statistical distributions, of which h is one, and 81 individual distributions (viz., $3 \times 3 \times 3 \times 3$), of which h is also one. Applying method I to division D_2, we found as the initial probability of h 1/16; if we apply it to D_3, we find 1/81; these two results are incompatible. Method II applied to D_2 led to the value 1/5; but applied to D_3 it yields 1/15. Thus this method likewise furnishes incompatible results.) We therefore restrict the use of either method to one division, viz. the one consisting of all properties which can be distinguished in the given universe of discourse (or which we wish to distinguish within a given context of investigation). If modified in this way, either method is consistent. We may still regard the examples in the diagram as representing the modified methods I and II, if we assume that the difference between black and white is the only difference among the given individuals, or the only difference relevant to a certain investigation.

How shall we decide which of the two methods to choose? Each of them is regarded as *the* reasonable method by prominent scholars. However, in my view, the chief mistake of the earlier authors was their failure to specify explicitly the main characteristic of a reasonable inductive method. It is due to this failure that some of them chose the wrong method. This characteristic is not difficult to find. Inductive thinking is a way of judging hypotheses concerning unknown events. In order to be reasonable, this judging must be guided by our knowledge of observed events. More specifically, other things being equal, a future event is to be regarded as the more probable, the greater the relative frequency of similar events observed so far under similar circumstances. This *principle of learning from experience* guides, or rather ought to guide, all inductive thinking in everyday affairs and in science. Our confidence that a certain drug will help in a present case of a certain disease is the higher the more frequently it has helped in past cases. We would regard a man's behavior as unreasonable if his expectation of a future event were the higher the less frequently he saw it happen in the past, and also if he formed his expectations for the future without any regard to what he had observed in the past. The principle of learning from experience seems indeed so obvious that it might appear superfluous to emphasize it explicitly. In fact, however, even some authors of high rank have advocated an inductive method that violates the principle.

Let us now examine the methods I and II from the point of view of the principle of learning from experience. In our earlier example we considered the evidence e saying that of the four balls drawn the first was B, the second W, the third B; in other words, that two B and one W were so far observed. According to the principle, the prediction h that the fourth ball will be black should be taken as more probable than its negation, non-h. We found, however, that method I assigns probability 1/2 to h, and therefore likewise 1/2 to non-h. And we see easily that it assigns to h this value 1/2 also on any other evidence concerning the first three balls. Thus method I violates the principle. A man following this method sticks to the initial probability value for a prediction, irrespective of all observations he makes. In spite of this character of method I, it was proposed as the valid method of induction by prominent philosophers, among them Charles Sanders Peirce (in 1883) and Ludwig Wittgenstein (in 1921), and even by Keynes in one chapter of his book, although in other chapters he emphasizes eloquently the necessity of learning from experience.

We saw earlier that method II assigns, on the evidence specified, to h the probability 3/5, hence to non-h 2/5. Thus the principle of learning from experience is satisfied in this case, and it can be shown that the same holds in any other case. (The reader can easily verify, for example, that with respect to the evidence that the first three balls are black, the probability of h is 4/5 and therefore that of non-h 1/5.) Method II in its modified, consistent form, was proposed by the author in 1945. Although it was often emphasized throughout the historical development that induction must be based on experience, nobody as far as I am aware, succeeded in specifying a consistent inductive method satisfying the principle of learning from experience. (The method proposed by Thomas Bayes (1763) and developed by Laplace – sometimes called 'Bayes' rule' or 'Laplace's rule of succession' – fulfills the principle. It is essentially method II, but in its unrestricted form; therefore it is inconsistent.) I found later that there are infinitely many consistent inductive methods which satisfy the principle (*The Continuum of Inductive Methods*, 1952). None of them seems to be as simple in its definition as method II, but some of them have other advantages.

Once a consistent and suitable inductive method is developed, it supplies the basis for a *general method of estimation*, i.e., a method for calculating, on the basis of given evidence, an estimate of an unknown value of any magnitude. Suppose that, on the basis of the evidence, there are n possibilities for the value of a certain magnitude at a given time, e.g., the amount of rain tomorrow, the number of persons coming to a meeting, the price of wheat after the next harvest. Let the possible values be $x_1, x_2, ..., x_n$, and their inductive probabilities with respect to the given evidence $p_1, p_2, ..., p_n$, respectively. Then we take the product $p_1 x_1$ as the expectation value of the first case at the present moment. Thus, if the occurrence of the first case is certain and hence $p_1 = 1$, its expectation value is the full value x_1; if it is just as probable that it will occur as that it will not, and hence $p_1 = 1/2$, its expectation value is half its full value $(p_1 x_1 = x_1/2)$, etc. We proceed similarly with the other possible values. As estimate or total expectation value of the magnitude on the given evidence we take the sum of the expectation values for the possible cases, that is, $p_1 x_1 + p_2 x_2 + ... + p_n x_n$. (For example, suppose someone considers buying a ticket for a lottery and, on the basis of his knowledge of the lottery procedure, there is a probability of 0.01 that the ticket will win the first prize of $200 and a probability of 0.03 that it will win $50; since there are no other prizes, the probability that it will win nothing is 0.96. Hence the estimate of the gain in dollars is $0.01 \times 200 + 0.03 \times 50 + 0.96 \times 0 = 3.50$. This is the value of the ticket for him and it would be irrational for him to pay more for it.) The same method may be used in order to make a rational decision in a situation where one among various possible actions is to be chosen. For example, a man considers several possible ways for investing a certain amount of money. Then he can – in principle, at least – calculate the estimate of his gain for each possible way. To act rationally, he should then choose that way for which the estimated gain is highest.

Bernoulli and Laplace and many of their followers envisaged the idea of a theory of inductive probability which, when fully developed, would supply the means for evaluating the acceptability of hypothetical assumptions in any field of theoretical research and at the same time methods for determining a rational decision in the affairs of practical life. In the more sober cultural atmosphere of the late nineteenth century and still more in the first half of the twentieth, this idea was usually regarded as a utopian dream. It is certainly true that those audacious thinkers were not as near to their aim as they believed. But a few men dare to think today that the pioneers were not mere dreamers and that it will be possible in the future to make far-reaching progress in essentially that direction in which they saw their vision.

Note

* Originally published by the Galois Institute of Mathematics and Art, Brooklyn, 1955. Copyright © 1955 Rudolf Carnap.

Bibliography

A survey of the various conceptions of probability is given by Ernest Nagel in *Principles of the Theory of Probability* (International Encyclopedia of Unified Science, Vol. I, No. 6, Chicago, 1939). This may serve as a first introduction to the original works listed below.

P.S. de Laplace, *A philosophical essay on probabilities*. (Orig. Paris, 1814) New York, 1902.

R. A. Fisher, 'On the mathematical foundations of theoretical statistics', *Phil. Trans. Royal Soc.*, Series A, Vol. 222, 1922. Reprinted in: *Contributions to mathematical statistics*, New York, 1950.

J. M. Keynes, *A treatise on probability*, London and New York, 1921.

R. von Mises, *Probability, statistics, and truth*. (Orig. 1928) New York, 1939. [Chapter 22 in this volume]

H. Reichenbach, *The theory of probability*. (Orig. Leiden, 1935). Berkeley, 1949.

H. Jeffreys, *Theory of probability*. Oxford (1939) 1950.

R. Carnap, *Logical foundations of probability*. Chicago, 1950.

R. Carnap, *The nature and application of inductive logic*. Chicago, 1951. (A reprint of six non-technical sections from *Logical Foundations* ... .)

R. Carnap, *The continuum of inductive methods*. Chicago, 1952.

20

IS THE THEORY OF LOGICAL
PROBABILITY GROUNDLESS?*

D. C. Stove

The General Suspicion of Logical Probability

I have identified two specific objections to the theory of logical probability, and tried to meet them. One was the objection arising from 'grue', that the theory of logical probability, being a form of non-deductive logic, is not formal. The other was that the theory of logical probability is not empirical.

But these objections, even taken together, do not make up the main component of that general 'suspicion of quackery' under which, with most philosophers, the theory of logical probability labours. What this main component is, is not very easy to say. It is an objection at once more damning, and less definite, than the two I have considered so far. It is, accordingly, more often met with in the oral tradition than in print. The best summary I can give of it is as follows. 'The theory of logical probability has not merely no empirical foundations, but no foundations of any kind: it is a completely arbitrary, groundless, free-floating intellectual construction. There is no reason to believe a word of it.'

This is not a very definite objection. But it is nonetheless very important that I should attempt to answer it, because it is an objection, which most philosophers *really* feel, to the theory of logical probability. They do not often let this feeling emerge fully in print, as I have said. Still, they sometimes do. Thus for example Professor I. Hacking says, in direct reference to theories of logical probability like Carnap's, that they are 'theories ... which *have no foundation at all*'.[1] And Professor T. S. Kuhn, without direct reference to Carnap's theory but undoubtedly intending to refer to it, says that such theories 'open the door to Cloudcuckoo-land'.[2]

As this objection to the theory of logical probability is so strongly and so widely felt, I must do my best, despite its indefiniteness, to show that it is wrong. First, however, I should make it clear that in a certain sense I believe it is *right*, only not an objection.

I maintain, with Carnap, that our knowledge of logical probability 'rests on intuition'. Now this may suggest that I regard *our intuitions* as reasons to believe statements of logical probability. It may suggest, for example, that if I were challenged to give a reason to believe the thesis of regularity (155), or a reason to believe an instance of it such as

(145) $P(\text{Abe is black}/T) < 1,$

because *according to my terminology*, the ascription of a numerical probability value such as 1/2 to a statement carries us beyond logic.

What I call the theory of logical probability may be compared with metrical geometry such as, say, Euclidean geometry. In Euclidean geometry, the only distance (or area or volume) whose numerical measure is defined by the theory itself is the zero distance (or area or volume). Other ascriptions of specific numerical values are extra-theoretical: they are not introduced by the theory, but by arbitrarily defining a yardstick. (If the theory is the geometry of the real world these ascriptions may be part of the physical theory, provided it contains a fundamental constant of length; but the choice of the Paris metre is not like this.) In the theory of logical probability we have not only 0 but also 1; all other ascriptions of specific numerical values are, in my terminology, extra-logical applications; although there may be, in the objective or physical interpretations of probability, ascriptions which are part of physical theory.[4]

Popper here allows as non-arbitrary, we see, only two kinds of statements of logical probability: the extreme numerical equalities, '$P(H/E) = 1$', '$P(H'/E') = 0$', etc. In fact, however, non-arbitrariness cannot possibly be confined to these. For *conjunctions* of propositions of these kinds entail some *comparative* equalities and inequalities, '$P(H/E) > P(H'/E')$', etc., which must therefore be non-arbitrary too. Again, if P is non-arbitrarily true or false, then so is its contradictory. Whence if '$P(H/E) = 1$' is non-arbitrary, so is '$P(H/E) < 1$'; and if '$P(H'/E') = 0$' is non-arbitrary, so is '$P(H'/E') > 0$'. Still, it is clear enough what Popper meant. He was evidently thinking only of the non-extreme numerical *equalities*, and his thesis was only that all of *these* are arbitrary.

But even that is false. There is nothing *arbitrary* about the instance of regularity

(137) $P(Ba.Bb. \sim Bc/T) > 0,$

in which the conjuncts abbreviate 'Abe is black', etc. On the contrary it is just obviously true. There is nothing arbitrary about the instance of the symmetry of individual constants

(136) $P(Ba.Bb. \sim Bc/T) = P(Ba. \sim Bb.Bc/T) = (\sim Ba.Bb.Bc/T).$

It is just obviously true. There is nothing arbitrary, either, about the *principles* of logical probability. But from (136), (137), and some of those principles (plus some other statements of logical probability all of the most impeccable non-arbitrariness, indeed triviality), it follows that

(121) $P(Ba/$Just two of the individuals $a, b, c,$ are $B) = 2/3.$

What follows from the non-arbitrary cannot be arbitrary. Yet (121) is a non-extreme numerical equality.

The assignment of a non-extreme number to a logical probability, then, is *not* always arbitrary. For we are *constrained* to some such assignments, if we believe two things: that a contingent non-quantified proposition is never certain or impossible in relation to a tautology; and that the logical probability of an argument is never changed by mere uniform exchange of one individual constant for another. And *these* beliefs are not arbitrary ones.

Regularity and the symmetry of individual constants do not suffice, of course, to fix the numerical value of all logical probabilities. The argument above does not show, therefore, that a numerical value can *always* be assigned non-arbitrarily to $P(H/E)$. But it does show that it sometimes can, and hence that the nearly universal conviction to the contrary is false. It therefore also shows, I may add, that it is sometimes entirely out of place, on account of its voluntaristic overtones, to speak of 'assigning' a number to a logical probability.

Truthmakers for Logical Probability

'But what in the world are the *truth-makers* for statements of logical probability? Perhaps you are right, and even some of the non-extreme numerical equalities are non-arbitrarily true or false. And of course you are able to prove, supposing some such statements to be true, that certain others are too: the principles of logical probability make sure of that. But *in virtue of what* is any of them true in the first place? The theory of logical probability really is a Laputan floating island, unless this question can be answered.'

Here I am trying once more to give a definite shape to the vague objection stated in the second paragraph of this chapter; and I am drawing, now, entirely on the oral tradition. The above is not one of the happier deliverances of that tradition.

It is a sufficient reason for being intensely suspicious of the 'truth-maker' terminology, that while being a brand-new piece of philosophical language, it is already found, by those who use it, virtually indispensable, and is thought by them to do great things. But there is also a much better reason for being suspicious of it. 'What is the truth-maker of p?', 'What makes it true that p?', or 'In virtue of what is p true?', is *always* a pseudo-question. For in every case the true answer to it, the whole truth, and nothing but the truth, is simply: the fact that p. But that, of course, is too transparently trivial to satisfy anyone, and the philosopher who asked the question demands some other answer. That only shows, however, that he ought to have asked some other questions. If he cannot frame another and more sensible question—if he finds the 'truth-maker' terminology nearly or absolutely indispensible—then he should conclude that he did not have a sensible question to ask in the first place.

But I do not need to insist on this, or to repudiate altogether our present version of the 'groundlessness' or 'no-foundations' objection. I can perfectly well afford to adopt for a while the vicious terminology of 'truth-makers', and I will do so for the rest of this section. For my answer to the present objection lies quite elsewhere.

I am asked what are the truth-makers for statements of logical probability; and I must confess that I cannot answer this question at once. I expect soon to be able to do so, however. For all I need to know first is, what the truth-makers are for the true propositions of *deductive* logic. Of course the two things will not be exactly the same: still, we know that deductive logic and the theory of logical probability are in the same epistemic boat. The answer to my question will therefore be a sufficient general guide to me in framing the answer to the question I am asked. I therefore ask my question: what are the truth-makers for *judgements of validity or of invalidity*?

I am asked, what in the world is the truth-maker for, for example,

(120)   P(Abe is black/Abe is a raven and just 95% of ravens are black) = 0.95.

I reply that, as (120) is not a contingent proposition, and still less an empirical one, there is, *in the world*, nothing that makes it true. If I am then asked what, even out of the world, makes (120) true, I promise to reply the moment my questioner tells me what, in the world or out of it, makes it true that an instance of *barbara* is valid: what makes it true, for example, that

(148)   'Abe is a raven and all ravens are black' entails 'Abe is black'.

(There might be some slight delay.)
   I am asked, what makes it true that

(145)   P(Abe is black/T) < 1.

I cannot reply, but promise to do so, as soon as my questioner tells me, what makes it true that the argument,

   T/Abe is black

is *invalid*. (After all, the thesis of regularity, (155), is only a certain general judgement of invalidity.)
   I am asked, in virtue of *what* is it true that

(146)   P(Abe is black/T) = P(Bob is black/T).

I cannot yet tell, but I will know as soon as I learn in virtue of what it is true that the two arguments.

   All men are mortal
   Socrates is mortal/Socrates is a man,

and

   All men are mortal
   Plato is mortal/Plato is a man,

are *both invalid or both valid*. (After all, even deductive logic cannot get along without a little help from the symmetry of individual constants.)
   The reader will easily recognize that we are dealing here with a generalization of something that occupied us repeatedly in Part One of *The Rationality of Induction*. That statements of logical probability require 'truth-makers', is just a generalized version of the idea that the rationality of inductive inference requires a 'ground': a ground *in nature*, according to the less sophisticated versions, but at any rate some ground or other. The idea is 'mere foolery' in the general case, as it is in the special case of induction. Still I fear, as I indicated in Part One, that nothing can loosen the grip that

it has on philosopher's minds, at least as far as induction is concerned. But if anything can do so, it is the following simple stratagem (already recommended in Part One). When someone asks you, what *makes* (some) inductive inferences rational, or what makes their conclusions probable in relation to the premises, do not quarrel with his language or logic: do not complain, for example, about misconditionalization. Instead, *close with his offer.* Pretend that his question is not a pseudo-question, and promise to answer it the moment he tells you what it is, in nature or out of it, that *makes* (all) inductive inferences *invalid.* If your logical *probability* requires a ground, his logical *possibility* requires a ground no less; and if he finds, as he will, that he must be content to let the fallibility of induction 'float', he cannot object if you let its rationality float too.

Those philosophers who ask to be told what are the 'truthmakers' for statements of logical probability say that their interest in the matter is an ontological one. But, partly because they evince no more interest than any other sensible person does in the 'ontology' of *deductive* logic, I believe that it is nothing of the kind. It is rather, I believe, purely epistemic, and even philosophical in the worst and most familiar sense. The man who asks the new-fangled question, 'what is the truth-maker?' for, say,

(120)   P(Abe is black/Abe is a raven and just 95% of ravens are black) = 0.95,

really means to ask the old-fashioned, philosophico-infantile, question,

(176)   *How do you know* that (120)?

But, such 'how do you know?' questions being in considerable disrepute, he has been obliged to find a new and more respectable way of asking it.

The question, 'How do you know that *p*?', ordinarily carries with it no suggestion that the person addressed does *not* know that *p*: quite the contrary, obviously. But the philosophico-infantile 'How do you know that *p*?' emphatically does carry that suggestion with it. Accordingly, if someone asks us (176), the first part of our reply to him should be: (a) 'I do know that (120)'. The rest of it should be as follows. '(b) You too know that (120). (c) So does everyone else. (d) I do not know *how* I know that (120), though I can tell you this much, that it is in essentially the same way as I know (140). (e) I do not care how I know that (120). (f) Neither do you care about that, despite your question. For if I *did* know how I know that (120), and told you, my answer being

(177)   ... ...,

your apparent interest in the question (176) would vanish on the instant to be instantly replaced, in the philosophico-infantile way, by an apparent interest in the question

(178)   How do you know that (177)?'

No person of sense would allow himself to be detained for long over the question, how he knows that (120). No person of sense, *a fortiori*, would allow himself to be detained for long over the still worse question, which is a surrogate of that one, what is the 'truth maker' of (120).

Some logical truths must 'float'

Reasons to believe a proposition of deductive logic, if they exist at all, are other propositions of deductive logic; and reasons to believe a statement of logical probability, if they exist at all, are other statements of logic probability. The only exceptions to this (noticed in Chapter X) are trivial in either case. Our logical knowledge, then, our knowledge of deductive as well as of non-deductive logic, really does float, in the sense that there is no epistemic anchorage for it *outside* logic.

This is apt to seem intolerable when one first thinks of it. The mass of our logical knowledge is certainly immense. It seems contrary to all physical analogy, to say nothing of biological common sense, to suppose that this whole huge mass is anchored only (and then only in parts) by itself: which is to say, is not anchored at all. Surely this 'floating island' picture of our logical knowledge cannot be right? It *must* be possible in principle, one feels, at least to *diminish* the number of logical truths which float: that is, for believing which there are either no reasons, or only reasons that are other logical truths.

But I believe that this is impossible, for a reason which might be called 'the spaghetti effect', from its resemblance to the way in which an inexperienced spaghetti-eater, when he tries to get a pendant string of the stuff into his mouth, is always *too* successful.

Suppose (what I believe is impossible) that you *did* find out a non-logical truth P which is in fact a reason to believe the logical truth Q. You will not, even so, have found a reason to believe Q, unless, when you come to know that P, or earlier, you come to know that

(R) P is a reason to believe Q.

Of course you would not need to *know* that you know that (R); but you would need to know it. (Otherwise it might even happen, say, that you positively believe (R) to be false; in which case you would certainly not have come to know a reason to believe Q, by coming to know that P.) And now the trouble is that (R), if it is true (as we are supposing), is itself a truth *of logic*. It will be a truth of deductive or of non-deductive logic, according as P is or is not a *completely* conclusive reason to believe Q; but in either case it will be a logical truth.

So if we *did* succeed, by finding a non-logical reason P to believe the logical truth Q, in diminishing by one, Q, the number of logical truths that float, we would also have *added* one logical truth (R), to the mass of those that still float. For the rope by which we attempt to connect our logical knowledge to a non-logical anchor, is always and instantly sucked up, like beginner's spaghetti, and added to the very body of logical knowledge which we are trying to anchor. The attempt, therefore, to modify the floating-island picture of our logical knowledge, or to find, outside logical truths, reasons for believing logical truths, is a mere labour of Sisyphus.

Notes

* Originally published as Chapter XI of D. C. Stove, *The Rationality of Induction*, Oxford University Press, Oxford, 1986, pp. 178–89. Copyright © 1986 D. C. Stove. Reprinted by permission of Oxford University Press.
1 Hacking (1975), p. 143. Italics in text.
2 Kuhn (1970), p. 264.

3 Keynes (1921), pp. 171 and 184.
4 Popper (1968), pp. 286–287.

Bibliography

Hacking (1975), *The Emergence of Probability*, Cambridge: Cambridge University Press.
Keynes, John Maynard (1921), *A Treatise on Probability*. London: Macmillan.
Kuhn (1970), 'Reflections on my Critics', in Imre Lakatos and Alan Musgrave (eds.) *Criticism and the Growth of Knowledge*, Cambridge: Cambridge University Press, pp. 231–278.
Popper, Karl R. (1968) 'Theories, Experience, and Probabilistic Intuitions', in Imre Lakatos (ed.) *The Problem of Inductive Logic*, Amsterdam: North-Holland, pp. 285–303.

Part V

PHYSICAL PROBABILITY
The frequency theory

21

INTRODUCTION

Physical probabilities and frequencies

While degrees of belief and logical probabilities are both prima facie plausible candidates for an account of evidential probability—how likely some claim is, given a body of evidence—there are uses of 'probable' that they seem ill-suited to capture. These are the uses we normally interpret as physical or empirical probabilities, such as:

(1) a The probability that a fair coin lands heads when tossed is one-half.
     b The probability that this uranium-238 atom will decay in the next 4.468 billion years is one-half.

Neither of these claims seems to be a report of subjective beliefs. Nor do they appear to be dictated by the evidence available, in part because they are perfectly comprehensible despite the fact that no evidence is mentioned. They seem rather to report empirical facts about the coins or uranium atoms in question, and are made true, if true, by the physical properties of fair coins and uranium atoms. The kind of probability mentioned in (1) we might call *empirical* or *physical*—these are probabilities featuring in empirical science, which are not discoverable a priori and do not have to hold of necessity. This kind of probability has also commonly been called *chance*.[1]

It is intuitively plausible that empirical physical probabilities exist. Take the coin mentioned in (1a). If we are betting on it, we may regard it as fair, while simultaneously noting that devious bookmakers do exist and swindlers might use subtly biased coins. In that case someone, A, may reasonably say

(2) I think this coin is fair, but it might not be.

The natural interpretation of (2) is that the coin has a real physical probability of landing heads that A estimates to be one-half, given their evidence. A correspondingly sets their degree of belief to that value. But A also recognises that the probability of the coin landing heads might have a real value that differs from their estimate. In that case, the probability cannot be identified with A's estimate, or the degree of belief A bases on that estimate. Neither logical probability, nor purely degrees of belief, can readily explain this; the view that there are physical probabilities, which derive from genuine features of the coin in question, can easily explain why (2) is appropriate and true. (If reference to fairness were to be explicated in terms of credence, (2) would be rather like Moore's paradox; yet it does not have any air of paradox about it.)

If physical probabilities aren't credences, what are they? One thing we do know is that they are somehow connected with how frequently an outcome occurs—other things being equal, outcomes with higher physical probability tend to occur more frequently. So coins biased in favour of heads tend to land heads more often, indeed, they tend to land heads in a proportion of the tosses which is fairly close to the probability. In many cases, it is these statistics of this *relative frequency* of an outcome in a collection of trials which provides our strongest evidence for the value of the physical probability.

There are at least two important connections between frequency and physical probability, related to the principles of 'ascertainability' and 'applicability' offered by Salmon (1966: 64). Firstly, if physical probabilities are to be legitimate entities, we should at least have some way of determining their values. A notion of physical probability that made it unknowable what the values were, and similarly unknowable whether there was a probability at all, would be useless and redundant—it wouldn't help us understand the behaviour of coins and radioactive nuclei, for example. Observed frequencies do provide us with reasonably compelling evidence about the value of physical probabilities. This is particularly important given the significant role assigned to probabilities in scientific theories; the values of probabilities must be constrained by the empirical evidence if theories that involve probabilities are to be supported by that evidence. Secondly, probabilities should predict future frequencies. A conception of physical probability according to which there is no reasonable inference from probabilities to at least the frequency of future outcomes would also be useless. If we couldn't be confident that more probable events would occur more often than less probable events, it would be difficult to see how probability could meet Bishop Butler's famous aphorism that 'probability is the very guide of life'. That is, we should be able to reasonably infer frequencies from probabilities. These connections are close to being platitudinous about probabilities and frequencies (see Hájek, Chapter 24, p. 395).

These two connections can be seen at work in our original examples. (1b) involves the concept of 'half-life', which is usually defined as the expected time at which the number of undecayed atoms in a sample of an element becomes half the original number of atoms. One natural way to characterise this is: the half-life is that elapsed time t after which half of all the atoms that ever exist of that substance will have decayed. The individual trials are thus the decaying or otherwise of each atom in t seconds. Empirical observation of the half-life of many samples will give a guide to the correct value of t for the half-life of the entire population.[2] There are many further cases where physical probabilities are closely tied to frequencies in large populations of outcomes. One nice case is in theoretical population genetics, which is concerned primarily with the frequency of traits in a population and the evolution of such frequencies over time. In a population which reproduces by random mating, 'the probability of two genotypes forming a mating pair is therefore equal to the product of their respective genotype frequencies' (Hartl, 2000: 26). Here there is obviously a very close connection between frequencies in a population and the probability of particular outcomes. This is a special case of the close connection between frequencies and probabilities in statistics more generally: the proportions of individuals in a population with a given property does and should correspond closely to the probability of a given individual in that population having the property, at least if the population is sufficiently homogenous. The success of mathematical statistics, as a branch of applied probability theory, is strong evidence of a genuine connection between probabilities and frequencies.

Motivations for frequentism

We have just seen that any acceptable conception of physical probability should explain the reasonableness of inferences from frequencies to probabilities, *and* from probabilities to frequencies. The simplest explanation is that probabilities *are* frequencies. This is the proposal known as *frequentism* about physical probability.

There are many kinds of thing for which there is reliable evidence that such things exist; yet we aren't often tempted to identify those things with the evidence. Frequentism does seem to identify the theoretical entity with the evidence for it, and so something needs to be said about why frequentism is attractive, wedded as it is to this prima facie implausible identification.

One of the main motives for early frequentists was a kind of *operationalism* about scientific theories. Von Mises gives expression to something like operationalism when he says 'the sole purpose of a scientific theory is to provide a mental image of objectively observable phenomena' (Chapter 22, p. 372); that is, a scientific theory gives a systematic presentation of the observed results, but good science need not ensure that the theoretical (non-observational) claims of the theory are themselves accurate representations. Theoretical concepts, like 'probability' or 'mass', have value only as they are linked to some specific observational experimental procedure; and the meaning of theoretical terms is fixed by their empirical tests. Philosophically, operationalism made clear how theoretical concepts could be empirically grounded. This was appealing in the case of probability, because if probability is a kind of graded possibility, as Leibniz said, then the empirical difficulties of investigating the merely possible seemed as if they might carry over to probability. But with an empirically straightforward operational definition, these difficulties were sidestepped. Scientifically, too, it was thought that one of the main reasons for the success of Einstein's special theory of relativity was his giving an operational definition of distant simultaneity in terms of measuring rods and clocks (Einstein 1905).

Operationalism did not last long as a general philosophical picture of science. Since the measurement procedure defines the term, there is no sense to be made of improving the accuracy of a measurement (see Hájek, Chapter 24, Objection 6, p. 403), or two different measurement procedures being found to measure the same quantity; yet actual science routinely makes use of both notions. Even the most devout early adherents of operationalism among the logical empiricists abandoned the view as ultimately unable to account for the banal fact that incremental improvement in laboratory equipment and procedures doesn't alter the reference of theoretical terms. While it is undoubtedly true that operationalism motivated some frequentists, frequentism survived the demise of operationalism; for frequency theories met a felt need to find an empirically respectable understanding of probability, whether motivated by operationalism or not.

Given this, perhaps the most substantial motive for frequentism was simply the desire to ground probability in genuine occurrent features of reality, and not in mere possibility. If a particular coin toss lands tails, the probability it had to land heads then must be grounded in something other than the merely possible outcome of it landing heads—frequentism tells us that it is grounded in the relative frequency of heads in *all* coin tosses, a perfectly respectable property of a collection of actual events. Moreover, this is a view which reduces probability to a complex property of patterns of occurrent events, and, as often in philosophy, reduction appears to explain a previously puzzling notion.

In motivating this view, it might be useful to consider an analogy. In the metaphysics of time, *eternalism* is the view that present, past and future objects exist in some tenseless sense, while *presentism* is the view that only present objects exist in that sense. When accounting for the present truth of past-tensed claims, the presentist view runs into considerable difficulties. For what presently existing things make it true that 'Many times in the past, philosophers have been wrong'? We cannot rest with 'merely past' but non-existent philosophers. The eternalist has a straightforward answer: the present truth of that claim depends on the existence of a number of times earlier than the present, at each of which times exist philosophers who are wrong. The eternalist appeals to the existence of other times than the present one to account for this present truth. By contrast, presentists end up appealing to rather more puzzling presently existing entities—'ways things used to be'—to make these past tensed claims true. The eternalist provides a reductive explanation of tense; the presentist clearly makes use of a tensed primitive. The analogy with frequentism is this: in explaining the truth of (1a), the frequentist too must appeal to outcomes other than the one directly under discussion, and appeals to facts about all the relevant outcomes taken together. In doing so they can offer a clear reductive explanation of probability; rival views, it may be thought, end up adopting probability as a new conceptual primitive, with all the attendant concerns such a primitive carries with it. This argument is persuasive so far as it goes, though this case for frequentism rests largely on the unintelligibility of its rivals. It would be undermined by a successful alternative characterisation of single-case chance—if propensities or chances were to be successfully shown to exist, it would hardly be advantageous to avoid reference to them in the way that the frequentist proposes. We will look at such *propensity* theories in part VI.

The fundamental motivation for all forms of frequentism, then, is an empiricist philosophical outlook. There are many views that can rightfully claim the name 'empiricist'; the one I'm interested in is the view that all contingent claims must make a potential difference to the course of experience. This view can be most naturally motivated within a certain metaphysical picture, *Humeanism*: 'the thesis that the whole truth about a world like ours supervenes on the spatiotemporal distribution of local qualities' (Lewis 1994: 473). If this thesis holds, then every contingent claim holds in virtue of the arrangement of local properties, so that any two situations which differ in any fact will differ in some local properties. Supposing that empirical science can discover these local facts, every truth is (at least potentially) empirically discoverable. This picture is deeply attractive to many philosophers, and frequentism very easily accommodates probabilities within this picture, in a way that many of its serious rivals cannot. For, frequentists say, it is the distribution of outcomes across a collection of events which grounds the probability. Some support for this can be found in the fact that we naturally expect the probability of an outcome to manifest in the frequency of that outcome. If we were confronted with a situation in which we had observed a certain frequency, we would not entertain the arbitrary hypothesis that the probability was far from that frequency, and would instead infer that the probability was at least close to the observed frequency. So our natural inclination with respect to probability is to connect it closely to empirically respectable local properties, like frequencies; the frequency theory elevates this connection to the status of a constitutive tie, cementing the empirical respectability of probability in the process.

Finite actual frequentism

Different versions of frequentism cash out their empiricism in different ways. The simplest form of frequentism, and the one that sticks most closely to empiricism, is *finite actual frequentism*. Russell introduces the theory this way:

> Let *B* be any finite class, and *A* any other class. We want to define the chance that a member of *B* chosen at random will be a member of *A*, e.g., that the first person you meet in the street will be called Smith. We define this probability as the number of *B*'s that are *A*'s divided by the total number of *B*'s.
>
> (Russell 1948: 368)

So the probability of *A* is the ratio of *A*-cases to all cases. Or, as Venn put it, after a discussion of proportions of male and female births:

> The probability *is* nothing but that proportion, and is derived from the statistics alone.
>
> (Venn 1876: 381)

One can see how this picture might fit with the motivations for frequentism just mentioned. The frequencies are evident in the statistics, so are not some mysterious further facts that float free of the particular goings on in our world. The explanation for our easy inferences between probabilities and observed frequencies is clear: those things are identical, so the inferences are entirely trivial. It is easy to see how objective probability could play a significant role in science—frequencies are obviously features of extra-mental reality, and clearly have some value in giving systematic presentations of the pattern of particular occurrent fact.

Von Mises introduces a technical term which is useful here. The *collective*

> denotes a sequence of uniform events or processes which differ by certain observable attributes, say colours, numbers, or anything else. ... All the throws of dice made in the course of a game form a collective wherein the attribute of the single event is the number of points thrown. Again, all the molecules in a given volume of gas may be considered as a collective, and the attribute of a single molecule might be its velocity. A further example of a collective is the whole class of insured men and women whose ages at death have been registered by an insurance office. The principle which underlies the whole of our treatment of the probability problem is that a collective must exist before we begin to speak of probability. The definition of probability which we shall give is only concerned with 'the probability of encountering a certain attribute in a given collective'. (p. 357)

In Venn's discussion, the set of all human births forms the collective against which the probability of male and female births is constituted by the proportion of the collective which satisfies each of those attributes. Von Mises is insistent that probability theory cannot sensibly be applied without the collective; he takes probability theory just to be the science of mass repetitive phenomena. So here we may indeed have another motivation for frequentism: empirical probability theory is the science of the properties of mass phenomena; probability theory thus applies only in cases where we do have a large class of similar events; in all such cases the probability exists and is close to the frequency value we observe in those parts of the collective we have observed. What else could the probability be but the frequency in the collective as a whole? Von Mises himself would reject this argument; the probability is not for him a directly observed property of a given empirical collective. But, for the finite frequentist, the physical probability of some outcome just is the proportion of elements of a given collective with that outcome.

Despite the attractive simplicity of the finite frequentist view, there are many difficulties with it. Hájek, in Chapter 24, provides a useful summary of these difficulties. He raises objections to all kinds of frequentism, but a particular focus is specifically on how a finite collective can misrepresent the probabilities, giving probabilities in various straightforward cases intuitively inappropriate values: undefined (Objection 8), trivial (Objection 9), biased (Objection 12) or restricted to rational numbers (Objection 14). Resulting from these misrepresentations are other problems, of spurious dependencies and correlations (Objection 13). These objections have particular force against finite frequentism and its identification of probability with frequency in a finite collective.

A second kind of objection is connected with explanation. Why do we see the frequencies we do? The natural answer: because the probabilities, in line with the laws of large numbers, lead to those frequencies. But, as Hájek observes, drawing on Armstrong's (1983) objection to regularity theories of laws, 'there is no explaining to be done if chance just *is* actual relative frequency: you can't explain something by reference to itself' (Objection 7, page 403). Of course, just as sophisticated regularity theories of law reject Armstrong's objection, so a sophisticated frequentism might be able to reject Hájek's; but it's not obvious that the kind of flat-footed denial of the need for explanation that an actual frequentist must offer will satisfy the objection.

These objections to finite frequentism arise because it seems that—for purely contingent and accidental reasons—the process which we expect to produce a certain stable frequency does not do so. If a symmetrical and unbiased coin is only tossed once, it seems that it is the paucity of tosses which prevents the right frequencies from appearing, and nothing to do with the probability. We are inclined to think: if only the coin had been tossed more times, then we would have seen the right frequency emerging. Or, as von Mises puts it (p. 356), the cases to which probability applies always in fact seem to be 'mass phenomena or repetitive events. The throwing of a pair of dice is an event which can theoretically be repeated an unlimited number of times ...' And when the event is repeated an unlimited number of times, 'for a sufficiently long time under conditions which do not change (insofar as this is practically possible), one would arrive at constant values' for the frequency (p. 359). Moreover, notice that this thought also opens a potential line of reply to the second kind of objection, for the fact that, if the event were repeated an unlimited number of times, we should expect to see a certain frequency, does seem as if it could explain why we do see an actual frequency close to that 'ideal' frequency. So abandoning these contingent limitations of the actual trials, and moving to an idealised—*hypothetical*—collective, may provide a better version of frequentism.

Hypothetical frequentism

The most sophisticated versions of frequentism, those of Reichenbach (1949) and von Mises, both identify probability with frequency in this kind of idealised hypothetical collective. Von Mises is explicit:

> We will say that a collective is a mass phenomenon or a repetitive event, or, simply, a long sequence of observations for which there are sufficient reasons to believe that the relative frequency of the observed attribute would tend to a fixed limit if the observations were indefinitely continued. This limit will be called *the probability of the attribute considered within the given collective.* (p. 360)

A finite collection of actual events is important only insofar as it provides reasons to believe that there is a suitable idealised collective to be obtained; the probability is not the actual frequency, but what the frequency *would be* if the collective were indefinitely continued. The empirical fact is that in most sequences of outcomes of chancy trials the frequency does, provided things are left to go on long enough, converge to the neighbourhood of some stable value. Left to go on indefinitely, the frequency would converge to a particular limiting value in the ideal collective, and this limit frequency would be the probability shorn of any contingency having to do with the actual number of trials. Adverting to what would happen in this way potentially overcomes the problems with actual frequentism.

The main objection people have raised to this part of von Mises' project is that this hypothetical collective doesn't have a sufficiently determinate character to permit it to have a well-defined frequency. To begin with, there doesn't seem to be a fact of the matter about how each individual toss would come out. As Jeffrey says,

> unless the coin has two heads or two tails (or the process is otherwise rigged), there is no telling whether the coin would have landed head up on a toss that never takes place. That's what probability is all about.
>
> A coin is tossed 20 times in its entire career. Would it have landed head up if it had been tossed once more? We tend to feel that there must be a truth of the matter, which could have been ascertained by performing a simple physical experiment, viz., toss the coin once more and see how it lands.
>
> (Jeffrey, Chapter 23, p. 389)

However, as Hájek points out when discussing his version of the same objection (Chapter 25, Argument 3, pp. 415–6), the hypothetical frequentist does have a response to this objection. There may be no fact of the matter about how each individual toss in the idealised collective would come out, but there is a fact of the matter about how the whole collective would look—it would consist of half heads and half tails. Since the frequentist only needs the limit frequency in the collective to be well defined, it doesn't matter that the individual tosses don't have determinate outcomes.

But this response is problematic, as Hájek goes on to argue. Why are we sure that the coin would land heads half the time? If we already had the probability, we could appeal to the law of large numbers (Primer, Theorem 19), which assures us (near enough)

345

that the frequency will be close to the probability. But, as Hájek points out (Chapter 25, pp. 420–1), it is not clear that the frequentist can or should help themselves to the law of large numbers here. We can add to what Hájek says. What is at issue here is precisely whether a coin will land heads half the time—we cannot assume that it will, giving us the probability p needed for the law of large numbers, and then establish on that basis that we should expect it to land heads half the time!

The point can be put another way, using the same example. On each toss, heads has some probability of occurring, so heads *might* occur on that toss; and if heads might occur on each toss, it might occur on *every* toss, because the tosses are causally independent of one another. But in that case an infinite sequence of heads might occur, seemingly undermining von Mises' claim that the infinite collective that would occur is one in which the limit frequency of heads is 1/2. For it can't be true both that the coin would land heads half the time if tossed infinitely, while also, if it had been tossed infinitely, it might have landed all heads. (Compare Hájek's Objection 6, Chapter 25, p. 410).

The hypothetical frequentist has a number of responses to this kind of objection. They could deny that the 'would' and 'might' counterfactual claims are inconsistent. This is a radical response; moreover, the usual way of implementing it to make the 'might' claim come out true involves the epistemic possibility of this counterfactual 'if the coin had been tossed infinitely, it would have landed all heads'. But the frequentist does not want to admit *that* as an epistemic possibility, at the risk of undermining our knowledge of probability claims—recalling that it was the possibility of giving empirical content to probability that was supposed to be an advantage for frequentism.

A second response would be to reject the move from 'heads might occur on each toss' to 'heads might occur on every toss'. The frequentist maintains that what gives the individual outcomes in the collective the probabilities they have is the frequency in the entire collective. Given this, it is not possible to keep the individual probabilities fixed while varying the overall outcome frequency. The probability really is just a disguised fact about the whole collective. As von Mises says of the single case chance of a given individual dying,

> We must not think of an individual, but of a certain class as a whole, e.g., 'all insured men forty-one years old living in a given country and not engaged in certain dangerous occupations'. A probability of death is attached to this class of men or to another class that can be defined in a similar way. We can say nothing about the probability of death of an individual even if we know his condition of life and health in detail. The phrase 'probability of death', when it refers to a single person, has no meaning at all for us. (p. 357)

So, for von Mises and other frequentists, all apparently singular chance ascriptions are in fact disguised references to a chance against the background of a collective. The tosses might be causally independent of each other, but the probability of a particular outcome is not counterfactually independent of the other outcomes in the collective, being in large part a fact about those other outcomes.

As Hájek emphasises, this response violates two very plausible principles about physical probability. One is that probability is an intrinsic feature of the particular chance trial:

The chance that this coin lands heads now does not depend on how the coin will land in the future—as it were, the coin doesn't have to 'wait and see' what it happens to do in the future in order to have a certain chance of landing heads now.

(Hájek, Chapter 24, p. 400)

Schaffer (2007: 125) calls this the 'Intrinsicness requirement', that duplicate trials have the same outcome chances. But making probability relative to a collective, as von Mises does, makes probability not intrinsic—what the chances are depends on which collective the event is part of, as well as how it intrinsically is. Of course, many probabilities attach to non-independent trials, in Markov processes, sampling without replacement, and so on. Here the intrinsicness requirement is too strong, neglecting as it does the context of the trial. But there is no succour for frequentism here (Chapter 25, Objection 12), as the paradigm for frequentism is those cases we would normally model as i.i.d. trials, in which the intrinsicness requirement does hold.

Making probability depend on a collective also undermines our apparently reasonable application of probability to essentially unrepeatable events:

Many experiments are most naturally regarded as being unrepeatable—a football game, a horse race, a presidential election, a war, a death, certain chancy events in the very early history of the universe. Nonetheless, it seems natural to think of non-extreme probabilities attaching to some of them.

(Hájek, Chapter 24, p. 404; see also Chapter 25, Argument 10)

If the frequentist cannot explain our ordinary use of objective probabilities attaching to unrepeated and unrepeatable events, so much the worse for frequentism.

The focus in this section has been on whether the idealised hypothetical collectives required by hypothetical frequentism exist with the right limiting frequencies. Hájek in Chapter 25 collects many other difficulties for these idealised collectives. In Part VI, especially in Popper's Chapter 28, we will see how the desire to give a more satisfactory answer to the question of what ensures the right limiting frequency would occur leads to the development of a quite different theory of probability, the propensity view.

Randomness

Though I have treated the collective above as simply an ordered collection of events of a certain homogenous kind in which a limit relative frequency exists, von Mises—though not Reichenbach—imposed an additional constraint for an idealised infinite collection to be a collective. This is because some such collections do not seem appropriately discussed in probabilistic terms.

Examples can easily be found where the relative frequencies converge towards definite limiting values, and where it is nevertheless not appropriate to speak of probability. Imagine, for instance, a road along which milestones are placed, large ones for whole miles and smaller ones for tenths of a mile. If we walk long enough along this road, calculating the relative frequencies of large stones, the value found in this way will lie around 1/10. The value will be exactly 0.1 whenever in each mile we are in that interval between two small milestones which corresponds to the one in which we started. The deviations from the value 0.1 will become smaller and smaller as the number of stones passed increases; in other words, the relative frequency tends towards the limiting value 0.1.

(Chapter 22, p. 365)

What is wrong with these apparent collectives? Von Mises argues that the frequencies are too regular to be properly part of the domain of probability theory, and imposes the further requirement that a true collective will be *random*. But what does it mean for a collective, a sequence of outcomes, to be random? One thing randomness is said commonly to involve is chanciness, but that is clearly no help as we are trying to define chance using randomness.

It was an old observation due to Laplace (1951) that, when tossing a coin, 'if heads comes up a hundred times in a row, then this appears to us extraordinary, because the almost infinite number of combinations that can arise in a hundred throws are divided into regular sequences, or those in which we observe a rule that is easy to grasp, and in irregular sequences, that are incomparably more numerous'. Modern theories of randomness take up two themes from Laplace—first, that random sequences are not governed by a simple rule; second, that random sequences are more numerous than non-random ones. There is a very considerable literature in *algorithmic randomness* devoted to spelling out these consequences. Following this literature, we will restrict our attention to binary sequences of outcomes, like sequences of outcomes of tosses of a fair coin.

Von Mises offers a characterisation of random sequences as those which are invariant under 'admissible place selections':

> these limiting values must remain the same in all partial sequences which may be selected from the original one in an arbitrary way. Of course, only such partial sequences can be taken into consideration as can be extended indefi-nitely, in the same way as the original sequence itself. Examples of this kind are, for instance, the partial sequences formed by all odd members of the orig-inal sequence, or by all members for which the place number in the sequence is the square of an integer, or a prime number, or a number selected accord-ing to some other rule, whatever it may be. The only essential condition is that the question whether or not a certain member of the original sequence belongs to the selected partial sequence should be settled independently of the result of the corresponding observation, i.e., before anything is known about this result. We shall call a selection of this kind a place selection. The limiting values of the relative frequencies in a collective must be independent of all possible place selections. By place selection we mean the selection of a partial sequence in such a way that we decide whether an element should or should not be included without making use of the attribute of the element, i.e., the result of our game of chance. (p. 366)

The notion of a place selection was not fixed by von Mises, who was inclined to allow the context of an experiment to fix which place selections were available to decide the applicability of probability theory. But too liberal a conception of place selections would trivialise the notion, as a completely 'arbitrary' place selection can always be found that selects just the heads in a random sequence of coin tosses. While place selections on infinite sequences are idealised, they correspond to an empirical phenomenon (just as the existence of a limit frequency in a hypothetical collective corresponds to the empirical phenomenon of increasingly stable frequencies as the number of actual outcomes increases). Von Mises notes that every system we actually think it appropriate to discuss probabilistically is not open to exploitation by a *gambling system*—a recipe for deciding when to bet on an outcome that ensures more successes than chance alone. (The 'gambler's fallacy' involves believing that a simple gambling system—bet on an outcome after a run of failures of that outcome, in the belief that it is 'due'—will do better than chance. von Mises' point is that all other gambling systems are equally unsuccessful, and that it would be equally fallacious to adopt them in the hope of beating chance.) To connect with the theme of Laplace, any simple rule governing a sequence would permit a gambling system. The fact that a gambling system is a recipe was an insight that allowed the first formal characterisation of place selections by Church:

> To a player who would beat the wheel at roulette a system is unusable which corresponds to a mathematical function known to exist but not given by explicit definition; and even the explicit definition is of no use unless it provides a means of calculating the particular values of the function. ... Thus a [gambling system] should be represented mathematically, not as a function, or even as a definition of a function, but as an effective algorithm for the calculation of the values of a function.
>
> (Church 1940: 133)

Where x is some infinite sequence, and x_i is the ith element of x, a place selection is any effectively computable function $\phi: (x_1, ..., x_{n-1}, n) \mapsto \{0, 1\}$ that takes the value 1 infinitely many times. A place selection chooses an index n based on the sequence elements at prior indices and the value of n, but, crucially, it does so in an effectively computable way. This captures von Mises' intent, since any place selection which will undermine a probabilistic description of some sequence (i.e., by permitting more effective description or prediction of the sequence) will at the very least have to correspond to a function we could compute and use to describe the sequence. By slight abuse of notation, let $\phi(x)$ be the infinite sequence consisting of all x_i such that i is a chosen index. According to von Mises, a sequence is random iff for every place selection ϕ, the limiting frequency of every outcome in $\phi(x)$ equals the limiting frequency of that outcome in x. More informally: a sequence is random iff there exists no effective method for choosing a subsequence of a random sequence that is biased with respect to the original frequencies.

The empirically demonstrated nonexistence of gambling systems assures us that there are actual systems that should be counted as random and appropriate to describe probabilistically. Similarly, Church observes that there are many infinite random sequences in the von Mises/Church sense; indeed, almost all infinite binary sequences have the feature of being frequency-invariant under place selections. This links up with the other theme from Laplace, because the von Mises/Church random sequences are much more numerous than the regular sequences.

While von Mises' condition of invariance under effective place selections is necessary for randomness, it is not now believed to be sufficient. Ville showed there are examples of sequences which are invariant and yet which have biased initial segments, so that while the limit frequency in the sequence and all infinite subsequences is 1/2, the limit is approached 'from above'—the frequency in every finite initial subsequence is > 1/2. This is a problem for von Mises' account of randomness, because it is thought that truly random sequences should also be random in how they approach the limit: the frequency in initial subsequences should be above 1/2 as much as it is below 1/2.

The obvious fix is to impose this 'symmetry' condition as an additional effectively determinable constraint on random sequences. And indeed it can be shown that almost all binary sequences also meet this symmetry condition, and almost all binary sequences meet both the symmetry condition *and* invariance under place selections. But, in fact, the next move in the debate was a spectacular generalisation of this fix. Rather than add additional intuitive randomness properties piecemeal to constrain the set of randomness sequences, Martin-Löf (1966) proposed to add *all* effectively determinable properties that almost all sequences have. Martin-Löf's proposal, in effect, was to suggest that the regular non-random sequences all exhibit some effectively determinable special mark, and to define the random sequences as those which exhibit no such mark. It turns out that almost all infinite binary sequences are irregular in Martin-Löf's sense, providing dramatic vindication of Laplace's intuition that random sequences should be both non-rule-governed and numerous in comparison to the rule-governed sequences.

The obvious problem with all this as an account of randomness more generally is that it does not apply to finite sequences. It would greatly bolster the hypothetical frequentist's position if there were some characterisation of randomness of the finite collectives we are actually presented with, so that an infinite collective would be the appropriate idealisation. As Jeffrey discusses in Chapter 23, the most popular approach to finite randomness is the *incompressibility* approach pioneered by Kolmogorov:

> a string of 1000000 1's is compressible, for the rule 'Write 1000000 ones' would be only some 100 binary digits long if letters, digits, and spaces were coded in some fairly simple way as blocks of binary digits. In detail, questions of compressibility are relative to (1) choice of one out of the infinity of universal systems of algorithms or programming schemes for generating binary sequences, and to (2) choice of one out of the infinity of measures of complexity of algorithms belonging to the same universal system – let us say, via length of representation in one of the infinity of effective binary coding schemes. Once these choices have been made, we have the means to define the *irregular* ('random') finite sequences as those *about as long as the shortest binary coded algorithms that generate them*. If we define the *algorithmic complexity* of a finite binary sequence as *the length of the shortest binary coded algorithms that generate it*, then the irregular sequences are those whose lengths are approximately equal to their algorithmic complexities. (p. 390)

Kolmogorov showed that this approach could be made robust, for he showed that, even though different codings compress different sequences by different amounts, there exists a universal coding that was approximately as good as every other coding, and this universal coding can be used to define a general notion of complexity of a string. For any coding, including the universal one, it is clear that very few binary strings can be usefully compressed. If the compression required is k (so if the original string has length l, the compressed description of the string has length $l - k$), then because there are only 2^{l-k}

strings of that length, at most $2^{l-k}/2^l = 1/2^k$ strings will compress. (Because we want to be able to unambiguously decode strings, there can be at most as many compressible strings as there are short descriptions.) Even if we adopt the most pitiful amount of compression, $k = 1$, only 1/2 of strings compress by even that much. As we increase k to useful values, we see that the incompressible—random—sequences come to be the vast majority of all sequences, once again conforming to Laplace's constraint. Moreover, since conforming to an effective rule permits a brief way of describing a sequence, the Kolmogorov random sequences will also not be governed by simple rules. As such, Kolmogorov randomness also supports von Mises' intuitions about randomness being linked to the impossibility of gambling systems, as there will be no way of effectively producing a given random sequence of outcomes using a set of initially given data any smaller than the sequence itself.

This agreement between Kolmogorov complexity and the Laplacean intuitions that also underlie the von Mises' and Martin-Löf's approaches to randomness is borne out by a theorem, due to Schnorr (1971), which shows that (modulo some mathematical subtleties in the formulation of Kolmogorov complexity) the Martin-Löf random sequences are exactly those, all of whose finite initial subsequences are Kolmogorov random. The convergence of these two quite different mathematical accounts of randomness on the same set of infinite sequences is some evidence that there is a robust notion here to be captured.

The development of the theory of algorithmic randomness briefly sketched here has gone far beyond the original use to which von Mises intended to put the notion, and has come to have an independent importance far outstripping the importance of frequentism in the philosophy of probability (one reason why I have covered it at length). In this, as in other topics, frequentism has been a rich source of suggestive and interesting ideas about probability. We shouldn't let the largely negative verdict on frequentism as an account of probability blind us to the intuitively compelling ideas that physical probability should be grounded in occurrent facts and be close in value to the frequency. While frequentism may have tried to make the connection too close, arguably some of the views of physical probability we encounter in the next part make the connection too loose. This opens the way to the sophisticated Humean account of chance offered by Lewis (and discussed by Loewer in Chapter 31), which goes beyond frequentism in many ways but is inspired by the same broad philosophical concerns.

Further reading

See the references at the end of Chapter 1, and the argument in Skyrms' paper (Chapter 32), for the view that degrees of belief can explain all apparent reference to physical probabilities. A general discussion of 'objective probability' (where that means physical probability), in frequentist and propensity versions, is Eells 1983; his discussion of frequentism is concentrated in sections 3–5.

Operationalism as a philosophy of science is related to logical positivism's verification principle, but its main defender was Bridgman (1927). Both the positivists and the operationalists took Einstein's 1905 discussion to be the ideal model for scientific definition, but Einstein's own views were more complicated, as Dieks (2010) makes clear. A helpful critique of operationalism is Gillies (1972). The literature on presentism and eternalism is extensive; a useful introduction and defence of an eternalist view is

Sider (2001: Ch. 2), while a presentist view that appeals to present traces of past events is defended by Bigelow (1996).

Humean motivations, for frequentism and other views in metaphysics, are widely defended. For the most influential contemporary version of Humeanism, see the Introduction to Lewis (1986), where Lewis introduces and sketches the doctrine of *Humean Supervenience*. It is further developed by Loewer (1996). The view is even more widely criticised: some particularly interesting attacks come from quantum mechanics (Maudlin 2007) and from the apparent possibility of rotating homogeneous discs, noted by Kripke and Armstrong (see Robinson (1989) and Callender (2001) for discussion).

The duality of 'would' and 'might' counterfactuals is defended by Lewis (1973), and criticised, with references to the literature, in DeRose (1999). The argument that the positive probability of some outcome undermines the claim that the outcome would not happen under the relevant circumstances is deployed in Hawthorne (2005); Williams (2008) offers a response to Hawthorne.

The literature on algorithmic randomness is vast and technical; useful surveys include those by Dasgupta (forthcoming), Earman (1986: Ch. VIII) and Downey and Hirschfeldt (2010). An account of the relationship between chance and randomness is Eagle (2010). Ville's counterexample to von Mises' account of randomness is discussed in van Lambalgen (1987), which also discusses the relationship between von Mises' and Martin-Löf's definitions of random sequences. The Kolmogorov complexity approach to randomness and incompressibility is thoroughly covered by Li and Vitanyi (1997); Chaitin (1975) gives an accessible presentation, and Smith (1998: Ch. 9) offers useful philosophical discussion. A view of randomness more inspired by randomness in science than in the mathematics of sequences, and so at odds with much of the literature on algorithmic randomness, is Eagle (2005).

A defence of frequentism from a Bayesian perspective is Howson (2000: Ch. 9).

Notes

1 None of this terminology is perfect. Often this is called 'objective' probability, and is contrasted with 'subjective' degrees of belief; but of course this distinction neglects logical probabilities. 'Chance' has often been reserved for single-case propensities, like those discussed in Part VI, rather than all physical probabilities. 'Empirical' suggests a particular epistemology of chance, empiricism, which tends to suggest frequencies rather more than more theoretical and less directly observable chances. And 'physical' tends to suggest that these probabilities are found only in physics; yet these probabilities are found throughout the sciences, including the social and behavioural sciences. It is hoped that by supplying many terms, the desired concept is readily triangulated.

2 This of course is a slightly unusual example, since we characterise the kind of trial in this case in order to obtain a certain frequency; in other cases we could set up a natural trial—e.g., the trial of an atom of Uranium-238 decaying in a minute—and then empirically determine the frequency.

Bibliography

Armstrong, D. M. (1983), *What is a Law of Nature?* Cambridge: Cambridge University Press.
Bigelow, John (1996), 'Presentism and Properties'. *Philosophical Perspectives*, vol. 10: pp. 35–52.
Bridgman, P. W. (1927), *The Logic of Modern Physics*. New York: Macmillan.
Callender, Craig (2001), 'Humean Supervenience and Rotating Homogeneous Matter'. *Mind*, vol. 110: pp. 25–43.

Chaitin, Gregory (1975), 'Randomness and Mathematical Proof'. *Scientific American*, vol. 232: pp. 47–52.

Church, Alonzo (1940), 'On the Concept of a Random Sequence'. *Bulletin of the American Mathematical Society*, vol. 46: pp. 130–135.

Dasgupta, Abhijit (forthcoming), 'Randomness Defined'. In Prasanta Bandyopadhyay and Malcolm Forster (eds.), *Handbook of the Philosophy of Science, vol. 7: Philosophy of Statistics*, Amsterdam: Elsevier.

DeRose, Keith (1999), 'Can it Be that it Would have Been even though it Might Not have Been?' *Philosophical Perspectives*, vol. 13: pp. 385–413.

Dieks, Dennis (2010), 'The Adolescence of Relativity: Einstein, Minkowski, and the Philosophy of Space and Time'. In Vesselin Petkov (ed.), *Minkowski Spacetime: a Hundred Years Later*, New York: Springer, pp. 225–245.

Downey, Rod and Hirschfeldt, Denis R. (2010), *Algorithmic Randomness and Complexity*. Berlin: Springer, URL https://www.mcs.vuw.ac.nz/~downey/randomness.pdf.

Eagle, Antony (2005), 'Randomness is Unpredictability'. *British Journal for the Philosophy of Science*, vol. 56: pp. 749–790.

—— (2010), 'Chance versus Randomness'. In Edward N. Zalta (ed.), *The Stanford Encyclopedia of Philosophy* (Fall 2010 Edition) http://plato.stanford.edu/archives/fall2010/entries/chance-randomness/.

Earman, John (1986), *A Primer on Determinism*. Dordrecht: D. Reidel.

Eells, Ellery (1983), 'Objective Probability Theory'. *Synthese*, vol. 57: pp. 387–442.

Einstein, Albert (1905), 'Zur Elektrodynamik bewegter Körper'. *Annalen der Physik*, vol. 17: pp. 891–921. English translation, 'On the Electrodynamics of Moving Bodies', available at http://www.csua.berkeley.edu/~ranga/papers/17_ADP_891/SR-en.pdf.

Gillies, Donald A. (1972), 'Operationalism'. *Synthese*, vol. 25: pp. 1–24.

Hartl, Daniel L. (2000), *A Primer of Population Genetics*. Cumberland, MA: Sinauer, 3 ed.

Hawthorne, John (2005), 'Chance and Counterfactuals'. *Philosophy and Phenomenological Research*, vol. LXX: pp. 396–405.

Howson, Colin (2000), *Hume's Problem: Induction and the Justification of Belief*. Oxford: Oxford University Press.

Laplace, Pierre-Simon (1951), *Philosophical Essay on Probabilities*. New York: Dover.

Lewis, David (1973), *Counterfactuals*. Oxford: Blackwell.

—— (1986), *Philosophical Papers*, vol. 2. Oxford: Oxford University Press.

—— (1994), 'Humean Supervenience Debugged'. *Mind*, vol. 103: pp. 473–490.

Li, Ming and Vitanyi, Paul M. B. (1997), *An Introduction to Kolmogorov Complexity and its Applications*. Berlin and New York: Springer Verlag, 2 ed.

Loewer, Barry (1996), 'Humean Supervenience'. *Philosophical Topics*, vol. 24: pp. 101–127.

Martin-Löf, Per (1966), 'The Definition of a Random Sequence'. *Information and Control*, vol. 9: pp. 602–619.

Maudlin, Tim (2007), 'Why be Humean?' In *The Metaphysics Within Physics*, Oxford: Oxford University Press, pp. 50–77.

Reichenbach, Hans (1949), *The Theory of Probability*. Berkeley: University of California Press.

Robinson, Denis (1989), 'Matter, Motion, and Humean Supervenience'. *Australasian Journal of Philosophy*, vol. 67: pp. 394–409.

Russell, Bertrand (1948), *Human Knowledge: Its Scope and Limits*. London: George Allen Unwin.

Salmon, Wesley C. (1966), *The Foundations of Scientific Inference*. Pittsburgh: University of Pittsburgh Press.

Schaffer, Jonathan (2007), 'Deterministic Chance?'. *British Journal for the Philosophy of Science*, vol. 58: pp. 113–140.

Schnorr, C. P. (1971), 'A unified approach to the definition of random sequences'. *Theory of Computing Systems*, vol. 5: pp. 246–258.

Sider, Theodore (2001), *Four-Dimensionalism: An Ontology of Persistence and Time*. Oxford: Oxford University Press.

Smith, Peter (1998), *Explaining Chaos*. Cambridge: Cambridge University Press.

van Lambalgen, Michiel (1987), 'Von Mises' Definition of Random Sequences Revisited'. *Journal of Symbolic Logic*, vol. 52: pp. 725–755.

Venn, John (1876), *The Logic of Chance*. London: Macmillan. 2 ed.

Williams, J. R. G. (2008), 'Chances, Counterfactuals, and Similarity'. *Philosophy and Phenomenological Research*, vol. 77: pp. 385–420.

22

THE DEFINITION OF PROBABILITY*

Richard von Mises

Limitation of scope

We now come to the description of our concept of probability. It follows from our previous remarks that our first task must be one of elimination. From the complex of ideas which are colloquially covered by the word 'probability', we must remove all those that remain outside the theory we are endeavouring to formulate. I shall therefore begin with a preliminary delimitation of our concept of probability; this will be developed into a more precise definition during the course of our discussion.

Our probability theory has nothing to do with questions such as: 'Is there a probability of Germany being at some time in the future involved in a war with Liberia?' Again, the question of the 'probability' of the correct interpretation of a certain passage from the *Annals* of Tacitus has nothing in common with our theory. It need hardly be pointed out that we are likewise unconcerned with the 'intrinsic probability' of a work of art. The relation of our theory to Goethe's superb dialogue on *Truth and Probability in Fine Art*[1] is thus only one of similarity in the sounds of words and consequently is irrelevant. We shall not deal with the problem of the historical accuracy of Biblical narratives, although it is interesting to note that a Russian mathematician, A. Markoff,[2] inspired by the ideas of the eighteenth-century Enlightenment, wished to see the theory of probability applied to this subject. Similarly, we shall not concern ourselves with any of those problems of the moral sciences which were so ingeniously treated by Laplace[3] in his *Essai Philosophique*. The unlimited extension of the validity of the exact sciences was a characteristic feature of the exaggerated rationalism of the eighteenth century. We do not intend to commit the same mistake.

Problems such as the probable reliability of witnesses and the correctness of judicial verdicts lie more or less on the boundary of the region which we are going to include in our treatment. These problems have been the subject of many scientific discussions; Poisson[4] chose them as the title of his famous book.

To reach the essence of the problems of probability which do form the subject-matter of this book, we must consider, for example, the probability of winning in a carefully defined game of chance. Is it sensible to bet that a 'double 6' will appear at least once if two dice are thrown twenty-four times? Is this result 'probable'? More exactly, how great is its probability? Such are the questions we feel able to answer. Many problems of considerable importance in everyday life belong to the same class and can be treated in the same way; examples of these are many problems connected with insurance, such

355

as those concerning the probability of illness or death occurring under carefully specified conditions, the premium which must be asked for insurance against a particular kind of risk, and so forth.

Besides the games of chance and certain problems relating to social mass phenomena, there is a third field in which our concept has a useful application. This is in the treatment of certain mechanical and physical phenomena. Typical examples may be seen in the movement of molecules in a gas or in the random motion of colloidal particles which can be observed with the ultramicroscope. ('Colloid' is the name given to a system of very fine particles freely suspended in a medium, with the size of the particles so minute that the whole appears to the naked eye to be a homogeneous liquid.)

Unlimited repetition

What is the common feature in the last three examples and what is the essential distinction between the meaning of 'probability' in these cases and its meaning in the earlier examples which we have excluded from our treatment? One common feature can be recognized easily, and we think it crucial. In games of chance, in the problems of insurance, and in the molecular processes we find events repeating themselves again and again. They are mass phenomena or repetitive events. The throwing of a pair of dice is an event which can theoretically be repeated an unlimited number of times, for we do not take into account the wear of the box or the possibility that the dice may break. If we are dealing with a typical problem of insurance, we can imagine a great army of individuals insuring themselves against the same risk, and the repeated occurrence of events of a similar kind (e.g., deaths) are registered in the records of insurance companies. In the third case, that of the molecules or colloidal particles, the immense number of particles partaking in each process is a fundamental feature of the whole conception.

On the other hand, this unlimited repetition, this 'mass character', is typically absent in the case of all the examples previously excluded. The implication of Germany in a war with the Republic of Liberia is not a situation which frequently repeats itself; the uncertainties that occur in the transcription of ancient authors are, in general, of a too individual character for them to be treated as mass phenomena. The question of the trustworthiness of the historical narratives of the Bible is clearly unique and cannot be considered as a link in a chain of analogous problems. We classified the reliability and trustworthiness of witnesses and judges as a borderline case since we may feel reasonable doubt whether similar situations occur sufficiently frequently and uniformly for them to be considered as repetitive phenomena.

We state here explicitly: The rational concept of probability, which is the only basis of probability calculus, applies only to problems in which either the same event repeats itself again and again, or a great number of uniform elements are involved at the same time. Using the language of physics, we may say that in order to apply the theory of probability we must have a practically unlimited sequence of uniform observations.

The collective

A good example of a mass phenomenon suitable for the application of the theory of probability is the inheritance of certain characteristics, e.g., the colour of flowers resulting from the cultivation of large numbers of plants of a given species from a given seed.

Here we can easily recognize what is meant by the words 'a repetitive event'. There is primarily a single instance: the growing of one plant and the observation of the colour of its flowers. Then comes the comprehensive treatment of a great number of such instances, considered as parts of one greater unity. The individual elements belonging to this unity differ from each other only with respect to a single attribute, the colour of the flowers.

In games of dice, the individual event is a single throw of the dice from the box and the attribute is the observation of the number of points shown by the dice. In the game 'heads or tails', each toss of the coin is an individual event, and the side of the coin which is uppermost is the attribute. In life insurance the single event is the life of the individual and the attribute observed is either the age at which the individual dies or, more generally, the moment at which the insurance company becomes liable for payment. When we speak of 'the probability of death', the exact meaning of this expression can be defined in the following way only. We must not think of an individual, but of a certain class as a whole, e.g., 'all insured men forty-one years old living in a given country and not engaged in certain dangerous occupations'. A probability of death is attached to this class of men or to another class that can be defined in a similar way. We can say nothing about the probability of death of an individual even if we know his condition of life and health in detail. The phrase 'probability of death', when it refers to a single person, has no meaning at all for us. This is one of the most important consequences of our definition of probability and we shall discuss this point in greater detail later on.

We must now introduce a new term, which will be very useful during the future course of our argument. This term is 'the collective', and it denotes a sequence of uniform events or processes which differ by certain observable attributes, say colours, numbers, or anything else. In a preliminary way we state: All the peas grown by a botanist concerned with the problem of heredity may be considered as a collective, the attributes in which we are interested being the different colours of the flowers. All the throws of dice made in the course of a game form a collective wherein the attribute of the single event is the number of points thrown. Again, all the molecules in a given volume of gas may be considered as a collective, and the attribute of a single molecule might be its velocity. A further example of a collective is the whole class of insured men and women whose ages at death have been registered by an insurance office. The principle which underlies the whole of our treatment of the probability problem is that a collective must exist before we begin to speak of probability. The definition of probability which we shall give is only concerned with 'the probability of encountering a certain attribute in a given collective'.

The first step towards a definition

After our previous discussion it should not be difficult to arrive at a rough form of definition of probability. We may consider a game with two dice. The attribute of a single throw is the sum of the points showing on the upper sides of the two dice. What shall we call the probability of the attribute '12', i.e., the case of each die showing six points? When we have thrown the dice a large number of times, say 200, and noted the results, we find that 12 has appeared a certain number of times, perhaps five times. The ratio $5/200 = 1/40$ is called the frequency, or more accurately the relative frequency, of the attribute '12' in the first 200 throws. If we continue the game for another

200 throws, we can find the corresponding relative frequency for 400 throws, and so on. The ratios which are obtained in this way will differ a little from the first one, 1/40. If the ratios were to continue to show considerable variation after the game had been repeated 2,000, 4,000, or a still larger number of times, then the question whether there is a definite probability of the result '12' would not arise at all. It is essential for the theory of probability that experience has shown that in the game of dice, as in all the other mass phenomena which we have mentioned, the relative frequencies of certain attributes become more and more stable as the number of observations is increased. We shall discuss the idea of 'the limiting value of the relative frequency' later on; meanwhile, we assume that the frequency is being computed with a limited accuracy only, so that small deviations are not perceptible. This approximate value of the relative frequency we shall, preliminarily, regard as the probability of the attribute in question, e.g., the probability of the result '12' in the game of dice. It is obvious that if we define probability in this way, it will be a number less than 1, that is, a proper fraction.

Two different pairs of dice

I have here two pairs of dice which are apparently alike. By repeatedly throwing one pair, it is found that the relative frequency of the 'double 6' approaches a value of 0.028, or 1/36, as the number of trials is increased. The second pair shows a relative frequency for the '12' which is four times as large. The first pair is usually called a pair of true dice, the second is called biased, but our definition of probability applies equally to both pairs. Whether or not a die is biased is as irrelevant for our theory as is the moral integrity of a patient when a physician is diagnosing his illness. 1,800 throws were made with each pair of these dice. The sum '12' appeared 48 times with the first pair and 178 times with the second. The relative frequencies are

$$\frac{48}{1,800} = \frac{1}{37.5} = 0.027$$

and

$$\frac{178}{1,800} = \frac{1}{10.1} = 0.099.$$

These ratios became practically constant towards the end of the series of trials. For instance, after the 1,500th throw they were 0.023 and 0.094, respectively. The differences between the values calculated at this stage and later on did not exceed 10%–15%.

It is impossible for me to show you a lengthy experiment in the throwing of dice during the course of this lecture since it would take too long. It is sufficient to make a few trials with the second pair of dice to see that at least one 6 appears at nearly every throw; this is a result very different from that obtained with the other pair. In fact, it can be shown that if we throw one of the dice belonging to the second pair, the relative frequency with which a single 6 appears is about 1/3, whereas for either of the first pair this frequency is almost exactly 1/6. In order to realize clearly what our meaning of probability implies, it will be useful to think of these two pairs of dice as often as possible; each pair has a characteristic probability of showing 'double 6', but these probabilities differ widely.

Here we have the 'primary phenomenon' (Urphänomen) of the theory of probability in its simplest form. The probability of a 6 is a physical property of a given die and is a property analogous to its mass, specific heat, or electrical resistance. Similarly, for a given *pair of dice* (including of course the total setup) the probability of a 'double 6' is a characteristic property, a physical constant belonging to the experiment as a whole and comparable with all its other physical properties. The theory of probability is only concerned with relations existing between physical quantities of this kind.

Limiting value of relative frequency

I have used the expression 'limiting value', which belongs to higher analysis, without further explanation.[5] We do not need to know much about the mathematical definition of this expression, since we propose to use it in a manner which can be understood by anyone, however ignorant of higher mathematics. Let us calculate the relative frequency of an attribute in a collective. This is the ratio of the number of cases in which the attribute has been found to the total number of observations. We shall calculate it with a certain limited accuracy, i.e., to a certain number of decimal places without asking what the following figures might be. Suppose, for instance, that we play 'heads or tails' a number of times and calculate the relative frequency of 'heads'. If the number of games is increased and if we always stop at the same decimal place in calculating the relative frequency, then, eventually, the results of such calculations will cease to change. If the relative frequency of heads is calculated accurately to the first decimal place, it would not be difficult to attain constancy in this first approximation. In fact, perhaps after some 500 games, this first approximation will reach the value of 0.5 and will not change afterwards. It will take us much longer to arrive at a constant value for the second approximation, calculated to two decimal places. For this purpose it may be necessary to calculate the relative frequency in intervals of, say, 500 casts, i.e., after the 500th, 1,000th, 1,500th, and 2,000th cast, and so on. Perhaps more than 10,000 casts will be required to show that now the second figure also ceases to change and remains equal to 0, so that the relative frequency remains constantly 0.50. Of course it is impossible to continue an experiment of this kind indefinitely. Two experimenters, co-operating efficiently, may be able to make up to 1,000 observations per hour, but not more. Imagine, for example, that the experiment has been continued for ten hours and that the relative frequency remained constant at 0.50 during the last two hours. An astute observer might perhaps have managed to calculate the third figure as well, and might have found that the changes in this figure during the last hours, although still occurring, were limited to a comparatively narrow range.

Considering these results, a scientifically trained mind may easily accept the hypothesis that by continuing this play for a sufficiently long time under conditions which do not change (insofar as this is practically possible), one would arrive at constant values for the third, fourth, and all the following decimal places as well. The expression we used, stating that the relative frequency of the attribute 'heads' tends to a limit, is no more than a short description of the situation assumed in this hypothesis.

Take a sheet of graph paper and draw a curve with the total number of observations as abscissæ and the value of the relative frequency of the result 'heads' as ordinates. At the beginning this curve shows large oscillations, but gradually they become smaller and smaller, and the curve approaches a straight horizontal line. At last the oscillations become so small that they cannot be represented on the diagram, even if a very large scale is used. It is of no importance for our purpose if the ordinate of the final horizontal line is 0.6, or any other value, instead of 0.5. The important point is the existence of this straight line. The ordinate of this horizontal line is the limiting value of the relative frequency represented by the diagram, in our case the relative frequency of the event 'heads'.

Let us now add further precision to our previous definition of the collective. We will say that a collective is a mass phenomenon or a repetitive event, or, simply, a long sequence of observations for which there are sufficient reasons to believe that the relative frequency of the observed attribute would tend to a fixed limit if the observations were indefinitely continued. This limit will be called *the probability of the attribute considered within the given collective*. This expression being a little cumbersome, it is obviously not necessary to repeat it always. Occasionally, we may speak simply of the *probability of 'heads'*. The important thing to remember is that this is only an abbreviation, and that we should know exactly the kind of collective to which we are referring. 'The probability of winning a battle', for instance, has no place in our theory of probability, because we cannot think of a collective to which it belongs. The theory of probability cannot be applied to this problem any more than the physical concept of work can be applied to the calculation of the 'work' done by an actor in reciting his part in a play.

The experimental basis of the theory of games

It will be useful to consider how the fundamental experiment of the determination of probability can be carried out in the other two cases mentioned: I mean in the case of life insurance, and that of molecules of a gas. Before doing this, I should like to add a few more words on the question of games of chance. People may ask, 'How do we know for certain that a game of chance will develop in practice along the lines which we have discussed, i.e., tending towards a stabilization of the relative frequencies of the possible results? Is there a sufficient basis for this important assumption in actual sequences of experiments? Are not all experiments limited to a relatively short initial stage?' The experimental material is, however, not as restricted as it may appear at first sight. The great gambling banks in Monte Carlo and elsewhere have collected data relating to many millions of repetitions of one and the same game. These banks do quite well on the assumption of the existence of a limiting value of the relative frequency of each possible result. The occasional occurrence of 'breaking the bank' is not an argument against the validity of this theory. This could only be questioned on the basis of a substantial decrease in the total earnings of the bank from the beginning of its operation to any specified date, or, even worse, by the transformation of a continued gain into a loss. Nobody who is acquainted with the balance sheets of gambling banks would ever consider such a possibility. The lottery belongs, from this point of view, to the same class as roulette. Lotteries have been organized by certain governments for decades, and the results have always been in complete agreement with the assumption of constant values of the relative frequencies.

We thus see that the hypothesis of the existence of limiting values of the relative frequencies is well corroborated by a large mass of experience with actual games of chance. Only processes to which this hypothesis applies form the subject of our subsequent discussion.

360

The probability of death

The 'probability of death' is calculated by the insurance companies by a method very similar to the one which we have used to define the probability in the case of the game of dice. The first thing needed is to have an exact definition of the collective for each single case. As an example, we may mention the compiling of the German Life Tables Based on the Experience of Twenty-three Insurance Companies. These tables were calculated on the basis of 900,000 single observations on persons whose lives were insured with one of the twenty-three companies.[6] The observations covered the period from the moment of conclusion of the insurance contract until the cessation of this contract by death or otherwise. Let us consider, in particular, the following collective: 'All men insured before reaching the age of forty after complete medical examination and with the normal premium, the characteristic event being the death of the insured in his forty-first year.' Cases in which the occurrence or non-occurrence of this event could not be ascertained, e.g., because of a discontinuation of the insurance, were excluded from calculation. The number of cases which could be ascertained was 85,020. The corresponding number of deaths was 940. The relative frequency of deaths or the death-rate is therefore $940:85,020 = 0.01106$. This figure was accepted, after certain corrections which we do not need to be bothered with, as the probability of death occurring in the forty-first year for members of the above-described class of insured persons, i.e., for an exactly defined collective.

In this case 85,000 observations have been assumed to be sufficient for the relative frequency of deaths to become practically equal to its limiting value, that is, to a constant which refers to an indefinitely long series of observations of persons of the same category. This assumption is an arbitrary one and, strictly speaking, it would be wrong to expect that the above relative frequency agrees with the true probability to more than the first three decimal places. In other words, if we could increase the number of observations and keep calculating the relative frequency of deaths, we can only expect that the first three decimal places of the original death-rate, namely 0.011, will remain unchanged. All concerned in insurance business would prefer the death-rates to be calculated on a broader basis; this, however, is difficult for obvious practical reasons. On the other hand, no figure of this kind, however exact at the moment of its determination, can remain valid for ever. The same is true for all physical data. The scientists determine the acceleration due to gravity at a certain place on the surface of the earth, and continue to use this value until a new determination happens to reveal a change in it; local differences are treated in the same way. Similarly, insurance mathematicians are satisfied with the best data available at the moment, and continue to use a figure such as the above 0.011 until new and more accurate calculations become possible. In other words, the insurance companies continue to assume that out of 1,000 newly insured men of the previously defined category, eleven will die in their forty-first year. No significance for any other category is claimed for this figure 0.011. It is utter nonsense to say, for instance, that Mr. X, now aged forty, has the probability 0.011 of dying in the course of the next year. If the analogous ratio is calculated for men and women together, the value obtained in this way is somewhat smaller than 0.011, and Mr. X belongs to this second collective as much as to that previously considered. He is, furthermore, a member of a great number of other collectives which can be easily defined, and for which the calculation of the probability of death may give as many different values. One might suggest that a correct value of the probability of death for Mr. X may be obtained by restricting the collective to which he belongs as far as possible, by taking into consideration more and more of his individual characteristics. There is, however, no end to this process, and if we go further and further into the selection of the members of the collective, we shall be left finally with this individual alone. Insurance companies nowadays apply the principle of so-called 'selection by insurance'; this means that they take into consideration the fact that persons who enter early into insurance contracts are on the average of a different type and have a different distribution of death ages from persons admitted to the insurance at a more advanced age. It is obviously possible to go further in this or other directions in the limitation of the collective. It is, however, equally obvious that in trying to take into account *all* the properties of an individual, we shall finally arrive at the stage of finding no other members of the collective at all, and the collective will cease to exist altogether.

First the collective—then the probability

I should like to dwell a little on this last point, which implies a characteristic difference between the definition of probability assumed in these lectures and that which has been generally accepted before. I have already stated this once in the following short sentence: 'We shall not speak of probability until a collective has been defined'. In this connection, it is of interest to consider the diametrically opposite viewpoint expressed by one of the older authors, Johannes von Kries,[7] in a once widely read book on the principles of the theory of probability. He declares: '... I shall assume therefore a definite probability of the death of Caius, Sempronius or Titus in the course of the next year. If, on the other hand, the question is raised of the probability of a general event, including an indefinite number of individual cases—for instance, of the probability of a man of 40 living another 20 years, this clearly means the use of the word 'probability' in another and not quite proper way—as a kind of abbreviation. If an expression of this kind should have any connection with the true meaning of probability at all, this connection may only consist in a comprehensive description of a certain number of single probabilities.'

My opinion is that the 'improper' use of the probability notion, as defined by von Kries, is in fact the only one admissible in the calculus of probability. This has been demonstrated in the foregoing paragraph by means of the same example of the death probability as was used by von Kries, and I have tried to show that any other conception is impossible. I consider, quite generally, the introduction of the expression 'probability in a collective' as an important 'improvement in word usage'. Two examples may help to elucidate this point further.

Consider a lottery with one million tickets. Imagine that the first prize has fallen to ticket No. 400,000. People will consider this an amazing and rare event; newspapers will discuss it, and everybody will think that this was a very improbable occurrence. On the other hand, the essence of a lottery is that all precautions have been taken to ensure the same probability for a win for all tickets, and No. 400,000 has therefore exactly the same chance of winning as all the other numbers, for instance No. 786,331—namely the probability 1/1,000,000. What shall we think about this paradox? Another example is given by Laplace[8] in his famous *Essai Philosophique*: In playing with small cards, on each of which is written a single letter, selecting at random fourteen of them and arranging them in a row, one would be extremely amazed to see the word 'Constantinople' formed. However, in this case again, the mechanism of the play is such as to ensure the same probability for each of the 26^{14} possible combinations of fourteen letters (out of the twenty-six letters of the alphabet). Why do we nevertheless assume the appearance of the word 'Constantinople' to be something utterly improbable?

The solution of these two seeming paradoxes is the same. The event that the first prize will fall to ticket No. 400,000 has, in itself, no 'probability' at all. A collective has to be defined before the word probability acquires a definite meaning. We may define this collective to consist of repeated draws of a lottery, the attribute of the particular draw being the number of the ticket drawn. In this collective each number has exactly the same probability as No. 400,000. However, in speaking of the 'improbability' of the number 400,000, we have in mind a collective of a different kind. The above-mentioned impression of improbability would be created not only by drawing the number 400,000, but all numbers of the same kind: 100,000, 200,000, etc. The collective with which we have to deal has therefore only the two following attributes—either the number does end with five 0's, or it does not. The first-named attribute has the probability 0.00001, the second 0.99999, i.e., nearly 100,000 times larger. In an alternative between the draw of a number containing five 0's and that of a number not having this property, the second result has indeed a very much larger probability.

Exactly the same considerations apply to the second example. What astonishes us in the case of the word 'Constantinople' is the fact that fourteen letters, taken and ordered at random, should form a well-known word instead of unreadable gibberish. Among the immense number of combinations of fourteen letters (26^{14}, or about 10^{20}), not more than a few thousand correspond to words. The elements of the collective are in this case all the possible combinations of fourteen letters with the alternative attributes 'coherent' or 'meaningless'. The second attribute ('meaningless') has, in this collective, a very much larger probability than the first one, and that is why we call the appearance of the word 'Constantinople'—or of any other word—a highly improbable event.

In many appropriate uses of the probability notion in practical life the collective can be easily constructed. In cases where this proves to be impossible, the use of the word probability, from the point of view of the rational theory of probability, is an illegitimate one, and numerical determination of the probability value is therefore impossible. In many cases the collective can be defined in several ways and these are cases in which the magnitude of the probability may become a subject of controversy. It is only the notion of *probability in a given collective* which is unambiguous.

Probability in the gas theory

We now return to our preliminary survey of fields in which the theory of probability can be applied, and consider the third example—that of molecular physics—rather more closely. In the investigation of the behaviour of molecules in a gas we encounter conditions not essentially different from those prevailing in the two applications of probability we have previously discussed. In this case, the collective can be formed, for instance, by all molecules present in the volume of gas enclosed by the walls of a cylinder and a piston. As attributes of the single elements (molecules), we may consider, for instance, the three rectangular components of their velocities, or the velocity vector itself. It is true that nobody has yet tried to measure the actual velocities of all the single molecules in a gas, and to calculate in this way the relative frequencies with which the different values occur. Instead, the physicist makes certain theoretical assumptions concerning these frequencies (or, more exactly, their limiting values), and tests experimentally certain consequences, derived on the basis of these assumptions. Although the possibility of a direct determination of the probability does not exist in this case, there is nevertheless no fundamental difference between it and the other two examples treated. The main point is that in this case, too, all considerations are based on the existence of constant limiting values of relative frequencies which are unaffected by a further increase in the number of elements concerned, i.e., by an increase in the volume of gas under consideration.

In order to explain the relation between this problem and the previous example of the probability of death established by direct counting, we may think of the following analogy. A surveyor may have to make calculations relating to a right-angled triangle, e.g., the evaluation of its hypotenuse by means of the Pythagorean theorem. His first step may be to establish by direct measurement that the angle in the triangle is sufficiently near to 90°. Another method which he can apply is to assume that this angle *is* 90°, to draw conclusions from this assumption, and to verify them by comparison with the experimental results. This is the situation in which the physicist finds himself when he applies statistical methods to molecules or other particles of the same kind. The physicists often say that the velocity of a molecule is 'in principle' a measurable quantity, although it is not possible to carry out this measurement in practice by means of the usual measuring devices. (At this stage we do not consider the modern development of the question of the measurability of molecular quantities.) Similarly, we can say that the relative frequency and its limiting value, the probability, are determined in the molecular collective 'in principle' in the same way as in the cases of the games of chance and of social statistics which we have previously discussed.

An historical remark

The way in which the probability concept has been developed in the preceding paragraphs is widely different from the one which the older textbooks of probability calculus used in formally defining their subject. On the other hand, our foundation of probability is in no contradiction whatsoever to the actual content of the probability concept used by these authors. In this sense, the first pages of Poisson's[9] famous textbook, *On the probability of the judgments of courts of justice*, are very instructive. Poisson says that a certain phenomenon has been found to occur in many different fields of experience, namely, the fact which we have described above as the stabilization of relative frequencies with the increase in the number of observations. In this connection, Poisson uses an expression which I have avoided up till now on account of a prevailing confusion regarding its interpretation. Poisson calls the fact that the relative frequencies become constant, after the sequence of experiments has been sufficiently extended, the Law of Large Numbers. He considers this law to be the basis of a theory of probability, and we fully agree with him on this point. In the actual investigations which follow the introduction, however, Poisson starts not from this law, but from the formal definition of probability introduced by Laplace.[10] (We shall have to speak about this definition later.) From it he deduces, by analytical methods, a mathematical proposition which he also calls the Law of Large Numbers. This mathematical proposition means something very different from the general empirical rule called by the same name at the beginning of Poisson's book. This double use of the same expression to describe two widely different things has caused much confusion.

Let me add that our conception of the *sequence of observations* as the cornerstone in the foundation of the theory of probability, and our definition of probability as the relative frequency with which certain events or properties recur in these sequences, is not something absolutely new. In a more dialectical form and without the immediate intention of developing a theory of probability calculus on this basis, the same ideas were presented as early as 1866 by John Venn[11] in his book *Logic of Chance*. The development of the so-called theory of finite populations by Theodor Fechner[12] and Heinrich Bruns[13] is closely related to our frequency theory of probability. Georg Helm,[14] who played a certain part in the foundation of the energy principle, expressed ideas very similar to ours in his paper on 'Probability Theory as the Theory of the Concept of Collectives', which appeared in 1902. These attempts, as well as many others which time does not allow us to enumerate, did not lead, and could not lead, to a complete theory of probability, because they failed to realize one decisive feature of a collective which we shall discuss in the following paragraph.

Randomness

The condition that the relative frequencies of attributes should have constant limiting values is not the only one we have to stipulate when dealing with collectives, i.e., with sequences of single observations, mass phenomena, or repetitive events which may appropriately serve as a basis for the application of probability theory. Examples can easily be found where the relative frequencies converge towards definite limiting values, and where it is nevertheless not appropriate to speak of probability. Imagine, for instance, a road along which milestones are placed, large ones for whole miles and smaller ones for tenths of a mile. If we walk long enough along this road, calculating the relative frequencies of large stones, the value found in this way will lie around 1/10. The value will be exactly 0.1 whenever in each mile we are in that interval between two small milestones which corresponds to the one in which we started. The deviations from the value 0.1 will become smaller and smaller as the number of stones passed increases; in other words, the relative frequency tends towards the limiting value 0.1. This result may induce us to speak of a certain 'probability of encountering a large stone'. Nothing that we have said so far prevents us from doing so. It is, however, worth while to inquire more closely into the obvious difference between the case of the milestones and the cases previously discussed. A point will emerge from this inquiry which will make it desirable to restrict the definition of a collective in such a way as to exclude the case of milestones and other cases of a similar nature. The sequence of observations of large or small stones differs essentially from the sequence of observations, for instance, of the results of a game of chance, in that the first sequence obeys an easily recognizable law. Exactly every tenth observation leads to the attribute 'large', all others to the attribute 'small'. After having just passed a large stone, we are in no doubt about the size of the next one; there is no chance of its being large. If, however, we have cast a double 6 with two dice, this fact in no way affects our chances of getting the same result in the next cast. Similarly, the death of an insured person during his forty-first year does not give the slightest indication of what will be the fate of another who is registered next to him in the books of the insurance company, regardless of how the company's list was prepared.

This difference between the two sequences of observations is actually observable. We shall, in future, consider only such sequences of events or observations, which satisfy the requirements of complete lawlessness or 'randomness' and refer to them as collectives. In certain cases, such as the one mentioned above, where there is no collective properly speaking, it may sometimes be useful to have a short expression for the limiting value of the relative frequency. We shall then speak of the 'chance' of an attribute's occurring in an unlimited sequence of observations, which may be called an improper collective. The term 'probability' will be reserved for the limiting value of the relative frequency in a true collective which satisfies the condition of randomness. The only question is how to describe this condition exactly enough to be able to give a sufficiently precise definition of a collective.

Definition of randomness: place selection

On the basis of all that has been said, an appropriate definition of randomness can be found without much difficulty. The essential difference between the sequence of the results obtained by casting dice and the regular sequence of large and small milestones consists in the possibility of devising a method of *selecting the elements* so as to produce a fundamental change in the relative frequencies.

We begin, for instance, with a large stone, and register only every second stone passed. The relation of the relative frequencies of the small and large stones will now converge towards 1/5 instead of 1/10. (We miss none of the large stones, but we do miss every second of the small ones.) If the same method, or any other, simple or complicated, method of selection is applied to the sequence of dice casts, the effect will always be nil; the relative frequency of the double 6, for instance, will remain, in all selected partial sequences, the same as in the original one (assuming, of course, that the selected sequences are long enough to show an approach to the limiting value). This impossibility of affecting the chances of a game by a system of selection, this uselessness of all systems of gambling, is the characteristic and decisive property common to all sequences of observations or mass phenomena which form the proper subject of probability calculus.

In this way we arrive at the following definition: A collective appropriate for the application of the theory of probability must fulfil two conditions. First, the relative frequencies of the attributes must possess limiting values. Second, these limiting values must remain the same in all partial sequences which may be selected from the original one in an arbitrary way. Of course, only such partial sequences can be taken into consideration as can be extended indefinitely, in the same way as the original sequence itself. Examples of this kind are, for instance, the partial sequences formed by all odd members of the original sequence, or by all members for which the place number in the sequence is the square of an integer, or a prime number, or a number selected according to some other rule, whatever it may be. The only essential condition is that the question whether or not a certain member of the original sequence belongs to the selected partial sequence should be settled *independently of the result* of the corresponding observation, i.e., before anything is known about this result. We shall call a selection of this kind a *place selection*. The limiting values of the relative frequencies in a collective must be independent of all possible place selections. By place selection we mean the selection of a partial sequence in such a way that we decide whether an element should or should not be included without making use of the attribute of the element, i.e., the result of our game of chance.

366

The principle of the impossibility of a gambling system

We may now ask a question similar to one we have previously asked: 'How do we know that collectives satisfying this new and more rigid requirement really exist?' Here again we may point to experimental results, and these are numerous enough. Everybody who has been to Monte Carlo, or who has read descriptions of a gambling bank, knows how many 'absolutely safe' gambling systems, sometimes of an enormously complicated character, have been invented and tried out by gamblers; and new systems are still being suggested every day. The authors of such systems have all, sooner or later, had the sad experience of finding out that no system is able to improve their chances of winning in the long run, i.e., to affect the relative frequencies with which different colours or numbers appear in a sequence selected from the total sequence of the game. This experience forms the experimental basis of our definition of probability.

An analogy presents itself at this point which I shall briefly discuss. The system fanatics of Monte Carlo show an obvious likeness to another class of 'inventors' whose useless labour we have been accustomed to consider with a certain compassion, namely, the ancient and undying family of constructors of 'perpetual-motion' machines. This analogy, which is not only a psychological one, is worth closer consideration. Why does every educated man smile nowadays when he hears of a new attempt to construct a perpetual-motion machine? Because, he will answer, he knows from the law of the conservation of energy that such a machine is impossible. However, the law of conservation of energy is nothing but a broad generalization—however firmly rooted in various branches of physics—of fundamental empirical results. The failure of all the innumerable attempts to build such a machine plays a decisive role among these. In theoretical physics, the energy principle and its various applications are often referred to as 'the principle of the impossibility of perpetual motion'. There can be no question of proving the law of conservation of energy—if we mean by 'proof' something more than the simple fact of an agreement between a principle and all the experimental results so far obtained. The character of being nearly self-evident, which this principle has acquired for us, is only due to the enormous accumulation of empirical data which confirm it. Apart from the unsuccessful attempts to construct a perpetual motion machine—the interest of which is now purely historical—all the technical methods of transformation of energy are evidence for the validity of the energy principle.

By generalizing the experience of the gambling banks, deducing from it the Principle of the Impossibility of a Gambling System, and including this principle in the foundation of the theory of probability, we proceed in the same way as did the physicists in the case of the energy principle. In our case also, the naïve attempts of the hunters of fortune are supplemented by more solid experience, especially that of the insurance companies and similar bodies. The results obtained by them can be stated as follows. The whole financial basis of insurance would be questionable if it were possible to change the relative frequency of the occurrence of the insurance cases (deaths, etc.) by excluding, for example, every tenth one of the insured persons, or by some other selection principle. The principle of the impossibility of a gambling system has the same importance for the insurance companies as the principle of the conservation of energy for the electric power station: it is the rock on which all the calculations rest. We can characterize these two principles, as well as all far-reaching laws of nature, by saying that they are restrictions which we impose on the basis of our previous experience, upon our expectation of the

367

further course of natural events. (This formulation goes back to E. Mach.) The fact that predictions of this kind have been repeatedly verified by experience entitles us to assume the existence of mass phenomena or repetitive events to which the principle of the impossibility of a gambling system actually applies. Only phenomena of this kind will be the subject of our further discussion.

Example of randomness

In order to illustrate the randomness in a collective, I will show a simple experiment. It is again taken from the field of games of chance; this is only because experiments on subjects belonging to other fields in which the theory of probability finds its application require apparatus much too elaborate to be shown here.

I have a bag containing ninety round discs, bearing the numbers 1 to 90. I extract one disc from the bag at random, I note whether the number it bears is an odd or an even one and replace the disc. I repeat the experiment 100 times and denote all the odd numbers by 1's, and all even numbers by 0's. The following table shows the result:

1	1	0	0	0	1	1	1	0	1
0	0	1	1	0	0	1	1	1	1
0	1	0	1	0	0	1	0	0	0
0	1	0	0	1	0	0	1	1	1
0	0	1	1	0	0	0	0	1	1
0	1	1	1	1	0	1	0	1	0
1	0	1	1	1	1	0	0	1	1
0	0	1	1	0	1	1	1	0	1
0	0	1	1	0	0	1	1	0	1
0	1	1	0	0	0	1	0	0	0

Among 100 experimental results we find fifty-one ones; in other words, the relative frequency of the result 1 is 51/100. If we consider only the first, third, fifth draw, and so forth, i.e., if we take only the figures in the odd columns of the table, we find that ones appear in twenty-four cases out of fifty; the relative frequency is 48/100. Using only the numbers in the odd horizontal rows of the table, we obtain, for the relative frequency of the result 1, the value 50/100. We may further consider only those results whose place in the sequence corresponds to one of the prime numbers, i.e., 1, 2, 3, 5, 7, 11, 13, 17, 19, 23, 29, 31, 37, 41, 43, 47, 53, 59, 61, 67, 71, 73, 79, 83, 89 and 97. These twenty-six draws have produced thirteen 1's, the relative frequency is thus again exactly 50/100. Finally, we may consider the 51 draws following a result 1. (A 'system' gambler might prefer to bet on 0 after 1 has just come out.) We find in this selection of results twenty-seven 1's, i.e., the relative frequency 27/51, or about 53/100. These calculations show that, in all the different selections which we have tried out, the 1's always appear with a relative frequency of about 1/2. I trust that this conveys the feeling that more extensive experiments, which I am not able to carry out here because of the lack of time, would demonstrate the phenomenon of randomness still more strikingly.

It is of course possible, after knowing the results of the hundred draws, to indicate a method of selection which would produce only 1's, or only 0's, or 1's and 0's in any desired proportion. It is also possible that in some other group of a hundred experiments, analogous to the one just performed, one kind of selection may give a result widely different from 1/2. The principle of randomness requires only that the relative frequency should converge to 1/2 when the number of results in an arbitrarily selected partial sequence becomes larger and larger.

Summary of the definition

I do not need to insist here on mathematical details and such considerations which are only necessary for making the definitions complete from a mathematical point of view. From the next section onwards, I will deal with various basic questions and with different objections to my definition of probability and these I hope to be able to refute. I trust that this discussion will dispel those doubts which may have arisen in your minds and further clarify certain points.

In closing this discussion, may I summarize briefly the propositions which we have found and which will serve as a basis for all future discussions. These propositions are equivalent to a definition of mathematical probability, in the only sense in which we intend to use this concept.

1   It is possible to speak about probabilities only in reference to a properly defined collective.
2   A collective is a mass phenomenon or an unlimited sequence of observations fulfilling the following two conditions: (i) the relative frequencies of particular attributes within the collective tend to fixed limits; (ii) these fixed limits are not affected by any place selection. That is to say, if we calculate the relative frequency of some attribute not in the original sequence, but in a partial set, selected according to some fixed rule, then we require that the relative frequency so calculated should tend to the same limit as it does in the original set.
3   The fulfilment of the condition (ii) will be described as the Principle of Randomness or the Principle of the Impossibility of a Gambling System.
4   The limiting value of the relative frequency of a given attribute, assumed to be independent of any place selection, will be called 'the probability of that attribute within the given collective'. Whenever this qualification of the word 'probability' is omitted, this omission should be considered as an abbreviation and the necessity for reference to some collective must be strictly kept in mind.
5   If a sequence of observations fulfills only the first condition (existence of limits of the relative frequencies), but not the second one, then such a limiting value will be called the 'chance' of the occurrence of the particular attribute rather than its 'probability'.

Objections to my theory

Since my first publications which appeared in 1919, an intensive discussion of the foundations of the theory of probability has started and is still in progress. Those authors who had worked in this field for many years and had been successful in the solution of a number of special problems could hardly be expected to agree at once to a complete revision of the very foundations of their work. Apart from this older generation,[15] there is scarcely a modern mathematician who still adheres without reservation to the classical theory of probability. The majority have more or less accepted the frequency definition. A small group, whom I call 'nihilists', insist that basic definitions connecting probability theory with the empirical world are unnecessary. I will deal with this point of view at the end of this lecture.

Even among those who agree that the subject of probability calculus is frequencies and who think that this should find its expression in the definition of probability, there are still many differences of opinion. In the first place, there are some mathematicians who begin their course by defining probability as the limit of relative frequency, but do not adhere consistently to this point of view in their further developments. Instead, they revert to the old ways of the classical theory. The French textbook by Fréchet and Halbwachs (1924),[16] and that by the American mathematician Julian Coolidge (1925),[17] belong to this group.

A more recent work by Harald Cramér,[18] which seems to represent the prevalent trend among American and British statisticians, completely adopts the point of view of the frequency definition. Cramér rejects the definition based on equally possible cases as inadequate and firmly opposes the standpoint of the modern subjectivists which will be further discussed later on. However, Cramér omits giving a clear definition of probability and in no way explains or derives in a logical manner the elementary operations of probability calculus. The reason why he and authors of the same school of thought are able to proceed in this way is that, for all of them, the fundamental questions which arise from the *simple* problems of the theory of chance do not exist. If one's attention is focused on the mathematical difficulties of complicated problems it is easily possible to pass over the difficulties of the fundamentals. The same holds true in the case of pure mathematics: the mathematician who is concentrating on the solution of intricate problems need not concern himself with the proposition that a times b equals b times a. The significant difference is that in this field scientific discipline is much further advanced and it is therefore no longer customary to deal with the foundations in a few casual words.

Another small group of mathematicians is opposed to the definition of the collective as an infinite sequence of elements; they prefer to deal exclusively with frequencies in long, but finite, sequences, i.e., to avoid the use of limits. A larger group accepts my first postulate, viz., the existence of limiting values of relative frequencies, but finds difficulties with the second one, the postulate of randomness. Certain suggestions concerning the possible alteration of these conditions have been made. I propose to deal with these questions in turn in the following sections, including also a brief discussion of new developments in the subjective concept of probability.

Finite collectives

There is no doubt about the fact that the sequences of observations to which the theory of probability is applied in practice are all finite. In the same way, we apply in practice the mechanics of particles to the treatment of problems concerned with bodies of finite size which are not geometrical points. Nevertheless, nobody will deny the utility and theoretical importance of the abstraction underlying the concept of a material point, and this despite the fact that we now have theories of mechanics which are not based on the consideration of discrete points. On the other hand, abstractions that originally belonged to the mechanics of particles permeate far into the mechanics of finite bodies. We need not enter into details here.

It is doubtless possible to avoid the notion of infinite sequences in dealing with mass phenomena or repetitive events. The question is, what would be the results of such a method? I do not know of any argument for using infinite sequences, apart from the greater simplicity of this method, and I have never claimed for it any other advantages. In 1934, Johannes Blume[19] set himself the task of transforming my theory in such a way as to use only finite sequences of observations, especially in the fundamental definitions. His procedure is this: Instead of the postulate concerning the limits of the relative frequencies, he assumes the existence of certain fixed numbers determining the distribution of the collective, and postulates that the values of the actual relative frequencies should differ from these numbers by no more than a small positive magnitude ε. Assuming that ε is sufficiently small, it is possible to perform certain operations on these finite collectives, constantly remaining within the limits of an approximation defined by the magnitude ε. As far as this method actually goes, it amounts to nothing more than a circumscription of the concept of a limiting value, which may be quite useful for certain purposes. This has been stressed already by A. Kolmogoroff[20] in his review of Blume's work. The word 'limit' is in fact used in mathematics only as a concise way of making certain statements concerning small deviations. On the other hand, neither Blume nor other authors working in the same direction have so far been successful in describing in the language of the 'finite' theory all properties of a collective and all connections between collectives, especially those relating to the principle of randomness. At the present time, therefore, I do not think that we can speak of the actual existence of a theory of probability based on finite collectives.[21]

Here I should like to insert an historical interpolation. The philosopher Theodor Fechner,[22] who had many-sided interests, created, under the name of 'Kollektiv-masslehre', a kind of systematic description of finite sequences of observations, which he called 'finite populations' (Kollektivgegenstände). This work was edited by Lipps in 1897, after the death of the author. Fechner probably did not think of the possibility of arriving at a rational concept of probability from such an abstraction as his 'finite population', but his views have served, at least for me, as a stimulus in developing the new concept of probability.

Returning to our subject, I must defend myself most emphatically against the recurring misunderstanding that in our theory infinite sequences are always substituted for finite sequences of observations. This is of course false. In an example discussed at the end of the preceding lecture, we spoke of the group of twenty-four throws of a pair of dice. Such a group can serve as the subject of our theory, if it is assumed that it has been repeated, as a whole, an infinite number of times and in this way has become an element of a collective. This leads us to certain statements about probability that apply to a *finite* number of observations, in this example, twenty-four. Similarly, if we consider, for instance, the birth rate of boys in a hundred different towns, our theory shows what can be expected, on the average, in the case of this finite number ($n = 100$) of observations. There is no question of substituting an infinite sequence for each group of 100 observations.

Testing probability statements

The problem of formulating a theory of finite collectives, in the sense explained above, must be clearly distinguished from that of the actual interpretation of the results of our probability calculations. Since we consider that the sole purpose of a scientific theory is to provide a mental image of objectively observable phenomena, the only test of such a theory is the extent to which it applies to actual sequences of observations, and these are always finite.

On the other hand, I have mentioned on many occasions that all the results of our calculations lead to statements which apply only to infinite sequences. Even if the subject of our investigation is a sequence of observations of a certain given length, say 500 individual trials, we actually treat this whole group as one element of an infinite sequence. Consequently, the results apply only to the infinite repetition of sequences of 500 observations each. It might thus appear that our theory could never be tested experimentally.

This difficulty, however, is exactly the same as that which occurs in all applications of science. If, for instance, a physical or a chemical consideration leads us to the conclusion that the specific weight of a substance is 0.897, we may try to test the accuracy of this conclusion by direct weighing, or by some other physical experiment. However, the weight of only a finite volume of the substance can be determined in this way. The value of the specific weight, i.e., the limit of the ratio weight/volume for an infinitely small volume, remains uncertain just as the value of a probability derived from the relative frequency in a finite sequence of observations remains uncertain. One might even go so far as to say that specific weight does not exist at all, because the atomic theory of matter makes impossible the transition to the limit of an infinitely small homogeneous volume. As a parallel to this difficulty we may consider, for instance, the fact that it is impossible to make an infinitely long sequence of throws with one and the same die, under unchanged conditions, because of the gradual wear of the die.

One could say that, after all, not all physical statements concern limits, for instance, that the indication of the weight of a certain finite volume of matter is likewise a physical statement. However, as soon as we begin to think about a really exact test of such a statement, we run into a number of conditions which cannot even be formulated in an exact way. For instance, the weighing has to be carried out under a known air pressure, and this notion of air pressure is in turn founded on the concept of a limit. An experienced physicist knows how to define conditions under which an experimental test can be considered as 'valid', but it is impossible to give a logically complete description of all these conditions in a form comparable, for instance, to that in which the premises of a mathematical proposition are stated. The assumption of the correctness of a theory is based, as H. Dubislav justly states, not so much on a logical conclusion (Schluss) as on a practical decision (Entschluss).

I quite agree with the view which Carl G. Hempel[23] put forward in his very clearly written article on 'The Content of Probability Statements'. According to Hempel, the results of a theory based on the notion of the infinite collective can be applied to finite sequences of observations in a way which is not logically definable, but is nevertheless sufficiently exact in practice. The relation of theory to observation is in this case essentially the same as in all other physical sciences.

Considerations of this kind are often described as inquiries into the 'problem of application'. It is, however, very definitely advisable to avoid the introduction of a 'problem of applicability', in addition to the two problems, the observations and their theory. There is no special theory, i.e., a system of propositions, deductions, proofs, etc., that deals with the question of how a scientific theory is to be applied to the actual observations. The connection between the empirical world and theory is established in each case by the fundamental principles of the particular theory, which are usually called its axioms. This remark is of special importance to us because occasional attempts have been made to assign to the theory of probability the role of such a general 'application theory'. This conception fails at once when we realize that a new problem of application would arise in connection with each single statement of the calculus of probability.

An objection to the first postulate

The majority of mathematicians now agree that the concept of an infinite sequence of observations or attributes is an appropriate foundation for a rational theory of probability. A certain objection, resulting from a vague recollection of the classical theory, is raised, however, by many who hear for the first time the definition of probability as the limiting value of the relative frequency. I will discuss this objection briefly, although it does not stand close examination.

The objection[24] refers in fact to the text of the theorem of Bernoulli and Poisson which I have mentioned previously. According to this proposition, it is 'almost certain' that the relative frequency of even numbers in a very long sequence of throws with a correct die will lie near to the probability value 1/2. Nevertheless, a certain small probability exists that this relative frequency will differ slightly from 0.5; it may be equal to 0.51, for instance, even if the sequence is a very long one. This is said to contradict the assumption that the limiting value of the relative frequency is exactly equal to 0.5.

In other words, so runs the objection, the frequency theory implies that, with a sufficient increase in the length of the sequence of observations, the difference between the observed relative frequency and the value 0.5 will certainly (and not *almost* certainly) become smaller than any given small fraction; there is no room for the deviation 0.01 from the value 0.50 occurring with a finite, although small, probability even in a sufficiently long sequence of observations.

This objection is based on nothing but an inexact wording and may be easily disposed of. The above-mentioned law does say something about the probability of a certain value of relative frequency occurring in a group of n experiments. We therefore have to know what probability means if we are to interpret the statement. According to our definition, the whole group of n consecutive throws has to be considered as one element in a collective, in the same way as this was done before with groups of four and of twenty-four throws. The attribute in the collective which we now consider is the frequency of the attribute 'even' in a group of n throws. Let us call this frequency x. It can have one of the $n+1$ values, 0, $1/n$, $2/n$, ... to $n/n = 1$. If 'even' appears m times in a series of n throws, the attribute is the fraction $x = m/n$. Each of these $n+1$ different values of x has a certain probability. The probability that x has a value greater than 0.51 may be, for example, 0.00001. According to our theory, this means that if we repeat these sets of n throws an infinite number of times, we shall find that, on the average, 1 in 100,000 of these sets contains more than 51% even results. The frequency which is considered in this example is that in a finite set of n casts and is obtained by the division of the m even numbers in the set by the fixed total number n of throws.

On the other hand, when defining the probability of 'even' we consider a relative frequency of a different kind. In fact, we consider the whole sequence of all experiments, without dividing it into sets of n, and count the number of even numbers from the beginning of the sequence. If N throws have been made altogether, and N_1 of them have given 'even' results, the quotient N_1/N is the frequency considered, and we assume that this fraction, in which both the denominator and the numerator increase indefinitely, tends to a constant limiting value. In our case this value would be 1/2. No immediate connection exists between the two propositions of which one postulates the existence of a limiting value of the ratio N_1/N, for N tending to infinity, and the other states the occurrence of certain sets of the given fixed length n which exhibit an unusual value of the frequency m/n. There is therefore no contradiction between the two statements. The idea of such a contradiction could only arise from an incomplete and inexact formulation of the problem. One of the purposes of our next lecture (Chapter 4 of *Probability, Statistics and Truth*) will be to inquire more closely into the relation between these two statements, and we shall find not only that they are reconcilable but that the Law of Large Numbers acquires its proper sense and full importance only by being based on the frequency definition of probability.

Objections to the condition of randomness

I shall now consider the objections which have been raised to my second condition, that of *randomness*. Let us restate the problem. We consider an infinite sequence of zeros and ones, i.e., the successive outcomes of a simple alternative. We say that it possesses the property of randomness if the relative frequency of 1's (and therefore also that of 0's) tends to a certain limiting value which remains unchanged by the omission of a certain number of the elements and the construction of a new sequence from those which are left. The selection must be a so-called place selection, i.e., it must be made by means of a formula which states which elements in the original sequence are to be selected and retained and which discarded. This formula must leave an infinite number of retained elements and it must not use the attributes of the selected elements, i.e., the fate of an element must not be affected by the value of its attribute.

Examples of place selection are: the selection of each third element in the sequence; the selection of each element whose place number, less 2, is the square of a prime number; or the selection of each number standing three places behind one whose attribute was 0.

The principle of randomness expresses a well-known property of games of chance, namely, the fact that the chances of winning or losing in a long series of games, e.g., of roulette, are independent of the system of gambling adopted. Betting on 'black' in each game gives the same result, in the long run, as doing so in every third game, or after 'black' has appeared five times in succession, and so on.

In my first publication, I gave much space to the discussion of the concept of randomness. Among other propositions, I derived the following 'Theorem 5': 'A collective is completely determined by the distribution, i.e., by the (limits of the) relative frequencies for each attribute; it is however impossible to specify which elements have which attributes.' In the discussion of this proposition, I said further that 'the existence of a collective cannot be proved by means of the actual analytical construction of a collective in a way similar, for example, to the proof of existence of continuous but nowhere differentiable functions, a proof which consists in actually writing down such a function. In the case of the collective, we must be satisfied with its abstract 'logical' existence. The proof of this 'existence' is that it is possible to operate with the concept of a collective without contradictions arising.'

Today, I would perhaps express this thought in different words, but the essential point remains: A sequence of zeros and ones which satisfies the principle of randomness cannot be described by a formula or by a rule such as: 'Each element whose place number is divisible by 3 has the attribute 1; all the others the attribute 0'; or 'All elements with place numbers equal to squares of prime numbers plus 2 have the attribute 1, all others the attribute 0'; and so on. If a collective could be described by such a formula, then, using the same formula for a place selection, we could select a sequence consisting of 1's (or 0's) only. The relative frequency of the attribute 1 in this selected sequence would have the limiting value 1, i.e., a value different from that of the same attribute in the initial complete sequence.

It is to this consideration, namely, to the impossibility of explicitly describing the succession of attributes in a collective by means of a formula that critics of the randomness principle attach their arguments. Reduced to its simplest form, the objection which we shall have to discuss first asserts that sequences which conform to the condition of randomness do not exist. Here, 'nonexistent' is equivalent to 'incapable of representation by a formula or rule'.

A variant of this objection counters the joint use of the second with the first axiom, that of randomness with that of limiting values. The argument runs, roughly, as follows.

The existence or nonexistence of limiting values of the frequencies of numbers composing a sequence, say 1's and 0's, can be proved only if this sequence conforms to a rule or formula. Since, however, in a sequence fulfilling the condition of randomness the succession of attributes never conforms to a rule, it is meaningless to speak of limiting values in sequences of this kind.

Restricted randomness

One way to avoid all these difficulties would seem to consist in effectively restricting the postulate of randomness. Instead of requiring that the limiting value of the relative frequency remain unchanged for *every* place selection, one may consider only a predetermined definite group of place selections.

In the example which we discussed at the end of the second lecture, we made use of a frequently recurring, typical place selection. Starting with an infinite sequence of elements, we first selected the 1st, 5th, 9th, 13th, ... elements; then the elements numbered 2, 6, 10, 14, ...; following this, the numbers 3, 7, 11, 15, ...; and finally 4, 8, 12, 16, ... We assumed that in each of these partial sequences the limiting frequencies of the various attributes were the same as in the original sequence, and furthermore that the four partial sequences were 'independent' in the sense required for the operation of combination, i.e., that the limiting frequencies in the new sequences which are formed by combination and whose attributes are four-dimensional could be computed according to the simple rule of multiplication. The same reasoning holds true if instead of the value $n = 4$ we consider any other integral value for n, such as $n = 24$, or $n = 400$. A sequence of elements which has the above-described property for *every* n is today generally called a Bernoulli sequence. The American mathematician A. H. Copeland[25] and later on myself,[26] in a simpler way, have shown how it is actually possible to construct Bernoulli sequences. By following explicitly prescribed rules, one can form an infinite sequence of 0's and 1's which satisfies the above-stated conditions for every n.

Copeland has also shown that Bernoulli sequences have other interesting properties. If a partial sequence is formed out of those elements which follow a predetermined group of results, e.g., a group of five elements consisting of four 1's with a 0 in the middle, then in such a sequence the limiting frequency of the 1 (and of course also of the 0) will remain unchanged. We may therefore say that Bernoulli sequences are those without aftereffects. This property is called 'freedom from aftereffect'.

These facts seem to indicate that it might be sufficient to require that a collective should be of the Bernoulli type. Since it is explicitly possible to construct Bernoulli sequences, this restriction would dispose of all arguments against the existence of such collectives. Let us, however, consider what we would lose by thus restricting the condition of randomness.

Whereas we would undoubtedly be able to deal with questions of the type of the problem of the Chevalier de Méré, discussed in the preceding lecture, and would be able to proceed in the same way, there is, on the other hand, no doubt that a number of other meaningful questions would now remain unanswered. What happens, for instance, if a player decides, at the beginning, that he will consider only the first, second, third, fifth, seventh, eleventh, ... casts of the die, that is to say, only those whose order number is a prime number? Will this change his chances of winning or not? Will the same rule of combination hold true in the sequence obtained through the place selection by prime numbers?

If, instead of restricting ourselves to Bernoulli sequences, we consider some differently defined class of sequences, we do not improve the state of affairs. In every case it will be possible to indicate place selections which will fall outside the framework of the class of sequences which we have selected. It is not possible to build a theory of probability on the assumption that the limiting values of the relative frequencies should remain unchanged only for a certain group of place selections, predetermined once and for all. All the same, we shall see that the consideration of sequences such as Bernoulli sequences and others, which satisfy conditions of restricted randomness, will prove valuable in solving certain questions in which we are interested.

Meaning of the condition of randomness

In our theory of probability we have given first place to the proposition that in the sequence of observations under consideration the relative frequency of each attribute has a limiting value independent of any place selection. Let us review once more what we mean by this postulate. To be sure, it is not possible to prove it. Even if it were possible to form infinite series of observations, we would not be able to test any one of them for its insensitivity against *all* place selections, if for no other reason, because we are not in a position to enumerate *all* place selections. The axioms of science are not statements of facts. They are rules which single out the classes of problems to which they apply and determine how we are to proceed in the theoretical consideration of these problems. If we say in classical mechanics that the mass of a solid body remains unchanged in time, then all we mean is that, in every individual problem of mechanics concerned with solid bodies, it will be assumed that a definite positive number can be attributed to the body under consideration; this number will be called its mass and will figure as a constant in all calculations. Whether this is 'correct' or not can be tested only by checking whether the predictions concerning the behaviour of the body made on the basis of such calculations coincide with observations. Another reason for rejecting the axiom of a constant mass would be, of course, that it presented a logical contradiction with other assumptions. This, however, would merely imply that calculations based on all assumptions together would lead to mutually contradictory predictions.

Let us now see what kind of prescriptions follow from the axiom of randomness. After all that has been said, it can only be this: We agree to assume that in problems of probability calculus, that is, in deriving new collectives from known ones, the relative frequencies of the attributes remain unchanged whenever any of the sequences has been subjected to one or more place selections. We do not ask, at this moment, whether such an assumption is appropriate, i.e., whether it will lead us to useful results. All we ask now is whether this procedure may cause contradictions. This question can be answered clearly, as I shall show below. But first, I must insert some words of explanation introducing an important mathematical concept.

A quantity which cannot be expressed by a number, in the usual sense of the word, is said to be infinite. However, following Georg Cantor, the great founder of the theory of sets, modern mathematics distinguishes between several kinds of infinity. I shall assume as known what is meant by the infinite sequence of natural numbers. If it is possible to establish a one-to-one correspondence between the elements of a given infinite set and the natural numbers, then we say that the set considered is enumerable or enumerably infinite. In other words, an infinite set is said to be enumerable whenever it is possible to number all its elements. The set of all numbers which represent squares of integers and also the set of all fractions having integers as numerators and denominators are enumerably infinite. On the other hand, the set of all numbers lying between two fixed limits, say, between 1 and 2, or the set of all points in a given interval are not enumerable. At least, it has not yet been possible to devise a theory of the set of points in an interval which would not use some other essential concept besides that of enumeration. The set of all points in an interval is said to be 'nonenumerable' or, more specifically, 'continuously infinite'. This distinction between enumerable and continuously infinite sets is of the greatest importance in many problems of mathematics. Using this concept, we will explain the present stage of our knowledge with respect to the consistency of the axiom of randomness.

Consistency of the randomness axiom

During the last twenty years, a number of mathematicians have worked on this question. I name here in particular, K. Dörge,[27] A. H. Copeland,[28] A. Wald,[29] and W. Feller.[30] Although both the starting points and the aims of their respective investigations vary, all of them unequivocally bring out this *same* result: Given a sequence of attributes, the assumption that the limits of the relative frequencies of the various attributes *are insensitive to any finite or enumerably infinite set of place selections* cannot lead to a contradiction in a theory based on this assumption. It is not necessary to specify the type or properties of the place selections under consideration. It can be shown that, whatever enumerably infinite set of place selections is used, there exist sequences of attributes which satisfy the postulate of insensitivity. It can even be stated that 'almost all' (and this expression has a precise meaning which I cannot go into here) sequences of attributes have the required property. This last statement implies that collectives are in a sense 'the rule', whereas lawfully ordered sequences are 'the exception', which is not surprising from our point of view.

I know of no problem in probability in which a sequence of attributes is subjected to more than an enumerably infinite number of place selections, and I do not know whether this is even possible. Rather, it might be in the spirit of modern logic to maintain that the total number of all the place selections *which can be indicated* is enumerable. Moreover, it has in no way been proved that if a problem should require the application of a continuously infinite number of place selections this would lead to a contradiction. This last question is still an open one.

But whatever the answer may be, from what we know so far, it is certain that the probability calculus, founded on the notion of the collective, will not lead to logical inconsistencies in any application of the theory known today. Therefore, whoever wishes to reject or to modify my theory cannot give as his reason that the theory is 'mathematically unsound'.

A problem of terminology

I must now say a few words about another question, which is solely one of terminology. It has sometimes been said that a deficiency of my theory consists in the exclusion of certain purely mathematical problems connected with the existence of limiting values of relative frequencies in sequences of numbers defined by formulæ. It is not my intention to exclude anything. I have merely introduced a *new name*, that of a *collective*, for sequences satisfying the criterion of randomness. I think further that it is reasonable to use the word 'probability' only in connection with the relative frequencies of attributes in sequences of this special kind. My purpose is to devise a uniform terminology for all investigations concerning the problems of games of chance and similar sequences of phenomena. It is open to everyone to use the term 'probability' with a more general meaning, e.g., to say that in going through the natural sequence of numbers the probability of encountering an even number is 1/2. It will, however, then be up to him to explain the difference existing, from his point of view, between, say, the natural sequence of integers and the sequence of the results of 'odd' and 'even' in a game of dice. This problem is not solved by a change in terminology.

Neither am I willing to concede that a theory is more general or superior because it is based on some notion of 'limited randomness', and therefore includes a greater variety of sequences. There still remains the essential difficulty of indicating the characteristics by which sequences such as those formed by the successive results of a game of chance differ from others. On the other hand, a probability theory which does not even try to define the boundaries of this special field, far from being superior to mine, fails, in my opinion, to fulfil the most legitimate demands.

I intend to show later, by certain examples, how sequences which do not possess the properties of collectives can be derived from collectives (in my sense) by means of operations which do not belong to the system of the four fundamental operations discussed above. In so far as sequences of this kind are of practical interest (e.g., certain so-called 'probability chains'), they belong within the framework of my theory; but I do not see any harm in denying the name 'probabilities' to the limiting values of the relative frequencies in such sequences. In my opinion, it is both convenient and useful to call these values simply 'limiting frequencies', or, as I have suggested earlier, to use a word such as 'chance'. Of course, there is no logical need for this cautious use of the word probability; it is quite possible that, once the frequency theory has been firmly established, more freedom can be allowed in the use of the terms.

Objections to the frequency concept

As I have mentioned previously, the frequency theory of probability has today been accepted by almost all mathematicians interested in the calculus of probability or in statistics. This is usually expressed by the phrase that probability means an 'idealized frequency' in a long sequence of similar observations. I believe that by introducing the notion of the collective I have shown how this 'idealization' is obtained and how it leads to the usual propositions and operations of probability calculus.

On the other hand, there have been in the past and there still are a few authors who recommend applying the theory of probability in cases which in no way deal with frequencies and mass observations. To cite an older example: Eduard v. Hartmann,[31] in the introduction to his *Philosophy of the Unconscious* (1869), derives mathematical formulæ for the probability of natural events being due to spiritual causes, and finds it to be equal to 0.5904. I have earlier mentioned the economist John Maynard Keynes,[32] a persistent subjectivist. According to his opinion, probability ceases to be a trustworthy guide in life if the frequency concept is adopted. It seems to me that if somebody intends to marry and wants to find out 'scientifically' if his choice will probably be successful, then he can be helped, *perhaps*, by psychology, physiology, eugenics, or sociology, but surely not by a science which centres around the word 'probable'. The point of view of the geophysicist Harold Jeffreys[33] is similar to that of Keynes. In his book *Scientific Inference* (1931), he goes even further and says that any probability, in the widest sense of the word, can be expressed by a number. If, for example, a newborn child has seen only blue and red objects so far in his life, there exists for this child a numerical probability of the next colour being yellow; this probability, however, is not supposed to be determined in any way by statistical observations. Other arguments of the subjectivists have been presented earlier in connection with the question of equally possible cases.

In recent years, the Keynes-Jeffrey point of view has found some support; efforts have been made to construct a rigorous system of subjective probability. Let us briefly describe these attempts.

Theory of the plausibility of statements

In an interesting paper (1941), the mathematician G. Pólya[34] takes as his starting point the following historical fact. Referring to a proposition concerning an unproved property of integers, Euler stated that this proposition was 'probably correct', since it was valid for the numbers 1 to 40 as well as for the numbers 101 and 301. Even though such inductive reasoning is not otherwise customary in mathematics, or perhaps just because of this fact, Pólya considers this argument worthy of further investigation. He proposes that in such instances one might speak of 'plausibility' instead of probability. We are quite willing from our point of view to accept this terminological suggestion. Pólya arrives essentially at the following conclusions: (1) There are objective rules, i.e., rules accepted by all, on how to judge plausibility; e.g., if the number of known instances which support a proposition is increased, the plausibility increases; if an hypothesis on which the proposition could be founded is shown to be incorrect, the plausibility is decreased. (2) A numerically non-determinable figure, between 0 and 1, corresponds to every plausibility. (3) The formulæ of the calculus of probability are *qualitatively* applicable to plausibility considerations.

RICHARD VON MISES

The first of the above conclusions, namely, that there are generally accepted rules for judging plausibility, will not be contended. What is meant by mathematical formulæ being qualitatively applicable is not quite clear to me. Perhaps this means that merely statements of inequalities and not of equalities can be made, though even that much would require that the plausibilities could be ordered in a sequence such as that of the real numbers. But my main objection to Pólya's plausibility theory is the following:

The plausibility of Euler's Theorem does not rest exclusively, or even essentially, on his forty-two particular instances. If it did, we might state equally well that all numbers of the decimal system could be represented by at most three digits, or that no number is the product of more than six prime numbers. The essential, or at least an essential, reason for the plausibility of Euler's theorem lies in the fact that it does not contradict any well-known and easily checked property of the integers. Moreover, if we pay attention to this theorem we do so because it was formulated by Euler and we know that he had a comprehensive knowledge of the theory of numbers. How are we to weigh these facts in judging the plausibility in question? Should we then count the number of properties which a theorem does not contradict? Would we have to conclude that plausibility will increase with every new property with which the theorem does not conflict?

As I have stated, Pólya does not attempt to express the plausibility of a statement by a definite number. Other authors are less reserved. R. Carnap,[35] who belonged to the Vienna Circle of Logical Positivism, now supports a theory of 'inductive logic' where he uses the expression 'probability 1' for the plausibility of a judgment, whereas the idealized frequency is called 'probability 2'. Both of these are said to follow the usual rules of probability calculus. In Carnap's opinion, the difference between Jeffrey's view and mine consists in the fact that one of us talks of 'probability 1' and the other of 'probability 2'. Within the framework of theory 1, Carnap formulates the following proposition: On the basis of today's meteorological data, the probability that it will rain tomorrow is 0.20. However, 'the value 0.20, in this statement, is not attributed to tomorrow's rain but to a definite logical relationship between the prediction of rain and the meteorological data. This relationship being a logical one ... does not require any verification by observation of tomorrow's weather or any other observation.' Carnap does not state how the figure 0.20 is to be derived from the meteorological data. No meteorologist would fail to say that such a deduction is ultimately based on statistical experience. This, however, would bring us right back to probability 2. Carnap's theory would need to indicate how, by starting with propositions expressing the meteorological data, we arrive, by means of logical operations, at the figure 0.20 (or any other figure). His theory is, however, unable to show this.

The same unbridgeable gap exists in other systems which seek to define 'a purely logical notion of the plausibility of an hypothesis on the basis of given facts', using in an elaborate way the formal tools of symbolic logic and large doses of mathematics. C. G. Hempel and P. Oppenheim,[36] who attempted to do this, had to resort in the end to the admission of statistical observations as an essential basis, thus recognizing that mass phenomena and repetitive events are actually the subject of their theory. I certainly do not wish to contest the usefulness of logical investigations, but I do not see why one cannot admit to begin with that any numerical statements about a probability 1, about plausibility, degree of confirmation, etc., are actually statements about relative frequencies.

380

The nihilists

Finally, it is necessary to say a few words about those contemporary mathematicians who profess, more or less explicitly, that there is no need to give any definition or explanation of the notion of probability: What probability is, everybody knows who uses everyday language; and the task of the theory of probability is only to determine the exact values of these probabilities in different special cases. Such mathematicians completely misunderstand the meaning of exact science. I think that I have already said in the first lecture all that need be said about this question. It is essentially true that, historically, such a conception forms the starting point of scientific development. All theories arise primarily from the wish to find relations between certain notions whose meaning seems to be firmly established. In the course of such investigations, it is often found that not every notion for which the usual language has a word is an appropriate basis for theoretical deductions. In all fields in which science has worked for a sufficiently long time, a number of new artificial or theoretical concepts have been created. We know that this process is an essential part of scientific progress. Everywhere, from the most abstract parts of mathematics to the experimental physical sciences, in so far as they are treated theoretically, the exact definition of concepts is a necessary step which precedes the statement of propositions or goes parallel to it.

We may find an example in the modern development of physics. In the whole history of theoretical physics until the beginning of the present century, the notion of two simultaneous events occurring at two different points was considered to be self-evident and in no need of further explanation. Today, every physicist knows, as an essential consequence of Einstein's special theory of relativity, that the notion of simultaneity requires a definition. A whole theory springs from this definition which is generally considered one of the most fruitful developments of modern physics. This theory must be simply non-existent for all who think that we know the meaning of simultaneity anyhow, i.e. 'from the usual sense of the word'.[37]

I think therefore that the refutation of those who consider every definition of probability to be superfluous can be left to follow its natural course. One reason for mentioning these 'nihilists' is the existence of certain intermediate opinions between their position and our point of view regarding the formation of concepts in an exact science. Some of these middle-of-the-road conceptions should not go unmentioned.

Restriction to one single initial collective

A point of view typical of the attitude of many mathematicians is represented in A. Kolmogoroff's attractive and important book on the *Foundations of the Theory of Probability*.[38] To understand this point of view, consider for a moment the purely mathematical aspect of the content of a textbook on the theory of probability. We soon notice that a great many of the calculations are of one and the same type; namely, 'Given the distribution in a certain collective; to determine the probability corresponding to a certain part of the total set of attributes'; this 'part' of the so-called 'attribute space' or 'label space' is often determined in a complicated way; problems of this kind, which in our terminology belong to the class of 'mixing' problems, are sometimes very complicated. The following is an example:

The given collective consists of a combination of n simple alternatives, n being a very large number. The attribute of an element is thus a sequence of n symbols, which are, e.g., 0 or 1, 'red' or 'blue', etc. The probability of each combined result, i.e., each of the 2^n possible combinations of n symbols is known. We now consider another large number m, smaller than n, together with a variable number x, lying between m and n, and a given function $f(x)$, (e.g., the square root of x). One may now ask, what is the probability for the number of 1's among the first x symbols to be smaller than $f(x)$, for all x lying between m and n? This question obviously singles out a certain part of the 2^n possible combinations, a part depending only on the number m and the function $f(x)$, and we are seeking the sum of the probabilities of all attributes belonging to this group. This is a 'mixing' problem. The mathematical solution of such a problem can be a very difficult and complicated one, even if it consists, as in this case, in the application of one single fundamental operation to one given initial collective. In the literature, we find the solution of this problem for the special case of $f(x)$ proportional to the product $\sqrt{x} \log(\log x)$ with m and n both becoming infinitely large.

Let us return to the general problem in which we are interested. It is quite understandable that mathematicians who are engaged in the solution of difficult problems of a certain kind become inclined to define probability in such a way that the definition fits exactly this type of problem. This may be the origin of the view (which is in general not explicitly formulated), that the calculus of probability deals each time merely with one single collective, whose distribution is subjected to certain summations or integrations. This kind of theory would not need any foundation or 'axioms' other than the conditions restricting the admissible distributions and integrations. The axioms of this theory therefore consist in assumptions concerning the admissible distribution functions, the nature of the sub-sets of the attribute space for which probabilities can be defined, etc.

In the case of probability calculus, these basic mathematical investigations were carried out by Kolmogoroff. They form an essential part of a complete course on the theory of probability. They do not, however, constitute the foundations of probability but rather the foundations of the mathematical theory of distributions, a theory which is also used in other branches of science.

According to our point of view, such a system of axioms cannot take the place of our attempt to clarify and delimit the concept of probability. This becomes evident if we think of the simple case of the die or the coin where the above-indicated mathematical difficulties do not exist or rather where their solution is immediate without drawing on the mathematical theory of sets.[39]

Our presentation of the foundations of probability aims at clarifying precisely that side of the problem which is left aside in the formalist mathematical conception.

Probability as part of the theory of sets

By consistently developing a theory which deals with only one collective in each problem of probability and merely with one type of operation applied to this collective, we would eventually arrive at the conclusion that there is no theory of probability at all. All that is left of it then are certain mathematical problems of real functions and point sets which in turn can be considered as belonging to other well-known mathematical domains. 'From this point of view', to quote from one of the reviews of Kolmogoroff's book,[40] 'the theory of probability appears to lose its individual existence; it becomes a part of the theory of additive set functions'.

In the same manner, some mathematicians proclaimed that hydrodynamics does not exist as a separate science since it is nothing but a certain boundary problem of the theory of partial differential equations. Years ago, when Einstein's theory first became known among mathematicians, some of them said that electrodynamics is from now on a part of the theory of groups.

To a logical mind this identification of two things belonging to different categories, this confusion of task and tool is something quite unbearable. A mathematical investigation, difficult as it may be, and much space as it may occupy in the presentation of a physical theory, is never, and can never be, identical with the theory itself. Still less can a physical theory be a part of a mathematical domain. The interest of the scientist may be concentrated on the mathematical, i.e., the tautological, side of the problem; the physical assumptions on which the mathematical construction is based may be mentioned extremely casually, but the logical relation of the two must never be reversed.

Here is an analogy from another field: A state is not identical with its government; it is not a part of the governmental functions. In certain cases all the external signs of the existence of a state are the actions of its government; but the two must not be identified.

In the same sense probability theory can never become a part of the mathematical theory of sets. It remains a natural science, a theory of certain observable phenomena, which we have idealized in the concept of a collective. It makes use of certain propositions of the theory of sets, especially the theory of integration, to solve the mathematical problems arising from the definition of collectives. Neither can we concede the existence of a separate concept of probability based on the theory of sets, which is sometimes said to contradict the concept of probability based on the notion of relative frequency.

All that remains after our study of the modern formal development of this problem is the rather unimportant statement that the theory of probability does not require in its summations (or integrations) other mathematical implements besides those already existing in the general theory of sets.

Development of the frequency theory

During the past decade, the frequency theory founded on the notion of the collective has given rise to a noteworthy development. This evolution seems most promising even though practically applicable formulations have so far not resulted from it. This new theory was founded in Germany (1936) by E. Tornier.[41] J. L. Doob[42] is today its chief proponent in America. I shall briefly explain its fundamental ideas, in so far as this is possible without presupposing familiarity with the theory of sets on the part of the reader.

At the outset, Tornier introduces in place of the 'collective' the concept of the 'experimental rule'. By that he means an infinite sequence of observations made according to a certain rule; for example, the consecutive results of a game of roulette. He expressly admits the possibility of the result of a certain observation depending on the preceding one or of other connections. My theory is based on the assumption that all that happens to *one* given die, or to *one* given roulette wheel forms one infinite sequence of events. In Tornier's theory, however, a given experimental rule admits of an infinite number of infinite sequences as its 'realizations'. Let us, for instance, think of a game of 'heads and tails' with the possible results described by the figures 0 (heads) and 1 (tails). One realization of this game may be an infinite sequence of 0's, another a sequence of alternating 0's and 1's, in short, any infinite sequence consisting of these two numbers. The total of all possible realizations forms a set in the mathematical sense of the word; each group of realizations which have a certain characteristic in common is a partial set.

383

If we assign the measure 1 to the total set, then the theory of sets teaches us how to attribute smaller numbers to the partial sets according to their frequencies; the sum of these numbers must be 1. In Tornier's theory, a given die, or rather the experimental rule referring to this die, is characterized by attributing to the partial sets of possible realizations certain measures as their probabilities. For instance, there may be a die such that the realizations containing more 1's than 6's predominate; for another die, sequences showing a certain regular alternation of results may occur frequently; and so on.

In Tornier's theory, there is not simply a probability of the 6 as such; there exists instead a probability of the 6 being, for instance, the result of the tenth cast, i.e., the relative frequency of the realizations which show a 6 on the tenth place. That means, of course, that the setup in Tornier's theory is much more general than that in my theory. His theory permits us, for instance, to stipulate that the probability of a 6 on the twentieth cast should be different from that on the tenth. It also leaves us free to make an arbitrary assumption concerning the probability of casting 1 in the eleventh trial after having cast 6 in the tenth one (this being the frequency of the group of realizations containing 6 in the tenth place and 1 in the eleventh place). Thus the multiplication rule does not follow from the fundamentals of this theory. Tornier's theory is also applicable to experimental rules whose results do not form collectives in the sense of my theory. To take into account the conditions which prevail in games of chance, it is necessary to make certain assumptions, e.g., that the multiplication rule holds, that the frequency of the realizations having a 6 in the nth place is independent of n, etc.

The greater generality of the Tornier-Doob theory is bought at the expense of a greatly complicated mathematical apparatus, but the logical structure of the system is perhaps more lucid and satisfactory. We will have to wait and see how the solutions of the *elementary* problems of probability calculus will be developed in the new system. This seems to me to be the test for judging the foundations of a theory.

It should be noted that in the American literature this development of the frequency theory is often referred to under the heading of 'Probability as a Measure of Sets'. I have earlier pointed out that probability can always be considered as a measure of a set even in the classical theory of equally likely cases. This is certainly not a speciality of the theory which we have just discussed, even though in it the principles of the theory of sets are used to a greater extent than in others.

Summary and conclusion

I have said all that I intended to say on the problem of the foundations of the theory of probability and the discussion which has arisen around it, and I am now at the end of this argument. In an attempt to summarize the results, I may conveniently refer to the content of the last paragraphs. My position may be described under the following five points:

1   The calculus of probability, i.e., the theory of probabilities, in so far as they are numerically representable, is the theory of definite observable phenomena, repetitive or mass events. Examples are found in games of chance, population statistics, Brownian motion, etc. The word 'theory' is used here in the same way as when we call hydrodynamics, the 'theory of the flow of fluids', thermodynamics, the 'theory of heat phenomena', or geometry, the 'theory of space phenomena'.

2   Each theory of this kind starts with a number of so-called axioms. In these axioms, use is made of general experience; they do not, however, state directly observable facts. They delineate or define the subject of the theory; all theorems are but deductions from the axioms, i.e., tautological transformations; besides this, to solve concrete problems by means of the theory, certain data have to be introduced to specify the particular problem.

3   The essentially new concept of our theory is the collective. Probabilities exist only in collectives and all problems of the theory of probability consist in deriving, according to certain rules, new collectives from the given ones, and calculating the distributions in these new collectives. This idea, which is a deliberate restriction of the calculus of probabilities to the investigation of relations between distributions, has not been clearly carried through in any of the former theories of probability.

4   The exact formulation of the necessary properties of a collective is of comparatively secondary importance and is capable of further modification. These properties are the existence of limiting values of relative frequencies, and randomness.

5   Recent investigations have shown that objections to the consistency of my theory are invalid. It is not possible to substitute for the general randomness requirement some postulate of randomness which is restricted to certain classes of place selections. The new setup of Tornier and Doob constitutes a promising development of the frequency theory.

Notes

*   Originally published in *Probability, Statistics and Truth*, Dover, New York, 1957, pp. 8–29 and pp. 81–103. Copyright © 1957 George Allen & Unwin Ltd. Reprinted by permission of Dover Publications, Inc.

1   GOETHE's article in *Propyläen*, Vol. I, No. 1 (Werke, Ausgabe letzter Hand 12°, Vol. 38, 1830, pp. 143–154) uses the word 'probability' in the sense of 'illusion'. In doing so, he shows a much finer sense of language than the philosophers previously quoted. 'Eine auf dem Theater dargestellte Szene muss nicht *wahr scheinen*, aber einen *Schein von Wahrheit* vermitteln'.

2   A. A. MARKOFF says in his textbook, *Theory of Probability* (German edition by H. Liebmann, Leipzig and Berlin 1912, p. 199): 'We do not agree at all with the academician Bunjakowski (*Foundations of the mathematical theory of probability*, p. 326) who says that a certain class of narratives must remain unconsidered, because it is not permitted to doubt their truth'.

3   PIERRE SIMON (later Marquis de) LAPLACE (1749–1827) published in 1814 his *Essai philosophique des probabilités*, which was reprinted as 'Introduction' in the later editions of his *Théorie analytique des probabilités*, (1st ed. 1812, 2nd ed. 1814, 3rd ed. 1820). The *Essai* represents the point of view of unlimited determinism and is a characteristic expression of the philosophical school of 18th century France. The *Essai* was republished in a convenient form in 1921 in the series *Les Maîtres de la Pensée scientifique*, Paris, 1921.

4   SIMÉON DENIS POISSON (1781–1840), published in 1837 a mathematical textbook of the theory of probability under the title *Recherches sur la probabilité des jugements en matière criminelle et en matière civile*. The subject mentioned in the title is only treated in the fifth chapter of the book, which is one of the most important works in the history of the mathematical theory of probability.

5   A mathematical definition of the concept of limiting value may be given in the following form: We say, that an infinite sequence of numbers a_1, a_2, ... lying between 0 and 1 approaches a limiting value if, no matter how large k may be, beginning with a certain number, a_N (where N depends on k) all those following have the same k first figures after the decimal point.

6   *Deutsche Sterblichkeitstafeln aus den Erfahrungen von 23 Lebensversicherungsgesellschaften*, Berlin 1883. Short remarks about this and other similar tables can be found in E. CZUBER, *Wahrscheinlichkeitsrechnung*, 3rd ed., Leipzig and Berlin 1921, Vol. 2, p. 140.

7 J. V. KRIES, *Die Prinzipien der Wahrscheinlichkeitsrechnung, eine logische Untersuchung* (1886), second reprint, Tübingen 1927, p. 130.

8 LAPLACE, *Essai* (see note 3), p. 15 of the 1921 French edition.

9 POISSON's textbook has been cited in footnote 4.

10 LAPLACE, see note 3.

11 JOHN VENN, *The logic of chance*, London and Cambridge 1866.

12 TH. FECHNER, *Kollektivmasslehre*, edited by A. F. Lipps, Leipzig 1897.

13 H. BRUNS, *Wahrscheinlichkeitsrechnung und Kollektivmasslehre*, Leipzig and Berlin, 1906.

14 G. HELM, 'Die Wahrscheinlichkeitslehre als Theorie der Kollektivbegriffe', *Annalen der Naturphilos.*, Vol. I, 1902, pp. 364–381.

15 In speaking of the 'older generation', I have in mind especially a group of Italian mathematicians who in several papers which appeared in 1916–17 (i.e., before the publication of my investigations) claimed to have proved the 'inadmissibility' of the assumption of limiting values of relative frequencies. See, for instance, F. P. CANTELLI, *Annal. de l'Institut Henri Poincaré*, Vol. 5, 1935, pp. 1–50. What is actually proved in this paper is the contradiction which arises if one assumes the existence of the limiting value of relative frequencies while using the term probability in calculations and applications without postulating its identity with limiting frequency. In answer, see: R. de Misès, Sul concetto di probabilità fondato sul limite di frequenze relative, *Giorn. dell'Istituto Ital, degli Attuari* 1936, pp. 235–255.

16 FRECHET et HALBWACHS, *Le calcul des probabilités à la portée de tous*, Paris 1924.

17 J. L. COOLIDGE, *An introduction to mathematical probability*, Oxford 1925.

18 HARALD CRAMÉR, *Mathematical methods of statistics*, Stockholm 1945 and Princeton 1946. See in particular p. 150ff.

19 HANS BLUME, *Zur axiomatischen Grundlegung der Wahrscheinlich-keitsrechnung*, 1934 (Dissert. Munster). Also two papers in *Zeitsch. f. Physik*, Vol. 92 (1934), pp. 232–252, and Vol. 94 (1935), pp. 192–203.

20 A. KOLMOGOROFF's criticism appeared in *Zentralblatt f. Mathem.*, Vol. 10 (1935), p. 172.

21 Subsequent to the author's last revision of this text, A. H. COPELAND published the following paper on this subject: A finite frequency theory of probability. *Studies in Math. and Mech.* Presented to Richard von Mises, New York, 1954.

22 THEODOR FECHNER, see note 12.

23 CARL G. HEMPEL, '*Erkenntnis*' (*Annalen der Philosophie*), Vol. 5 (1935), pp. 228–260.

24 This objection forms the main content of the criticism of CANTELLI and other Italians referred to in note 15.

25 A. H. COPELAND, Independent event histories, *Am. J. of Math.*, 51 (1929), pp. 612–618; The theory of probability from the point of view of admissible numbers, *Ann. of Math. Stat.*, 3 (1932), pp. 143–156; Admissible numbers in the theory of geometrical probability, *Am. J. of Math.*, 53 (1931), pp. 153–162.

26 R. V. MISES, Über Zahlenfolgen die ein kollektiv-ähnliches Verhalten zeigen, *Math. Ann.*, Vol. 108 (1933), pp. 757–772. On the subject of Bernoulli-sequences cf. also H. REICHENBACH, *Wahrscheinlichkeitslehre*, Leiden 1935. Engl. ed., *The theory of probability*, Berkeley and Los Angeles 1945.

27 K. DÖRGE, Eine Axiomatisierung der von Misesschen Wahrscheinlichkeitstheorie, *Jahresb. d. deutschen Mathematiker-Vereinigung*, 43 (1934), pp. 39–47. Also, by the same author, *Mathem. Zeitsch.*, 32 (1930), pp. 232–258 and 40 (1935), pp. 161–193.

28 A. H. COPELAND, besides the papers indicated in note 25 above, see also, Point set theory applied to the random selection of the digits of an admissible number, *Amer. J. of Mathem.*, 58 (1936), pp. 181–192.

29 A. WALD, Über die Wiederspruchsfreiheit des Kollektivbegriffes, *Ergebnisse eines mathem. Kolloquiums*, Wien No. 8, pp. 38–72.

30 W. FELLER, Über die Existenz sogenannter Kollektive, *Fundamentæ Mathematicæ*, 32 (1939), pp. 87–96.

31 ED. V. HARTMANN, *Philosophie des Unbewussten*, 11th ed., Leipzig 1904, Vol. 1, pp. 36–47.

32 J. M. KEYNES, *Treatise on Probability*, London 1921.

33 HAROLD JEFFREYS, *Scientific Inference*, Cambridge 1931; esp. pp. 8–35.

34 G. PÓLYA, Heuristic reasoning and the theory of probability, *Amer. Mathem. Monthly*, 48 (1941), pp. 450–465. More recent works by the same author on this subject are: On patterns of plausible inference, *Courant Anniversary Volume*, 1948, pp. 277–288. Preliminary remarks

on a logic of plausible inference, *Dialectica*, Vol. 3 (1949), pp. 28–35. On plausible reasoning, *Proc. Intern. Congr. of Math.*, 1950, Vol. I, pp. 739–747. *Mathematics and Plausible Reasoning*, Vols. I and II, Princeton University Press 1954; note esp. Chs. XIV and XV.

35 R. CARNAP, *Logical foundations of probability*, University of Chicago Press, Vol. 1, 1950.

36 C. G. HEMPEL and P. OPPENHEIM, A definition of 'degree of confirmation', *Philosophy of Science*, 12 (1945), pp. 98–115.

37 In a paper, 'Über die J. v. Neumann'sche Theorie der Spiele', *Mathem. Nachrichten*, 9 (1953), von Mises comments: 'In the detailed presentation given in the book of v. Neumann and Morgenstern (*Theory of games and economic behaviour*, Princeton 1944) where every arithmetic or geometric concept is analyzed down to its last element, the words 'probability' and 'expected value' are used without any definition.'

38 A. KOLMOGOROFF, Grundbegriffe der Wahrscheinlichkeitsrechnung, *Ergebnisse der Mathematik und ihrer Grenzgebiete*, Vol. 2, No. 3, Berlin 1933. Engl. transl. *Foundations of the Theory of Probability*, New York 1950.

39 Here some ten lines of the text were replaced by the original editor by other material taken from the author's writings which, in her opinion, render more clearly v. Mises' point of view in his last years; see particularly: *Sur les fondéments du calcul des probabilités* ....

40 Review by DOETSCH, *Jahresber. d. deutsch. Mathem. Verein.*, Vol. 45 (1935), p. 153.

41 From E. TORNIER's writings we may cite here: Wahrscheinlichkeitsrechnung und Zahlentheorie, *Journal f. die reine und angewandte Mathem.*, Bd. 160 (1929), pp. 177–198; Die Axiome der Wahrscheinlichkeitsrechnung, *Acta Mathematica*, 60 (1939), pp. 239–280; *Wahrscheinlichkeitsrechnung und Integrationstheorie*, Leipzig 1936; *Theorie der Versuchsvorschriften der Wahrscheinlichkeitsrechnung*, by ERHARD TORNIER and HANS DOMIZLAFF, Stuttgart 1952.

42 J. L. DOOB, Note on probability, *Annals of Mathematics*, 37 (1936), pp. 363–367.

23

MISES REDUX*

Richard C. Jeffrey

> Once one has clarified the concept of random sequence, one can define the
> probability of an event as the limit of the relative frequency with which this
> event occurs in the random sequence. This concept of probability then has a
> well defined physical interpretation.
>
> (Schnorr, 1971, pp. 8–9)

Mises' (1919) concept of *irregular* ('random') *sequence* resisted precise mathematical
definition for over four decades. (See Martin-Löf, 1970, for some details). This circumstance led many to see the difficulty of defining 'irregular' as *the* obstacle to success of
Mises' programme, and to suppose that the solution of that difficulty in recent years has
finally set probability theory on the sure path of a science along lines that Mises had
envisaged. To the contrary, I shall argue that since stochastic processes do not go on
forever, Mises' identification of each such process with *the infinite sequence of outputs
it would produce if it ran forever* is a metaphysical conceit that provides no physical
interpretation of probability.

Bernoulli trials

Martin-Löf (1966) showed how to overcome the distracting technical obstacle to
Mises' programme, and Schnorr (1971) and others have continued his work. The air is
clear for examination of the substantive claim that probabilities can be interpreted in
physical terms as limiting relative frequencies of attributes in particular infinite sequences
of events.

The simplest examples are provided by binary stochastic processes such as coin-
tossing. Here, Mises conceives of an unknown member, h, of the set of all functions
from the positive integers to the set $\{0, 1\}$ as representing *the* sequence of outputs that
the process would produce if it ran forever. He then identifies the physical probabilities
of attributes as the limiting relative frequencies of those attributes in that sequence; e.g.,
in the case of tosses of a particular coin, h is defined by the condition

(1) $h(i) = 1$ *iff the ith toss (if there were one) would yield a head,*

and the probability of the attribute *head* is defined,

(2) $p(head) = \lim_{n \to \infty} \frac{1}{n} \sum_{i=1}^{n} h(i)$

Both parts of this definition are essential to Mises' attempt to interpret $p(head)$ as a physical magnitude.

In their algorithmic theory of randomness for infinite sequences, Martin-Löf, Schnorr, et al. have provided satisfactory abstract models within which part (2) of the definition makes mathematical sense. Thus, Martin-Löf (1968) proposes a model in which Mises' irregular collectives are represented by the set of all functions h that belong to all sets of Lebesgue measure 1 that are definable in the constructive infinitary propositional calculus, e.g., the set of sequences for which p(head) = 1/2 in (2). In proving that the intersection of all such sets has measure 1, he shows that his definition escapes the fate of von Mises' (according to which there would be no random sequences) and yields the desired result, that 'almost' all infinite binary sequences are random. The condition $p(head)$ = 1/2 is inessential: The same approach works for Bernoulli trials with any probability of *head* on each.

But the brilliance of this abstract model of Bernoulli trials is far from showing how probability is connected with physical reality: Rather, it deepens the obscurity of Mises' condition (1), which purports to provide that connection. For most coins are never tossed, and those that are, are never tossed more than finite numbers of times. No infinite sequence of physical events determines the function h of (2): For all but a finite number of values of 'i', the clause following 'iff' in (1) must be taken quite seriously as a counterfactual conditional. But unless the coin has two heads or two tails (or the process is otherwise rigged), there is no telling whether the coin would have landed head up on a toss that never takes place. That's what probability is all about.

A coin is tossed 20 times in its entire career. Would it have landed head up if it had been tossed once more? We tend to feel that there must be a truth of the matter, which could have been ascertained by performing a simple physical experiment, viz., toss the coin once more and see how it lands. But there is no truth of the matter if there is no 21st toss. The impression that there *is* a truth of the matter arises through the analogy between (a) extending a series of tosses of a coin, and (b) extending a series of measurements of a physical parameter, e.g., mass of a certain planet. If $p(head)$ is a physical parameter on a par with m(Neptune), then – the argument goes – (a) really is just like (b). But the analogy is a false one because while Neptune exists, and has a mass whether or not we measure it to a certain accuracy, the 21st toss of a coin that is tossed only 20 times does not exist and has no outcome: Neither *head* nor *tail*. A truer analogy would compare p(head) with $m(x)$ where x is a nonexistent planet, e.g., the 10th from the Sun. Mises defines $p(head)$ as the limiting relative frequency of heads in an infinite sequence that has no physical existence. If one could and did toss the coin forever (without changing its physical characteristics) one would have brought such a sequence into physical existence, just as one would have brought an extra planet into existence by suitable godlike feats, if one were capable of them and carried them out. But in the real world, neither the sequence nor the planet exists, and the one is as far from having a limiting relative frequency of heads as the other is from having a mass.

Granted: There is a telling difference between the two cases. In the case of the nonexistent 10th planet we are at a loss to say what its mass would be if it had one, while in the case of the coin that is tossed just 20 times we are ready enough to name a probability for heads. If the coin is a short cylinder with differently marked ends and homogeneous mass distribution, we are confident that heads have probability 1/2. But this difference tells against Mises: It identifies the probability of heads as a physical parameter of the coin, whether or not it is ever tossed, in terms of which we explain and predict actual finite sequence of events – directly, and not by reference to a nonexistent infinite sequence of tosses. It is because the probability of heads is 1/2 that we grant: If the coin *were* tossed ad infinitum without changing its physical characteristics, the limiting relative frequency of heads would be 1/2. But since there is no infinite sequence of tosses, 'its' characteristics cannot explain why heads have probability 1/2.

Irregular finite sequences

In the 1960s, Kolmogorov and others (Chaitin, Solomonoff) founded a theory of algorithmic complexity of finite sequences that sheds fresh light on probability. In showing that the sequences irregular in Kolmogorov's sense are those that pass a certain universal test for randomness, Martin-Löf (1966) provided an alternative definition of irregularity that he was able to extend quite naturally to the case of infinite sequences. In deprecating the foundational importance of the infinite case, I am far from denying the importance and foundational relevance of the finite case as treated by Kolmogorov, Martin-Löf, and others. What I do wish to deny is that by continuity with the finite case, or by mathematical infection from it, the infinite case gets the importance it would have if ours were a world in which each Bernoulli process went on forever (and in which each Markov process, infinitely replicated, went on forever). To get a sense of the importance and autonomy of the finite case, let us review it briefly.

Tables of 'random numbers' are long, irregular sequences of digits – binary digits, let us suppose. The easiest and surest way to generate such sequences is by Bernoulli processes with equiprobability for the two outcomes on each trial, e.g., by repeated tosses of a coin, with heads recorded as 1's and tails as 0's. In principle, such a process could yield a table of a million 1's, but in practice, no one would buy such a table or give it shelf space.

Why? Well, why spend the money? The table is utterly regular, the relevant rule being, 'Write 1 000 000 ones'. It is not only cheaper but easier to use that rule in your head than to buy and consult the table. *Moral*: We use 'equi-Bernoulli' processes to generate tables of 'random numbers' not because we have use for the outputs of such processes no matter what they may prove to be, but because we expect such outputs to be irregular, and it is irregularity of the sequence that we seek, irrespective of its provenance.

Kolmogorov (1962) pointed to *incompressibility* as a definitive characteristic of irregularity of finite sequences. Thus, a string of 1 000 000 1's is compressible, for the rule 'Write 1 000 000 ones' would be only some 100 binary digits long if letters, digits, and spaces were coded in some fairly simple way as blocks of binary digits. In detail, questions of compressibility are relative to (1) choice of one out of the infinity of universal systems of algorithms or programming schemes for generating binary sequences, and to (2) choice of one out of the infinity of measures of complexity of algorithms belonging to the same universal system – let us say, via length of representation in one of the infinity of effective binary coding schemes. Once these choices have been made, we have the means to define the *irregular* ('random') finite sequences as those *about as long as the shortest binary coded algorithms that generate them*. If we define the *algorithmic complexity* of a finite binary sequence as *the length of the shortest binary coded algorithms that generate it*, then the irregular sequences are those whose lengths are approximately equal to their algorithmic complexities.

Locally (i.e., for each particular sequence) the relativity of algorithmic complexity to choices (1) and (2) is problematical [cf. Goodman's (1955) 'grue' paradox], but globally its effect is negligible, for if k_1 and k_2 are two particular measures of algorithmic complexity, there will be a finite bound on the absolute differences between $k_1(s)$ and $k_2(s)$ as 's' ranges over all finite binary sequences. Thus, one proves that the percentage of irregular sequences among all sequences of the same length approaches 100 as the length of the sequences increases without bound: *For large n, practically all sequences of length n are irregular.*

Why do we turn to equi-Bernoulli processes as sources of irregular finite sequences? Kolmogorov's theory provides a clear answer, as follows. (1) For such processes, all output sequences of length n have probability 2^{-n}. (2) For large n, practically all sequences of length n are irregular. Therefore: (3) For large n, the probability is practically 1 that the output of such a process will be irregular. Then devices lie ready to hand that, with practical certainty, generate long irregular sequences. But mathematical certainty about irregularity is far more difficult to attain: (4) For universal systems of algorithms, the halting problem is unsolvable, and therefore there is no effective test for irregularity of finite sequences. In principle, one might nevertheless be able to prove that particular finite sequences are irregular, but in practice we do well to rest content with high probability.

Mixed Bayesianism

Suppose that a coin is tossed 40 times, and the process yields nothing but heads. There is a dim argument to the effect that this should not surprise us, for the sequence of 40 heads is no less probable than any other sequence of that length, be it ever so irregular. Of course, this argument must be wrong if we rightly see in such an output compelling evidence that the source was not as we had supposed it to be, e.g., if we see the output as overwhelming evidence that the source, far from being equi-Bernoullian, is one that yields heads with probability 1 on each toss. But what is the rationale behind this sensible view of the evidence? Here I give a mixed Bayesian answer to this question – 'mixed' in the sense that while statistical hypotheses about the source are treated objectivistically (as hypotheses about physical magnitudes), probabilities of those hypotheses are treated judgmentalistically ('subjectivistically').

(1) Consciously or not, we do or should entertain various hypotheses H_1, H_2, ... about the source, where (in the present example) initially we judge H_1 (the equi-Bernoullian hypothesis) to be overwhelmingly more probable than H_2 (the hypothesis that heads have probability 1 on each toss), in some such sense as this:

$$\frac{p(H_1)}{p(H_2)} = 2^{20} \approx 1\ 000\ 000.$$

(2) After seeing the output sequence and so verifying the evidence-statement E = 'The output is a string of 40 heads', we revise our judgment via the probability calculus, changing our degree of belief in each hypothesis H from its prior value, $p(H)$, to its posterior value,

$$p(H|E) = p(E|H) \times \frac{p(H)}{p(E)} \quad \text{(Bayes' Theorem)}.$$

391

so that now H_1 is overwhelmingly less probable than H_2, in the sense that

$$\frac{p(H_1|E)}{p(H_2|E)} = \frac{p(E|H_1)p(H_1)}{p(E|H_2)p(H_2)} = 2^{20}2^{-40} \approx 0.000\ 001.$$

In this Bayesian answer, the probabilities of the hypotheses are 'subjective' in the sense that they are degrees of belief, which need not be 'subjective' in the sense of being ill-founded, arbitrary, or idiosyncratic. But the statistical hypotheses H_1 and H_2 themselves are treated objectivistically. Some Bayesians – notably, de Finetti – would treat all probabilities as degrees of belief, and others would treat all of them objectivistically. The mixed position represented here is the commonsensical version of Bayesianism that Bayesian extremists must explain away or reproduce within their own terms of reference.

'Bayesians' are so called because of their willingness to use Bayes' theorem in cases where most thoroughgoing objectivists would reject as senseless the prior probabilities $p(H)$ and $p(E)$ of evidence and hypothesis that appear in it. The affinity of Bayesianism with 'subjectivism' (judgementalism) derives from the fact that we may have broadly shared judgements in the form of degrees of belief in H and E even in cases like the present example, where prior inspection of the coin is supposed to have led us to think the equi-Bernoullian hypothesis overwhelmingly more probable than the other, but where we envisage no definite stochastic process of which the coin is the product – a process of which the ratio of *physical* probabilities would be $p(H_1)/p(H_2) \approx 1\ 000\ 000$. Pure objectivists who would be Bayesian must envisage some such higher-level process, and treat the prior probability function p as the probability law of that process. Thus, commonsense objectivists sometimes speak (without conviction) of urns containing assortments of coins, some normal, some bent, some two-headed, etc., out of one of which the coin actually used is imagined to have been drawn. In that vision, $p(H_1)$ is the proportion of normal coins in the urn.

Observe that where the 'subject' thinks she knows the objective probability of an event (e.g., the event that all 40 tosses yield heads) and thinks she knows nothing else that bears on the matter, (e.g., perhaps, that the first toss yielded a tail!), she will adopt what she takes to be the objective probability as her degree of belief. Then 'subjective' does not mean *whimsical*. To call a probability 'subjective' is simply to say that it is somebody's degree of belief. One does not thereby deny that the belief has a sound objective basis. Furthermore, the 'events' to which subjective probabilities can be attributed need have no special character (e.g., 'unique', weird, etc.), for they are simply the events concerning which people can have degrees of belief, viz., all events whatever. [These remarks are directed in part to the comments on subjective probability in Schnorr (1971, p. 10).]

Nonfrequentist objectivism

Frequencies are important: The laws of large numbers tell us why; e.g., they tell us that in stationary binary processes, the relative frequency of 'success' will in all probability be very close to the probability of success on the separate trials. Notice that here, the notion of probability appears along with that of relative frequency in the formulation of the law itself. (The notion of probability appears as well in the definition of 'stationary', viz., invariance of probability of specified outcomes on specified trials, under translation of trials). Frequentism is a doomed attempt to define probability in such a way as to turn the laws of large numbers into tautologies.

The lure of von Mises' programme lies in its goal of providing a uniform, general definition of probability as a physical parameter – a definition that can be applied prior to the scientific discoveries that reveal the detailed physical determinants of stochastic processes, as e.g., the discoveries by Mendel, Crick, and many others revealing the mechanisms underlying the mass phenomena encountered in genetics. Mises sought to found probability as an independent science, on the basis of imaginary infinite sequences of events. Taxed with the unreality of those foundations, he replied that they are as real as the foundations of physics: To measure the physical parameter $p(head)$ to a desired accuracy it suffices to toss the coin often enough, for $p(head)$ is the limit of such a sequence of measurements just as surely as m(Neptune) is the limit of another sequence of measurements. Shall we hold the foundations of probability to a higher standard of physical reality than that to which we hold physics itself?

Surely not; but here, Mises holds physics itself to a remarkably low standard of reality, i.e., essentially, the idealist standard to which Bishop Berkeley held it: *Esse percipi est.* The suggestion is that the mass of Neptune exists to the extent to which we measure it, just as the sequence of outcomes exists to the extent to which we toss the coin. As was suggested on page 389, the limiting relative frequency of heads in the 'ideal' (i.e., nonexistent) infinite sequence of tosses is more properly compared with the mass of some nonexistent planet, e.g., the 10th from the Sun.

But if probabilities are not limiting relative frequencies, what are they? If there is no uniform, general definition of probability that is independent of other scientific inquiries, how shall we define probability as an objective magnitude? I would answer these questions as follows.

The physical determinants of probabilities will vary from class to class of cases; there is no telling a priori what they will prove to be. In the case of die-casting, the experience of gamblers and tricksters joins with physical and physiological theory to point to the shape, mass distribution, and (most important) markings of the die itself, as the determinants of the probabilities of the possible outcomes on each toss, and these considerations also join to say that different tosses are probabilistically independent. The case is similar for coin-tossing (where the point about markings is that there *are* two-headed coins about). In lotteries, by design, the determinants are the numbers of tickets of each sort (or the numbers of balls of different colors in the urn), but design is not enough: Empirical and theoretical inquiry may show the design to have been defective, e.g., because the balls of one color share a palpably distinct texture. As with games of chance, so with social, biological, and physical probabilities, but even more so: We look to experience, informed with theory, to identify the objective determinants of the probability laws of types of stochastic processes.

The easiest cases are lotteries and urn processes. There, we identify objective statistical hypotheses with the makeup of (say) the urn, and, by a happy accident, the probability of drawing a ball of a certain color is numerically equal to the proportion of balls of that color in the urn. In practically all other cases, such a numerical coincidence is lacking. The 'classical' view tried to generalize that coincidence to all stochastic processes. The frequentist view tries to generalize a different coincidence – one that is probable where the law of large numbers holds. On a nonfrequentist objectivistic view, one must face the fact that typically, no such coincidence will be forthcoming – not uniformly in all cases, and not even differentially, on a case-by-case basis. Still, we are often in a position where we can be fairly sure that the relevant determinants, difficult as they may be to describe explicitly and in detail, are the same in two processes, as when we ascertain that two coins were cast in the same mold under similar conditions: Believing that the determinants are shape, mass distribution, and markings, and having good reason to think that these determinants were determined in the same way for the two coins, we have good reason to think that the same probability law will govern the two processes of tossing them – even though we are at a loss to specify the common shape or the common mass distribution except ostensively.

No pure objectivist, I think it important to use judgmental probabilities, e.g., as illustrated in my remarks on mixed Bayesianism above (in an extreme, simplified example). The present suggestion is that the objective statistical hypotheses to which judgemental probabilities are attributed in such cases will be hypotheses about various kinds of physical magnitudes, which we shall seldom be in a position to specify explicitly and in detail, but which we can often identify ostensively, well enough for our purposes, once we understand what the *kinds* of magnitudes are that determine the process at hand – kinds like shape, mass distribution, and marking.

This is a far cry from Mises' uniform, general identification of probability with a particular physical magnitude, found in all cases; but that magnitude does not exist.

Note

* Originally published as Chapter 11 of R. E. Butts and J. Hintikka (eds.), *Basic Problems in Methodology and Linguistics*, Kluwer Academic Publishers: Dordrecht, 1977, pp. 213–22. Copyright ©1977 Kluwer Academic Publishers. Reprinted by permission of Springer Science+Business Media.

Bibliography

Chaitin, G. J.: 1966, 'On the Length of Programs for Computing Finite Binary Sequences', *J. Assn. Computing Machinery* **13**, 547–569.

Chaitin, G. J.: 1969, 'On the Length of Programs for Computing Finite Binary Sequences: Statistical Considerations', *J. Assn. Computing Machinery* **16**, 145–159.

DeFinetti, B.: 1974, 1975, *Theory of Probability*, Wiley, 2 vols.

Goodman, N.: 1955, *Fact, Fiction, and Forecast*, Harvard.

Kolmogorov, A. N.: 1963, 'On Tables of Random Numbers', *Sankhyā*, Ser. A **25**, 369–376.

Kolmogorov, A. N.: 1965, 'Three Approaches to Definition of the Concept of Information Content' (Russian), *Probl. Peredači Inform.* **1**, 3–11.

Martin-Löf, P.: 1966, 'The Definition of Random Sequences', *Information and Control* **6**, 602–619.

Martin-Löf, P.: 1970, 'On the Notion of Randomness', in A. Kino et al. (eds.), *Intuitionism and Proof Theory* (Proc. of Summer Conf., Buffalo, N.Y., 1968), North-Holland.

Mises, R. v.: 1919, 'Grundlagen der Wahrscheinlichkeitstheorie', *Math. Z.* **5**, 52–99.

Mises, R. v.: 1928, 1951, *Probability, Statistics, and Truth* (2nd revised English ed.), Macmillan, 1957.

Mises, R. v.: 1964, *Mathematical Theory of Probability and Statistics*. Academic Press.

Schnorr, C. P.: 1971, *Zufälligkeit und Wahrscheinlichkeit*, Springer Lecture Notes in Mathematics **218**.

Solomonoff, R. J.: 1964, 'A Formal Theory of Inductive Inference', *Information and Control* **7**, 1–22.

24

'MISES REDUX'-REDUX

Fifteen arguments against finite frequentism*

Alan Hájek

Introduction[1]

The most widely accepted interpretation of probability is *frequentism*. Roughly, frequentism says: the probability that a coin lands heads when tossed is the number of times that the coin lands heads, divided by the total number of times that the coin is tossed; the probability that a radium atom decays in 1500 years is the number of radium atoms that so decay, divided by the total number of radium atoms; and so on. This should sound familiar – all too familiar – for somehow this notion still pervades much scientific thinking about probability. But it should be rejected, as I will argue here – fifteen times over.

To philosophers or philosophically inclined scientists, the demise of frequentism is familiar, I admit, even though it hasn't quite been universally accepted.[2] Familiar too are many of the arguments that I will present here – indeed, some of them were inspired by Richard Jeffrey's 'Mises *Redux*' (1977) – though I hope it will be useful to have them gathered in one place. Other arguments in this paper are new, as far as I am aware. So even if the fact that there is bad news for frequentism is old news, I hope it is newsworthy just *how much* bad news there really is.

The stance that one takes on issues of philosophical methodology is important here. I will begin by saying some friendly things about the role of intuition in the philosophical analysis of objective probability, by way of preparation for the unfriendly things that I will say about frequentism as such an analysis. I will distinguish two frequentist analyses – *finite frequentism* and *hypothetical frequentism*. Although space limitations require me to confine my discussion to the former, many of the arguments that I will adduce will count equally against both.

Objective probability: intuitions and analysis

Probability is, I claim, a concept of both commonsense and science. The person on the street recognizes and understands it (at least to some extent) in locutions such as 'the probability that this coin lands heads is 1/2'; the scientist recognizes and understands it (at least to some extent) in locutions such as 'this electron is measured to be spin 'up' with probability 1/2'. Commonsense and science are joined by a two-way street: scientific theories are, after all, invented by people who share the folk's conceptual apparatus, and who seek to refine it; and commonsense, in turn, partly incorporates some of these refinements, as scientific ideas become popularized. The concept of gravity, for example, was once a part of neither commonsense nor science, and now it is part of both. I believe the same is true of the concept of probability.

Many computer scientists, statisticians, physicists, economists ... seem to speak as if probability simply *is* relative frequency – no ifs or buts, end of story.[3] This is surely mistaken. We would do better to think of it as a putative *analysis* of our pretheoretical notion of probability, one which both informs and is informed by a more sophisticated scientific notion of probability. 'Probability', after all, is not just a technical term that one is free to define as one pleases. Rather, it is a concept whose analysis is answerable to our intuitions, a concept that has various associated platitudes (for example: 'if X has probability greater than 0, then X can happen'). Thus, it is unlike terms like 'complete metric space' or 'Granger causation' or 'material conditional', for which there are stipulative definitions with which there is no sensible arguing, and no associated platitudes. What 'probability' is like, instead, are concepts like 'space' or 'causation' or 'if ... then', concepts that can be the subject matter of analyses. It is fair game to dispute such analyses; and it is certainly fair game to dispute frequentism. I say this early on, to forestall any possible puzzlement about my project here (a puzzlement that I have already encountered from various computer scientists, statisticians ...).

Furthermore, frequentism is at best an analysis of *objective* probability, sometimes called objective *chance* (to be distinguished, for example, from subjective probability, or degree of belief.) As we will see, however, it cannot be even that.

This is not to deny that probability and relative frequency have *some* sort of close connection. Subjectivists, propensity theorists, logical probabilists, and so on presumably all agree, for example, that an event with probability half should be expected to occur roughly half of the time, in some senses of the words 'should', 'expected', and 'roughly' (I would say this is another platitude). Moreover, I concede that finding out a relative frequency can often be the best – and sometimes even the only – way of finding out the value of a probability. I do not deny the existence of some interesting relationship between the two; I am only disputing their identification.

So far I have taken as a starting point our commonsensical notion of probability, and I have regarded frequentism as an analysis of that (a bad one). But we could come to frequentism from another direction. Frequentism is, as I said at the outset, an *interpretation* of probability. More precisely, it is a putative interpretation of the axioms of probability theory – traditionally, those provided by Kolmogorov. So starting with a primitive, uninterpreted function P, defined over a certain set-theoretic substructure, which is non-negative, normalized, and additive, we might come to a frequentist understanding of P. Here again, intuitions have a role to play. For *many* quantities that have nothing to do with our intuitive notion of probability conform to Kolmogorov's axioms, and so in some sense provide an interpretation of them – think of mass, or length, or volume, which are clearly non-negative and additive, and which can be suitably normalized. They are not even in the running, however, because commonsense tells us that probability is simply something *else*. (Just try substituting any of them into the platitudes above!) Incidentally, this also shows that it is too glib to say that a satisfactory understanding of probability is provided as long as we find a concept of importance to science that conforms to the axioms—for that does not narrow down the field enough. In any case, the more strictly *philosophical* project of analysing our commonsensical concept would remain, much as the project of analysing our commonsensical concept of causation, say, would remain even if we had already done the job for the concept as it appears in science.

Versions of frequentism

It is necessary to distinguish two variants of *actual* frequentism, and these from *hypothetical* frequentism. According to actual frequentism, the probability of an event or attribute is to be identified with its actual relative frequency: there is no need to 'leave the actual world', for all the requisite facts are right here. Now, if there happen to be infinitely many events or attributes of the requisite sort, then we cannot simply count the number of 'successes' and divide this by the total number of trials, since this will take the indeterminate form ∞/∞. In that case, we take the limit of the relative frequency up to the nth trial, as n tends to infinity. Hypothetical frequentism keeps the intuition that probability is such limiting relative frequency, but applies when the actual world does not furnish the infinitely many trials required. It thus identifies probability with a *counterfactual* limiting relative frequency: the limiting relative frequency *if* there were infinitely many trials.

I cannot discuss the problems with hypothetical frequentism here; and since the infinite variant of actual frequentism suffers from many of the same problems, my discussion of it is best left for another occasion also.[4] So let me focus solely, then, on the version of actual frequentism in which there are only finitely many trials of the relevant sort – for short, *finite frequentism*:

> FINITE FREQUENTISM: The probability of an attribute *A* in a finite reference class *B* is the relative frequency of actual occurrences of *A* within *B*.

Venn (1876), in his discussion of the proportion of births of males and females, concludes: 'probability *is* nothing but that proportion' (p. 84, his emphasis). This I take to be finite frequentism at its purest. Reichenbach had such inclinations also, although his account in the end looked more like hypothetical frequentism; finite frequentist accounts were pursued in more detail by Cramér, Hempel and Putnam among others.

Of course, all of this was a long time ago. It might thus be thought that frequentism is at best of historical interest as far as the philosophical literature is concerned – its currency elsewhere I have already emphasized – unworthy of much scrutiny in these more enlightened times. Up to a point, this is true enough, I guess; but only up to a point. As I indicated earlier, frequentism still has its proponents among philosophically inclined statisticians, and even philosophers. Furthermore, some of the criticisms presented here have some force against more sophisticated accounts that have grown out of frequentist soil, for example Lewis' (1994) 'best system' approach to objective chance, as I will argue at the appropriate point. Indeed, one wonders if an empiricist account of objective chance could be given that didn't look a lot like frequentism, and I suspect that many of these arguments could be adapted accordingly against any such account.

Any aspiring frequentist with serious empiricist scruples should not give up on finite frequentism lightly. The move to hypothetical frequentism, say, comes at a considerable metaphysical price, one that an empiricist should be unwilling to pay. Finite frequentism is really the only version that upholds the anti-metaphysical, scientific inclinations that might make frequentists of us in the first place. In any case, at first blush, it is an attractive theory. It is a reductive analysis, whose primitives are well understood; it apparently makes the epistemology of probability straightforward; unlike the classical and logical theories of probability, it appears to be about the world; and it seems to be inspired by actual scientific practice.

However, at second blush, it does not look nearly so good: it runs afoul of many important intuitions that we have about probability. Or so I will argue.

The arguments

We are almost ready for the arguments. Why so many of them? It might make you suspicious that I am uneasy about them, substituting quantity for quality. It recalls Flew's 'leaky buckets' metaphor for philosophical arguments: to paraphrase him, one watertight one is better than fifteen leaky ones. Suffice to say that I think the arguments here are pretty watertight, and some of them are pretty decisive on their own.

One reason for giving so many arguments is this. You might agree with me that frequentism cannot be an analysis of our concept of (objective) probability; however, you might think that it is, so to speak, a successful *partial* analysis of the concept, one that captures an important and central strand in our thinking about probability (even if there are other such strands). In my ecumenical moments, even I feel some temptation to concede this: perhaps we should let a thousand flowers bloom, with frequentism being one of them. Or you might think that frequentism is a good *explication* of the concept of probability – a cleaned-up surrogate for a messy, ambiguous, vague, and even confused concept, one suitable for use in science and clear-headed discourse. But I do think that the many arguments here successively chip away at frequentism's possible domain, steadily reducing its interest.

Another reason for giving so many arguments is that it shows just how dim are the prospects for retrenching frequentism in favor of some close relative of it. A single class of counterexamples to it might prompt one to add a single epicycle in order to save it. What I hope to make clear, by piling on ever more arguments against frequentism, is that the problems are not an artifact of some particular presentation of it, ones that would go away with a little clever cosmetic surgery. No – the problems with frequentism run deep.

Despite the title and fanfare, I don't want to be too fussy about how the arguments are counted. Not all of the arguments are completely independent of each other; in fact, several of them might be regarded as stemming from a single intuition (that probability statements can obey a certain sort of 'counterfactual independence'). On the other hand, elsewhere I might combine under the one heading two or more arguments that could be separated. I will distinguish the arguments in a way that I hope is natural.

I will begin with some general arguments that I think are telling against any form of frequentism; then, arguments specifically against finite frequentism.

General problems concerning any version of frequentism

1. The reference class problem

We think that various events straightforwardly have unconditional probabilities, and indeed we even have theories that tell us what some of these probabilities are. But it seems that frequentism delivers only conditional probabilities – or in any case, relativized probabilities.[5] Von Mises (1957) writes: 'It is only the notion of *probability in a given collective* which is unambiguous' (p. 365 in this volume). Suppose I am interested in my probability of dying by age 60. What I want is an *unconditional* probability. I can be placed in various reference classes: the set of all living things; the set of all humans; the set of all males; the set of all non-smoking males who exercise occasionally; the set of all philosophers; the set of all Woody Allen fans ... Each of these reference classes will have its own associated relative frequency for death by age 60. But I'm not interested in my probability of death *qua* philosopher, say. To repeat, I want an unconditional probability.

Here we confront the notorious 'reference class problem': a given event or attribute has more than one relative frequency; and according to the frequentist, this means that the event or attribute has more than one probability.

There is some irony here. Frequentists have been quick to mock Carnapian logical probability on the grounds that it must always be relativized to a choice of language, and no single language seems to be the canonical one. But a parallel problem is practically alluded to in the very name '*relative* frequency' – frequencies must always be relativized to a choice of reference class, and no single reference class seems to be the canonical one.

I see only one possible way out for the frequentist. He should insist that *all* probability is really conditional; and that a putative unconditional probability statement is really elliptical for a conditional probability statement in which the condition is tacit. He could maintain that probability theory could still do a lot of work for us. For example, knowledge of inequalities between conditional probabilities might be all that we need in order to control our environment in desirable ways, modifying our behavior beneficially. (When you see that the conditional probability of death by age 60, given smoking, is substantially greater than it is given non-smoking, you see a good reason to quit smoking – at least when you have ruled out other explanations for this correlation, such as the existence of a common cause, also on the sole basis of conditional probability information.) In short, rather than seeing the reference class problem as a problem, the frequentist could embrace it.

Perhaps this gives the frequentist a way out of the reference class problem. But he should admit that this 'eliminativism' regarding unconditional probability is somewhat radical, if only because science seems to abound with statements of unconditional probability. And of course he can no longer pretend to be giving an interpretation of Kolmogorov's axioms.

2. Typing events may change the probability

Every event, in all its myriad detail, is unique. This is just Leibniz's principle of the identity of indiscernibles, applied to events. So if you are going to group an event with others, you will have to allow differences between them. But there needs to be a guarantee that these differences make no difference to the probability. The thought must be that whatever the differences are, they are not relevant. The bulge in the carpet then moves over to the notion of 'relevance'. It had better not be probabilistic relevance, on pain of circularity. But what is it, then?

Plausibility drains from finite frequentism especially when the putative reference class is too heterogeneous, or too small. Unfortunately for the frequentist, these problems work in tandem, so that solving one tends to exacerbate the other. Homogeneity can be enhanced by raising the admission standards into a reference class, demanding greater similarity between the individuals or events; but that reduces the number of individuals or events that can be admitted.[6]

3. Probabilities of local events can be counterfactually independent of distant events

Let me first continue my plea on behalf of commonsense, with a little homily on philosophical argumentation. Sometimes arguments against a philosophical position attempt to show that the position has *internal* difficulties (and some of my arguments against frequentism are of this form). On the other hand, sometimes arguments begin with commonsensical intuitions that are supposed to be dear to us, and then deploy these intuitions against a philosophical position with which they clash. For example, we might begin with the following commonsensical intuition: this fire's burning my hand is a matter solely involving a small region of space-time containing the fire, my hand, and little else; and then deploy this intuition against Hume's regularity account of causation. 'Intuition-based' arguments are often not as damaging as 'internal-difficulty' arguments; and when faced with an intuition-based argument, a proponent of the philosophical position in question might simply retort that the argument is question-begging, and that we should revise our intuitions. Nevertheless, depending on the strength of those intuitions, and the weight that we attach to commonsense, such arguments can still have some pull on us. Much philosophy – the greater part of it, I would say – proceeds in just this way. (Think especially of philosophy's famous thought experiments: the Chinese Room, Twin Earth, and so on.) The argument that I want to turn to now is of this form.

Here is a radium atom; its probability of decaying in 1,500 years is 1/2. If radium atoms distant from it in space and time had behaved differently, this probability would still have been 1/2. I submit that probability statements about things can be (and perhaps typically are) counterfactually independent of what other things of that kind happen to do; and probability statements about local events can be (and perhaps typically are) counterfactually independent of distant events of the same kind. But according to relative frequentism, this is not so.

And I submit that probability statements about a thing at a time can be counterfactually independent of the behavior of that thing at other times. The chance that this coin lands heads *now* does not depend on how the coin will land in the future – as it were, the coin doesn't have to 'wait and see' what it happens to do in the future in order to have a certain chance of landing heads now. To put the point crudely, though vividly: it's almost as if the frequentist believes in something like backward causation from future results to current chances. Put more carefully: the frequentist believes that the *future* behavior of the coin places constraints on the chance that the coin lands heads *now*, and in that sense, that chance is counterfactually dependent on the future behavior. Indeed, if the coin has yet to be tossed, the future behavior fully determines that current chance, according to the finite frequentist.[7] I think the frequentist has things backwards: surely it is the coin's probability of landing heads that gives rise to its statistics, rather than the other way round.

And so it is in general. Frequentism suffers much the same fate as Hume's theory of causation. The fact that *this* flame burned my hand does not depend on whether *other* flames happen to be contiguous with *other* hands getting burned. The intuition behind this argument is that probability, like causation, is a far more private matter than that.

Digressing briefly: I said earlier that some of my arguments have force against certain more sophisticated analyses of objective probability that could be thought of as refinements of frequentism, notably Lewis' (1994). It runs roughly as follows. The laws of nature are those regularities that are theorems of the *best theory:* the true theory of the universe that best balances simplicity, strength, and likelihood (that is, the probability of the actual course of history, given the theory). If any of the laws are probabilistic, then the chances are whatever these laws say they are. It seems that according to Lewis, the probability that this radium atom decays in 1500 years does depend on what other, perhaps distant atoms (and perhaps not just radium atoms) happen to do – at least this will be so under the assumption that there are sufficiently many such atoms. For if many such atoms had decayed, say, much earlier than they actually did (something the best theory will admit has positive chance), then plausibly the best theory would have had different radioactive decay laws – it would have needed to in order to have reasonable likelihood. In particular, plausibly the decay law for radium would have been different, and hence so too the decay probability for this particular radium atom.

I think that the next two arguments also carry some weight against the Lewis analysis, and perhaps even the two after that (with some smallish modifications); but let us return to our discussion of (finite) frequentism.

4. An argument from concern

Let me pursue a variation on the 'counterfactual independence' theme. I am inspired here by Kripke's (1980) famous 'argument from concern' against Lewis' counterpart theory, according to which entities cannot be genuinely identified across possible worlds:

> [According to Lewis] if we say 'Humphrey might have won the election (if only he had done such-and-such)', we are not talking about something that might have happened to *Humphrey* but to someone else, a 'counterpart'. Probably, however, Humphrey could not care less whether someone *else*, no matter how much resembling him, would have been victorious in another possible world. (p. 45)

Arguments from concern have the form: 'If A were the correct analysis of B, then our concerns would be such-and-such; they are not; hence A cannot be the correct analysis of B'. To be sure, such arguments are defeasible, and what our concerns happen to be is, I suppose, a highly contingent matter. Still, much as thought experiments can be a source of philosophical insight – even though our responses to them are surely highly contingent – I believe such arguments can be also. And they may serve a distinctive function, trading as they do not only on our beliefs, but also on our desires (fears, regrets, ...).

It is natural to think that my probability of dying by a certain age is a property of *me* (or perhaps me plus my immediate environment). Natural, though von Mises goes out of his way to deny it: 'We can say nothing about the probability of death of an individual even if we know his condition of life and health in detail. The phrase 'probability of death', when it refers to a single person, has no meaning at all for us' (p. 357 of this volume). Also: 'It is utter nonsense to say, for instance, that Mr. X, now aged forty, has the probability 0.011 of dying in the course of the next year' (p. 361). But surely it is just such 'nonsense' that Mr. X really cares about, when he is concerned about his probability of death. Of course, he may well unselfishly care about his fellow citizens too, and he may be concerned to find out how high the death rate is among people of his type. But to the extent that his concerns are directed to himself, the other people can drop out of the picture (much as Kripke would say that Humphrey's counterparts can drop out of the picture when it comes to Humphrey's concern about losing the election). The statistics about others like him may give him good *evidence* as to his own chance of dying, but the *fact* that he ultimately cares about is a fact about himself – one expressed by a meaningful 'probability of death' statement that refers to a single person.

General problems concerning actual frequentism
(both finite and infinite)

5. Actual frequentism commits one to a surprisingly rich ontology

Here is another variant of the 'counterfactual independence' argument, though sufficiently different to merit separate treatment, I think. Nicolas of Autrecourt once said words to the effect that, from the existence of one object, one cannot deduce the existence of others. But according to finite frequentism, the existence of a non-trivial probability for an event *does* imply the existence of other, similar events in the actual world. The fact that I have a non-trivial probability for dying by age 60 proves that I am not alone in the world, according to the frequentist. Or consider some probability statement about my own mind: for example, that it will deteriorate by age 60 with probability 0.1. According to the finite frequentist, this means that a tenth of the people out there with minds like mine experience such deterioration by age 60 – which of course implies that there *are* other such minds. Now there's a quick argument against solipsism for you!

I'm being a little facetious here. It's not that implying the falsehood of solipsism is a bad thing – on the contrary. And of course the would-be solipsist-frequentist will simply deny that there are any non-trivial probabilities about my mind. What's troubling, though, is that statements of probability about a mind, an object, or an event, seem to be simply irrelevant to the existence of *other* minds, *other* objects, *other* events of the same sort, right here in the actual world. Moreover, we can even put lower bounds on *how many* such entities there are – for example, at least 9 other minds in the case just considered, and of course some multiple of 10 minds in total. It is often true that the required things do indeed exist, and in the numbers required (at least 9 other minds, for example). But sometimes they do not – see the problem of the single case below; and in any case, these things simply don't seem to be *implied* by the corresponding probability statements.

6. Actual frequentism = operationalism about probability

The finite frequentist definition of probability sounds a lot like an *operational* definition. Like the operational definitions of temperature in terms of actual thermometer measurements, or mental states in terms of actual behaviour, we have probability being defined in terms of the results of some actual 'measurement' (put in scare quotes, since the results might not always be observed): in this case, the results of trials of the relevant sort. 'Measurement' of the probability is mistaken for the probability itself.

Operationalism has hit hard times, of course. And rightly so – the arguments are well known. To rehearse just one of these arguments: we want to be able to say that

402

measurements can be misleading ('the thermometers were poorly calibrated'), but an operational definition doesn't let us say that. Likewise, if the frequentist has his way, we can't say that the chance of the coin landing heads really was 1/2, but that there was an unusually high proportion of tails in the actual sequence of tosses. And yet that could be a very natural thing to say.

7. Chance is supposed to explain stable relative frequencies

Why do we believe in chances? Because we observe that various relative frequencies of events are stable; and that is exactly what we would expect if there are under-lying chances with similar values. We posit chances in order to explain the stability of these relative frequencies. But there is no explaining to be done if chance just *is* actual relative frequency: you can't explain something by reference to itself. Here I am echoing a well-known argument due to Armstrong (1983) against the 'naive regular-ity theory' of lawhood (that laws are simply true universal generalizations). Compare: we posit laws of nature in order to explain regularities, so they had better not simply *be* those regularities, as a naive regularity theory of lawhood would have it. (Indeed, the demise of frequentism is parallel to that of the naive regularity theory in many respects.)

I have presented firstly some general arguments that work equally well against any of the versions of frequentism that I have mentioned – and indeed, in some cases, even against more sophisticated refinements thereof; and then some further arguments against actual frequentism, irrespective of the size of the reference classes. But finite frequentism also has its own characteristic problems, all really stemming from simple mathematical facts about ratios of (finite) natural numbers.

Problems specific to finite frequentism

8. Attributes with no occurrences have undefined relative frequencies. chance gaps

Relative frequencies are undefined for attributes that have no occurrences: 0/0 has no determinate value. But I contend that such attributes can have probabilities nonetheless.

Imagine two different worlds, each with a single die. In the first world, the die is tossed a number of times, but in the second it is never tossed. There's a sense in which both dice can be said to have well-defined probabilities for landing 6, say, but according to finite frequentism, only the first does. By analogy, in the first world, the die is weighed, but in the second it is never weighed; nonetheless, both dice have masses.

Ironically, von Mises adduces considerations similar to mine about dice in order to argue for his *opposite* conclusion that probability is relative frequency: 'The probability of a 6 is a physical property of a given die and is a property analogous to its mass, specific heat, or electrical resistance' (p. 358 of this volume). Exactly! But taking the analogy at face value, the conclusion ought to be that probability is an intrinsic prop-erty of chance devices (such as dice) – something a propensity theorist might say. The analogy to those other properties presumably appealed to von Mises because of his thor-oughgoing positivism, bordering on operationalism. He regarded the mass of a die, for example, as the limit of a sequence of ever improving measurements of the mass. But who among us now would want to say *that*?

All this may devolve into a clash of intuitions, as so many philosophical debates do (which is not to say that the debates are worthless); but I think that the intuitions on my side are perhaps even more compelling in the examples in the next section.

9. If B occurs once, A has probability 0 or 1: local determinism

Now suppose that we toss a certain coin exactly once. It lands heads. Then the relative frequency of heads is 1. But we don't want to be committed to saying that the probability of heads is 1, since we want to allow that it could be an indeterministic device. (Change the example to Stern-Gerlach measurements of electron spin, if you think that coin tosses are deterministic; and imagine a world in which there is only the one coin, if you think that the results of tossing other coins, when there are any, are relevant.) And in general, an event that only happens once (according to any sensible standard for typing it) does not automatically do so with probability 1. Such an *a priori* argument for local pockets of determinism is surely too good to be true![8]

Of course it isn't true. Consider now a radioactive atom that obeys an indeterministic decay law, but as it so happens, there is exactly one such atom in the entire history of the universe (cf. Lewis' (1994) 'unobtainium'). Are we to say that its probability of decay is 0 or 1, over any time interval, simply because for each such interval the relative frequency of decays is either 0 or 1? So with probability 1 it decays exactly when it does? This contradicts our supposition that it obeys an indeterministic decay law. An innocuous supposition, surely.

Many experiments are most naturally regarded as being unrepeatable – a football game, a horse race, a presidential election, a war, a death, certain chancy events in the very early history of the universe. Nonetheless, it seems natural to think of non-extreme probabilities attaching to some of them. This, then, is another notorious problem for frequentism: the so-called *problem of the single case*.

10. Universal generalizations and existential statements

Certain statements are 'single case' in virtue of their very logical form: for example, universal generalizations and existential claims. Some people think that non-trivial (objective) probabilities attach to such statements – as it might be, 'the probability that all ravens are black is 0.9', or 'the probability that there exist tachyons is 0.1'. If there is sense to be made of such probabilities, then it is not the frequentist who can make it, for such statements only get one opportunity to be true or false. How do you count cases in which a universal generalization, or an existential statement, is true? What is the reference class, 0.9 of whose instances are 'all ravens are black' instances? I suppose one could imagine counting possible worlds: (in the limit?) 10% of all possible worlds are 'there exist tachyons'-worlds. But this is hardly an attractive proposal, and in any case, it is certainly not finite frequentism.

An ecumenical frequentist might acknowledge some further, non-frequentist sense of probability that covers such cases ('let a thousand flowers bloom ...'), insisting that frequentism still holds sway elsewhere. The point of this argument is to identify certain sorts of probability statements that people have found quite intelligible, even though they are (virtually) unintelligible on a frequentist analysis. And various real-life frequentists are not so ecumenical.[9]

So far, the problems have involved very low numbers of instances of the attributes in question, namely 0 or 1. So the reaction might be: 'frequentism was never meant to handle cases in which there are no statistics, or only a single data point; but in decent-sized samples it works just fine'. This is the intuition encapsulated in the catchy but all-too-vague slogan 'Probability is *long run* relative frequency'. The reaction is wrong-headed: problems remain even if we let our finite number of trials be as large as we like.

11. Intermediate 'probabilities' in a deterministic world

The problem of the single case was that certain relative frequencies are guaranteed to be extreme (0 or 1), even when they are the results of indeterministic processes. This is an embarrassment for frequentism, because such indeterminism is thought to be incompatible with extreme (objective) probabilities – hence those relative frequencies cannot be probabilities. Now let's turn this thought on its head: *determinism*, it would seem, is incompatible with *intermediate* (objective) probabilities: in a deterministic world, nothing is chancy, and so all objective chances are 0 or 1. But determinism is no obstacle to there being relative frequencies that lie between these values. Remember Venn's example: the probability of a male birth is simply the proportion of male births among all births. This proportion is presumably roughly 1/2; but the process that determines a baby's sex could well be deterministic nonetheless.

12. Finite frequentism generates spurious biases

Consider a coin that is perfectly fair, meaning by this that it lands heads with probability equal to 1/2, and likewise for tails. Yet it might not come up heads exactly 1/2 of the time in actual tossing. In fact, it would be highly unlikely to do so in a huge number of tosses, say 1,000,000.

If the number of tosses is 1,000,001, it would be more than unlikely to do so – it would be downright impossible. So the finite frequentist thinks that we would then be wrong in saying that the coin is perfectly fair. Put simply: according to finite frequentism, it is an *analytic* truth that any coin that is tossed an odd number of times is biased. Now there's a startling bit of *a priori* reasoning for you.

Likewise, we do not need to leave our finite frequentist arm-chairs to 'discover' the biasedness of all *n*-sided dice that are tossed a number of times that is not divisible by *n* (a coin can be regarded, after all, as just the special case in which $n = 2$). And so on for other chance processes. If only all empirical matters could be settled so easily!

Furthermore, there is a 'graininess' to the possible biases of the coin, or the dice. Toss them *n* times; the relative frequencies must all be multiples of $1/n$. So not only can the finite frequentist assure us that various coins and dice are biased – he can even put severe constraints on the possible extents of the biases!

He should resist the temptation to reply to all of this: 'When we say that the coin is fair, we really mean that it lands heads with probability *approximately* equal to 1/2, and likewise for tails'.[10] First, there is no guarantee that the fair coin will land heads even approximately half the time. Secondly, we can at least *imagine* a genuinely fair coin, one that moreover is tossed an odd number of times; but the finite frequentist thinks that this is on a par with imagining an uncolored red object – namely, imagining gibberish. Finally, we should not let too much hinge on the choice of the example. Consider if you prefer certain Stern-Gerlach spin measurements, which are perhaps 'fairer' than the coin is; or consider the half-life of radium; or whatever your favorite example might be.

Ironically, the longer the finite run of coin tosses (or whatever), the more *unlikely* it is that the relative frequency exactly equals the value that it 'should'. To be sure, the probability that the relative frequency is *near* the value that it 'should' equal increases. But if frequentism is supposed to be an analysis of probability, near enough is not good enough.

13. Finite frequentism generates spurious correlations

Let us say that A is *spuriously correlated* with B if $P(A|B) \neq P(A)$, and yet A and B are not causally related. The finite frequentist will see spurious correlations all over the place. We can be pretty sure that, say, the relative frequency of people who die by the age of 60 is not exactly the same in general as it is among people who wear green shirts. In fact, we can be absolutely sure that this is so if the smaller sample size happens not to divide the larger one. To see the point, pretend that there are 10 people in our sample reference class, and that 7 of them wear green shirts. (Note that 7 does not divide 10.) Then all relative frequencies within the whole sample must be a multiple of 1/10, while within the green shirt sample they must be a multiple of 1/7. Now, there is no way for a multiple of 1/10 to equal a multiple of 1/7 (apart from the trivial cases of 0 and 1, which are uninteresting). The finite frequentist translates this as: there is no way for the probabilities to agree. In other words, a correlation – presumably, a spurious one – between death by the age of 60, and the wearing of green shirts, is guaranteed in this case. Again, it is startling that such results can be derived *a priori*!

14. All irrational probabilities, and infinitely many rational probabilities, 'go missing'

There's a good sense in which most of the numbers between 0 and 1 are irrational (uncountably many are, only countably many aren't). Yet a finite relative frequency can never take an irrational value. Thus, any theory which gives such values to probabilities is necessarily false, according to finite frequentism, irrespective of its subject matter. That's certainly a quick refutation of quantum mechanics! For example, according to finite frequentism, the radioactive law for radium is false for all time periods that have irrational probabilities for decay – which is to say that it is false almost everywhere.

Reply number 1 (à la Reichenbach, and very similar to one that we saw above): we can approximate an irrational value as closely as we like, provided we have a sufficiently large (finite) number of trials.

Counter-reply: again, this misses the point. The thesis before us is not that probability is approximately relative frequency, but that it *is* relative frequency. We have an *identification* of probability with relative frequency. Of course, it implies that we can approximate probability values as closely as we like with relative frequency values – anything approximates itself as closely as we like! – but it is a much stronger claim. The point about approximation might be appropriate in justifying relative frequentism as good methodology for discovering probabilities; but our topic is the analysis of probability, not its methodology.

Reply number 2: Bite the bullet, and deny that there are such things as irrational probabilities. No experiment could ever reveal their existence.

Counter-replies: Firstly, this would mean that the truth about various probabilistic laws is more complicated than we think. For instance, the radioactive decay laws would involve step functions, rather than smooth exponential curves. Secondly, the reply smells of positivism. Thirdly, we can imagine possible worlds that instantiate irrational probabilities, even if the actual world turns out not to be one of them. We surely do not want to say that quantum mechanics is not only false, but *logically* false.[11]

(By the way, *a fortiori* infinitesimal probabilities are ruled out by finite frequentism – and indeed, by any version of frequentism – yet such probabilities may nonetheless have an important role to play. For sympathetic discussion of infinitesimal probabilities, see for example Skyrms (1980), pp. 177–187.)

Moreover, according to finite frequentism, infinitely many rational probabilities 'go missing' also. This is related to the point I made earlier about the 'graininess' of finite relative frequencies, for a given sample size. All rational values that fall between the endpoints of the grains will be ineligible as probability values, according to the finite frequentist.

Note that the last few arguments did not require any assumptions about what we take to be the relevant reference classes. As I indicated before, I have misgivings about including in the reference class of a certain coin, the results of tossing *other*, very different or distant coins. But even waiving those misgivings, the last arguments still go through. Include if you like the results of various other coins when determining the probability for *this* coin; indeed, include if you like the results of all coins that ever were tossed, are tossed, and ever will be tossed. Since there will still be only finitely many trials in the reference class, still the frequentist will have to say: all probabilities will be guaranteed to be rational, and in fact, all multiples of a certain finite fraction; spurious correlations with other appropriately chosen factors can be guaranteed; and it is discoverable from the arm-chair that if the total number of tosses is odd, the coins are biased.

15. Non-frequentist considerations enter our probabilistic judgments: symmetry, derivation from theory ...

We should regard the various cases above as fatal for finite frequentism, because they provide bullets that cannot easily be bitten. We know that coins and dice cannot so easily be 'shown' to be biased, because we sometimes have independent grip on what their various chances are. We know that probabilities of radioactive decay cannot so easily be 'shown' to be rational, because quantum mechanics says otherwise. There are other sources of our probability judgments besides relative frequencies – for example, symmetry considerations, and derivation from scientific theories that we already subscribe to. When there's a conflict between relative frequency and one of these other sources, the latter often wins.

Conclusion

In this space, I could not give voice to various responses to these arguments on behalf of finite frequentists (although I did give voice to quite a few). They would doubtless reject the starting points of some of the arguments, particularly those that were 'intuition-based'; other arguments they would perhaps grant me, remaining untroubled by their conclusions. That should hardly be surprising: most philosophical debates seem to go the same way.

I do, however, think that finite frequentism is about as close to being refuted as a serious philosophical position ever gets. This becomes clear once we have separated the question of how probabilities are discovered from the question of what probabilities *are*. (A good way to find out if a man is a bachelor is to ask him; but we wouldn't want to analyse 'bachelor' as one who answers 'yes' to the question.) To put my position in the form of a slogan: 'Finite frequentism: reasonable methodology, bad analysis'.[12]

Notes

* Originally published in *Erkenntnis*, **45** (1997), pp. 209–27. Copyright © 1997 Kluwer Academic Publishers. Reprinted by permission of Springer Science+Business Media.
1 This paper is an edited version of the first half of my talk 'Thirty Arguments Against Frequentism', presented at the Luino Conference. I wanted this paper to reflect that talk, while meeting the reasonable length constraints that this volume required. So I have omitted my lengthy discussion of hypothetical frequentism, hoping to present that on another occasion (It can be found as Chapter 25 of this volume). I thank the editors for their forbearance.
2 I know this from various conversations I have had, though catching such frequentists out of the closet and in print is not so easy. Shafer (1976) comes close in his definition of chance: '... the proportion of the time that a particular one of the possible outcomes [of a random experiment] tends to occur is called the chance of that outcome' (p. 9), and closer still when he drops the qualification 'tends to' four pages later.
3 Witness Frieden (1991): 'The word "probability" is but a mathematical abstraction for the intuitively more meaningful term "frequency of occurrence"' (p. 10).
4 The discussion takes place in my manuscript 'Fifteen Arguments Against Hypothetical Frequentism', the second half of my talk at Luino, printed as Chapter 25 in this volume.
5 The distinction, I take it, is between a conditional probability of the form $P(B|A)$ and a relativised probability of the form $P_A(B)$. The former presupposes that $P(A)$ is defined, the latter does not.
6 This resembles somewhat the tension between simplicity and strength in the competition for the 'best' theory of the universe, central to Lewis' (1994) account of chance: raising the standards for admission is like an increase in strength, with a corresponding loss in simplicity. More on that shortly.
7 It is hardly better to propose instead that the chances evolve over time exactly as the corresponding relative frequencies evolve over time: for that would mean that the yet-to-be-tossed coin has an undefined chance of landing heads – see the 'chance gap' objection below.
8 I cannot pause for further discussion on the connection between determinism and objective chance. I admit that the connections I assume here are not uncontroversial. See Lewis (1986) pp. 117–121 for a fuller treatment.
9 Frieden, for example – see footnote 3.
10 I suppose we already knew that no actual coin lands heads with probability 1/2 *exactly*, and tails with probability 1/2 *exactly*, if only because some tiny amount of probability goes to the coin landing on its edge; and perhaps even some (tinier still) amounts of probability go to the coin landing on each of the two edges of its edge.
11 Here I construe logic broadly to include analytic truths.
12 I am grateful to many people for discussions of this material, especially Jim Bogen, Alex Byrne, Fiona Cowie, Ned Hall, David Hilbert, Marc Lange, Brian Skyrms, Nigel Thomas, Jim Woodward, and Lyle Zynda.

Bibliography

Armstrong, D. M.: 1983, *What is a Law of Nature?* Cambridge University Press.
Frieden, B. R.: 1991, *Probability, Statistical Optics, and Data Testing*, Springer-Verlag.

Jeffrey, Richard: 1977, 'Mises *Redux*', in R. E. Butts and J. Hintikka (eds.), *Basic Problems in Methodology and Linguistics*, reprinted as Chapter 23 in this volume.

Kripke, Saul: 1980, *Naming and Necessity*, Oxford University Press.

Lewis, David: 1986, *Philosophical Papers*, vol. II, Oxford University Press.

Lewis, David: 1994, 'Humean Supervenience Debugged', *Mind* 103, 473–490.

Reichenbach, Hans: 1949, *The Theory of Probability*, University of California Press.

Shafer, Glenn: 1976, *A Mathematical Theory of Evidence*, Princeton University Press.

Skyrms, Brian: 1980, *Causal Necessity*, Yale 1980.

Venn, John: 1876, *The Logic of Chance*, 2nd ed., Macmillan and Co.

von Mises, Richard: 1957, *Probability, Truth and Statistics*, Macmillan, relevant extracts reprinted as Chapter 22 in this volume.

25

FIFTEEN ARGUMENTS
AGAINST HYPOTHETICAL
FREQUENTISM*

Alan Hájek

Prologue

Over a decade ago, in a flurry of youthful zeal, I wrote a paper called 'Thirty Arguments Against Frequentism' for the wonderful 3rd Luino Conference on Probability, Dynamics and Causality, organized by Domenico Costantini and Maria-Carla Galavotti. The conference was held in honor of Richard Jeffrey, and his paper 'Mises Redux' (Chapter 23 in this volume), a famous critique of the frequentist interpretation of probability, provided the inspiration for mine. The conference proceedings eventually appeared in *Erkenntnis* Vol. 45 (1997), and they were reprinted in Costantini and Galavotti (1997). In my original paper I distinguished two versions of frequentism—what I called *finite* frequentism, and *hypothetical* frequentism, and I marshaled fifteen arguments against each. Unfortunately, my paper was roughly twice the length allowed for the publications. Fortunately, this problem was easily solved—I simply cut the paper into two halves, one on each version of frequentism, and I submitted the first half! (Chapter 24 of this volume.) The second half remained on my computer's hard drive and in the hands of a few interested folk who solicited copies of it—until now.

It's a slightly curious feeling revisiting and revising that paper. It's like co-authoring a paper with someone with whom I agree mostly but not entirely, and with the co-author denied the right of reply. Perhaps I have mellowed in the intervening years, but I now see some frequentist responses that I didn't see then, as this version of the paper shows. I even offer the frequentist a positive proposal, *hyperhypothetical frequentism*, which I argue avoids several of the problems with hypothetical frequentism. That said, I stand by all the main points of the original article, so I am happy to reprise them here. Anyway, I hereby appoint my current time-slice as the senior author; but all mistakes should be blamed on my younger self!

Hypothetical frequentism

Probability is *long run* relative frequency—or so it is said. Here is a well-known engineering textbook saying so: 'The probability of an event (or outcome) is the proportion of times the event would occur in a long run of repeated experiments' (Johnson 1994, p. 57). So the probability that the coin lands Heads is the relative frequency of

Heads in a long run of tosses of the coin, the probability that the radium atom decays in 1,600 years is the relative frequency of such atoms that so decay in a long sequence of such atoms, and so on. What if the world is not generous enough actually to provide a long run of the relevant sequence of events? And how long is 'long', in any case? We can circumvent both concerns with a single stroke, by going *hypothetical*—by considering what things *would* be like if the run in question were of any length that we care to specify. (Notice the 'would' in the quote above.) And since we are going hypothetical, we might as well make the most of it and consider the longest run possible: an infinite run. After all, whatever vagueness there may be in 'long run', an infinite run surely counts. So let us give as broad a characterization of hypothetical frequentism as we can, consistent with this commitment. It asserts:

> (HF) *The probability of an attribute A in a reference class B is p*
>
> *iff*
>
> *the limit of the relative frequency of occurrences of A within B would be p if B were infinite.*

This characterization is meant to subsume various more specific accounts—for example, those of Reichenbach (1949) and von Mises (1957), the latter endorsed by Howson and Urbach (1993).

This account of probability will be my target—15 times over. Why so many arguments? Is this an exercise in overkill? Or worse, is it an exercise in *under*kill, my deployment of so many arguments betraying a lack of faith that any one of them actually does the job? On the contrary, as in *Murder On the Orient Express*, I think that many of the blows may well be fatal on their own (although in the book, the victim only received twelve of them). But there is good reason to accumulate the arguments: they successively cut off hypothetical frequentism's escape routes, making the addition of an epicycle here or a further clause there less and less promising. For example, some of the arguments work in tandem, setting up dilemmas for hypothetical frequentism: if it dodges one argument by retreating one way, another argument awaits it there.[1] Moreover, different frequentists may have different ambitions for their theory. Some might offer it as an analysis of the concept of 'objective probability'. Others might regard it as an explication, allowing that it might precisify or otherwise slightly revise a messy, pre-scientific concept so that it is fit for science. Still others might be content to identify a core usage of the words 'objective probability' in our theorizing, or some central strand of our thinking about it, and seek just to capture that. And so on. By piling on argument after argument, we thwart more and more of these ambitions. When we are done, I hope to have shown that probability is not recognizably a frequentist notion, however we squint at it.

Despite its eventual and overdetermined demise, hypothetical frequentism is a worthy target. It is certainly entrenched, arguably the most entrenched of all the major interpretations of probability. Just ask your typical physicist or engineer what *they* think probability is, if you need any convincing of this. It still has some currency among philosophers nowadays—I have already mentioned Howson and Urbach's endorsement of it. It seems to render precise our folk understanding of probability as having a close connection to long run frequencies, even when those long runs are not actualized.

It resonates with the class of limit theorems known as the 'laws of large numbers'—more on that shortly. Moreover, hypothetical frequentism is recognizable in more recent frequency-based philosophical accounts of probability—notably van Fraassen's (1980) 'modal frequency' account. And there are ghosts of hypothetical frequentism in Lewis's (and his followers') 'best systems' accounts (Lewis 1994). They say, roughly, that objective probabilities ('chances') are given by indeterministic laws as stated by the theory of the universe that best combines simplicity, strength, and fit to the data. I believe that collectively the arguments here cast some doubt on the viability of these more recent accounts, too, so I hope the interest of the arguments extends beyond the narrower focus of this paper.

Since the target is worthy, it is worth pursuing at least some of the epicycles or further clauses, to see how they play out. Along the way I will suggest ways in which frequentism can be buttressed in the face of the problems that I point out. However, buttressing frequentism is one thing, saving it another.

I will present first some more broadly philosophical arguments, then more precise, mathematical arguments. Not all of them are original to me, although when they are not I think at least I have something original to say about them. And I hope it will be useful to have them gathered alongside more original arguments, so that the case against hypothetical frequentism can be assessed in its entirety.

Enough preliminaries; onwards to

The arguments

1. An abandonment of empiricism

Frequentism has laudable empiricist motivations, and frequentists have typically had an eye on scientific applications of probability. Finite frequentism, the target of this paper's predecessor, admirably respected those motivations, its other failings notwithstanding. It says:

> The probability of an attribute A in a finite reference class B is the relative frequency of actual occurrences of A within B.

But hypothetical frequentism makes two modifications of that account that ought to make an empiricist uneasy: its invocation of a *limit*, and of a *counterfactual*. Regarding the limit, any finite sequence—which is, after all, all we ever see—puts no constraint whatsoever on the limiting relative frequency of some attribute. Limiting relative frequencies are unobservable in a strong sense: improving our measuring instruments or our eyesight as much as we like would not help us ascertain them. Imagine what it would take to observe the limiting relative frequency of Heads in an infinite sequence of coin tosses—the observers would have to live forever, or be able to complete successive tosses in exponentially shorter intervals, Zeno-like, so that all the tosses are completed in a finite period of time. Hume would turn in his grave.

Related, finite frequentism made congenial the *epistemology* of probability. One can easily know the relative frequency of Heads in some finite sequence—it's as easy as watching, counting, and dividing. But how can one know what the limiting relative frequency of Heads would be in a hypothetical infinite sequence? To be sure, science appeals to quantities that are defined in terms of limits—think of velocity, or acceleration, or

412

power—and we take ourselves to be able to know the values of such quantities, well enough. But the value of a limiting hypothetical relative frequency is unknowable in the strongest sense, for the reasons in the previous paragraph, and also since there is necessarily no fact of the matter of this value (as I will shortly argue), and knowledge is factive.

A commonly made criticism of one early version of Carnapian logical probability (1950), $c^\dagger$, is that it 'does not learn from experience': evidence regarding the properties of certain individuals does not change prior probabilities for other individuals having those properties. But to the extent that this is a problem, it affects frequentism—the interpretation whose very motivation is to take evidence seriously. Indeed, finite frequentism takes evidence *so* seriously that it conflates a certain kind of good evidence for a probability claim for the truth-maker of the claim itself. But ironically, hypothetical frequentism seems to suffer from $c^\dagger$'s problem more than $c^\dagger$ itself does. For while Carnap's $c^\dagger(h, e)$ is a function of e, and in that sense surely *does* take the evidence seriously, finite strings of data put absolutely no constraint on the hypothetical frequentist's probability. But again, finite strings of data are all that we ever see.

The frequentist could try to relieve this problem by restricting his account, only according probabilities to attributes whose relative frequencies converge *quickly* (in some sense to be spelled out more precisely). For such attributes, finite strings of data could be a good guide to the corresponding limiting behavior after all.[2] For example, there are many hypothetical sequences of coin tosses for which the relative frequency of Heads beyond the 100th toss never deviates by more than 0.1 from 1/2. In those sequences, the first 100 tosses reflect well the limiting behavior. More generally, the frequentist might choose an $\varepsilon > 0$ and an N such that the only attributes that have probabilities are those whose hypothetical relative frequencies beyond N remain within ε of their limiting values. This proposal arguably would help with the epistemological problem that I have raised: if a probability exists at all, then it can be ascertained fairly accurately with a comparatively small number of observations. But the proposal renders worse the problem, which we will see shortly, of probabilities being undefined when intuitively they should be defined—see argument 5. And it shifts the epistemological problem to one of knowing *whether* a probability exists at all, which finite frequentism at least made tractable.

Nor should the appeal to HF's counterfactual sit well with frequentism's forefathers: frequentism has gone modal. The frequentist can no longer obviously take the philosophical high ground when compared to a propensity theorist, who sees probabilities as certain dispositions. After all, dispositions are typically closely linked to counterfactuals about behavior under appropriate circumstances: to say that a piece of salt is soluble is (roughly[3]) to say that it would dissolve if it were placed in water, and so on. Hypothetical frequentism's counterfactual has a similar ring to it. In fact, it has a worse ring to it, by empiricist lights—a death knell.

2. The counterfactuals appealed to are utterly bizarre

For HF isn't just some innocent, innocuous counterfactual. It is infinitely more far-fetched than the solubility counterfactual. To focus our discussion, let us think of counterfactuals as being analyzed in terms of a Stalnaker/Lewis-style possible worlds semantics (Stalnaker 1968, Lewis 1973). Taking hypothetical frequentism's statement literally—and I don't know how else to take it—we are supposed to imagine a world in which an infinite sequence of the relevant attribute occurs. But for almost any attribute you can think of, any world in which *that* is the case would have to be *very* different from the actual world. Consider the radium atom's decay. We are supposed to imagine infinitely many radium atoms: that is, a world in which there is an infinite amount of matter (and not just the 10^{80} or so atoms that populate the actual universe, according to a recent census). Consider the coin toss. We are supposed to imagine infinitely many results of tossing the coin: that is, a world in which coins are 'immortal', lasting forever, coin-tossers are immortal and never tire of tossing (or something similar, anyway), or else in which coin tosses can be completed in ever shorter intervals of time... In short, we are supposed to imagine *utterly bizarre* worlds—perhaps worlds in which entropy does not increase over time, for instance, or in which special relativity is violated in spectacular ways. In any case, they sound like worlds in which the laws of physics (and the laws of biology and psychology?) are quite different to what they actually are. But if the chances are closely connected to the laws, as seems reasonable, and the laws are so different, then surely the chances could then be quite different, too.[4]

Note also a further consequences for the world that we are supposed to consider here. If there are infinitely many events of a given sort in a single world, then either time is continuous (as opposed to quantized), or infinite in at least one direction, or infinitely many events are simultaneous, or we have a Zeno-like compression of the events into smaller and smaller intervals. In any case, I find it odd that there should be such extravagant consequences for the truth-makers of probability statements in the actual world.

So what goes on in these worlds seems to be entirely irrelevant to facts about this world. Moreover, we are supposed to have intuitions about what happens in these worlds—for example, that the limiting relative frequency of Heads would be 1/2 in a nearest world in which the coin is tossed forever. But intuitions that we have developed in the actual world will be a poor guide to what goes on in these remote worlds. Who knows what would happen in such a world? And our confidence that the limiting relative frequency really would be 1/2 surely derives from actual-worldly facts—the actual symmetry of the coin, the behavior of other similar coins in actual tosses, or what have you—so it is really *those* facts that underpin our intuition.

Readers of Kripke (1980) will recognize a parallel here to his famous argument against a dispositional analysis of meaning. Kripke's skeptic challenges you to come up with a fact that determines that you should now compute the *plus* function rather than the *quus* function in order to accord with your past intentions. Response: your past *dispositions* constrain what you should now do. But as Kripke points out, you had only a finite set of dispositions, being a mortal being with a finite mind, so that underdetermines what you should do now. Response: then let's imagine away those limitations, considering instead what would be true if you had an infinite brain ... But Kripke replies—and now the parallel should be clear—who knows what would be the case under such a bizarre supposition? It seems that any plausibility the infinite-case counterfactual has, it derives from the finite case.

Now, it may be objected to Kripke that the infinite brain is an idealization, much like an ideal gas or a frictionless plane, and that such idealization is a familiar part of science.[5] So it is; but I don't see how talk of idealization rescues hypothetical frequentism, regarded as an *analysis* of probability. HF asserts a biconditional (one which presumably is supposed to be necessarily true). According to it, the coin in my pocket lands Heads with probability 1/2 *if and only if* a certain bizarre counterfactual about a very different coin is true. I am puzzled by the claim that the two sides of this biconditional (necessarily) have the same truth value; indeed, I flatly deny it. Is my puzzlement supposed to vanish when I am told that HF involves an *idealization*? Does the biconditional suddenly become true if we think of it as an *idealization*? I don't know that would even mean.

Perhaps I am not doing justice to the role that idealization might play in hypothetical frequentism; I did, after all, allow that different frequentists might have different ambitions for their theory. Very well then; perhaps they have an answer to this argument. But I also said that I have other arguments as backup, poised to scotch those ambitions. So let me continue.

3. There is no fact of what the hypothetical sequences look like

In fact the problem for the hypothetical frequentist's counterfactual is still worse than it was for the 'infinite brain' counterfactual. Here is a coin that is tossed exactly once, and it lands Heads. How would it have landed if tossed infinitely many times? Never mind that—let's answer a seemingly easier question: how would it have landed on the second toss? Suppose you say 'Heads'. Why *Heads*? The coin equally could have landed Tails, so I say that it would have. We can each pound the table if we like, but we can't both be right. More than that: neither of us can be right. For to give a definite answer as to how a chancy device would behave is to misunderstand chance.

Here I am echoing one of Jeffrey's (1992) main arguments against frequentism. In his words, 'there is no telling whether the coin would have landed head up on a toss that never takes place. That's what probability is all about' (193). He says that it's like asking: what would be the mass of a tenth planet?[6] There's no fact of the matter. In fact, I would go further than him on this point: it's *worse* than asking that question. At least it's consistent with the concept of mass that we could answer the question about the tenth planet; and perhaps cosmologists could point to facts about the distribution of nearby matter, or what have you, that would dictate a sensible answer. But to say that there is a fact of the matter of how the second toss would land is to deny that the coin is a chancy system, whereas the point of the example is exactly that.

The frequentist will be quick to point out that what matters is not what the next toss would be, but rather what the limiting relative frequency would be. He might even add: while there may be no fact of the matter of how the coin would land on any given trial, there *is* a fact of the matter of what the limiting relative frequency would be, namely one half. After all, he continues, all the nearest possible worlds in which the coin is tossed forever agree on that fact.[7]

I contend that this is not so. This is the upshot of the next few arguments.

A good strategy for arguing against an analysis that involves a definite description of the form '*the F* such that ...' is to argue against the presupposition that there is exactly one such *F*. There are two ways to do this:

1) argue that there could be more than one such *F*; and
2) argue that there could be less than one.

Sometimes one can do both, and one can here. HF invokes a definite description: *the* limit of the relative frequency of *A*'s among the *B*'s ... I will now challenge it in both these ways.

415

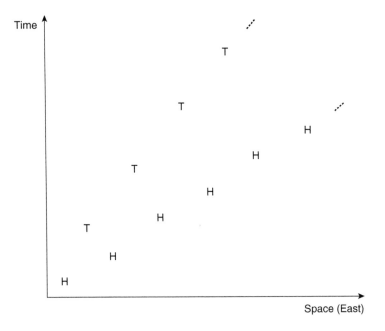

4. There could be more than one limiting relative frequency: the problem of ordering

Suppose that I am tossing a coin on a train that is moving back and forth on tracks that point in a generally easterly direction. Suppose that the results happen to fall in a pattern as depicted in the 'space-time' diagram below. Think of the horizontal axis as the west-east spatial dimension, and the vertical axis as the temporal dimension.

Moving from left to right (west to east), we see the pattern: HTHTHTHTH... Moving upwards (earlier to later), we see the pattern: HHTHHTHHT... Imagine, as we can, that these patterns persist forever. What is the limiting relative frequency of Heads? Taking the results in their temporal order, the answer is 2/3, and I suppose this is the answer that the frequentist would be tempted to give. But taking them in their west-east spatial order, the answer is 1/2. Now, why should one answer have priority over the other? In other words, we have more than one limiting relative frequency, depending on which spatio-temporal dimension we privilege.

We can imagine making matters still worse for the frequentist. Now suppose that the train has an elevator inside, and that the results taken in the up-down spatial dimension happen to follow the pattern HTTHTTHTT... (I won't attempt to draw a picture of this!) Then the limiting relative frequency of Heads in that dimension is 1/3. Yet that is apparently an equally natural ordering of the results.

It is arbitrary to select, say, the temporal ordering of the results as the one for which the limiting relative frequency is to be ascertained. Indeed, it seems worse than arbitrary: for we often think of chances as themselves evolving over time—more on that later—but if we privilege the temporal ordering, there is a worry that the limiting relative frequencies will not so evolve. Moreover, suppose that all the trials of some experiment are simultaneous—there is a world, for example, in which infinitely many radium atoms are created at once, setting up infinitely opportunities for them to decay within 1,600 years, side by side. In that case they don't have a temporal ordering at all; how, then, should they be ordered? And as Einstein has taught us, one should really say 'simultaneous in a certain *reference frame*'. But that only confounds the frequentist further: by changing reference frame, one can change temporal orders of events—and possibly the limiting relative frequency, much as I did by changing the choice of dimension above.

The upshot is this. *Limiting relative frequency depends on the order of trials, whereas probability does not. They therefore cannot be the same thing.*

Frequentism has long been regarded as foundering on the reference class problem: its probability assignments must be relativized to a *reference class* of outcomes. Hypothetical frequentism founders on a further problem: even after we have settled upon a reference class, there is the further problem of ordering it. We might call this the *reference sequence problem*. Hypothetical frequentism turns the one-place property 'having probability p' of an event, into the *three*-place relation 'having limiting relative frequency p relative to reference class R, according to ordering O'.

The reference sequence problem also brings home how serious is the problem with HF's counterfactual: it makes no sense in general to say what the limiting relative frequency of some attribute *would* be, because different orderings will yield different answers.

In Argument 2 I argued that HF requires the frequentist to countenance utterly bizarre worlds in which infinitely many trials take place. The frequentist could, I suppose, modify his account so that the infinitely many trials are not confined to a single world, but rather are taken *across* infinitely many worlds.[8] That might solve the problem raised in that section: none of the worlds need have an extravagant ontology. However, it would do so by making the problem raised in *this* section worse: trivial cases aside, different *orderings* of the worlds will yield different limiting relative frequencies for a given attribute, and it is hard to see how any particular ordering could be privileged.

5. There could be less than one limiting relative frequency: the limit may not exist

Suppose that we have a privileged ordering of the results of tossing a fair coin—as it might be, the temporal ordering in our frame of reference. Then, despite its fairness—or better, *because* of its fairness—there is no ruling out the sequence of results:

HT HHTT HHHHTTTT HHHHHHHHTTTTTTTT...

Here we have sequences of 2^n Heads followed by sequences of 2^n Tails. There is no limiting relative frequency for Heads here: the relative frequency sequence oscillates wildly, growing steadily through each run of Heads, then decreasing steadily through each run of Tails; and the runs are always long enough to counterbalance all that has come before. The hypothetical frequentist has to say that the probability of Heads does not exist. But I told you that it is a fair coin, so the probability is 1/2, and I do not appear to have contradicted myself.

It is no solution to rule this sequence out as impossible. For if this sequence is impossible, then surely all sequences are impossible: all sequences are equal cohabitants of the infinite product space, and they all have exactly the same probability. So this sequence is no more impossible than your favorite 'well-mixed' sequence. In short, there is no guarantee that the limit of the relative frequency of Heads is defined.

6. The limit may equal the wrong value

There are still further sequences—indeed, uncountably many of them, exactly as many as the 'well-behaved' sequences—in which the limit exists, but does not equal what it 'should' (namely 1/2). The fair coin could land Heads forever: HHHHH ... Now, ironically, no reordering of the results (temporal, east-west, up-down, or anything else) will save it: on any ordering the limiting relative frequency of Heads is 1. Again, this cannot be ruled out any more than your favorite nicely mixed sequence of Heads and Tails.

The frequentist might bite the bullet and say 'if that is really the sequence of results, then the probability of Heads really is 1. The coin sure looks like it deterministically yields only Heads'. But then let the sequence be a single Tail, followed by Heads forever: THHHHH. ... Or a finite sprinkling of Tails, followed eventually by Heads forever. Or the sequence TH THH THHH THHHH THHHHH, in which a single tail is always followed by ever-lengthening sequences of Heads. Perhaps this still looks too patterned to be indeterministic; so randomize where the T's appear. We can still see to it that the limiting relative frequency of Heads is 1.

The upshot is that the hypothetical limit of the relative frequency of Heads may not be what the frequentist wants it to be. In fact, the limit may exist, but equal any value between 0 and 1: this is one way of demonstrating that the cardinality of the set of 'badly-behaved' sequences is exactly the same as the cardinality of the set of 'well-behaved' sequences. The data could be misleading in every possible way.[9] Not only is this compatible with our hypothesis that the coin is fair—*it is implied by it!*

Interlude: three replies on behalf of the frequentist

At this stage, the frequentist that dwells deep inside you may want to fight back. In the years that have passed since writing this paper's predecessor, even I have found my inner frequentist (I told you that I may have mellowed!)—up to a point. I will now let him speak, offering three responses to the last four objections. They all imagined various ways in which the hypothetical limiting relative frequency for some attribute could be badly behaved: by there not being a fact regarding its value, by having different values on natural reorderings, by being undefined, or by being defined but having the wrong value. The three responses will each challenge the claim that these things could happen, in the relevant sense of 'could', insisting that these cases pose no real threat to frequentism.

But fear not; I have not lost my nerve. In each case, I think the response can be safely rebutted, as I will argue.

Frequentist response #1: in the nearest possible worlds the limiting relative frequency is what it 'should' be

The frequentist responds:

> Granted, the errant sequences that have been imagined are possible—there are possible worlds in which they occur. But as Stalnaker and Lewis have taught us, what matters to the truth conditions of counterfactuals are the *nearest*

possible worlds in which the antecedents are realized. And in each imagined case, the nearest possible worlds would display the limiting relative frequency that they 'should'. For example, in all the nearest worlds in which we toss a fair coin infinitely often, its limiting relative frequency of Heads is 1/2. To be sure, there are other worlds in which the limiting relative frequency is something else, or is undefined; but those worlds are *less similar* to the actual world. After all, something anomalous, probabilistically speaking, is going on in those worlds, and they are more remote for that very reason.

I reply: I began with a coin that was tossed exactly once, and that landed Heads, and I asked how it would behave on its hypothetical subsequent trials. For all that has been said so far, it may be reasonable to think that the nearest possible world in which it is tossed forever is one in which it lands Heads forever. After all, what could be more similar to the coin's actual behavior than a continuation of that behavior? Perhaps this is not so compelling after just a single trial; so consider instead the result of actually tossing the coin 1,000 times. It is extremely unlikely to land Heads exactly 500 times; for definiteness, suppose that it does so 471 times. The hypothetical frequentist may want to claim that the limiting relative frequency of Heads would not be 0.471, but rather 1/2, if the sequence were infinitely extended: in all possible worlds in which the sequence is so extended, the limiting relative frequency is 1/2. But why think this? There is a sense in which 'correcting' what was observed in this way involves a gratuitous modification of the facts, an uncalled-for extra departure from actuality.[10] If the hypothetical frequentist insists that the coin is fair, I ask him what makes him so sure. Is it something about the coin's physical make-up, for example its near-perfect symmetry? Then he starts sounding like a propensity theorist. Is it the fact that the relative frequency in 1,000 trials was roughly 1/2? Then he starts sounding like a finite frequentist—except he has no business rounding off the decimal of 0.471. Perhaps he is more of a Lewisian 'best systems' theorist, insisting that rounding off the decimal provides a gain in simplicity that more than offsets the loss in fit—but again that is to favor a rival theory. He surely does not directly intuit that the nearest infinitely-tossed worlds are all limiting-relative-frequency-equals-1/2 worlds. Rather, that intuition (if he has it at all) must be based on belief that the probability of Heads is 1/2, grounded in some *other* fact about the coin. But then it seems that the truth-maker for his probability claim is this other fact, rather than the limiting relative frequency.

In any case, in insisting that if the coin were tossed infinitely often, the limiting relative frequency *would* be 1/2, the hypothetical frequentist is apparently denying that it *might not* be 1/2—for I take it that the 'would' and 'might not' counterfactuals are contraries. But now it is my turn to insist on something: the chanciness of the coin implies that the limiting relative frequency *might not* be 1/2—it might be something other than 1/2, or it might not exist at all. That's what probability is all about.

Frequentist response #2: the strong law of large numbers underwrites the 'would' counterfactuals

The frequentist responds:

The strong law of large numbers tells us that a fair coin *would* land Heads with limiting relative frequency 1/2. In general, it says:

For a sequence of independent trials, with probability p of a 'success' on any given trial, $Pr(\text{limiting relative frequency of successes} = p) = 1$.

Said another way: those 'badly behaved' sequences that do not have the correct limiting relative frequency have collectively probability 0, and they are in this sense pathological. That's why we may safely ignore them.

I reply: This move won't work, for a number of reasons:

First, whether or not a sequence is pathological is not immediately read off its probability. For as I have said, all sequences, including the patently well-behaved ones (whatever that exactly means) have the same probability, namely 0.

Secondly, the law of large numbers itself has several probabilistic references in it, both tacit and explicit. The notion of 'independent' trials is tacitly probabilistic: it means that the probability of conjunctions of trials equals the corresponding product of probabilities. p is a probability, the constant probability of a success from trial to trial. So is Pr, the 'meta'-probability whose value is 1. How are these probabilities to be understood? As limiting relative frequencies? Take for instance the meta-probability statement, that essentially says that a set of sequences of a particular sort has probability 1. Should we give a frequentist translation of this: the limiting relative frequency, within an infinite meta-sequence of sequences, of sequences of that sort, is 1? But that is not quite right, for even the frequentist should admit that this limit is not *certain* to be 1—that statement in turn is true only 'with probability 1'. So we have a meta-meta-probability, whose value is 1. Should we give a frequentist translation of this? Not unless we are fond of infinite regresses.

Thirdly, an appeal to the law of large numbers from a frequentist should strike one as quite odd. Jeffrey notes that according to the frequentist, the law of large numbers is a tautology. To be sure, tautologies are true, and we often appeal to the 'tautologies' of mathematics and logic in our theorizing. So I would put the point a little differently: according to the frequentist, the law of large numbers admits of a one-line proof! Little wonder that the limiting relative frequency equals the true probability, with probability one. According to the frequentist, it is an analytic truth that the limiting relative frequency and the true probability are one and the same!

In fact, the frequentist should regard the law of large numbers as strangely coy. The law is stated cautiously: the convergence to the true probability happens *only* with probability one, while the frequentist thinks that it happens with certainty. And, as probability textbooks are fond of reminding us, 'probability one' is weaker than 'certainty'.

The frequentist might put up some resistance at this point: 'Granted, the required convergence must be qualified: the limiting relative frequency equals the true probability *with probability one*. And that means in turn that, in an infinite meta-sequence of sequences of such trials, the limiting relative frequency of 'good' sequences is 1—again, with the qualification *with probability one*. And so on. But each step in this regress adds further information. The regress is not vicious, but informative'. In response to this, it might be helpful to reflect on why the hypothetical frequentist believes in probability in the first place. Presumably it is because he can't predict with certainty the outcomes of certain experiments (and maybe he thinks that these outcomes are unpredictable in principle). He wishes that at least he could predict with certainty their relative frequency in a finite sequence of observations; but he still can't do that. So he tries to comfort himself with the thought that at least he could make the prediction with certainty in a hypothetical infinite sequence; but even that is not quite right. So he retreats to the true statement that the relative frequency does what it is supposed to in this hypothetical sequence 'with probability one'. (He just can't get rid of those wretched modalities, can he?!) The strong things that he wants to say are not true, and the true things that he ends up saying are not strong enough for his purposes.

Frequentist response #3: probabilities are only defined in collectives

The frequentist responds:

HF is on the right track, but following von Mises (1957) and Church (1940), an extra detail is required. Probabilities are hypothetical relative frequencies in *collectives*. A collective is an infinite sequence in which limiting relative frequencies are well-behaved in a particular way. More formally, a collective is an infinite sequence $\varpi = (\varpi 1, \varpi 2, \ldots,)$ of attributes (thought of as all the outcomes of a repeatable experiment), which obeys two axioms:

Axiom of Convergence: the limiting relative frequency of any attribute exists.

Axiom of Randomness: the limiting relative frequency of each attribute is the same in any recursively specifiable infinite subsequence of ϖ.

The latter axiom is meant to capture the idea that the individual results in the collective are in a strong sense unpredictable: there is no gambling system for betting on or against the various possibilities that would improve the gambler's odds. For example, the sequence:

HTHTHTHTHTHT...

is not a collective, since it violates the axiom of randomness. The limiting relative frequency of 'H' in the infinite subsequence of odd-numbered trials is 1, while in the infinite subsequence of even-numbered trials it is 0. This corresponds to a predictability in the sequence that a gambler could exploit: she could guarantee wins by betting on 'H' on exactly the odd-numbered trials.

Now we can answer some of the arguments to hypothetical frequentism of the previous sections. In the train example (argument 4), the spatial ordering of outcomes was exactly this sequence, hence it was not collective; nor was the temporal ordering of outcomes, for that matter. And a sequence in which the limiting relative frequency of an attribute does not exist (argument 5) is not a collective, since it violates the first axiom. So hypothetical frequentist probabilities should not be defined in these cases.

I reply: The axiom of randomness both excludes and includes too much. It excludes too much: one may speak of a *process* as being random, irrespective of its outcomes. Repeatedly tossing a fair coin is a paradigmatically random process, but its outcomes may not form a collective. (Make the example quantum mechanical if you prefer.) And it includes too much: it judges as random the sequence HHHHHH... After all, the limiting relative frequency of H is the same in *every* subsequence (namely, 1), so *a fortiori* it is the same in every infinite recursively specifiable subsequence. But if you ask me, that is as *non*-random as a sequence can be.[11] And more to the point, I appealed to exactly this sequence in argument 6, so it was certainly fair game to do so. Moreover, I could change the train example so that the spatial and temporal orderings of the outcomes are *both collectives*, but with different limiting relative frequencies for Heads. Admittedly, I would not be able to convey to you exactly what the orderings look like—to do so would require my giving a recursive specification of the Heads outcomes, which the axiom of randomness rules out. But nor was von Mises able to give us an example of a collective (for the same reason)—apart from examples that are surely *counter* examples, degenerate cases such as HHHH...

According to a von Mises-style hypothetical frequentist, we know that for any coin that has a well-defined probability of landing 'Heads', the following counterfactual is true:

> if the coin were tossed infinitely often, it would either yield a sequence in which the placement of Heads outcomes is not recursively specifiable, or else a degenerate sequence in which all infinite subsequences have the same limiting relative frequency (0 or 1).

I claim that we don't know that. If the coin were tossed infinitely often, it *might not* yield either kind of sequence—the 'might' here being epistemic, signifying what is consistent with all that we know. We are in no position to rule out other things that such a coin could do—see my previous arguments for some examples!

This ends the interlude; back to main arguments.

7. Hypothetical frequentism's order of explanation is back-to-front

Von Mises introduced collectives because he believed that the regularities in the behavior of certain actual sequences of outcomes are best explained by the hypothesis that those sequences are initial segments of collectives. This seems curious to me: we *know* for any actual sequence of outcomes that they are *not* initial segments of collectives, since we know that they are not initial segments of infinite sequences—period. In fact, often we know rather more than that—e.g., I can know that this coin will only ever be tossed once (I can destroy it to make sure of that). But even if, completely implausibly, we believed that an actual sequence *was* an initial segment of a collective, how would that explain, let alone *best* explain, the regularity in this initial segment? It is not as if facts about the collective impose some constraint on the behavior of the actual sequence. Something that *would* impose such a constraint—probabilistic, to be sure—is a single case probability that is fixed from trial to trial. For example, we explain the fact that our coin landed Heads roughly half the time in 1,000 tosses with the hypothesis that its single case probability of Heads is roughly 1/2, constant across trials, and that the trials are independent of each other. We then appeal to the usual Binomial model of the experiment, and show that such a result is highly probable, given that model. But this is not the hypothetical frequentist's explanation. Von Mises famously regarded single case probabilities as 'nonsense' (this volume, p. 361). I leave it to you to judge whether that epithet is better reserved for the explanation of the coin's behavior that adverts to the wild fiction of its results belonging to a collective.

Generalizing to any hypothetical frequentist account: I maintain that its order of explanation is back to front. The fact that we have IID trials of a random experiment explains their long run frequency behavior, rather than the other way round. Compare the case of repeated sampling from a fixed population with mean μ, and the sample mean $\overline{X}$ for large samples. We do not account for μ being what it is on the basis of $\overline{X}$ being what it is; rather, the order or explanation is the other way around.

8. The limit might exist when it should not

In Argument 5 I considered cases in which a given probability exists, but the limiting relative frequency does not. Now consider reverse cases: a given probability does *not* exist, but the limiting relative frequency does (as it so happens).

One way of making this point involves an appeal to a result from measure theory. It turns out that, given certain plausible assumptions, it is impossible to assign a uniform probability distribution across the [0, 1] interval, such that every subset receives a probability value. Certain subsets remain as probability gaps: so called 'non-measurable' sets. Let N be such a set. Imagine throwing an infinitely thin dart at random at the [0, 1] interval, and consider the probability that the dart lands inside N. Let us agree that N has no probability (for to say otherwise would be to attribute a measure to a non-measurable set). Now imagine performing this experiment infinitely often, and consider whether the limiting relative frequency of landings inside N exists or not. It had better not, according to the frequentist, since we have agreed that the probability does not.

What does it mean for a limiting relative frequency not to exist? The only way that this can happen is if the relative frequency sequence oscillates forever, the oscillations never damping to arbitrarily small levels. This in turn only happens when successively longer and longer runs of one result predominating are followed by successively longer and longer runs of one result predominating. (Recall the HT HHTT HHHHTTTT HHHHHHHHTTTTTTTT... sequence.) But what reason do we have to think that our sequence of dart-landings inside and outside N will display such persistent instability? I challenge the frequentist to make sense of probability distributions such as the usual Lebesgue measure over [0, 1], with its corresponding non-measurable sets.

My strategy here is to find objective probability gaps that hypothetical frequentism wrongly fills. Perhaps other, less esoteric examples will do the job. For example, *free acts* may be the sorts of things to which objective probabilities simply don't attach. Nevertheless, in virtue of their very freedom, they may have stable relative frequencies. Suppose that I repeatedly may choose to raise my left hand or right hand. I can drive the relative frequency of each to whatever value I like—and if you are happy to entertain staggering counterfactuals about my making these choices infinitely often, then you should be happy to allow the innocuous further assumption that I can freely steer the limiting relative frequency anywhere I want. And yet my free choice may lack an objective probability. The frequentist sees objective probability values, when there may be none. If you don't like this example, but you like some other example of a probability gap, then I am sure that I can run my argument using it instead.

Another way of making my point is to consider gerrymandered sequences of trials of highly heterogeneous events. Let the first trial determine whether the next person to cross the New South Wales border has an even number of hairs. Let the second trial determine whether Betelgeuse goes supernova or not in the next million years. Let the third trial determine whether my dog Tilly catches the next ball I throw to her or not ... Consider the highly disjunctive 'event type' D that occurs when any of these events occur, and imagine keeping a tally of D's relative frequency as each trial is completed. For all we know, D could have a well-defined limiting relative frequency; the hypothetical frequentist then regards that as D's objective probability. But it is not clear that D is the sort of event type that could have an objective probability at all. Unlike, say, repeated tosses of a coin, there is nothing *projectible* about it. If the relative frequencies happen to stabilize, that is by fluke, and not because of some stable feature of the event type itself. I take objective probabilities to be such stable features.

A brief aside. I said earlier that I believe that collectively my fifteen arguments also threaten Lewisian 'best systems' accounts of chance. I can now be more specific about that claim: I believe that the last five arguments (Arguments 4–8) can easily be rewritten to target such accounts.

9. Subsequences can be found converging to whatever value you like

For each infinite sequence that gives rise to a non-trivial limiting relative frequency, there is an infinite *subsequence* converging in relative frequency to any value you like (indeed, infinitely many such subsequences). And for each subsequence that gives rise to a non-trivial limiting relative frequency, there is a sub-subsequence converging in relative frequency to any value you like (indeed, infinitely many sub-subsequences). And so on. There are, moreover, subsequences converging to no value at all (again, infinitely many). This is reminiscent of the problem of ordering discussed earlier: infinite sequences provide an embarrassment of riches. It is another way in which hypothetical frequentism faces a reference sequence problem. It is also another way of making the point that there is no such thing as 'the' infinite counterfactual extension of a given finite sequence. Far from there being a single such extension, there are infinitely many; and far from them agreeing on the limiting relative frequency, they collectively display every disagreement possible.

10. Necessarily single-case events

A fatal problem for finite frequentism is the notorious problem of the single case, and I discussed it in my previous paper. For example, a coin that is tossed exactly once necessarily has a relative frequency of either 1 or 0 of Heads, yet the probability of Heads can surely be intermediate. Hypothetical frequentism appears to solve the problem by going hypothetical—by sending us to other possible worlds in which the coin is tossed repeatedly. However, consider an event that is *essentially* single case: it *cannot* be repeated. For instance, some cosmologists regard it as a genuinely chancy matter whether our universe is open or closed—apparently certain quantum fluctuations could, in principle, tip it one way or the other—yet whatever it is, it is 'single-case' in the strongest possible sense. Either we can make no sense of the limiting relative frequency in HF for this case, or it trivially collapses to 1 or 0.

424

11. *Uncountably many events*

The previous problem involved cases where there are *too few* events of the requisite kind; now I want to consider cases where there are *too many*. HF assumes a *denumerable* sequence of results. It runs into trouble if we have *non*-denumerably many events of the relevant sort; how are we to form a merely denumerable sequence of them? For instance, each space-time point may have a certain property or not—say, the property of having a field strength of a certain magnitude located there. What is the probability that a given point has this property? The trouble is that there are uncountably many such points.

I suppose the frequentist might imagine a denumerable sequence of 'random' selections of points (whatever that might mean) and the limiting relative frequency with which the points have the property. But my question was not about such a sequence, which forms only a tiny subset of the set of all points. It's as if the frequentist wants to pay heed to the evidence—the pattern of instantiation of the property—but only a *little* heed. After all, he identifies the probability of the property's instantiation at a point with its relative frequency of instantiation in a very small set (comparatively speaking) of representative points. And which denumerable subset is to form this set? As in the problem of reordering (argument 4) and of subsequences (argument 9), the frequentist faces an embarrassment of riches. Any limiting relative frequency will be instantiated by *some* denumerable sequence, trivial cases aside.

The problem of necessarily single-case events, and of uncountably many events, are two ends of a spectrum. HF speaks only to the 'middle' cases in which denumerable sequences of trials of the relevant kind are both possible and exhaustive. But probabilities should not be held hostage to these seemingly extraneous facts about event cardinality.

12. *Exchangeability, and independent, identically distributed trials*

Consider a man repeatedly throwing darts at a dartboard, who can either hit or miss the bull's eye. As he practices, he gets better; his probability of a hit increases:

$$P(\text{hit on } (n+1)\text{th trial}) > P(\text{hit on } n\text{th trial}).$$

Hence, the trials are not *identically distributed*. Still less are they *exchangeable* (meaning that the probability of any sequence of outcomes is preserved under permutation of finitely many of the trials). And he remembers his successes and is fairly good at repeating them immediately afterwards:

$$P(\text{hit on } (n+1)\text{th trial} \mid \text{hit on } n\text{th trial}) > P(\text{hit on } (n+1)\text{th trial})$$

Hence, the trials are not *independent*.

For all these reasons, the joint probability distribution over the outcomes of his throws is poorly modeled by relative frequencies—and the model doesn't get any better if we imagine his sequence of throws continuing infinitely. More generally, in attributing the probabilities to the outcomes that are blind to trial number, the frequentist regards the trials as being identically distributed and indeed exchangeable. And the probability he assigns to the outcome of a given trial is insensitive to the outcomes of any finite

ALAN HÁJEK

number of *other* trials. To be sure, this probability is sensitive to the outcomes of *all* the other trials. All too sensitive—the individual trial completely loses its autonomy, its probability entirely determined by what *other* trials do.

The hypothetical frequentist might reply that we should 'freeze' the dart-thrower's skill level before a given throw, and imagine an infinite sequence of hypothetical tosses performed at exactly that skill level.[12] For example, the probability that he hits the bull's eye on the 17th throw is putatively the limiting relative frequency of hits in an infinite sequence, on every trial of which he has exactly the ability that he actually has on the 17th throw. But this really is to give up on the idea that relative frequencies in the actual world have anything to do with probabilities. Indeed, this seems like a convoluted way of being a propensity theorist: all the work is being done by the thrower's 'ability', a dispositional property of his, and the hypothetical limiting relative frequency appears to be a metaphysically profligate add-on, an idle wheel.

Our dart-thrower is hardly far-fetched (unlike the counterfactuals that our frequentist will deploy in describing him). He can't be easily dismissed as a 'don't care' for an account of probability. On the contrary, I would have thought that systems that have memories, that self-regulate, and that respond to their environments in ways that thwart IID probabilistic models, are the norm rather than the exception.

13. Limiting relative frequency violates countable additivity

Kolmogorov's axiom of countable additivity says: given a countable sequence of disjoint propositions, the probability of their union equals the sum of their individual probabilities. Hypothetical frequentism violates this axiom: there are cases in which the limiting relative frequency of the union does not equal the sum of the limiting relative frequencies. For anyone who holds sacred Kolmogorov's full set of axioms of probability, this is a serious blow against frequentism: it means that frequentism is not an interpretation of the entire Kolmogorov probability calculus.

To see this, start with a countably infinite event space—for definiteness, consider an infinite lottery, with tickets 1, 2, 3, ... Let A_i = 'ticket i is drawn'. Suppose that we have a denumerable sequence of draws (with replacement), and as it happens, each ticket is drawn exactly once. Then the limiting relative frequency of each ticket being drawn is 0; and so according to the hypothetical frequentist, $P(A_i) = 0$ for all i, and so

$$\sum_{n=1}^{\infty} P(A_n) = 0.$$

But $A_1 \cup A_2 \cup A_3 \cup \ldots$ is an event that happens every time, so its limiting relative frequency is 1. According to the hypothetical frequentist, this means that

$$P\left(\bigcup_{n=1}^{\infty} A_n\right) = 1,$$

a violation of countable additivity.

The hypothetical frequentist cannot help himself to various important limit theorems of probability theory that require countable additivity for their proof. The failure of countable additivity also gives rises to failures of conglomerability (Seidenfeld et al.

426

1998), which is perhaps more troubling for credences than for objective probabilities, but still troubling enough, especially since credences are supposed to coordinate with objective probabilities à la Lewis' Principal Principle (1980). And at least *some* objective probabilities seem to be countably additive, since they are parasitic on lengths, areas, or volumes of regions of space, which are themselves countable additive. As van Fraassen (1980) points out, for events of the form 'the outcome is in Q', where Q is a measurable region of n-dimensional Euclidean space, we may define a probability that is proportional to the 'volume', or Lebesgue measure of Q; and Lebesgue measure is countably additive (hence, so is anything proportional to it). These probabilities, then, cannot be limiting relative frequencies.

14. The domain of limiting relative frequencies is not a field

Probabilities are usually defined on a *field* on some set Ω—a collection of subsets of Ω closed under complementation and intersection. (Indeed, Kolmogorov went further, defining probabilities on a *sigma*-field, which is closed under complementation and *countable* intersection.) However, the domain of limiting relative frequencies is not a field. There are cases in which the limiting relative frequency of A is defined, the limiting relative frequency of B is defined, but the limiting relative frequency of the intersection AB is undefined.

De Finetti (1972) writes:

> Two people, A and B, are gambling on the same sequence of coin tossings; A bets always on Heads, B changes between heads and tails at intervals of increasing length. Things may be arranged (proof omitted in this translation) so that the [relative] frequency of successes for A and for B tends to 1/2, but the [relative] frequency of joint success AB oscillates between the lower limit 0 and the upper limit 1. (75)

Let's clean up de Finetti's infelicitous notation—'A' and 'B' start out as people, but end up as events that can be conjoined. Let A be the event 'the first person succeeds' and B be the event 'the second person succeeds'. It's unfortunate that the proof is omitted. In fact, there is surely a mistake here: the relative frequency of joint success AB cannot oscillate as high as 1 in the long run, since the relative frequency of AB is bounded above by the relative frequency of A, and its limit is 1/2. But the relative frequency of AB *can* oscillate between roughly 0 and 1/2 in the long run, and that suffices to show that the domain of limiting relative frequencies is not a field.

For example, suppose that the first person bets on H on each toss. The second person bets on oscillating runs of length 10^n, as follows: H on the first trial; T for the next 10 trials; H for the next 10^2 trials, T for the next 10^3 trials, etc. In fact, the coin lands HTHTHTHT.... Then we have:

$$\text{relative frequency}(A) \to 1/2.$$
$$\text{relative frequency}(B) \to 1/2.$$

But

$$\text{relative frequency}(AB) \text{ has no limit,}$$

since it oscillates between roughly 0 and 1/2 forever. For joint successes happen *none* of the time throughout a particular run of the second person betting on T, and eventually these amount to nearly all of the trials; but joint successes happen *half* the time during a particular run of her betting on H, and eventually *these* amount to nearly all of the trials.

I will conclude with one further argument based on the mathematics of limiting relative frequencies. In the prequel to this paper, I noted that according to finite frequentism, there are no irrational probabilities. To be sure, the move to hypothetical frequentism solves this problem. But an analogue of this problem holds even for hypothetical frequentism.

15. According to hypothetical frequentism, there are no infinitesimal probabilities

A positive infinitesimal is a number greater than zero, but smaller than every positive real number. The hypothetical frequentist's probabilities are always either rational numbers, or the limits of sequences of rational numbers. In either case, they are real-valued. This means that they cannot be (positive) infinitesimal-valued. Yet infinitesimal probabilities have appealed to, and have been appealed to by, various philosophers—e.g. Lewis (1980), Skyrms (1980), McGee (1994), and Elga (2004). If a probability function over an uncountable space is to be 'regular'—it assigns 0 only to the empty set—it must make infinitesimal probability assignments. (See Hájek 2003 for a proof.) Moreover, infinitesimal probability assignments seem to be well motivated by various random experiments with uncountably many possible outcomes—e.g., throwing a dart at random at the [0, 1] interval. And infinitesimal probabilities can apparently help to solve a variety of problems—for example, the 'shooting room problem' (Bartha and Hitchcock 1999). To be sure, in some of these applications the probabilities in question may be regarded as subjective. But it is somewhat troubling that they *cannot* be objective, if objective probabilities are understood along frequentist lines.

A parting offering: hyper-hypothetical frequentism

The last objection prompts me to end with a tentative positive proposal as to how hypothetical frequentism might be refined, so as to evade this objection and several others besides. The objections I have in mind turned on certain mathematical facts about the limits of infinite sequences of rational numbers (arguments 4, 5, 13, 14, and 15). The proposal, then, is to appeal to something that preserves the idea of having such infinite sequences, but for which the mathematics 'looks' finite: namely the theory of *hyper-real numbers*. I can only sketch the idea here—but I hope that someone familiar with the theory will see how the details might be filled in further.

Non-standard models give us a way handling infinite and infinitesimal quantities in a way that makes them behave just like finite quantities: these are so-called *hyperfinite* models. One construction that I find particularly user-friendly treats hyper-real numbers as equivalence classes of sequences of reals. *What is the equivalence relation?* Two sequences are regarded as equivalent iff they agree term by term almost everywhere. *What does 'almost everywhere' mean?* We must impose an additive measure on the positive integers $\mathbf{N}$, which takes just the values 0 and 1, and which assigns $\mathbf{N}$ measure 1, and all finite sets measure 0. But there are infinitely many such measures—*which one are we talking about?* That just means that there are as many different ways of defining the hyper-reals as there are ways of making this arbitrary choice of the measure. So imagine this choice being made. Among the hyper-reals so chosen are infinite numbers, such as this one: the set of all sequences equivalent to {1, 2, 3,...}. Call that number K. Among them are also infinitesimals, such as this one: the set of all sequences equivalent to {1, 1/2, 1/3,...}. This will turn out to be $1/K$. For further details, see Lindstrom (1989).

We want to have most of our cake, and to eat most of it too: we want a genuinely infinite sequence of trials, yet we want to avoid some of the problems, encountered previously, that were artifacts of our use of infinite sequences. The trick, I suggest, is to suppose that we have a hyperfinite number of appropriate trials; and now define probability as simply relative frequency (note: *not* limiting relative frequency) among these. More precisely, let us introduce *hyper-hypothetical frequentism* as follows[13]:

(HHF) *The probability of an attribute A in a reference class B is p*

iff

the relative frequency of occurrences of A within B would be p if B were hyperfinite.

We not only recover irrational probabilities this way—we even recover infinitesimal probabilities. For example, suppose that our B consists of K trials, and consider an event that happens exactly once. Its relative frequency is $1/K$, which is infinitesimal. And we can distinguish it in probability from another event that happens twice, hence whose relative frequency is $2/K$. And so on for any event that happens a finite number of times. But standard hypothetical frequentism conflates the probabilities of events that happen finitely many times: they all are regarded as having probability 0.

The mathematics of hyper-hypothetical frequentism in other respects looks finite, and this gives it several further advantages over hypothetical frequentism. Now, one cannot change the relative frequency by reordering the trials (just as one cannot in finite sequences). Probabilities are now *guaranteed* to exist (and not just 'almost certain' to), just as they were for finite actual frequentism: after all, we are simply counting and taking ratios, not taking limits as well. The taking of subsequences is no more allowed than it was for finite actual frequentism: I said that we are to take the relative frequency among the K trials, and not some smaller number of trials. So probabilities will always be uniquely defined. They are hyperfinitely additive—that is, given a sequence of j disjoint propositions, where j is a non-standard integer which may even be infinite, their probabilities add in a finite-looking way. And their domain of definition is a field, as it should be; indeed, probability assignments are closed under hyperfinite unions and intersections.

That's the good news; now I should be forthright about the bad news. It begins with what I breezily called the 'arbitrary choice' of measure when constructing our hyper-real model: demons lurk behind the words 'arbitrary' and 'choice'. It is often a sign of a weakness in a philosophical position when it requires an arbitrary choice, particularly if that choice seems not to correspond to any natural property or distinction that we might care about. I imagined *choosing a measure* over **N**; but what could favor

ALAN HÁJEK

one choice over another one? (Arbitrariness entered again when I imagined a hyperfinite set of *K* trials; why *K* rather than some other hyperfinite number?) Moreover, I *imagined* choosing a measure over **N**; but in fact we cannot fully specify this measure, even in principle. Cognoscenti will recognize this problem as the indefinability of the ultrafilter that corresponds to the 'measure 1' sets in the construction that I sketched above—see my 2003 for further discussion. Hyper-real numbers are in this sense *ineffable*. To be sure, this seems to be a general cause for concern about the use of hyper-real probabilities, the enthusiasm for infinitesimal probabilities that I reported notwithstanding. My final argument above, then, is weakened to that extent. That said, at least the problem of arbitrariness for my proposal has a counterpart for hypothetical frequentism that is worth highlighting now. After all, that account privileged *denumerable* reference classes among all the infinite cardinalities—why that order type rather than another? Exposing the arbitrariness inherent in this would give us a close variant of argument 11.

And what about all my other objections to hypothetical frequentism? Well may you ask. They remain, as far as I am concerned. My proposal is still a complete abandonment of empiricism; it has us imagine utterly bizarre counterfactuals (even more so than HF does); there is no fact of what the counterfactual hyper-hypothetical sequences will look like; and so on. I offer my proposal as an improvement on hypothetical frequentism, not as a rescue of it. I believe it is beyond rescuing.

Conclusion

Finite frequentism confuses good methodology concerning probability for probability itself: while it respects the practice of experimental science, it disrespects too many of our central intuitions about probability. Hypothetical frequentism strives to have the best of both worlds: the scientific spirit of finite frequentism, yet with an injection of the modality that our commonsensical notion of probability seems to require. However, in the final analysis, it runs afoul of both science and commonsense. Its abandonment of finite frequentism's empiricism is costly, and it fails to pay its way with corresponding benefits; moreover, it suffers from other technical difficulties of its own. I have suggested a way to refine hypothetical frequentism so as to avoid some of these difficulties, with hyper-hypothetical frequentism—but in the end I think it amounts only to a little cosmetic surgery.[14]

Notes

* Originally published in *Erkenntnis*, 70 (2009), pp. 211–35. Copyright © 2009 Springer Science+Business Media B.V. Reprinted by permission of Alan Hájek.
1 Kenny Easwaran suggested that I might offer instead 'Seven and a Half Dilemmas for Hypothetical Frequentism'!
2 Thanks here to Kenny Easwaran.
3 I ignore various subtleties—e.g. so called 'finkish' dispositions.
4 It only adds to the bizarreness if we add that the counterfactually repeated trials are to be '*identically prepared*', a phrase one sometimes hears the frequentist add. Actual repeated events differ in so many ways from each other—removing all of these respects of difference takes us still further from actuality. We can countenance probabilities involving certain supernova explosions, for instance; but can we even imagine the 'identical preparation' of a sequence of supernova explosions—let alone an infinite sequence of them? In fact, if the identity of indiscernibles is a necessary truth, then such identical preparation may be downright impossible.

430

5 Thanks here to Darren Bradley.

6 Jeffrey wrote before Pluto arguably lost its title of being a planet; and before Eris arguably gained *its* title.

7 The frequentist's idea here is somewhat reminiscent of the supervaluational treatment of vagueness. Even though there might be no determinate fact of the matter of which hair makes the difference between baldness and non-baldness, with different 'valuations' disagreeing on it, it is determinately true that everyone is bald-or-not-bald, since this is true on *all* valuations. But as we will shortly see, the analogy to supervaluating does not go through, much as the frequentist might like it to: it is *not* true that the limiting relative frequency is the same in *all* the nearest possible worlds.

8 Thanks here to Kenny Easwaran.

9 This recalls the problems with 'operationalism', mentioned in my previous paper's discussion of finite frequentism.

10 I thank Daniel Nolan for suggesting a version of this point to me.

11 Now perhaps you may reply that it *is* random: it is the degenerate case of a random sequence of outcomes of a coin that is guaranteed to land Heads (e.g. it is two-headed). Then let the sequence be a single tail, followed by Heads forever: THHHHH. ... Or the sequence TH THH THHH THHHH THHHHH, in which a single tail is always followed by ever lengthening sequences of Heads. These sequences are also *non*-random, yet they are still collectives.

12 Thanks to Kenny Easwaran and Aidan Lyon for suggesting versions of this reply.

13 I thank Aidan Lyon for suggesting this name.

14 There are many people to thank for discussions of this material over its many years of gestation. My younger self thanks especially Fiona Cowie, Peter Gerdes, Ned Hall, David Hilbert, Carl Hoefer, Richard Jeffrey, Marc Lange, David Lewis, Daniel Nolan, Brian Skyrms, Bas van Fraassen, Jim Woodward, and Lyle Zynda. My current self thanks especially Paul Bartha, Darren Bradley, Kenny Easwaran, Branden Fitelson, Aidan Lyon, Ralph Miles, and Daniel Nolan.

Bibliography

Bartha, P., & Hitchcock, C. (1999). The shooting-room paradox and conditionalizing on 'measurably challenged' sets. *Synthese, 118*, 403–437. doi:10.1023/A:1005100407551.

Carnap, R. (1950). *Logical foundations of probability*. Chicago: University of Chicago Press.

Church, A. (1940). On the concept of a random sequence. *Bulletin of the American Mathematical Society, 46*, 130–135. doi:10.1090/S0002–9904–1940–07154–X.

Costantini, D., & Galavotti, M. (Eds.). (1997). *Probability, dynamics and causality-essays in honor of R. C. Jeffrey*, Dordrecht: Kluwer.

de Finetti, B. (1972). *Probability, induction and statistics*. London: John Wiley & Sons.

Elga, A. (2004). Infinitesimal chances and the laws of nature. *Australasian Journal of Philosophy, 82*, (March), 67–76. (Reprinted from *Lewisian themes: The philosophy of David K. Lewis*, by F. Jackson, G. Priest (Eds.), 2004, Oxford: Oxford University Press.)

Hájek, A. (1997). 'Mises Redux'—Redux: Fifteen arguments against finite frequentism, *Erkenntnis 45*, 209–227, reprinted as Chapter 24 in this volume.

Hájek, A. (2003). What conditional probability could not be. *Synthese, 137*(3), 273–323. doi:10.1023/B:SYNT.0000004904.91112.16.

Howson, C., & Urbach, P. (1993). *Scientific reasoning: The Bayesian approach* (2nd ed.). La Salle: Open Court.

Jeffrey, R. (1992). Mises Redux. In *Probability and the art of judgment*. Cambridge: Cambridge University Press, reprinted as Chapter 23 in this volume.

Johnson, R. A. (1994). *Miller & Freund's probability & statistics for engineers* (5th ed.). New Jersey: Prentice Hall.

Kripke, S. A. (1980). *Wittgenstein on rules and private language*. Cambridge, MA: Harvard University Press.

Lewis, D. (1973). *Counterfactuals*. Oxford/Cambridge, MA: Blackwell/Harvard University Press.

Lewis, D. (1980). A subjectivist's guide to objective chance. In Richard C. Jeffrey (Ed.), *Studies in inductive logic and probability* (Vol. 2, pp. 263–293). Berkeley and Los Angeles: University of California Press. Reprinted as Chapter 27 in this volume.

Lewis, D. (1986). *Philosophical papers* (Vol. 2). Oxford: Oxford University Press.

Lewis, D. (1994). Humean supervenience debugged. *Mind, 103*, 473–490. doi:10.1093/mind/103.412.473.

Lindstrom, T. (1989). An invitation to nonstandard analysis. In N. J. Cutland (Ed.), *Nonstandard analysis and its applications* (pp. 1–105). Cambridge: Cambridge University Press.

McGee, V. (1994). Learning the impossible. In Ellery Eells & Brian Skyrms (Eds.), *Probability and conditionals*. Cambridge: Cambridge University Press.

Reichenbach, H. (1949). *The theory of probability*. Berkeley: University of California Press.

Seidenfeld, T., Schervish, M. J., & Kadane, J. B. (1998). Non-conglomerability for finite-valued, finitely additive probability. *Sankhya Series A, 60*(3), 476–491.

Skyrms, B. (1980). *Causal necessity*. New Haven: Yale University Press.

Stalnaker, R. (1968). *A Theory of Conditionals*. Studies in logical theory, *American philosophical quarterly monograph series* (Vol. 2). Oxford: Blackwell.

van Fraassen, B. (1980). *The scientific image*. Oxford: Clarendon Press.

von Mises, R. (1957). *Probability, statistics and truth*, revised English edition. New York: Macmillan, relevant extracts reprinted as Chapter 22 in this volume.

Part VI

PHYSICAL PROBABILITY
Objective chance and propensities

26

INTRODUCTION

The chance role

In the discussion of frequentism in Chapter 21, appeals were made to principles that capture the 'chance role'. It was clear in Hájek's two chapters (24 and 25) that frequencies do not easily satisfy the chance role. But what exactly is going on with these appeals?

Giving a philosophical account of something like chance is a balancing act. One wants to respect the things we already take ourselves to know about chance, which are the starting points of inquiry, but not be enslaved by them. One way this balancing act can be carried out is to add what we know about chance to other plausible prior considerations in the hope that something satisfies enough of them well enough to deserve the name. This procedure will not generally deliver a 'conceptual analysis' or definition of the target notion; rather, the various things we know about chance, collectively, will provide a reference-fixing description.[1] In the case of chance, the hope is that the referent of 'chance' can be fixed as the thing—if such a thing exists—that best fits the role picked out by the various things we take ourselves to know about it.

Many claims have been proposed that would partly constrain the chance role:

> Chance is connected to such further notions as *credence, possibility, futurity, intrinsicness, lawhood,* and *causation.* To characterize the role of chance is to trace such connections.
>
> (Schaffer 2007: 123)

So, for example, it is one of the truths about chance that Schaffer mentions that *chance should only concern future events*; if something is chancy, then its happening or not happening is an open possibility in a way that nothing about the past is (non-epistemically) open.[2] (See also Lewis's remarks about the evolution of chances over time as one passes through the labyrinth, Chapter 27).

The connection between chance and the openness of the future in some sense doesn't by itself constrain very much what chance is. But, it is hoped, by looking at other things we know about chance, we can get a detailed enough conception of what chances are like that we can sensibly evaluate more substantive proposals about what fills the chance role—what is picked out by the description.

The Principal Principle

Lewis suggests that there is a principle which captures 'all we know about chance' (p. 460), which he therefore calls the Principal Principle (PP). The PP is a *probability coordination* principle, connecting chance and credence. (Compare the reflection principle considered by van Fraassen in Chapter 8). Let p be some proposition which has a chance assigned to it by the chance function at time t, $Ch_t(\cdot)$, C be a reasonable initial credence function and e be the background evidence at t, where e crucially doesn't include information that pertains to the truth of p except through its chance (Chapter 27, p. 464)—evidence which meets this condition is said to be *admissible*. It is standardly assumed that, at least, historical information prior to t and information about how possible histories and possible laws bear on possible chances is admissible. Then the Principal Principle is

$$C(p|\ulcorner Ch_t(p) = x \urcorner \wedge e) = x. \tag{PP}$$

Assuming one updates credences by conditionalising, this form of the Principal Principle then entails that when rational agents come to know the chances, their credences are equal to the chances when they have no inadmissible information about the outcome. Even when an agent never becomes certain of any claim about the chances, and so never adopts a chance function as their credence function, if they obey the Principal Principle their credence will be equal to their subjective expectation of the chances. As foreshadowed in Chapter 1, chance thus plays the role of an 'expert' probability function, a norm for the credences of rational agents. The expertise of the chance function in the original Principal Principle is unconditional—rational credences should simply adopt values equal to the chances. When the evidence e is ordinary, this is unproblematic; but if there are ever cases where the evidence trumps the chances, a more nuanced principle is required—the New Principle, of which more below.

Lewis shows that much of what we know about chance follows from the Principal Principle. For example, if it is accepted, we needn't add as a separate constraint that chances are probabilities. Suppose one knew all the propositions stating the chances at some particular time of all future outcomes. Suppose one had rational credence before learning the chances. Then, in accordance with the Principal Principle, one would assign the same value to conditional credence in each future proposition as the value of its chance. Since rational conditional credences are probabilities, so too must chances be (Chapter 27, p. 458). Furthermore, the chance of past events is always 1. Suppose A has already happened; since historical information is admissible, the Principal Principle implies that the chance of A, at t, is 1. It does not imply that the chance of A was always 1, and typically it will not have been; so chances change over time in accordance at least with the common belief that only the future is chancy and the past is fixed. So the Principal Principle subsumes the connection between chance and the open future. And finally, since an agent's credences guide their actions—that's partly what makes them that agent's credences—if the agent updates their credences rationally and in line with the Principal Principle, then their beliefs about chances will guide their credences. Chance, then, is the kind of probability which 'is the very guide of life' (Butler 1736: Introduction).

Most interestingly from the perspective of Part V, Lewis shows that the Principal Principle predicts a close connection between frequency and chance. If chances are just frequencies, the PP is an instance of the principle of *direct inference*, that we should set our credences equal to the frequencies. The failings of frequentism make direct inference of credences from frequencies problematic, because many of the problems raised by Hájek and others turn on the fact that in many cases of unrepresentative outcomes it is unreasonable to be guided by the frequencies. Lewis shows (Chapter 27, pp. 471–76) that even if frequency and chance come apart, evidence from frequencies still governs credence, via supporting various hypotheses about the chances involved in generating those frequencies. Likewise, chances will govern expectation about frequencies. The appeal of frequentism, and part of its downfall, is simultaneously explained.

Of course, someone who didn't believe in credences wouldn't accept the principal principle (Kyburg, Chapter 3), and there have been modifications and amendments proposed to respond to various problems some have perceived with the Principal Principle (see below). But the former group is vanishingly small in number, and even those who propose modifications agree that the Principal Principle is an extremely good approximation to the correct principle. Even if PP turns out to be not exactly right, the commonsense belief to which it gives precise form would still remain as a guiding constraint for any theory that could reasonably be considered a theory of chance:

> A feature of Reality deserves the name of chance to the extent that it occupies the definitive role of chance; and occupying the role means obeying the old Principle [PP], applied as if information about present chances, and the complete theory of chance, were perfectly admissible. Because of undermining [see below], nothing perfectly occupies the role, so nothing perfectly deserves the name. But near enough is good enough. If nature is kind to us, the chances ascribed by the probabilistic laws of the best system will obey the old Principle to a very good approximation in commonplace applications. They will thereby occupy the chance-role well enough to deserve the name. To deny that they are really chances would be just silly.
>
> (Lewis, 1994: 489)

There is thus widespread agreement that the Principal Principle, or something close to it, captures a basic truth about chance.[3]

As Lewis states, it is the problem of 'undermining' which has come to be seen as most problematic for the Principal Principle. This is the problem that knowing the chances itself seems to provide trumping evidence about the chances! According to reductionist theories of chance, like frequentism or Lewis's own Humean view of objective chance (discussed by Loewer, Chapter 31), the values of the chances are fixed by the total history of occurring events. A simple view of this sort is the modified frequentist view that says the chances are just the occurrent frequencies, rounded to give simple values. So if a coin is repeatedly tossed and lands heads *about* half the time, round the frequency to one-half exactly—that is the chance of heads. But if the chance of heads is now 1/2, the chance of one million consecutive heads is $1/2^{10^6} > 0$. Supposing the coin has only been tossed a reasonably small number of times, a million further heads will swamp the currently observed frequencies; in other words, if that very surprising but nevertheless possible event were to occur, the chance of heads would be 1, or very close to it—not 1/2. Such a possible future, which has some chance of making the actual theory of chances false, is called an *undermining* future. The problem arises because the current chance of an undermining future is positive; but since, if the undermining future came to pass, the current chances would not be what they are, they would be different. So we know that given the actual theory of chances, the undermining future will *not* come to pass. So we can know a priori that if the chances are as we think they are, the undermining future is impossible, and we should assign no credence in the undermining future conditional on the chances being as they are. But the PP entails that we should place some positive credence in the undermining future conditional on the chances being as they are. Contradiction.

In response, Lewis (1994), adopting suggestions of Hall and Thau, advocates moving to another principle. Hall diagnoses the problem as arising because the present chances involve, on this reductionist picture, information which interacts problematically with the chances assigned to undermining futures—they aren't independent of one another. So the chances aren't an unconditional expert. But the chances are still expert for you, not in the sense that you should slavishly adopt the chances as your credences, but in the sense that, given your current information, the chance of some outcome is still a better guide to what you should set your credence to be than any alternative. That is, Hall (2004: 101) argues, chance is an *analyst-expert*, which 'earns [its] epistemic status because [it] is particularly good at evaluating the relevance of one proposition to another'—in this case, evaluating the relevance of your evidence (even evidence about the chances) to future outcomes. In that case, we should adopt only something like this principle connecting chance and credence (Hall 2004, Equation 3.9):

$$C(p|\ulcorner Ch(p|e) = x \urcorner \wedge e) = x.$$ (Chance-Analyst)

If we adopt this something like this principle instead of PP (modulo some important qualifications that Hall (2004: pp. 102–5) discusses), we can avoid the problem of undermining futures. Consider now an undermining future f, and fix on any proposition e which does not entail currently inadmissible evidence, but which does specify the present chances (note that e, so specified, will entail claims of the form $Ch(p|e) = x$). It remains true that f has some chance of coming to pass, so that there is some chance that the chances are otherwise. Earlier we used the PP to show that rational agents should therefore have some positive credence in f conditional on e, even though they are a priori inconsistent. That is, as e specifies the current chances (and no further inadmissible information), then $C(f|e) = 0$, because f and e are inconsistent; but the PP entails that $C(f|e) = Ch(f) > 0$, whence the contradiction. But the above principle only tells us that

$$C(f|\ulcorner Ch(f|e) = x \urcorner \wedge e) = x.$$

Since it follows immediately because e includes facts about the present chances that e and f are inconsistent, the chance of f conditional on e is zero and therefore $x = 0$—we cannot derive from the analyst-expert role of chance the problematic claim. This is just to say that if the present evidence suffices to establish the chances, it also suffices to rule out undermining futures which would falsify what e says about the present chances (though, since undermining futures are possible, evidence about chances, including e as specified above, is not perfectly admissible).

For various reasons, Chance-Analyst hasn't been thought to perfectly capture the full sense in which we should epistemically defer to chance. For one thing, that principle permits credence to be conditionalised on a proposition about chance, that the chance function is itself not conditionalised upon (the case above, where e included information about the chances, is a special one). It seems perhaps odd that one would count as failing to defer to chance if the chance function did not assign chance 1 to the proposition about chance that you are conditionally certain of, and yet that is a consequence of Chance-Analyst. In this sense, an overall better formulation of the New Principle that Lewis and others invoke to respond to the problem of undermining futures might be the version proposed by Joyce (2007). This is a 'global' principle, because it involves conditioning on a claim about an entire probability function at once. Let **chance** be a non-rigid designator of the actual chance function (varying from world to world), and let **P** rigidly designate some particular probability function. Then, Joyce proposes, this principle captures what it means for someone to defer their credence to the chances:

> (NP) Let C be the credence function for someone whose evidence is limited to the past and present. Then, if the chances are given by probability function P, then $C(p|\ulcorner\text{chance} = \mathbf{P}\urcorner) = P(p|\ulcorner\text{chance} = \mathbf{P}\urcorner)$.

(Joyce, 2007: 198)

Joyce notes that an aspect of his principle NP is a commitment to the earlier principle Chance-Analyst, in cases like that considered above, so adopting NP as one's conception of deference to chances allows the reductionist to block the problem of undermining in the way sketched above.

The general inadmissibility of evidence about the chance is a problem for Humeans, since we won't have inadmissible evidence generally. It will be difficult to apply either of these principles, NP or Chance-Analyst, in a way that generates unconditional credences by conditionalisation. Credence will still be the expectation of conditional chance according to NP, even if information about chance is inadmissible. But it will be very complicated in general to work this out, whereas working out the expectation of chance under the original PP was relatively easy. For that reason, it is useful to see under what circumstances the original PP remains an accurate guide to the credences we should have. One answer, that the PP is accurate to the extent that present chances are independent of possible undermining futures, is not very helpful. The further observation that most future events, even if they make some small contribution to the coming to pass of an undermining future, can be treated *as if* they are independent of the present chances without risk of significant error, is more helpful. It shows that, for most particular localised future events, we can treat chance as if it were governed by the PP (as what Hall calls a 'database expert'), as Chance-Analyst closely approximates the original PP. So reductionists and non-reductionists alike can accept the new principle, knowing in the latter case that the chances are independent of the future and so the original PP is fine, and in the former case that for all practical purposes the original PP is fine.

Others have argued that the original puzzle only arises because even the original PP inappropriately conditionalises the credence on evidence e which includes information about the chances. Ismael (forthcoming) argues that the real principle to adopt is the following, where h_t is just the history up to t

$$C(p|h_t) = \text{Ch}_t(p). \tag{UPP}$$

This principle also is not susceptible to undermining, because one never conditionalises on the theory of chance (assuming that the past history itself does not fix the chances). One won't ever in general know the right-hand side of this equation; but, by the theorem of total probability and general principles about current estimates of unknown quantities, it can be estimated as the weighted sum of the chances assigned by various future histories, weighted by your credences in those histories. Ismael's final recommendation is 'that you should adjust credence in A to your best estimate of the chances'.

Other principles about chance

Contrary to Lewis's contention, however, the Principal Principle (or its successors) does not capture all we know about chance. As Arntzenius and Hall (2003) have pointed out (in connection with the problems for reductionism about chance), some probability functions that obey the Principal Principle perfectly are very *unlike* chances. They conclude that we know more about chance than is captured by the Principal Principle alone, because we know that these functions, constructed simply to meet the Principal Principle but with no independent claim to be classified as chances, are not chances. This conclusion has been widely accepted. So while the Principal Principle captures a lot of what we know about chance, there are other truths about chance that help to narrow the field of probability functions which could be chances still further.

Another central principle connects chance and possibility, the *Basic Chance Principle* (BCP) of Bigelow, Collins and Pargetter (1993). They offer this informal argument for the existence of such a connection:

> In general, if the chance of A is positive there must be a possible future in which A is true. Let us say that any such possible future *grounds* the positive chance of A. But what kinds of worlds can have futures that ground the fact that there is a positive present chance of A in the actual world? Not just any old worlds ... [T]he positive present chance of A in this world must be grounded by the future course of events in some A-world sharing the history of our world and in which the present chance of A has the same value as it has in our world. That is precisely the content of the BCP.
>
> (Bigelow *et al.* 1993: 459)

In other words, if the chance of p is non-zero in some world w at some time, then p will in fact happen in some possible world which shares the history and chances with w—if not w itself, then a situation very like w. If Ch_{tw} is the chance distribution at t in world w, their formulation of the BCP is this:

> Suppose $x > 0$ and $\mathrm{Ch}_{tw}(p) = x$. Then p is true in at least one of those worlds w' that matches w up to time t and for which $\mathrm{Ch}_t(p) = x$.
>
> (Bigelow *et al.* 1993: 459)

Again, in accepting the connection between chance and possibility expressed by the BCP, we needn't endorse this precise formulation. Schaffer, for example, motivates it by this informal gloss: 'if there is a non-zero chance of p, this should entail that p is possible, and indeed that p is compossible with the circumstances' (Schaffer 2007: 124).[4] And still other conceptions of modality also turn out to support the broad thrust of the BCP.

The BCP is not a trivial truth, and it is not universally accepted. One objection is that the BCP is inconsistent with the existence of undermining futures, as discussed in the previous section. The present chance of tossing a fair coin one million times and it landing heads every time is $1/2^{10^6}$; this is small but non-zero. If this event were to occur in some possibility, the chance of heads for that coin in that world would not—or so the story goes—be 1/2; so there is no world with the same chances and history as ours in which this event occurs, contrary to the BCP. As above, the key to the existence of undermining futures is the broadly Humean (or reductionist) principle that whatever the chances are, they should supervene on the total arrangement or pattern of occurrent events. So if the counterfactual pattern of events can be so as to undermine the actual chance, the BCP will fail. Thus commitment to the BCP prima facie involves a commitment to a non-Humean conception of chance, one on which undermining is impossible.

This objection only has force if one accepts Humean reductionism about chance, and while that has a strong pull for many broadly empiricist metaphysicians and philosophers of science, it cannot be thought to have as much direct intuitive support as the BCP itself (indeed, Bigelow *et al.* (1993) are explicit in using the BCP to argue against Humeanism). A rejection of Humeanism would certainly be a welcome conclusion to some; it is arguably a requirement for the success of *propensity* accounts of what fills the chance role, like those offered by Popper (Chapter 28) and Giere (Chapter 29).

However, some accounts of the connection between chance and possibility, particularly of course those that begin with a Humean conception of possibility, will not have the strong anti-Humean consequences of the original Bigelow *et al.* version. For example, Schaffer (2003: sect. 4) has argued that, despite appearances, there is a conception of chance according to which the BCP and a broadly Humean account of chance are together consistent (and moreover consistent with the PP).[5] So this objection isn't conclusive.

*

Recall von Mises' insistence that probability only applies to 'mass phenomena' (Chapter 22). This was explicitly defined so as to require 'repetitive' events, not an arbitrary collection of events. (It is this requirement, effectively, that Popper starts from in developing his frequentist-inspired propensity theory—Chapter 28, pp. 493–4). This requirement on usable frequencies, that they come from repeated trials of the same experiment, points us towards another constraint on theories of chance, that chances should depend on the properties of the chance setup. The chance of a single outcome might well be measured by the frequencies in similar trials, but the connection between the trial of interest and the other trials is not merely incidental—what makes those trials evidentially relevant is the fact that they share underlying physical similarities.

One way of capturing this idea is at least that duplicate trials, precisely similar in all respects, in the same world (and thus subject to the same laws of nature) should have the same outcome chances. This is roughly the 'stable trial principle' as defended by Schaffer (2003: 37) (later slightly varied as the 'intrinsicness requirement' in Schaffer 2007: 125). Pretty much all conceptions of chance, reductionist and non-reductionist alike, respect this constraint, it has been argued:

> [any reductionist] recipe for how total history determines chances should be sensitive to basic symmetries of time and space—so that if, for example, two processes going on in different regions of spacetime are exactly alike, your recipe assigns to their outcomes the same single-case chances. (It is not that a non-reductionist will have no place for such a constraint: it is just that she will likely not view it as a substantive metaphysical thesis about chance, but as a substantive methodological thesis about how we should, in doing science, theorize about chance.)
>
> (Arntzenius and Hall, 2003: 178)

441

Even quite exotic views about chance respect the stable trial principle. Consider the view that robust objective chances are unnecessary, and can be replaced entirely by credences with certain formal properties (a view, as we will see further below, closely associated with de Finetti's famous proof (1964) that exchangeable—order-invariant—credences about the outcomes of many individual trials will behave as if there was a real unknown chance guiding the agent's overall credence in the pattern of those outcomes). This theory of 'chance', minimal as it is, nevertheless seems to respect something like the stable trial principle, because exchangeable credences demand the same credences about cases that are (credal) duplicates. This kind of observation is made by Skyrms (Chapter 32, p. 534), when he hints at something like this entirely subjectivist view about chance. And certainly views of chance according to which chance is a real objective phenomenon, grounded in the chance setup of mass phenomena, will endorse the stable trial principle. Indeed, many such views will even endorse stronger principles, such as that the chances supervene on the physical properties of the trial device alone, or that the chance depends on some particular dispositional property of the chance setup (as in propensity theories). But the controversies around propensities, which envelop these stronger claims, don't significantly undermine the original stable trial principle, and the original intuition that the underlying physical process that generates a chancy outcome is of primary importance for grounding the value of a chance under a given set of laws.

Reductionism and the occupants of the chance role

With those remarks about the chance role in hand, we can now look to a variety of theories about what exactly fills it. These are substantive ontological theses about the kinds of things that inhabit the world. Of course the frequency theory is such a theory too, one that makes only very minimal additional ontological commitments (though the ideological commitment to sensible counterfactuals about infinite sequences of coin tosses is severe); but it fails to provide something that can meet the chance role at all plausibly. The genuine contenders will be those that fill all roles more or less satisfactorily. But there is some tension between the different aspects of the role, which can be brought out as follows. Note that the BCP rules out undermining futures, because for any sequences of outcome that collectively have positive chance there is a world where the chances remain the same and that outcome occurs. So even an unlikely future course of events u takes place in a world with our chances. But of course there is an alternative set of chances too—chances that make u likely. (So there is a world where the coin is fair but lands heads one million times consecutively; and another world with the same pattern of outcomes but where the coin is biased heavily to heads.) Of course a kind of epistemic undermining still exists, where the future course of events becomes evidence for us about what the chances really have been all along, correcting an earlier mistake. But the sort that poses a problem for reductionists is not possible. The BCP thus fits most comfortably with the rejection of the possibility of reducing chance to patterns of outcomes.

On the other hand, the PP seems to fit well with reductionism. Non-reductionism would permit the primitive chance and the observed pattern of outcomes to diverge. But would this new primitive entity deserve the name? Lewis thinks not:

> Be my guest—posit all the primitive unHumean whatnots you like. … But play
> fair in naming your whatnots. Don't call any alleged feature of reality 'chance'

442

unless you've already shown that you have something, knowledge of which could constrain rational credence. I think I see, dimly but well enough, how knowledge of frequencies and symmetries and best systems could constrain rational credence.

But it is not clear that supposed 'chances' that can diverge arbitrarily from the observed patterns of outcomes, which are our only evidence about the chances, could really guide our credences in the right way. Suppose we lived in one of the worlds countenanced by the BCP, where a coin is fair but where an unlikely sequence of one million consecutive heads has occurred. Is it rational to have credence 1/2 in heads despite the wealth of evidence against it, conditional on knowing whatever specific feature it is that the envisaged coin has in common with an actual coin and which, it is proposed, grounds the chance? (Don't call it 'chance' yet, for that is exactly what's at issue.) The difficulty of plausibly satisfying the PP arises for many substantive non-reductive accounts of the occupant of the chance role, when that occupant is described independently of the chance role it is intended to fill.

Of course, the objection can be resisted. While Lewis sees 'dimly' how the reductionist resources of frequencies, etc., can constrain credence, it nevertheless remains true that 'no reductionist has in fact ever provided an exact recipe that would show how categorical facts fix the facts about objective chance' (Hall 2004: 111). And the non-reductionist can take PP to be a conceptual truth, which would obviate the need for any justification. Nevertheless, it remains helpful to use the apparent tension between these two sides of the chance role to look at the debate over which things fill it.

All theories of chance are impressed by the appearance of chance in physics, particularly its appearance in the spectacularly successful theories of quantum mechanics and statistical accounts of thermodynamics. It is a desideratum on a theory of chance that the chances proposed by fundamental or near-fundamental physical theories should turn out to genuinely exist. Popper (pp. 489–90) certainly seems to have been convinced by the apparent oddity of some aspects of quantum mechanics that a reductionist theory like the frequency theory wasn't 'realist enough' about chances—the only way that the behaviour of entangled systems could be explained was to posit propensities. It's not entirely clear how this argument is supposed to work (I think Popper believes that, in entanglement, the chances literally interfere with one another, so must be [grounded in] physical entities), but it is indicative at least of the main ground for believing in chances. Let us proceed for now, then, on the assumption that chances do exist, and look at some views of what they are.

Propensities

Propensity theories are non-reductive accounts of chance. The propensities which ground the chances, it is proposed, are a new kind of entity, not seen in non-probabilistic theories, but required to understand how chance functions if we take physics seriously. The primary insight is closely connected to something like the stable trial principle, that chance is somehow a feature of the 'generating conditions' of an event that happens by chance. It seems that the feature should be dispositional, rather than categorical; for the characteristic behaviour of a chance system only occurs when it is trialled in a certain way, and not invariably. The propensity theory, in its barest outlines, is the view that chance is grounded in a dispositional property of the chance setup. An early proponent was Peirce:

> I am, then, to define the meanings of the statement that the *probability*, that if a die be thrown from a dice box it will turn up a number divisible by three, is one-third. The statement means that the die has a certain 'would-be'; and to say that a die has a 'would-be' is to say that it has a property, quite analogous to any *habit* that a man might have.
>
> (Peirce, 1910: 169)

It is quite clear that taking chances to be grounded in dispositions can remove many difficulties for the frequency theory, which is how Popper initially motivates the adoption of a propensity theory. Accidents of the manifestation of the disposition in actual outcomes needn't undermine the intuitively correct value of the chances; and it is clear that the disposition can be present even in the single case.

Popper is not entirely clear, however, on what the manifestation and individuation conditions of propensities are. This gives rise to two candidate propensity theories (Kyburg 1974). One is the *long-run* view, according to which a propensity is a sure-fire disposition of a kind of trial to produce an outcome sequence with a certain (limit) frequency. The way in which Popper introduces the propensity theory as only a slight modification of frequentism suggests something like this interpretation: that the probability is grounded in the disposition of the generating conditions to support a certain infinite relative frequency. (As Giere notes, p. 501, Popper's later views make his commitment to this kind of view explicit.) The individuation conditions will involve the constraint that, if there is a case which gives rise to different frequencies, there must be different propensities involved.

The alternative view makes a more radical departure from frequentism. This is the *single-case tendency* version of the propensity theory. Rather than taking the propensity as a sure-fire disposition to produce a certain total outcome sequence with a certain frequency property, the propensity is a non-sure-fire disposition to produce a particular outcome—heads, for example. This kind of 'causal tendency' view is suggested by Popper's remark that '[W]e do interpret probability measures, or weights attached to the possibility, as measuring its disposition, or tendency, to realise itself ...' (p. 495). But the view is obviously present in Giere, who takes care to distance himself from the long-run view. In part this is because Giere is sceptical of the ability of the long-run view to adequately characterise the constant features of a repeated trial; in his view, the single case, in all its particularity, is the only appropriate ground on the probability on this occasion. Too much is potentially relevant to the chance to try and provide an invariable ground for a constant chance wherever it appears.

Both kinds of view have been primarily developed in ways that are explicitly anti-reductionist. Defenders of the propensity theory have maintained that there can be two possible worlds which differ with respect to the chances but do not differ in the non-chance patterns of occurrences. One could imagine, however, a kind of reductionist propensity theory, where the propensities were reduced to physical symmetries or to something else that wasn't in turn reduced to the patterns of occurrence. This kind of view hasn't been much developed, perhaps because it is difficult to see any viable candidates for the reduction. In any case, no propensity theory will reduce chance to Humean facts about the patterns of local occurrences, including facts about frequency.

The long-run view permits a possibility in which there is a certain pattern of long-run frequencies by accident; a world without chances that nevertheless has well-defined frequencies, because things just happen to turn out that way. The single-case view permits even more obvious examples of the failure of Humean reduction: we can have a single-case tendency of a biased coin to land heads, and a single-case tendency of a fair coin to land heads, where each coin is tossed only once and thus yields two worlds which are indistinguishable with respect to non-chance outcomes; the first kind of example can also exist if propensities are single-case. So both views take a step away from reductionism and empiricism; a step that seems at least intuitively to be warranted, at least in light of platitudes like the BCP and the stable trial principle, but nevertheless a step.

Problems for propensities

The two varieties of propensity theory face somewhat different hurdles. The long-run view faces considerable difficulties in giving an independent specification of what exactly the disposition involved is. It needs to be some property X, present in every trial, even the single case, which makes it true that any system with X, if it were trialled infinitely many times, would yield a certain limit frequency. So stated, many of the problems for hypothetical frequentism seem to plague this view. One example is Hájek's argument concerning order (Chapter 25, Argument 4, p. 416). Since the limit frequency depends on the order of the trials, it looks as though the long-run propensity must ensure that the trials occur in a certain order. (Otherwise there could be different frequencies, implying different propensities, but with the same underlying dispositions.) But it is more than remarkable that the individual trials in an infinite sequence of independent, identically distributed coin tosses should place constraints like this on one another.

But the main problem for this view isn't the puzzling metaphysics it requires. It is that the view seems to be devoid of substantial content. It is part of the chance role that it constrains credence, explains frequency and so on. We are told that what explains these things is the existence of a propensity; that then fills the chance role. But when we ask what the propensity is, we are given individuation conditions in terms of frequencies—it is the property which ensures that the frequencies come out right. But it is legitimate to ask at this point whether that is information about the *occupant* of the role, which explains the frequencies (and our attitudes to outcomes which take those frequencies as evidence), or whether it is merely another presentation of a constraint on the chance role itself. Of course, the propensity theory says that the propensity guarantees the hypothetical frequency, and the intuition about chances is that the hypothetical frequency is only very likely in the hypothesised circumstances; but insofar as this is an argument that 'propensity' isn't merely another name for chance, it is an argument that propensities aren't chances. The non-reductive aspect of propensities might provide another reason to think that it is not merely a notational innovation; yet, on reconsidering the example given above, it seems to turn simply on the direct non-reductive intuition we have about the chance role, that there could be two worlds which differ in the existence of chances yet agree in outcomes. Insofar as this kind of case exists, it could be perfectly described without ever making use of the term 'propensity', suggesting again that the real content of the long-run propensity theory is a commitment to non-reductive realism as a constraint on the chance role, and a hope that the expression 'the dispositional property which explains the frequency' is a non-defective definite description. Since we are given no independent characterisation of the supposed disposition, it is very hard to feel that genuine explanation is provided by this theory, at least in part because it is hard to see how any non-reductive realist about chance wouldn't automatically count as accepting something like the long-run propensity theory.

The single-case propensity theory, by contrast, does provide a substantive independent characterisation of the relevant property. We are told that propensities are a generalisation of causation, and that does provide information about the kinds of occupants in question—they are, at the very least, those properties such that, if they were absent, the causal factors leading to the outcome would have been different (and the outcome may not have been caused to happen at all). It is plausible to think that, as we are told this much about how propensities interact with causes, we have an independent enough specification of the occupant of the chance role for the view to have some teeth. Giere certainly thinks so. Consider his discussion of determinism (Chapter 29, pp. 502–4): the reason that determinism trivialises chance is because determinism ensures that the causal antecedents of any event guarantee it, so that the propensity (among these causal antecedents) must be trivial too.

Single-case causal tendencies, intrinsic to a particular system and causing to a greater or lesser degree the outcomes of that system, appear to be well suited to satisfy the stable trial principle and the BCP. There is a question obviously about the PP, as Giere notes and attempts to address in his discussion of statistical inference (pp. 504–6). But, as Humphreys points out (Chapter 30), all such views face a far more basic challenge—can they provide a conception of chance in which chance is a probability?

His argument can be put quite simply. The interpretation of chance should not require actual backwards causation for every well-defined conditional chance $Ch(p|q)$ where p occurs causally prior to q. Yet if the chance role is occupied by causal tendencies, this is precisely what is required. The argument that this is so runs as follows. Probabilities, as we saw in the primer, obey Bayes' theorem, which relates the conditional probability $P(p|q)$ to the conditional probability $P(q|p)$ (which Humphreys calls the 'inverse' probability) and to unconditional probabilities. The most natural interpretation of conditional chance as a propensity is to consider the conditioning event as a type of experiment, and to consider the propensity of the conditioned event in that experiment. Humphreys considers an experiment with an electron source and a half-silvered mirror. There is an overall chance of electrons passing through the entire apparatus; there is a chance of the electron passing the mirror, given that it impinged on the mirror, and this is most naturally construed as a conditional chance. But even if it made sense to consider the event of impinging on the mirror to have a propensity to bring about the event of the electron passing through the mirror, the converse does not hold; the event of passing the mirror does not have a propensity to bring it about that the electron hit the mirror. So the conditional propensity for the electron to impinge upon the mirror is unaffected by whether or not it passes through the mirror, and should be equal to the unconditional propensity for the electron to hit the mirror. But it follows from Bayes' theorem, applied to the assumptions about the case, that the conditional probability of an electron impinging on the mirror, given that it passed the mirror, will be 1. So there is an asymmetry in causal propensities that is not present in chance; so chances cannot be propensities.

Humphreys himself is fairly sanguine about the consequences of his argument; in the final section of his chapter, he argues that the propensity interpretation, because of its connection with the independently grasped concept of causation, might be epistemically secure enough not to need the connection with the probability calculus that his example severs. Others have agreed; Fetzer and Nute offer a non-standard probability calculus that is expressly designed to allow for Humphreys-style examples. But, given the existence of an argument that chances are probabilities from the PP, it seems that causal propensities can't satisfy the PP, and hence cannot be chances after all. Other responses that attempt to avoid the problematic conclusion have been given, usually by ascribing all of the relevant propensities to the initial state of the system. But this is apparently to abandon the causal understanding of propensities, and it is not clear what is being offered to replace it.

Reductionism about chance

If frequentism was the only reductionist alternative, these objections to the propensity theory and other non-reductive theories would not matter—whatever their problems, I suspect, the difficulties for frequentism are worse. However, scattered through Lewis's writings on chance are the hints of a reductionist alternative, able to overcome the difficulties for frequentism.

Frequency theories define chance as relative frequency in some collection of trials. This is admirably simple. As Hájek showed, however, this simplicity has a price. For there are cases where our judgements about chance, formed by consideration of factors *other* than the bare frequencies, conflict with the deliverances of frequentism. This suggests that a successful reductive account will say that chance supervenes on more than just the bare frequencies, as long as everything on which chance supervenes is an occurrent non-chance fact. (Note that Hájek claims that several of his arguments are problematic even for these more sophisticated reductive accounts; this is more contentious than his claim to offer problems for simple frequentist accounts.)

As we saw in Chapter 21, many of the problems with actual frequentism seemed to derive from the way that the actual frequencies might misrepresent the chances. Hypothetical frequentism is predicated on the hope that the problems might disappear if only we idealised the frequencies in some way. But, once the possibility that chance supervenes on more than just frequency is raised, this strategy seems in retrospect bizarre. A coin is tossed a few times, and lands heads roughly half the time. It is bizarre to correct this actual frequency in light of an infinite idealisation, because insofar as the idealisation is compelling at all, it presupposes the chances to constrain it, and we could more easily have corrected the frequency in light of the chances. Lewis notes that if we permit ourselves to draw on other things we know, for example, that the coin has a symmetrical mass distribution, we can correct the actual frequency without resorting to this problematic hypothetical frequency.

As Loewer (Chapter 31) observes, Lewis embeds this observation in a much more general framework. Lewis had argued previously, following earlier hints found in Ramsey (1990: sect. 12), that the laws of nature could be given a reductive analysis as

> [T]here exist ... innumerable true deductive systems: deductively closed, axiomatizable sets of true sentences. Of these true deductive systems, some can be axiomatized more *simply* than others. Also, some of them have more *strength*, or *information content*, than others ... [A] contingent generalization is a *law of nature* if and only if it appears as a theorem (or axiom) in each of the true deductive systems that achieves a best combination of simplicity and strength.
>
> (Lewis 1973: 73)

This theory is entirely reductive—the laws are no different than other contingent generalisations, except that they play a central role in all good ways of organising the truths of our world. By way of illustration, consider Newton's equations of motion, in a world where they are true. They are very simple. They are also quite strong—they rule out a lot of the ways that things could have gone, so have a lot of content. In conjunction with the initial conditions, a fact about the state of the world at one time, they serve to entail every (or almost every) truth about the world. So it looks as though they are at least laws. Are they the only laws? We could add the statement of initial conditions as a law, but that statement will be much less simple that the other laws, specifying as it does the complete and possibly highly nonhomogenous state of the world in full particularity. So while that augmented system is stronger, given that the original system was still strong and far simpler, only the three original laws deserve the name. And this seems to accord with intuition.

Lewis's account still apparently gives laws a special status—they can explain (by entailing) many particular matters of fact, they can support counterfactuals (since our standards hold them fixed while letting the accidents of the initial conditions vary, at least in many cases) and they can avoid vacuity (unlike less sophisticated reductive accounts). If simplicity and strength are objective enough, and Lewis is inclined to believe that they are (particularly because he takes simplicity to involve complexity of expression in a privileged language that invokes perfectly natural properties), and the best system is better enough than its rivals, then the theory will even give a set of laws that is robust enough to genuinely appear to be a species of 'natural necessity'. But the account is entirely reductive—laws are simply systematic representations of the actual patterns of outcomes.

For Lewis, chance enters the story through laws about chances. A law about chance will be something like a statement of frequency that *fits* the actual frequencies best, or best given the other constraints. Consider a very simple coin toss world, where a symmetrical coin is tossed 100 times and lands heads 47 times. The law that the chance is 0.5 fits quite well, and it meshes nicely with the symmetry claim to yield a simple and strong theory. It is simpler than the theory with perfect fit (chance is 0.47), and at least as strong (both theories assign the observed evidence a high probability, but only the former gives the symmetry of the coin an important role). This shows how the best systems account can adjudicate between hypotheses that each involve chance. But the main role for chance is that it permits the construction of better systems than are available without it; as Loewer says, 'by assigning chances systems sacrifice strength for fit but may also make great gains in simplicity' (p. 523). Chances enter the laws just in case a theory with chances, summarising in a more structural way the facts about outcome patterns, is simpler and not much less strong than a theory with a complete and full description of those outcome patterns in a way that gives more than merely structural information. (The contrast is between the structural information that there were about fifty heads in a given sequence, and the detailed information given by a list of the actual outcomes.) A strong and well-fitted chance theory can be much simpler than a rival stronger theory that does not involve chance; indeed, as Loewer goes on to argue, fit can be seen as just that dimension of informativeness which is appropriate for assessing probabilistic information (it is something like a probabilistic analogue of truth), so that strength and fit together should characterise a single dimension of informativeness. The point then is that systems involving chances can be simpler and nearly as informative as systems without chance, and thus better overall.

Loewer argues that, on this view, the PP is an entirely natural consequence of the conception of chance laws. Someone who adopts the PP agrees to set their credences by the best information available about the global pattern of outcomes of a given system, in the guise of the chances. But of course it is rational to have one's credences guided by the best information available; so it is rational to adopt the PP.

The reductionist alternative to the propensity theory, sketched by Lewis and developed by Loewer, is a promising one—if it can be made to work. It depends on the best system account of laws being correct; of further being able to specify the notion of fit correctly; and further on whether the resulting laws give the chances that can play the right role. Note, for one thing, that Lewisian chances seem to be derived from the laws of nature, which in turn depend on systematising everything about a world. So there is no sense in which what grounds the chance of this coin landing heads on this toss is something entirely intrinsic to the coin and toss. Embedding that very same coin and toss in a world with radically different patterns for that coin at other times will vary the chances without varying the intrinsic nature of the coin. Of course, even non-reductive accounts can share that intuition, if the laws of chance are contingent. But the sensitivity to circumstances of Lewisian chances is of an altogether more extreme sort. And again, because the chance-making facts are partly in the future, the BCP is not altogether easy to satisfy for the reductionist.

Radical subjectivism: what if there are no objective probabilities?

At this point, both Lewisian reductionism and non-reductionist propensity theories seem to face difficulties. This may make what seems initially to be a truly eccentric option more palatable: what if there are no chances? This is the radical subjectivism about chance, associated with de Finetti's radical probabilist slogan 'probability does not exist' (de Finetti 1974). Such a view may seem absurd, given the role of chance in science; what de Finetti shows, and what Skyrms draws on in Chapter 32, is that certain features of a subjective credence function can make it appear *as if* the credence is sensitive to some objective constraints. Maybe, therefore, the objective aspects of chance are, as Hume might have it, a projection of certain features of credence onto the world.

De Finetti's own explanation of the apparent objectivity of certain credence assignments depended on the notion of *exchangeability*. Suppose a credence function C is defined over an event space of sequences of 0 and 1 of arbitrary length—this might represent sequences of coin tosses, or the presence or absence of a property in a population of unknown size. If the credence in a certain sequence being actual is a function, not of the order in which the 1s and 0s appear, but only of the number of 1s and 0s in that sequence, then the credence is exchangeable: it is invariant under changes in the order of the outcomes. (This kind of probability assignment should remind one somewhat of Carnap's measure over structure descriptions, Chapter 19). If $X_1, ..., X_n, ...$ are random variables taking the value of a given sequence at the nth point, they are said also to be exchangeable relative to C. By way of illustration: if the X_is are independent and identically distributed, then they are exchangeable. But exchangeability is strictly weaker than independence.[6]

Given a sequence of exchangeable random variables, de Finetti (1975: 211–24) showed that, if your credences about a case are exchangeable, then your credence in any particular sequence of n variables taking the value 1 r times behaves exactly as if you believed that there was a real but unknown and constant chance p that $X_i = 1$ for

449

any i. That is, you behave as if you have a subjective credence distribution over the propositions $\ulcorner p = x \urcorner$, for $x \in [0, 1]$, and your credence (in line with the PP) is the expectation of how likely the given outcome sequence is given a particular chance hypothesis, weighted by how likely you believe it is that the chance hypothesis is true.

The lesson that de Finetti drew was this: if your credences meet the condition of exchangeability, then you act just as if you had a credence distribution over the chances. But since this follows merely from a condition on credences in outcomes, the introduction of real chances for us to be ignorant with respect to is otiose. If we wish to explain, for example, our judgements of the chances of sequences of coin tosses of unknown bias, we need not invoke objective chance at all, since we would have the same credences if our credences were exchangeable. Of course, if one looks for an *explanation* of why one's credences should be exchangeable, it is natural to look at the objective chances as providing that justification. As Howson and Urbach (1993: 350) point out, if you had exchangeable credences, a highly orderly sequence of length n like 0101010101...0 should have equal probability to a highly disorderly sequence of equal overall proportion of 1s and 0s; and, conditional on either of these sequences, the value of the $(n + 1)$th place will be independent and equal to the frequency 1/2. But, unless one was *already* convinced that the sequence was of independent outcomes (and correspondingly that the orderly sequence was an accident), one's credence in the next outcome being 1 should be close to 1 conditional on the orderly sequence, and 1/2 conditional on the disorderly one. So exchangeability seems to be a sensible constraint on credences which are appropriately sensitive to the evidence only in cases where one is antecedently convinced of genuine chance independence.

Skyrms (Chapter 32) invokes the notion of *resiliency* towards a similar but more modest end than de Finetti. One's credences are resilient to the extent that they remain constant after one updates on *any* potential piece of evidence. This dynamic property, about how credences could change, isn't exhausted by one's synchronic credence in a given hypothesis, as Skyrms illustrates with the example of two cases where one may have credence of 0.5 that a coin will land heads; one where one has no knowledge at all of the possible bias, and another where one is certain that the coin is fair. In the second case, but not the first, whatever the prior tosses are, one will not shift one's credence much, hence they are resilient. But in the first case, various biased sequences will confirm for you the hypothesis that the coin is biased, and can shift your credences arbitrarily close to 1 and 0. Skyrms shows that various claims made by realists about probability, mostly of the long-run propensity variety in his account, will give rise to corresponding properties concerning the resiliency of credences. What is of interest to us in the present context is the idea in Skyrms that these various features of chances have an impact on credences almost entirely characterised by the resiliency or otherwise of a credence function. So, he maintains, 'probabilistic resiliency of 1 does not require belief in the existence of an objective, physically random, sequence of events' (p. 534), though it is consistent with it. Moreover, strong enough belief in the existence of objective chance will guarantee resiliency, whether or not the belief is true. So, as long as we believe there are chances of independent and identically distributed events, we will act exactly as if we obeyed the Principal Principle, because the resiliency of our credences will secure immunity to revision on updating on observed outcomes.

Exactly how far resiliency and the belief in chance can substitute for the real existence of chances is not clear. But consider the following case (Lewis 1986: 120–21). There are no chances; the laws of nature entirely determine the future course of events, given suitably detailed information about the past and present. But suppose we don't have, and can't get, suitably detailed information; we only know in quite a coarse way what the current and previous states of the world are. In that case, we start with a reasonable credence and update on information which we can get, which suffices to tell us which coarse-grained way of characterising the state of the world we are in, but nothing more specific. After sufficient investigation, we should expect to converge to having credence 1 in being in a given coarse-grained state, and to be uniform over all the finer states consistent with it. Credences over this cell in the partition will act like chances—they will be resilient, as no information we can get will enable us to narrow the space of possibilities more finely in advance. But such 'counterfeit' chances are relative to the partition; if we can somehow extend our discriminatory abilities, we can gain perfectly admissible information which trumps these prior resilient credences, showing that these things aren't chances obeying the PP in any full-blooded sense. But if the coarse-graining of the states is natural enough, and admissible information is information that doesn't discriminate finer possibilities, resilient credences in Skyrms's sense will act as if they obeyed the PP.

Chance and physics

One natural question that arises here is: why do we not think those numbers, which guide credence conditional on the partition, are chances? Lewis's thought seems to be: there exists inaccessible but nevertheless admissible information which would trump these chances, so they can at best be measures introduced to help us deal with our ignorance of this information. In a case with genuine chance, on the contrary, there is no such further admissible information at all; so the structurally similar fine-grained partition in a case of genuine chance is untrumpable and thus really does meet the PP.

This depends, of course, on what we want chance to help explain. One problem with Lewis's view, and the views of all those who tie chance to indeterminism (the chapters of Giere and Skyrms also make this connection), is that it can seem to undermine one of the original arguments for being a realist about chance in the first place, namely, the role of chance in physics. This is because the chances introduced in classical statistical mechanics seem to be genuinely objective, to guide credence, to give substantive predictions and explanations about the behaviour of thermodynamic systems—and to be trumped by information about the underlying Newtonian microstate. So either chance in physics doesn't actually support realism about chance; or it is false that the existence of admissible trumping information shows that resilient credences aren't everywhere equal to a relevant chance function. Much of the recent interesting debate over *deterministic chance* aims to weigh up these options, with Loewer (2001) arguing that the naturalness of a certain 'macroscopic' partition of the states of the world into macroscopically indistinguishable equivalence classes yields a species of resilient probability, which guides correspondingly resilient credence in line with the PP, that can be trumped only by information that is macroscopically indistinguishable. And these resilient probabilities are themselves objectively fixed initially, because the simplest best theory of the initial conditions is one on which there is a uniform distribution over all microstates of the system. So we have objectively constrained macroscopic chances in deterministic physics. Schaffer (2007) argues against Loewer, and other conceptions of deterministic chance, arguing that whatever the naturalness of the relevant partition, nevertheless there always remains trumping admissible information, which cannot be systematically excluded while continuing to satisfy all the constraints on the chance role. Moreover, there is no need to posit an objective initial probability function, because we can introduce an objectively informed resilient credence to do exactly the same job without again violating anything we know about chance. This debate, as will be evident from the further reading, is ongoing.

The status of chance in quantum mechanics is not apparently threatened by determinism. But it is threatened by the difficulties philosophers have in understanding exactly what the ontology of the theory is. On the 'orthodox' collapse interpretation, a picture rather like Giere's emerges: a system in a given quantum state has a propensity to collapse, on being measured, into a given classical state, which is measured by the Born rule. But the deep conceptual problems with understanding measurement, particularly those unattractive views in which it essentially involves the imposition of a conscious observer, have meant that few serious philosophers of physics continue to advocate this view. But most of the views which give an objective understanding of a measurement process end up giving rather different pictures of the grounds of chances. So, for example, the Everett (many worlds) interpretation ends up (in effect) characterising the entire system in terms of the entirely deterministic evolution of the quantum state in accordance with the Schrödinger equation. On the de Broglie-Bohm theory, the entirely classical positions of the particles involved, plus a 'pilot wave' that is mathematically just like an instantaneous quantum state on the Everett interpretation, suffice once again to perfectly deterministically govern the evolution of the system. A theory on which there is something genuinely indeterministic and involving irreducible probabilities of collapse is the GRW theory; but some tricky mathematical issues mean that even this view doesn't ascribe *exactly* the probabilities we would expect, since collapse never *exactly* happens in quite the way we'd expect. This absurdly brief survey can't hope to resolve these issues. But it does suggest that the status of chance in even the most apparently hospitable part of physics is far from straightforward; the further reading indicates where you might go next to find out more.

Further reading

Some of this chapter draws on Eagle (2010: Supplement 1).

The locution 'probability coordination' is also found in Strevens (1999); there he argues that coordination principles like the Principal Principle cannot be derived non-circularly from other claims, but must be taken as basic truths about chance. Useful discussions of the principle of direct inference include those by Eells (1983) and Hacking (1965). The problem of undermining and the move to the new principle are discussed in two papers which guided Lewis's own thinking, by Hall (1994) and Thau (1994). The necessity of the shift from the old to the new principle has been questioned by Loewer (Chapter 31), Roberts (2001), Strevens (1995) and in two papers by Vranas (2002; 2004); Briggs (2009) argues that Humeans need to take the 'bug' of undermining more seriously than they have heretofore. Ismael (1996) argues that the possibility of undermining shows that standard conceptions of chances in quantum mechanics, as something like causal propensities, cannot be sustained. Strevens (1996) offers a reply to Ismael. Hoefer (2007) defends a version of the old Principal Principle which, he argues, is immune to the problem of undermining, through being rather less committed than Lewis himself about giving an explicit characterisation of the notion of admissibility.

Other views which posit a close connection between chance and possibility, motivated by similar considerations to those motivating the BCP, include Mellor (2000),

452

who argues that there is a 'necessity condition' on chance, ensuring that chances behave just like modalities. Eagle (forthcoming) agrees with Mellor that 'qualitative' chances behave like modalities, but argues that chance is closely related to dynamic (ability) modals like 'can' rather than metaphysical possibility (Kratzer, 1977). An earlier defender of an account of chance which involves a similar connection between chance and abilities is Levi (1980: Ch. 11–2).

Gillies (2000) addresses the two kinds of propensity theory, while Sklar (1970) examines the role of dispositions in characterising the grounds of chance. The long-run propensity view, in a more sophisticated version than that sketched either by Popper or in the text above, is defended by Mellor (1971); this theory is critically addressed by Salmon (1979). The single-case tendency view has come to characterise the majority of propensity theories; see those offered by Fetzer (1971), Jackson and Pargetter (1982), and Weiner and Belnap (2006). The branching possibilities account of chance and laws, defended by Vallentyne (1988) and McCall (1994: Ch. 5), while not explicitly invoking propensities, share many of the logical features of the single-case propensity theory and face many of the same difficulties. Giere (1976) offers a semantics of chance ascriptions which is explicit in providing a construction invoking a distribution over worlds that share a history to ground a present chance; this kind of construction is very similar to those offered by Vallentyne and McCall, and straightforwardly satisfies the BCP. The question of whether these branching possibilities conceptions of chance can satisfactorily ground the PP is posed in a telling form by van Fraassen (1989: 84–5), which he calls the 'horizontal/vertical' problem. An objection closely related to Humphreys' is posed by Milne (1985). The Fetzer-Nute causal calculus is presented by Fetzer (1981: 59–67). Miller (2002) and McCurdy (1996) both offer initial-state propensity theories in response to Humphreys' problem; Miller is explicit that he believes we 'have to discard altogether the lazy idea that propensities are generalized dispositions or partial causes' (p. 115). Eagle (2004) offers a compendium of both greater and lesser challenges to the propensity theory.

The best system analysis of laws is also advocated by Lewis (1994), Loewer (1996) and Cohen and Callender (2009). Criticisms of the proposal include Carroll (1994: 60–68), van Fraassen (1989: Ch. 3), Lange (2009: 49–59) and Tooley (1977: 669–72). The possibility that, if the initial conditions are simple enough (or if they have some very simple feature), facts about them might count as laws is canvassed by Albert (2000) and Loewer (2007) (they are particularly concerned whether the fact that our initial conditions were low entropy should count as a law); a criticism is made by Callender (2009). Hoefer (2007) offers an account of objective chance that is closely related to Lewis's. The notion of 'fit' used in the best systems analysis when extended to chances is put under pressure by Elga (2004). Black (1998) argues that the Humean justification of the PP Loewer offers on Lewis's behalf cannot be sustained by the reductionist. Sturgeon (1998) raises a number of tricky issues for the reductionist. A theory with reductionist aspirations, but of a rather different kind, is that sketched by Eagle (forthcoming).

The notion of exchangeability is introduced with further detail by Diaconis and Freedman (1980), Howson and Urbach (1993: 347–51) and Jeffrey (2004: Ch. 5). Galavotti (1989) discusses de Finetti's use of exchangeability to motivate his radical subjectivism; Howson and Urbach demur. The notion of resilient credence is connected to the notion of objectified credence in Jeffrey (1983: sect. 12.7); Skyrms (1980) provides more detail.

A considerable literature on objective chance, much of it stimulated by the debate over classical statistical mechanics, has grown up. The natural but largely tacit assumption is that chance and determinism are incompatible, as Lewis and Schaffer explicitly urge, along with Frigg (2008). Those advocating with Loewer the possibility of deterministic chance, whether or not they adapt resilient credence to their needs, include Clark (1987), Eagle (forthcoming), Glynn (2010), Hoefer (2007), Ismael (2009), Levi (1990) and Sober (2010).

A good introduction to philosophical issues around quantum mechanics is Albert (1992); see also van Fraassen (1991) and Hughes (1989). The Bohm theory is further discussed in Bell (1987). There is a significant and ongoing debate about the status of probability in the many-worlds/many-minds theory; see Barrett (1999) for a general overview of these theories. Wallace (2006; 2007) and Greaves (2007a) offer an argument that chance can be explained in the context of the deterministic Everettian theory; Peter Lewis (2007) and David Lewis (2004) disagree; Greaves (2007b) provides an overview.

Notes

1 As such, even if a principle involving belief—such as the Principal Principle—is part of the description, it cannot be said to be part of the definition. This is relevant to a claim Howson (2000: 222) makes about Lewis's theory of chance, that it 'implicitly defines chance ... in terms of its relation to beliefs'. Howson takes this to be an objectionable feature, but from the present perspective, and from Lewis's own, his claim is misguided, as no definition is on offer. 'The thing that regulates beliefs in line with PP' is no more a *definition* of chance than 'the thing measured by the scales' is a definition of mass.

2 This doesn't commit one to any substantive theses about what it means for the future to be open, such as a denial of eternalism; just that whatever one says about chances had better yield some kind of asymmetry between the past and the future.

3 One recent objection to PP worth noting arises from apparent direct counterexamples to the PP, derived from the existence of contingent a priori truths which illustrate the possibility of a formal mismatch between chance functions and credence functions (Hawthorne and Lasonen-Aarnio 2009; Williamson 2006). This example (due to Moritz Schulz) gives the flavour of both arguments: consider the sentence 'actually p iff p'. This sentence is a priori true, and so should presumably get credence 1. Yet the sentence is contingent. Suppose that p is actually true; then, according to the standard logic of the 'actually' operator (Davies and Humberstone,1980), 'Actually p iff p' is true in exactly the same possibilities as p (this is because 'Actually p' is necessarily true if true). So if p is a statement with a non-trivial chance, 'actually p iff p' also has that same non-trivial chance, differing from its credence. The natural response to this kind of argument is to take the entities in the domain of the chance and credence functions to be propositions rather than sentences (as Lewis originally did in formulating the PP); the problem does not arise because the contingent a priori only emerges at the level of sentences. Whether this response succeeds remains a matter for debate.

4 Schaffer endorses a strengthened version of the BCP, which he calls the realization principle: this is the claim that if the present chance of p is greater than zero, there is a world where p is true which matches ours in history and natural laws (not just laws of chance, but all laws).

5 The downside is that his theory of 'L*-chance' is subject to the objections raised by Arntzenius and Hall (2003) that we discussed above.

6 Consider *Polya's urn*: an urn containing b black balls and w white balls. A ball is drawn at random and its colour noted, then replaced *along with another ball of the same colour*. Repeat the procedure ad infinitum. Let $X_i = 1$ if a black ball is drawn on the ith draw, and 0 otherwise. The sequence $X_1, ..., X_n, ...$ is exchangeable. For example (by simple rearrangement):

$$C(101) = \frac{b}{b+w} \frac{w}{b+w+1} \frac{b+1}{b+w+2} = \frac{w}{b+w} \frac{b}{b+w+1} \frac{b+1}{b+w+2} = C(011).$$

But clearly these events are not independent.

Bibliography

Albert, David Z. (1992), *Quantum Mechanics and Experience*. Cambridge, MA: Harvard University Press.

—— (2000), *Time and Chance*. Cambridge, MA: Harvard University Press.

Arntzenius, Frank and Hall, Ned (2003), 'On What we Know about Chance'. *British Journal for the Philosophy of Science*, vol. 54: pp. 171–179.

Barrett, Jeffrey A. (1999), *The Quantum Mechanics of Minds and Worlds*. Oxford: Oxford University Press.

Bell, J. S. (1987), 'On the Impossible Pilot Wave'. In *Speakable and Unspeakable in Quantum Mechanics*, Cambridge: Cambridge University Press, pp. 159–168.

Bigelow, John, Collins, John and Pargetter, Robert (1993), 'The Big Bad Bug: What are the Humean's Chances?' *British Journal for the Philosophy of Science*, vol. 44: pp. 443–462.

Black, Robert (1998), 'Chance, Credence, and the Principal Principle'. *British Journal for the Philosophy of Science*, vol. 49: pp. 371–385.

Briggs, Rachael (2009), 'The Anatomy of the Big Bad Bug'. *Noûs*, vol. 43: pp. 428–449.

Butler, Joseph (1736), *The Analogy of Religion, Natural and Revealed, to the Constitution and Course of Nature*. London.

Callender, Craig (2009), 'Thermodynamic Asymmetry in Time'. In Edward N. Zalta (ed.), *The Stanford Encyclopedia of Philosophy*, spring 2009 ed.

Carroll, John (1994), *Laws of Nature*. Cambridge: Cambridge University Press.

Clark, Peter (1987), 'Determinism and Probability in Physics'. *Proceedings of the Aristotelian Society, Supplementary Volume*, vol. 61: pp. 185–210.

Cohen, Jonathan and Callender, Craig (2009), 'A Better Best System Account of Lawhood'. *Philosophical Studies*, vol. 145: pp. 1–34.

Davies, Martin and Humberstone, Lloyd (1980), 'Two Notions of Necessity'. *Philosophical Studies*, vol. 38: pp. 1–30.

de Finetti, Bruno (1964), 'Foresight: its Logical Laws, its Subjective Sources'. In Henry E. Kyburg, Jr. and Howard E. Smokler (eds.), *Studies in Subjective Probability*, New York: Wiley, pp. 93–158.

—— (1974), *Theory of Probability*, vol. 1. New York: Wiley.

—— (1975), *Theory of Probability*, vol. 2. New York: Wiley.

Diaconis, Persi and Freedman, David (1980), 'Finite Exchangeable Sequences'. *Annals of Probability*, vol. 8: pp. 745–764.

Eagle, Antony (2004), 'Twenty-One Arguments against Propensity Analyses of Probability'. *Erkenntnis*, vol. 60: pp. 371–416.

—— (2010), 'Chance versus Randomness'. In Edward N. Zalta (ed.), *The Stanford Encyclopedia of Philosophy*.

—— (forthcoming), 'Deterministic Chance'. *Noûs*, DOI 10.1111/j.1468-0068.2010.00771.x.

Eells, Ellery (1983), 'Objective Probability Theory Theory'. *Synthese*, vol. 57: pp. 387–442.

Elga, Adam (2004), 'Infinitesimal Chances and the Laws of Nature'. *Australasian Journal of Philosophy*, vol. 82: pp. 67–76.

Fetzer, James H. (1971), 'Dispositional Probabilities'. In R. Buck and R. Cohen (eds.), *PSA 1970*, Dordrecht: D. Reidel, pp. 473–482.

—— (1981), *Scientific Knowledge: Causation, Explanation, and Corroboration*. Dordrecht: D. Reidel.

Frigg, Roman (2008), 'Chance in Boltzmannian Statistical Mechanics'. *Philosophy of Science*, vol. 75: pp. 670–681.

Galavotti, Maria Carla (1989), 'Anti-Realism in the Philosophy of Probability: Bruno de Finetti's Subjectivism'. *Erkenntnis*, vol. 31: pp. 239–261.

Giere, Ronald N. (1976), 'A Laplacean Formal Semantics for Single Case Propensities'. *Journal of Philosophical Logic*, vol. 5: pp. 321–353.

Gillies, Donald (2000), 'Varieties of Propensity'. *British Journal for the Philosophy of Science*, vol. 51: pp. 807–835.

Glynn, Luke (2010), 'Deterministic Chance'. *British Journal for the Philosophy of Science*, vol. 61: pp. 51–80.

Greaves, Hilary (2007a), 'On the Everettian Epistemic Problem'. *Studies in History and Philosophy of Modern Physics*, vol. 38: pp. 120–152.

—— (2007b), 'Probability in the Everett Interpretation'. *Philosophy Compass*, vol. 2: pp. 109–128.

Hacking, Ian (1965), *The Logic of Statistical Inference*. Cambridge: Cambridge University Press.

Hall, Ned (1994), 'Correcting the Guide to Objective Chance'. *Mind*, vol. 103: pp. 505–517.

—— (2004), 'Two Mistakes about Credence and Chance'. In Frank Jackson and Graham Priest (eds.), *Lewisian Themes*, Oxford: Oxford University Press, pp. 94–112.

Hawthorne, John and Lasonen-Aarnio, Maria (2009), 'Knowledge and Objective Chance'. In Patrick Greenough and Duncan Pritchard (eds.), *Williamson on Knowledge*, Oxford: Oxford University Press, pp. 92–108.

Hoefer, Carl (2007), 'The Third Way on Objective Probability: A Sceptic's Guide to Objective Chance'. *Mind*, vol. 116: pp. 549–596.

Howson, Colin (2000), *Hume's Problem: Induction and the Justification of Belief*. Oxford: Oxford University Press.

Howson, Colin and Urbach, Peter (1993), *Scientific Reasoning: the Bayesian Approach*. Chicago: Open Court, 2 ed.

Hughes, R. I. G. (1989), *The Structure and Interpretation of Quantum Mechanics*. Cambridge, MA: Harvard University Press.

Ismael, Jenann (1996), 'What Chances Could Not Be'. *British Journal for the Philosophy of Science*, vol. 47: pp. 79–91.

—— (2009), 'Probability in Deterministic Physics'. *Journal of Philosophy*, vol. 106: pp. 89–109.

—— (forthcoming), 'Raid! The Big Bad Bug Dissolved'. *Noûs*.

Jackson, Frank and Pargetter, Robert (1982), 'Physical Probability as a Propensity'. *Noûs*, vol. 16: pp. 567–583.

Jeffrey, Richard C. (1983), *The Logic of Decision*. Chicago: University of Chicago Press, 2 ed.

—— (2004), *Subjective Probability (The Real Thing)*. Cambridge: Cambridge University Press.

Kratzer, Angelika (1977), 'What "must" and "can" Must and Can Mean'. *Linguistics and Philosophy*, vol. 1: pp. 337–355.

Kyburg, Jr., Henry E. (1974), 'Propensities and Probabilities'. *British Journal for the Philosophy of Science*, vol. 25: pp. 358–375.

Lange, Marc (2009), *Laws and Lawmakers*. Oxford: Oxford University Press.

Levi, Isaac (1980), *The Enterprise of Knowledge*. Cambridge, MA: MIT Press.

—— (1990), 'Chance'. *Philosophical Topics*, vol. 18: pp. 117–149.

Lewis, David (1973), *Counterfactuals*. Oxford: Blackwell.

—— (1986), *Philosophical Papers*, vol. 2. Oxford: Oxford University Press.

—— (1994), 'Humean Supervenience Debugged'. *Mind*, vol. 103: pp. 473–490.

—— (2004), 'How Many Lives has Schrödinger's Cat?' *Australasian Journal of Philosophy*, vol. 82.

Lewis, Peter (2007), 'Uncertainty and Probability for Branching Selves'. *Studies in History and Philosophy of Modern Physics*, vol. 38: pp. 1–14.

Loewer, Barry (1996), 'Humean Supervenience'. *Philosophical Topics*, vol. 24: pp. 101–127.

—— (2001), 'Determinism and Chance'. *Studies in History and Philosophy of Modern Physics*, vol. 32: pp. 609–620.

—— (2007), 'Counterfactuals and the Second Law'. In Huw Price and Richard Corry (eds.), *Causation, Physics, and the Constitution of Reality: Russell's Republic Revisited*, Oxford: Oxford University Press, pp. 293–326.

McCall, Storrs (1994), *A Model of the Universe: Space-Time, Probability, and Decision*. Oxford: Oxford University Press.

McCurdy, C. S. I. (1996), 'Humphreys' Paradox and the Interpretation of Inverse Conditional Probability'. *Synthese*, vol. 108: pp. 105–125.

Mellor, D. H. (1971), *The Matter of Chance*. Cambridge: Cambridge University Press.

—— (2000), 'Possibility, Chance and Necessity'. *Australasian Journal of Philosophy*, vol. 78: pp. 16–27.

Miller, David (2002), 'Propensities May Satisfy Bayes's Theorem'. In Richard Swinburne (ed.), *Bayes' Theorem*, vol. 113 of *Proceedings of the British Academy*, Oxford: Oxford University Press, pp. 111–116.

Milne, P. (1985), 'Can there be a Realist Single Case Interpretation of Probability?' *Erkenntnis*, vol. 25: pp. 129–132.

Peirce, Charles Sanders (1910), 'On the Doctrine of Chances, with Later Reflections'. In Justus Buchler (ed.), *Philosophical Writings of Peirce*, New York: Dover, pp. 157–173.

Ramsey, F. P. (1990), 'Universals of Law and of Fact'. In *Philosophical Papers*, Cambridge: Cambridge University Press, pp. 140–144.

Roberts, John (2001), 'Undermining Undermined: Why Humean Supervenience Never Needed to be Debugged (Even if it's a Necessary Truth)'. *Philosophy of Science*, vol. 68: pp. S98–S108.

Salmon, Wesley C. (1979), 'Propensities: a Discussion Review of Mellor (1971)'. *Erkenntnis*, vol. 14: pp. 183–216.

Schaffer, Jonathan (2003), 'Principled Chances'. *British Journal for the Philosophy of Science*, vol. 54: pp. 27–41.

—— (2007), 'Deterministic Chance?' *British Journal for the Philosophy of Science*, vol. 58: pp. 113–140.

Sklar, Lawrence (1970), 'Is Probability a Dispositional Property?' *Journal of Philosophy*, vol. 67: pp. 355–366.

Skyrms, Brian (1980), *Causal Necessity*. New Haven: Yale University Press.

Sober, Elliott (2010), 'Evolutionary Theory and the Reality of Macro Probabilities'. In Ellery Eells and James H. Fetzer (eds.), *The Place of Probability in Science*, Dordrecht: Springer, pp. 133–161.

Strevens, Michael (1995), 'A Closer Look at the "New" Principle'. *British Journal for the Philosophy of Science*, vol. 46: pp. 545–561.

—— (1996), 'Quantum Mechanics and Frequentism: A Reply to Ismael'. *British Journal for the Philosophy of Science*, vol. 47: pp. 575–577.

—— (1999), 'Objective Probability as a Guide to the World'. *Philosophical Studies*, vol. 95: pp. 243–275.

Sturgeon, Scott (1998), 'Humean Chance: Five Questions for David Lewis'. *Erkenntnis*, vol. 49: pp. 321–335.

Thau, Michael (1994), 'Undermining and Admissibility'. *Mind*, vol. 103: pp. 491–503.

Tooley, Michael (1977), 'The Nature of Laws'. *Canadian Journal of Philosophy*, vol. 7: pp. 667–698.

Vallentyne, Peter (1988), 'Explicating Lawhood'. *Philosophy of Science*, vol. 55: pp. 598–613.

van Fraassen, Bas C. (1989), *Laws and Symmetry*. Oxford: Oxford University Press.

—— (1991), *Quantum Mechanics: An Empiricist View*. Oxford: Oxford University Press.

Vranas, Peter B. M. (2002), 'Who's Afraid of Undermining? Why the Principal Principle Might Not Contradict Humean Supervenience'. *Erkenntnis*, vol. 57: pp. 151–174.

—— (2004), 'Have your Cake and Eat it Too: The Old Principal Principle Reconciled with the New'. *Philosophy and Phenomenological Research*, vol. 69: pp. 368–382.

Wallace, David (2006), 'Epistemology Quantised: circumstances in which we should come to believe in the Everett interpretation'. *British Journal for the Philosophy of Science*, vol. 57: pp. 655–689.

—— (2007), 'Quantum Probability from Subjective Likelihood: Improving on Deutsch's Proof of the Probability Rule'. *Studies in History and Philosophy of Modern Physics*, vol. 38: pp. 311–332.

Weiner, Matthew and Belnap, Nuel (2006), 'How Causal Probabilities might Fit into our Objectively Indeterministic World'. *Synthese*, vol. 149: pp. 1–36.

Williamson, Timothy (2006), 'Indicative versus Subjunctive Conditionals, Congruential versus Non-Hyperintensional Contexts'. *Philosophical Issues*, vol. 16: pp. 310–333.

27

A SUBJECTIVIST'S GUIDE TO OBJECTIVE CHANCE*†

David Lewis

Introduction

We subjectivists conceive of probability as the measure of reasonable partial belief. But we need not make war against other conceptions of probability, declaring that where subjective credence leaves off, there nonsense begins. Along with subjective credence we should believe also in objective chance. The practice and the analysis of science require both concepts. Neither can replace the other. Among the propositions that deserve our credence we find, for instance, the proposition that (as a matter of contingent fact about our world) any tritium atom that now exists has a certain chance of decaying within a year. Why should we subjectivists be less able than other folk to make sense of that?

Carnap (1945) did well to distinguish two concepts of probability, insisting that both were legitimate and useful and that neither was at fault because it was not the other. I do not think Carnap chose quite the right two concepts, however. In place of his 'degree of confirmation' I would put *credence* or *degree of belief*; in place of his 'relative frequency in the long run' I would put *chance* or *propensity*, understood as making sense in the single case. The division of labor between the two concepts will be little changed by these replacements. Credence is well suited to play the role of Carnap's probability$_1$, and chance to play the role of probability$_2$.

Given two kinds of probability, credence and chance, we can have hybrid probabilities of probabilities. (Not 'second order probabilities', which suggests one kind of probability self-applied.) Chance of credence need not detain us. It may be partly a matter of chance what one comes to believe, but what of it? Credence about chance is more important. To the believer in chance, chance is a proper subject to have beliefs about. Propositions about chance will enjoy various degrees of belief, and other propositions will be believed to various degrees conditionally upon them.

As I hope the following questionnaire will show, we have some very firm and definite opinions concerning reasonable credence about chance. These opinions seem to me to afford the best grip we have on the concept of chance. Indeed, I am led to wonder whether anyone *but* a subjectivist is in a position to understand objective chance!

Questionnaires

First question. A certain coin is scheduled to be tossed at noon today. You are sure that this chosen coin is fair: it has a 50% chance of falling heads and a 50% chance

458

of falling tails. You have no other relevant information. Consider the proposition that the coin tossed at noon today falls heads. To what degree would you now believe that proposition?

Answer. 50%, of course.

(Two comments. (1) It is abbreviation to speak of the coin as fair. Strictly speaking, what you are sure of is that the entire 'chance set-up' is fair: coin, tosser, landing surface, air, and surrounding together are such as to make it so that the chance of heads is 50%. (2) Is it reasonable to think of coin-tossing as a genuine chance process, given present-day scientific knowledge? I think so: consider, for instance, that air resistance depends partly on the chance making and breaking of chemical bonds between the coin and the air molecules it encounters. What is less clear is that the toss could be designed so that you could reasonably be sure that the chance of heads is 50% exactly. If you doubt that such a toss could be designed, you may substitute an example involving radioactive decay.)

Next question. As before, except that you have plenty of seemingly relevant evidence tending to lead you to expect that the coin will fall heads. This coin is known to have a displaced center of mass, it has been tossed 100 times before with 86 heads, and many duplicates of it have been tossed thousands of times with about 90% heads. Yet you remain quite sure, despite all this evidence, that the chance of heads this time is 50%. To what degree should you believe the proposition that the coin falls heads this time?

Answer. Still 50%. Such evidence is relevant to the outcome by way of its relevance to the proposition that the chance of heads is 50%, not in any other way. If the evidence somehow fails to diminish your certainty that the coin is fair, then it should have no effect on the distribution of credence about outcomes that accords with that certainty about chance. To the extent that uncertainty about outcomes is based on certainty about their chances, it is a stable, resilient sort of uncertainty—new evidence won't get rid of it. (The term 'resiliency' comes from Skyrms (1977); see also Jeffrey (1965), §12.5.)

Someone might object that you could not reasonably remain sure that the coin was fair, given such evidence as I described and no contrary evidence that I failed to mention. That may be so, but it doesn't matter. Canons of reasonable belief need not be counsels of perfection. A moral code that forbids all robbery may also prescribe that if one nevertheless robs, one should rob only the rich. Likewise it is a sensible question what it is reasonable to believe about outcomes if one is unreasonably stubborn in clinging to one's certainty about chances.

Next question. As before, except that now it is afternoon and you have evidence that became available after the coin was tossed at noon. Maybe you know for certain that it fell heads; maybe some fairly reliable witness has told you that it fell heads; maybe the witness has told you that it fell heads in nine out of ten tosses of which the noon toss was one. You remain as sure as ever that the chance of heads, just before noon, was 50%. To what degree should you believe that the coin tossed at noon fell heads?

Answer. Not 50%, but something not far short of 100%. Resiliency has its limits. If evidence bears in a direct enough way on the outcome—a way which may nevertheless fall short of outright implication—then it may bear on your beliefs about outcomes otherwise than by way of your beliefs about the chances of the outcomes. Resiliency under all evidence whatever would be extremely unreasonable.

We can only say that degrees of belief about outcomes that are based on certainty about chances are resilient under *admissible* evidence. The previous question gave examples of admissible evidence; this question gave examples of inadmissible evidence.

Last question. You have no inadmissible evidence; if you have any relevant admissible evidence, it already has had its proper effect on your credence about the chance of heads. But this time, suppose you are not sure that the coin is fair. You divide your belief among three alternative hypotheses about the chance of heads, as follows.

> You believe to degree 27% that the chance of heads is 50%.
> You believe to degree 22% that the chance of heads is 35%.
> You believe to degree 51% that the chance of heads is 80%.

Then to what degree should you believe that the coin falls heads?

Answer. $(27\% \times 50\%) + (22\% \times 35\%) + (51\% \times 80\%)$; that is, 62%. Your degree of belief that the coin falls heads, conditionally on any one of the hypotheses about the chance of heads, should equal your unconditional degree of belief if you were sure of that hypothesis. That in turn should equal the chance of heads according to the hypothesis: 50% for the first hypothesis, 35% for the second, and 80% for the third. Given your degrees of belief that the coin falls heads, conditionally on the hypotheses, we need only apply the standard multiplicative and additive principles to obtain our answer.

The Principal Principle

I have given undefended answers to my four questions. I hope you found them obviously right, so that you will be willing to take them as evidence for what follows. If not, do please reconsider. If so, splendid—now read on.

It is time to formulate a general principle to capture the intuitions that were forthcoming in our questionnaire. It will resemble familiar principles of direct inference except that (1) it will concern chance, not some sort of actual or hypothetical frequency, and (2) it will incorporate the observation that certainty about chances—or conditionality on propositions about chances—makes for resilient degrees of belief about outcomes. Since this principle seems to me to capture all we know about chance, I call it.

THE PRINCIPAL PRINCIPLE. Let C be any reasonable initial credence function. Let t be any time. Let x be any real number in the unit interval. Let X be the proposition that the chance, at time t, of A's holding equals x. Let E be any proposition compatible with X that is admissible at time t. Then

$$C(A/XE) = x.$$

That will need a good deal of explaining. But first I shall illustrate the principle by applying it to the cases in our questionnaire.

Suppose your present credence function is $C(-/E)$, the function that comes from some reasonable initial credence function C by conditionalizing on your present total evidence E. Let t be the time of the toss, noon today, and let A be the proposition that the coin tossed today falls heads. Let X be the proposition that the chance at noon (just before the toss) of heads is x. (In our questionnaire, we mostly considered the case that x is 50%). Suppose that nothing in your total evidence E contradicts X; suppose also that it is not yet noon, and you have no foreknowledge of the outcome, so everything that is included in E entirely admissible. The conditions of the Principal Principle are met. Therefore $C(A/XE)$ equals x. That is to say that x is your present degree of belief that

460

the coin falls heads, conditionally on the proposition that its chance of falling heads is x. If in addition you are sure that the chance of heads is x—that is, if $C(X/E)$ is one—then it follows also that x is your present unconditional degree of belief that the coin falls heads. More generally, whether or not you are sure about the chance of heads, your unconditional degree of belief that the coin falls heads is given by summing over alternative hypotheses about chance:

$$C(A/E) = \Sigma_x C(X_x/E)C(A/X_x E) = \Sigma_x C(X_x/E)x,$$

where X_x, for any value of x, is the proposition that the chance at t of A equals x.

Several parts of the formulation of the Principal Principle call for explanation and comment. Let us take them in turn.

The initial credence function C

I said: let C be any reasonable initial credence function. By that I meant, in part, that C was to be a probability distribution over (at least) the space whose points are possible worlds and whose regions (sets of worlds) are propositions. C is a non-negative, normalized, finitely additive measure defined on all propositions.

The corresponding conditional credence function is defined simply as a quotient of unconditional credences:

$$C(A/B) =_{df} C(AB)/C(B).$$

I should like to assume that it makes sense to conditionalize on any but the empty proposition. Therefore, I require that C is *regular*: $C(B)$ is zero, and $C(A/B)$ is undefined, only if B is the empty proposition, true at no worlds. You may protest that there are too many alternative possible worlds to permit regularity. But that is so only if we suppose, as I do not, that the values of the function C are restricted to the standard reals. Many propositions must have infinitesimal C-values, and $C(A/B)$ often will be defined as a quotient of infinitesimals, each infinitely close but not equal to zero. (See Bernstein and Wattenberg (1969).) The assumption that C is regular will prove convenient, but it is not justified only as a convenience. Also it is required as a condition of reasonableness: one who started out with an irregular credence function (and who then learned from experience by conditionalizing) would stubbornly refuse to believe some propositions no matter what the evidence in their favor.

In general, C is to be reasonable in the sense that if you started out with it as your initial credence function, and if you always learned from experience by conditionalizing on your total evidence, then no matter what course of experience you might undergo your beliefs would be reasonable for one who had undergone that course of experience. I do not say what distinguishes a reasonable from an unreasonable credence function to arrive at after a given course of experience. We do make the distinction, even if we cannot analyze it; and therefore I may appeal to it in saying what it means to require that C be a reasonable initial credence function.

I have assumed that the method of conditionalizing is *one* reasonable way to learn from experience, given the right initial credence function. I have not assumed something more controversial: that it is the *only* reasonable way. The latter view may also be right (the cases where it seems wrong to conditionalize may all be cases where one departure from ideal rationality is needed to compensate for another) but I shall not need it here.

(I said that C was to be a probability distribution over *at least* the space of worlds; the reason for that qualification is that sometimes one's credence might be divided between different possibilities within a single world. That is the case for someone who is sure what sort of world he lives in, but not at all sure who and when and where in the world he is. In a fully general treatment of credence it would be well to replace the worlds by something like the 'centered worlds' of Quine (1969), and the propositions by something corresponding to properties. But I shall ignore these complications here).

The real number x

I said: let x be any real number in the unit interval. I must emphasize that 'x' is a quantified variable; it is not a schematic letter that may freely be replaced by terms that designate real numbers in the unit interval. For fixed A and t, 'the chance, at t, of A's holding' is such a term; suppose we put it in for the variable x. It might seem that for suitable C and E we have the following: if X is the proposition that the chance, at t, of A's holding equals the chance, at t, of A's holding—in other words, if X is the necessary proposition—then

$$C(A/XE) = \text{the chance, at } t, \text{ of } A\text{'s holding.}$$

But that is absurd. It means that if E is your present total evidence and $C(-/E)$ is your present credence function, then if the coin is in fact fair—whether or not you think it is!—then your degree of belief that it falls heads is 50%. Fortunately, that absurdity is not an instance of the Principal Principle. The term 'the chance, at t, of A's holding' is a non-rigid designator; chance being a matter of contingent fact, it designates different numbers at different worlds. The context 'the proposition that ...', within which the variable 'x' occurs, is intensional. Universal instantiation into an intensional context with a non-rigid term is a fallacy. It is the fallacy that takes you, for instance, from the true premise 'For any number x, the proposition that x is nine is non-contingent' to the false conclusion 'The proposition that the number of planets is nine is non-contingent'. See Jeffrey (1970) for discussion of this point in connection with a relative of the Principal Principle.

I should note that the values of 'x' are not restricted to the standard reals in the unit interval. The Principal Principle may be applied as follows: you are sure that some spinner is fair, hence that it has infinitesimal chance of coming to rest at any particular point; therefore (if your total evidence is admissible) you should believe only to an infinitesimal degree that it will come to rest at any particular point.

The proposition X

I said: let X be the proposition that the chance, at time t, of A's holding equals x. I emphasize that I am speaking of objective, single-case chance—not credence, not frequency. Like it or not, we have this concept. We think that a coin about to be tossed has a certain chance of falling heads, or that a radioactive atom has a certain chance of decaying within the year, quite regardless of what anyone may believe about it and quite regardless of whether there are any other similar coins or atoms. As philosophers we may well find the concept of objective chance troublesome, but that is no excuse to deny its existence, its legitimacy, or its indispensability. If we can't understand it, so much the worse for us.

Chance and credence are distinct, but I don't say they are unrelated. What is the Principal Principle but a statement of their relation? Neither do I say that chance and frequency are unrelated, but they are distinct. Suppose we have many coin-tosses with the same chance of heads (not zero or one) in each case. Then there is some chance of getting any frequency of heads whatever; and hence some chance that the frequency and the uniform single-case chance of heads may differ, which could not be so if these were one and the same thing. Indeed the chance of difference may be infinitesimal if there are infinitely many tosses, but that is still not zero. Nor do hypothetical frequencies fare any better. There is no such thing as *the* infinite sequence of outcomes, or *the* limiting frequency of heads, that *would* eventuate if some particular coin-toss were somehow repeated forever. Rather there are countless sequences, and countless frequencies, that *might* eventuate and would have some chance (perhaps infinitesimal) of eventuating. (See Jeffrey (1977), Skyrms (1977), and the discussion of 'might' counterfactuals in Lewis (1973)).

Chance is not the same thing as credence or frequency; this is not yet to deny that there might be some roundabout way to analyze chance in terms of credence or frequency. I would only ask that no such analysis be accepted unless it is compatible with the Principal Principle. We shall consider how this requirement bears on the prospects for an analysis of chance, but without settling the question of whether such an analysis is possible.

I think of chance as attaching in the first instance to propositions: the chance of an event, an outcome, etc. is the chance of truth of the proposition that holds at just those worlds where that event, outcome, or whatnot occurs. (Here I ignore the special usage of 'event' to simply mean 'proposition'). I have foremost in mind the chances of truth of propositions about localized matters of particular fact—a certain toss of a coin, the fate of a certain tritium atom on a certain day—but I do not say that those are the only propositions to which chance applies. Not only does it make sense to speak of the chance that a coin will fall heads on a particular occasion; equally it makes sense to speak of the chance of getting exactly seven heads in a particular sequence of eleven tosses. It is only caution, not any definite reason to think otherwise, that stops me from assuming that chance of truth applies to any proposition whatever. I shall assume, however, that the broad class of propositions to which chance of truth applies is closed under the Boolean operations of conjunction (intersection), disjunction (union), and negation (complementation).

We ordinarily think of chance as time-dependent, and I have made that dependence explicit. Suppose you enter a labyrinth at 11:00 a.m., planning to choose your turn whenever you come to a branch point by tossing a coin. When you enter at 11:00, you may have a 42% chance of reaching the center by noon. But in the first half hour you may stray into a region from which it is hard to reach the center, so that by 11:30 your chance of reaching the center by noon has fallen to 26%. But then you turn lucky; by 11:45 you are not far from the center and your chance of reaching it by noon is 78%. At 11:49 you reach the center; then and forevermore your chance of reaching it by noon is 100%.

Sometimes, to be sure, we omit reference to a time. I do not think this means that we have some timeless notion of chance. Rather, we have other ways to fix the time than by specifying it explicitly. In the case of the labyrinth we might well say (before, after, or during your exploration) that your chance of reaching the center by noon is 42%. The understood time of reference is the time when your exploration begins. Likewise we might speak simply of the chance of a certain atom's decaying within a certain year, meaning the chance at the beginning of that year. In general, if A is the proposition that something or other takes place within a certain interval beginning at time t, then we may take a special interest in what I shall call the *endpoint chance* of A's holding: the chance at t, the beginning of the interval in question. If we speak simply of the chance of A's holding, not mentioning a time, it is this endpoint chance—the chance at t of A's holding—that we are likely to mean.

Chance also is world-dependent. Your chance at 11:00 of reaching the center of the labyrinth by noon depends on all sorts of contingent features of the world: the structure of the labyrinth and the speed with which you can walk through it, for instance. Your chance at 11:30 of reaching the center by noon depends on these things, and also on where in the labyrinth you then are. Since these things vary from world to world, so does your chance (at either time) of reaching the center by noon. Your chance at noon of reaching the center by noon is one at the worlds where you have reached the center; zero at all others, including those worlds where you do not explore the labyrinth at all, perhaps because you or it do not exist. (Here I am speaking loosely, as if I believed that you and the labyrinth could inhabit several worlds at once. See Lewis (1968) for the needed correction.)

We have decided this much about chance, at least: it is a function of three arguments. To a proposition, a time, and a world it assigns a real number. Fixing the proposition A, the time t, and the number x, we have our proposition X: it is the proposition that holds at all and only those worlds w such that this function assigns to A, t, and w the value x. This is the proposition that the chance, at t, of A's holding is x.

The admissible proposition E

I said: let E be any proposition that is admissible at time t. Admissible propositions are the sort of information whose impact on credence about outcomes comes entirely by way of credence about the chances of those outcomes. Once the chances are given outright, conditionally or unconditionally, evidence bearing on them no longer matters. (Once it is settled that the suspect fired the gun, the discovery of his fingerprint on the trigger adds nothing to the case against him.) The power of the Principal Principle depends entirely on how much is admissible. If nothing is admissible it is vacuous. If everything is admissible it is inconsistent. Our questionnaire suggested that a great deal is admissible, but we saw examples also of inadmissible information. I have no definition of admissibility to offer, but must be content to suggest sufficient (or almost sufficient) conditions for admissibility. I suggest that two different sorts of information are generally admissible.

The first sort is historical information. If a proposition is entirely about matters of particular fact at times no later than t, then as a rule that proposition is admissible at t. Admissible information just before the toss of a coin, for example, includes the outcomes of all previous tosses of that coin and others like it. It also includes every detail—no matter how hard it might be to discover—of the structure of the coin, the tosser, other parts of the set-up, and even anything nearby that might somehow intervene. It also includes a great deal of other information that is completely irrelevant to the outcome of the toss.

A proposition is *about* a subject matter—about history up to a certain time, for instance—if and only if that proposition holds at both or neither of any two worlds that match perfectly with respect to that subject matter. (Or we can go the other way: two worlds match perfectly with respect to a subject matter if and only if every proposition about that subject matter holds at both or neither.) If our world and another are alike point for point, atom for atom, field for field, even spirit for spirit (if such there be) throughout the past and up until noon today, then any proposition that distinguishes the two cannot be entirely about the respects in which there is no difference. It cannot be entirely about what goes on no later than noon today. That is so even if its linguistic expression makes no overt mention of later times; we must beware lest information about the future is hidden in the predicates, as in 'Fred was mortally wounded at 11:58'. I doubt that any linguistic test of aboutness will work without circular restrictions on the language used. Hence it seems best to take either 'about' or 'perfect match with respect to' as a primitive.

Time-dependent chance and time-dependent admissibility go together. Suppose the proposition A is about matters of particular fact at some moment or interval t_A, and suppose we are concerned with chance at time t. If t is later than t_A, then A is admissible at t. The Principal Principle applies with A for E. If X is the proposition that the chance at t of A equals x, and if A and X are compatible, then

$$1 = C(A/XA) = x.$$

Put contrapositively, this means that if the chance at t of A, according to X, is anything but one, then A and X are incompatible. A implies that the chance at t of A, unless undefined, equals one. What's past is no longer chancy. The past, unlike the future, has no chance of being any other way than the way it actually is. This temporal asymmetry of chance falls into place as part of our conception of the past as 'fixed' and the future as 'open'—whatever that may mean. The asymmetry of fixity and of chance may be pictured by a tree (as in Figure 27.1). The single trunk is the one possible past that has any present chance of being actual. The many branches are the many possible futures that have some present chance of being actual. I shall not try to say here what features of the world justify our discriminatory attitude toward past and future possibilities, reflected for instance in the judgement that historical information is admissible and similar information about the future is not. But I think they are contingent features, subject to exception and absent altogether from some possible worlds.

That possibility calls into question my thesis that historical information is invariably admissible. What if the commonplace *de facto* asymmetries between past and future break down? If the past lies far in the future, as we are far to the west of ourselves, then it cannot simply be that propositions about the past are admissible and propositions about the future are not. And if the past contains seers with foreknowledge of what chance will bring, or time travelers who have witnessed the outcome of coin-tosses to come, then patches of the past are enough tainted with futurity so that historical information about them may well seem inadmissible. That is why I qualified my claim that historical information is admissible, saying only that it is so 'as a rule'. Perhaps it is fair to ignore this problem in building a case that the Principal Principle captures our

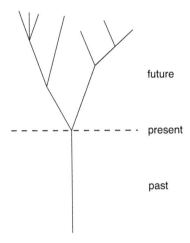

Figure 27.1 The asymmetry of fixity and chance.

common opinions about chance, since those opinions may rest on a naive faith that past and future cannot possibly get mixed up. Any serious physicist, if he remains at least open-minded both about the shape of the cosmos and about the existence of chance processes, ought to do better. But I shall not; I shall carry on as if historical information is admissible without exception.

Besides historical information, there is at least one other sort of admissible information: hypothetical information about chance itself. Let us return briefly to our questionnaire and add one further supposition to each case. Suppose you have various opinions about what the chance of heads would be under various hypotheses about the detailed nature and history of the chance set-up under consideration. Suppose further that you have similar hypothetical opinions about other chance set-ups, past, present, and future. (Assume that these opinions are consistent with your admissible historical information and your opinions about chance in the present case.) It seems quite clear to me—and I hope it does to you also—that these added opinions do not change anything. The correct answers to the questionnaire are just as before. The added opinions do not bear in any overly direct way on the future outcomes of chance processes. Therefore they are admissible.

We must take care, though. Some propositions about future chances do reveal inadmissible information about future history, and these are inadmissible. Recall the case of the labyrinth: you enter at 11:00, choosing your turns by chance, and hope to reach the center by noon. Your subsequent chance of success depends on the point you have reached. The proposition that at 11:30 your chance of success has fallen to 26% is not admissible information at 11:00; it is a giveaway about your bad luck in the first half hour. What is admissible at 11:00 is a conditional version: if you were to reach a certain point at 11:30, your chance of success would then be 26%. But even some conditionals are tainted: for instance, any conditional that could yield inadmissible information about future chances by *modus ponens* from admissible historical propositions. Consider also the truth-functional conditional that if history up to 11:30 follows a certain course, then you will have a 98% chance of becoming a monkey's uncle before the year is out. This conditional closely resembles the denial of its antecedent, and is inadmissible at 11:00 for the same reason.

I suggest that conditionals of the following sort, however, are admissible; and indeed admissible at all times. (1) The consequent is a proposition about chance at a certain time. (2) The antecedent is a proposition about history up to that time; and further, it is a complete proposition about history up to that time, so that it either implies or else is incompatible with any other proposition about history up to that time. It fully specifies a segment, up to the given time, of some possible course of history. (3) The conditional is made from its consequent and antecedent not truth-functionally, but rather by means of a strong conditional operation of some sort. This might well be the counterfactual conditional of Lewis (1973); but various rival versions would serve as well, since many differences do not matter for the case at hand. One feature of my treatment will be needed, however: if the antecedent of one of our conditionals holds at a world, then both or neither of the conditional and its consequent hold there.

These admissible conditionals are propositions about how chance depends (or fails to depend) on history. They say nothing, however, about how history chances to go. A set of them is a theory about the way chance works. It may or may not be a complete theory, a consistent theory, a systematic theory, or a credible theory. It might be a miscellany of unrelated propositions about what the chances would be after various fully specified particular courses of events. Or it might be systematic, compressible into generalizations to the effect that after any course of history with property J there would follow a chance distribution with property K. (For instance, it might say that any coin with a certain structure would be fair.) These generalizations are universally quantified conditionals about single-case chance; if lawful, they are probabilistic laws in the sense of Railton (1978). (I shall not consider here what would make them lawful; but see Lewis (1973), §3.3, for a treatment that could cover laws about chance along with other laws.) Systematic theories of chance are the ones we can express in language, think about, and believe to substantial degrees. But a reasonable initial credence function does not reject any possibility out of hand. It assigns some non-zero credence to any consistent theory of chance, no matter how unsystematic and incompressible it is.

Historical propositions are admissible; so are propositions about the dependence of chance on history. Combinations of the two, of course, are also admissible. More generally, we may assume that any Boolean combination of propositions admissible at a time also is admissible at that time. Admissibility consists in keeping out of a forbidden subject matter—how the chance processes turned out—and there is no way to break into a subject matter by making Boolean combinations of propositions that lie outside it.

There may be sorts of admissible propositions besides those I have considered. If so, we shall have no need of them in what follows.

This completes an exposition of the Principal Principle. We turn next to an examination of its consequences. I maintain that they include all that we take ourselves to know about chance.

The Principle reformulated

Given a time t and world w, let us write P_{tw} for the *chance distribution* that obtains at t and w. For any proposition A, $P_{tw}(A)$ is the chance, at time t and world w, of

467

A's holding. (The domain of P_{tw} comprises those propositions for which this chance is defined.)

Let us also write H_{tw} for the *complete history* of world w up to time t: the conjunction of all propositions that hold at w about matters of particular fact no later than t. H_{tw} is the proposition that holds at exactly those worlds that perfectly match w, in matters of particular fact, up to time t.

Let us also write T_w for the *complete theory of chance* for world w: the conjunction of all the conditionals from history to chance, of the sort just considered, that hold at w. Thus T_w is a full specification, for world w, of the way chances at any time depend on history up to that time.

Taking the conjunction $H_{tw}T_w$, we have a proposition that tells us a great deal about the world w. It is nevertheless admissible at time t, being simply a giant conjunction of historical propositions that are admissible at t and conditionals from history to chance that are admissible at any time. Hence the Principal Principle applies:

$$C(A/XH_{tw}T_w) = x$$

when C is a reasonable initial credence function, X is the proposition that the chance at t of A is x, and $H_{tw}T_w$ is compatible with X.

Suppose X holds at w. That is so if and only if x equals $P_{tw}(A)$. Hence we can choose such an X whenever A is in the domain of P_{tw}. $H_{tw}T_w$ and X both hold at w, therefore they are compatible. But further, $H_{tw}T_w$ implies X. The theory T_w and the history H_{tw} together are enough to imply all that is true (and contradict all that is false) at world w about chances at time t. For consider the strong conditional with antecedent H_{tw} and consequent X. This conditional holds at w, since by hypothesis its antecedent and consequent hold there. Hence it is implied by T_w, which is the conjunction of all conditionals of its sort that hold at w; and this conditional and H_{tw} yield X by *modus ponens*. Consequently, the conjunction $XH_{tw}T_w$ simplifies to $H_{tw}T_w$. Provided that A is in the domain of P_{tw} so that we can make a suitable choice of X, we can substitute $P_{tw}(A)$ for x, and $H_{tw}T_w$ for $XH_{tw}T_w$, in our instance of the Principal Principle. Therefore we have

THE PRINCIPAL PRINCIPLE REFORMULATED. Let C be any reasonable initial credence function. Then for any time t, world w, and proposition A in the domain of P_{tw}

$$P_{tw}(A) = C(A/H_{tw}T_w).$$

In words: the chance distribution at a time and a world comes from any reasonable initial credence function by conditionalizing on the complete history of the world up to the time, together with the complete theory of chance for the world.

This reformulation enjoys less direct intuitive support than the original formulation, but it will prove easier to use. It will serve as our point of departure in examining further consequences of the Principal Principle.

Chance and the probability calculus

A reasonable initial credence function is, among other things, a probability distribution: a non-negative, normalized, finitely additive measure. It obeys the laws of mathematical probability theory. There are well-known reasons why that must be so if credence is to rationalize courses of action that would not seem blatantly unreasonable in some circumstances.

Whatever comes by conditionalizing from a probability distribution is itself a probability distribution. Therefore a chance distribution is a probability distribution. For any time t and world w, P_{tw} obeys the laws of mathematical probability theory. These laws carry over from credence to chance via the Principal Principle. We have no need of any independent assumption that chance is a kind of probability.

Observe that although the Principal Principle concerns the relationship between chance and credence, some of its consequences concern chance alone. We have seen two such consequences. (1) The thesis that the past has no present chance of being otherwise than it actually is. (2) The thesis that chance obeys the laws of probability. More such consequences will appear later.

Chance as objectified credence

Chance is an objectified subjective probability in the sense of Jeffrey (1965), §12.7. Jeffrey's construction (omitting his use of sequences of partitions, which is unnecessary if we allow infinitesimal credences) works as follows. Suppose given a partition of logical space: a set of mutually exclusive and jointly exhaustive propositions. Then we can define the *objectification* of a credence function, with respect to this partition, at a certain world, as the probability distribution that comes from the given credence function by conditionalizing on the member of the given partition that holds at the given world. Objectified credence is credence conditional on the truth—not the whole truth, however, but exactly as much of it as can be captured by a member of the partition without further subdivision of logical space. The member of the partition that holds depends on matters of contingent fact, varying from one world to another; it does not depend on what we think (except insofar as our thoughts are relevant matters of fact) and we may well be ignorant or mistaken about it. The same goes for objectified credence.

Now consider one particular way of partitioning. For any time t, consider the partition consisting of the propositions $H_{tw}T_w$ for all worlds w. Call this the *history-theory partition* for time t. A member of this partition is an equivalence class of worlds with respect to the relation of being exactly alike both in respect of matters of particular fact up to time t and in respect of the dependence of chance on history. The Principal Principle tells us that the chance distribution, at any time t and world w, is the objectification of any reasonable credence function, with respect to the history-theory partition for time t, at world w. Chance is credence conditional on the truth—*if* the truth is subject to censorship along the lines of the history-theory partition, and *if* the credence is reasonable.

Any historical proposition admissible at time t, or any admissible conditional from history to chance, or any admissible Boolean combination of propositions of these two kinds—in short, any sort of admissible proposition we have considered—is a disjunction of members of the history-theory partition for t. Its borders follow the lines of the partition, never cutting between two worlds that the partition does not distinguish. Likewise for any proposition about chances at t. Let X be the proposition that the chance at t of A is x, let Y be any member of the history-theory partition for t, and let C be any reasonable initial credence function. Then, according to our reformulation of the

Principal Principle, X holds at all worlds in Y if $C(A/Y)$ equals x, and at no worlds in Y otherwise. Therefore X is the disjunction of all members Y of the partition such that $C(A/Y)$ equals x.

We may picture the situation as follows. The partition divides logical space into countless tiny squares. In each square there is a black region where A holds and a white region where it does not. Now blur the focus, so that divisions within the squares disappear from view. Each square becomes a grey patch in a broad expanse covered with varying shades of grey. Any maximal region of uniform shade is a proposition specifying the chance of A. The darker the shade, the higher is the uniform chance of A at the worlds in the region. The worlds themselves are not grey—they are black or white, worlds where A holds or where it doesn't—but we cannot focus on single worlds, so they all seem to be the shade of grey that covers their region. Admissible propositions, of the sorts we have considered, are regions that may cut across the contours of the shades of grey. The conjunction of one of these admissible propositions and a proposition about the chance of A is a region of uniform shade, but not in general a maximal uniform region. It consists of some, but perhaps not all, the members Y of the partition for which $C(A/Y)$ takes a certain value.

We derived our reformulation of the Principal Principle from the original formulation, but have not given a reverse derivation to show the two formulations equivalent. In fact the reformulation may be weaker, but not in any way that is likely to matter. Let C be a reasonable initial credence function; let X be the proposition that the chance at t of A is x; let E be admissible at t (in one of the ways we have considered) and compatible with X. According to the reformulation, as we have seen, XE is a disjunction of incompatible propositions Y, for each of which $C(A/Y)$ equals x. If there were only finitely many Y's, it would follow that $C(A/XE)$ also equals x. But the implication fails in certain cases with infinitely many Y's (and indeed we would expect the history-theory partition to be infinite) so we cannot quite recover the original formulation in this way. The cases of failure are peculiar, however, so the extra strength of the original formulation in ruling them out seems unimportant.

Kinematics of chance

Chance being a kind of probability, we may define conditional chance in the usual way as a quotient (leaving it undefined if the denominator is zero):

$$P_{tw}(A/B) =_{\mathrm{df}} P_{tw}(AB)/P_{tw}(B).$$

To simplify notation, let us fix on a particular world—ours, as it might be—and omit the subscript 'w'; let us fix on some particular reasonable initial credence function C, it doesn't matter which; and let us fix on a sequence of times, in order from earlier to later, to be called $1, 2, 3,. \ldots$ (I do not assume they are equally spaced.) For any time t in our sequence, let the proposition I_t be the complete history of our chosen world in the interval from time t to time $t+1$ (including $t+1$ but not t). Thus I_t is the set of worlds that match the chosen world perfectly in matters of particular fact throughout the given interval.

A complete history up to some time may be extended by conjoining complete histories of subsequent intervals. H_2 is H_1I_1, H_3 is $H_1I_1I_2$, and so on. Then by the Principal

Principal we have:

$$P_1(A) = C(A/H_1T),$$
$$P_2(A) = C(A/H_2T) = C(A/H_1I_1T) = P_1(A/I_1),$$
$$P_3(A) = C(A/H_3T) = C(A/H_1I_1I_2T) = P_2(A/I_2) = P_1(A/I_1I_2),$$

$$\vdots$$

and in general

$$P_{t+n+1}(A) = P_t(A/I_t \ldots I_{t+n}).$$

In words: a later chance distribution comes from an earlier one by conditionalizing on the complete history of the interval in between.

The evolution of chance is parallel to the evolution of credence for an agent who learns from experience, as he reasonably might, by conditionalizing. In that case a later credence function comes from an earlier one by conditionalizing on the total increment of evidence gained in the interval in between. For the evolution of chance we simply put the world's chance distribution in place of the agent's credence function, and the totality of particular fact about a time in place of the totality of evidence gained at that time.

In the interval from t to $t + 1$ there is a certain way that the world will in fact develop: namely, the way given by I_t. And at t, the last moment before the interval begins, there is a certain chance that the world will develop in that way: $P_t(I_t)$, the endpoint chance of I_t. Likewise for a longer interval, say from time 1 to time 18. The world will in fact develop in the way given by $I_1 \ldots I_{17}$, and the endpoint chance of its doing so is $P_1(I_1 \ldots I_{17})$. By definition of conditional chance

$$P_1(I_1 \ldots I_{17}) = P_1(I_1) \cdot P_1(I_2/I_1) \cdot P_1(I_3/I_1I_2) \ldots P_1(I_{17}/I_1 \ldots I_{16}),$$

and by the Principal Principle, applied as above,

$$P_1(I_1 \ldots I_{17}) = P_1(I_1) \cdot P_2(I_2) \cdot P_3(I_3) \ldots P_{17}(I_{17}).$$

In general, if an interval is divided into subintervals, then the endpoint chance of the complete history of the interval is the product of the endpoint chances of the complete histories of the subintervals.

Earlier we drew a tree to represent the temporal asymmetry of chance. Now we can embellish the tree with numbers to represent the kinematics of chance (see Figure 27.2). Take time 1 as the present. Worlds—those of them that are compatible with a certain common past and a certain common theory of chance—lie along paths through the tree. The numbers on each segment give the endpoint chance of the course of history represented by that segment, for any world that passes through that segment. Likewise, for any path consisting of several segments, the product of numbers along the path gives the endpoint chance of the course of history represented by the entire path.

Chance of frequency

Suppose that there is to be a long sequence of coin tosses under more or less standardized conditions. The first will be in the interval between time 1 and time 2,

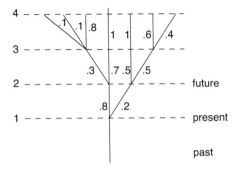

Figure 27.2 The kinematics of chance.

the second in the interval between 2 and 3, and so on. Our chosen world is such that at time 1 there is no chance, or negligible chance, that the planned sequence of tosses will not take place. And indeed it does take place. The outcomes are given by a sequence of propositions A_1, A_2, ... Each A_t states truly whether the toss between t and $t+1$ fell heads or tails. A conjunction A_1 ... A_n then gives the history of outcomes for an initial segment of the sequence.

The endpoint chance $P_1(A_1 \ldots A_n)$ of such a sequence of outcomes is given by a product of conditional chances. By definition of conditional chance,

$$P_1(A_1 \ldots A_n) = P_1(A_1) \cdot P_1(A_2/A_1) \cdot P_1(A_3/A_1A_2) \ldots \cdot P_1(A_n/A_1 \ldots A_{n-1}).$$

Since we are dealing with propositions that give only incomplete histories of intervals, there is no general guarantee that these factors equal the endpoint chances of the A's. The endpoint chance of A_2, $P_2(A_2)$, is given by $P_1(A_2/I_1)$; this may differ from $P_1(A_2/A_1)$ because the complete history I_1 includes some relevant information that the incomplete history A_1 omits about chance occurrences in the first interval. Likewise for the conditional and endpoint chances pertaining to later intervals.

Even though there is no general guarantee that the endpoint chance of a sequence of outcomes equals the product of the endpoint chances of the individual outcomes, yet it may be so if the world is right. It may be, for instance, that the endpoint chance of A_2 does not depend on those aspects of the history of the first interval that are omitted from A_1—it would be the same regardless. Consider the class of all possible complete histories up to time 2 that are compatible both with the previous history H_1 and with the outcome A_1 of the first toss. These give all the ways the omitted aspects of the first interval might be. For each of these histories, some strong conditional holds at our chosen world that tells what the chance at 2 of A_2 would be if that history were to come about. Suppose all these conditionals have the same consequent: whichever one of the alternative histories were to come about, it would be that X, where X is the proposition that the chance at 2 of A_2 equals x. Then the conditionals taken together tell us that the endpoint chance of A_2 is independent of all aspects of the history of the first interval except the outcome of the first toss.

In that case we can equate the conditional chance $P_1(A_2/A_1)$ and the endpoint chance $P_2(A_2)$. Note that our conditionals are of the sort implied by T, the complete theory

472

of chance for our chosen world. Hence A_1, H_1, and T jointly imply X. It follows that A_1H_1T and XA_1H_1T are the same proposition. It also follows that X holds at our chosen world, and hence that x equals $P_2(A_2)$. Note also that A_1H_1T is admissible at time 2. Now, using the Principal Principle first as reformulated and then in the original formulation, we have

$$P_1(A_2/A_1) = C(A_2/A_1H_1T) = C(A_2/XA_1H_1T) = x = P_2(A_2).$$

If we also have another such battery of conditionals to the effect that the endpoint chance of A_3 is independent of all aspects of the history of the first two intervals except the outcomes A_1 and A_2 of the first two tosses, and another battery for A_4, and so on, then the multiplicative rule for endpoint chances follows:

$$P_1(A_1 \ldots A_n) = P_1(A_1) \cdot P_2(A_2) \cdot P_3(A_3) \ldots P_n(A_n).$$

The conditionals that constitute the independence of endpoint chances mean that the incompleteness of the histories A_1, A_2, ... doesn't matter. The missing part wouldn't make any difference.

We might have a stronger form of independence. The endpoint chances might not depend on *any* aspects of history after time 1, not even the outcomes of previous tosses. Then conditionals would hold at our chosen world to the effect that if any complete history up to time 2 which is compatible with H_1 were to come about, it would be that X (where X is again the proposition that the chance at 2 of A_2 equals x). We argue as before, leaving out A_1: T implies the conditionals, H_1 and T jointly imply X, H_1T and XH_1T are the same, X holds, x equals $P_2(A_2)$, H_1T is admissible at 2; so, using the Principal Principle in both formulations, we have

$$P_1(A_2) = C(A_2/H_1T) = C(A_2/XH_1T) = x = P_2(A_2).$$

Our strengthened independence assumption implies the weaker independence assumption of the previous case, wherefore

$$P_1(A_2/A_1) = P_2(A_2) = P_1(A_2).$$

If the later outcomes are likewise independent of history after time 1, then we have a multiplicative rule not only for endpoint chances but also for unconditional chances of outcomes at time 1:

$$P_1(A_1 \ldots A_n) = P_1(A_1) \cdot P_1(A_2) \cdot P_1(A_3) \ldots P_1(A_n).$$

Two conceptions of independence are in play together. One is the familiar probabilistic conception: A_2 is independent of A_1, with respect to the chance distribution P_1, if the conditional chance $P_1(A_2/A_1)$ equals the unconditional chance $P_1(A_2)$; equivalently, if the chance $P_1(A_1A_2)$ of the conjunction equals the product $P_1(A_1) \cdot P_1(A_2)$ of the chances of the conjuncts. The other conception involves batteries of strong conditionals with different antecedents and the same consequent. (I consider this to be *causal* independence, but that's another story.) The conditionals need not have anything to do with probability; for instance, my beard does not depend on my politics since I would have such a beard whether I were Republican, Democrat, Prohibitionist, Libertarian, Socialist Labor, or whatever. But one sort of consequent that can be independent of a range of alternatives, as we have seen, is a consequent about single-case chance. What I have done is to use the Principal Principle to parlay battery-of-conditionals independence into ordinary probabilistic independence.

If the world is right, the situation might be still simpler; and this is the case we hope to achieve in a well-conducted sequence of chance trials. Suppose the history-to-chance conditionals and the previous history of our chosen world give us not only independence (of the stronger sort) but also uniformity of chances: for any toss in our sequence, the endpoint chance of heads on that toss would be h (and the endpoint chance of tails would be $1 - h$) no matter which of the possible previous histories compatible with H_1 might have come to pass. Then each of the A_t's has an endpoint chance of h if it specifies an outcome of heads, $1 - h$ if it specifies an outcome of tails. By the multiplicative rule for endpoint chances,

$$P_1(A_1 \dots A_n) = h^{fn} \cdot (1 - h)^{n - fn}$$

where f is the frequency of heads in the first n tosses according to $A_1 \dots A_n$.

Now consider any other world that matches our chosen world in its history up to time 1 and in its complete theory of chance, but not in its sequence of outcomes. By the Principal Principle, the chance distribution at time 1 is the same for both worlds. Our assumptions of independence and uniformity apply to both worlds, being built into the shared history and theory. So all goes through for this other world as it did for our chosen world. Our calculation of the chance at time 1 of a sequence of outcomes, as a function of the uniform single-case chance of heads and the length and frequency of heads in the sequence, goes for any sequence, not only for the sequence $A_1, A_2, \dots$ that comes about at our chosen world.

Let F be the proposition that the frequency of heads in the first n tosses is f. F is a disjunction of propositions each specifying a sequence of n outcomes with frequency f of heads; each disjunct has the same chance at time 1, under our assumptions of independence and uniformity; and the disjuncts are incompatible. Multiplying the number of these propositions by the uniform chance of each, we get the chance of obtaining some or other sequence of outcomes with frequency f of heads:

$$P_1(F) = \frac{n! \cdot h^{fn} \cdot (1 - h)^{n - fn}}{(fn)! \cdot (n - fn)!}.$$

The rest is well known. For fixed h and n, the right hand side of the equation peaks for f close to h; the greater is n, the sharper is the peak. If there are many tosses, then the chance is close to one that the frequency of heads is close to the uniform single-case chance of heads. The more tosses, the more stringent we can be about what counts as 'close'. That much of frequentism is true; and that much is a consequence of the Principal Principle, which relates chance not only to credence but also to frequency.

On the other hand, unless h is zero or one, the right hand side of the equation is non-zero. So, as already noted, there is always some chance that the frequency and the single-case chance may differ as badly as you please. That objection to frequentist analyses also turns out to be a consequence of the Principal Principle.

Evidence about chances

To the subjectivist who believes in objective chance, particular or general propositions about chances are nothing special. We believe them to varying degrees. As new evidence arrives, our credence in them should wax and wane in accordance with Bayesian confirmation theory. It is reasonable to believe such a proposition, like any other, to the degree given by a reasonable initial credence function conditionalized on one's present total evidence.

If we look at the matter in closer detail, we find that the calculations of changing reasonable credence involve *likelihoods*: credences of bits of evidence conditionally upon hypotheses. Here the Principal Principle may act as a useful constraint. Sometimes when the hypothesis concerns chance and the bit of evidence concerns the outcome, the reasonable likelihood is fixed, independently of the vagaries of initial credence and previous evidence. What is more, the likelihoods are fixed in such a way that observed frequencies tend to confirm hypotheses according to which these frequencies differ not too much from uniform chances.

To illustrate, let us return to our example of the sequence of coin tosses. Think of it as an experiment, designed to provide evidence bearing on various hypotheses about the single-case chances of heads. The sequence begins at time 1 and goes on for at least n tosses. The evidence gained by the end of the experiment is a proposition F to the effect that the frequency of heads in the first n tosses was f. (I assume that we use a mechanical counter that keeps no record of individual tosses. The case in which there is a full record, however, is little different. I also assume, in an unrealistic simplification, that no other evidence whatever arrives during the experiment.) Suppose that at time 1 your credence function is $C(-/E)$, the function that comes from our chosen reasonable initial credence function C by conditionalizing on your total evidence E up to that time. Then if you learn from experience by conditionalizing, your credence function after the experiment is $C(-/FE)$. The impact of your experimental evidence F on your beliefs, about chances or anything else, is given by the difference between these two functions.

Suppose that before the experiment your credence is distributed over a range of alternative hypotheses about the endpoint chances of heads in the experimental tosses. (Your degree of belief that none of these hypotheses is correct may not be zero, but I am supposing it to be negligible and shall accordingly neglect it.) The hypotheses agree that these chances are uniform, and each independent of the previous course of history after time 1; but they disagree about what the uniform chance of heads is. Let us write G_h for the hypothesis that the endpoint chances of heads are uniformly h. Then the credences $C(G_h/E)$, for various h's, comprise the *prior distribution* of credence over the hypotheses; the credences $C(G_h/FE)$ comprise the *posterior distribution*; and the credences $C(F/G_hE)$ are the likelihoods. Bayes' Theorem gives the posterior distribution in terms of terms of the prior distribution and the likelihoods:

$$C(G_h/FE) = \frac{C(G_h/E) \cdot C(F/G_hE)}{\Sigma_h[C(G_h/E) \cdot C(F/G_hE)]}.$$

(Note that 'h' is a bound variable of summation in the denominator of the right hand side, but a free variable elsewhere.) In words: to get the posterior distribution, multiply the prior distribution by the likelihood function and renormalize.

In talking only about a single experiment, there is little to say about the prior distribution. That does indeed depend on the vagaries of initial credence and previous evidence.

Not so for the likelihoods. As we saw in the last section, each G_h implies a proposition X_h to the effect that the chance at 1 of F equals x_h, where x_h is given by a certain function of h, n and f. Hence G_hE and X_hG_hE are the same proposition. Further, G_hE and X are compatible (unless G_hE is itself impossible, in which case G_h might as well be omitted from the range of hypotheses). E is admissible at 1, being about matters of particular fact—your evidence—at times no later than 1. G_h also is admissible at 1. Recall from the last section that what makes such a proposition hold at a world is a certain relationship between that world's complete history up to time 1 and that world's history-to-chance conditionals about the chances that would follow various complete extensions of that history. Hence any member of the history-theory partition for time 1 either implies or contradicts G_h; G_h is therefore a disjunction of conjunctions of admissible historical propositions and admissible history-to-chance conditionals. Finally, we supposed that C is reasonable. So the Principal Principle applies:

$$C(F/G_hE) = C(F/X_hG_hE) = x_h.$$

The likelihoods are the endpoint chances, according to the various hypotheses, of obtaining the frequency of heads that was in fact obtained.

When we carry the calculation through, putting these implied chances for the likelihoods in Bayes' theorem, the results are as we would expect. An observed frequency of f raises the credences of the hypotheses G_h with h close to f at the expense of the others; the more sharply so, the greater is the number of tosses. Unless the prior distribution is irremediably biased, the result after enough tosses is that the lion's share of the posterior credence will go to hypotheses putting the single-case chance of heads close to the observed frequency.

Chance as a guide to life

It is reasonable to let one's choices be guided in part by one's firm opinions about objective chances or, when firm opinions are lacking, by one's degrees of belief about chances. *Ceteris paribus*, the greater chance you think a lottery ticket has of winning, the more that ticket should be worth to you and the more you should be disposed to choose it over other desirable things. Why so?

There is no great puzzle about why credence should be a guide to life. Roughly speaking, what makes it be so that a certain credence function is *your* credence function is the very fact that you are disposed to act in more or less the ways that it rationalizes. (Better: what makes it be so that a certain reasonable initial credence function and a certain reasonable system of basic intrinsic values are both yours is that you are disposed to act in more or less the ways that are rationalized by the pair of them together, taking into account the modification of credence by conditionalizing on total evidence; and further, you would have been likewise disposed if your life history of experience, and consequent modification of credence, had been different; and further, no other such pair would fit your dispositions more closely.) No wonder your credence function tends to guide your life. If its doing so did not accord to some considerable extent with your dispositions to act, then it would not be your credence function. You would have some other credence function, or none.

If your present degrees of belief are reasonable—or at least if they come from some reasonable initial credence function by conditionalizing on your total evidence—then the Principal Principle applies. Your credences about outcomes conform to your firm beliefs and your partial beliefs about chances. Then the latter guide your life because the former do. The greater chance you think the ticket has of winning, the greater should be your degree of belief that it will win; and the greater is your degree of belief that it will win, the more, *ceteris paribus*, it should be worth to you and the more you should be disposed to choose it over other desirable things.

Prospects for an analysis of chance

Consider once more the Principal Principle as reformulated:

$$P_{tw}(A) = C(A/H_{tw}T_w).$$

Or in words: the chance distribution at a time and a world comes from any reasonable initial credence function by conditionalizing on the complete history of the world up to the time, together with the complete theory of chance for the world.

Doubtless it has crossed your mind that this has at least the form of an analysis of chance. But you may well doubt that it is informative as an analysis; that depends on the distance between the analysandum and the concepts employed in the analysans.

Not that it has to be informative *as an analysis* to be informative. I hope I have convinced you that the Principal Principle is indeed informative, being rich in consequences that are central to our ordinary ways of thinking about chance.

There are two different reasons to doubt that the Principal Principle qualifies as an analysis. The first concerns the allusion in the analysans to reasonable initial credence functions. The second concerns the allusion to complete theories of chance. In both cases the challenge is the same: could we possibly get any independent grasp on this concept, otherwise than by way of the concept of chance itself? In both cases my provisional answer is: most likely not, but it would be worth trying. Let us consider the two problems in turn.

It would be natural to think that the Principal Principle tells us nothing at all about chance, but rather tells us something about what makes an initial credence function be a reasonable one. To be reasonable is to conform to objective chances in the way described. Put this strongly, the response is wrong: the Principle has consequences, as we noted, that are about chance and not at all about its relationship to credence. (They would be acceptable, I trust, to a believer in objective single-case chance who rejects the very idea of degree of belief.) It tells us more than nothing about chance. But perhaps it is divisible into two parts: one part that tells us something about chance, another that takes the concept of chance for granted and goes on to lay down a criterion of reasonableness for initial credence.

Is there any hope that we might leave the Principal Principle in abeyance, lay down other criteria of reasonableness that do not mention chance, and get a good enough grip on the concept that way? It's a lot to ask. For note that just as the Principal Principle yields some consequences that are entirely about chance, so also it yields some that are entirely about reasonable initial credence. One such consequence is as follows. There is a large class of propositions such that if Y is any one of these, and C_1 and C_2 are any two reasonable initial credence functions, then the functions that come from C_1 and C_2 by conditionalizing on Y are exactly the same. (The large class is, of course, the class of members of history-theory partitions for all times.) That severely limits the ways that reasonable initial credence functions may differ, and so shows that criteria adequate to pick them out must be quite strong. What might we try? A reasonable initial credence function ought to (1) obey the laws of mathematical probability theory; (2) avoid dogmatism, at least by never assigning zero credence to possible propositions and perhaps also by never assigning infinitesimal credence to certain kinds of possible propositions; (3) make it possible to learn from experience by having a built-in bias in favor of worlds where the future in some sense resembles the past; and perhaps (4) obey certain carefully restricted principles of indifference, thereby respecting certain symmetries. Of these, criteria (1)–(3) are all very well, but surely not yet strong enough. Given C_1 satisfying (1)–(3), and given any proposition Y that holds at more than one world, it will be possible to distort C_1 very slightly to produce C_2, such that $C_1(—/Y)$ and $C_2(—/Y)$ differ but C_2 also satisfies (1)–(3). It is less clear what (4) might be able to do for us. Mostly that is because (4) is less clear *simpliciter*, in view of the fact that it is not possible to obey too many different restricted principles of indifference at once and it is hard to give good reasons to prefer some over their competitors. It also remains possible, of course, that some criterion of reasonableness along different lines than any I have mentioned would do the trick.

I turn now to our second problem: the concept of a complete theory of chance. In saying what makes a certain proposition be the complete theory of chance for a world (and for any world where it holds), I gave an explanation in terms of chance. Could these same propositions possibly be picked out in some other way, without mentioning chance?

The question turns on an underlying metaphysical issue. A broadly Humean doctrine (something I would very much like to believe if at all possible) holds that all the facts there are about the world are particular facts, or combinations thereof. This need not be taken as a doctrine of analyzability, since some combinations of particular facts cannot be captured in any finite way. It might be better taken as a doctrine of supervenience: if two worlds match perfectly in all matters of particular fact, they match perfectly in all other ways too—in modal properties, laws, causal connections, chances, ... It seems that if this broadly Humean doctrine is false, then chances are a likely candidate to be the fatal counter-instance. And if chances are not supervenient on particular fact, then neither are complete theories of chance. For the chances at a world are jointly determined by its complete theory of chance together with propositions about its history, which latter plainly are supervenient on particular fact.

If chances are not supervenient on particular fact, then neither chance itself nor the concept of a complete theory of chance could possibly be analyzed in terms of particular fact, or of anything supervenient thereon. The only hope for an analysis would be to use something in the analysans which is itself not supervenient on particular fact. I cannot say what that something might be.

How might chance, and complete theories of chance, be supervenient on particular fact? Could something like this be right: the complete theory of chance for a world is that one of all possible complete theories of chance that somehow best fits the global pattern of outcomes and frequencies of outcomes? It could not. For consider any such global pattern, and consider a time long before the pattern is complete. At that time, the pattern surely has some chance of coming about and some chance of not coming about. There is surely some chance of a very different global pattern coming about; one which, according to the proposal under consideration, would make true some different complete theory of chance. But a complete theory of chance is not something that could have some chance of coming about or not coming about. By the Principal Principle,

$$P_{tw}(T_w) = C(T_w/H_{tw}T_w) = 1.$$

If T_w is something that holds in virtue of some global pattern of particular fact that obtains at world w, this pattern must be one that has no chance at any time (at w) of not obtaining. If w is a world where many matters of particular fact are the outcomes of chance processes, then I fail to see what kind of global pattern this could possibly be.

But there is one more alternative. I have spoken as if I took it for granted that different worlds have different history-to-chance conditionals, and hence different complete theories of chance. Perhaps this is not so: perhaps all worlds are exactly alike in the dependence of chance on history. Then the complete theory of chance for every world, and all the conditionals that comprise it, are necessary. They are supervenient on particular fact in the trivial way that what is non-contingent is supervenient on anything—no two worlds differ with respect to it. Chances are still contingent, but only because they depend on contingent historical propositions (information about the details of the coin and tosser, as it might be) and not also because they depend on a contingent theory of chance. Our theory is much simplified if this is true. Admissible information is simply historical information; the history-theory partition at t is simply the partition of alternative complete histories up to t; for any reasonable initial credence function C

$$P_{tw}(A) = C(A/H_{tw}),$$

so that the chance distribution at t and w comes from C by conditionalizing on the complete history of w up to t. Chance is reasonable credence conditional on the whole truth about history up to a time. The broadly Humean doctrine is upheld, so far as chances are concerned: what makes it true at a time and a world that something has a certain chance of happening is something about matters of particular fact at that time and (perhaps) before.

What's the catch? For one thing, we are no longer safely exploring the consequences of the Principal Principle, but rather engaging in speculation. For another, our broadly Humean speculation that history-to-chance conditionals are necessary solves our second problem by making the first one worse. Reasonable initial credence functions are constrained more narrowly than ever. Any two of them, C_1 and C_2, are now required to yield the same function by conditionalizing on the complete history of any world up to any time. Put it this way: according to our broadly Humean speculation (and the Principal Principle) if I were perfectly reasonable and knew all about the course of history up to now (no matter what that course of history actually is, and no matter what time is now) then there would be only one credence function I could have. Any other would be unreasonable.

It is not very easy to believe that the requirements of reason leave so little leeway as that. Neither is it very easy to believe in features of the world that are not supervenient on particular fact. But if I am right, that seems to be the choice. I shall not attempt to decide between the Humean and the anti-Humean variants of my approach to credence and chance. The Principal Principle doesn't.

Postscript (1986): Laws of chance

Despite the foundational problems of quantum mechanics, it remains a good guess that many processes are governed by probabilistic laws of nature. These laws of chance, like other laws of nature, have the form of universal generalizations. Just as some laws concern forces, which are magnitudes pertaining to particulars, so some laws concern single-case chances, which likewise are magnitudes pertaining to particulars.

For instance, a law of chance might say that for any tritium atom and any time when it exists, there is such-and-such chance of that atom decaying within one second after that time.[1] What makes it at least a regularity—a true generalization—is that for each tritium atom and time, the chance of decay is as the law says it is. What makes it a law, I suggest, is the same thing that gives some others regularities the status of laws: it fits into some integrated system of truths that combines simplicity with strength in the best way possible.[2]

This is a kind of regularity theory of lawhood; but it is a collective and selective regularity theory. Collective, since regularities earn their lawhood not by themselves, but by the joint efforts of a system in which they figure either as axioms or as theorems. Selective, because not just any regularity qualifies as a law. If it would complicate the otherwise best system to include it as an axiom, or to include premises that would imply it, and if it would not add sufficient strength to pay its way, then it is left as a merely accidental regularity.

Five remarks about the best-system theory of lawhood may be useful before we return to our topic of how this theory works in the presence of chance.

(1) The standards of simplicity, of strength, and of balance between them are to be those that guide us in assessing the credibility of rival hypotheses as to what the laws are. In a way, that makes lawhood depend on us—a feature of the approach that I do not at all welcome! But at least it does not follow that lawhood depends on us in the most straightforward way: namely, that if our standards were suitably different, then the laws would be different. For we can take our actual standards as fixed, and apply them in asking what the laws would be in various counterfactual situations, including counterfactual situations in which people have different standards—or in which there are no people at all. Likewise, it fortunately does not follow that the laws are different at other times and places where there live people with other standards.

(2) On this approach, it is not to be said that certain generalizations are *lawlike* whether or not they are true, and the laws are exactly those of the lawlikes that are true. There will normally be three possibilities for any given generalization: that it be false, that it be true but accidental, and that it be true as a law. Whether it is true accidentally or as a law depends on what else is true along with it, thus on what integrated systems of truths are available for it to enter into. To illustrate the point: it may be true accidentally that every gold sphere is less than one mile in diameter; but if gold were unstable in such a way that there was no chance whatever that a large amount of gold could last long enough to be formed into a one-mile sphere, then this same generalization would be true as a law.

480

(3) I do not say that the competing integrated systems of truths are to consist entirely of regularities; however, only the regularities in the best system are to be laws. It is open that the best system might include truths about particular places or things, in which case there might be laws about these particulars. As an empirical matter, I do not suppose there are laws that essentially mention Smith's garden, the center of the earth or of the universe, or even the Big Bang. But such laws ought not to be excluded *a priori*.[3]

(4) It will trivialize our comparisons of simplicity if we allow our competing systems to be formulated with just any hooked-up primitives. So I take it that this kind of regularity theory of lawhood requires some sort of inegalitarian theory of properties: simple systems are those that come out formally simple when formulated in terms of perfectly natural properties. Then, sad to say, it's useless (though true) to say that the natural properties are the ones that figure in laws.[4]

(5) If two or more systems are tied for best, then certainly any regularity that appears in all the tied systems should count as a law. But what of a regularity that appears in some but not all of the tied systems? We have three choices: it is not a law (take the intersection of the tied systems); it is a law (take the union); it is indeterminate whether it is law (apply a general treatment for failed presuppositions of uniqueness). If required to choose, I suppose I would favor the first choice; but it seems a reasonable hope that nature might be kind to us, and put some one system so far out front that the problem will not arise. Likewise, we may hope that some system will be so far out front that it will win no matter what the standards of simplicity, strength, and balance are, within reason. If so, it will also not matter if these standards themselves are unsettled. To simplify, let me ignore the possibility of ties, or of systems so close to tied that indeterminacy of the standards matters; if need be, the reader may restore the needed complications.

To return to laws of chance: if indeed there are chances, they can be part of the subject matter of a system of truths; then regularities about them can appear as axioms or theorems of the best system; then such regularities are laws. Other regularities about chances might fail to earn a place in the best system; those ones are accidental. All this is just as it would be for laws about other magnitudes. So far, so good.

But there is a problem nearby; not especially a problem about laws of chance, but about laws generally in a chancy world. We have said that a regularity is accidental if it cannot earn a place in the best system: if it is too weak to enter as an axiom, and also cannot be made to follow as a theorem unless by overloading the system with particular information. That is one way to be accidental; but it seems that a regularity might be accidental also for a different and simpler reason. It might hold merely by chance. It might be simple and powerful and well deserve a place in the ideal system and yet be no law. For it might have, or it might once have had, some chance of failing to hold; whereas it seems very clear, *contra* the best-system theory as so far stated, that no genuine law ever could have had any chance of not holding. A world of lawful chance might have both sorts of accidental regularities, some disqualified by their inadequate contribution to simplicity and strength and others by their chanciness.

Suppose that radioactive decay is chancy in the way we mostly believe it to be. Then for each unstable nucleus there is an expected lifetime, given by the constant chance of decay for a nucleus of that species. It might happen—there is some chance of it, infinitesimal but not zero—that each nucleus lasted for precisely its expected lifetime, no more and no less. Suppose that were so. The regularity governing lifetimes might well qualify to join the best system, just as the corresponding regularity governing *expected* lifetimes does. Still, it is not a law. For if it were a law, it would be a law with some chance—in fact, an overwhelming chance—of being broken. That cannot be so.[5]

(Admittedly, we do speak of defeasible laws, laws with exceptions, and so forth. But these, I take it, are rough-and-ready approximations to the real laws. There real laws have no exceptions, and never had any chance of having any.)

Understand that I am not supposing that the constant chances of decay are *replaced* by a law of constant lifetimes. That is of course possible. What is not possible, unfortunately for the best-system theory, is for the constant chances to remain and to coexist with a law of constant lifetimes.

If the lifetimes chanced to be constant, and if the matter were well investigated, doubtless the investigators would come to believe in a law of constant lifetimes. But they would be mistaken, fooled by a deceptive coincidence. It is one thing for a regularity to be a law; another thing for it to be so regarded, however reasonably. Indeed, there are philosophers who seem oblivious to the distinction; but I think these philosophers misrepresent their own view. They are sceptics; they do not believe in laws of nature at all, they resort to regarded-as-law regularities as a substitute, and they call their substitute by the name of the real thing.

So the best-system theory of lawhood, as it stands, is in trouble. I propose this correction. Previously, we held a competition between all true systems. Instead, let us admit to the competition only those systems that are true not by chance; that is, those that not only are true, but also have never had any chance of being false. The field of eligible competitors is thus cut down. But then the competition works as before. The best system is the one that achieves as much simplicity as is possible without excessive loss of strength, and as much strength as is possible without excessive loss of simplicity. A law is a regularity that is included, as an axiom or as a theorem, in the best system.

Then a chance regularity, such as our regularity of constant life-times, cannot even be included in any of the competing systems. *A fortiori*, it cannot be included in the best of them. Then it cannot count as a law. It will be an accidental regularity, and for the right reason: because it had a chance of being false. Other regularities may still be accidental for our original reason. These would be regularities that never had any chance of being false, but that don't earn their way into the best system because they don't contribute enough to simplicity and strength. For instance suppose that (according to regularities that do earn a place in the best system) a certain quantity is strictly conserved, and suppose that the universe is finite in extent. Then we have a regularity to the effect that the total of this quantity, over the entire universe, always equals a certain fixed value. This regularity never had any chance of being false. But it is not likely to earn a place in the best system and qualify as a law.

In the paper, I made much use of the history-to-chance conditionals giving hypothetical information about the chance distribution that would follow a given (fully specified) initial segment of history. Indeed, my reformulation of the Principal Principle involves a 'complete theory of chance' which is the conjunction of all such history-to-chance conditionals that hold at a given world, and which therefore fully specifies the way chances at any time depend on history up to that time.

It is to be hoped that the history-to-chance conditionals will follow, entirely or for the most part, from the laws of nature; and, in particular, from the laws of chance. We might indeed impose a requirement to that effect on our competing systems. I have chosen not to. While the thesis that chances might be entirely governed by law has some plausibility, I am not sure whether it deserves to be built into the analysis of lawhood. Perhaps rather it is an empirical thesis: a virtue that we may hope distinguishes our world from more chaotic worlds.

At any rate, we can be sure that the history-to-chance conditionals will not conflict with the system of laws of chance. Not, at any rate, in what they say about the outcomes and chances that would follow any initial segment of history that ever had any chance of coming about. Let H be a proposition fully specifying such a segment. Let t be a time at which there was some chance that H would come about. Let L be the conjunction of the laws. There was no chance, at t, of L being false. Suppose for *reductio* first that we have a history-to-chance conditional 'if H, then A' (where A might, for instance, specify chances at the end-time of the segment); and second that H and L jointly imply not-A, so that the conditional conflicts with the laws. The conditional had no chance at t of being false—this is an immediate consequence of the reformulated Principal Principle. Since we had some chance at t of H, we had some chance of H holding along with the conditional, hence some chance of H and A. And since there was no chance that L would be false, there was some chance that all of H, A, and L would hold together, so some chance at t of a contradiction. Which is impossible: there never can be any chance of a contradiction.

A more subtle sort of conflict also is ruled out. Let t, L, and H be as before. Suppose for *reductio* first that we have a history-to-chance conditional 'if H, then there would be a certain positive chance of A'; and second that H and L jointly imply not-A. This is not the same supposition as before: after all, it would be no contradiction if something had a positive chance and still did not happen. But it is still a kind of conflict: the definiteness of the law disagrees with the chanciness of the conditional. To rule it out, recall that we had at t some chance of H, but no chance of the conditional being false; so at t there was a chance of H holding along with the conditional; so at t there was a chance that, later, there would be a chance of A following the history H; but chanciness does not increase with time (assuming, as always, the normal asymmetries); an earlier chance of a later chance of something implies an earlier chance of it; so already at t there was some chance of H and A holding together. Now we can go on as before: we have that at t there was no chance that L would be false, so some chance that all of H, A, and L would hold together, so some chance at t of a contradiction; which is impossible.

The best-system theory of lawhood in its original form served the cause of Humean supervenience. History, the pattern of particular fact throughout the universe, chooses the candidate systems, and the standards of selection do the rest. So no two worlds could differ in laws without differing also in their history. But our correction spoils that. The laws—laws of chance, and other laws besides—supervene now on the pattern of particular chances. If the chances in turn somehow supervene on history, then we have Humean supervenience of the laws as well; if not, not. The corrected theory of lawhood starts with the chances. It does nothing to explain them.

Once, *circa* 1975, I hoped to do better: to extend the best-system approach in such a way that it would provide for the Humean supervenience of chances and laws together, in one package deal. This was my plan. We hold a competition of deductive systems, as before; but we impose less stringent requirements of eligibility to enter the competition, and we change the terms on which candidate systems compete. We no longer require a candidate system to be entirely true, still less do we require that it never had any chance of being false. Instead, we only require that a candidate system be true in what it says about history; we leave it open, for now, whether it also is true in what it says about chances. We also impose a requirement of coherence: each candidate system must imply that the chances are such as to give that very system no chance at any time of being false. Once we have our competing systems, they vary in simplicity and in strength, as before. But also they vary in what I shall call *fit*: a system fits a world to the extent that the history of that world is a comparatively probable history according to that system. (No history will be very probable; in fact, any history for a world like ours will be very improbable according to any system that deserves in the end to be accepted as correct; but still, some are more probable than others.) If the histories permitted by a system formed a tree with finitely many branch points and finitely many alternatives at each point, and the system specified chances for each alternative at each branch point, then the fit between the system and a branch would be the product of these chances along that branch; and likewise, somehow, for the general, infinite case. (Never mind the details if, as I think, the plan won't work anyway.) The best system will be the winner, now, in a three-way balance between simplicity, strength, and fit. As before, the laws are the generalizations that appear as axioms or theorems in the best system; further, the true chances are the chances as they are according to the best system. So it turns out that the best system is true in its entirety—true in what it says about chances, as well as in what it says about history. So the laws of chance, as well as other laws, turn out to be true; and further, to have had no chance at any time of being false. We have our Humean supervenience of chances and of laws; because history selects the candidate systems, history determines how well each one fits, and our standards of selection do the rest. We will tend, *ceteris paribus*, to get the proper agreement between frequencies and uniform chances, because that agreement is conducive to fit. But we leave it open that frequencies may chance to differ from the uniform chances, since *ceteris* may not be *paribus* and the chances are under pressure not only to fit the frequencies but also to fit into a simple and strong system. All this seems very nice.

But it doesn't work. Along with simpler analyses of chance in terms of actual frequency, it falls victim to the main argument in the last section of the paper. Present chances are determined by history up to now, together with history-to-chance conditionals. These conditionals are supposed to supervene, via the laws of chance of the best system, on a global pattern of particular fact. This global pattern includes future history. But there are various different futures which have some present chance of coming about, and which would make the best system different, and thus make the conditionals different, and thus make the present chances different. We have the actual present chance distribution over alternative futures, determined by the one future which will actually come about. Using it, we have the expected values of the present chances: the average of the present chances that would be made true by the various futures, weighted by the chances of those futures. But these presently expected values of present chances may differ from the actual present chances. A peculiar situation, to say the least.

And worse than peculiar. Enter the Principal Principle: it says first that if we knew the present chances, we should conform our credences about the future to them. But it says also that we should conform our credences to the expected values of the present chances.[6] If the two differ, we cannot do both. So if the Principle is right (and if it is possible to conform our credences as we ought to), the two cannot differ. So a theory that says they can is wrong.

That was the strategy behind my argument in the paper. But I streamlined the argument by considering one credence in particular. Let T be a full specification of history up to the present and of present chances; and suppose for *reductio* that F is a nonactual future, with some positive present chance of coming about, that would give a different present distribution of chances. What is a reasonable credence for F conditionally on T? Zero, because F contradicts T. But not zero, by the Principal Principle, because it should equal the positive chance of F according to T. This completes the *reductio*.

This streamlining might hide the way the argument exploits a predicament that arises already when we consider chance alone. Even one who rejects the very idea of credence, and with it the Principal Principle, ought to be suspicious of a theory that permits discrepancies between the chances and their expected values.

If anyone wants to defend the best-system theory of laws and chances both (as opposed to the best-system theory of laws, given chances), I suppose the right move would be to cripple the Principal Principle by declaring that information about the chances at a time is *not*, in general, admissible at that time; and hence that hypothetical information about chances, which can join with admissible historical information to imply chances at a time, is likewise inadmissible. The reason would be that, under the proposed analysis of chances, information about present chances is a disguised form of inadmissible information about future history—to some extent, it reveals the outcomes of matters that are presently chancy. That crippling stops all versions of our *reductio* against positive present chances of futures that would yield different present chances.[7] I think the cost is excessive; in ordinary calculations with chances, it seems intuitively right to reply on this hypothetical information. So, much as I would like to use the best-system approach in defense of Humean supervenience, I cannot support this way out of our difficulty.

I stand by my view, in the paper, that if there is any hope for Humean supervenience of chances, it lies in a different direction: the history-to-chance conditionals must supervene trivially, by not being contingent at all. As noted, that would impose remarkably stringent standards on reasonable belief. To illustrate: on this hypothesis, enough purely historical information would suffice to tell a reasonable believer whether the half-life of radon is 3.825 days or 3.852. What is more: enough purely historical information *about any initial segment of the universe*, however short, would settle the half-life! (It might even be a segment before the time when radon first appeared.) For presumably the half-life of radon is settled by the laws of chance; any initial segment of history, aided by enough noncontingent history-to-chance conditionals, suffices to settle any feature of the world that never had a chance to be otherwise; and the laws are such a feature. But just how is the believer, however reasonable, supposed to figure out the half-life given his scrap of ancient history? We can hope, I suppose, that some appropriate symmetries in the space of possibilities would do the trick. But it seems hard to connect these hoped-for symmetries with anything we now know about the workings of radioactive decay!

Notes

* Originally published in Richard C. Jeffrey (ed.), *Studies in Inductive Logic and Probability*, volume II, University of California Press, Berkeley, 1980. Copyright © David Lewis. Postscript originally published in David Lewis, *Philosophical Papers*, volume II, Oxford University Press, Oxford, 1986, pp. 121–31. Reprinted with kind permission from Stephanie Lewis.
† I am grateful to several people for valuable discussions of this material; especially John Burgess, Nancy Cartwright, Richard Jeffrey, Peter Railton, and Brian Skyrms. I am also much indebted to Mellor (1971), which presents a view very close to mine; exactly how close I am not prepared to say.

1 Peter Railton employs laws of chance of just this sort to bring probabilistic explanation under the deductive-nomological model. The outcome itself cannot be deduced, of course; but the single-case chance of it can be. See Railton, 'A Deductive-Nomological Model of Probabilistic Explanation', *Philosophy of Science* 45 (1978): 206–26; and the final section of my 'Causal Explanation' in David Lewis, Philosophical Papers, Oxford University Press, Oxford, 1986, pp. 214–40.

2 I advocate a best-system theory of lawhood in *Counterfactuals* (Oxford: Blackwell, 1973), pp. 73–75. Similar theories of lawhood were held by Mill and, briefly, by Ramsey. See John Stuart Mill, *A System of Logic* (London: Parker, 1843), Book III, Chapter IV, Section 1; and F. P. Ramsey, 'Universals of Law and of Fact', in his *Foundations* (London: Routledge & Kegan Paul, 1978). For further discussion, see John Earman, 'Laws of Nature: The Empiricist Challenge', in *D. M. Armstrong*, ed. by Radu J. Bogdan (Dordrecht: Reidel, 1984).

Mill's version is not quite the same as mine. He says that the question what are the laws of nature could be restated thus: 'What are the fewest general propositions from which all the uniformities which exist in the universe might be deductively inferred?'; so it seems that the ideal system is supposed to be complete as regards uniformities, that it may contain only general propositions as axioms, and that its theorems do not qualify as laws.

It is not clear to me from his brief statement whether Ramsey's version was quite the same as mine. His summary statement (after changing his mind) that he had taken laws to be 'consequences of those propositions we should take as axioms if we knew everything and organized it as simply as possible into a deductive system' (*Foundations*, p. 138) is puzzling. Besides Ramsey's needless mention of knowledge, his 'it' with antecedent 'everything' suggests that the ideal system is supposed to imply everything true. Unless Ramsey made a stupid mistake, which is impossible, that cannot have been his intent; it would make all regularities come out as laws.

3 In defense of the possibility that there might be a special law about the fruit in Smith's garden, see Michael Tooley, 'The Nature of Laws', *Canadian Journal of Philosophy* 7 (1977): 667–98, especially p. 687; and D. M. Armstrong, *What is a Law of Nature?* (Cambridge: Cambridge University Press, 1983), Sections 3.I, 3.II, and 6.VII. In 'The Universality of Laws', *Philosophy of Science* 45 (1978): 173–81, John Earman observes that the best-system theory of lawhood avoids any *a priori* guarantee that the laws will satisfy strong requirements of universality.

4 See my 'New Work for a Theory of Universals', *Australasian Journal of Philosophy* 61 (1983): 343–77, especially pp. 366–68.

5 At this point I am indebted to correspondence and discussion with Frank Jackson, arising out of his discussion of 'Hume worlds' in 'A Causal Theory of Counterfactuals', *Australasian Journal of Philosophy* 55 (1977): 3–21, especially pp. 5–6. A Hume world, as Jackson describes it, is 'a possible world where every particular fact is as it is in our world, but there are no causes or effects at all. Every regular conjunction is an accidental one, not a causal one'. I am not sure whether Jackson's Hume world is one with chances—lawless chances, of course—or without. In the former case, the bogus laws of the Hume world would be like our bogus law of constant lifetimes, but on a grander scale.

6 Let A be any proposition; let $P_1, P_2, \ldots$ be a partition of propositions to the effect that the present chance of A is $x_1, x_2, \ldots$, respectively; let these propositions have positive present chances of $y_1, y_2, \ldots$, respectively; let C be a reasonable initial credence function; let E be someone's present total evidence, which we may suppose to be presently admissible. Suppose that $C(-/E)$ assigns probability 1 to the propositions that the present chance of P_1 is y_1, the present chance of P_2 is $y_2, \ldots$. By additivity,

$$(1) \quad C(A/E) = C(A/P_1E)C(P_1/E) + C(A/P_2E)C(P_2/E) + \ldots$$

By the Principal Principle,

$$(2) \quad C(P_1/E) = y_1,$$
$$C(P_2/E) = y_2,$$
$$\ldots$$

and

$$(3) \quad C(A/P_1E) = x_1,$$
$$C(A/P_2E) = x_2,$$

(Since the $C(P_i/E)$'s are positive, the $C(A/P_iE)$'s are well defined.) So we have the prescription

$$(4) \quad C(A/E) = y_1x_t + y_2x_2 + \ldots$$

that the credence is to be equal to the expected value of chance.

7 As to the version in the paper: declaring hypothetical information about chances inadmissible blocks my reformulation of the Principal Principle, and it was this reformulation that I used in the *reductio*.

As to the version in the previous footnote: if information about present chances is inadmissible, then it becomes very questionable whether the total evidence E can indeed be admissible, given that $C(-/E)$ assigns probability 1 to propositions about present chance.

As to the streamlined version in this postscript: T includes information about present chances, and its partial inadmissibility would block the use of the Principal Principle to prescribe positive credence for F conditionally on T.

Bibliography

Bernstein, Allen R. and Wattenberg, Frank, 'Non-Standard Measure Theory', in *Applications of Model Theory of Algebra, Analysis, and Probability*, ed. by W. Luxemburg, Holt, Reinhart, and Winston, 1969.

Carnap, Rudolf, 'The Two Concepts of Probability', *Philosophy and Phenomenological Research* 5 (1945), 513–532.

Jeffrey, Richard C., *The Logic of Decision*, McGraw-Hill, 1965.

Jeffrey, Richard C., review of articles by David Miller *et al.*, *Journal of Symbolic Logic* 35 (1970), 124–127.

Jeffrey, Richard C., 'Mises Redux', in *Basic Problems in Methodology and Linguistics: Proceedings of the Fifth International Congress of Logic, Methodology and Philosophy of Science*, Part III, ed. by R. Butts and J. Hintikka, D. Reidel, Dordrecht, Holland, 1977. Reprinted as Chapter 23 in this volume.

Lewis, David, 'Counterpart Theory and Quantified Modal Logic', *Journal of Philosophy* 65 (1968), 113–126.

Lewis, David, *Counterfactuals*, Blackwell, 1973.

Mellor, D. H., *The Matter of Chance*, Cambridge University Press, 1971.

Quine, W. V., 'Propositional Objects', in *Ontological Relativity and Other Essays*, Columbia University Press, 1969.

Railton, Peter, 'A Deductive-Nomological Model of Probabilistic Explanation', *Philosophy of Science* 45 (1978), 206–226.

Skyrms, Brian, 'Resiliency, Propensities, and Causal Necessity', *Journal of Philosophy* 74 (1977), 704–713. Reprinted as Chapter 32 in this volume.

28

THE PROPENSITY
INTERPRETATION OF
PROBABILITY*

Karl Popper

Introduction

In this paper I intend to put forward some arguments in favour of what I am going to call the propensity interpretation of probability.

By an interpretation of probability—or, more precisely, of the theory of probability—I mean an interpretation of such statements as,

'The probability of *a* given *b* is equal to *r*'

(where *r* is a real number); a statement which we can put in symbols as follows:

$$`p(a, b) = r.`$$

There have been many interpretations of these probability statements, and years ago I have divided these interpretations into two main classes—the subjective and the objective interpretations.[1]

The various subjective interpretations have all one thing in common: probability theory is regarded as a means of dealing with the *incompleteness of our knowledge*, and the number $p(a, b)$ is regarded as a measure of the degree of rational assurance, or of rational belief, which the knowledge of the information *b* confers upon *a* (*a* is in this context often called 'the hypothesis *a*').

The objective interpretations may also be characterised by a common feature: they all interpret

$$p(a, b) = r$$

as a statement that can, in principle, be objectively *tested*, by means of statistical tests. These tests consist in sequences of experiments: *b* in '$p(a, b) = r$', describes the experimental conditions; *a* describes some of the possible *outcomes* of the experiments; and the number *r* describes the *relative frequency* with which the outcome *a* is estimated to occur in any sufficiently long sequence of experiments characterised by the experimental conditions *b*.

It is my conviction that most of the usual applications of subjective interpretation of probability are untenable. There may be something like a measurable degree of the rationality of a belief in *a*, given the information *b*; but I assert that this belief cannot be adequately measured by a measure that satisfies the laws of the calculus of probability.[2] (I think it likely, however, that 'degree of confirmation or corroboration'—the latter term is preferable—will turn out to furnish, under certain circumstances, an adequate measure of the rationality of a belief; see my notes on 'Degree of Confirmation', *British Journal for the Philosophy of Science*, 1954, 5, 143, 334, 359; 1957, 7, 350, and 1958, 8, 294.)

As to the objective interpretations, the simplest seems to be *the purely statistical or the frequency interpretation*. (I take these two designations as synonymous.) This interpretation regards the statement

$$p(a, b) = r$$

as an estimate, or a hypothesis, asserting *nothing but* that the relative frequency of the event *a* in a sequence defined by the conditions *b* is equal to *r*. Or in other words, the statement '$p(a, b) = r$' is interpreted to mean: 'events of the kind *a* occur, in sequences characterised by *b*, with the frequency *r*'. Thus, for example, '$p(a, b) = 1/2$' may mean 'the relative frequency of tossing heads with a normal penny equals 1/2' (where *a* is getting heads upmost, and *b* is a sequence of tosses with a normal penny).

The frequency interpretation has been often criticised, but I believe that it is possible to construct a frequency theory of probability that avoids all the objections which have been raised and discussed. I have sketched such a theory many years ago (it was a modification of the theory of Richard von Mises), and I still believe that (after some minor improvements which I have made since) it is immune to the usual objections. Thus the reason why I changed my mind in favour of the propensity interpretation was not that I felt I had to give way to these objections (as has been suggested by W. C. Kneale in a discussion of a paper of mine[3]). Rather, I gave up the frequency interpretation of probability in 1953 for two reasons.

(1) The first was connected with the problem of the interpretation of quantum theory.

(2) The second was that I found certain flaws in my own treatment of the probability of *single events* (in contrast to sequences of events), or 'singular events', as I shall call them in analogy to 'singular statements'.

Propensities and the quantum theory

Although the bulk of the present paper is devoted to a discussion of the second of these two points, I wish to mention first very briefly the reasons connected with the first point, because it was the first point in time and importance: it was only after I had developed, and tried out, the idea that probabilities are *physical propensities*, comparable to Newtonian forces, that I discovered the flaw in my treatment of the probability of singular events.

I had always been convinced that the problem of the interpretation of the quantum theory was closely linked with the problem of the interpretation of probability theory in general, and that the Bohr-Heisenberg interpretation was the result of a subjectivist interpretation of probability. My early attempts to base the interpretation of quantum theory upon an objective interpretation of probability (it was the frequency interpretation) had led me to the following results.

(1) The so-called 'problem of the reduction of the wave packet' turns out to be a problem inherent in every probabilistic theory, and creates no special difficulty.

(2) Heisenberg's so-called indeterminacy relations must not be interpreted subjectively, as asserting something about our possible knowledge, or lack of knowledge, but objectively, as scatter-relations. (This removes an asymmetry between p and q which is inherent in Heisenberg's interpretation unless we link it with a phenomenalist or positivist philosophy; see my *Logic of Scientific Discovery*, p. 451.)

(3) The particles have paths, i.e., momentum and positions, although we cannot predict these, owing to the scatter relations.

(4) This was also the result of the imaginary experiment ('thought-experiment') of Einstein, Podolski, and Rosen.

(5) I also produced an explanation of the interference experiments ('two-slit-experiments'), but I later gave this up as unsatisfactory.

It was this last point, the interpretation of the two-slit-experiment, which ultimately led me to the propensity theory: it convinced me that probabilities must be 'physically real'—that they must be physical propensities, abstract relational properties of the physical situation, like Newtonian forces, and 'real', not only in the sense that they could influence the experimental results, but also in the sense that they could, under certain circumstances (coherence), interfere, i.e. interact, with one another.

Now these propensities turn out to be *propensities to realise singular events*. It is this fact which led me to reconsider the status of singular events within the frequency interpretation of probability. In the course of this reconsideration, I found what I thought to be independent arguments in favour of the propensity interpretation. It is the main purpose of the present paper to present this line of thought.[4]

From the frequency theory to the propensity theory

The subjective interpretation of probability may *perhaps* be tenable as an interpretation of certain gambling situations—horse racing, for example—in which the objective conditions of the event are ill-defined and irreproducible. (I do not really believe that it is applicable even to situations like these, because I think that a strong case could be made—if it were worth making—for the view that what a gambler, or a 'rational better', tries to find out, in order to bet upon it, is always and invariably the *objective* propensities, the *objective* odds of the event: thus the man who bets on horses is anxious to get more information about horses—rather than information about his own state of belief, or about the logical force of the total information in his possession.) Yet in the typical game of chance—roulette, say, or dicing, or tossing pennies—and in all physical experiments, the subjective interpretation fails completely. For in all these cases probabilities depend upon the *objective conditions of the experiment*.[5]

In the remaining sections of this paper, the discussion will be confined solely to the problem of interpreting the probability of 'singular events' (or 'occurrences'); and it is the frequency theory of the probability of *singular events* which I have in mind whenever I speak here of the frequency interpretation of probability, in contradistinction to the propensity interpretation.

From the point of view of the frequency interpretation, the probability of an *event of a certain kind*—such as obtaining a six with a particular die—can be *nothing but* the relative frequency of this kind of event in an extremely long (perhaps infinite) sequence of events. And if we speak of the probability of a *singular* event such as the probability of obtaining a six in the third throw made after nine o'clock this morning with this die, then, according to the purely statistical interpretation, we mean to say *only* that this third throw may be regarded as a member of a sequence of throws, and that, in its capacity as a member of this sequence, it shares in the probabilities of that sequence. It shares, that is to say, those probabilities which are *nothing but the relative frequencies* within that sequence.

In the present section I propose to argue against this interpretation, and in favour of the propensity interpretation. I propose to proceed as follows. (1) I will first show that, from the point of view of the frequency interpretation, objections must be raised against the propensity interpretation which appear to make the latter unacceptable. (2) I will next give a preliminary reply to these objections; and I will then present, as point (3), a certain difficulty which the frequency interpretation has to face, though it does not, when first raised, look like a serious difficulty. (4) Ultimately I will show that in order to get over this difficulty, the frequency interpretation is forced to adopt a modification which appears to be slight at first sight; yet the adoption of this apparently slight modification turns out to be equivalent to the adoption of the propensity interpretation.

(1) From the point of view of a purely statistical interpretation of probability it is clear that the propensity interpretation is unacceptable. For propensities may be explained as possibilities (or as measures or 'weights' of possibilities) which are endowed with tendencies or dispositions to realise themselves, and which are taken to be responsible for the statistical frequencies with which they will in fact realise themselves in long sequences of repetitions of an experiment. Propensities are thus introduced in order to help us to explain, and to predict, the statistical properties of certain sequences; and *this is their sole function.* Thus (the frequency theorist will assert) they do not allow us to predict, or to say, *anything whatever* about a single event, except that its repetition, under the same conditions, will generate a sequence with certain statistical properties. All this shows that the propensity interpretation can add nothing to the frequency interpretation except a new word—'propensity'—and a new image or metaphor which is associated with it—that of a tendency or disposition or urge. But these anthropomorphic or psychological metaphors are even less useful than the old psychological metaphors of 'force' and of 'energy' which became useful physical concepts only to the extent to which they lost their original metaphysical and anthropomorphic meaning.

This, roughly, would be the view of the frequency theorist. In defending the propensity interpretation I am going to make use of two different arguments: a preliminary reply (2), and an argument that amounts to an attempt to turn the tables upon the frequency theorist; this will be discussed under (3) and (4).

(2) As a preliminary reply, I am inclined to accept the suggestion that there is an analogy between the idea of propensities and that of forces—especially fields of forces. But I should point out that although the labels 'force' or 'propensity' may both be psychological or anthropomorphic metaphors, the important analogy between the two ideas does not lie here; it lies, rather, in the fact that both ideas draw attention to *unobservable dispositional properties of the physical world*, and thus help in the interpretation of physical theory. Herein lies their usefulness. The concept of force—or better still, the concept of a field of forces—introduces a dispositional physical entity, described by certain equations (rather than by metaphors), in order to explain observable accelerations. Similarly, the concept of propensity, or of a field of propensities, introduces a dispositional property of singular physical experimental arrangements—that is to say, of singular physical events—in order to explain observable frequencies in sequences of

repetitions of these events. In both cases the introduction of the new idea can be justified only by an appeal to its usefulness for physical theory. Both concepts are 'occult', in Berkeley's sense, or 'mere words'.[6] But part of the usefulness of these concepts lies precisely in the fact that they suggest that the theory is concerned with the properties of an *unobservable* physical reality and that it is only some of the more superficial effects of this reality which we can observe, and which thus make it possible for us to test the theory. The main argument in favour of the propensity interpretation is to be found in its power to eliminate from quantum theory certain disturbing elements of an irrational and subjectivist character—elements which, I believe, are more 'metaphysical' than propensities and, moreover, 'metaphysical' in the bad sense of the word. It is by its success or failure in this field of application that the propensity interpretation will have to be judged.

Having stressed this point I proceed to my main argument in favour of the propensity interpretation. It consists in pointing out certain difficulties which the frequency interpretation must face. We thus come to the point (3), announced above.

(3) Many objections have been raised against the frequency interpretation of probability, especially in connection with the idea of infinite sequences of events, and of limits of relative frequencies. I shall not refer to these objections here because I believe that they can be adequately met. Yet there is a simple and important objection which has not, to my knowledge, been raised in this form before.

Let us assume that we have a loaded die, and that we have satisfied ourselves, after long sequences of experiments, that the probability of getting a six with this loaded die very nearly equals 1/4. Now consider a sequence *b*, say, consisting of throws with this loaded die, but including a few throws (two, or perhaps three) with a homogeneous and symmetrical die. Clearly, we shall have to say, with respect to each of these few throws with this correct die, that the probability of a six is 1/6 rather than 1/4, in spite of the fact that these throws are, according to our assumptions, *members of a sequence* of throws with the statistical frequency 1/4.

I believe that this simple objection is decisive, even though there are various possible rejoinders.

One rejoinder may be mentioned only in passing, since it amounts to an attempt to fall back upon the subjectivist interpretation of probability. It amounts to the assertion that it is our special *knowledge*, the special *information* we have concerning these throws with the correct die, which changes the probability. Since I do not believe, for many reasons, in the subjective theory of probability, I am not inclined to accept this assertion. Moreover, I believe that the case before us even suggests a new argument (although not a very important one) against the subjective theory. For we may not know which of the throws are made with the correct die, although we may know that there are only two or three such throws. In this case it will be quite reasonable to bet (provided we are determined to bet on a considerable number of throws) on the basis of a probability 1/4 (or very close to 1/4), even though we do know that there will be two or three throws on which we should not accept bets on these terms, if only we could identify them. We know that, in the case of these throws, the probability of a six is less than 1/4—that it is, in fact, 1/6; but we also know that we cannot identify these throws, and that their influence must be very small if the number of bets is large. Now it is clear that, as we nevertheless attribute to these unknown throws a probability of 1/6, we do not mean by the word 'probability', and cannot possibly mean by it, a 'reasonable betting quotient in the light of our total actual knowledge' as the subjective theory has it.

But let us now leave the subjective theory entirely aside. What can the frequency theorist say in reply to our objection?

Having been a frequency theorist myself for many years, I know fairly well what my reply would have been.

The description given to us of the sequence b shows that b shows that b is composed of throws with a loaded die and of throws with a correct die. We estimate or, rather, we conjecture (on the basis of previous experience, or of intuition—it never matters what is the 'basis' of a conjecture) that the side six will turn up in a sequence of throws of the loaded die with the frequency 1/4, and in a sequence of throws with the correct die with the frequency 1/6. Let us denote this latter sequence, that of throws with the correct die, by 'c'. Then our information as to the composition of b tells us (i) that $p(a, b) = 1/4$ (or very nearly so), because almost all throws are with the loaded die, and (ii) that bc—that is to say the class of throws belonging to both b and c—is not empty; and since bc consists of throws belonging to c, we are entitled to assert that the singular probability of a six, among those throws which belong to bc, will be 1/6—by virtue of the fact that these singular throws are members of a sequence c for which we have $p(a, c) = 1/6$.

I think that this would have been my reply, by and large; and I now wonder how I could ever have been satisfied with a reply of this kind, for it now seems plain to me that it is utterly unsatisfactory.

Of course there is no doubt as to the compatibility of the two equations

(i) $p(a, b) = 1/4$,
(ii) $p(a, bc) = 1/6$,

nor is there any question that these two cases can be realised within the frequency theory: we *might* construct some sequence b such that equation (i) is satisfied, while in a selection sequence bc—a very long and virtually infinite sequence whose elements belong both to b and to c—equation (ii) is satisfied. *But our case is not of this kind.* For bc is not, in our case, a virtually infinite sequence. It contains, according to our assumption, at most three elements. In bc the six may come up not at all, or once, or twice, or three times. But it *certainly* will not occur with the frequency 1/6 in the sequence bc because we *know* that this sequence contains at most three elements.

Thus there are only two infinite, or very long, sequences in our case: the (actual) sequence b and the (virtual) sequence c. The throws in question belong to both of them. And our problem is this. Although they belong to both of these sequences, and although we only know that these particular throws bc occur somewhere in b (we are not told where, and we are therefore not able to identify them), we have no doubt whatever that in their case the proper, the true singular probability, is 1/6 rather than 1/4. Or in other words, although they belong to both sequences, we have no doubt that their singular probability is to be estimated as being equal to the frequency of the sequence c rather than b—simply because they are throws with a different (a correct) die, and because we estimate or conjecture that, in a sequence of throws with a correct die, the six will come up in 1/6 of the cases.

(4) All this means that the frequency theorist is forced to introduce a modification of his theory—apparently a very slight one. He will now say that an admissible sequence of events (a reference sequence, a 'collective') must always be a sequence of repeated experiments. Or more generally, he will say that admissible sequences must be either virtual or actual sequences which are *characterised by a set of generating*

493

conditions—by a set of conditions whose repeated realisation produces the elements of the sequence.

If this modification is introduced, then our problem is at once solved. For the sequence *b* will not be any longer an admissible reference sequence. Its main part, which consists only of throws with the loaded die, will make an admissible sequence, and no question arises with respect to it. The other part, *bc*, consists of throws with a regular die, and belongs to a virtual sequence *c*—also an admissible one—of such throws. There is again no problem here. It is clear that, once the modification has been adopted, the frequency interpretation is no longer in any difficulty.

Moreover, it seems that what I have here described as a 'modification' only states explicitly an assumption which most frequency theorists (myself included) have always taken for granted.

Yet, if we look more closely at this apparently slight modification, then we find that it amounts to a transition from the frequency interpretation to the propensity interpretation.

The frequency interpretation always takes probability as relative to a sequence which is assumed as given; and it works on the assumption that a probability is *a property of some given sequence*. But with our modification, the sequence in its turn is defined by its set of *generating conditions*; and in such a way that probability may now be said to be *a property of the generating conditions*.

But this makes a very great difference, especially to the probability of a singular event (or an 'occurrence'). For now we can say that the singular event *a* possesses a probability $p(a, b)$ owing to the fact that it is an event produced, or selected, in accordance with the generating conditions *b*, rather than owing to the fact that it is a member of a sequence *b*. In this way, a singular event may have a probability even though it may occur only once; for its probability is a property of its generating conditions.

Admittedly, the frequency theorist can still say that the probability, even though it is a property of the generating conditions, is equal to the relative frequency within a virtual or actual sequence generated by these conditions. But if we think this out more fully it becomes quite clear that our frequency theorist has, inadvertently, turned into a propensity theorist. For if the probability is a property of the generating conditions— of the experimental arrangement—and if it is therefore considered as depending upon these conditions, then the answer given by the frequency theorist implies that the virtual frequency must also depend upon these conditions. But this means that we have to visualise the conditions as endowed with a tendency, or disposition, or propensity, to produce sequences whose frequencies are equal to the probabilities; which is precisely what the propensity interpretation asserts.

Propensities and possibilities

It might be thought that we can avoid the last step—the attribution of propensities to the generating conditions—by speaking of mere possibilities rather than of propensities. In this way one may hope to avoid what seems to be the most objectionable aspect of the propensity interpretation: its intuitive similarity to 'vital forces' and similar anthropomorphisms which have been found to be barren pseudo-explanations.

The interpretation of probabilities in terms of possibilities is of course very old. We may, for the sake of the argument, suppress the well known objections (exemplified by the case of the loaded die) against the classical definition of probability, in terms of *equal* possibilities, as the number of the favourable possibilities divided by the number of all the possibilities; and we may confine ourselves to cases such as symmetrical dies or pennies, in order to see how this definition compares with the propensity interpretation.

The two interpretations have a great deal in common. Both refer primarily to singular events, and to the possibilities inherent in the conditions under which these events take place. And both consider these conditions as reproducible in principle, so that they may give rise to a sequence of events. The difference, it seems, lies merely in this: that the one interpretation introduces those objectionable metaphysical propensities, while the other simply refers to the physical symmetries of the conditions—to the equal possibilities which are left open by the conditions.

Yet this agreement is only apparent. It is not difficult to see that mere possibilities are inadequate for our purpose—or that of the physicist, or the gambler—and that even the classical definition assumes, implicitly, that equal *dispositions, or tendencies, or propensities to realise the possibilities in question,* must be attached to the equal possibilities.

This can be easily shown if we first consider equi-possibilities very close to zero. An example of an equi-possibility very close to zero would be the probability of any definite sequence of 0's (heads) and 1's (tails) of the length n: there are 2^n such sequences, so that in the case of equi-possibility, each possibility has the value $1/2^n$ which for a large n is very close to zero. The complementary possibility is, of course, just as close to one. Now these possibilities close to zero are generally interpreted as 'almost impossible', or as 'almost never realising themselves', while, of course, the complementary possibilities, which are close to one, are interpreted as 'almost necessary', or as 'almost always realising themselves'.

But if it is admitted that possibilities close to zero and close to one are to be interpreted as predictions—'almost never to happen' and 'almost always to happen'—then it can easily be shown that the two possibilities of getting heads or tails, assumed to be exhaustive, exclusive and equal, are also to be interpreted as predictions. They correspond to the predictions 'almost certain to realise themselves, in the long run, in about *half* of the cases'. For we can show, with the help of Bernoulli's theorem (and the above example of sequences of the length n) that this interpretation of possibilities 1/2 is *logically equivalent* to the interpretation, just given, of possibilities close to zero or to one.

To put the same point somewhat differently, mere possibilities could never give rise to any prediction. It is possible, for example, that an earthquake will destroy tomorrow *all* the houses between the 13th parallels north and south (and *no* other houses). Nobody can calculate this possibility, but most people would estimate it as exceedingly small; and while the sheer possibility as such does not give rise to any prediction, the estimate that it is exceedingly small may be made the basis of the prediction that the event described will not take place ('in all probability').

Thus the estimate of the *measure* of a possibility—that is, the estimate of the probability attached to it—has always a predictive function, while we should hardly predict an event upon being told no more than that this event is possible. In other words, we do not assume that a possibility as such has any tendency to realise itself; but we do interpret probability measures, or 'weights' attributed to the possibility, as measuring its disposition, or tendency, or propensity to realise itself; and in physics (or in betting) we are interested in such measures, or 'weights' of possibilities, as might permit us to make predictions. We therefore cannot get round the fact that we treat measures of possibilities as dispositions or tendencies or propensities. My reason for choosing the label *'propensity interpretation'* is that I wish to emphasise this point which, as the history of probability theory shows, may easily be missed.

This is why I am not intimidated by the allegation that propensity is an anthropomorphic conception, or that it is similar to the conception of a vital force. (This conception has indeed been barren so far, and it seems to be objectionable. But the disposition, or tendency, or propensity, of most organisms to struggle for survival is not a barren conception, but a very useful one; and the barrenness of the idea of a vital force seems to be due to the fact that it promises to add, but fails to add, something important to the assertion that most organisms show a propensity to struggle for survival.)

To sum up, the propensity interpretation may be presented as retaining the view that probabilities are conjectured or estimated statistical frequencies in long (actual or virtual) sequences. Yet by drawing attention to the fact that these sequences are defined by the manner in which their elements are generated—that is, by the experimental conditions—we can show that we are bound to attribute our conjectured probabilities to these experimental conditions: we are bound to admit that they depend on these conditions, and that they may change with them. This modification of the frequency interpretation leads almost inevitably to the conjecture that probabilities are dispositional properties of these conditions—that is to say, propensities. This allows us to interpret the probability of a *singular* event as a property of the singular event itself, to be measured by a conjectured *potential or virtual* statistical frequency rather than by an *actual* one.

Like all dispositional properties, propensities exhibit a certain similarity to Aristotelian potentialities. But there is an important difference: they cannot, as Aristotle thought, be inherent in the individual *things*. They are not properties inherent in the die, or in the penny, but in something a little more abstract, even though physically real: they are relational properties of the experimental arrangement—of the conditions we intend to keep constant during repetition. Here again they resemble forces, or fields of forces: a Newtonian force is not a property of a thing but a relational property of at least two things; and the actual resulting forces in a physical system are always a property of the whole physical system. Force, like propensity, is a relational concept.

These results support, and are supported by, my remarks about the role of *b*—the second argument—in '*p(a, b)*'; and they show that, although we may interpret '*b*' as the name of a (potential or virtual) sequence of events, we must not admit every possible sequence: only sequences which may be described as repetitions of an experiment are admitted, and which may be defined by the method of their generation, that is to say, by a generating set of experimental conditions.

The (meta)physical character of the propensity hypothesis

There is a possibility of misinterpreting my arguments, and especially those of the preceding two sections. For they might perhaps be taken as illustrating the method of *meaning analysis*: what I have done, or tried to do, it could be said, is to show that the word 'probability' is used, in certain contexts, to denote propensities. I have perhaps even encouraged this misinterpretation (especially in the third section) by suggesting that the frequency theory is, partly, the result of a mistaken meaning analysis, or of an incomplete meaning analysis. Yet I do not suggest putting another meaning analysis in its place. This will be clearly seen as soon as it is understood that what I propose is *a new physical hypothesis* (or perhaps a metaphysical hypothesis) analogous to the hypothesis of Newtonian forces. It is the hypothesis that every experimental arrangement (and therefore every state of a system) generates physical propensities which can be tested by frequencies. This hypothesis is testable, and it is corroborated by certain quantum experiments. The two-slit experiment, for example, may be said to be something like a crucial experiment between the purely statistical and the propensity interpretation of probability, and to decide the issue against the purely statistical interpretation.

Notes

* Originally published in *British Journal for the Philosophy of Science*, 10 (1959), pp. 25–38 (omitting the note and appendix). Copyright © 1959 The British Society for the Philosophy of Science. Reprinted by permission of Oxford University Press.

1 See my *Logic of Scientific Discovery* (1934, 1959), Section 48, and Appendix* ii

2 The most characteristic laws of the calculus of probability are (1) the addition theorems, pertaining to the probability of $a \vee b$ (that is, of *a-or-b*); (2) the multiplication theorems, pertaining to the probability of ab (that is, of *a-and-b*); and (3) the complementation theorems, pertaining to the probability of $\bar{a}$ (that is, of non-*a*). They may be written

(1) $p(a \vee b, c) = p(a, c) + p(b, c) - p(ab, c)$
(2) $p(ab, c) = p(a, bc)p(b, c)$
(3) $p(\bar{a}, c) = 1 - p(a, c)$, provided $p(\bar{c}, c) \neq 1$.

The form of (3) here given is somewhat unusual: it is characteristic of a probability theory in which

(4) $p(a, \bar{a}) = 1$

is a theorem. The first axiom system for a theory of this kind was presented, as far as I know, in *BJPS*, 1955, 6, 56. See also my *Logic of Scientific Discovery*, appendix* iv.

3 W. C. Kneale said in this discussion: 'More recently the difficulties of the frequency interpretation, i.e. the muddles, if not the plain contradictions, which can be found in von Mises, have become well known, and I suppose that these are the considerations which have led Professor Popper to abandon that interpretation of probability.' See *Observation and Interpretation*, edited by S. Körner, 1957, p. 80. I am not aware of any 'muddles' or 'contradictions' in the frequency theory which have become well known more recently; on the contrary, I believe that I have discussed all objections of any importance in my *Logic of Scientific Discovery* when it was first published in 1934, and I do not think that Kneale's criticism of the frequency theory in his *Probability and Induction*, 1949, presents a correct picture of the situation prevailing at any time since 1934. One objection of Kneale's (see especially p. 80 of his book) was not discussed in my book—that, in the frequency theory, a probability equal to one does not mean that the event in question will occur without exception (or 'with certainty'). But this objection is invalid; it can be shown that every adequate theory of probability (if applicable to infinite sets) must lead to the same result.

4 The remaining sections of this paper follow closely a section of my forthcoming book, *Postscript: After Twenty Years*. See also my paper 'The Propensity Interpretation of the Calculus of Probability and The Quantum Theory', in *Observation and Interpretation*, edited by S. Körner, 1957.

5 A criticism of the subjective theory of probability will be found in my notes in *BJPS*, quoted above, and in my paper 'Probability Magic, or Logic out of Ignorance', *Dialectica*, 1957, 354–374.

6 See my 'Note on Berkeley as a Precursor of Mach', *British Journal for the Philosophy of Science*, 1953, 4, 21 (4).

29

OBJECTIVE SINGLE-CASE
PROBABILITIES AND THE
FOUNDATIONS OF STATISTICS*

Ronald N. Giere

Introduction

Probability is becoming ever more important in all areas of science. Yet although there is widespread agreement concerning the mathematical development of probability theory, there are still fundamental disputes as to what further interpretation (or interpretations) of probability are needed both for a clear understanding of scientific inquiry and for sound scientific practice. Fortunately there are only a few significantly different interpretations with any substantial following. One interpretation, which goes back at least to LAPLACE (1814), takes probability to be a relation between a body of evidence and a hypothesis. One modern branch of this tradition, represented by CARNAP (1950; also this volume, Chapter 19) and HINTIKKA (1965), JEFFREYS (1939), KEYNES (1921), holds this relation to be purely *logical* (or, more precisely, semantical). Another branch, represented by DE FINETTI (1937), GOOD (1950, 1965), RAMSEY (1931, this volume, Chapter 2), and SAVAGE (1954, 1962a, 1962b), takes the relation to be *subjective*, so that a probability is always someone's degree of belief in a hypothesis given some evidence. The other major alternative interpretation of probability, first explored in detail by VENN (1866) and later developed by REICHENBACH (1949), SALMON (1966) and VON MISES (1919, 1957, this volume, Chapter 22), takes a probability to be a limiting relative frequency of an attribute in an infinite sequence of objects or events. Other important authors, e.g., CRAMÉR (1946) and KOLMOGOROV (1933), interpret probabilities in terms of relative frequencies but do not strictly identify probabilities with relative frequencies.

As CARNAP has argued (1950, Ch. 2), it is possible to reconcile the major opposing traditions by insisting that science utilizes *both* interpretations. The statistical hypotheses of physics, biology, etc., may be interpreted as statements about relative frequencies while all scientific hypotheses, whether statistical or not, are said to have an inductive (for Carnap, logical) probability relation with their respective bodies of evidence. Thus Carnap distinguishes sharply between the content of physical probability statements and the inductive probability relations they bear to a body of evidence.

Unfortunately Carnap's neat resolution cannot be applied to the present situation in the foundations of statistics. On the one hand, the objectivists, who associate probabilities with frequencies, i.e., FISHER (1950), NEYMAN (1967), and just about everyone else but the subjectivists, do not employ anything like an inductive probability relation in their theories of statistical inference (including testing and estimation).[2] At the same time, advocates of the main systematic rival account of statistical inference, i.e., the subjective Bayesians, or Bayesian personalists to use Savage's term, insist that the *only* probabilities involved in scientific inquiry are subjective. For them, probabilities as independent, external facts do not exist, and Carnap's distinction between physical probabilities and inductive probabilistic relations disappears.[3]

Current opposition to standard methods of testing and estimation is by no means confined to the personalists.[4] Only the personalists, however, have made the frequency interpretation of probability a special focus of their discontent. Thus anyone wishing to uphold some form of objectivist approach to statistics must answer current objections to objectivist interpretations of statistical probabilities. This is just what I hope to do here. My strategy, however, will not be to defend a frequency interpretation of probability but to develop a different interpretation which, while objective and empirical, applies primarily to individual events rather than to sequences of events. This will turn out to be a version of what has been called the *propensity interpretation of probability*.

The following section of this paper summarizes the shortcomings of frequency interpretations, thus providing a basis for judging the advantages of a propensity interpretation. I then introduce the single-case propensity interpretation, paying particular attention to the indeterministic nature of propensities. Next it is shown that the relation between propensities and frequencies makes the existence of propensities incompatible with a Humean metaphysics and epistemology. Finally, I indicate how a single-case propensity interpretation may illuminate typical examples of statistical practice.

Frequency interpretations

There are at least two recognizably different interpretations going under the title 'the frequency interpretation of probability'. The older theory, and the one most discussed by philosophers, defines the probability of an attribute as the *limiting relative frequency* of that attribute in an *infinite sequence* of observations. There are many objections to the limiting frequency interpretation, e.g., that the probability depends on the *order* of the events in the sequence (BRAITHWAITE, 1953, p. 125), or that developing statistical theory rigorously in terms of limiting frequencies is prohibitively complex (SUPPES, 1970). The primary traditional objection, however, is that limiting frequency interpretations cannot handle applications of probability to *single events*. As personalists now inquire, 'What good is it to know that a certain method will give a correct estimate 95% of the time on the average?' The problem is to know what to think about the particular case before use (SMITH, 1965, p. 471). VON MISES (this volume, p. 356) forthrightly insisted that since a probability has a value only relative to an infinite sequence, the empirical concept of probability simply *does not apply* to individual events. But while agreeing that the concept of probability is not strictly applicable to single events, some frequency theorists, notably Venn, Reichenbach and Salmon, insist that 'the problem of the single case', as it is called, can be solved. As SALMON (1966) explains it, the basic strategy is to use the limiting relative frequency of an attribute as the rational betting rate for its occurrence in an individual case. But of course any single event may be a member of many infinite sequences with different limiting relative frequencies for the attribute in question. The residual task of designating a suitable unique sequence is known as 'the problem of the reference class'.

RONALD N. GIERE

In his latest publication, SALMON (1970) has to admit that his modification of Reichenbach's reference class rule is not guaranteed to associate a unique limiting frequency with every single event. But even if a satisfactory rule were devised, one still must explain why the limit of an infinite sequence should determine the rational expectation (expressed as a betting rate or 'weight') in the single case. Why should what happens in the limit be relevant (HACKING, 1965, Ch. 4)? Sufficient attention to this question may lead one to seek the basis of rational single-case expectations in the individual events themselves. This is just what a single-case propensity interpretation tries to do.

The second frequency interpretation seems to have originated with KOLMOGOROV (1933) and until recently (HEMPEL, 1965; LEVI, 1967) has been the almost exclusive possession of statisticians and mathematicians. As developed by CRAMÉR (1946, Ch. 13), Kolmogorov's views may be expressed as follows. Let *CSU* be a chance setup (random experiment) with a finite set, S, of possible outcomes. Let F be an algebra of events, E_i, defined on S, and define a real-valued function $P(E)$ over F such that: (i) $P(E) \geq 0$, (ii) $P(S) = 1$, (iii) $P(E \cup F) = P(E) + P(F)$ if $E \cap F = \emptyset$. Then, according to Cramér, the statement that $P(E) = r$ is to have the following 'concrete' meaning:

In a long series of repetitions of *CSU*, it is practically certain that the frequency of E will be approximately equal to r. (1946, p. 148)

For Cramér, this statement constitutes 'the frequency interpretation of probability'. In addition, Cramér takes pains to argue that a probability value 'provides a conceptual counterpart of the empirical frequency ratios' in the way that the points and lines of pure geometry provide a conceptual counterpart of empirical chalk marks, rulers, etc. (1946, p. 148). In short, Cramér seems to hold that probability is a 'theoretical' concept which is made 'concrete' or, as some would say, 'operationalized', in terms of frequencies in a long but finite series of trials.

Now the Kolmogorov-Cramér interpretation is incomplete in several respects. It is not stated whether the trials in the series of repetitions are independent or not; nor is independence defined except in terms of probability. Also, the notion of 'practical certainty' is hardly less in need of interpretation than that of probability. But this interpretation is not merely incomplete; it is, I think, fundamentally mistaken due to its tacit adherence to an overly rigid operationist or verificationist approach to theoretical concepts. The interpretation conflates the problem of saying what it *is* for a probability to have a certain value with the problem of saying when one may be *justified in claiming* (practically certain) that a probability has a certain value. Unfortunately I am not prepared to provide a general account of the semantics of theoretical terms. Thus I will simply insist that this must be done in such a way that the *ontological* question, 'What *are* statistical probabilities?', be logically distinct from the *epistemological* question, 'When may one legitimately *assert* the existence of a certain statistical probability?' By keeping these two issues separate one may hope to give a satisfactory interpretation in which statistical probabilities are truly objective and empirical as well as theoretical.

Physical probabilities as single-case propensities

Many shortcomings of the Kolmogorov-Cramér interpretation, which invokes only *finite* series, may be overcome by moving to a *limiting* frequency interpretation. But the limiting frequency interpretation has considerable shortcomings of its own. I propose

500

to move, so to speak, in the other direction, i.e., to the *individual trial*, thereby avoiding the problems of both frequency interpretations.

Consider again a chance setup, *CSU*, with a finite set of outcomes and an associated probability function $P(E)$ with the usual formal properties. The following is then a simple statement of the desired physical interpretation of the statement $P(E) = r$:

The strength of the *propensity* of *CSU* to produce outcome *E* on trial *L* is *r*.

This statement clearly refers to a particular trial. Given this single-case interpretation, one may of course generalize to any number of trials. Indeed, the statement $P(E) = r$ may often be intended to express the generalization,

For every trial of *CSU*, the propensity of *CSU* to produce outcome *E* is *r*.

Nevertheless, whether or not the latter generalization happens to be true, it is the single case that is fundamental for understanding what physical probabilities are.

The term 'propensity' ('tendency', 'disposition', or even 'dispositional tendency' would do), as well as some general inspiration for this type of interpretation, comes from recent papers by SIR KARL POPPER (1957, 1959, 1967). Yet in spite of some similarities, there are fundamental differences between what appears to be Popper's propensity interpretation and the above *single-case* propensity interpretation. Explicit mention of these differences will help to clarify my view.

I assume that a propensity must be a propensity of something (*X*) to produce something else (*Y*). On this assumption, it seems that I differ with Popper regarding the nature of both *X* and *Y*. Concerning *Y*, an early discussion of Popper's includes the statement that 'propensities turn out to be *propensities to realize singular events* [this volume, p. 490, Popper's italics]'. This parallels my view that propensities are tendencies to produce specific outcomes on particular trials. Yet in the same article Popper describes his propensity interpretation as asserting precisely that experimental conditions are 'endowed with a ... propensity to produce *sequences* whose *frequencies* are equal to the probabilities [this volume, p. 494, my italics]'. Now if 'propensities to realize singular events' are fundamental, then propensities to produce certain frequencies in sequences of trials follow naturally. The reverse, however, is not true, and in his later writings Popper seems to make the production of *sequences* fundamental. Thus in his most recent discussion Popper writes as follows concerning the occurrence of a '6' on the toss of a die:

We may agree to take as our measure of that propensity the (virtual) *relative frequency* with which the side turns up in a (virtual, and virtually infinite) sequence of repetitions of the experiment.

[1967, p. 32, Popper's italics]

This is followed immediately by the simple statement that we 'interpret' propensities 'as tendencies to produce frequencies'.

Popper's choice of *Y*, i.e., what is produced, has immediate consequences for his choice of *X*, i.e., what does the producing. Propensities, he says are '*properties of the repeatable experimental arrangement* [1967, p. 38, Popper's italics]'. The arrangement must be *repeatable*, of course, if it is to produce a *sequence*, even a 'virtual' sequence.

501

But then the description of the propensity must include a specification of what counts as a repetition of *the* experiment. Popper accepts this '*relativity to specification*' [1967, p. 39, Popper's italics], but seems not to realize that it destroys his earlier claim to have solved the problem of the single case. To take his own example: What is the propensity for heads on a particular toss of a coin? This depends, of course, on the experimental arrangement. But what counts as a repetition of the same experiment? For example, should the maximum height of the coin be specified? If it is not, then the toss in question may be a member of many virtual sequences, e.g., one in which the height is 10' and one in which it is 9'. But if the limiting frequency of heads is different in these two virtual sequences, as it might be, then, following the line of argument POPPER (1959) himself employs against the limiting frequency interpretation, it would be wrong to assign to this single case the virtual frequency of the sequence of 10' tosses if it were in fact a 9' toss. Thus Popper fails to solve the problem of the single case for the old-fashioned reason that he provides no solution to the problem of the reference class.[5]

By contrast, a single-case propensity interpretation, which makes no essential reference to any sequence (virtual or real), automatically avoids the problem of the single case and the problem of the reference class as well. The propensities associated with a trial of a setup are no more relative to any description than any other physical characteristics, e.g., mass, specific gravity, or electrical conductivity. The prima facie objections to the single-case propensity interpretation are entirely different.

Initially one may think that the single-case interpretation is quite empty; it largely just substitutes the word 'propensity' for the word 'probability'. This, I shall argue, is not so. In the first place, although it is of course not necessary, a new word is both desirable and appropriate because the word 'probability' is commonly used to describe the abstract relations of formal probability theory while the word 'propensity' is intended to designate a *physical realization* (or physical model) of the abstract structure. But not only are propensities physical, they are, as Popper and also Cramér would insist, *theoretical*. Thus the appropriate analogy for the relation between abstract probability spaces and physical propensities is that between, for example, an abstract structure for particle mechanics and the actual masses, forces, etc., which might be physically realized. Indeed, the analogy between propensities and forces is quite illuminating. Just as one might argue that force in classical particle mechanics is not reducible to, i.e., definable in terms of, less theoretical concepts like mass and acceleration, so I would claim that propensities are not reducible to less theoretical concepts like relative frequency. I will return to this point below.

Determinism and single-case propensities

The classical argument connecting interpretations of probability with determinism was given by LAPLACE (1814) who argued that since everything that happens does so according to deterministic laws, the probability of an event can only be a measure of our knowledge or ignorance of conditions relevant to that event. This is the background of the principle of indifference.[6] Mill, who had little use for LAPLACE's mathematical theory or for the principle of insufficient reason, nevertheless gave in on this point. Having withdrawn earlier objections to LAPLACE's view, he concludes:

> Every event is in itself certain, not probable; if we knew all, we should either know positively that it will happen or positively that it will not. But its

probability to us means the degree of expectation of its occurrence which we are warranted in entertaining by our present evidence.

The role of the assumption of determinism in this argument is clear enough.[7]

One will not find the above argument in the writings of LAPLACE's contemporary heirs, the subjective Bayesians, but they are tacitly committed to a similar position. The most prominent personalists, e.g., Savage and de Finetti, insist that there is only one legitimate concept of probability, that which identifies probability with subjective uncertainty. Once this identification is made, however, one lacks the conceptual apparatus to distinguish uncertainty due to lack of information from uncertainty which no physically possible increase in present knowledge could eliminate. But this is just the distinction between physical determinism and physical indeterminism. Not being able to make the distinction, Bayesians are forced to assume that all uncertainty is due to lack of information, i.e., to assume determinism. Indeed, to admit the possibility of uncertainty not due to lack of information would be to admit the possibility of physical, i.e., non-subjective, probabilities—an admission personalists refuse to make.

For my part, I agree with the implication of LAPLACE's position that *if* the world is deterministic, then all single-case propensities have value 0 or 1. For under determinism, any physical process has only one physically possible outcome. Note that this result does not hold for limiting frequency interpretations since limiting frequencies other than 0 or 1 may exist in either a deterministic or indeterministic universe.

If we knew our world to be deterministic, discussion of single-case propensities would be quite academic. Fortunately, however, there are good grounds for claiming that determinism does not hold, at least not at the micro-level. Consider an ensemble of identically prepared micro-systems, each of which is subjected to the same measuring process to determine the value of some physical parameter. Unlike the case in classical physics, it is a consequence of quantum theory itself that the measured values will exhibit a dispersion which cannot in principle be eliminated by any physical means. In his classic work on the foundations of quantum theory, VON NEUMANN (1955, p. 302) considers two possible explanations of this result:

I The individual systems $S_1, ..., S_n$ of our ensemble can be in different states, so that the ensemble $[S_1, ..., S_n]$ is defined by their relative frequencies. The fact that we do not obtain sharp values for the physical quantities in this case is caused by our lack of information: we do not know in which state we are measuring, and therefore we cannot predict the results.

II All individual systems $S_1, ..., S_n$ are in the same state, but the laws of nature are not causal. Then the cause of the dispersions is not our lack of information, but is nature itself, which has disregarded the 'principle of sufficient cause'.

'Case I', he goes on to say, 'is generally well known while Case II is important and new'. It is the latter interpretation that invites consideration of single-case propensities.[8]

As a concrete example, consider a single isolated radioactive nucleus. Pick a time t_0 at which the nucleus has not yet decayed. Then there is a time period T, the 'half-life' of the nucleus, such that the propensity of the nucleus to decay between t_0 and $t_0 + T$ is 1/2. Moreover, if the Ψ-function provides a complete physical description

503

of the nucleus, then there is no variable x such that the value of x uniquely determines the time of decay. The indeterminacy is in nature itself, not in our knowledge. I take this example to be a paradigm realization of a single-case propensity. Just how this interpretation may be applied in fields other than microphysics will be discussed below.

Taking quantum phenomena as paradigm examples of propensities makes it possible to be somewhat more precise about the analogy between propensities and theoretical quantities like classical forces. Standard formalizations of classical mechanics contain a term whose physical realizations we call forces. At the moment there are no rigorous, widely accepted formalizations of quantum theory, but it is a good bet that such a formalization will contain a term with the basic formal characteristics of a probability. The physical realizations of these quantities will be propensities.[9] Thus in principle the status of propensities as theoretical empirical quantities is just like that of classical forces. And just as forces are related to 'observables' such as position and velocity, so quantum propensities may be related to 'observables' like energy level and nuclear structure. The fact that the one theory is deterministic and the other indeterministic seems to me of little consequence here. To resolve this question, however, would require a satisfactory general account of the semantic relations between 'theory' and 'observation'.

Propensities and relative frequencies

Single-case propensities are not to be interpreted in terms of relative frequencies, but there are other important relations between propensities and frequencies. Some discussion of these relations will further illuminate the advantages and (for some) disadvantages of a single-case propensity interpretation of probability.

A preliminary point worth emphasizing is that a single-case propensity interpretation provides an extremely natural understanding of the standard formalism for dealing with series of trials. Indeed, it provides a natural interpretation for the whole mathematical theory of probability and statistics since KOLMOGOROV (1933).[10] Thus, for example, a series of trials is conventionally represented by a sequence of random variables X_1, X_2, ..., X_n. On my interpretation, the density function, $P(X_i = x)$, gives the propensity distribution on the ith trial. It is as simple as that. There is no need for vague talk about 'virtual' infinite sequences, etc. Independence of trials just means that there is no causal interaction between the outcome of one trial and the propensity distribution on any other trial. Similarly, time dependent trials, which already worried Venn, have a completely natural single-case propensity interpretation. In this respect the contrast with the limiting frequency interpretation, which necessitates many mathematical complexities, e.g., in the definition of a random sequence, is striking.

A central question concerning the relation between single-case propensities and frequencies is whether it is possible to *deduce* values of one from values of the other. The answer, as one would expect since propensities are theoretical, is negative. Consider a series of Bernoullian trials in which the propensity for success is r on each trial. Let f_n be the relative frequency of successes after n trials. In this case the strongest connection one can establish between r and f_n is given by the Bernoulli theorem, namely:

$$(\varepsilon > 0)(\delta > 0)(\exists N)[(n > N) \supset P(|f_n - r| > \varepsilon) > (1 - \delta)]$$

504

where P measures a propensity of the compound trial which consists of n trials of the original chance setup. It does *not* follow that the sequence of values of f_n has limit r in the ordinary sense, i.e., that,

$$(\varepsilon > 0)(\exists N)[(n > N) \supset |f_n - r| < \varepsilon].$$

Thus the sequence need not be a probability sequence in the sense of von Mises or Reichenbach. Indeed, it is *logically* possible, for example, that $r = 1/2$ and that $f_n = 1$ for any n, although of course the propensity for this outcome approaches zero. The limiting frequency interpretation rules out all such possibilities by convention.

It follows from the lack of direct entailment between frequencies and propensities that the existence of single-case propensities is inconsistent with a Humean metaphysics. For Hume the objective existence of a universal causal connection consists solely in de facto conjunction, past, present, and future. Extending this conception to probabilistic laws, the probabilistic connection, for a Humean, can only consist in the de facto relative frequency. But since there is no direct logical connection between single-case propensities and relative frequencies, not even 'in the limit', the relation expressed by propensity statements cannot be a Humean probability law.

The same point can be made in epistemological terms as well. The Humean insists that one cannot *know* the truth of a law (universal or probabilistic) on partial evidence. But if one somehow could know the whole actual history of the universe, one would know all the laws. Interpreting the actual history of the universe in terms of standard limit concepts, it is clear that one could know the limits of sequences and not know the values of the single-case propensities which generated the sequences. Thus, it is concluded, single-case propensities are 'metaphysical' because unverifiable in principle, even in the long run.

In spite of their non-Humean character, I would insist that relative frequencies may provide *evidence* for propensity hypotheses. Indeed, in the absence of a well-developed theoretical background, observed relative frequencies may provide the only evidence for propensity statements. Let us briefly explore this relationship through a simple example. Suppose one wishes to test a hypothesis concerning the half-life of a radio-active nucleus Z. The standard procedure, as any physics text reveals, is to obtain a large number, say 10^{18}, of such nuclei and to count the relative numbers decaying within specified time intervals. This procedure, however, assumes that each nucleus in the sample has the *same* half-life, whatever its value. Thus the test assumes the truth of some propensity statements, though of course not the truth of the hypothesis being tested. This example of testing propensity hypotheses using relative frequencies raises several philosophically interesting questions: Is it possible to test a single-case propensity hypothesis without assuming the truth of some *other* propensity statement? If not, does this make such an account of physical probabilities unacceptable?

These questions show that one cannot completely isolate the problem of interpreting probability from other issues in the foundations of statistics. An answer to the first question, for example, presupposes a detailed theory of statistical inference. As this is no place to launch a discussion of inference, I will simply state my belief that any scientifically legitimate inference concerning physical probabilities must presuppose the truth of some probability hypothesis. That this admission does not render all probability conclusions ultimately unjustifiable requires further argument. Here, however, I can only appeal once again to the analogy between propensities and classical forces.[11]

Consider the concept of an individual (as opposed to total) force in classical physics. Any attempt to determine the value of a particular force requires assumptions concerning other forces, e.g., that there are none operative or that their influence has been taken into account. Thus if one regards the concept of an individual force as a legitimate empirical concept, one cannot dismiss single-case propensities solely on the ground that empirical tests of propensity hypotheses assume the truth of other propensity hypotheses. This argument is hardly conclusive since strict empiricists have often sought to banish the concept of force from science. It does show, however, that the problem of testing propensity hypotheses is not scientifically unique.

Propensities and statistical practice

Fundamental issues in the foundations of statistics will only be resolved, I think, through the self-conscious application of rival approaches in a wide variety of actual scientific contexts. Here I can only indicate briefly the benefits of a single-case propensity interpretation for statistical practice.

Consider the familiar case of cigarette smoking and cancer. Examination of the medical histories of large numbers of men selected at random shows that the percentage of smokers contracting cancer is significantly higher. The question is how to interpret this result, both as scientists and as individuals facing the choice of smoking or not. Suppose as scientists we were to say merely that the relative frequency of cancer victims among smokers is greater than among non-smokers. Then, following a familiar line of argument, an individual may well ask what this tells him about his individual chances of contracting cancer if he smokes. Might he not be one of those who do not get cancer even if they are heavy smokers?

The propensity interpretation at least makes clear the relevance of the observed frequencies to the individual in a natural manner. Here each person is regarded as a chance setup which at each moment has a definite propensity to contract cancer under certain conditions.[12] The many studies, therefore, provide strong evidence that, on the average, a man's propensity to contract cancer is greater if he smokes than if he does not. Of course one may still wonder whether his particular propensities are above or below the average, but at least the relation between an individual's propensities and an average propensity is fairly straightforward. Furthermore, it is clear what stopping smoking accomplishes. It changes the individual's physical system in such a way as to lower his individual propensity for developing cancer.[13]

The classical model for sampling problems is an urn filled with colored balls. This is clearly a deterministic model in that the possibility of the balls being indeterministic systems which change colors is not considered. Thus, if one insists on assigning a propensity, e.g., to an individual ball's being red, the value can only be 0 or 1. There is, however, a class of somewhat different propensity statements that might be made. Suppose the ratio of red balls in the (finite) urn is r. Then the propensity for a random sampling mechanism to select a red ball is r. Here, however, the propensity belongs not to any individual ball, but to the sampling mechanism which is assumed indeterministic.

What, finally, can be said about macro phenomena which are, to a very good approximation, deterministic systems throughout, though the relevant variables may be unknown and practically uncontrollable? This class contains the mechanisms used in many classical games of chance, e.g., roulette and dice. Due to the operation of many uncontrollable variables, series of trials of such mechanisms are often experimentally indistinguishable from series that would be generated by a sequence of genuinely indeterministic individual trials. This empirical fact justifies our using probability theory in such cases, and even makes it natural to apply probability language to individual trials. But it must be realized that this is only a convenient way of talking and that the implied physical probabilities really do not exist. To forget this is to invite conceptual confusion.[14]

One might object in principle to any interpretation of probability which takes abstruse and even controversial micro phenomena as its paradigms while relegating traditionally paradigm phenomena and games of chance to the status of fictional, 'pseudoprobabilities' (SKLAR, 1970). This blanket objection, however, is ill advised. Such a radical reordering of paradigms may be just what is needed to resolve years of inconclusive debate over the possibility of an adequate physical interpretation of probability.

Notes

* Originally published in P. Suppes, L. Henkin, G. C. Moisil, and A. Joja (eds.), *Logic, methodology, and philosophy of science IV: Proceedings of the Fourth International Congress for Logic, Methodology and Philosophy of Science, Bucharest, 1971*, Amsterdam: North-Holland, 1973, pp. 467–83. Reprinted by permission of Ronald N. Giere.

1 This work was completed during the author's tenure as associate research scientist at the Courant Institute of Mathematical Sciences (New York University), and has been supported by the National Science Foundation under Grants GS 2525 and GS 28628 and the National Institutes of Health under Grant GM 16202.

2 Fisher's fiducial probability might best be understood as a logical probability (KYBURG, 1964). But even if true, this claim would not invalidate my statement. Those contemporary statisticians who have been sympathetic toward the fiducial argument, e.g., TUKEY (1957), seem to have given it up, though HACKING (1965) has attempted a revival.

3 For a recent statement of the personalist's viewpoint see SAVAGE (1973). It is possible, of course, to be a subjectivist and still agree with Carnap's general thesis that two concepts of probability are needed. One could simply argue that the inductive probability relations between evidence and objective probability hypotheses are subjective. I would ascribe this more modest Bayesian view to GOOD (1965), SHIMONY (1970), and SUPPES (1973). Perhaps it is significant that the latter two authors have also devoted considerable thought to the foundations of quantum mechanics where physical probabilities may seem quite objective indeed.

4 Thus BIRNBAUM (1962, 1969), COX (1958), and TUKEY (1961) all reject aspects of standard methods of testing and estimation, preferring an eclectic form of 'data analysis'. Another group, e.g., BARNARD (1949), EDWARDS (1969) and HACKING (1965) wishes to interpret statistical evidence solely in terms of likelihoods.

5 Interpreting Popper's view in terms of counterfactuals, i.e., what frequencies *would* be generated if the arrangement *were* repeated, SKLAR (1970) has reached similar conclusions, though by different arguments. Popper, of course, is not the only, or even the clearest, advocate of a propensity interpretation, though he is the best known. Other propensity theorists include HACKING (1965), LEVI (1967) and MELLOR (1971). Even BRAITHWAITE (1953), CRAMÉR (1946) and HEMPEL (1965) might be placed in this camp. Except for Mellor, however, none of the above authors focuses on the single case.

6 Thus LAPLACE:

> Given for one instant an intelligence which could comprehend all the forces by which nature is animated and the respective situation of the beings who compose it—an intelligence sufficiently vast to submit these data to analysis—it would embrace in the same formula the movements of the greatest bodies of the universe and those of the lightest atom; for it, nothing would be uncertain and the future, as the past, would be present to its eyes.

This famous passage occurs not in the *Méchanique Céleste*, but in the introduction to the *Théorie analytique des probabilités* (1814, p. 4). It is followed a few paragraphs later by the assertion: 'Probability is relative, in part to [our] ignorance, in part to our knowledge'.

7 In the first edition of his *Logic*, MILL (1843) insisted that one can take two kinds of events to be equally probable only if they have been found to occur with roughly *equal frequency* in nature. By the eighth edition, however, he explicitly gave up his earlier view. The above quote is from the eighth edition, Book III, Ch. XVIII, Sec. 1.

8 The view von Neumann rejects is not without able adherents such as MARGENAU (1967) and his students. For a sympathetic recent review of this approach see BALLENTINE (1970). If Margenau and Ballentine are correct, there are no reasons for thinking that any single-case propensities exist. This does not mean that they *could* not exist, but lacking any extant cases, the development of a single-case propensity interpretation would become rather academic.

9 Whether or not quantum mechanical propensities have *all* the formal properties of classical probabilities is a problem for those working in the foundations of quantum theory. For an introduction to the literature on this issue see BALLENTINE (1970), MARGENAU and PARK (1967) and SUPPES (1966).

10 POPPER (1957) has remarked that the shift from a frequency interpretation to a propensity interpretation reflects a shift from the formalism of VON MISES (1919) to that of KOLMOGOROV (1933).

11 I have dealt at length with the ultimate justification of physical probability assertions in GIERE (1975).

12 I assume that the correct degree of expectation (expressible as a betting rate) in an outcome equals the propensity for that outcome. Moreover, this identification seems to me not to need any further explanation—just as one need not explain why it is correct to believe that the causally necessary result of a deterministic process will occur. Indeed, I am inclined to think that any attempt to explain the identification will be circular. For an opposing view, however, see MELLOR (1971, Ch. 4). Note that Bayesians have difficulty distinguishing the correct degree of belief from merely coherent degrees of belief. The best that can be done in a subjective framework is to define the correct expectation as that on which a given community agrees (coherently) after examining considerable evidence (SMITH, 1965). But this definition is incompatible with what I take to be a minimal requirement of scientific realism, namely, that everyone *could* be wrong irrespective of the amount of evidence at hand.

13 It may be that the human body is effectively a deterministic system so that there really is no such thing as a propensity to contract cancer. For my analysis of this case see the following paragraph. But even if this propensity does exist, there is no reason to suppose it is fundamental. Rather, it would seem to be explainable in terms of propensities of cells and genes and perhaps even of elementary particles.

14 Speaking more generally, the application of probability theory, for example, to classical statistical mechanics and standard games of chance, is *instrumentalistic*. The theory gives highly accurate results even though, strictly speaking, the entities and processes referred to are known not to exist. This claim should not be taken pejoratively. All applications of Newtonian mechanics, e.g., in civil engineering and in space programs, have the same status.

Bibliography

BALLENTINE, L. E., 1970, 'The statistical interpretation of quantum mechanics', *Reviews of Modern Physics*, vol. 42, pp. 358–381.

BARNARD, G. A., 1949, 'Statistical inference', *Journal of the Royal Statistical Society*, B, vol. 11, pp. 115–149.

BIRNBAUM, A., 1962, 'On the foundations of statistical inference', *Journal of the American Statistical Association*, vol. 57, pp. 269–306.

BIRNBAUM, A., 1969, 'Concepts of statistical evidence', in: *Philosophy, Science and Method*, eds. S. Morgenbesser, P. Suppes and M. White (St. Martins, New York), pp. 112–143.

BRAITHWAITE, R.B., 1953, *Scientific explanation* (Cambridge University Press, Cambridge).

CARNAP, R., 1950, *Logical foundations of probability* (University of Chicago Press, Chicago; 2nd edition, 1962).

Cox, D. R., 1958, 'Some problems connected with statistical inference', *Annals of Mathematical Statistics*, vol. 29, pp. 357–372.

Cramér, H., 1946. *Mathematical methods of statistics* (Princeton University Press, Princeton; 2nd edition 1961).

Edwards, A. W. F., 1969, 'Statistical methods in scientific inference', *Nature*, vol. 222, pp. 1233–1237.

de Finetti, B., 1937, 'La prévision: Ses lois logiques, ses sources subjectives', *Annales de l'Institut Henri Poincaré*, vol. 7, pp. 1–68. English translation in: Studies in Subjective Probability, ed. H. E. Kyburg, Jr., and H. E. Smokler (Wiley, New York, 1964), pp. 93–158.

Fisher, Sir R. A., 1950. *Contributions to mathematical statistics* (Wiley, New York).

Giere, R. N., 1975, 'Epistemological Roots of Scientific Knowledge'. In *Induction, Probability, and Confirmation*, Minnesota Studies in the Philosophy of Science, Vol. VI. Ed. G. Maxwell and R. M. Anderson, Jr. Minneapolis: University of Minnesota Press, pp. 212–261.

Good, I.J., 1950, *Probability and the weighing of evidence* (Griffin, London).

Good, I.J., 1965, *The estimation of probabilities* (Massachusetts Institute of Technology, Cambridge).

Hacking, I., 1965, *Logic of statistical inference* (Cambridge University Press, Cambridge).

Hempel, C. G., 1965, 'Aspects of scientific explanation', in: *Aspects of Scientific Explanation* (Free Press, New York), pp. 331–496.

Hintikka, J. K., 1965, 'On a combined system of inductive logic', *Acta Philosophica Fennica*, vol. 18, pp. 21–30.

Jeffreys, H., 1939, *Theory of probability* (Oxford University Press, Oxford; 3rd edition 1961).

Keynes, J. M., 1921. *A treatise on probability* (Macmillan, London).

Kolmogorov, A., 1933, *Grundbegriffe der Wahrscheinlichkeitsrechnung* (Springer, Berlin) English translation: *Foundations of the Theory of Probability*, ed. N. Morrison (Chelsea, New York, 1950).

Kyburg, H. E., Jr., 1964, 'Logical and fiducial probability', *Bulletin of the International Statistical Institute, Proceedings of the Thirty-Fourth* Session, Ottawa (University of Toronto Press, Toronto).

Laplace, P. S., Marquis de, 1814, *A philosophical essay on probabilities*, Translated from the Sixth French Edition by F. W. Truscatt and F. L. Emory (Dover, New York, 1951).

Levi, I., 1967, *Gambling with truth* (Knopf, New York).

Margenau, H. and J. L. Park, 1967, 'Objectivity in quantum mechanics', in: *Delaware Seminar in the Foundations of* Physics, ed. M. Bunge (Springer, New York), pp. 161–187.

Mellor, D. H., 1971, *The matter of chance* (Cambridge University Press, Cambridge).

Mill, J. S., 1843, *Logic* (London).

Neyman, J., 1967, *A selection of early statistical papers of J. Neyman* (University of California, Berkeley).

Popper, K. R., 1957, 'The propensity interpretation of the calculus of probability and the quantum theory', in: *Observation and Interpretation in the Philosophy of Physics*, ed. S. Körner (Butterworth, London).

Popper, K. R., 1959, 'The propensity interpretation of probability', *British Journal for the Philosophy of Science*, vol. 10, pp. 25–42, reprinted as Chapter 28 in this volume.

Popper, K. R., 1967, 'Quantum mechanics without "the observer"', in: *Quantum Theory and Reality*, ed. M. Bunge (Springer, New York).

Ramsey, F. P., 1931, 'Truth and probability', in: *The Foundations of Mathematics*, ed. R. B. Braithwaite (Routledge and Kegan Paul, London), pp. 156–198, reprinted as Chapter 2 in this volume.

Reichenbach, H., 1949, *The theory of probability*, (University of California Press, Berkeley).

Salmon, W. C., 1966, *The foundations of scientific inference* (University of Pittsburgh Press, Pittsburgh).

Salmon, W. C., 1970, 'Statistical explanation', in: *The Nature and Function of Scientific Theories*, ed. R. G. Colodny (University of Pittsburgh Press, Pittsburgh), pp. 173–231.

SAVAGE, L. J., 1954, *The foundations of statistics* (Wiley, New York).

SAVAGE, L. J., 1962a, 'Bayesian statistics', in: *Recent Developments in Decision and Information Processes*, eds. R. E. Machol and P. Gray (Macmillan, New York), pp. 161–194.

SAVAGE, L. J., 1962b, 'Subjective probability and statistical practice', in: *The Foundations of Statistical Inference*, ed. M. S. Bartlett (Methuen, London), pp. 9–35.

SAVAGE, L. J., 1973, 'Probability in science: a personalistic account', in Suppes et al. (eds.) *Logic, Methodology and Philosophy of Science IV*, Amsterdam: North-Holland, pp. 417–428.

SHIMONY, A., 1970, 'Scientific inference', in: *The Nature and Function of Scientific Theories*, ed. R. G. Colodny (University of Pittsburgh Press, Pittsburgh), pp. 79–172.

SKLAR, L., 1970, 'Is probability a dispositional property?', *Journal of Philosophy*, vol. 67, pp. 355–366.

SMITH, C. A. B., 1965, 'Personal probability and statistical analysis', *Journal of Royal Statistical Society*, A, vol. 128, pp. 469–489.

SUPPES, P., 1966, 'The probabilistic argument for a non-classical logic in quantum mechanics', *Philosophy of Science*, vol. 33, pp. 14–21.

SUPPES, P., 1970, *Set-theoretical structures in science* (Institute for Mathematical Studies in the Social Sciences, Stanford).

SUPPES, P., 1973, 'New foundations of objective probability: Axioms for propensities', in Suppes et al. (eds.) *Logic, Methodology and Philosophy of Science IV*, Amsterdam: North-Holland, pp. 515–529.

TUKEY, J. W., 1957, 'Some examples with fiducial relevance', *Annals of Mathematical Statistics*, vol. 28, pp. 687–695.

TUKEY, J. W., 1961, 'The future of data analysis', *Annals of Mathematical Statistics*, vol. 33, pp. 1–67.

VENN, J., 1866, *The logic of chance* (Macmillan, London).

VON MISES, R., 1919, 'Grundlagen der Wahrscheinlichkietsrechnung', *Mathematische Zeitschrift*, vol. 5, pp. 52–99.

VON MISES, R., 1957, *Probability, statistics and truth*, (Allen and Unwin, London), relevant extracts reprinted as Chapter 22 in this volume.

VON NEUMANN, J. 1955, *Mathematical foundations of quantum mechanics*, (Princeton University Press, Princeton).

30

WHY PROPENSITIES CANNOT BE PROBABILITIES*

Paul W. Humphreys

The notion that probability theory is the theory of chance has an immediate appeal. We may allow that there are other kinds of things to which probability can address itself, things such as degrees of rational belief and degrees of confirmation, to name only two, but if chance forms part of the world, then probability theory ought, it would seem, to be the device to deal with it. Although chance is undeniably a mysterious thing, one promising way to approach it is through the use of propensities—indeterministic dispositions possessed by systems in a particular environment, exemplified perhaps by such quite different phenomena as a radioactive atom's propensity to decay and my neighbor's propensity to shout at his wife on hot summer days. There is no generally accepted account of propensities, but whatever they are, propensities must, it is commonly held, have the properties prescribed by probability theory. My contention is that they do not and, that rather than this being construed as a problem for propensities, it is to be taken as a reason for rejecting the current theory of probability as the correct theory of chance.

The first section of the paper will provide an informal version of the argument, indicating how the causal nature of propensities cannot be adequately represented by standard probability theory. In the second section a full version of the argument will be given so that the assumptions underlying the informal account can be precisely identified. The third section examines those assumptions and deals with objections that could be raised against the argument and its conclusion. The fourth and final section draws out some rather more general consequences of accepting the main argument. Those who find the first section sufficiently persuasive by itself may wish to go immediately to the final section, returning thereafter to the second and third sections as necessary.

The informal argument

Consider first a traditional deterministic disposition, such as the disposition for a glass window to shatter when struck by a heavy object. Given slightly idealized circumstances, the window is certain to break when hit by a rock, and this manifestation of the disposition is displayed whenever the appropriate conditions are present. Such deterministic dispositions are, however, often asymmetric. The window has no disposition to be hit by a rock when broken, and similarly, whatever disposition there is for the air temperature to go above 80°F is unaffected by whether my neighbor loses his

511

temper, even though the converse influence is certainly there. The reason for this asymmetry is that many dispositions are intimately connected with causal relationships, and as a result they often possess the asymmetry of that latter relationship. Thus we might expect propensities, as particular kinds of dispositions, to possess a similar asymmetry and indeed they do, although because propensities come in degrees, the situation is understandably somewhat different.

The point can be illustrated by means of a simple scientific example. When light with a frequency greater than some threshold value falls on a metal plate, electrons are emitted by the photoelectric effect. Whether or not a particular electron is emitted is an indeterministic matter, and hence we can claim that there is a propensity p for an electron in the metal to be emitted, conditional upon the metal being exposed to light above the threshold frequency. Is there a corresponding propensity for the metal to be exposed to such light, conditional on an electron being emitted, and if so, what is its value? Probability theory provides an answer to this question if we identify conditional propensities with conditional probabilities. The answer is simple—calculate the inverse probability from the conditional probability. Yet it is just this answer which is incorrect for propensities and the reason is easy to see. The propensity for the metal to be exposed to radiation above the threshold frequency, conditional upon an electron being emitted, is equal to the unconditional propensity for the metal to be exposed to such radiation, because whether or not the conditioning factor occurs in this case cannot affect the propensity value for that latter event to occur. That is, with the obvious interpretation of the notation, $\Pr(R/\overline{E}) = \Pr(R/E) = \Pr(R)$. However, any use of inverse probability theorems from standard probability theory will require that $\Pr(R/E) = \Pr(E/R)\,P(R)/\,P(E)$ and if $P(E/R) \neq P(E)$, we shall have $P(R/E) \neq P(R)$. In this case, because of the influence of the radiation on the propensity for emission, the first inequality is true, but the lack of reverse influence makes the second inequality false for propensities. To take another example, heavy cigarette smoking increases the propensity for lung cancer, whereas the presence of (undiscovered) lung cancer has no effect on the propensity to smoke, and a similar probability calculation would give an incorrect result. Many other examples can obviously be given.

Thus a necessary condition for probability theory to provide the correct answer for conditional propensities is that any influence on the propensity which is present in one direction must also be present in the other. Yet it is just this symmetry which is lacking in most propensities. We can hence draw this conclusion from our informal argument: the properties of conditional propensities are not correctly represented by the standard theory of conditional probability; in particular any result involving inverse probabilities, including Bayes' Theorem, will, except in special cases, give incorrect results.

This short argument needs refinement, and so I turn to a fuller version which has a structure similar to the one just given but which is, of necessity, somewhat more complex.

The detailed argument

Any standard axiomatic system for conditional probability[1] will contain this multiplication principle:

(MP) $P(AB/C) = P(A/BC)P(B/C) = P(B/AC)P(A/C) = P(BA/C)$

512

I emphasize here that this relationship appears not only as a direct consequence of the traditional definition of conditional probability, *viz* $P(A/B) = P(AB)/P(B)$ but also as an axiom in probability calculi which take conditional probability as a primitive relation.[2] If we assume also the additivity axiom for conditional probabilities:

(Add)   If A and B are disjoint, then $P(A \vee B/C) = P(A/C) + P(B/C)$

then as an easy consequence we have the theorem on total probability for binary events:

(TP) $P(A/C) = P(A/BC)P(B/C) + P(A/\overline{B}C)P(\overline{B}/C)$

and also Bayes' Theorem for binary events:

(BT) $P(B/AC) = P(A/BC)P(B/C)/[P(A/BC)P(B/C) + P(A/\overline{B}C)P(\overline{B}/C)]$

I note here for future reference that the only additional assumption needed to derive these second two from the first two is distributivity.

Consider now the conditional propensity function $Pr(A/B)$, the propensity for A to occur, conditional on the occurrence of B.[3] This propensity will be interpreted initially as a single case propensity, where A and B are specific instances of event types, but nothing that is said here entails that either A or B has actually occurred or will occur. Dispositions being relatively permanent properties, they can be attributed to a system irrespective of whether the test condition, B, or the display, A, actually occurs. I shall assume throughout that the specific system which possesses the propensity remains the same, and hence omit notational devices representing the system or the structural basis of the propensity. Propensities are, however, often time-dependent, and so a fuller notation $Pr_{t_i}(A_{t_j}/B_{t_k})$ is needed, interpreted as 'the propensity at t_i for A to occur at t_j, conditional upon B occurring at t_k'. I shall now show that both the multiplication principle and Bayes' Theorem fail for conditional propensities. A specific example will be referred to for illustrative purposes, but the argument could be given for any case which possesses the kind of asymmetry present in the particular example. Take, then, the case of a well-known physical phenomenon, the transmission and reflection of photons from a half-silvered mirror. A source of spontaneously emitted photons allows the particles to impinge upon the mirror, but the system is so arranged that not all the photons emitted from the source. Hit the mirror, and it is sufficiently isolated that only the factors explicitly mentioned here are relevant. Let I_{t_2} be the event of a photon impinging upon the mirror at time t_2, and let T_{t_3} be the event of a photon being transmitted through the mirror at time t_3 later than t_2. Now consider the single-case conditional propensity Pr_{t_1} $(\cdot/\cdot)$ where t_1 is earlier than t_2, and take these assignments of propensity values:

i) $Pr_{t_1}(T_{t_3}/I_{t_2}B_{t_1}) = p > 0$
ii) $1 > Pr_{t_1}(I_{t_2}/B_{t_1}) = q > 0$
iii) $Pr_{t_1}(T_{t_3}/\overline{I}_{t_2}B_{t_1}) = 0$

where, to avoid concerns about maximal specificity, each propensity is conditioned on a complete set of background conditions B_{t_1} which include the fact that a photon was emitted from the source at t_0, which is no later than t_1. The parameters p and q can have any values within the limits prescribed. We need one further assumption for the argument. It is:

$$(\text{CI}) \quad \text{Pr}_{t_1}(I_{t_2}/T_{t_3}B_{t_1}) = \text{Pr}_{t_1}(I_{t_2}/\bar{I}_{t_3}B_{t_1}) = \text{Pr}_{t_1}(I_{t_2}/B_{t_1})$$

That is, the propensity for a particle to impinge upon the mirror is unaffected by whether the particle is transmitted or not. This assumption plays a crucial role in the argument, and will be discussed in the next section.

Argument 1: MP fails for propensities

From TP we have

$$\text{Pr}_{t_1}(T_{t_3}/B_{t_1}) = \text{Pr}_{t_1}(T_{t_3}/I_{t_2}B_{t_1})\text{Pr}_{t_1}(I_{t_2}/B_{t_1}) + \text{Pr}_{t_1}(T_{t_3}/\bar{I}_{t_2}B_{t_1})\text{Pr}_{t_1}(\bar{I}_{t_2}/B_{t_1})$$

and substituting in the values of the propensities from i), ii), iii) above,

$$\text{Pr}_{t_1}(T_{t_3}/B_{t_1}) = pq + 0 = pq$$

From CI we have

$$\text{Pr}_{t_1}(I_{t_2}/T_{t_3}B_{t_1}) = \text{Pr}_{t_1}(I_{t_2}/B_{t_1}) = q$$

Hence using MP we have

$$\text{Pr}_{t_1}(I_{t_2}T_{t_3}/B_{t_1}) = \text{Pr}_{t_1}(I_{t_2}/T_{t_3}B_{t_1})\text{Pr}_{t_1}(T_{t_3}/B_{t_1}) = pq^2$$

But from MP directly we have

$$\text{Pr}_{t_1}(I_{t_2}T_{t_3}/B_{t_1}) = \text{Pr}_{t_1}(T_{t_3}I_{t_2}/B_{t_1}) = \text{Pr}_{t_1}(T_{t_3}/I_{t_2}B_{t_1})\text{Pr}_{t_1}(I_{t_2}/B_{t_1}) = pq$$

We thus have

$$pq^2 = pq$$

i.e. $p = 0$, $q = 0$, or $q = 1$, which is inconsistent with i) or with ii).

Argument 2: Bayes Theorem fails for propensities

Take as assumptions BT and i), ii), iii) above. Then substituting in those values to BT we have

$$\text{Pr}_{t_1}(I_{t_2}/T_{t_3}B_{t_1}) = pq/[pq + 0] = 1$$

But from CI we have

$$\text{Pr}_{t_1}(I_{t_2}/T_{t_3}B_{t_1}) = \text{Pr}_{t_1}(I_{t_2}/B_{t_1}) = q < 1.$$

These arguments clearly suggest that inversion theorems of the classical probability calculus are inapplicable in a straightforward way to propensities. I shall now consider some of the most important ways which might be suggested for avoiding the arguments given above.

Objections, replies and discussion

Objection: The argument depends crucially upon the assumption CI. Rejecting a substantial part of classical probability theory is too great a price to pay, and hence we should abandon CI.

Reply. It is clearly not enough to rely upon the intuitive plausibility of CI. That principle can, however, be justified directly in the following way. The particle has a certain propensity within the given system to impinge upon the mirror. Suppose that we were to manipulate the system's conditions so that no particle hitting the mirror was in fact transmitted, say by rendering opaque the rear of the mirror. Would that alter the propensity for the particle to impinge upon the mirror? Given what we know about such systems, it clearly would not, and we could, if desired, support that claim by showing that the relative frequency of particles impinging on the mirror was unaffected by manipulations in the conditioning factor T when all other factors were kept constant as far as possible. Similarly, were we to manipulate the conditions so that all particles hitting the mirror were transmitted, say by rendering the mirror transparent, this too would leave the propensity for impinging unaltered. Given these facts, the events T_{t_3} and $\overline{T}_{t_3}$ are irrelevant to the propensity for I_{t_2}, and they can be omitted from the factors upon which the propensity is conditioned without altering its value. Some further remarks are required here. It is essential not to impose an epistemological interpretation on CI. It is undoubtedly true that in our example transmission of the particle is *evidence for* the earlier incidence of the particle on the mirror, but we are not concerned with evidential connections, nor with any other epistemological relationships. The conditional propensity constitutes an objective relationship between two events and any increase in our information about one when we learn of the other is a completely separate matter. The tendency to interpret CI evidentially must therefore be resisted. Nor should we think of CI in terms of the relative frequencies with which one event is accompanied by another. Propensity values can, in many cases, be measured by relative frequencies, but the essence of a propensity account is that it puts primary emphasis upon the system and conditions which generate the frequencies and only secondarily upon the frequencies themselves. The issues of interest for a propensity calculus are not ones stemming from the passive observation of frequencies, but the activist ones of which frequency values remain unchanged under actual or hypothetical experimental interventions. No distinction is made within frequency interpretations of probability theory between mere associations of events and genuine causal connections, but this distinction is critical for propensities and cannot be ignored.

One final point needs to be discussed in this connection. In order to avoid having to justify the assumption CI for each case individually, we might want to refer to a general principle of the form:

> (CI′) If Y is causally independent of X,
>
>   then $\Pr(Y/XZ) = \Pr(Y/Z)$ for all Z.

My own view is that such a general principle can be justified and used in place of the special assumption CI. To do this would, however, require a lengthy excursion into some controversial issues in probabilistic causality which are not central to the point under discussion here. In particular, it would require a general justification of a variational account of causation which is applicable to indeterministic systems. I am confident that the argument given above in favor of CI is sufficiently compelling for our present purposes, and so I shall remain with it.

Objection. The asymmetry present in the example is due to temporal asymmetry and is not therefore a property of the propensities themselves.

Reply. It is true that it is difficult to separate the asymmetry of single-case propensities from the asymmetry of temporally ordered events. However, a precisely similar argument to that above can be given for propensities having event types as relata, and within which no temporal ordering occurs essentially. Consider the example mentioned earlier of the neighbor who harangues his wife on hot summer days. If we let T = tirade at wife and I = intensely hot day, where now no temporal subscripts are required, and retain the propensity assignments (i), (ii) and (iii), then it is possible to repeat the arguments above *mutatis mutandis*, and show that the multiplication principle and Bayes' Theorem fail for general propensities as well. The failures thus clearly stem from the nature of propensities and not from the nature of time.

This response also shows that one cannot avoid the argument by insisting that it is meaningless or inadmissible to condition upon future events. For that objection would not dispose of the argument as applied to general propensities which are not temporally dependent. Furthermore, for temporally dependent single-case propensities, given any meaningful propensity assertion under this view which is conditioned only upon earlier events, there will exist an application of Bayes' Theorem, and an application of the multiplication axiom, which take that meaningful propensity assertion and transform it into a meaningless claim. Indeed, any application of Bayes' Theorem to temporally ordered events will fail the meaning-preservation criterion, and the restriction of probability theory required to satisfy that criterion would eliminate use of the theorem entirely for single-case propensities.

Objection. The problem lies with the use of conditional probabilities $P(B/A)$ to represent propensities. Instead probability conditionals of the form $P(A \to B)$ should be used. As we know,[4] the two behave differently outside trivial cases and so the fault lies in the mode of representation and not in the probability calculus.

Reply. This response can, I think, best be construed as a positive suggestion for an alternative approach to representing propensities. For example, some versions of causal decision theory have used the difference between conditional probabilities and the probability of conditionals to avoid Newcomb problems, by invoking a principle of causal independence which is similar to CI' above, so that when A has no causal influence on B, $P(A \to B) = P(B)$.[5] If such an approach is taken, however, it would have to be sharply separated from the subjectivist interpretations of the probability function with which it is usually associated, for as I construe them, propensity values are objective properties of physical and social systems.[6] Because the properties of conditional propensities are so intimately connected with those of probabilistic causality, and there is currently available no comprehensive theory of the latter for the singular case, I am unfortunately unable at present to offer a positive account of the nature of conditional propensities.

Discussion. How do we arrive at the propensity assignments (i), (ii) and (iii)? Because the argument depends only upon whether the propensities do or do not have extremal values, we can invoke the following two special principles both of which appear to be correct for single case propensities, (although each would be subject to measure theoretic nuances within a Kolmogorovian framework). The first principle is: if an instance $X_{t'}$ of an event type X never occurs with an instance Y_t of an event type Y, then the conditional propensity of $X_{t'}$ conditional on Y_t is zero, for any such pair of instances. The second principle is: if an instance of an event type X occurs together with an instance of an event type Y, and an instance of event type Y occurs without an instance of event type X, then the propensity for X_t conditional on Y_t lies strictly between zero and one, for any such pair of instances. (Both principles assume that all other background factors have been conditioned into $\Pr(\cdot/\cdot)$.) The first principle secures (iii), the second principle secures (ii) and the first half of the second principle secures (i).

Would it be possible to reject some assumption other than CI and preserve MP and BT? The only other candidates are finite additivity and distributivity (which is needed to derive TP and BT). Although there are well-known reasons for doubting the universal application of distributivity to quantum probabilities there is, I think, no good reason for supposing that it fails for propensities in general. The failure of finite additivity would be as conclusive a reason as the failure of the multiplication axiom to reject the classical probability calculus, and its failure would merely compound the difficulties for the traditional theory. However, the argument given above is so clearly directed against inversion principles that any considerations involving other parts of the calculus seem to be quite separate. The account thus ought not to be viewed as a pragmatic argument based on considerations of simplicity or convenience, but as showing directly the falsity of the multiplication principle and Bayes' theorem.

It is perhaps ironic that the first fully general version of Bayes' Theorem was formulated by Laplace in order to calculate the probability of various causes which may have given rise to an observed effect.[7] Laplace was concerned with legitimizing a probabilistic version of Newtonian induction, of inferring causes from their effects, and given his deterministic views, only an epistemic interpretation of the theorem made sense for him. But when our concern is with objective chance, such inductive interests are of secondary importance, and once the metaphysical aspects of chance are separated from the epistemological, Laplace's interpretation no longer seems quite so compelling.

Consequences

What is the epistemological status of probability theory? It seems to occupy a peculiar position somewhere between the purely mathematical and the obviously scientific. The subject matter of the theory, if matter there be, has been identified with, among other things, finite class frequencies, degrees of rational belief, limiting relative frequencies, propensities, degrees of logical confirmation and measures on abstract spaces, to name only some of the most important. This diversity of interpretations has been matched by the range of views on the nature of the theory itself. It has been taken as a generalization of classical logic, as an abstract mathematical theory, as an empirical scientific theory, as a theory of inference perhaps distinct from but certainly underpinning the theory of statistical inference, as a theory of normative rationality, as the source of models for irregular phenomena, as an interpretative theory for certain parameters in scientific theories, as the basis for an analysis of causality and as the reference point for definitions of randomness. Yet underlying this remarkable range of views is an equally remarkable agreement about the correct structure of the calculus itself. In particular, empiricists and rationalists may differ about the source of the probability values used in applications of the theory, but there is little disagreement about the truth of the theory—indeed, it would not be an exaggeration to say that the theory of probability is commonly regarded as though it were necessarily true.

If the arguments given in the first three sections of this paper are correct, this perception of probability theory is profoundly mistaken. It is thus worth recalling how it arose. Historically, the success of Kolmogorov's axiomatization, published in German in 1933, quickly eclipsed for scientific purposes Reichenbach's axiomatization of 1932 and the frequency theories of von Mises and of Popper, published in 1928 and 1934, respectively. Philosophically, the hegemony of standard probability theory has been reinforced by its affinities with logic. The view that probability theory is an extension of classical logic was adopted by Bolzano, Boole, Venn, Lukasiewicz, Reichenbach, Carnap and Popper, and has been supported by results showing that, in some cases, the logical structure of the probability space can be derived from the axioms of probability theory, indicating that classical sentential logic is a special case of the structure imposed upon proposition by the theory of probability.[8] This, together with the application of the theory in a manner seemingly independent of subject matter, reinforces the conception that the theory has an epistemological status akin to that of logic. Hence one arrives at the position that the correct way to utilize probability theory within science is to first separately axiomatize a purely formal theory of probability, and non-probabilistic axioms for specific scientific theories can then be added to this fixed set of probability axioms in exactly the same way that non-logical axioms are standardly added to logical axioms or rules.

This approach naturally leads to the project of 'providing an interpretation for probability theory' and the widespread use of the criterion of admissibility as a condition of adequacy for any interpretation of the theory. The criterion asserts that in order to be acceptable as an interpretation of the term 'probability', at least within scientific contexts, the interpretation must satisfy a standard set of axioms of abstract probability theory or a close variant thereof. This approach of considering 'probability' as a primitive term to be interpreted by means of an implicit definition is now so widespread as to be considered mandatory for any new account of probability, to the extent that we tend to automatically lapse into calling such accounts new interpretations rather than new theories of probability.

It is time, I believe, to give up the criterion of admissibility. We have seen that it places an unreasonable demand upon one plausible construal of propensities. Add to this the facts that limiting relative frequencies violate the axiom of countable additivity and that their probability spaces are not sigma-fields unless further constraints are added; that rational degrees of belief, according to some accounts, are not and cannot sensibly be required to be countably additive; and that there is serious doubt as to whether the traditional theory of probability is the correct account for use in quantum theory. Then the project of constraining semantics by syntax begins to look quite implausible in this area.[9] I do not wish to deny that the project of axiomatizing probability theory has had an enormously clarifying effect upon investigations into probability. What I do deny is that the concept of chance, as represented by propensities, is so obscure, or so abstract, that its properties are accessible only by means of a theory whose origins in equi-possible outcomes and finite frequencies can all too easily be forgotten.[10]

Notes

* Originally published in *Philosophical Review*, **94** (1985), pp. 557–70. Copyright © 1985 Sage School of Philosophy at Cornell University. Reprinted by permission of Duke University Press.

1 I take standard axiom systems for conditional probability to be those containing at least axioms of additivity, normalization, non-negativity and the multiplication principle.

2 For example, K. Popper, *The Logic of Scientific Discovery* (London: Hutchinson and Company, 1959), Appendix iv, *v; R. Stalnaker, 'Probability and Conditionals', *Philosophy of Science 37* (1970), pp. 64–80, especially p. 70.

3 Throughout this paper, the notation '*P*' will denote probability, and 'Pr' propensity.

4 See D. Lewis, 'Probabilities of Conditionals and Conditional Probabilities', *The Philosophical Review 85* (1976), pp. 297–315, in particular pp. 300–302.

5 For example, A. Gibbard and W. Harper, 'Counterfactuals and Two Kinds of Expected Utility', pp. 125–162 in *Foundations and Applications of Decision Theory, Volume 1*, C. Hooker, J. Leach, and E. McClennen, eds., (Dordrecht: D. Reidel 1978).

6 David Lewis, in his 'A Subjectivist's Guide to Objective Chance' in *Studies in Inductive Logic and Probability, Volume 2*, R. C. Jeffrey, ed., (Berkeley: University of California Press, 1980) reprinted as Chapter 27 in this volume, has provided what is probably the most fully developed theory relating chance and credence. One brief point should be made in connection with Lewis' theory. For him, chance is credence objectified and (hence) chance obeys the laws of probability theory. Conditional chance is then defined in the usual manner. This entails, I believe, that such an account of chance based on subjective probabilities cannot capture the causal aspects of conditional propensities, even with the restrictions of admissible evidence imposed by Lewis. I certainly do not want to claim that the very rough sketch I have provided here of propensities is the only one possible, but it does suggest that carrying over the properties of subjective probability to chances will result in certain characteristic features of the latter being lost. A similar point can be made about the suggestion that we can define an absolute propensity measure as $c(A) =_{df} Pr(A/T)$, where T is any certain event, and then define a conditional probability measure in the usual way using c.

7 In Pierre Simon, Marquis de Laplace, *Theorie Analytique des Probabilites* (Paris: Courcier, 1820) (3rd Edition), pp. 183–184.

8 See, for example, K. Popper, op. cit., and H. Leblanc, 'On Requirements for Conditional Probability Functions', *Journal of Symbolic Logic 25* (1960), pp. 238–242. It should be noted that Popper is somewhat ambiguous about the status of these results, for having asserted earlier that his calculus '… is formal; that is to say, it does not assume any particular interpretation, although allowing for at least all known interpretations' (ibid, p. 326) he then qualifies the results with 'in its logical interpretation, the probability calculus is a genuine generalization of the logic of derivation' (ibid, p. 356).

9 For a discussion of the flaws in the relative frequency interpretation, and a suggested repair, see B. van Fraassen, *The Scientific Image* (Oxford: The Clarendon Press, 1980), Chapter 6, section 4; on subjective probability see B. de Finetti 'On the Axiomatization of Probability Theory' in his *Probability, Induction, and Statistics* (New York: Wiley and Sons, 1972), and for the quantum-theoretical case, see A. Fine 'Probability and the Interpretation of Quantum Mechanics' *British Journal for the Philosophy of Science 24* (1973), pp. 1–37, for a discussion and dissenting view.

10 This paper has benefitted greatly from the comments and criticisms of Robert Almeder, James Cargile, James Fetzer, Ronald Giere, Donald Gillies, Clark Glymour, Richard Otte, Sir Karl Popper, Wesley Salmon, Robert Stalnaker and an anonymous referee for this Journal. It should not be assumed that they endorse the conclusions which I have drawn above. Brief mention of the main point can be found in my paper 'Is "Physical Randomness" Just Indeterminism in Disguise'? in *PSA 1978, Volume 2*, P. Asquith and I. Hacking, eds., Philosophy of Science Association, East Lansing, 1981, p. 102, and early responses are in W. Salmon 'Propensities: A Discussion Review', *Erkenntnis 14* (1979), pp. 213–214; and J. Fetzer, *Scientific Knowledge* (Dordrecht: D. Reidel, 1981), pp. 283–286.

31

DAVID LEWIS'S HUMEAN
THEORY OF OBJECTIVE
CHANCE*†

Barry Loewer

In David Lewis's framework, described in his paper 'A Subjectivist's Guide to Objective Chance' (this volume, Chapter 27) chances are given by propositions in the language of fundamental physics that specify that a type of event will (or won't) occur at a specific time (or during a particular time interval) in a specific location (or region)). Such chances are 'single case' since they apply to token fundamental events. The chance of an event A occurring at time t may itself change during the time prior to t so chances are time indexed. At t the chance of A occurring at $t+2$ may be 1/2. But at $t+1$ the chance of A occurring at $t+2$ may increase to .9. At t the chance of every proposition about times entirely prior to t is either 0 or 1. If we think of time as discrete then the assignment of chances gives rise to a tree structure branching toward the future. At each node the branches are the possible futures from that node each weighted by its chance from the time of that node. If at each node there is a chance (or chance density) for every possible subsequent state the chances of each possible future (sequence of states) is determined.

In Lewis's framework all chances fall under what he calls 'history to chance conditionals'. These are laws of the form 'if h is the actual history up to and including t the chance at t of S at t' $(t' > t)$ is x'.[1] In all the candidates for fundamental theories I know the dynamical chances at t are determined by the state at t. So the history to chance laws are state to chance conditionals of the form 'if the state at t is S^* then the chance at t of the state at t' being S is x'. The chance at t of a proposition R is the sum of the chances of the possible histories branching from the actual history at t at which R is true.

Chances are involved in the causal nexus. Chancy events are caused by events that raise their chances and chances are involved in explaining the events they are chances of. It is difficult to see how chances can play their roles in laws, explanation, and causation unless they are *objective*; i.e. their existence and values are independent of our beliefs. But objective chance is related to belief in a special way; chances rationally *guide* belief. It is not just that our beliefs ought to track truths about chance (as they ought track truths about various other matters) but that beliefs about the chance of an event rationally constrain beliefs about that event itself. Lewis proposes a principle which he thinks captures how chance should guide belief called 'the *Principal Principle*' (PP).

520

The (PP) says, roughly, that a person M's degree of belief (at t) that A conditional on the proposition that the chance of A (at t) is x should be equal to x; with the qualification that at t she has no information about A that is *inadmissible*. Information about A is inadmissible if it is information about A over and above information about A's chance.

PP: $C(A/P(A) = x \,\&\, T) = x$ (where T is any information admissible wrt A).

So, for example, if you believe that the coin in front of you has a chance of 1/2 of landing heads when flipped then your degree of belief conditional on that and any other information that doesn't tell you anything about the outcome of the flip (except what its chance is) should also be 1/2. While Lewis initially glosses admissibility as above he later suggests that any information about times prior to the time of A and any laws of nature—including laws that specify chances—are always admissible relative to A.[2]

The PP enables one to infer credences about frequencies from credences about chance. So, for example if you think that the chance of an event of type A in circumstances of type E is x and repetitions of E are independent then the PP implies that if there are many repetitions of E your degree of belief that the frequency with which A events occur in E situations is approximately x should be close to 1. Lewis shows how PP fits into Bayesian inference to yield an epistemology for chance propositions. If H and H^* are exclusive and exhaustive hypotheses that specify chances for experimental outcomes then the PP says that one's conditional credences $(C(e|H), C(e|H^*))$ should be the chances H and H^* respectively, assign to e. Given prior credences for H and H^* Bayes theorem yields the posterior credences $C(H|e)$ and $C(H^*|e)$.

We have seen that chances are Janus-faced. On the one hand, they are objective features of reality involved in laws and causation and, on the other hand, they rationally constrain degrees of beliefs via the (PP). We would like an account that explains both of these aspects and shows us how one property can possess both kinds of features. That is, how an *objective* feature of a situation S (the chance of S resulting in event e) which is part of the causal order and is metaphysically distinct from e (it is possible for it to occur without e) *rationally* constrain what degree of belief we should have in e's occurring? That something can possess both features can appear very puzzling; as puzzling as the Mackie found ethical facts that allegedly are part of the causal order and also normatively constrain what we should value.[3]

Lewis's framework seems designed for so called 'propensity chances'.[4] But toward the end of the paper he suggests a novel account which is quite different from standard propensity accounts. In a longer version of this paper I survey the standard interpretations of probability—actual and modal frequency accounts, propensity accounts of various sorts, and subjectivist accounts—with an eye to evaluating whether any yields a notion of chance capable of playing its role in physical theories and also as guiding belief via the PP. My conclusion is that none of the usual suspects measure up. Those which interpret chance as an objective feature of fundamental events may account for its role in physics but make it utterly mysterious why chances so construed should guide our beliefs in conformity with the PP. Subjectivist accounts have no trouble with PP but are not credible as accounts of the chances that occur in physics. This opens the field for Lewis's novel account.

521

Lewis's account of chance is part of his more general Humean account of laws including laws of chance; the Best System Account (BSA). The account is 'Humean' in that it characterizes laws as certain regularities and which regularities are laws is determined by the total pattern of instantiation of categorical properties.[5] Here is how the BSA works. Let L be a language whose atomic predicates express only fundamental properties (Lewis calls these 'perfectly natural properties'), spatio-temporal predicates (e.g. distances among points) and mathematics/logic. The truths of L specify the geometrical structure of space-time and the fundamental properties that are instantiated at each point. Lewis thinks that it is the job of fundamental physics to inventory these properties and suggests that they are or are similar to quantities like mass, charge, electromagnetic field values and so forth. All truths supervene on the totality of truths expressible in L (that is what makes L fundamental). A deductive system in L is a set of sentences of L. The laws are defined as follows:

> Take all deductive systems whose theorems are true. Some are simpler, better systematized than others. Some are stronger, more informative than others. These virtues compete: An uninformative system can be very simple, an unsystematized compendium of miscellaneous information can be very informative. The best system is the one that strikes as good a balance as truth will allow between simplicity and strength. How good a balance that is will depend on how kind nature is. A regularity is a law IFF it is a [contingent] theorem of the best system. (1994: 478)

There may be further conditions that should be put on the law giving systems. For example, that it counts against a system if it is compatible with events that are not covered by its laws.

Chances enter the picture by letting deductive systems include sentences that specify the chances of events.

> Consider deductive systems that pertain not only to what happens in history, but also to what the chances are of various outcomes in various situations—for instance the decay probabilities for atoms of various isotopes. Require these systems to be true in what they say about history. ... Require also that these systems aren't in the business of guessing the outcomes of what, by their own lights, are chance events; they never say that A without also saying that A never had any chance of not coming about. (1994: 480)

The axiom systems that vie for the title 'Best' are supplemented with a so far uninterpreted function Pt that is thought of as assigning chances to certain propositions at times. All candidates for Best system must be true. The virtues that make for a good system are simplicity, strength, and fit. Simplicity is measured in terms of order of differential equations, number of parameters, length of the conjunction of axioms etc. Strength is measured in terms of informativeness (possibilities characterized in terms of natural predicates excluded). Lewis suggests evaluating 'fit' in terms of the likelihood of truths. The higher the chance a system assigns to the true history (or to segments of it given part of the history) the better its fit. So understood fit is a kind of informativeness appropriate for chance. The better a theory fits the facts the more it says about those facts. I will later discuss just how a chance theory provides information. For now let us just observe that these various virtues will typically trade off. Strength and fit can often be improved at the cost of simplicity and visa versa. By assigning chances systems sacrifice strength for fit but may also make great gains in simplicity. Lewis's account assumes that there is a set of fundamental natural properties and that there is a unique Best System and that it is both pretty simple and pretty informative.[6] Assuming he is right about this the BSA will deliver a determinate collection of true generalizations. Let's call the contingent ones the 'L-laws' and the chances entailed by the L-laws 'L-chances'.

Lewis's BSA is a big improvement over previous Humean accounts. Among its improvements are that it connects L-laws and L-chances with the criteria (simplicity, informativeness, and so forth) physicists actually employ. Further, it is able to distinguish lawful from accidental regularities and allow for vacuous laws. L-chances apply both to token events (the chance that this photon will pass through a that polarizer in the next second) and to type chances (the chance that a photon with polarization of type X will pass through a polarizer of type Y). Also, while L-chances are connected to actual frequencies they can diverge arbitrarily from them.

Despite its attractions Lewis's account is not lacking in critics. The main worry is that Humean regularities—even the special ones given by the Best System of the world—are two weak to do the work of *real* laws. It has been claimed that Humean regularities (and specifically L-laws) are too anemic to support counterfactuals, provide explanations, be inductively confirmed as so forth. All of these objections have been adequately rebutted by Lewis and others.[7] Even so it is not difficult to produce thought experiments that provoke non-Humean intuitions.[8] I think that the most effective reply for the Humean is to grant the point but argue that L-laws can play the role of laws and that non-Humean laws are metaphysically and epistemologically problematic. The main non-Humean competitor to Lewis's account claims that laws and chances involve facts over and above the history of the distribution of fundamental properties that in some way *govern* or *guide* the evolution of events. Call these M-laws. The trouble with M-laws is that it is hard to understand what the metaphor of *governing* comes to. How can the M-law, which is one thing, govern or produce other events? It is especially problematic when the fundamental laws involve propensity chances. How does a propensity guide the development of subsequent events? And, even more puzzling, why should degrees of propensity guide rational belief? I think that critics of Lewis's account have no adequate answers to these questions. If there were no alternatives to positing laws and chances we might have to accept ('with natural piety' as Armstrong puts it) the existence of M-law and propensities. But Lewis's account is a less metaphysical alternative and also, as we will see, has some very interesting further advantages over its metaphysical rivals.

But first, I need to discuss what Lewis called 'a big bad bug' in his account of chance. The problem is that the Best Theory of a world may assign a non-zero L-chance at time t to a possible future $F(t)$ which is *logically* incompatible with that L-chance. He calls such a future 'undermining' since it undermines the theory that assigns it a positive chance. For example, suppose that world w consists entirely of a sequence of 1000 'coin flips' occurring at discrete times about half of which are h and half t so that the Best Theory $BT(w)$ for w says that the flips form a Bernoulli sequences with equal chances of h and t on each flip. Suppose the history to time 500 $H(500)$ consists of an equal number of hs and ts. At time 500 a future $F(500)$ consisting of 500 heads has, according to $BT(w)$, a chance of 1/2 to the 500 power. $F(500)$ is an undermining future relative to $BT(w)$. By the PP $C(F(500)/H(500)BT(w)) = 1/2$ to the

500th power. Let w' be the world composed of $H(500) + F(500)$. $BT(w')$ is certainly different from $BT(w)$. So $BT(w)$ is (supposedly) logically incompatible with w'. But then $C(F(500)/H(500)BT(w)) = 0$. Since this is correct the PP is false for L-chance.[9] One can avoid an outright contradiction by claiming that $BT(w)$ is not admissible. This is reasonable since $BT(w)$ provides information about the future. But this is of little comfort since in general $BT(w)$ provides information about the future. If it is never admissible then PP will be useless. Lewis observed that the problem is not specific to the BSA account but will arise on any account of chance compatible with Humean Supervenience on which chances are contingent. Since Lewis thought that the PP encapsulates 'all we know about chance' this supposed incompatibility caused him to despair that his BSA could be defended.[10]

Lewis eventually proposed to solve the problem by replacing the PP with

$$\text{NP: } C(A/T) = P(A/T).$$

Since $P(F(500)/BT(w)) = 0$ the problem (as given in the example but the point is general) doesn't arise. The NP give almost the same results as the PP for L-chances and exactly the same results on any account of chance on which the true chance theory has chance $= 1$.[11] Lewis seems content to think that by adopting the NP the BSA is saved. The fact that L-chances almost satisfy the NP (since the NP and the PP are quite close) allows us to count L-chances as genuine chances, at least as long as there is nothing that plays the chance role any better. A defense of that claim would of course involve showing that propensity chances don't exist.

Let's return to the question of why we should accept the PP or the NP? Lewis says, somewhat mysteriously, 'I can see, dimly but well enough, how knowledge of frequencies and symmetries and best systems could constrain rational credence ...' (Lewis 1994: 484). He seems to be suggesting that on the BSA account chances involve symmetries and frequencies and that these constrain rational degrees of belief. Unlike propensities but like actual frequencies L-chances supervene on non-chance propositions so a principle of rationality that constrains rational degrees of belief with respect to non-chance propositions can entail that chance propositions rational constrain belief. But it is not clear how the principle of indifference can support the PP with respect to L-chance (in fact it seems to conflict with it) and, in any case, the principle of indifference has little to recommend it.[12] But I think that we can see how L-chances can constrain degrees of belief if we recall how they are characterized in terms of Best Theory. Recall that a Best System is one that best combines simplicity, informativeness, and fit. The fit of a theory is measured by the probability that it assigns to true propositions. Fit can be understood as a kind of *informativeness*—the information that probabilistic propositions provide concerning the propositions they attribute probability to. The higher the probability assigned to true propositions the more informative the theory (the higher the probability to false propositions the less informative and the more misleading the theory). But these probabilities are informative only to someone who is willing to let them constrain her degrees of belief. Now, suppose that someone decides to let the PP constrain her degrees of belief. Then for her the Best Theory will be one that best combines simplicity and informativeness—including informativeness as evaluated in terms of the degrees of belief she assigns to true propositions. On this proposal the PP is 'built into' the account of L-chance. It can constrain belief because that is part of the account of how a theory earns its title as 'Best System'.

Suppose that instead of adopting the PP someone decides to set her degrees of belief by a different principle; say the anti-PP; $C(A) = 1 - P(A)$. When this principle is used to evaluate the informativeness of theories we will count a theory as more informative the lower the probability it assigns to true proposition. Of course the system that will be counted as Best when using this principle will differ from the Best Theory characterized using the PP and the probabilities it defines then will differ (systematically) from the L-chances. Let's call them anti-L-chances. Anti-L-chances exist just as much as L-chances. The important point is that someone who sets her degrees of belief by the anti-PP applied to anti-L-chances will have degrees of belief that are exactly the same as someone who uses the PP as applied to L-chances. And, of course, there are countless other principles that characterize alternative chance like notions ('chance like' because they characterize functions that satisfy the probability calculus) but which recommend more or less the same degrees of belief (when applied to the chance notion they help characterize) as the PP does for L-chance. Perhaps we could use one of these other principles and one of these other notions of chance. The PP (and L-chance) recommends itself because it is the simplest.

The preceding considerations shows that a Humean who values possessing the Best Theory of the world (because that theory specifies by his Humean lights the nomological structure of the world) and whose Best Theory contains probability statements must adopt some principle that extracts information about the Humean mosaic from these statements. The PP is a way of doing that. In the process it provides an interpretation (i.e., truth conditions) for probability statements. So a Humean who values possessing the Best Theory has a reason to adopt the PP (or its correction the NP). It is worth nothing what these considerations don't show. They don't establish that degrees of belief that fail to conform to the PP for L-chances are incoherent (i.e. violate the probability calculus). There are coherent credence functions that violate the PP for L-chance. Nor do they show that violation of the PP is a violation of some version of the principle of indifference. On natural construals the principle of indifference is incompatible with the PP. And of course we haven't shown that failure to set one's degrees of belief by the PP will lead to failure in one's decisions (say gambles on the outcomes of quantum experiments) in either the short or the long run. The most that could ever by shown is that failure would be probable but that is only significant given the PP. However, someone who violates the PP is, in a fairly straightforward sense, being irrational. On the one hand she accepts that a theory T provides the best combination of simplicity and informativeness and that T recommends that she have a degree of belief of p in a proposition A (as long as she has no inadmissible information wrt A) and yet she opts for a different degree of belief. Such a person is in the position of accepting that a certain person is the best source on what degrees of belief to have regarding certain matters and then opting for different degrees of belief. Notice that this rationale for the PP is not available for propensity chances. Without replying on the PP there is no non-question begging reason to think that setting one's degrees of belief by propensity chances will result in having high degrees of belief in truths and low degrees of belief in falsehoods. And since propositions about propensity chances are facts logically completely distinct from the propositions they assign chances to it is utterly mysterious why they should tell us anything about what degrees of belief to have in those propositions.

There are important theories in physics that assign chances to events even though the dynamical laws that occur in these theories are thoroughly deterministic. Two examples are statistical mechanics and Bohmian mechanics. Both contain principles or laws that specify probability distributions over initial conditions. There is a tradition of attempting to interpret these probabilities *subjectively*, as degrees of belief. But, for pretty much the reasons mentioned in our earlier discussion of subjective probabilities it is hard to see how subjective probabilities can underwrite the use of probabilities in explanation and laws. For example, within Bohmian mechanics the prohibition on super-luminal signaling follows from the specific Bohmian probability assumption over initial conditions. Other probability distributions permit super-luminal signaling. The failure of super-luminal signaling seems about as lawful as any generalization. But it would be awkward at best to maintain that its status as a law is due to our degrees of belief—*to our ignorance!*

It is not difficult to extend L-chances to cover initial condition probability distributions. If by adding such a proposition to a theory one makes a great gain in informativeness with little cost in simplicity than that probability distribution has earned its status as a law and the chances it specifies are as objective as dynamical L-chances. Arguably this is just the case with respect to the micro-canonical distribution in statistical mechanics and the Bohmian probability distribution within Bohmian mechanics. By adding the micro-canonical distribution to Newtonian laws the resulting system (and the proposition that the entropy in the distant past was much lower than currently) entails all of statistical mechanics. By adding the quantum equilibrium distribution $(P(x) = \Psi^2)$ to the Bohmian dynamical laws the resulting system entails standard quantum mechanics. In both cases enormous information gain is achieved with very little cost in simplicity.[13]

Even believers in propensity chances and metaphysical laws should grant (assuming that simplicity and informativeness are clear) that L-chances and L-laws exist.[14] The issue between them and advocates of the BSA account is whether L-laws and chances are the chances and laws that are posited by fundamental theories like GRW and Bohmian Mechanics? Whether or not L-chances are the subject of these theories depends in part on whether L-laws are good candidates for being fundamental laws. If scientific laws can be identified with L-laws then the L-chances they may specify do, I think, play the role of chances in science. They are objective, governed by laws (L-laws), enter into explanations, and underwrite a rationale for the PP. Of course this is a big 'IF'. The main competition for L-laws and L-chances are from more metaphysical views about laws and chance. It must be admitted that these metaphysical accounts fit some of our intuitions concerning law and chance better than the L-versions do. In particular the intuition that very different systems of laws and chances can give rise to the same total history of occurrent events is quite strong. If the requirement that anything worthy of the names 'law' and 'chance' satisfy this intuition then HS accounts are dead in the water. But until it can be shown that this requirement is essential if laws and chances are to play the roles that science requires of them then I think we have little reason to give such deference to the intuition. And that is especially so for those who, like myself, find metaphysical laws and chances that are at once metaphysically independent of events and yet govern and their evolution and rationally guide our beliefs utterly mysterious.

Notes

* Originally published in *Philosophy of Science*, 71 (2004), pp. 1115–25. Copyright © 2004 by the Philosophy of Science Association. Reprinted by permission of University of Chicago Press.

† Thanks to David Albert, Tim Maudlin, Frank Arntzenius, and David Papineau for comments on various versions of this paper.
1 Lewis says that the conditionals are stronger than material conditionals. If the chances are fundamental then it follows from Lewis's account of chances and laws that these conditionals are nomologically necessary.
2 What is admissible for a given person will in general depend on her credence function. Lewis can be understood as suggesting that rational credence functions are ones in which information about the past and about laws are relevant to a proposition A only by being relevant to the chance of A.
3 This analogy between chances and values is also made by Black (1998) who thinks it poses a problem for propensity accounts of chance and at least as great a problem for Lewis's account of chance that I discuss later. As the reader will soon see I agree with the first but not the second of these claims.
4 On the propensity account the chance at t of situation S result in E is a measure of the degree of the disposition (or propensity) of S at t to bring about E.
5 A property are categorical just in case its involvement in laws is not essential to it. Lewis characterizes 'Humean Supervenience' as the doctrine that (i) all the fundamental natural properties instantiated in the world are categorical and (ii) all truths supervene on the pattern of instantiation of fundamental properties.
6 Lewis suggests that if there is a tie then the laws are the generalizations common to both and that given the enormity of our world makes it unlikely that there are ties. If there is no very good systematization then the Humean should say that there are no laws.
7 Objections along these lines are made by Armstrong, Dretske, Foster, among others. Lewis (1983) and Loewer (1996) contain responses.
8 These thought experiments involve describing situations in which it appears that the occurrent facts (and so regularities) are held fixed while the laws and chances vary. See for example Carroll (1994) and Tooley (1977). I discuss these and explain why they don't tell much against Lewis's account in my (1996).
9 As we will see this argument is fallacious. One also needs to add to FH the statement that FH is the entire history of the world.
10 Propensity accounts of chance don't conflict with PP since chances are logically compatible with any histories. The very feature of propensity accounts that makes them metaphysically and epistemologically suspect (that worlds can completely agree with respect to their non-chance facts but differ in their chances and disagree enormously yet agree on their chances) is what allows them to conform to the PP.
11 On Lewis's account a chance theory will assign itself a chance less than 1. A propensity account typically will not assign chances to chance statements but it is compatible with those accounts to extend the chance distribution so that the chance theory obtains chance = 1.
12 Hoefer provides an example in which the PP applied to L-chance and the principle of indifference conflict and suggests that a Humean should go with the latter.
13 See my 'Determinism and Chance' (2001) for a development and defense of the idea that L-chances are compatible with determinism.
14 An interesting question is whether metaphysical laws and propensity chances will match or are likely to match the L versions. It is hard to see how to argue that it is likely that they will match without appealing to the PP but, as I have argued, it is hard to see what justifies the PP for propensity chances.

Bibliography

Black, Robert (1998), 'Chance, Credence and the Principal Principle', *British Journal for the Philosophy of Science* 49: 371–385.
Carroll, John (1994), *Laws of Nature*. Cambridge: Cambridge University Press.
Lewis, David (1983), 'New Work for a Theory of Universals', *Australian Journal of Philosophy* 61: 343–377.
——(1986), 'A Subjectivist's Guide to Objective Chance', in *Philosophical Papers*, vol. 2. Oxford: Oxford University Press, 83–132; reprinted in this volume, Chapter 27.

——(1994), 'Chance and Credence: Humean Supervenience Debugged', *Mind* 103: 473–490.

Loewer, Barry (1996), 'Humean Supervenience', *Philosophical Topics* 24: 101–127.

——(2001), 'Determinism and Chance', *Studies in History and Philosophy of Modern Physics* 32: 609–620.

Tooley, Michael (1977), 'The Nature of Laws', *Canadian Journal of Philosophy* 7: 667–698.

32

RESILIENCY, PROPENSITIES, AND CAUSAL NECESSITY*†

Brian Skyrms

Consider laws of the form: 'If a physical system is in state x then the probability that it has property ϕ is α'; or 'The probability that a physical system has property ϕ given that it has property $x = \alpha$'. These laws may be generated by statistical treatment of an underlying deterministic process (e.g., statistical mechanics) or may be, to the best of our knowledge, basic (e.g., quantum mechanics). The physical system with property x is said to have a *propensity to exhibit ϕ with probability α*. Propensities arising from the first sort of law (e.g., the propensity of a Brownian particle to migrate a certain distance in a certain time) are not essentially different from propensities generated by roulette wheels, etc.

Statistical laws and resultant statements of propensity cannot simply be saying that the limiting relative frequency of ϕ within the ensemble of systems that exhibit x is α any more than a universal law 'All Fs are Gs' can simply be saying that '100% of the Fs are Gs'. There are the considerations of lawlikeness. We might get a relative frequency *by accident*. What is worse, we might not only get a relative frequency where there is no statistical law operative (a 'spurious correlation') but we might get the *wrong* relative frequency even where a statistical law *is* operative. To make the point bluntly, suppose a statistical law sets $\alpha = 1/2$ and only one physical system ever exhibits x and it is destroyed after one trial (for vividness, you might imagine a special roulette wheel built to oddball specifications). Then the limiting relative frequency is either 0 or 1. Less extreme examples of the same phenomenon emerge when we calculate *from* the law that there is a positive probability that in a finite number of trials the relative frequency will diverge from the probability.

To attempt to escape these embarrassments by conjuring up large ensembles is of a piece with trying to rescue lawlikeness for universally quantified material conditionals by appeal to 'unrestricted scope'—and just as vain.

To avoid these unacceptable consequences, some writers have suggested that propensities be construed counterfactually, as hypothetical relative frequencies; or as dispositions to manifest those relative frequencies. Thus, $\Pr(\phi \text{ given } x) = \alpha$, if an infinite number of physical systems were put into state x, the limiting relative frequency of ϕ among them would be α.

This view runs into some of the same difficulties as the foregoing, although in attenuated form. I believe that the probability of heads on a fair flip of a fair coin is 1/2. Does this logically *entail* that if I were to flip a fair coin (by a fair flipping process) an infinite number of times I would not get one head after another? Again, I think not. Granted that the probability of 'all heads' gets smaller as the number of trials increases and approaches 0 as the number of trials goes to infinity (hence the attenuation). *But we must not take zero probability as tantamount to impossibility in these contexts.* After all, the same assumptions that got us zero probability for 'all heads' get us zero probability for *each* infinite sequence of heads and tails, and we cannot very well hold that they are *all* impossible! Therefore, appeal to laws of large numbers, and appeal to hypothetical situations to assure those large numbers, is not enough to guarantee a correct representation of propensities.

I want here to introduce a technical notion, the *resiliency* of a probability claim. Let a belief state be represented by a probability distribution $[Pr_i]$ over a language, and let p be a sentence of the language. Then:

> *Def. Probabilistic Resiliency:* The resiliency of $Pr(p) = a$ in $[Pr_i]$ is 1 − the maximum over j of $|Pr_j(p) - \alpha|$ where the $[Pr_j]$s are the probability distributions got from $[Pr_i]$ by conditionalizing on some sentence of the language consistent with p; $\sim p$.

Resiliency is a stability property, akin to the concept of robustness in statistics. A resilient probability is one that is relatively insensitive to perturbations in our belief structure. A treatment of conditional probabilities in the same spirit is possible:

> *Def. Resiliency for Conditional Probabilities:* The resiliency of Pr (q given p) $= a$ in $[Pr_i]$ is 1 − the maximum over j of Pr_j (q given p), where the $[Pr_i]$s are the probability distributions got from $[Pr_i]$ by conditionalization on some sentence that entails neither $p \supset q$ nor $p \supset \sim q$.

The concept of probabilistic resiliency is nicely illustrated by Richard Jeffrey's solution to Karl Popper's 'paradox of ideal evidence'.

Popper proposes the following problem. You are presented with a coin and are to assign rational degrees of belief to the probability that it will come up heads and the probability that it will come up tails. You are not sure that the coin is fair. You believe that there is some chance that it is biased, either toward heads or toward tails. But you have no more reason to think it is biased one way than the other. From 'symmetry of ignorance', so to speak, you arrive at the conclusion that $Pr(tails) = 1/2$. Now compare this with the situation in which you toss the coin a great number of times and get about 50% tails; you examine the coin and find it physically symmetrical, etc. You now have a great deal of knowledge available that you did not have in the first case, and yet when asked your rational degree of belief that the coin will come up tails on the next toss, you will give the same answer: $Pr(tails) = 1/2$. The conclusion appears to be that your added knowledge is *simply not reflected* in your degrees of belief in the outcomes of the coin-tossing experiments. (Popper then wants to conclude that they can be reflected only in degrees of belief about *objective* probabilities: at this stage he is thinking about relative frequencies).

In a slightly different context, Leonard Savage flirts with the idea of explaining the difference between subjective probabilities that we are 'sure of' and those we are not sure of, by introducing second-order subjective probabilities:

> To approach the matter in a somewhat different way, there seems to be some probability relations about which we are relatively 'sure' as compared

with others. When our opinions, as reflected in real or envisaged action, are inconsistent we sacrifice the unsure opinions to the sure ones. The notion of 'sure' and 'unsure' introduced here is vague, and my complaint is precisely that neither the theory of personal probability as developed in this book, nor any other device known to me renders the notion less vague. There is some temptation to introduce probabilities of the second order.[1]

We appear to have a quite intuitive picture here of the situation in the Popper examples. In both situations the first-order probability of tails is 1/2. But in the ignorance situation the *second-order* probabilities are spread out all over the spectrum for Pr(tails) = x [though we may plausibly assume that the second-order probability weighed average for values of Pr(tails) = x; i.e., the second-order expectation, is 1/2]. In the 'ideal-evidence' situation, the second-order probabilities can be thought of as concentrated sharply at Pr(tails) = 1/2, so that Pr(Pr(tails) = 1/2) = 1 (or some close approximation to that situation). (Notice that *mathematically* the Savage picture may not be so different from what Popper has in mind. Savage thinks of both first- and second-order probabilities as subjective, while Popper thinks of second-order as subjective and first-order as objective). Jeffrey points out, however, that we do not even need to ascend to second-order probabilities, in order to find the imprint of the additional evidence:

> I suggest at this point that your attention is being misdirected to A_n (the nth toss comes up heads) as a proposition to which your old and new belief functions must surely assign different values, if there be such a proposition. But as you both agree, prob(symmetric ignorance) and PROB(ideal evidence) shall both assign the value 1 here. Then this cannot be the locus of the difference. Nevertheless, there *is* a difference: prob and PROB will assign different values to any proposition $A(n)$ that asserts, concerning $n \geq 2$ distinct tosses, that all of them yield heads. To any such proposition PROB assigns the value $1/2^n$; but to the same proposition prob must assign a higher value, if you hope to learn from experience.[2]

In other words, the difference shows up in the first-order *conditional* probabilities. In the ignorance case, Pr(tails on toss 100) = 1/2, but Pr(tails on toss 100 given heads on tosses 1 through 99) is nearer 0. In the ideal-evidence case, this conditional probability would stay at (or very near) 1/2. Our 'sureness' that Pr(tails) = 1/2 is manifest as a reluctance to change Pr(tails) on various evidence, and this is mirrored by the constancy of value of Pr(tails on a given q) for various q. In a word, the ideal evidence has changed not the *probability* of tails on toss a, but rather the *resiliency* of the probability of tails on toss a.[3]

Now in the first 'symmetric ignorance' case, our rational degree of belief in the proposition that the coin has a *propensity* to come up tails with probability 1/2 is quite small, but in the 'ideal-evidence' case, it is quite high. Let x be a description of the kind of trial involved, and let ϕ be the property that it has a propensity to exhibit (e.g., tails). Then it seems plausible to take as our degree of confirmation that x has a propensity to exhibit ϕ with Probability = α, as the instantial resiliency with respect to an unexamined trial, a:

$$\text{Resiliency} \quad \text{Pr}(\phi \text{ a given } x \text{ a}) = \alpha$$

531

Likewise, a statistical law (or consequence of a statistical law) of the form: 'The probability that a physical system has property ϕ given that it is in state χ is α' may be taken to be well confirmed to its degree of instantial resiliency, as specified above.

Resiliency over the whole language may be a requirement of unrealistic stringency. There is no unique answer as to which sublanguage resiliency must be evaluated over, for lawlikeness. Rather, we must again say that *the larger* the sublanguage over which we have high instantial resiliency, the more *lawlike* the statistical law. At one end of the scale we have statements like 'the probability of death within a year given that one is an American male of age $65 = d$', which is extremely sensitive to auxiliary information, and whose resiliency is limited indeed. At the other end we have laws of radioactive decay, which have been tested under an enormous variety of circumstances and whose resiliency extends over a language of impressive scope.

We can, however, say something more about how broadly the language is taken over which resiliency is to be evaluated. It so happens that different choices of 'scope' of resiliency correspond to different statistical properties which play an important role in the discussion of propensities.

Let us first compare the pre-quantum-mechanical status of the laws of statistical mechanics and their consequences (e.g., the random walk of a Brownian particle) with the current status of the laws of quantum mechanics and their results (e.g., laws of radioactive decay). In the former case we are thought to have a statistical situation only in virtue of our ignorance of the initial conditions of the system involved. Given the initial position and momentum of each particle involved, Newton's laws predict the evolution of the system deterministically. The quantum-mechanical laws on the other hand are thought to be basic (hidden-variable aficionados aside), and the statistical situation with respect to them is due not to ignorance of initial conditions, but to a 'genuine metaphysical indeterminism'. Some writers regard the propensities involved in the first sort of situation as bogus. They believe that in a deterministic universe there are no real propensities. Let us call this school the *indeterminists*. Pre-quantum-mechanics, the universe *was* thought to be deterministic. According to the indeterminists, then, in that knowledge situation we should *not* have thought of statistical mechanics as giving us *genuine propensities or genuine statistical laws*. Likewise, we should not have thought of roulette wheels, etc. as chance set-ups having genuine propensities. Other writers find the concepts of propensity and physical law equally applicable in both sorts of case.

Now, from the standpoint of the present treatment, the dispute can be seen as a dispute over how broadly to evaluate resiliency. The indeterminist is worried about the fact that, once we introduce descriptions of the microstate of the system into the language, the resiliency of the appropriate probability drops drastically. But those of us who are happy about talking about statistical laws and propensities with regard to classical statistical mechanics, are presumably impressed enough by resiliency over descriptions of the macro-state of the system. Similar remarks apply, *mutatis mutandis* to roulette wheels and other homely paradigm chance set-ups. At this point, it is not clear that *determinism* should be the point at issue here, rather than macro-description vs. micro-description or rough, everyday description vs. precise mechanical description (for the roulette wheel). But if indeterminism is *really* what the indeterminist wants, then it is clear that he should evaluate Resiliency of $\Pr(\phi a \text{ given } \chi a) = \alpha$ over a language that includes resources for a complete description of the history of the world up to the time of occurrence of *a* (but not after that time). But this requirement is *very* strict, and its temporal asymmetry strikes me as a little odd in this context.

Another bone of contention among propensity theorists is whether the various trials produced by a chance set up must be independent. Some wish to assume independence of trials, in order to use the strong law of large numbers in the aforementioned justification of limiting relative frequency. (The strong law of large numbers is that, if the trials are independent and identically distributed, the limiting probability that relative frequency of an outcome diverges from its probability is zero). Independence is also a special case of resiliency; that is, resiliency of 1 over the results of other trials.

Finally, there is the question of whether the sequence of trials should be *random*. Randomness was introduced into the theory of physical probabilities by Richard von Mises. An infinite sequence (e.g., tosses of a coin) is to be *random with respect to its outcomes* (e.g., heads, tails) just in case the relative frequency of the outcomes remains unchanged in all subsequences got from the original sequence by 'place selection'. The intuitive idea behind place selection is:

> By place selection, we mean the selection of a partial sequence in such a way that we decide whether an element should or should not be included without making use of the attribute of the element.[4]

Von Mises tried to make this idea precise by identifying place selection as selection by a characteristic function: a function that takes as arguments initial segments of the sequence and as values 0 (signifying 'next member not selected for the subsequence' and 1 (signifying 'next member selected'). Of course, with the set-theoretic sense of function this will not do, for there are enough functions around to upset the claims to randomness of *all* sequences (excepting a few degenerate ones). Take an infinite sequence of heads and tails. Consider the function that maps an initial segment of the sequence onto 1 just in case the next element is Heads. There *is* such a function in the set-theoretic sense, although the way I have specified it may seem a little underhanded. And, provided there were an infinite number of heads in the original sequence, it will select out an infinite subsequence consisting entirely of heads. Likewise with tails. The problem is that the epistemic clause: 'without making use of the attribute of the element' has no restrictive role to play in this account.

What one can have in a non-vacuous way is a notion of randomness relativized to a certain class of place-selection functions. George Wald showed that, relative to an arbitrary denumerable class of place-selection functions, there is a continuum of random sequences. Alonzo Church suggests taking a particularly natural set of place-selection functions, the recursive ones.

It should be clear that these ideas of randomness are also closely connected with probabilistic resiliency. For every place-selection function there is a corresponding property that selects out the subsequence (e.g., the property of following the initial segment TTT or the initial segment TTTH or the initial segment TTTHHT or ...) Resiliency of 1 over the instantiations of this class of properties will guarantee randomness relative to the associated class of place-selection functions. (And will coincide with it provided that the class of properties has the appropriate Boolean closure property). The fact that so many key concepts are special cases of probabilistic resiliency should not be surprising. Resiliency of 1 comprises a very general and very fundamental concept of *invariance*.

If resiliency of Pr(p) is 1 over a language, then Pr(p) is invariant over any situation consistent with p describable in the language (or, in other words, over all partitions of that region of logical space within which p is true, that can be generated by the language).

Looking at the other side of the coin, we might say that probabilistic resiliency is a natural generalization of von Mises' original definition of randomness. In fact, Hans Reichenbach objects that the direction suggested by Church construes the invariance too narrowly for the intended physical applications: 'if a sequence possesses randomness of the von Mises-Church type there may still be *physical* selections that lead to a deviating frequency'.[5] That is, some physical property (e.g., temperature below -200 degrees C) might select out a subsequence, or sub-ensemble, which changed the frequency (and thus called for qualification of the associated physical law or propensity statement). Let us call Reichenbach's idea of invariance under selection of subsequence by an arbitrary physical property *physical randomness.*

The *absolute* concept of physical randomness is clearly in as much trouble as von Mises' original definition. Just what physical properties *exist* is a tricky physical question. If we take the extensional route of identifying physical properties with classes of physical events, we will have a bit of difficulty finding physically random sequences. But even without indulging in such dubious metaphysical identifications, we can see that the concept of absolute physical randomness is suspect. Consider the paradigm case of radioactive decay. We can select out subsequences with different relative frequencies simply by referring to the readings of detectors placed in the vicinity. There seems to me to be no reason to believe that we could not always, by referring to the results of physical measurements, select out subsequences with variant relative frequencies. The only sort of physical randomness that makes sense, then, is randomness *relative* to a given set of physical properties (in other words, randomness relative to a given language).

Of course, physical randomness as thought of by Reichenbach is a property of objective sequences of events in the world, and I have been presenting probabilistic resiliency as a property of our system of beliefs about the world. This is not to say that the account presented here is *anti*-objectivist. Probabilistic resiliency of 1 does not *require* belief in the existence of an objective, physically random, sequence of events. But it does not exclude the possibility that the resiliency is based in the belief *in* such a sequence. And, in fact, strong enough belief in physical randomness *will* guarantee the corresponding probabilistic resiliency.

The key tool in investigating these questions is the De Finetti representation theorem. A probability distribution is said to be *symmetric* for a sequence of trials just in case the probabilities are invariant over permutations of trials; equivalently, the trials are said to be *exchangeable.* (We have been assuming all along that 'new' individuals—individuals not in our evidence base—are exchangeable). De Finetti showed that the probabilities of an exchangeable series of events can be represented as a mixture (i.e., a weighted average) of probabilities of independent series of events. One way of using this mathematical result is to think of my subjective probabilities of events in such sequences as being weighted averages of objective probabilities; with the weights being our subjective probabilities that the corresponding objective probabilities are the true ones. Then my subjective resiliency of Pr(Fa) $= \alpha$ will approach 1 as my belief in the physical randomness of the corresponding sequence of events with Pr(Fa) $=$ Pr(Fb) $= \ldots = \alpha$ approaches 1.

The concept of resiliency has connections with a whole cluster of concepts associated with lawlikeness and causality. I can here only briefly indicate a few of these.

(1) *Shielding-off:* Suppose that e_1 and e_2, though not independent, became independent after conditionalizing on c, that is,

$$\Pr(e_2 \text{ given } e_1 \,\&\, c) = \Pr(e_2 \text{ given } c)$$

Then c is said to *shield-off* e_1 from e_2. In a wide range of contexts it is plausible to assume that *shielding-off* holds the key to causal order: e.g., the current atmospheric conditions shield-off the dropping barometer from the impending rain.

To say that c *shields-off* e_2 from e_1 is to say that $\Pr(e_2 \text{ given } c)$ has resiliency of 1 over e_1.

The plausibility of the connection between resiliency and causal ordering depends on the same sorts of assumptions that are required for the legitimacy of the second law of thermodynamics. But this reservation should increase rather than decrease the importance that resiliency has in this area.

(2) *Resiliency of Nonprobabilistic Statements and Rules of Acceptance:* The resiliency of a nonstatistical statement, p, can be identified with the limiting case of the resiliency of a statistical statement $\Pr(p) = 1$. Then, the resiliency of p is the minimum of $\Pr(p \text{ given } q_i)$ where the q_is are the propositions consistent with p in the language in question.

It is of some interest to see whether we can find probabilistic rules of acceptance that are *strongly consistent*, that is, which always lead to a consistent set of accepted sentences. The lottery paradox shows that high probability alone will not do. However, it is possible to show that:

> *Th.* For any compact language, with a strictly coherent probability distribution on it, any rule of acceptance that requires resiliency > .5 will yield a consistent set of accepted statements.

(3) *Simple Nonstatistical Laws:* Some new light can be thrown on old issues concerning the confirmation of simple nonstatistical laws of the form 'All Fs are Gs'. Let us say that a numerical quantity M on laws of this form *supports prediction* iff $\Pr(Ga$ given $Fa)^5 \geq M$ (All Fs are Gs). A quantity that *supports prediction* is one that certifies only those laws which issue good inference tickets. Let us say that a quantity M *satisfies the equivalence condition* iff all logically equivalent laws[6] receive the same M values. Then, subject to certain restrictions, it can be shown that there is a unique quantity M which supports prediction and satisfies the equivalence condition, and that it is the resiliency of the material conditional which instantiates the law R $(Fa \supset Ga)$ over a suitable instantial language.

Thus two prima facie alternative positions:

I   That a law is expressible in terms of the material conditional, $\supset$, but that being well confirmed qua law involves a different *status* from merely high probability; and

II   That a law is *a bundle of conditionals which are not material* conditionals; e.g., a bundle of conditional probabilities,

can be seen to be compatible.

Notes

* Originally published in *The Journal of Philosophy*, **74** (1977), pp. 704–713. Copyright © 1977 Journal of Philosophy, Inc. Reprinted by permission of Brian Skyrms and The Journal of Philosophy.
† Presented at an APA symposium on Causation and Conditionals. Patrick Suppes and Robert Stalnaker commented; see *The Journal of Philosophy*, **74** (1977), pp. 713–714, for Suppes' comments.
1 *The Foundations of Statistics* (New York: Wiley, 1954), pp. 57–58.
2 *Logic of Decision* (New York: McGraw-Hill, 1965), p. 184.
3 These facts are not unrelated to the second-order approach. See discussions of the De Finetti representation theorem in Bruno de Finetti, 'Foresight: Its Logical Laws, Its Subjective Sources', in H. E. Kyburg and H. E. Smokler, eds., *Studies in Subjective Probability* (New York: Wiley, 1963), in Savage, *op. cit.*, sec. 3.7., and in I. J. Good, *The Estimation of Probabilities*, Research Monograph No. 30 (Cambridge, Mass.: MIT Press, 1965).
4 Chapter 22 in this volume, p. 355.
5 *Theory of Probability* (Berkeley: University of California Press, 1949), p. 150; I learned of this through Jose Alberto Coffa.

INDEX

Academy of Sciences, Paris 299
actual frequentism 343–4, 397, 402–3
Adams, Ernest 42
Adams, John Couch 240–2
ad hoc theories and hypotheses 213, 218, 223,
    238–45; Bayesian view of 243–4; examples
    of 239–40
additivity applied to degrees of belief 97;
    see also countable additivity
admissability of information and propositions
    436, 464–5, 479, 521
Airy, Sir George 242–3
Albert, David Z. 453
Alchourrón, Carlos E. 127
analysis experts 40–2, 438
arbitrary shifts, rationality of 179–80
Aristotle 48, 496
Armendt, Brad 128, 180
Armstrong, D.M. 344, 403, 523
Arntzenius, Frank 43, 126–7, 439, 441;
    author of Chapter 11
articulable propositions 120
assumption-free and *assumption-laden* cases
    212–13
Augustine, St. 159
avowal 162
axioms of science 376–7, 382, 385, 518

Babbage, Charles 227
Bacon, Sir Francis 239, 241, 245
Bartha, Paul 292–3
basic chance principle (BCP) 439–42, 445,
    448, 452
Bayes, Thomas 325
Bayes' theorem 85–6, 222–6, 232–6, 244–5,
    255, 445–6, 476, 512–13, 516–17
Bayesian theory 43, 137, 150–1, 163, 179–80,
    194–5, 209–11, 214–19, 222–39, 243–8,
    252–65; ad hoc 243–4; objections to
    214–16, 255, 266; reasons for the appeal of
    256; *see also* mixed Bayesianism; normative
    decision theory; objective Bayesianism;
    subjective Bayesianism

belief: measurement of 53–60; in theory
    151–2; *see also* degrees of belief; full belief;
    partial belief
Bell, J.S. 454
Berkeley, George 393, 492
Bernoulli, Daniel 299–300
Bernoulli, Jacob 319, 325
Bernoulli sequences 375–6, 524
Bernoulli theorem 64, 69, 495, 504
Bernoulli trials 388–90, 504
Bertrand, Joseph 303–9, 312–14
best system account (BSA) of laws of change
    522–5
betting 28–31, 39, 56–62, 73–4, 77, 253–4
biases, spurious 405–6
Bigelow, John 292, 352, 439–40
Black, Robert 453
Blackwell, David 44
Blake, W. 48
Blume, Johannes 371
Bohmian mechanics 526
Bohr, Niels 150
Bovens, Luc 218
Bradley, Darren *co-author of Chapter 12*
Bridgman, P.W. 351
Brier, George 93
Brier scores 90, 93
Briggs, Rachael 128, 452
Bruns, Heinrich 365
Buffon, George-Louis Leclerc 299–303,
    309–10
Butler, Joseph 340, 436

calibration 37–8, 90, 101–3, 156–7
calibration theorem 102
Callender, Craig 453
Cantor, Georg 377
Carnap, Rudolph 73–4, 86, 148, 152, 154–5,
    251, 253, 256–7, 284, 287–9, 293, 305,
    327, 330, 380, 399, 413, 449, 458, 498–9;
    author of Chapter 19
categorical scales for accuracy of beliefs 97
causality, law of 69
Chadwick, J.A. 52